HITLER AND HIS GOD

Georges Van Vrekhem (1935-2012) was a Flemish speaking Belgian who was known in his country as a journalist, poet and playwright. He was the artistic manager of a professional theatre company, the Nederland Toneel te Gent. He lived in Auroville, the international township in south India.

Georges Van Vrekhem's notable works include *Beyond Man*; *The Mother*; *Overman*; and *Patterns of the Present*. Translations of his books have been published in many languages like Dutch, French, Russian and Spanish.

HITLER AND HIS GOD
The background of the Hitler phenomenon

Georges Van Vrekhem

RUPA

I dedicate this book to my true family.
GVV

Published by
Rupa Publications India Pvt. Ltd 2006
7/16, Ansari Road, Daryaganj
New Delhi 110002

Sales centres:
Allahabad Bengaluru Chennai
Hyderabad Jaipur Kathmandu
Kolkata Mumbai

Copyright © Sudha Mohanty 2006, 2012
The works of Sri Aurobindo © Sri Aurobindo Ashram

The views and opinions expressed in this book are the author's own and the facts are as reported by him which have been verified to the extent possible, and the publishers are not in any way liable for the same.

All rights reserved.
No part of this publication may be reproduced, transmitted, or stored in a retrieval system, in any form or by any means, electronic, mechanical, photocopying, recording or otherwise, without the prior permission of the publisher.

ISBN: 978-81-291-0953-8

Fifth impression 2016

10 9 8 7 6 5

The author asserts the moral right to be identified as the author of this work.

This edition is for sale in Indian subcontinent only.

Printed at Gopsons Papers Ltd., Noida

This book is sold subject to the condition that it shall not, by way of trade or otherwise, be lent, resold, hired out, or otherwise circulated, without the publisher's prior consent, in any form of binding or cover other than that in which it is published.

Contents

PART ONE: WHEN HITLER BECAME THE FÜHRER   1

1. Turnabout   3
    A corporal watching mice   3
    Germany in turmoil   7
    Like a worn out stray dog   11
    Captain Mayr's discovery   13

2. Masters   21
    Austrian visionaries   22
    The Germanenorden [Order of Germanic people]   27
    Rudolf von Sebottendorff   32
    The Thule Society   36

3. Mentor   46
    Thule reaches out   46
    The corporal joins a party   49
    Dietrich Eckart   55

4. Wolf   65
    A mental make-up   65
    Persisting memories   68
    A sudden burst of energy   73

Turmoil	78
The corporal becomes the Führer	81
Mayhem and murder	86
"Fortunate Wolf"	94

5. **Settling accounts** — 98
   - Annus terribilis — 98
   - A putschist in tail coat — 102
   - "Bolshevism from Moses to Lenin" — 107
   - RIP — 112

6. **Mein Kampf** — 119
   - The Landsberg retreat — 119
   - Hitler bares his mind — 126
   - Mortal enemy France — 129
   - "The System" — 135
   - "Germany, awake!" — 138
   - The leader and the masses — 144
   - Blind faith — 148
   - A militant movement — 152
   - "Great master of the lie" — 156
   - The Protocols of the Wise Men of Zion — 161
   - Living space for the master race — 165

PART TWO: THE ROOTS OF NAZISM — 173

7. **Superior people** — 175
   - Hitler was no accident — 175
   - Superior people — 178
   - The quest for world domination — 181
   - Hitler's global ambitions — 183
   - Renaissance and Reformation — 189
   - Romanticism (1770-1840) — 194
   - List and Lanz — 200

A place in the sun	203
The First World War	208

8. Long skulls and broad skulls — 211
- The white man's pride — 211
- Social Darwinism — 214
- Treitschke, Fritsch, Haeckel — 220
- Gobineau and Vacher de Lapouge — 226
- Chamberlain and Rosenberg — 233
- Hitler's racism — 240

9. The volkisch movement — 249
- Volkisch romanticism — 252
- Back to nature — 259
- A German religion — 266
- The light of Apollo, the frenzy of Wotan — 275
- In defiance of reason — 287
- A path apart — 292

10. The Jewish Question — 297
- The Jewish stereotype — 297
- 'Cargo' — 300
- 'Without Christianity no anti-Semitism' — 304
- The crusades and the Black Death — 307
- Luther, the anti-Semite — 312
- A less prejudiced attitude — 315
- 'The Jews are our misfortune' — 317
- Assimilation — 328
- The Jewish menace — 330
- 'The Jew' — 332
- A Jewish race? — 335
- Money — 336
- Intelligence — 340
- Socialists and Communists — 344

Front soldiers 348
World conspiration 351
War and extermination 354
The unwritten order 359

11. The German aspiration 364
The search for meaning 364
The 1880 watershed 369
Things visible and invisible 374
The living and the dead 380
Waiting for Godot 387
A new human being 393
Schwabing 403
'A devil or a god' 406
Claus von Stauffenberg 409
A higher and a lower choice 416

PART THREE: HITLER AND HIS GOD 423

12 The vision of Adolf Hitler 425
Nazism 425
Hitlerism 430
The Messiah 437
Faith 446
A new world 447
'National Socialism is a religion' 453
A new man 458
The Order of the Death's Head 464

13. Medium 475
Magnetism 480
Blue eyes 486
'A little guy yelled himself into a fit' 491
'Near-ultimate evil' 498

Evil unexplained	501
On the mountain	507
Rienzi	510
Convergences	514

14. Sri Aurobindo's vision — 525
A double ladder	525
Man is a transitional being	528
'In Matter lies the crux'	530
Humanity is one	533
Scholar and revolutionary	534
A lady from Paris	540
'The Titan kings attack …'	548
The human cycle	552
Parallels and contrasts	556
A higher and a lower choice: what went wrong	559

15. 'The Lord of the Nations' — 562
The four asuras	563
Fallen angels	569
A charmed life	572
Convergences (continued)	576
A friend	586
More friends	591

16. Two poems — 598
'The Dwarf Napoleon'	600
Four-in-one	612
Suffering	616
'The Children of Wotan'	624

17. A world in the balance — 627
The Munich Agreement	630
The beginning of the Second World War	634

Objective India — 650
The Sri Aurobindo Ashram in peril — 653
'Where is Hitler now…?' — 661

Acknowledgements — 667

Index — 669

A race possessed inhabited those parts.
A force demoniac lurking in man's depths
That heaves suppressed by the heart's human law,
Awed by the calm and sovereign eyes of Thought,
Can in a fire and earthquake of the soul
Arise and, calling to its native night,
Overthrow the reason, occupy the life
And stamp its hoof on Nature's shaking ground...
>   Sri Aurobindo, *Savitri*

Who, if I screamed, might hear me from the realms
of the angels? And supposed one touched
of a sudden my heart: I would perish because of
his stronger presence. For Beauty is but
the dawning of Terror, hardly endurable,
and we admire it so because, impassive, it spurns
to undo us. Every angel is terrible.
>   Rainer Maria Rilke, *Duineser Elegien*

Possessions die, clans die;
You will die like them.
One thing, I know, lives forever:
The fame and the deeds of the dead.
>   Hávamál, old-Nordic saga

PART ONE
When Hitler became the Führer

1

Turnabout

> *"I guarantee you, gentlemen, that the impossible always succeeds. What is most improbable is most certain".*
>
> Adolf Hitler

A corporal watching mice

The corporal woke up rather early in the morning, before the start of his daily routine. As he had nothing else to do, he amused himself by throwing bread crumbs at the mice which were the regular visitors of his small room, and watched them playing with the crumbs or fighting for them. The First World War – the so-called "Great War" – was over, and the future of the corporal, who had no ties with relatives or friends, looked very bleak indeed.

He had not come back marching among the endless grey, weary throngs of soldiers carrying the smell of mud, gun powder and rotten human flesh in the folds of their uniforms. For shortly before the armistice he had been blinded by gas near Wervik, on the French-Belgian border, and transported far northwards to a military hospital at Pasewalk, in Pommerania. There he had touched the depths of his ordeal when hearing the announcement that the fighting had stopped on 11 November, that Germany had lost the war, that the

Kaiser and all German princes had abdicated, and that a German republic had been proclaimed. Now he was waiting in Munich, in the barracks of what remained of his regiment, to be demobilized.

Although Austrian by birth and still by nationality, Adolf Hitler had, in August 1914, been allowed to enlist in the 16th Bavarian Reserve Infantry Regiment, the "List Regiment". He had served most honourably from the first weeks of the war until the last days, a full four years. As a battle dispatch runner (*Gefechtsmeldegänger*, to use his own designation) in the regimental headquarters he had participated in a great number of murderous battles in France and Belgium; he had escaped death narrowly on several occasions, and was awarded the Iron Cross Second and First Class for bravery. "Nobody who has known [Hitler] from nearby will doubt his courage", testified the Adjutant of the Regiment later on. "In the field he has proved himself to be a brave, exceptionally reliable dispatch runner who really deserved the Iron Cross First Class, and who several times had been mentioned for it before he was awarded with it. He was the example of the unknown soldier who quietly and unassumingly performed his duty".[1]

The war had been "the most unforgettable and greatest time of his earthly life"[2]; as Hitler himself would write, he had been "passionately happy to be a soldier". He was now twenty-nine years old. What would become of him? He had no prospects, no future. Therefore he did everything possible to postpone his demobilization, for the army still gave him a bunk to sleep on and a chunk of bread to eat. Once on his own, he could only slide back into his dreams of becoming a great architect, while having to earn a living selling water colour paintings of picturesque buildings and monuments. For that was what he had done in Munich before the outbreak of the war, as it was what he had done in Vienna, where he had led the

---

All translations of non-English texts are by the author.
[1] Anton Joachimsthaler: *Hitlers Weg begann in München 1913-1923*, p. 154.
[2] Christian Zentner: *Adolf Hitlers 'Mein Kampf' – Eine kommentierte Auswahl*, p. 65.

life of a tramp. "He always looked so starved", remembered people who had known him at the time.

He might have to change into civilian clothes any day now. War heroes there were aplenty. Nobody cared for the columns of bedraggled soldiers, ill-fed and shabbily clothed, still carrying their weapons, with the reflection of unspeakable horrors and death in their eyes, moving through a civilian world they no longer recognized and deeply despised. The food situation in Germany remained so bad that nobody cared about the starvation of others. A few crumbs could be spared for the mice, though. "Since I regularly woke up before five o' clock in the morning", wrote Hitler in *Mein Kampf*, "I had got into the habit of putting a few left-overs or crusts of bread on the floor for the mice which amused themselves in my little room, and watching the droll little beasts chasing around after these choice morsels. I had known so much poverty in my life that I was well able to imagine the hunger, and hence also the pleasure, of the little creatures".[3]

But, lo and behold ... not that many years later there stood that selfsame Adolf Hitler, triumphantly, as the new Chancellor of Germany on the balcony of the Reich Chancellery in Berlin, acclaimed by thousands of enthusiastic German citizens! And then he stood, all by himself and with the Iron Cross First Class on his chest, high above huge, neatly drawn up columns of uniformed Germans on the Zeppelin Field in Nuremberg. They hailed and revered him as their Leader, their *Führer*, even as their Messiah, who had come to make them great again, greater than they had ever been before in their history, rulers of the earth. *Deutschland über alles, über alles in der Welt.* The one-time desperate corporal-without-a-future had become "Leader of the nation, Supreme Commander of the Armed Forces,

---

[3] Adolf Hitler: *Mein Kampf*, p. 199. The English translation of this book here used as the basic text is the early but anonymous translation published by Jaico Publishing, New Delhi. However, all quotations have been checked against a copy of the 1939 German impression by the *Zentralverlag der NSDAP*, Munich.

Head of Government and Supreme Executive Chief, Supreme Judiciar and Leader of the [NSDAP] Party".[4]

Not only had he become master of life and death in the country he ruled, where his will was law and his word gospel truth, he also "changed the map of Europe, destroyed empires, and promoted the rise of new powers, evoked revolutions, and brought the colonial age to an end".[5] The "man from nowhere" united Austria with Germany and entered as conqueror into Prague, Warsaw and Paris. He conquered, enslaved and killed – and intended to conquer more, kill more and enslave more.

How had this come to pass? How had the former Austrian corporal, once compared to a worn out stray dog, reached such a pinnacle of power that Joachim Fest could write: "If Hitler had succumbed to an assassination or an accident at the end of 1938, few would hesitate to call him one of the greatest German statesmen, the consummator of Germany's history"?[6]

Libraries have been written about Hitler and Nazi Germany, yet several of the best-known and most widely read historians agree that he remains enigmatic. "The more extensive the material at our disposal and the greater the historical distance, the more puzzling Hitler seems to become", writes Christian von Krockow.[7] Allan Bullock, author of such essays like *Hitler – A Study in Tyranny* and *Hitler and Stalin – Parallel Lives*, admits in a conversation: "The more I learn about Hitler, the harder I find it to explain ... I can't explain Hitler. I don't believe anybody can."[8] And to H.R. Trevor-Roper "after fifty years Adolf Hitler remains a frightening mystery".[9]

---

[4] J.P Stern: *Hitler – The Führer and the People*, p. 4.
[5] Joachim Fest: *Hitler* (1974 ed.), p. 754.
[6] Id., p. 9.
[7] Christian von Krockow: *Hitler und seine Deutschen*, p. 7.
[8] Ron Rosenbaum: *Explaining Hitler – The Search for the Origins of His Evil*, pp. xv and 68.
[9] Id., p. xv.

"At one time I have within myself chosen my way in spite of totally inimical surroundings", said Adolf Hitler, "and I, an unknown and nameless man, have kept walking until the final success. Often declared no longer existent and always wished to be non-existent, in the end I was the victor."[10]

There must have been a time "when Hitler became Hitler", when the nonentity turned into a seer and a politician who, in a very short time, accomplished feats deemed impossible: wipe out the humiliation of the Versailles Treaty, build up a prostrate and despondent Germany, and unify the country into an efficient war machine for his megalomaniac and criminal overt and covert goals. There must have been a source of the power supporting this rootless, often ridiculed and always underestimated man to build up a powerful and ruthless political party, inspiring him to overcome the most critical situations, and impelling him to take his stand above all those superior to him inside and outside Germany. There must have been a fountainhead of the evil that through this man tried to ravage humanity and make it regress into a state of barbarism supposed to belong definitively to the past.

Germany in turmoil

"Caste" is generally associated with India and fossilized backwardness. Little does the common awareness in the West realize that caste did, and to a considerable extent still does, determine the patterns of its social structures. In the Middle Ages – not so very long ago – caste was a fact of life. There was the Catholic Church with its clergy (*brahmins*); there was the nobility with its feudal hierarchy (*kshatriyas*); there was the upcoming and very diligent class of the merchants (*vaishyas*); and last and very much least there was the class of the workers (*shudras*), mostly serfs without any rights, on a par with the animals and other possessions.

---

[10]In Joachim Köhler: *Wagners Hitler – Der Prophet und sein Vollstrecker*, p. 418.

Because of the Renaissance this social pyramid, which had shaped the Western outlook on life for centuries, was put into question, together with everything else in life. Acquiring the ideals of the Enlightenment – among them equal rights for all human beings – the "third estate", the merchant or bourgeois class, grew conscious of itself. The French Revolution would be the revolution of this "third estate". To work out the impetus of its ideas the revolution of 1789 needed subsequent revolutions in the nineteenth century, the high time of the bourgeoisie, of reason, liberalism, materialism and progress. These subsequent revolutions (in 1830, 1848 and 1870) were made necessary by the resistance of the clergy and the nobility, fighting for their survival, and because of the resistance to any kind of change in the nature of the human being.

But what about the "fourth estate", the class of labourers, servants and peasants, of the workers of all kinds? They too were human beings, after all, and therefore entitled to equal rights like anybody else. When in parallel with the unexpected French Revolution a no less surprising Industrial Revolution came about, the role of the workers, of the *shudras*, grew in importance: they were the manpower with which to make that gigantic industrial development possible. Fed up with their peasants' existence, the toilers of the land left their ploughs and their cows and migrated to the towns, expecting heaven but stumbling into a hell worse than their soil-bound labour. They became the "proletariat". Only the blind could fail to see that this down-trodden, struggling, exploited human masses would soon arise in an effort to take their due place in humanity, that they would strive for an equal footing with those who had for so long used and abused them.

After a preparation and build-up of almost a century, the "proletariat" resolutely took the fore of the stage of history in the Russian Revolution of 1917. The German Army High Command, by that time de facto rulers of the country, had supported the Russian revolutionaries in the hope that the collapse of tsarist Russia would free them from the burden of their eastern front, and allow them to deal a decisive blow to the Allies in the west. Their calculations proved almost correct, for the German "spring offensive" in 1918, made possible because of the Peace Treaty of Brest-Litovsk, threw the Allies back and even threatened Paris again, creating the exhilaration of impending victory among the population in Germany. But the Allies recovered, partly thanks to the fresh American troops, and from 8 August, Germany's "black day", the Hindenburg-Ludendorff duo knew that defeat was inevitable and informed their Kaiser accordingly.

All this has a direct impact on our story. The German proletariat, represented by the "German Socialist Party" and the more radical Marxist "German Independent Socialist Party" – which would soon become the "German Communist Party" – formed a considerable part of the population. The German Socialist Party had in the 1912 general election, just before the war, won the highest number of votes. This had caused unease and fear among the traditional classes who were, in that Prussian dominated country, extremely aware of their social status, in other words, class-conscious. There was place for the workers beneath them, not beside them, and surely not above them as members of a government, administrators, or whatever. Germany had not assimilated the ideals of the Enlightenment; it had remained a Prussian, autocratic, hierarchically structured society where all looked up to those above and down on those below.

Yet the war had shattered many a certainty. The Germans felt that the Bolshevik revolution in Russia threatened their existence directly. Had the Marxist doctrine not predicted that Germany, the foremost industrialized country in Europe with a massive proletariat, would be the country best prepared for the great proletarian revolution? And did the Russian Bolshevik leaders not do everything in their might to light the fuse of revolution in other countries, especially in Germany? Russian refugees arrived in droves in Berlin, Hamburg, Leipzig, Munich, every one of them with his or her tales of horror about the Reds, and with dire warnings. Along with them infiltrated Bolshevist agents, teleguided by the Third International, and in the eyes of the German Marxists adorned with the halo of heroes who had accomplished a historical feat that would change the world.

The traditional German higher and middle classes were, in the last months of 1918, more fanatically nationalistic than ever, misled as they were by the propaganda of the Supreme Army Command and the narrowness of their own convictions. The hell of the battlefields they knew only from hearsay. But so many young men would not come home anymore; the food was scarce and procuring it often the main occupation in life; the tension of the war was hard to bear and gnawed at the roots of all certainties. The Left, less socially inhibited and incited by the events in Russia, no longer hesitated to go on strike at the end of October and in the beginning of November 1918.

Then came the coup in Munich: Kurt Eisner, a Jewish journalist, proclaimed Bavaria a Socialist Republic on 7 November. The Wittelsbach king, Ludwig III, abdicated that very day, the first of all eighteen still ruling German princes to do so. (Kaiser Wilhelm II would follow suit on 9 November. It had been one of the peace conditions formulated by the American President, Woodrow Wilson, that all authoritarian and military structures and institutions in Germany should be abolished.) Eisner, a bearded intellectual who did not look the part of a revolutionary, was not a fanatic; he was a pacifist, idealistic-humanitarian socialist, carried forward by the enthusiasm of his comrades and the war-weariness of many different-minded but starving citizens. Bavaria would be governed by a council of inexperienced workers, soldiers and farmers who had to improvise an administration in harsh circumstances. The most inexperienced was Eisner himself. This he proved soon at a socialist congress in Bern, where before the world he declared Germany guilty of starting the war, thereby pronouncing his own death sentence.

Like a worn out stray dog

This was the Munich corporal Hitler arrived in on 21 December 1918, discharged from the hospital at Pasewalk. He was assigned to the Reserve Battalion of the 2nd Infantry Regiment, a battalion marked for immediate demobilization. But demobilization was what Hitler tried to prevent by any means for, as we have seen, he really "stood before the Void".[11] He managed to be detailed to a prisoners of war camp in Traunstein, between Munich and Salzburg, to guard the last Russian and French soldiers there before they were sent home. Towards the end of January 1919 Hitler was back in Munich, where he joined a military guard unit at the Central Railway Station.

He was also elected *Vertrauensmann*, i.e. representative, of the lower ranks of his battalion. This is not surprising considering his war record and the impression made by his occasional outbursts of oratory, when provoked, which testified to a certain level of intellectual capability. But his election is startling because the whole army garrison in Munich was governed by Eisner's socialists, which means that Hitler went along with the Leftists, something diametrically opposed to his later beliefs. He even became a member of the propaganda section of the Soldiers Council. And when Kurt Eisner had been murdered, on 21 February, *Vertrauensmann* Hitler was one of the hundred thousand mourners following the remains of the Jewish prime minister to the burial ground.[12]

"With a probability bordering on certainty Hitler has, till May 1919, chosen the side of the people [i.e. the socialists] of whom he later untruthfully said 'that already in November 1918 he had found out that they possessed no honour'".[13] Many students of Hitler's life have been surprised by these recently discovered facts because they took for granted Hitler's statement in *Mein Kampf* that "the

---

11 Anton Joachimsthaler, op. cit., p 184.
12 Ralph Reuth: *Hitler – Eine politische Biographie*, p. 79.
13 Anton Joachimsthaler, op. cit., p. 203.

granite foundation" of his world view had already been laid in his years in Vienna (from 1907 till 1913). But Brigitte Hamann and others in her tracks have shown "how much *Mein Kampf* is political propaganda and how little a biography".[14] In the beginning of 1919 corporal Hitler would have done anything to stay another day in the army, for he had nowhere else to go.

"He was after the First World War one of the many thousands of ex-soldiers who roamed the streets looking for work ... At that time Hitler was willing to accept a job from anybody who was kind towards him. He would have worked as eagerly for a Jewish or French employer as for an Aryan", a certain ex-captain Mayr remembered later on. And he added: "When I first met him he resembled a worn out stray dog looking for a master"[15] – words he would come to regret.

The Russian Revolution had been a two-phase event: in February 1917 the socialist, humane Menshevik revolution with Alexander Kerensky as its leader; in October of the same year the Marxist, ruthless, Bolshevik takeover led by Lenin. A similar evolvement was tried out in Berlin, where the radical Spartacists led by Karl Liebknecht and Rosa Luxemburg tried to take over from the socialist government. But the Spartacist coup was put down by the socialist government with the help of *Freikorps*, independent and ultra rightist armed units mainly consisting of war veterans and commanded by charismatic officers with condottiere allures. In Munich, though, the communist follow-up to Eisner's socialist government succeeded, albeit only for a short time. The "dictatorship of the proletariat" was proclaimed on 7 April 1919 and a government of army and workers councils installed, after the Russian example of the "soviets". A "Red Army", under a twenty-three year old sailor, would be this government's power base to change German society into a proletarian paradise.

---

[14] Brigitte Hamann: *Hitlers Wien – Lehrjahre eines Diktators*, p. 22.
[15] Anton Joachimsthaler, op. cit., p. 184.

It should be kept in mind that Germany in those early post-war months was in complete distress. The shock of the unexpected defeat, the thousands of jobless, aimless military men hanging about everywhere, the new social-democratic regime, called "The System", felt as foreign to the body of the "real" Germany and resented from the very beginning, and above all, the food shortage undiminished because of the continuing Allied blockade – all this contributed to the mental and physical disarray. Like Eisner and his political amateurs the young communist leaders proved too small for their boots. At first it was an enjoyable game for them to scare and steal from the clergy, the rich, the petty bourgeois and all those who were considered enemies of the people. But soon the blundering councils succeeded in causing such confusion that the *Reichswehr* (the national Army), supported by several Free Corps units, had little trouble defeating them. By 3 May the last Red resistance was crushed, often brutally.

This object lesson in "dictatorship of the proletariat" so much increased the fear and passionate rejection of Communism, and of Leftism in general, that Catholic Bavaria now became a haven for all factions, ideologies, groupings and individuals of the Right. Moreover, and not less important: Bavaria would never forget that, like Eisner, several of the most active leaders of the Red Councils had been Jews, and that at the command of those Jews German nationalist hostages had been murdered. This was at a time that the leadership of the Russian Revolution, including Lenin, was generally (but incorrectly) supposed to be entirely Jewish, that the Jew Bela Kun had started a short-lived Marxist revolution in Hungary, that the Jews Rosa Luxemburg, Leo Jogisches and others had sparked off the Spartacist revolt, and that Marxist revolts were brewing throughout Germany. The more the stomachs hungered, the more the ingrained German anti-Semitism found abundant nourishment.

Captain Mayr's discovery

After the obliteration of the Munich Republic of Councils, an officer appeared in the city who was to play an important part in the making of Adolf Hitler: Staff Captain Karl Mayr. It was the intention of the central government in Berlin as well as of the Army High Command to wipe out all Leftist indoctrination in the minds of the soldiers and to replace it with correct patriotic, nationalist ideas. To this end an "information service", in fact an intelligence and propaganda section, was created by Army Group 4 which covered the whole of Bavaria under the command of the powerful General Arnold von Möhl. Captain Mayr was appointed chief of this propaganda section.

Mayr, "very much radical Right", was "ambitious, intelligent, a talented organizer and politically involved"; he was also an opponent of the Weimar Republic and an anti-Semite.[16] His network of connections seems to have extended to the most influential centres of German society. He was extraordinarily active, brimming with ideas and initiatives, and his influence was much greater than his rank and function would suggest. Not only did he have access to the highest levels of the Army through General von Möhl, with whom he stood on a confidential footing, he undoubtedly had direct links with the mighty Pan-German League and the *Germanenorden*, two organizations we will meet further on.

Soon Mayr's attention was drawn to Corporal Hitler. Not only had Hitler been elected representative of his battalion under the socialist regime, he had also been elected "deputy battalion representative" under the regime of the communist soldier councils. Then, after the Republic of Councils was crushed, in a new turnabout Hitler surprisingly became a member of a commission of inquiry, whose task it was to report on the patriotic fidelity of the soldiers of his battalion under the ephemeral communist regime, to which he himself had acquiesced! No doubt, he was able to turn with the wind and go to any end in order to stay in the army. But his comrades in arms undeniably looked up to him; and as he also had the gift of the gab, Mayr put his name on the list of participants in a "oratory

---

[16]Id., p. 225.

course" for army propagandists, to be held at Munich University from 5 till 12 June 1919.

The teachers of the course were learned doctors and professor-doctors like Karl Alexander von Müller, Karl von Bothmer and Michael Horlacher. Their themes were "the political history of the war"; "Socialism in theory and practice"; "our agricultural situation and the peace conditions"; and "the relation between internal and external politics".[17] It was there that Hitler for the first time heard educated intellectuals speak on subjects which interested him, and that he learned how those opinions could be fitted together into something like a coherent opinion or world view. The general trend of the lectures was obligatorily social-democratic, as the government was social-democratic, but the deeper tendency was doubtlessly nationalistic, pan-German and anti-Semitic.

Hitler's mind, at the age of thirty, was not a blank sheet, of course. During his youth in Austria he had imbibed the pan-Germanic ideas of his father, of his history teacher Leopold Pötsch and of Georg von Schönerer, and anti-Semitism was part of the air one breathed there. Besides, young Adolf had always been interested in politics, mainly to voice his spiteful disagreement. In Vienna he had attended sessions of the Austrian parliament and avidly read the newspapers in the cafés, as well as any tract or pamphlet he could lay his hand on. Now the physical presence and the discourse of the esteemed doctors and professors made a lasting impression upon him and put many of his opinions into context.

The lectures were followed by discussion groups. Here Hitler came into his own. He had always been what one might call a profuse "monologist" when agitated, unstoppably pouring the flood of his words over any individual listener as if addressing a crowd. His one close friend during the days in Linz and Vienna, August Kubizek, tells in his reminiscences about Adolf's frequent outbursts of oratory,

---

[17]Id., p. 229.

and many of Hitler's companions in the asylum and in the trenches recalled how easily he could be egged on into a thundering diatribe when his opinions were contradicted. Hitler now got the occasion to express his newly acquired knowledge in the discussion groups. Speaking was no longer an idiosyncrasy; it became his assigned duty as an army propagandist who had to educate wrong-thinking leftists into right-thinking German patriots.

K.A. von Müller has narrated how, after one of his lectures, his attention was drawn to a group "spellbound by a man in their midst who, with an unusually guttural voice, talked to them uninterruptedly and with increasing passion. I had the strange feeling that their excitement was caused by him and simultaneously caused him to speak in return. I saw a pale, lean face under an unmilitary strand of hair, with a clipped moustache and striking big, light blue, fanatically cold eyes".[18] When Müller pointed the man out to Mayr, the captain said casually: "Oh, that's Hitler from the List Regiment".

Hitler became Mayr's star orator. In the middle of August he was sent to Lechfeld, where there was a camp with German soldiers who had been brainwashed in Russian captivity; they were to be mentally turned around before being released into civilian life. The camp had a permanent unit of Mayr's "information service" under another trained propagandist, Rudolf Beyschlag, a non-commissioned officer who was to be Hitler's superior for the duration of this assignment. The themes of the lectures were essentially the same as those taught to Mayr's trainees during the course in oratory. Hitler was praised by his audiences as "a very good and passionate speaker", "an outstanding and temperamental orator".[19] It was to this period that he himself referred when he wrote in *Mein Kampf* the often quoted words: "I could speak". What he meant was not that he could formulate and orally express his thoughts, for he had done that in

---

[18] Christian von Krockow, op. cit., p. 52.
[19] Anton Joachimsthaler, op. cit., p. 243.

countless monologues since his early youth. He meant that he was able to carry along an audience, and this would be of crucial importance for his and Germany's future.

Another noteworthy fact during his mission in Lechfeld was that Hitler, for the first time, began to attack the Jews, so vehemently that he had to be restrained by his superiors, who, however much they might agree with him, were after all serving a social-democratic government. The commandant of the Lechfeld camp wrote to Army Group 4: "Concerning a very beautiful, clear and temperamental lecture on capitalism by Corporal Hitler, who on this occasion touched upon the Jewish question ... The thought was uttered that the [propaganda] section had been founded by Gruppenkommando Möhl to function as a military unit. Yet as the Jewish problem was very clearly expounded [by Hitler] with special consideration of the Germanic standpoint, then such a discussion could easily give the Jews a pretext to label the lectures anti-Jewish propaganda. I found it therefore necessary to instruct that the utmost care should be taken in the discussion of the problem, and that too explicit references to the race that is foreign to the German people should be omitted as much as possible".[20]

Although anti-Semitism was imprinted upon the German mind, the subject was not mentioned by the instructors at Munich University. It has, moreover, been shown by Brigitte Hamann that Hitler was not an actively conscious anti-Semite during his Vienna years, where he had friendly relations with Jews among the inmates of the men's hostel and among the shopkeepers who sold his water colour paintings. Where, then, or by whom had he been infected with these vehement anti-Judaic feelings?

That by that time he was regarded an authority on anti-Semitic matters is documented by a short letter written to him by Captain Mayr on 10 September 1919. In this letter Mayr asks Hitler to

---

[20] Id., p. 244.

answer a question put to him in writing by Adolf Gemlich, another of Mayr's military propagandists. The question was: "What is the attitude of the social-democratic government towards the Jews? Are the Jews also included in the socialist programme of "equal rights" of the peoples, even so when one considers them to be a threat to the *Volkstum* [the people as a race]"?[21] In his request to answer in his place Captain Mayr addresses his subordinate, a corporal, as *Sehr verehrter Herr Hitler*. This is usually translated as "Dear Sir". But the tone of the German formula is much more reverential, for it says literally: "Very respected Mister Hitler". Joachim Fest, a German, finds this "an unusual salutation from a captain to a corporal",[22] and so does Werner Maser, also a German, who writes that it is "unusually respectful".

Hitler's answer not only reflects the sources of his newly acquired thoughts, it also documents the fact that his thinking had now been ordered into a pattern which will remain, as far as the Jews are concerned, the basis of his ideology, his real "granite foundation", till the last day of his life. There is the foreignness and the danger represented by the Jewish people; there is the affirmation that the Jews are a race, not a religious community; and there is the statement that the ultimate aim of the struggle against the Jews must be, "unshakeably", their elimination – whatever this word my have meant to Hitler in 1919.[23]

Mayr has written that he had daily contact with Hitler for more than fifteen months, ie from June 1919 till September of the next year. Hitler, acting on his innate despotic impulse, had already managed to push Beyschlag aside. He was "a frequent visitor to the War Ministry and ranked as a member of Mayr's political staff ... Mayr decided to use his discovery for greater things".[24] Indeed, on

---

[21]Id., p. 232 (facsimile).
[22]Joachim Fest, op. cit., 115.
[23]Werner Maser: *Adolf Hitler – Legende, Mythos, Wirklichkeit*, p. 177.
[24]Heinz Höhne: *The Order of the Death's Head*, p. 17.

12 September 1919, Hitler was sent to a conference room in a Munich beer house to report on a small loge-like group that called itself "German Workers Party" (DAP). As the saying goes: The rest is history.

A comparison of the dates is telling. Mayr's respectful request to his corporal was written on 10 September; Hitler's answer was sent to Gemlich on 17 September; Hitler's first contact with the DAP, founded by the Thule Society, took place on 12 September. Clearly Hitler had covered a considerable stretch on the road of his ambitions since 6 June, the day Captain Mayr had reacted so casually: "Oh, that's Hitler from the List Regiment" and the day he treated his corporal with such respect. "The process [of the formation of Hitler's ideology] started in the year 1919, or becomes for the first time discernible in this year. In no earlier notes does one find even the smallest hint of the later concepts ... One may even conclude that Hitler did not have any interest in politics [before 1919] ... One is not even sure that at that time he was already an anti-Semite ..." (Eberhard Jäckel[25])

It is evident that in the summer months of 1919 an important change took place in Hitler's life. Sebastian Haffner calls this period "an unexplainable gap". Konrad Heiden writes: "In these months a transformation took place in Hitler", and he wonders about "the mysterious circumstances that transformed him".[26] John Lukacs is of the same opinion: "The year 1919 was a decisive milestone, indeed a turning point in [Hitler's] life".[27] While Ian Kershaw writes that "without Captain Mayr's 'talent spotting' Hitler might never have been heard of".[28] "In this period in Munich lies the key of Hitler's entrance into politics",[29] confirms Joachim Fest. Finally, there is

---

[25]Eberhard Jäckel: *Hitlers Weltanschauung*, pp. 130-31.
[26]Konrad Heiden: *The Führer* (1999 ed.), p. 77.
[27]John Lukacs: *The Hitler of History*, p. 49.
[28]Ian Kershaw, *Hitler – 1889-1936 Hubris*, p. 128.
[29]Joachim Fest, op. cit., p. 177.

Hitler's own confirmation in 1941, in the course of a conversation in which he unwittingly contradicted several untruthful statements in *Mein Kampf*: "My programme originated in 1919".[30] By "programme" he did not mean the NSDAP party programme, which was composed in 1920, but the basics of his personal thinking, his ideology.

---

[30]Henry Picker: *Hitlers Tischgespräche im Führerhauptquartier*, p. 76.

2

Masters

The Thule people were the first to sacrifice their lives for the swastika.

Hermann Gilbhard

"It was to members of Thule that Hitler first came, and Thule members were the first who allied themselves with Hitler".[1] Rudolf von Sebottendorff wrote this statement in his book *Before Hitler Came*, published in Germany in 1933, shortly after Hitler had become Chancellor. Many years before, in 1917, Sebottendorff had founded the Thule Society in Munich and been its Grand Master till 1919, during the eventful months of the Red governments of Eisner and the Republic of Councils. He had then left Germany and found a new home in Turkey. That Sebottendorff had not followed Hitler's ascent to power from nearby may have been the reason for the ignorance or candour with which he published *Before Hitler Came*. He should have known that Hitler never acknowledged any debt

---

[1] Rudolf von Sebottendorff: *Bevor Hitler kam*, Roland Faksimile edition (2000), p. 8.

towards a former helper, guide, teacher or superior – with the exception of Richard Wagner and Dietrich Eckart. Those who dared to remind him of such a kind of relationship soon found themselves muzzled and in some cases, dumped into a concentration camp. Which is what happened to Sebottendorff. But he was lucky: Rudolf Hess, once a member of Thule and now a man near the top in the Third Reich, saw to it that his former Grand Master was set free, with the suggestion that the air outside Germany might be better for his health.

The *Thule-Gesellschaft* was a secret society, extensively and sometimes fancifully treated in books on the occult side of Nazism. This must be the reason that until recently academic historians have approached the subject which caution. Peter Levenda writes: "To hear most historians speak of the *Thule-Gesellschaft*, one would think that it was a slight aberration, an anomaly that does not deserve close scrutiny".[2] Yet the body of historical facts concerning the Thule Society is so large that it must be accorded its proper place in any history of Hitler's life and of Nazism. Without this information an indispensable episode in Hitler's life remains lacking. It may therefore be apposite to state at this point of our tale that the facts in the present chapters are historical, not the result of freewheeling fancy.

Austrian visionaries

Around 1880 a remarkable change took place in the European consciousness. The acquisitions of the Enlightenment had already been questioned by the Romantic Movement at the beginning of the century. Now a powerful wave of vitalism and intuitionalism restated the rights of the emotional components of human nature. This change was initiated in the arts, foremost by the Impressionist "light

---

[2] Peter Levenda: *Unholy Alliance*, p. 46.

explosion". In quick succession Nietzsche, Freud, Bergson and Proust – to name only a few of the important innovators – appeared on the cultural scene. All contended the sole rule of reason; the human being burst out of the straitjacket of the rational mind. The result was that it felt, in some ways, disoriented in its newly acquired liberty, while in other ways it felt dizzy because of the new perspectives and possibilities. It was the time that the coming of one kind of "superman" after another was proclaimed to be the destiny of humanity. Nietzsche's "re-evaluation of all values" created a euphoria and simultaneously a deep fear, for most customary and trusted beacons seemed to vanish.

An important role in this cultural upheaval – which would create the tension that led to the First World War – was played by the Theosophical Society, founded by H.P. Blavatsky and H.S. Olcott in 1875. That Theosophy spread so fast, and so widely, proves that it provided some answers to deep and unfulfilled needs in the human being. The human being is more complex than thought by Descartes and his philosophical progeny: rationalism, materialism, positivism, scientism, reductionism. In the human being there is of course the material part, but there is also the vital part with the life forces, the mental part (considered no more than an "epiphenomenon" by Descartes) and a soul. Theosophy borrowed from the Eastern wisdom a view of the multi-layered nature of our being, of the corresponding layers of the cosmos, and of a history of mankind going back much further than the improbably short time span accepted by the academic sciences at present. Reincarnation gave a new value to the small number of years of the human life, suggesting that it had meaning after all. And, not least, Theosophy proposed a new, no longer anthropomorphic image of God, asserting that all was "That" and that That could be directly contacted and even realized, for that That was the living Presence in the soul.

"The modern German [and Austrian] occult revival owes its inceptions to the popularity of Theosophy in the Anglo-Saxon world during the 1880s", writes Nicholas Goodrick-Clarke.[3] He situates this revival in the period 1880-1910 and notes that Theosophy "made a deeper impression in Germany than in other European countries". The reason was that in Germany a strong opposition was growing against the ideals of the Enlightenment due to the particular development of a German nationalistic spirit, in the margin as it were and even contrary to modern cultural acquisitions in other West-European countries. This specifically German path is sometimes called *Sonderweg*, Germany's "road apart".

In Austria were invented some fundamental beliefs and convictions which would lead to Nazism. This is not always recognized because this beautiful country is usually associated with Tyrolean hats, yodelling and *Gemütlichkeit*, and also because in the tense political situation between the post-war occupying powers Austria escaped its own Nuremberg trial. The feeling of cultural and racial superiority in the Austrian Germans, leading to pan-German fanaticism, was the result of the hostile relations between the various races and language communities in the ever less governable empire-cum-kingdom of Austria-Hungary. There the German speaking population had to fight for the preservation of their leadership status against no less patriotic or racist Czechs, Slovaks, Poles, Ruthenians, Slovenes, Serbo-Croats, Italians, and others. "In Vienna there lived at the time more Czechs than in Prague, more Jews than in Jerusalem and more Croats than in Zagreb".[4]

The new ideas of Theosophy together with the growing self-awareness of the Austrian Pan-Germans explain in part a figure like Guido von List (1848-1919). List was a romantic visionary whose writings glorified a mythic Germanic past. The Ario-Germanic god-man was the highest type humanity had ever produced and would

---

[3] Nicholas Goodrick-Clarke: *The Occult Roots of Nazism – Secret Aryan Cults and Their Influence on Nazi Ideology*, p. 18.
[4] Anton Joachimsthaler: *Hitlers Weg began in München*, p. 40.

again become "the highest form of life ever to evolve in the universe".[5] The Ario-Germanics had known an exoteric and an esoteric form of religious practice, the former Wotanist, the latter Armanist. In the far North the line of Armanist initiates had continued to exist uninterruptedly from times immemorial until the present day. This elite, the *Armanenschaft*, had to be revived and made conscious of its sacred task to create the future race of god-men.

List supported his visions with pseudo-historical narrations, created interest in the remains of the great Ario-Germanic past in the monuments, landscapes and archaeological discoveries of central and northern Europe, wrote volumes about the sacred runes – and doing all that revivified the anti-Roman, anti-Catholic sentiments which had been present in the German conscience from times before Luther. The titles of his books are instructive: *German Mythological Landscapes; The Original Language of the Ario-Germanics and the Language of Their Mysteries; The Religion of the Ario-Germanics – Its Esoterics and Exoterics; The Armanenhood of the Ario-Germans; The Secret of the Runes* ...

List's influence spread widely; List Societies and secret Armanen loges were founded in many towns in Austria and still more in Germany. No doubt, his books bolstered the Germanic ego by the evocation of a glorious past and a radiant future. And in List many read for the first time about reincarnation and karma. Much that the brutish imposition of the Christian faith had suppressed in the German psyche found resonance and expression in List's visionary writings, which would become a substantial element in the *völkisch*, i.e. Germanic racist, movement. "List became virtually the guru of the pan-Germans", writes Peter Orzechowski. "In a contemporary biography he was lauded as 'the rediscoverer of age-old Aryan wisdom'. With such publicity there could be little delay before the mythical glorification of Germanhood was also spread, through the members of the List Society, in the empire of William II".[6]

---

[5]Nicholas Goodrick-Clarke, op. cit., p. 54.
[6]Peter Orzechowski: *Schwarze Magie – Braune Macht*, p. 79.

List's revelations were supported and in a way complemented by the publications of another Austrian, Jörg Lanz von Liebenfels (1874-1954). Not only was Lanz acquainted with List, Brigitte Hamann sees Lanz as his "closest disciple and follower".[7] It was Lanz who coined the term "ariosophy", applicable to his own and List's teachings (and showing the influence of theosophy). Ex-monk Lanz was also a learned student of the Bible, for the "true" understanding of which he invented a new key, and he felt a deep longing to realize the ideals of the Knights Templar, or what he supposed those ideals to have been. In later years he would found the "Order of the New Templars".

He wrote books with titles like *Theo-Zoology or the Lore of the Sodom-Apelings and the Electron of the Gods* (1905). But his most influential essays appeared in his periodical *Ostara*, actually a series of brochures on single themes. Some titles of these booklets are: *Race and Woman, and Her Preferences for the Male of the Lower Species*; *The Dangers of Women's Rights and the Necessity of a Superior Morality Based on the Right of Men*; *The Sexual and the Love Life of the Blonds and the Dark Skinned*; *Introduction to Sexual Physics*; *The Blonds as Creators of Language*... As these titles tell us, the obsessions of the former monk were more vicious than List's. He seems to have been a badly frustrated man. No wonder that one of the reasons for his expulsion from the Cistercian Order was formulated as *amori carnati captus*, meaning that he was taken by carnal love, apparently homosexual.

Lanz's fundamental revelation was the existence of an unbridgeable gap between the higher, noble, god-like beings, and the lower, monstrous, animal-like beings whom he called Chandalas, apelings or *Schrättlinge*, i.e. mongrels, monstrosities. The higher beings were "the blond Ario-heroic races of all peoples and nations". Alas, the women of these exalted beings let themselves be seduced by the mongrels who delighted in thus contaminating the blood of the

---

[7] Brigitte Hamann: *Hitlers Wien*, p. 308.

noble races. They steadily degraded all that was blond, and consequently noble, pure and creative, into the transmogrified image of themselves, nearer to the animal than to the human being. It was through the women that sin had come into the world, for they were far more prone to bestial lust than men.

The ravings of Lanz did not remain confined within an obscure group or sect. The *Ostara* was printed in great numbers and widely read. In Lanz's ideas, as in those of List, resounded the feelings of racial superiority, supported by Darwinism, but also inspired by the longing for the realization of higher ideals that were rife at that time in Germany and Austria. Such feelings were among the driving forces of the multifarious volkisch* movement, and they will form an integral part of Nazism.

It should be mentioned here that several authoritative writers give credence to Lanz's statement that Hitler was a reader of *Ostara* during his years in Vienna. Lanz himself wrote in 1932: "Hitler is one of our pupils".[8] He was, just like Sebottendorff, silenced for his impudence. The saddest fact, however, is that so many of Lanz's ideas were put into practice by Nazism, especially by Himmler's Black Knights, the SS. Lanz von Liebenfels even found pleasure in imagining that his quasi-human mongrels would be sacrificed as a holocaust, a burnt offering, to the gods. And he wrote: "Amid the jubilation of the god-men we will conquer the whole planet".[9]

The *Germanenorden* [Order of Germanic people]

It was around 1880 – an axis in European cultural history – that the self-consciousness of the Germans, not to say their superiority

---

*The German term *völkisch* is not adequately translatable. It is closely associated with "race" and with things belonging to the past, and evokes English words like "folklore", "folk music", etc. In this book a simplified spelling is adopted which leaves no doubt about the provenance and the meaning of the word.
8 Nicholas Goodrick-Clarke, op. cit., p. 192.
9 Id., p. 98.

complex, took on inflated proportions. Thanks to the statesmanship of Bismarck they had finally succeeded, in 1871, to build a German nation, which they considered to be the Second Reich. (The First Reich, the Holy Roman Empire of the German Nation, had ended in 1806.) But the more the Germans became convinced of their exceptional qualities as a nation, and more particularly as a race, the more they felt inclined to look down on peoples who were in their opinion less favoured by the Creator. These were also the years in which Darwinism became accepted even by religious persons, who managed to combine an outlook based on chance with the omnipotence of their God and with Providence. Social Darwinism suited racism admirably and gave it a new impetus.

That this is not one jot exaggerated may be shown by a paragraph from a propaganda leaflet of the Germanenorden: "The most highly talented and gifted race is the Nordic-Ariogermanic race, of which the main external characteristics, in their purest form and distinguishing them from all other human races, are: blond hair, blue eyes, and a rosy-white colour of the skin, together with a noble stature. This race has been, according to the most recent research, from olden times the one and only originator and owner of the noblest moral notions and of all highly developed forms of culture. It is the age-old noble race of humanity that, because of its innate gift of intelligence, richness of feeling and honour, because of its sense of justice and human benevolence, and because of its creative capacity and power of execution, is chosen to be the leader of humanity".[10] This was the fundamental belief of all German nationalists and Pan-Germans, as it was the conviction that impelled the Nazis to power and the German armies to conquer the world.

If the Germans were the best, the divinely chosen people, then one should understand that they had reason to feel annoyed by people foreign to the body of their Germanic, or Nordic, or Nordic-

---

[10] Facsimile in Detlev Rose: *Die Thulegesellschaft – Legende, Mythos, Wirklichkeit*, p. 90.

Germanic, or Ario-Germanic race. Such non-Germans there had been among them for centuries, industrious, intelligent, even occupying high places in their society: they were the Jews, now representing about one person out of every hundred in the country. Like the populations of other European nations, the Germans had a long-standing tradition of deep-seated anti-Semitism, centuries ago transmitted to them by Christianity, which taught that the Jews had killed their incarnated God, and that they had been dispersed throughout the world by way of punishment. The bigger the German ego, the less place there was for "foreigners" and the more ardent, or virulent, their anti-Semitic feelings grew.

On this well-prepared soil the *Germanenorden* was born, the brainchild of a mechanical engineer, Theodor Fritsch (1852-1933). Some consider him to have been "the most important anti-Semitic before Hitler".[11] It was Fritsch who compiled, in 1887, the *Catechism of the Anti-Semite;* its twenty-seventh impression in 1907 was renamed *Handbook of the Jewish Question* and remained till the end of the Third Reich a source of reference and inspiration for all Jew-haters. Fritsch launched the "Anti-Semitic People's Party" in 1889. In 1902 he started a periodical, the *Hammer*, which became such a success that Hammer Associations sprang up everywhere in Germany. And it was with these associations as a basis that Fritsch founded, in 1912, the *Germanenorden*. "The most important carriers of Listian ideas across the border [between Austria and Germany] were the members of the List Society in the German Reich who were involved in the founding of the *Reichshammerbund* and the *Germanenorden*", writes Goodrick-Clarke.[12] Fritsch's multiple initiatives, which found broad resonance in Germany, leave no doubt that his influence was enormous; he was the person who undertook the step to convert the vague though widespread anti-Semitic sentiments into clearly formulated anti-Semitic concepts, slogans and actions.

---

11 Words of Reginald Phelps quoted in Detlev Rose, op. cit., p. 16.
12 Nicholas Goodrick-Clarke, op. cit., p. 45.

The *Germanenorden* was a sister-organization of the *Hammerbund*; it was, in fact, its secret twin. Detlev Rose tells us: "The activists in the *Germanenorden* founded the first anti-Semitic lodge, a secret association which would consciously counteract the Jewish secret associations ... They tried to gain influence through information and instruction, in order that the control of the destiny of the Germanic countries would return into German hands".[13] For there was supposed to exist a Jewish conspiracy to obtain the mastery of the world and more specifically of Germany. This was a popular rumour long before the fake *Protocols of the Wise Men of Zion* started on its devastating career.

It is rather amazing that the Germanenorden was structured in lodges, for Freemasonry would be one of the main targets of all Germanic-minded organizations, most of all of the Nazis. The reason for this enmity was that the sources of inspiration of Freemasonry were the ideals of the Enlightenment, and that the Masons were consequently internationalist in principle. From this the Germanic zealots concluded that Freemasonry could not but be an instrument of Jewish world power. For, firstly, the Enlightenment had been a Jewish bid for power over the peoples' minds through the imposition of the rule of Reason. And secondly, internationalism was an offshoot of the Enlightenment, as were individualism, democracy, liberalism and socialism – all of which were directly or indirectly under the control of World-Jewry. Given such logic, it would not take long before the Jews would be the cause of all that ached in the world. The revered Herr Professor Treitschke had already coined the formula: "The Jews are our misfortune".

Still further went the Germanenorden in its imitation of Freemasonry by prescribing rituals which an outsider might find slightly bizarre. Such a ritual was, for instance, "The Return of the Wayward Aryan to the German Halgadom".[14] The master of the

---

[13] Detlev Rose, op. cit., pp. 19 and 25.
[14] Id., p. 24.

lodge which was to receive the wayward Aryan in its lap had to sit under a baldachin, flanked by two knights in white robes, wearing a helmet with horns and leaning on their swords. The brothers of the lodge stood before him in a semi-circle, while in the background music was played on a harmonium or piano, accompanying a choir of forest elves. The brothers sang the "Pilgrim's Choir" from Wagner's *Tannhäuser*. The ritual had to take place by candle light. And so on. This goes to show that the Germanenorden was still deeply stuck in the naïve imaginings of a romantic past. It is not that simple to create a new culture with new myths. Hitler will do much better.

Still, if a certain aspect of the Germanenorden may appear jejune, its anti-Semitism was fanatical, aggressive and malignant. The order has been the breeding ground of the horrors committed by the Nazis. And it will be in the secrecy of the order that killer commandos will be formed. According to Hermann Gilbhard: "From the ranks of the Germanenorden extremely dangerous terrorists have gone out, as proved by the murder of Matthias Erzberger. For both murderers who shot the former finance minister in August 1921 belonged, together with Manfred von Killinger who gave the order of the murder, not only to the *Organisation Consul* in Munich, but beyond it to the Germanenorden in Regensburg ..."[15]

Occult organizations are prone to splits and schisms. The reason seems to be that perception of the occult reality is a subjective experience – and who is to say who has the highest or the most powerful subjective experiences among the decision makers of the organisation? In autumn 1916 the Germanenorden broke up into two separate orders, one under Philipp Stauff, who had been a personal disciple of Guido von List, the other under Hermann Pohl. Pohl called his fiefdom "Germanenorden-Walvater" after Wotan (or Odin), "the Nordic All-Father or Walvater who determines the

---

[15] Hermann Gilbhard: *Die Thulegesellschaft – Vom okkulten Mummenschanz zum Hakenkreuz*, p. 48.

heroic death of the humans on the *Walstatt*, the battle field".[16] And it is here that we meet another of the main personages in our tale: Rudolf von Sebottendorff. For Sebottendorff came into contact with Pohl, and seems to have had such impressive credentials that shortly after the schism he was appointed Grand Master of the Bavarian province of the Germanenorden-Walvater in Munich.

Rudolf von Sebottendorff

Adam Glauer, alias Rudolf Freiherr von Sebottendorff von der Rose, was born in 1875 as the son of a locomotive driver. Machinery and all kinds of technical gadgets interested the son as much as the father, for Adam became a skilled technician; he even undertook engineering studies but never brought them to a successful end. He wanted to see the world and signed on for various technical jobs on ships with destination New York, Naples and Australia. He did not hesitate to desert one ship for another if he found the new destination more alluring. In Australia, in the year 1900, he even went on an adventurous search for gold, but had to abandon the project because of the sudden death of his partner. Soon Glauer found a new job on a ship which took him to Egypt. And it was in Cairo that a new leaf in the book of his life was turned over: in the presence of the pyramids he became interested in the reality behind the surface of things, in matters which are called by the generic name "occultism".

"Glauer began a serious study of occultism", writes Goodrick-Clarke. "His interest in exotic religions had been kindled when he saw the Mevlevi sect of whirling dervishes and visited the Cheops pyramid at El-Giza in July 1900. His companion Ibrahim told him of the cosmological and numerological significance of the pyramids and aroused Glauer's curiosity about the occult gnosis of ancient

---

[16]Otto Holzapfel: *Die Germanen – Mythos und Wirklichkeit*, p. 53.

theocracies. Hussein Pasha, his wealthy and learned host, practiced a form of Sufism and discussed these matters with Glauer. At Bursa he made the acquaintance of the Termudi family ... Old Termudi had retired from business to devote himself to a study of the Cabbala and collecting alchemical and Rosicrucian texts ... The Termudis were Freemasons ... Glauer was initiated into the lodge by old Termudi and subsequently inherited his occult library. In one of these books Glauer discovered a note from Hussein Pasha, describing the secret mystical exercises of traditional Islamic alchemists, still practised by the Baktashi sect of dervishes".[17]

In 1902 Glauer was back in Germany, but Turkey remained on his mind, the more so because his marriage and some financial matters did not turn out well. By the end of 1908 he was back in Turkey, where he "continued to study Islamic mysticism, which in his opinion shared a common Aryan source with the Germanic runes". One result of his study an essay on the Baktashi dervishes, "an antinomian mystical order widely spread and influential in Turkey and connected by legend with the origin of the Janissaries".[18] The secret organization of the Baktashi resembled that of the Freemasons; they played an important role in the transition from Ottoman absolutism to a modern Turkish state, for the revolution of the Young Turks had now established a constitutional monarchy and the rule of parliament. Glauer was, according to his own attestation, naturalized as a Turkish citizen in 1911 and adopted by a German baron who lived in Turkey, Heinrich von Sebottendorff von der Rose, whose name he would bear.

Sebottendorff returned to Germany in 1913, a year before the outbreak of the First World War. What he found there "was a materialistic land without any orientation, and that seemed to be on the verge of spiritual collapse ... the disappearance of the former simple manners and customs, seeking consolation in consumption,

---

[17] Nicholas Goodrick-Clarke, op. cit., p. 138.
[18] Id., p. 140.

empty churches from which nobody drew any confirmation of his faith anymore, the venom of jealousy and hatred ... a boom of false prophets and spiritist circles where 'hysterical women' and 'anaemic men' desperately looked for help, but became the victims of nothing but cheats. 'Nothing was too stupid not to be believed'. ..."[19]

What was it that made Sebottendorff a fervent German nationalist and anti-Semite – he who had been steeped into the occult tradition of the Near East? Maybe it was the very discipline of inner values, of concentration and the awareness of an invisible but elementary hierarchy, peculiar to all true spiritual exploration. In his reaction to the superficial Western way of living and his rejection of it, Sebottendorff actually joined the mentality of the adherents of the volkisch movement, turning back towards the past and concentrating inwardly on the glow of "the German soul". "Sebottendorff's political views were primarily inspired by a religious orientation: the antimaterialism of pan-Ottoman mysticism, alchemy, and Rosicrucianism, combined with a post-war hatred of Bolchevism, which he identified as the acme of materialism, led him to embrace anti-democratic ideas".[20] It was this kind of mental make-up which rendered Sebottendorff receptive to the writings of Guido von List and Jörg Lanz von Liebenfels (whose actual names were Guido List, without the ennobling "von", and Georg Lanz, *tout court*).

Sebottendorff, like List, was fascinated by the runes. Knowledgeable people write that the phonetic runic alphabet dates from the first centuries CE, and that it may be derived from the Etruscan script. Yet numerous runic inscriptions from prehistoric times have been found, especially in Scandinavia. "Prehistorians generally accept that the runes had possessed a symbolism over and above their phonetic value and use in writing, so that they were accordingly used for divination, the casting of lots, magical

---

[19]Rüdiger Sünner: *Schwarze Sonne – Entfesselung und Missbrauch der Mythen in Nationalsozialismus und rechter Esoterik*, p. 29.
[20]Nicholas Goodrick-Clarke, op. cit., p. 140.

invocations, and the preparation of amulets and charms".[21] List had written extensively on the runes and declared them to be sacred glyphs of the Armanen, the Ario-Germanic initiates and god-men of yore. It was this subject that brought Sebottendorff together with Philipp Stauff, a Listian and, as we have seen, since recently Grand Master of the Germanenorden-Walvater.

We have now an idea of the credentials which made Stauff place Sebottendorff at the head of the Bavarian province of the Order. Sebottendorff would go on to write two semi-autobiographical novels and no less than seven astrological textbooks between 1921 and 1923. He was one of the most looked up to astrologers at a time that "Germany counted more astrologers per square mile than anywhere else in the world". If one adds to these publications his essay on the Baktashi dervishes and his articles in the publications under his supervision, then one cannot but conclude that Sebottendorff was a person out of the ordinary. This is confirmed by the fact that so many prominent members of Munich society joined the Germanenorden. In this light, one takes with a pinch of salt statements like: "[Sebottendorff] was a political adventurer with a rather unsavoury past" (Fest[22]) and Detlev Rose's title of his chapter on Sebottendorff: "The Adventurer from Hoyerswerda"[23] (the name of his birthplace). Such partial statements put a label on Sebottendorff which hampers understanding him. Goodrick-Clarke's conclusion is much more objective, because better informed, when he writes: "Without this man it is likely that the Germanenorden and Ariosophy would have been condemned to oblivion".[24]

---

[21] See Hans von See: *Barbar, Germane, Arier – Die Suche nach der Identität der Deutschen*, p. 217, and Otto Holzapfel, op. cit., p. 138.
[22] Joachim Fest: *Hitler*, p. 115.
[23] Detlev Rose, op. cit., p. 27.
[24] Nicholas Goodrick-Clarke, op. cit., p. 133.

The Thule Society

The Germanenorden-Walvater was not in good shape when Sebottendorff took charge of the Bavarian province in 1916. This was in the middle of "the Great War" which the Germans at the outset had expected to last only a few weeks or months, but which had turned into unending hell at the front and dire hardship in the homeland. Many of the members of the Germanenorden were bearing arms, and everyone's ideals were put severely to the test. Goodrick-Clarke says that the Germanenorden was then "moribund"; one finds this confirmed in Sebottendorff, for he writes that the members who had stayed behind in the homeland must make an effort "to bring the order to life again".[25] Sebottendorff, though, proved to be a vigorous and inspirational organizer, and soon the order numbered 1500 members in Bavaria, of whom 250 were residents of Munich.

Grand Master Sebottendorff chose a new seat for the Munich chapter: the prestigious *Hotel Vier Jahreszeiten* (Four Seasons). (This hotel is still one of the topmost in the city.) The new rooms of the order were inaugurated on Christmas Day 1917. On this occasion Sebottendorff launched two periodicals, one typically titled *Runes*, for the friends and sympathizers of the order, the other called *General News of the Order*, for initiated members. Sebottendorff, who had come into money by marrying the daughter of a wealthy businessman, also bought a barely surviving newspaper, the *Münchener Beobachter*. This newspaper would later be retitled the *Völkische Beobachter* and be the flagship of the Nazis. As the emblem of the Thule Society was chosen a swastika backed by a sword and crowned with oak leafs.

The directives and goals of the Germanenorden were the following: 1. One had to be a German "who could prove the purity of his blood up to the third degree; by this would be prevented that

---

[25]Rudolf von Sebottendorff, op. cit., p. 34.

descendants from Jews would infiltrate the order"; 2. "Special value would be attached to the propaganda of racial science", understood in the Darwinian sense; 3. "The principles of the pan-Germans were to be extended to the whole Germanic race; a unification of all peoples of Germanic blood should be prepared"; 4. "The battle against everything un-German, a fight against internationalism, against the Jewishness in the Germans, should be stimulated with all possible energy". Members of the order also had to sign an attestation concerning their blood: "The signatory assures, to the best of his knowledge and conscience, that no Jewish or coloured blood flows in his veins and in those of his wife, and that there are no members of the coloured races among his forebears".[26]

On the occasion of the inauguration Sebottendorff revealed the new name of the Munich chapter of the order: *Thule-Gesellschaft*, Thule Society. From then onwards the secret Germanenorden would act in the open under this assumed name. "Since the ritual Germanenorden activities were supplemented by overt right-wing meetings the term Thule Society was adopted as a cover-name for the order to spare it the unwelcome attentions of socialist and pro-Republican elements", explains Good-Clarke.[27] This cover name sounded "sufficiently mysterious", found Sebottendorff, and at the same time "told those-who-knew what it was about".[28] The lineage of the Thule Society leaves not a shadow of doubt: Fritsch's Reichshammerbund had created a secret twin-organization, the Germanenorden, of which the Munich chapter of the Bavarian province was named "Thule Society". In Bavaria the Germanenorden and the Thule Society were one and the same.

"Thule", mentioned by some ancient historians, was a legendary country beyond the British Isles, somewhere in the misty regions of eternal ice and snow near, or at the, North Pole. The romantic

---

[26]Id., p. 42.
[27]Nicolas Goodrick-Clarke, op. cit., p. 144.
[28]Rudolf von Sebottendorff, op. cit., p. 52.

volkisch imagination turned that country into "*the* myth of the North"²⁹. It was "the homeland of the soul of the Nordic race ... the remembrance of paradise ..." (Sünner³⁰); it was "the mysterious country of origin of the Aryans, a superhuman race with god-like capacities and knowledge no longer accessible to modern man".³¹ In short, all dreams and frustrations were projected back onto that legendary country in a mythic past, with the deep longing that they might be realized again in the future of the Germanic people. "Thule was concurrently the expression of a spiritual aspiration with which many Germans reacted to the modern tendencies, experienced as puzzling and frightening, to economic liberalism, materialistic utilitarianism and scientific positivism ... Thule represented a symbolism of life-denial, eternity and solace, a symbolism of death and conquest of death at the origin of the race".³²

Thule was inevitably mixed up with the memory of Atlantis, time and again resurgent if not from the waves of the ocean then from the eddies of humanity's memory. "All Germans stand in the depth of their unconscious with one leg on Atlantis", according to Chris Amery. And Franz Wegener writes: "The Nordic-racist myth of Atlantis was understood to be the common starting point of German culture".³³ The importance of these matters for our tale will be apparent in the following lines by Sebottendorff: "One has tried to convince us, and the world still believes it today, that the place of origin of the [Aryan] people is the Asiatic highlands or Mesopotamia. The light is supposed to have come out of the East. But more recent research has shown that this supposition is wrong: Northern Europe, North Germany is the rootplace of the bearers of culture. It is there

---

[29] Detlev Rose, op. cit., p. 57.
[30] Rüdiger Sünner, op. cit., p. 41.
[31] Detlev Rose, op. cit., p. 7.
[32] Id., p. 37.
[33] Franz Wegener: *Das Atlantidische Weltbild*, pp. 11, 80. See also Jocelyn Godwyn: *Arktos – The Polar Myth in Science, Symbolism and Nazi Survival*.

that, from the dark prehistoric times till the present, streams of fertilizing German blood have poured forth, that waves upon waves have gone out to bring culture to the whole world".[34] This was much more than a personal opinion. This kind of thought was given currency in the nineteenth century by a succession of esteemed publicists, scientists as well as litterateurs, and became gospel truth to all volkisch-oriented, racist Germans in the first decennia of the twentieth century. Hitler, for one, held exactly the same opinion, as did Alfred Rosenberg, the ideological supervisor of the Third Reich and consequently of the official ideology of the Nazis.

Thule had also become familiar in the imagination of the volkisch Germans by another way: the publisher Eugen Diederichs had chosen the word "Thule" as the title of a series of twenty-four volumes of translations of the Nordic myths and sagas, the *Sammlung Thule*, published from 1911 onwards. Few means are so powerful for the spreading of an idea as the publication of a carefully selected book or collection of books at an affordable price. The Eddas and other Nordic myths, legends, songs and epics could for the first time be read and studied by a large public. Diederich's initiative strongly influenced "the turn northwards" of the German mind, away from the Orient but still more away from southern Europe, more specifically from Rome, symbol of the ancient Roman empire and its culture, and of the Catholic Church. "Thule is not the past: Thule is the eternal German soul", proclaimed a prospectus of Diederich's collection.[35]

"In the Thule Society it was like in a dovecote", reminisces Sebottendorff, "there was in Munich no association representing some national interest or other which did not find shelter in Thule".[36] As Munich, with its beer halls and its beer culture, was (and is) the

---

[34]Rudolf von Sebottendorff, op. cit., p. 47.
[35]Stefanie von Schnurbein and Justus Ulbricht (ed.): *Völkische Religion und Krisen der Moderne*, p. 245.
[36]Rudolf von Sebottendorff, op. cit., p. 62.

kind of city where social interrelation is a way of life and "everybody knows anybody else" – an important factor in the emergence of the Nazi movement – the influence of the Thule Society in the Bavarian capital must have been considerable.

Besides meetings of the nationalistic and anti-Semitic associations, Thule organized a great variety of activities of its own, for it was after all registered as "Study group of Germanic antiquity". There were lectures on runes, on German history and prehistory, on the Eddas and the Song of the Nibelungs, on other volkisch subjects accepted and promoted by the Germanenorden. Astrology, numerology, and the use of the pendulum and the dowsing-rod were studied. There were artistic evenings with vocal and instrumental recitals. The highlights of the Germanic calendar, especially the summer and winter solstices, were celebrated – all this taking place in clouds of cigar and cigarette smoke and cheered up with sausages and beer.

But there was another side to the Thule: the occult activities, covered up by the outward bustle. Thule was after all a secret society whose members were sworn to silence.[37] In the first place there were the sessions of the pseudo-masonic Germanenorden-Walvater: the return of a "wayward Aryan into Halgadom', the routine meetings of instruction and proposal of activities *extra muros*, or the promotion of a member to a higher grade within the order. And there were the meetings of Thule members interested in occultism of various sorts". We know about Sebottendorff's Middle Eastern background and he will have sought or been requested to share his knowledge. The readings of Walter Nauhaus, a close collaborator of his, "ranged from Guido von List's 'researches' to astrology, chiromancy, and the writings of Peryt Shou. In a letter to List he admitted to an interest in the Cabbala, and in Hindu and Egyptian

---

[37]See e.g. Dietrich Bronder: *Bevor Hitler kam*, p. 243. Bronder's book should not be confused with Sebottendorff's, as both have the same title.

beliefs. Like Sebottendorff, Nauhaus was fascinated by the mystical ideologies of ancient theocracies and secret cults".[38]

We find another echo of the goings-on in Thule in the memoirs of Walter Schellenberg, the SS chief of foreign intelligence: "Hitler's racial mania was one of his characteristic features. I discussed this several times with Dr. Gutbarlett [correctly: Gutberlet], a Munich physician who belonged to the intimate circle around Hitler. Gutbarlett believed in the 'sidereal pendulum', an astrological contraption, and claimed that this had given him the power to sense at once the presence of any Jew or persons of partial Jewish ancestry, and to pick them out in any group of people. Hitler ... had many discussions with him on racial questions".[39] Wilhelm Gutberlet, a medical doctor, is mentioned in Sebottendorff's list at the end of *Before Hitler Came* as a member of Thule's *Kampfbund*, one of its two Free Corps to which belonged also a certain Rudolf Hess.

Taking all this into consideration, there can hardly be any doubt that another focus of interest in Thule was spiritism. Philipp Stauff, one of the founders of the Germanenorden, "was involved in a series of spiritualist séances which claimed to have communicated with long-dead priest-kings of the old religion".[40] In Germany the evocation of otherworldly spirits was then at an all-time high because so many sought consolation in a contact with their son, father or brother killed on the battlefield. Spiritism was, moreover, more than what it is now commonly supposed to be, namely a pursuit of hair-raising sensationalism: it was the search for "a new form of transcendental experience" based on a holistic interpretation of reality.[41]

---

[38]Nicholas Goodrick-Clarke, op. cit., p. 143.
[39]Walter Schellenberg: *The Labyrinth*, p. 95.
[40]Nicholas Goodrick-Clarke, op. cit., p. 132.
[41]Moritz Bassler and Hildegard Châtelier (ed.): *Mystique, mysticisme et modernité en Allemagne autour de 1900*, pp. 115 ff.

In *Before Hitler Came*, Sebottendorff reproduces some of his writings in the Thule publications. Some brief quotations will have to do: "The German needs a *Führer* who imposes himself on him ... We don't acknowledge any international brotherhood, but only the interests of our race; we don't acknowledge the brotherhood of men, but only the brotherhood of the blood ... Struggle is the father of everything ... We don't want to be the anvil anymore, we want to be the hammer [an allusion to Fritsch's Hammerbund] ... Democracy is Jewish, any kind of democratic revolution is Jewish ... There are higher and lower races. If one attributes the same value to racial bastards, the Chandalas, as one does to the Aryans, the noble people, one commits a crime against humanity. Humanity needs leaders and leading races for its upward evolution ..."[42] Sebottendorff's own proud comment: "This was a language one had not yet heard in Munich until then." The position taken by Thule represented "a fundamental change in the attitude of the Germans towards the Jews ... Now research and proven facts leave no more doubt that the Jewish problem is a racial problem which has nothing to do with religion. The question is the following: shall we, German companions-in-race [*Volksgenossen*] let ourselves in the future be dominated politically, economically and culturally by a decreasing minority of a people of a foreign race, that feels itself as such and keeps itself carefully apart and of pure blood through law and religion, which to the Jews are one and the same?"[43]

In the first days of November 1918 sailors of the German fleet at Kiel and Wilhelmshaven, following the example of the Russian Kronstadt Revolt, rose against their officers and thereby started the German revolution. They spread through the country, inciting the population to join them in their protest against the war, the war mongers and the catastrophic consequences for Germany. They raised the red flag and preached the international revolution of the

---

[42]Rudolf von Sebottendorff, op. cit., pp. 16, 24, 25 and 47.
[43]Id., p. 179.

proletariat. On 7 November, Kurt Eisner, before a huge crowd on the *Theresienwiese* (a large open space) in Munich, declared Bavaria a social-democratic republic. The Wittelsbach king abdicated and went into exile. On 11 November Germany put down its weapons. Its "grasp for the world power" had failed, its "war of illusions" had been lost. The shock to the psyche of the Germans and their feelings of superiority was numbing. This was a chance for the Thule Society to prove that it could do more than promulgate grandiloquent proclamations.

Sebottendorff reacted immediately to the revolutionary situation in a speech to the members of Thule: "My Brothers and Sisters: Yesterday we experienced the collapse of all we were used to, of all we loved and valued. In the stead of our princes, related to us by blood, reigns our deadly enemy Juda. We do not yet know what will develop out of this chaos. We can guess it ... All of us who are involved in this struggle are in danger, for the enemy hates us with the boundless hate of the Jewish race. Now it is an eye for an eye, a tooth for a tooth ... It will be my aim as long as I am holding this iron hammer [as Grand Master] to involve the Thule in this struggle ... From today we will act ..."[44]

And act they did. Hermann Gilbhard writes: "The Thule represented, at the time of the [German] revolution, the umbrella organization of nearly all nationalistic and anti-Semitic forces in Munich".[45] Detlev Rose agrees: "The Thule Society became a centralising organization for pan-German, patriotic and similar associations and tried to harbour all groupings which became threatened by the political upheaval ... The significance of the Society in this phase of turmoil cannot be overestimated ... Many invisible threads met in the *Vier Jahreszeiten*."[46]

---

[44]Rudolf von Sebottendorff, op. cit., pp. 57 ff.
[45]Hermann Gilbhard, op. cit., p. 12.
[46]Detlev Rose, op. cit., pp. 42-43, 67.

The Thule Society ran an active propaganda campaign against the Reds and printed tens of thousands of leaflets, one of the principal means of political action at a time that the "media" were not what they have become today. Weapons, massively available after the return of the armies from the front, were bought and stacked in hidden places. The Thule Society formed its *Kampfbund Thule* in the very first days of the Republic, and the Society would equip a second fighting unit, the *Freikorps Oberland*. Both Free Corps units were commanded by demobilized officers with years of front experience; they would distinguish themselves in the liberation of Munich from the communist Republic of Councils as well as in the battles against the Russian Bolsheviks in the Baltic region. When Kurt Eisner was murdered on 21 February 1919, he was on his way to step down as president. His murderer, a young student Anton von Arco auf Valley, was allegedly connected with Thule.

Thule's anti-revolutionary endeavours became still more intensive after the communist Republic of Councils had succeeded Eisner's socialists and increased the general confusion. The Bolsheviks were a direct challenge to every single article of the Thulean creed, and they did not hesitate to requisition, ransack, imprison and kill. In a tragicomedy of errors, seven Thule members were arrested and executed, some say in a gruesome manner. One of them was Walter Nauhaus, who had proposed the swastika as Thule's emblem; others were Baron Karl von Teuchert, Countess Heila von Westarp and Prince Gustav Maria von Thurn und Taxis. The eighth person to be executed together with those anti-Semites was a Jew, professor Ernst Berger, arrested by mistake; he had insisted on being led to his execution thinking that they were taken to be interrogated and that he would be able to prove his identity. The news of those executions quickly reached the units of the *Reichswehr* (the national army) and the Free Corps who had encircled Munich and who, when executing their attack, took bloody revenge on the communists.

As Grand Master of the Thule Society, Sebottendorff did not survive very long the six months of the revolutionary events in

Munich (from November 1918 till May 1919). As he himself puts it: the socialist newspaper the *Münchener Post* had printed a pamphlet accusing him of living under a false name; of having deserted the Thule cowardly at the time of the murders; of having acquired the Turkish nationality to be exempt of military service and thus escape being sent to the front; of having embezzled certain sums of money; etc.[47] Sebottendorff claims that he refused to defend himself to prevent that the Order's secrets would be exposed, and that he preferred to take his leave: "He had to go so that the delicate plant would not be smothered" – the delicate plant, that is, of the political movement he had initiated. But this brings us to our following chapter.

---

[47]Rudolf von Sebottendorff, op. cit., p. 169.

3

MENTOR

The German soul, like the light of the suns,
Conquers the night with a new dawn!

DIETRICH ECKART

Thule reaches out

Bismarck had not been able to suppress the social-democratic upsurge, feared and hated by the reactionaries. In 1912 the Socialists obtained 110 seats in parliament, more than any other party. In 1914, carried on the wave of general euphoria with which the war was greeted, the social-democrats temporarily put aside, or betrayed, their internationalist principles, but most of them, under pressure from the Communists and the 1917 events in Russia, reverted to their original ideals when the war turned sour. Since the 1918 revolution, which made Germany from a monarchy into a republic, the country was fissured into two hostile blocks and "the menace of civil war hung like a black cloud over Germany".[1]

The Thule Society, "probably the most powerful secret organization in Germany",[2] had become aware of the potentially

---

[1] Konrad Heiden: *The Führer*, p. 89.
[2] Joachim Köhler: *Wagners Hitler – Der Prophet und sein Vollstrecker*, p. 215.

catastrophic gap between Right and Left, and decided to do something about it by trying to win over the workers for the nationalist ideas. In the following words of Hitler, in *Mein Kampf*, one hears an echo of Thule's concerns: "The bourgeoisie has misjudged the importance of the mass and therefore of the social problem. Because of this the bourgeoisie has estranged the workers from their own *Volkstum* [racehood] and driven them into the arms of their Judeo-Marxist leaders. This has been an unforgivable mistake ... It is decisive for the success of the Party to reach out in the first place to the large masses".[3]

Thule's awareness of the necessity to gain the workers for the nationalist (and anti-Semitic) cause may have been prompted by politically active elements in the Reichswehr like General Arnold von Möhl and Captain Karl Mayr. "There was a personal and ideological relationship between the Reichswehr and the Thule",[4] according to Orzechowski. This is corroborated by Joachim Köhler: "Mayr was a confidant of the Order".[5] There was, in fact, a close interaction between all rightist activists to whatever organization they belonged, be it the Germanenorden or the Reichswehr, the Pan-German League, the Free Corps, etc. In the confused and tense atmosphere of those years the Right felt that they, and with them German culture, were besieged from within by "Bolshevism". The civil war was rarely fought out in the open, but for the most part on countless fronts by secret associations in hidden ways.

To gain the proletariat for their cause, the Thule Society founded towards the end of 1918 two front organizations. The first was named "German Socialist Party", for which the propaganda was launched on Christmas Day. This was meant to be a political party

---

[3]Christian Zentner: *Adolf Hitlers 'Mein Kampf' – Eine kommentierte Auswahl*, p. 79.
[4]Peter Orzechowski: *Schwarze Magie – Braune Macht*, p. 34.
[5]Joachim Köhler, op. cit., p. 215.

in the classical sense of the word, "German-volkisch and socialist", but not accessible for Jews. Its newspaper would be the *Münchener Beobachter und Sportblatt* – a title intended to allure the lower classes by the addition of *Sportblatt*, which means "sports magazine". The president of the new party, Hans Grassinger, was a member of the Thule Kampfbund.

The Thule Society was less ambitious at the cradle of its second offspring, the "German Workers' Party", German initials *DAP*, founded on 5 January 1919. The president of the DAP, Karl Harrer, a member of Thule, conceived his party more like a lodge, a secret volkisch club where members of the working class would be introduced to the Thule ideals. Thus the DAP would be something like a proletarian annexe of the more select Thule Society. Ironically, it was the DAP which grew into the NSDAP, Hitler's National Socialist Workers' Party, and which would swallow up its fledgling sister organization, the German Socialist Party.

"Brother" Karl Harrer (1890-1926), "untiring fighter for justice and truth", was a sports journalist by profession. The evening paper for which he worked, the *München-Augsburger Abendzeitung*, had once published an article in favour of continuing the war by one Anton Drexler. In March 1918 Drexler had founded a "Worker's Committee for a Just Peace" in Bremen, and had invited Harrer to one of the meetings. And so it happened that, when Harrer was entrusted with his assignment by the leadership of the Order to create an instrument "to win the workers for the volkisch politics"[6], he sought out Drexler, who was now employed as a locksmith with the German Railways in Munich.

Anton Drexler (1884-1942) certainly was no ordinary proletarian, taking into consideration his previous activities in Bremen, his writings, including *My Political Awakening*, and his political initiatives. He became a "guest" of the Thule – the designation of persons who

---

[6]Hermann Gilbhard: *Die Thule-Gesellschaft*, p. 148.

had close dealings with the Order without being initiated – and founded in collaboration with Harrer "a workers' circle" of which he was the president for Munich and Harrer the "national president", and of which at first most of the members were recruited among Drexler's co-workers. "The persons who were accepted as members by the executive committee were sworn to silence about the activities and membership of the group."[7] This circle soon became the DAP. "While the political workers' circle was clearly meant to be a creation of Thule, the German Workers' Party, for tactical reasons, had to be presented as an initiative of Drexler's".[8] "The German Workers' Party gained no great influence at first and remained mainly limited to Munich. Only when through an intervention of Destiny Adolf Hitler joined the still thinly populated ranks of the Party, in the autumn of 1919, came the turnabout which gained great historical significance for the whole German people".[9]

The corporal joins a party

In *Mein Kampf* Hitler tells his first and fateful contact with the DAP, on 12 September 1919, as follows: "One day I received an order from my superiors to investigate the nature of an association which was apparently political. It called itself 'The German Labour Party' and was soon to hold a meeting at which Gottfried Feder would speak. I was ordered to attend this meeting and report on the situation ... I decided to attend the meeting of this Party which had hitherto been entirely unknown to me".[10] These few lines have lived on as part of the Hitler myth, suggesting that his first contact with the DAP was coincidental. Yet there are sound reasons to see Hitler's debut in politics in a very different way.

---

[7]Id., p. 149.
[8]Ibid.
[9]Rudolf von Sebottendorff: *Bevor Hitler kam*, p. 184.
[10]Adolf Hitler: *Mein Kampf*, pp. 186-87.

The Thule was a secret society and so was, as we just saw, its "workers' circle" which had become the DAP, contrived by Harrer more as a lodge than as an ordinary political party. A footnote in Ralph Manheim's English translation of *Mein Kampf* reads: "As part of the party's policy deliberately to restrict membership so as to maintain its esoteric quality, attendance at its meetings was usually by invitation ..."[11] Hitler was now no longer only a Reichswehr propagandist, he was also an agent in military intelligence, commissioned to spy on the frenzied and often shady political hustle and bustle in Munich. How had he been informed about the date and venue, the Sterneckerbräu, of the secret DAP's meeting on 12 September? Moreover, how could he enter that meeting without an introduction? He was but a corporal still wearing uniform. And he was accompanied by three other military men, for we find in Joachimsthaler: "On that day, Friday 12 September 1919, 43 persons were present, according to the attendance list, among whom, as companions of Hitler, Sergeant Alois Grillmeier and two propagandists of the Gruko [*Gruppenkommando*], Ewald Bolle and Alois Knodn".[12]

The chief speaker at the meeting in question was Gottfried Feder, author of a *Manifest for the Breaking of the Interest Slavery of Money*, a cranky theory which at the time made a deep impression on the German anti-Semites, including Hitler, who remarks: "Feder's lecture was known to me from the courses [for propagandists at Munich University]". In fact, Feder was standing in for Dietrich Eckart, a "guest" of Thule who had recently become a member of the DAP and was well known to Captain Mayr. "The speaker was to have been Eckart, but he was ill".[13] And here we meet again with an old acquaintance, the inventor of the sidereal pendulum, Wilhelm Gutberlet. "Dr. Wilhelm Gutberlet (1870-1933), medical doctor at

---

[11]Ralph Manheim's translation of *Mein Kampf*, p. 200, footnote.
[12]Anton Joachimsthaler: *Hitlers Weg begann in München*, p. 252.
[13]Ian Kershaw: *Hitler – 1889-1936 Hubris*, p. 126.

Munich, member of Thule and eminent astrologer, sat by the side of Hitler [at the 12 September meeting], and wrote a long report on him for Dietrich Eckart".[14]

Hitler's flaming retort towards the end of the meeting to a certain professor Baumann, who had dared to defend the idea of an alliance between Bavaria and Austria, both Catholic, against Protestant Prussia, may have been less impromptu than Hitler himself would have us think. "At this juncture I felt bound to ask for permission to speak and to tell the learned gentleman what I thought. The result was that the honourable gentleman who had last spoken slipped out of his place, like a whipped cur, without uttering a sound. While I was speaking the audience listened with an expression of surprise on their faces".[15] The corporal had demonstrated his oratory skill and passed muster. He was invited to become a member of the DAP and joined the party a few days later.

Most of the recently published experts on this period in Hitler's life agree that he, in his appearance on the political scene, was supported by the Reichswehr and by the Thule Society. "Hitler wanted to conceal", in his chapter on the German Worker's Party in *Mein Kampf*, "that the initiative of his joining the DAP had not been taken by himself", writes Ralph Reuth.[16] Ian Kershaw, in this connection, refers to Captain Mayr: "In a little noticed piece of evidence, [Hitler's] Reichswehr boss Captain Mayr later claimed that he had *ordered* Hitler to join the German Worker's Party to help foster its growth. For this purpose, Mayr went on, [Hitler] was provided at first with funds ... and, contrary to normal practice about members of the Reichswehr joining political parties, was allowed to stay in the army".[17] Anton Joachimsthaler also says that Hitler was ordered by Mayr to have a look at the DAP "and even to

---

[14] André Brissaud: *Hitler et l'Ordre noir*, p. 67, footnote.
[15] Adolf Hitler, op. cit., p. 187.
[16] Ralph Reuth: *Hitler – Eine politische Biographie*, p. 100.
[17] Ian Kershaw, op. cit., p. 127.

establish contact with them ... One may accept that Captain Mayr has advised Hitler to join the DAP, if he has not instigated him to do so, that he generously supported him in his subsequent political activities in the DAP, and that he gave him further assignments".[18] "Hitler was as representative of the Reichswehr smuggled into the DAP", according to Orzechowski, who also writes: "The members of the occult Thule Society helped Hitler into the saddle".[19]

All this is undeniably confirmed in letters from Captain Mayr to Wolfgang Kapp, the front man of the rightist "Kapp Putsch" in 1920. (The letters, by the way, prove again that Captain Karl Mayr was one link in a wide nationalist network, and that there existed a coordinated interaction between the nationalist organizations against the social-democratic government.) It is here that Mayr writes that he had daily contact with Hitler for more than fifteen months. And he continues: "We are building the organization of national radicalism. The national worker's party (DAP) must constitute the foundation of the strong storm troop we hope to form ... I have been trying to strengthen the movement since July [1919] ... I have set going very tough young people ... Hitler has become a moving force ... I agree fully with Mister Hitler that what is called the social-democracy of the government is completely at the mercy of the Jews ... All harmful elements must, like breeders of illness, be expelled or isolated — which goes for the Jews too ..."[20]

Hitler's first visit to the DAP was not the casual occurrence it is still generally supposed to have been. This can also be deduced from some statements in his autobiography in spite of the smokescreen with which he tries to conceal the truth. The last words of chapter 7, "The Revolution", are the often quoted: "As to me, I decided to become a politician".[21] This decision is supposed to have

---

[18] Anton Joachimsthaler, op. cit., pp. 251, 255.
[19] Peter Orzechowski, op. cit., pp. 22, 205.
[20] Anton Joachimsthaler, op. cit., p. 255.
[21] Adolf Hitler, op. cit., p. 187.

been taken in the Pasewalk hospital, at the end of the deep depression which overtook him on learning that Germany had lost the war and that the country had become a republic overnight. Hitler's statement is untrue and even nonsensical. At Pasewalk his social isolation was nearly absolute; at the age of twenty-nine his heroic years as a soldier were wiped out by the German defeat; he had no future, no professional competence, no relatives or friends who could help him, and no means whatsoever. He himself confesses: "That I was poor and without means seems to me the most bearable part, but it was harder that I was numbered among the nameless, that I was one of the millions whom chance permits to live or summons out of existence without even their closest neighbours condescending to take any notice of it. In addition, there was the difficulty which eventually arose from my lack of schooling".[22] We may find a clue to what really happened at Pasewalk further on in our story.

But then the providential turnabout happened to Hitler, and now, in September 1919, he *was* entering politics. Surprisingly, "on joining the DAP he had very concrete ideas about the aims he was going to pursue".[23] "This absurd little group with its few members [the DAP] seemed to me to possess one advantage", he writes, "that it had not frozen into an 'organization', but left the individual an opportunity for real personal activity. Here it was still possible to work, and the smaller the movement, the more readily it could be put into the proper form. Here the context, the goal and the road could still be determined, which in the existing great parties was impossible from the outset".[24] And he declares: "I had no intention of joining a ready-made party, but wanted to found one of my own".[25] Max Amann, who had been Hitler's sergeant in the army, met the corporal by chance "somewhere in the spring of 1920". "He

---

[22]Id., p. 203.
[23]Christian Zentner, op. cit., p. 76.
[24]Adolf Hitler, op. cit., p. 203.
[25]Id., p. 200.

was still wearing his military uniform", remembers Amann. "To my question what he was becoming, he answered that he was now an educational officer in the Reichswehr ... He did, however, not find any satisfaction in this occupation. It was his intention to enter the political life and to found his own political party".[26] (What we have seen before allows us to adjust Amann's recollection and to place the encounter in early autumn 1919.)

Where had Hitler got the idea to found a party – he who was "a man from nowhere", and who was himself very much aware of the fact? "The so-called 'intelligentsia' still looks down with infinite superciliousness on anyone who has not been through the prescribed schools and allowed them to pump the necessary knowledge into him. The question of what a man can do is never asked, but rather: what has he learned? 'Educated' people look upon any imbecile who is plastered with a number of academic certificates as superior to the ablest young fellow who lacks these precious documents". (*Mein Kampf*[27]) This feeling of social inferiority was ingrained in Hitler and he will, in spite of his authoritarian predispositions, always bear a grudge against 'educated people'.

From where did he have the idea that "it was a new ideology and not a new election slogan that had to be proclaimed"? How came that he, who initially participated in meetings attended by no more than thirty, forty people, "thought from the very beginning on the scale of a party for the masses"?[28] There are secrets in between the lines of *Mein Kampf* which are part of the "enigma" that keeps the historians guessing. Why would, for Hitler, joining an insignificant group of rightist fanatics and their sympathizers be "the hardest question of my life" – he for whom survival from one day to the next had been the most urgent problem on his mind? And has joining a political party, especially one hidden in the dingy darkness

---

[26] Anton Joachimsthaler, op. cit., p. 260.
[27] Adolf Hitler, op. cit., 191.
[28] Joachim Fest: *Hitler*, p. 175.

of a second-rate beer hall, ever been for anybody "a decision that would be for good, with no turning back", as Hitler says it was for him?[29] A man who had some answers to these questions was Dietrich Eckart.

Dietrich Eckart

Brigitte Hamann, in her highly rated *Hitlers Wien* (1998), calls Dietrich Eckart the "closest friend and mentor" of Hitler.[30] In this she is not alone. Actually, most students of Hitler's life say the same and use identical words. A "mentor", according to the dictionaries, is "a wise and trusted adviser and guide", "a wise and trusted counsellor or teacher".

One obtains a somewhat different impression about Eckart from Joachim Fest: "A roughhewn and comical figure, with his thick round head, his partiality for good wine and crude talk, Eckart had missed the great success he hoped for as a poet and a dramatist ... In compensation he had thrown himself into that bohemian group which indulged in politics".[31] And John Toland writes: "Dietrich Eckart – poet, playwright, coffeehouse intellectual – was a tall, bald, burly eccentric who spent much of his time in cafés and beer halls giving equal attention to drink and talk".[32] The correspondent for the *Frankfurter Zeitung* Konrad Heiden, though, who was an eye-witness and an opponent of the rise of the NSDAP in Munich, reports: "... The recognized spiritual leader of the small group [around Hitler] was Eckart, the journalist and poet, twenty-one years older than Hitler ... He had a strong influence on the younger man, probably the strongest anyone ever has had on him".[33]

---

[29] Adolf Hitler, op. cit., p. 202.
[30] Brigitte Hamann: *Hitlers Wien*, p. 332.
[31] Joachim Fest, op. cit., p.132.
[32] John Toland: *Adolf Hitler* (1977 ed.), p. 106.
[33] Konrad Heiden, op. cit., p. 85.

In *The Crisis of German Ideology*, George Mosse agrees that Dietrich Eckart was "the man who exercised the greatest influence on Adolf Hitler in the immediate postwar years". In his opinion "this important figure in the volkisch movement played the key role in crystallizing Hitler's attitudes ... The two formed a team in which Hitler was the avid and quickly learning disciple". And Mosse adds quite rightly: "Thus it is indeed surprising that historians have failed to give Eckart due credit for his contribution to the viability of National Socialism".[34] François Delpla puts it bluntly: "History has not been interested in Eckart".[35] In their Hitler biographies Fest (1973) dedicates to Eckart one page, Toland (1976) one and a half paragraph, Steinert (1991) two paragraphs, and Kershaw (1998) also two paragraphs, although he thinks that "Eckart's role was crucial.

This gaping lacuna in the life of Adolf Hitler and the history of Nazism is still more amazing as there is no lack of documents. Eckart's considerable literary and journalistic oeuvre could have been studied if sought for; Ernst Nolte, one of the dominant German historians, has drawn attention to the relevance of Eckart's *Zwiegespräch*, a so-called dialogue with Hitler, in 1969; and Margarete Plewnia's biography of Eckart was published in 1970. But the main source indicating Eckart's historical importance was Adolf Hitler himself. Here the abundance of references is really overwhelming, taking into account that Hitler as a rule blotted out all traces leading towards his pre-public past and in many cases eliminated the persons connected with it. ("A Führer can never admit that what he advocates, he got from others."[36])

The greatest honour Hitler did to Eckart was highlighting his name as the last two words of *Mein Kampf*: "Here at the end of this

---

34 George Mosse: *The Crisis of German Ideology – Intellectual Origins of the Third Reich* (1998 ed.), pp. 26, 296, 297.
35 François Delpla: *Hitler*, p. 74.
36 Quoted in Geoffrey Stoakes: *Hitler and the Quest for World Dominion – Nazi Ideology and Foreign Policy in the 1920s*, p. 52.

second volume* let me again bring those men to the memory of the adherents and champions of our ideals, as heroes who, in the full consciousness of what they were doing, sacrificed their lives for us all ... Together with those, and as one of the best of all, I should like to mention the name of a man who devoted his life to reawakening his and our people, through his writing and his ideas, and finally through positive action: *Dietrich Eckart*".[37]

Hitler bought, with funds provided by an industrialist supporter, the Barlow Palace on Briennerstrasse in Munich and had it renovated into the local Nazi headquarters by his favourite architect, who was soon to die, Paul Troost. Two busts were installed in what was called the "Senate Hall": the one of Otto von Bismarck, the other of Dietrich Eckart. In the canteen of that building was a seat permanently reserved for the Führer, under a bust of Eckart.

The person most often mentioned in Hitler's monologues at his Head Quarters in Rastenburg, on the eastern front, was Dietrich Eckart, some twenty years after his death. One of Hitler's secretaries has said that tears would well in Hitler's eyes every time he remembered the man he once called his "fatherly friend". "Eckart's merits are imperishable", he said, and: "It is deeply tragic that Dietrich Eckart has not lived to see the rise [of the Nazi Party]".[38] He reminisced about his discovery, thanks to Eckart, of the Obersalzberg and the house there that would become his villa *Berghof*, and how one night he had woken Eckart up unannounced, and how Eckart had opened the door in his night-shirt, showing his hairy legs. "Today, we have all come a step further; therefore we do not realize what [Eckart] was at the time: a polar star".

---

*Mein Kampf was originally written in two parts, the first in the prison at Landsberg, the second after Hitler's discharge from prison on the Obersalzberg. From 1931 onwards the two parts were published as one volume.
[37] Adolf Hitler, op. cit., p. 559.
[38] *Monologe im Führerhauptquartier 1941-1944*, pp. 161, 173.

When the Reichstag building had burned and the Reichstag, the German parliament, met for the first time in the Kroll Opera House, its president Hermann Göring opened the session with a memorial address on Dietrich Eckart. A statue of the poet was inaugurated in his birthplace, Neumarkt, by the Führer himself, as was an open air theatre, named after Eckart, in Berlin. There were Dietrich Eckart Societies and Dietrich Eckart Homes in Dortmund and in many other places. His poems were learned by heart in the schools and university students wrote theses on his oeuvre; his birthday was commemorated in the press; his plays were, sometimes at the instigation of the Führer, revived in many theatres. Eckart was made posthumously into "the symbolic figure of the young [NSDAP] Party".[39]

Dietrich Eckart was born in Neumarkt in 1866 as the son of a royal notary.[40] He studied medicine – and also law for some time, according to Hitler – but he never finished his studies because of illness. Delicate health will remain a factor throughout his life and be the cause of his dependence on pain-killing morphine. In 1899 Eckart went to live in Berlin, where he tried to realize his literary ambitions and led the bohemian life in literary circles and cafés. This and the fact that he was a generous, uncalculating man, at times even a spendthrift, soon finished the money he had inherited after his father's death and turned his Berlin period into "twelve hungry years". It was then that he wrote most of his plays, such as *Father of a Family*, *A Fellow who Speculates* and *King of the Frogs*. The plays were put on the stage but met with no more than moderate success. In the meantime, he kept himself afloat with journalistic work and by writing literary and political essays – besides his production as a poet, which he essentially was.

---

[39] Michael Rissmann: *Hitlers Gott – Vorsehungsglaube und Sendungsbewusstsein des deutschen Diktators*, p. 131.
[40] Most of the data in the following paragraphs are from Margarete Plewnia's biography of Eckart: *Auf dem Weg zu Hitler – Der 'völkische' Publizist Dietrich Eckart*.

However, one of his plays, *The Hereditary Count*, was attended by Emperor Wilhelm II, who liked it so much that he went to enjoy the next performance. It was at this time that Eckart's adaptation of Ibsen's *Peer Gynt* obtained an unprecedented success and became the most often performed play of the *Hofbühne*, the Court Theatre, of which the emperor was the protector. As a consequence the emperor commissioned Eckart to write a play for the marriage of his daughter with the Duke of Brunswick. The play, *Heinrich the Hohenstauffer*, had its premiere in 1915.

1915, the second year of the Great War, was also the year that Eckart shifted from Berlin to Munich, where he felt much more at home and where he became involved in political circles and in journalistic skirmishes with Leftist newspapers, for during the first war years he had turned into a fervent nationalist and a rabid anti-Semite. The reasons for this portentous change in his mental outlook are not clear. A spiteful reaction to the non-acceptance or the critical failure of some of his plays does not seem a sufficient explanation. Contact with circles like the Thule Society may have been a more adequate reason. Eckart is mentioned as a "guest" of Thule in *Before Hitler Came*, and many of the new features of Eckart's thought fit closely with those of the Thule as presented by Sebottendorff in the same book. That both men knew each other is confirmed by Sebottendorff's words about the publication of Eckart's magazine *In Plain German*: "The launching of this magazine was the cause of Eckart's enmity towards Sebottendorff" (Sebottendorff writes here in the third person), because the latter could or would not provide the former with the necessary finance.[41] The underlying cause of the friction may have been that both strong characters refused to cede part of their turf to each other.

The first issue of *In Plain German* came out on 7 December 1918, less than a month after the armistice and during the short-

---

[41]Rudolf von Sebottendorff, op. cit., p. 77.

lived presidency of Kurt Eisner. Among the first well-wishers of the new magazine, in principle a fortnightly but reflecting Eckart's character by its irregularity, were, significantly, Wolfgang Kapp and Captain Karl Mayr. Mayr bought clandestinely a great number of copies for distribution among the military. How well-known Eckart actually was is shown by the names of the collaborators to his magazine. They included many prominent nationalist and anti-Semitic writers, and *In Plain German* was praised by Theodor Fritsch himself, the founder and supreme Grand Master of the Germanenorden. The main themes of the polemical publication were: 1. the spreading of the *Dolchstosslegende*: Germany had not been defeated but stabbed in the back by the internal enemy, Jewish Bolshevism; 2. the Jews, who in a worldwide conspiracy were striving for world hegemony and were focusing particularly on Germany; 3. democracy, socialism and communism, all Jewish inventions and machinations to bring chaos into the world and destroy the German soul; 4. Germany, which had to become a strong and self-conscious unified nation; therefore the traditional Bavarian tendency towards separatism was to be condemned and the feeling of national unity promoted.[42] All four themes would become pillars of Hitler's thought. (It was the fourth point which provoked Hitler's fiery intervention on the occasion of his first contact with the DAP.)

It is difficult to say who determined the political course of the Thule Society – probably to a great extent Sebottendorff himself. Yet it is striking that the goals of the Society intimately agreed with those of an independent personality like Eckart. The exchange of opinions between the dominating Thule members must have been frequent and intense. Eckart also vividly felt the need to reach out to the workers and convert them from socialist internationalists into nationalistic Germans, because the primordial requirement of a unified Volk and nation could not be attained otherwise. He did not see the body of the German Volk as consisting of *Volksgenossen* (racial

---

[42] Margarete Plewnia, op. cit., pp. 37 ff.

compatriots) but of *Bürger*, a body of "citizens" forming a natural hierarchy, based upon the individual state of psychological perfection, which would constitute the nation of all Germans. To that end Eckart founded a "Citizens' Association" for the unification of all "workers of the head and the hand". The association never took off. Still Eckart tried to make himself useful by participating in the Thule resistance against the communist Republic of Councils. The result was that the Reds caught him, and that his name could very well have been on the list of the executed Thule members, had he not managed to talk himself out of a risky and totally unnecessary situation.

It was around this time that Alfred Rosenberg, a German Balt who had emigrated from Russia and arrived in Munich in November 1918, went knocking on Eckart's door, looking for support and possibly a job. Rosenberg describes Eckart on that occasion: "From behind a desk covered with papers rose a tall man with a shaven head, a deeply furrowed forehead and horn-rimmed spectacles before blue eyes. The slightly curved nose was rather short and fleshy. He had a full mouth and a broad, one might say aggressive chin".[43] Eckart took Rosenberg under his wing, improved his knowledge of the German language, made him a collaborator of *In Plain German*, and got in return a fanatical anti-Semite who would be the main advocate of the *Protocols of the Wise Men of Zion*, the faked, widespread anti-Semitic pamphlet which has done so much damage.

This brief biographical sketch of Dietrich Eckart would remain incomplete without mentioning another aspect of his personality, the side turned towards the philosophical, the occult and the spiritual. He was, like Hitler, an admirer of the philosopher Arthur Schopenhauer (1788-1860). (Hitler has said that during the war he always carried in his knapsack the five small volumes of the Reclam edition of Schopenhauer's work.) The thought of this philosopher

---

[43]Id., p. 35.

is one long but well-written lamento on the misery of all existence, supported and ever impelled by Desire, which he names "Will". Because of his stress on the Life Force and his disparagement of reason, Schopenhauer became an inspirer of the volkisch movement. He was also the philosopher who, as one of the first Westerners, discovered Buddhism and its techniques of world-negation as a means of escape from an absurd, blindly desire-driven world subjected to *Maya*.

Eckart was, moreover, a devoted admirer of Angelus Silesius (1624-77), of whom he could quote whole passages by heart. Eckart was of the opinion that what counted in life was "to wake up the Divinity in man", and that nobility was not a matter of birth but of the spirit. In his hierarchical view of humanity he was strongly anti-materialistic, and therefore against the ideals of the Enlightenment, modernity, industrialization and progress. (Plewnia defined him in the title of her book as "a volkisch publicist".) The more spiritual and the greater the portion of the Divine in man, the higher the degree he will occupy in the human hierarchy. Eckart, like others at that time, conceived of a higher, internalized man, a "superman", ie a chosen being, child of the Light, who would react against all forms of materialism. If the Germans became aware of their superior soul quality, they would become such supermen. They had to fight against the increasing materialism and cultivate their superior Aryan soul. The German people were destined to redeem the world.

As high as the Aryan Germans stood on the hierarchical ladder of humanity, so low stood the Jews. "The Jew has no sense of the experience of what is eternal or of the need of immortality. Ergo: he has no soul, and is therefore the opposite pole of the Germans, who are always striving for something higher. They are as light is to darkness".[44] The Jews are materialistic, intellectual, world-bound,

---

[44]Id., p. 47.

egoistic, children of darkness; the Aryans (read: Germans) are noble, pure, idealistic, aspiring for the light, selfless world-negators, worthy of ruling the world.

This kind of thinking was common among the German nationalists and volkists, whose sources were Luther, Wagner, Houston Chamberlain and Theodor Fritsch, to name only four of the most influential. Less common was Eckart's "dualism", his conviction that idealism and materialism, light and darkness, the Aryan and the Jewish side of the scale, were present in humanity since its beginning and therefore in every individual. In the eternal struggle between good and evil for dominion over the world the Germans constituted the vanguard. This battle must not only be fought in the open, between the opponents in society, but first of all in every individual, for only mastery *within himself* of the Aryan over the Jew could lead to mastery over the world. The Jews "belong to 'the organism of humanity' as certain bacteria do to the human body. ... We have to endure the Jews among us as a necessary evil, who knows for how many millennia more".[45] Hitler will take over Eckart's ideas to a certain degree and speak about an "anti-Semitism of the reason" in contrast to the impulsive anti-Semitism of the pogroms, but he will found his eschatological world view on a crude racist, Darwinian theoretical basis.

All this makes one see Eckart in a way quite different from the usual manner of depicting him as a Bavarian *Stammtisch* hero. This he was also, but this aspect of his character would certainly not suffice to explain his influence on Hitler and on the budding Nazist movement. A crude, impulsive and comical beer swiller would not have built up the wide network of prominent people throughout Germany which could be contacted by Eckart. Nor would a cultured man-of-the-world like Ernst Hanfstängl have written: "[Eckart] was a man of education, a poet, whose German version of *Peer Gynt*

---

[45]Ibid.

remains the standard translation ... He it was who had first taken Hitler under his wing in the Party ... Eckart has always been one of my favourites, a big bear of a man with sparkling eyes and a genuine sense of humour".[46]

Eckart made the existential choice to try out the realization of world-negation *in* the world. We will follow him there for a while.

---

[46]Ernst Hanfstängl: *Hitler – The Missing Years*, pp. 45, 80.

4

WOLF

The best would be if one could liquidate all pessimists.
ADOLF HITLER

A mental make-up

Hitler is still often represented in the popular media as a madman obsessed by a few fixed ideas. There is truth in the obsession, but he was not a madman. "Hitler was not mad", writes John Lukacs, "he was responsible for what he did and said and thought ... He had very considerable intellectual talents".[1] He had, for one, an excellent memory, which was a principal instrument in his exercise of authority in all phases of his political career, and which he used to impress his interlocutors. He had also the gift of simplifying and summarizing complex matters. As Fest puts it: "Hitler had the knack of translating into simple images the abstract character of political and functional relationships".[2]

When reading some biographies one might gain the impression that Hitler studied, in his Viennese years, some of the most influential

---

[1] John Lukacs: *The Hitler of History*, p. 43.
[2] Joachim Fest: *Hitler*, p. 429.

philosophers – an impression furthered by Hitler himself by dropping their names in his writings and speeches. Yet it is hardly believable that a twenty year old, unsystematic autodidact could grasp the intricacies of philosophers like Nietzsche, Marx and Schopenhauer. Hitler would no doubt be able to quote striking sayings and passages from philosophers which accorded with his prejudices, but this is not exactly the same as insight into a philosopher's thinking. "It must be understood that young Hitler in no way drew from primary sources, which means that mostly he did not have his knowledge from let us say Darwin, Chamberlain, Dühring, Le Bon, Nietzsche, Schopenhauer or Schiller. He drew his knowledge in the first place from articles about all this in newspapers, brochures and popular writings". (Brigitte Hamann[3]) "In actual fact, knowledge meant nothing to Hitler; he was not acquainted with the pleasure or struggle that go with its acquisition; to him it was merely useful, and 'the art of correct reading' of which he spoke was nothing more than the hunt for formulations to borrow and authorities to cite in support of his own preconceptions ..." (Joachim Fest[4]) "Ideas held no interest for Hitler as abstractions. They were important as tools of mobilization". (Ian Kershaw[5])

"Books, always books! I cannot think of Adolf Hitler without books. Books were his world",[6] writes August Kubizek, Hitler's close friend in Linz and Vienna until somewhere in 1909, when Hitler failed his entrance examination to the Academy of Fine Arts for the second time and disappeared into the anonymity of the metropolis. Hitler read about the subjects that interested him: Richard Wagner, the theatre, the technical aspects of stagecraft, architecture, military equipment and war, German history, and the political background of the events he witnessed in Vienna. But another, and

---

[3]Brigitte Hamann: *Hitlers Wien*, p.333.
[4]Joachim Fest, op. cit., p. 201.
[5]Ian Kershaw: *Hitler – 1889-1936 Hubris*, p. 137.
[6]August Kubizek: *Adolf Hitler, mein Jugendfreund*, p. 188.

not less important, source of his mental make-up were the newspapers, at present still a familiar feature in the Viennese cafés, where it was warm and where Hitler could pass hours reading behind a cup of coffee. "He learned especially from newspapers", writes Hamann, and Hitler himself mentions "so much reading of the newspapers when I was quite young". "Earlier Hitler biographers tended to confine their surveys of Hitler's supposed sources of inspiration to intellectually respectable writers on racial superiority and anti-Semitism such as Gobineau, Nietzsche, Wagner and Chamberlain. But there is no evidence that Hitler read their scholarly works. It is altogether more likely that he would have picked up ideas to rationalize his own dualist outlook and fixation on Germany from cheap and accessible pamphlets in contemporary Vienna".[7]

André François-Poncet, the French ambassador in Berlin who knew Hitler well and who was the only foreign diplomat to gain his esteem, writes in his memoirs: "He is an autodidact whose curiosity goes out to the subjects which catch the attention of the public mind, the attention of the man in the street ... Hitler's talent consists in absorbing what the brain of the common man might absorb, in linking the various elements with one another by apparent logic, and in presenting them in a simple and vivid way, comprehensible to a rudimentary intelligence".[8] "[Hitler] read not for knowledge or enlightenment, but for confirmation of his own perceptions",[9] writes Kershaw echoing Kubizek's remark: "He found in the books only what suited him".[10] "Amateurishness was one of Hitler's dominant traits", remembers architect Albert Speer. "He never learned a profession and basically always remained an outsider to all fields of endeavour. Like many self-taught people, he had no idea what real specialized knowledge meant".[11] And Speer writes in another context:

---

[7] Nicholas Goodrick-Clarke: *The Occult Roots of Nazism*, p. 194.
[8] André François-Poncet: *Souvenirs d'une ambassade à Berlin*, pp. 84, 85.
[9] Ian Kershaw, op. cit., p. 240.
[10] August Kubizek, op. cit., p. 191.
[11] Albert Speer: *Inside the Third Reich*, p. 320.

"We all knew that he firmly believed in reading only the end of a book, because everything important was to be found there".[12]

All of the above is confirmed in the passage in *Mein Kampf* where Hitler lectures his readers on the art of reading. "I know people who read interminably, book after book, from page to page, and yet I would not call them 'well-read'. Of course they 'know' an immense amount, but their brain seems incapable of assorting and classifying the material which they have gathered from books. They lack the faculty of distinguishing between what is useful and useless in a book ... For reading is not an end in itself, but a means to an end. Its chief purpose is to help towards filling in the framework which is made up of the talents and capabilities that each individual possesses. Thus each one procures for himself the implements and materials necessary for the fulfilment of his calling in life ..."[13]

There was, however, another side to Hitler's mind: a kind of intuition which made him remarkably perceptive and able to react instantly to the attitudes and arguments of the persons or situations he had to deal with, using the mental material at his disposal and charging it with the power of conviction. SS-General Walter Schellenberg, who worked with him, writes: "There was his extraordinary dialectical ability which enabled him to out-argue even the most expert authorities in any field of discussion ... He threw them so off balance that they did not think of the appropriate replies until afterwards".[14] Few were Hitler's interlocutors who could keep a clear mind in his presence and did not leave him convinced or at least impressed.

Persisting memories

Hitler's mind was certainly not a tabula rasa when, after the war, Captain Mayr picked him out, aged thirty, for the course at Munich

---

[12] Albert Speer: *Spandau: the Secret Diaries*, p. 118.
[13] Adolf Hitler, op. cit., p. 42.
[14] Walter Schellenberg: *The Labyrinth*, p. 94.

University. He had lived through many very strong experiences, stronger than those of an average person, especially in turbulent, overcrowded, decaying Vienna and in the unending hell of the trenches. His authoritarian father, whom Adolf hated but who as a customs inspector was a uniformed official (in that society a matter of importance), may have communicated to him his fanatical preference for all things German, although the customs inspector always remained faithful to his supreme superior, the Austrian Emperor. "Racial hatreds dominated politics in the Hapsburg Empire, where both Hitler and Adolf Eichmann spent their formative years. From 1882 through 1914 constant demonstrations and riots were mounted by ethnic groups fighting for power within the multinational Austrian state. Already in 1848 Catholic anti-Semitism flourished among Austro-Germans … In 1911, the last election before 1914, two-thirds of all Austro-Germans voted for anti-Semites. It is not surprising that Austro-German participation in the Holocaust was higher than that of Germans in general". (John Weiss[15])

The pages in *Mein Kampf* written on Georg von Schönerer and Karl Lueger, mayor of Vienna, bear testimony to the influence both men had on Hitler. Karl Lueger (1844-1910), mayor of Vienna, impressed Hitler because of his oratorial skill and his power over the masses, capacities which appealed to Hitler's own, as yet latent, capabilities. Lueger was not only the mayor, he was also "the Lord of Vienna", an uncrowned king powerful enough to stand up to Emperor Franz Joseph. It was not so much Lueger-the-politician and his party, the Christian-Socialists – by 1895 the most powerful anti-Semitic party in Europe – who attracted Hitler, as his towering personality, an example of what young Hitler dreamed of becoming.

More concrete was the influence of Georg von Schönerer (1842-1921), the proclaimed *Führer* of the Austrian Pan-Germans, who strove for unification of their country with Germany. "Schönerer

---

[15]John Weiss: *Ideology of Death – Why the Holocaust Happened in Germany*, p. 156.

held no brief for either Catholicism or the Empire. Leader of the Austrian pan-German movement, a racist pure and simple, supporter of *Anschluss* [the joining of Austria with Germany] and an enemy to the death of both Slavs and Jews, he would become Hitler's ideological model".[16] A failure Hitler would never make, though, was Schönerer's open belligerence against the Catholic Church in anti-Semitic but predominantly Catholic Austria. Schönerer's "Away from Rome" movement cost him the adherence of so many supporters that he fell from power.

A young vagabond like Adolf Hitler during his Vienna years could never meet with a rich and revered pan-German Führer, but "the young Hitler experienced with certainty the cult of the idol of the Pan-Germans, especially in the newspapers of their party".[17] Schönerer's speeches, moreover, were printed as brochures, and the terror exerted by the Pan-Germans against Jews and Czechs in the streets of Vienna was a fact of everyday life. Schönerer had become "the idol of German shopkeepers, artisans and clerks, his photo was displayed in countless shops, his paper was available for reading in nearly every pub. A brisk business was done in watch chains with images of hanged Jews ... The party program was depressingly familiar: Jews must not teach or serve in the army or the civil service, and there should be quotas in law and medicine ... Artisans and peasants must be protected [against the Jews] and Jews kept out of the empire; those already there were to be treated as aliens with special legal and tax burdens".[18] "It is indeed beyond question that Hitler not only took over Schönerer's political principles, but that he nearly copied them", writes Hamann.[19]

Another pronounced influence on Hitler's mind, preceding the role of Schönerer and Lueger, was that of his history teacher Leopold

---

[16] Id., p. 165.
[17] Brigitte Hamann, op. cit., p. 337.
[18] John Weiss, op. cit., pp. 168, 169.
[19] Brigitte Hamann, op. cit., p. 361.

Pötsch at the Linzer *Realschule* (gymnasium), which young Adolf left without finishing his studies. The beloved history teacher made an indelible impression on Hitler – headstrong and rebellious towards the other members of the teaching staff – so much so that he dedicated to his memory no less than two and a half pages of *Mein Kampf*. "To study history means to search for and discover the forces that are the causes of those results which appear before our eyes as historical events ... Perhaps my whole future life was determined by the fact that I had a teacher of history who understood, as few others understand, how to make this viewpoint prevail in teaching and in examining. This teacher was Dr Leopold Pötsch, of the *Realschule* in Linz. He was the ideal personification of the qualities necessary to a teacher of history in the sense I have mentioned above. An elderly gentleman with a decisive manner but a kindly heart, he was a spellbinding speaker and was able to inspire us with his own enthusiasm".[20]

Hitler, when in power, honoured Pötsch in many ways. "You have no idea what I owe that man", he said to his entourage after having met privately with his old teacher at Klagenfurt in 1938.[21] One of the effects of Pötsch's influence upon Hitler, together with that of his veneration for Wagner, was his love of the German myths and legends, often held to be historical fact. "The volumes of the *Sagas of the German Heroes* were his favourite reading which he never lent to anyone else", remembers Kubizek. "He identified always anew with the great men of that bygone world ... It remains a fact that Adolf Hitler did not find during his lifetime another ground on which he, with something like pious devotion, could dwell than the world to which the sagas of the German heroes had opened the gate."[22]

---

[20] Adolf Hitler, op. cit., pp. 25-26.
[21] August Kubizek, op. cit., p. 61.
[22] Id., p. 82.

All these influences were stored in Hitler's memory when he was "discovered" by Captain Mayr, who soon afterwards introduced him into the DAP. But the process of Hitler's mental development in matters of pan-Germanism, nationalism and anti-Semitism seems less articulated and rectilinear than Brigitte Hamann would have it with so much certainty. If Hitler's mental make-up had already been configured to the degree she suggests, then it would be incomprehensible that several people he was acquainted with at the men's hostel in the Meldemannstrasse were Jews, as Hamann herself found out. She also writes: "The decisive question when anti-Semitism became for Hitler the crucial point cannot be answered from his time in Linz and Vienna".[23]

When Hitler, in the hostel and in the frontline dugouts, launched into one of his rhetorical outbursts, his vehemence was not directed against the Jews; he was angered because Germany and his pan-German feelings had been offended by a scathing remark sometimes expressly made to get him going. Some officers in his regiment were Jews, one of them the captain who cited him for his Iron Cross First Class. And there is also the fact that Corporal Hitler wore the red armband under Eisner and the Republic of Councils. The influence of Schönerer and Lueger, as well as that of List and Lanz von Liebenfels, must have been revived and reformulated at the time of his instruction and his activities as a propagandist. And here all the evidence converges on the well-read, well-informed, well-connected and fanatic anti-Semite Dietrich Eckart.

Before carrying on with our story, a last and rather surprising source of influence on Hitler's mind should be mentioned: the German author Karl May, fertile writer of some seventy adventure stories for the youth. "Adi" (Hitler's pet name) had also liked *Don Quichote*, *Robinson Crusoe*, *Gulliver's Travels*, *Uncle Tom's Cabin* and *The Arabian Nights*, but May remained his favourite author even

---

[23]Brigitte Hamann, op. cit. p. 502.

in adulthood. "Hitler's cult of May weathered time unscathed. It is said that even when Chancellor of the Reich he took the time to read May's complete works. In 1943 he had, in spite of the paper shortage, 300,000 copies of a Winnetou book printed for the soldiers, this notwithstanding the undeniable fact that May's heroes belonged to a foreign race, for they were 'Redskins', [American] Indians".[24] "He might well mention Napoleon and Old Shatterhand in one sentence", writes Speer.[25]

Karl May belonged to the Christian faction of the German volkisch movement. He gave in March 1912, shortly before his death, a talk in Vienna which Hitler, if he knew about it, will not have missed. May's subject was *Empor ins Reich der Edelmenschen*,[26] which means something like "Up towards the Reign of the Noble Human Beings". *Edelmensch* was an often used synonym of the Arian-Nordic-German in his purest state – one of the many forms of expectation of the "superman" around the previous turn of the century. Whatever the ideology behind his literary production, Karl May's fantasies have kept innumerable children spellbound, not only in Germany. His suggestive writings – especially about the skills of Winnetou and Old Shatterhand in dangerous situations – may have contributed to saving Hitler's life in the First World War when he was a dispatch runner, one of the most risky assignments in battle.

A sudden burst of energy

After the collapse of the Republic of Councils and still more under the rightist regime of Gustav von Kahr, Bavaria became "a haven for right-wing extremists from all over Germany, including many under order of arrest elsewhere in the country".[27] There were "the *Bund*

---

[24] Id. p. 547.
[25] Albert Speer: *Spandau: the Hidden Diaries*, pp. 59, 347.
[26] There is a facsimile of the poster in Brigitte Hamann, op. cit., p. 545.
[27] Ian Kershaw, op. cit., p. 171.

Oberland (Oberland League), the officers' association *Eiserne Hand* (Iron Hand), the *Escherich Organization*, the *Deutschvölkische Schutz- and Trutzbund* (Defense and Defiance League of the German Race), the *Verband Altreichsflagge* (Flag of the Old Reich Association), the Bayreuth, Würzburg and Wolf Free Corps, and a variety of other organizations" – including the Thule Society and the (NS)DAP.

The ranks of the rightists in Bavaria were swelled by the defeated participants in the Kapp Putsch (March 1920) who had to flee Berlin, among them the figurehead of the putsch Wolfgang Kapp himself, the national German hero Erich von Ludendorff, and some very dangerous elements of the Ehrhardt Brigade, including its commander Captain Ehrhardt and his right-hand man Lieutenant Klintzsch, respectively founder and leading member of the murderous *Organization Consul*. There were "vigilante killers, adventurous and nationalist revolutionaries of various ideological shades ... They were able to exploit the traditional Old Bavarian separatism, for the [Catholic] Bavarians had a long history of intense dislike for Prussian Protestant Berlin",[28] lasting to this day. It was on such a scene, still more garbled by the disoriented and dispirited social conditions in post-war Germany, that Dietrich Eckart met Corporal Hitler.

Anton Drexler, with Karl Harrer founder of the DAP, "knew the volkisch-nationalistic and aggressively anti-Semitic [Eckart] ... since early summer 1919". Eckart himself remembered later: "At the beginning of 1919 I received the visit of Anton Drexler shortly after he had founded the National Socialist German Workers' Party" – it was, in fact, still only the German Workers' Party – "and who acquainted me with the ideas. I found them at once interesting and decided to make myself useful for the young movement to the measure of my possibilities. A few weeks or months later I met with Hitler for the first time".[29]

---

[28]Joachim Fest, op. cit., pp. 112, 131.
[29]Anton Joachimsthaler: *Hitlers Weg begann in München*, p. 276.

Taking into account that Wilhelm Gutberlet had to report to Eckart about Hitler's doings at the DAP meeting on 12 September, when illness prevented Eckart from speaking, it stands to reason that the first Eckart-Hitler encounter took place before that date, probably several weeks before. We recall that Captain Mayr became interested in Corporal Hitler from the List Regiment in the last days of May or the first of June, before the start of the oratory course for army propagandists. Mayr knew Eckart, from whom he bought copies of *In Plain German* for distribution among the military. We may presume that Mayr introduced Hitler to Eckart in June or at the latest in July, and that both agreed that this Austrian Corporal with the Iron Cross and the gift of the gab might be an asset for the Thule Society's floundering DAP.

Hitler was not an anti-Semite (at least not outspoken) in May, under the Republic of Councils, when he wore the red armband; the course he attended at Munich University was not openly and still less expressly anti-Semitic, for it was an initiative of the social-democratic government. As towards the end of July Hitler was told at Lechfeld to tone down his anti-Semitic diatribes, and as on 10 September Captain Mayr considered him an authority on the Jewish question, sufficiently so to illumine an army propaganda colleague on the subject, the simple conclusion is that Hitler's mind was turned during the months of June and July in 1919, and that the person under whose influence this happened was his "mentor" Dietrich Eckart.

With Eckart, Hitler came into his own. The loner who had been living in hostels, dugouts and barracks was suddenly accepted into the warmth and cosiness of a civilian home by a well-known man who was a poet, dramatist, journalist and the publisher and editor of a magazine. Hitler's interests concurred with the main themes of *In Plain German*: Germany's greatness and revenge, and the battle against the ideals of the Enlightenment which, according to the volkisch-German view, were turning the world into a nightmare of crass materialism. Moreover, Eckart knew so much; he had read all the books and was able to knit ideas together. And he was an outgoing man, a jovial character who felt at home in Munich and particularly in Schwabing, the bohemian part of the city frequented by half of the then living writers and artists. "The two formed a team in which Hitler was the avid and quickly learning disciple",[30] writes Mosse. Reuth agrees, saying that Eckart imparted to Hitler the coherence of the ideas he had acquired until then, and that Hitler's theory of a worldwide conspiracy took shape "under Eckart's influence".[31]

Now the seeds germinated which were stored in Hitler's subconscious mind. "Eckart was very influential in the development of the anti-Semitic dynamic within the ranks of the Workers' Party", writes Mosse. "He reinforced Hitler's abhorrence of Jews as a mysterious, strange and conspiring people, supplementing Hitler's ideas in some areas, while creating a more fanatical foundation for their development in others. While Hitler had already shared some of Eckart's beliefs, most of them were as yet only vague, unformulated convictions. Eckart plumbed deeper and connected the removal of the Jewish menace with the resuscitation of the Volk. He was to make Hitler view the problem as he himself viewed it: it transcended all others in importance, and its solution would bring to an end the Volk's period of trial. Or, as he stated it: 'The Jewish question is the chief problem of humanity, in which, indeed, every one of its other problems is contained. Nothing on earth could remain darkened if one could throw light on the secret of the Jews'".[32]

What happened between Eckart and Hitler during their frequent meetings remains unknown. It is nonetheless undeniable that Hitler generated a sudden burst of energy which would make him, within a short time, the undisputed leader of a dynamic party out of what had been a tame affair when he was introduced to it. This is the more

---

[30]George Mosse: *The Crisis of German Ideology*, p. 297.
[31]Ralph Reuth: *Hitler*, p. 123.
[32]George Mosse, op. cit., p. 297.

astonishing because Adolf Hitler was an outsider and apparently a rather laughable or pitiable figure, still wearing his grey army uniform (until the end of March 1920), with uncouth manners, a submissive air when not aroused into eloquence, a deep-throated voice, a waxen, hungry face, and a moustache he would soon reduce to "a ridiculous little smudge". From the moment he took him under his aegis, Eckart, "who played the key role in crystallizing Hitler's political ideas",[33] stood always beside or behind him and steered his career as a true mentor or "godfather" would do.

When Hitler became a member of Drexler and Harrer's DAP, he was given the innocuous post of *Werbeobmann*, i.e., in charge of propaganda. Little did the leadership realize that they had taken a wolf into their pen, and that it was Hitler's intention from the start to change the small political club into a dynamic political party. He set to work at once, increased the number of invitations to the meetings (the average attendance had been from thirty to forty), had defiant red posters printed to show that the DAP was taking up the gauntlet against the leftists, and hired ever greater venues for the meetings till they were held in the centrally located Hofbräuhaus and he could fill Circus Krone to capacity.

Hitler's drive inevitably created friction within the DAP, especially between him and Karl Harrer. Harrer had always seen his creation as a quiet, civil club more or less after the example of a masonic lodge. He could in no way agree with Hitler's approach and even belittled the oratorical gifts of the *Werbeobmann*. But the other DAP members realized that they did not mean much without Hitler, and Harrer, the "national chairman", had to give way. "The problem 'loge' or active party was decided already on 5 January 1920. On that day Karl Harrer left the German Workers' Party." (Gilbhard[34]) It did not take Hitler more than four months to push him out of the nest.

---

[33]Id., p. 296.
[34]Hermann Gilbhard: *Die Thule-Gesellschaft*, p. 152.

The twenty-five points of the party programme, formulated by Hitler and Drexler, were presented to the public on 24 February 1920. The *Lexikon Nationalsozialismus* mentions the four main points as follows: "1. the unification of all Germans into a Greater Germany; 2. the abolition of the Treaties of Versailles and St Germain; 3. the right of Germany to the necessary territories and colonies; 4. the expulsion of all Jews from Germany".[35] Before long the name of the German Workers' Party (DAP) was changed into "National Socialist German Workers' Party" (NSDAP) – quite a mouthful, but no problem in a language in which words like *Bauchspeicheldrüsenentzündung* (inflammation of the pancreas) are common. Hitler, from his Schwabing headquarters in "Café Heck", "Osteria Bavaria", "Bratwürstglockl" and "Schelling Salon", planned, organized, created symbols, standards and labels, wrote articles, decided authoritatively on propositions and choices made by others, and sought for means to collect funds. Most of this he did on the advice of Captain Mayr and Dietrich Eckart, or after consulting them.

Turmoil

In a Germany in turmoil and with something like half the population inimical towards its social-democratic government, there was a spate of national and local coups by the Far Right as well as by the Far Left. Besides the revolutions in Munich there were other leftist bids for power in Berlin (the Spartacus Revolt), Hamburg, the Rhineland, Swabia, Thuringia and elsewhere. The "Kapp Putsch" in March 1920 was a right-wing, reactionary revolt against the Weimar Republic. The pan-German journalist Wolfgang Kapp (1868-1922), whom we have met as an acquaintance of Mayr and Eckart, was its figurehead, but its military leader was General von Lüttwitz, supported by one of the most ruthless Free Corps, Captain Ehrhardt's Marine Brigade.

The Ehrhardt Brigade marched into Berlin; the government troops refused to fire on the Free Corps soldiers who had been their

---

[35]Hilde Kammer & Elisabeth Bartsch: *Lexikon Nationalsozialismus*, p. 168.

comrades during the war; the government fled and Lüttwitz proclaimed a new, revolutionary government with Kapp as Chancellor. But the legal government called for a general strike of all workers against the right-wing putschists: "Strike, stop working, prevent the return of bloody reaction. Not a hand must move, not a single worker must help the military dictatorship. General strike all along the line! Workers, unite!"[36] For once *all* the workers, Socialists as well as Communists, took heed and acted in unison. Berlin was paralyzed. Five days later Kapp announced his resignation and fled to Sweden, as did Erich Ludendorff who had supported him, while most of the other putschists trekked southwards, to Bavaria.

The relevance of this event to our story is that Mayr and Eckart deemed the putsch sufficiently important to contact Kapp in Berlin, with the intention to coordinate with his coup an eventual rightist revolt in Bavaria. Mayr borrowed a light airplane from the Reichswehr, and Eckart, with "his collaborator" Hitler, flew to Berlin on 16 March. (Toland writes: "The weather was so turbulent that despite the pilot's skill Hitler kept vomiting ... When they touched down at Berlin the wan Hitler vowed that he would never, never fly again".[37]) But on their arrival at the centre of the capital the coup was already fizzling out and the Ehrhardt Brigade was marching in the opposite direction, back to their quarters on the outside of the city. Eckart profited of the occasion to introduce Hitler for the first time to some influential friends in Berlin. Afterwards they will travel there on several occasions.

When in December 1923 the financial situation of the *Völkische Beobachter* became so critical that the newspaper had to be sold, Hitler jumped to the occasion. He alerted Drexler, but the person who directed the operation of gathering the necessary funds was again Dietrich Eckart. The *Völkische Beobachter* (a title sometimes translated as "Racial Observer") will later on be the main organ of

---

[36]Louis Snyder: *Encyclopedia of the Third Reich*, p. 191.
[37]John Toland: *Adolf Hitler*, p. 133.

the Nazi party till the very end. Its first editor was – who else? – Dietrich Eckart.

In Rosenbaum's *Explaining Hitler* we obtain a glimpse of the political atmosphere in Munich at the time of Hitler's rising. The written histories of Hitler's life and of the Nazi party always zoom in so closely on their subject that it seems to occupy the whole stage, or at least centre stage, of life in Germany at the time. But the movement launched by Mayr, Eckart, Hitler and others was one of the many irrational undertakings in an irrational time – irrational not only in matters of politics but also in matters sociological, ideological and religious. The times were out of joint, not only in Germany, but all the same very much so in the land of Goethe and Kant. Hitler, driven by the power of his "obsessions", was an intriguing figure of the kind which fascinated the masses. And the more his fame spread, the more he was attacked by the enemy on the left, in Munich particularly by a socialist newspaper, the *Münchener Post*.

The Nazis called the *Münchener Post* "the poison kitchen". "The journalists of this newspaper were the first to focus sustained critical attention on Hitler from the very first moment this strange spectre emerged from the beer-hall back rooms", writes Rosenbaum. "They were the first to tangle with him, the first to ridicule him, the first to investigate him, the first to expose the seamy underside of his party, the murderous criminal behaviour masked by its pretensions to being a political movement. They were the first to attempt to alert the world to the nature of the rough beast slouching toward Berlin ... Their duel with Hitler lasted a dozen years and produced some of the sharpest, most penetrating insights into his character, his mind and method, then or since. Much of their work has been forgotten, but not much has been surpassed. And, as the name Poison Kitchen suggests, they succeeded in getting under Hitler's skin".[38] One of

---

[38] Ron Rosenbaum: *Explaining Hitler – The Search for the Origins of His Evil*, pp. 37, 38.

the first actions of the Nazis during the putsch of 1923 was the destruction of the offices and presses of the *Münchener Post*, as it was again in 1933 as soon as Hitler had become Chancellor.

The corporal becomes the Führer

It was in the *Münchener Post* that in July 1921 the text of a pamphlet was printed with the title *Adolf Hitler, Traitor*, accusing Hitler of all kinds of misbehaviour within the NSDAP, and of acting in the same fashion as the people he ranted against in his speeches and articles, the Jews. The pamphlet was written as an angry reaction against Hitler by a group of NSDAP members. The broader background was that Drexler and others, during a prolonged absence of Hitler in Berlin, had approached other small nationalist parties with the intent of an amalgamation in order to increase their political effectiveness. Hitler had not been consulted and reacted, "primadonna-like", with a fit of rage. He had already in those days "rapid resorts to extraordinary outbursts of uncontrolled temper".[39] He resigned brusquely from the party on 11 July.

For a person without other means of support, who had been convinced on entering the party that "there was no turning back", this resignation was a risky move. Or was it? Hitler knew full well that "the loss of its sole star performer would be a major, perhaps fatal, blow to the NSDAP".[40] His apparently impulsive resignation looks more like a well-planned manoeuvre to obtain the absolute power in the party – which was entrusted to him thanks to the mediation of, once again, Dietrich Eckart: Hitler re-entered the party on 26 July and was elected "chairman with dictatorial power" three days later. He obtained, moreover, that the party programme would be regarded as inviolate and that there would be no more merger attempts with other parties or organizations.

---

[39] Ian Kershaw, op. cit., p. 162.
[40] Id., p. 165.

Here the real Hitler stood up for the first time. He alone knew what he had been missioned to accomplish (and what he will never reveal to anyone); he considered the NSDAP his instrument; and he would never let anyone, under any condition, thwart his mission. In his inner mind Adolf Hitler was an absolute autocrat from those days in the summer of 1919, when an as yet unexplained change took place in him, till the moment he put a bullet through his head. Only the circumstances of his improbable rise made him temporarily hide or adapt his constant ambition. "Hitler is the extreme example of a politician who put his personal conviction of being missioned above everything else and practised politics according to the norms of his personal biography", writes Sebastian Haffner.[41]

One of the legends abroad in the land of Historia is that Hitler, in the first years of his public life, thought of himself as an announcer, a precursor, a "drummer", assembling the people for the coming of "the Strong One from Above", the *Führer* who, at the head of the German Volk, would at last lead them toward their glorious future as the Master Race. The legend that Hitler was a "drummer" until the time of his imprisonment at Landsberg and the writing of *Mein Kampf* originated in works like Albrecht Tyrell's *From 'Drummer' to 'Führer'* (1975) and had Ian Kershaw as its chief promulgator.

It is true that Hitler called himself a "drummer" on a few occasions, but these occasions were always public addresses or conversations with outsiders, especially journalists. The reason of these acts of apparent humility is simple: at that time Hitler was to the general public no more than an upstart, a funny-looking, pretentious, fanatical newcomer on a crowded political scene in Munich, a place somewhere in the south-eastern corner of Germany. At that time the country's Right had no shortage of leaders with dictatorial aspirations. There were the business and press magnate Alfred Hugenberg, the pan-German eminence Heinrich Class, and the commander of the

---

[41]Sebastian Haffner: *Anmerkungen zu Hitler*, p. 186.

Reichswehr General Hans von Seeckt. And there was, above all, Field Marshall Erich von Ludendorff, hero of Tannenberg and, with Paul von Hindenburg, co-dictator of Germany during the last half of the war, "who within the volkisch-nationalist camp was generally seen in the role of a future dictator" (Peter Longerich[42]).

"Hitler was elaborately modest when it came to comparing his position in [the unsuccessful 1923 putsch] with Ludendorff's. It was Ludendorff who held first place, he told the court [during the trial following the putsch], while he, Adolf Hitler, only led the political battle. For him to pretend to first place in a common enterprise with Ludendorff at his side was 'unthinkable'".[43] And so it was indeed. Hitler was obsessed but not crazy, not to the degree of proclaiming himself publicly as the Führer of the German people when he was still "a lonely wanderer out of nothingness" (his own words), a practically unknown Austrian, a lowly former corporal, a political backstreet adventurer and beer hall orator – while Ludendorff "was regarded as the symbol of the national struggle".[44]

But Hitler's attitude was quite different *within* the Party: there, from July 1921 onwards, he acted throughout as the Führer, the one and only person in the last instance responsible for all decisions. "... By a unanimous vote at a general meeting [of the NSDAP on 29 July] the entire direction of the party was entrusted to my own hands. At the same time a new statute was passed which invested the sole responsibility in the chairman of the movement ..." wrote Hitler in *Mein Kampf*. "When the new statute was approved and I was appointed as president, I had the necessary authority in my hands and also the corresponding right to make short shrift of all that nonsense [i.e. the democratic process]. In the place of decisions by the majority vote of the committee, the principle of absolute

---

[42]Peter Longerich: *Geschichte der SA*, p. 39.
[43]Eugene Davidson: *The Making of Adolf Hitler – The Birth and Rise of Nazism*, p. 210.
[44]Ian Kershaw, op. cit., 199.

responsibility was introduced".[45] He had obtained, thanks to the mediation of Dietrich Eckart, the "dictatorial powers" which suited his ambitions, and he would never let go of them. "With a mixture of cold-bloodedness, cunning, and resolution, with that readiness to take great risks even for small goals, which he was to exhibit time and again in crucial circumstances, he succeeded in gaining control of the NSDAP while strengthening his claim to leadership of the entire national-racist movement". (Fest[46]) Kershaw himself writes: "[The July coup within the NSDAP] was the first step on transforming the NSDAP into a new-style party, a 'Führer-party'".[47] This is confirmed by Heiden: "From that day", 29 July 1921, "Hitler was the leader of Munich's National Socialist Movement".[48]

"That same evening, at the Krone Circus, Hermann Esser hailed Hitler as 'our leader' – *unser Führer*. It was Esser, too, who held forth with cynical sentimentality in restaurants and taverns as the most zealous preacher of the Führer myth. Simultaneously, Dietrich Eckart in the *Völkische Beobachter* began a well-orchestrated campaign to purvey the same myth. On 4 August he sketched a profile of Hitler as a 'selfless, self-sacrificing, devoted and sincere' man, forever 'purposeful and alert'. A few days later came another account, this one written by Rudolf Hess, which further spiritualized the manly picture. It glorified Hitler's 'purest intent', his strength, his oratory, his admirable fund of knowledge and clear intellect. The fantastic growth of the Hitler cult is evidenced by another essay, written by Hess a year later, in connection with a contest on the subject: 'What will be the nature of the man who will lead Germany back to the summit?' Hess' piece took first prize …"[49]

As such it was, as "the man who one day will set Germany free", that Eckart introduced his protégé to the higher strata of Munich

---

[45] Adolf Hitler, op. cit., pp. 479, 480.
[46] Joachim Fest, op. cit., p. 139.
[47] Ian Kershaw, op. cit., p. 165.
[48] Konrad Heiden: *The Führer*, p. 95.
[49] Joachim Fest, op. cit., p. 134.

society. Some of its well-heeled members were Brothers and Sisters of the Thule Society; others were prominent and moneyed nationalists and Pan-Germans, like the publisher Julius Lehmann; still others belonged to the wealthy circles to which Eckart had access in his personal name and in the name of Ernst Hanfstängl, an admirer and supporter of Hitler who had studied at Harvard, was acquainted with T.S. Eliot, Walter Lippman and President Franklin Roosevelt, and ran an international arts business.

It was at the house of Hanfstängl's sister Erna that the historian K.A. von Müller saw Hitler arrive one day: "... The bell rang. Through the open door I could see him in the narrow hallway politely and almost servilely greeting our hostess, laying aside riding whip, velour hat and trench coat, finally unbuckling his cartridge belt with revolver attached and likewise hanging it on the clothes hook. It all looked very odd, reminiscent of Karl May's novels. As yet we did not know how precisely each of these trivialities in clothing and behaviour was even then calculated for effect, as were the strikingly close-cropped moustache, which was narrower than the unpleasantly wide-nostriled nose".[50]

Eckart introduced Hitler to the same kind of circles in Berlin and to the Wagner clan in Bayreuth, whom he knew well, for he had been a newspaper critic at the *Festspiele* for several years. Hamann, in her recent book *Winifred Wagner, or Hitler's Bayreuth*, calls Eckart "a Wagnerian", which reveals another interest he shared with Hitler. Winifred Wagner, the Englishwoman married to Siegfried Wagner, had spent several years of her youth in the house of the Bechsteins, the manufacturers of the famed pianos, whom she considered her step-parents. The Bechsteins had provided Eckart with funds for his magazine *In Plain German*. In June 1921 he introduced Adolf Hitler to them and they became "passionate friends of Hitler", sticking by him through thick and thin. What Hitler during his climb to power owed to supporters like the Bechsteins, the Bruckmanns and the

---

[50]Id., pp. 134-35.

Wagners is for the greatest part still unwritten history. And at every stage of that climb, behind every move of his pupil, we perceive the hand of Dietrich Eckart, who kept up a front of the rowdy Bavarian beer drinker, jumping on tables and bellowing his poem: *Sturm! Sturm! Sturm!* – but who seems to have seen the real Hitler in the corporal long before anybody else did, and who guided his first steps on his fateful way.

"As Führer we need a man who does not run away when he hears the sound of a machine gun", Eckart is reported to have exclaimed at a *Stammtisch* one night in early 1919. "We cannot use an officer: the people do not respect them any more! The best would be a worker with the gift of the gab – surely not a learned professor who shakes like a leaf and does it in his pants when the Reds start brandishing table legs. He does not need much brains: politics is the stupidest business in the world, and every market-woman in Munich knows more than the gentlemen in Weimar [the seat of the social-democratic government]. And he must be a bachelor, then we will get the women."[51] In later years the existence of Hitler's mistress, Eva Braun, was kept a secret from the German people. To them their Führer was that lonely figure perorating on the rostrum of the Zeppelin Field in Nuremberg or reviewing, with his right arm raised, an endless armed parade. Hitler fitted Eckart's prerequisites, but the mentor could not suspect – or could he? – that his pupil would exceed them beyond all human bonds.

Mayhem and murder

In post-war Munich one of the very first necessities for the propagation of an idea in public was protection from the rowdy beer hall mores, intensified by a nervous, explosive political situation. One of the traits of the Bavarian character, besides a maudlin

---

[51] Peter Orzechowski: *Schwarze Magie – Braune Macht*, pp. 30-31.

sentimentality when in a romantic mood or drunk, is its physical exuberance often bordering on violence. In the time under consideration violence was in the air everywhere in Germany. The thousands of battle-hardened soldiers had brought the atmosphere of the front into the fatherland, with violence and death still marching by their side. Nothing could be more alien and despicable to them than the bourgeois world of civil "decency". This was a generation of nihilists, whether the exalted, literary nihilism of an Ernst Jünger or the crude, physical nihilism of the street fighter whose only loyalty was to his comrades-in-desperation.

Moreover, Germany was a divided country where the tension of a possible civil war was almost palpable and where it ignited at times in the revolutionary bids for power mentioned before. It was impossible to take a public stand, and still more to propagate a new political party, without the physical force to confront any opposition. Hitler's awareness of this fact from the very beginning may be ascribed to the obvious circumstances, but behind his stress on the necessity of physical force there was something more profound, something "metaphysical". "While the programme of the ordinary political parties is nothing but the recipe for cooking up favourable results out of the next general elections", he wrote in *Mein Kampf*, "the programme of a Weltanschauung [like his] represents a declaration of war against an existing order of things, against present conditions, in short, against the established Weltanschauung ... In order to carry a Weltanschauung into practical effect it must be incorporated in a fighting movement ... Any Weltanschauung, though a thousand times right and supremely beneficial to humanity, will be of no practical service for the maintenance of a people as long as its principles have not yet become the rallying point of a militant movement".[52]

From the beginning this man was convinced that he was bringing a new "Weltanschauung", a new world vision, and still more a new

---

[52]Adolf Hitler, op. cit., pp. 380, 381, 319.

Faith to Germany and the world; he had seen at once that the insignificant DAP might be used as the seed-bed of a mass party to dominate all of society; and he knew that only physical force, in other words violence, was able to bring about the realization of his aspirations. "Since the first day of our foundation", he wrote, "we were resolved to secure the future of the movement by fighting our way forward in a spirit of blind faith and reckless determination ... We, by our aggressive policy, are setting up a new Weltanschauung which we shall defend with indomitable devotion ... Terror cannot be overcome with the weapons of the mind, but only by counter-terror".[53] Here is the origin of the barbarism, terror and cruelty which will be the hallmarks of the Third Reich. "Though these were violent times, this was from its inception an exceptionally violent movement", observes Laurence Rees.[54] Konrad Heiden heard Hitler shout: "We may be inhuman! But if we save Germany, we have accomplished the greatest deed in the world. We may do wrong. But if we save Germany, we have ended the greatest wrong in the world. We may be immoral. But if our people is saved, we have reopened the road for morality!"[55]

The need for a gang of muscular bodyguards was obvious from the first occasions on which the NSDAP stepped into the open. Just like the Socialist and Communists, and like their Rightist rivals, the Nazis needed at their meetings a *Saalschutz*, a trained guard to silence the hecklers or throw them into the street, if need be, with bloody harshness. The use of beer mugs and table and chair legs was part of the political customs of that period. In this the Nazis were as industrious as their opponents, and Hitler himself received a prison sentence for breaking up, with the assistance of his cronies, a meeting of Bavarian monarchists at the Löwenbräukeller.

---

[53] Id., pp. 305, 317, 299.
[54] Laurence Rees: *The Nazis – A Warning from History*, p. 23.
[55] Konrad Heiden, op. cit., pp. 124-25.

Many years later Hitler will reminisce in his monologues: "I could use only people who knew how to brawl. It was the same everywhere: people who were not ready to use their fists, but could only make plans, were of no use. I needed people who were ready to do what had to be done"[56] – which may mean anything. "What we needed and need", he wrote in *Mein Kampf*, "were and are not a hundred or two hundred hot-headed conspirators, but hundreds of thousands and more hundreds of thousands fanatical fighters for our ideology. It is not in secret circles that one should work, but in gigantic mass manifestations, and the road of the movement cannot be cleared by dagger or pistol, but by the conquest of the street. We must teach Marxism that the future lord of the street is National Socialism, just as one day it will be the lord of the nation".[57]

And so it was that the *Sturmabteilung* (literally "attack section"), SA for short, came into being. At first these desperados were recruited under the cover of a sports club, but things changed when professionals took matters in hand, more specifically the Ehrhardt Brigade. The full name of this notorious Free Corps, which fought after the war in Brunswick, Munich and Silesia, was "Marine Brigade Ehrhardt", after its founder and leader, *Korvettenkapitän* (equivalent to Commander) Hermann Ehrhardt. "At the time of the mutiny in Kiel", the event which at the beginning of November 1918 sparked off the German revolution, "the spade-bearded Ehrhardt had begun mobilizing antirevolutionary soldiers into a five-thousand man brigade, which one impartial expert later called the best combat unit he had ever seen".[58]

Still, this Free Corps was only one of many "which sprang up like mushrooms after the rain", and which numbered in the whole of Germany about 400,000 men. (Germany had demobilized six million soldiers.) "The Free Corps were latter-day condotierri", writes

---

[56] *Monologe im Führerhauptquartier 1941-1944*, p. 146.
[57] In Christian Zentner: *Adolf Hitlers 'Mein Kampf'*, p. 94.
[58] Otto Friedrich: *Before the Deluge – A Portrait of Berlin in the 1920s*, p. 59.

Burleigh, "consisting of former shock troops, junior and temporary officers, university students who had missed the war experience and anyone still spoiling for blood or incapable of psychological demobilization".[59] "Like the old mercenaries, they were possessed with an 'insatiable restlessness, a determination to burn themselves out; they felt the primeval male urge permanently to court danger. As soldiers of fortune, they accepted the disdain of the corpulent sedentary bourgeoisie and returned it in full measure round their camp fires and in their quarters, in battle or on the march'", writes Heinz Höhne, quoting Ernst Jünger.[60] Konrad Heiden called them "the armed human scum of five destructive years".[61]

The link between the Ehrhardt Brigade and the Hitler movement was Captain Ernst Röhm, one of those, with Mayr and Eckart, who made Hitler possible. Longerich calls him the "foster father" of the SA. "His conceptions of society were dominated by military categories; he shared the contempt of everything civil and looked with expectation for the outbreak of a war".[62] The military and the war, in which he had been wounded several times – part of his nose was shot away – were his life, and his mentality was that of the Free Corps toughs, with this difference that he was an officer in the legal Reichswehr, according to the Treaty of Versailles reduced to 100,000 men. Röhm was an amazingly influential officer, considering his captain's grade. He could take decisions on a political level over the heads of his superiors, in the first place because he was the lynchpin in the movement of illegal stocks of weapons in Bavaria, so much so that he was called "machine-gun king". "Röhm possessed the key to the weapons arsenal".[63] Like Captain Mayr, Röhm had connections in many organizations, overt and covert. He was himself the head

---

[59] Michael Burleigh: *The Third Reich*, p. 36.
[60] Heinz Höhne: *The Order of the Death's Head*, p. 63.
[61] Konrad Heiden, op. cit., p. 280.
[62] Peter Longerich, op. cit., p. 17.
[63] Id., p. 16.

of the *Reichkriegsflagge*, the War Banner of the Reich, and played a dominant role in the *Eiserne Faust*, the Iron Fist. And there was, in addition, the homosexual boys' network, an at the time most scandalous eruption of the latent homoeroticism in the youth movement and the *Männerbünde*, the men's leagues, including Army and Free Corps.

Röhm had become a member of the DAP shortly after Hitler. Again the jovial Eckart played a role in attracting this powerful and capable officer who would organize the fighting troops of the Party and provide them with arms when the situation so required. In fact, officer Ernst Röhm will never unreservedly submit to ex-corporal Hitler, even if for a time they addressed each other with the familiar *du*; between them there remained an unresolved conflict which will lead ultimately to Röhm's physical elimination. "Though Röhm had great hopes in the NSDAP leader, he felt in no way inclined to submit to Hitler unconditionally. On the contrary, to him Hitler, as the 'political' leader of the *Kampfbund* [a temporary coalition of nationalist organizations], was in the first place the publicly active 'drummer', who within the movement had to take his stand behind the military men. To the extremely self-conscious Röhm it was, in the relation between army and politics, always the soldier who took precedence over the politician".[64]

"Röhm enrolled Ehrhardt's soldiers in Hitler's SA, of which they formed the real nucleus", writes Heiden.[65] "The Ehrhard Brigade simply turned into the *Sturmabteilung Hitler*", confirms Heinz Höhne.[66] Of this fact we have an eyewitness, Ernst Hanfstängl: "Hitler worked more or less openly with the Ehrhardt Brigade people ... When I first started going to the *Beobachter* offices, which was the headquarters of the plot, the two men on guard at Hitler's door were not SA men at all, but members of the Organization

---

[64] Peter Longerich, op. cit., p. 39.
[65] Konrad Heiden, op. cit., p. 120.
[66] Heinz Höhne, op. cit., p. 20.

Consul, that section of the Ehrhardt group which had been behind the murders of Erzberger and Rathenau ... The SA usually marched together with the *Viking Bund*, who were Ehrhardt's militarized formations".[67] "Then there was a slightly mysterious man named Lieutenant Klintzsch", remembers Hanfstängl, "who was one of the storm trooper leaders and had been and probably still was a member of the Organization Consul".[68] Klintzsch, the right-hand man of Ehrhardt, was involved in the murder of Matthias Erzberger. "Organization Consul" was a secret cabal within the Ehrhardt Brigade charged with the execution of vehmic murders; "Consul" was the code name of Ehrhardt himself. Knowledgeable from personal observation about the association of the Hitler movement with this band of professional killers, journalist Konrad Heiden puts Erzberger's murder squarely at Hitler's door: "Erzberger was killed by Hitler's own men".[69]

Ron Rosenbaum's search for an explanation of "Hitler's evil" led him back to stains of blood and brains on the walls, to the residues of death. "After immersing myself in their reportage [of the *Munich Post*] on Hitler and the Hitler Party", writes Ron Rosenbaum, "I came to see that 'political criminal' was not an empty epithet but a carefully considered encapsulation of a larger vision: that Hitler's evil was not generated from some malevolent higher abstraction or belief, from an ideology that descended into criminality and murder to achieve its aims; rather, his evil *arose* from his criminality and only garbed itself in ideological belief. One sees this in the paper day by day, not so much in the big scandals, the head-line making events, but in the daily log of murders. "Vehme Murder in Thuringia', 'Brown Murder in Stuttgart', 'S.A. Killing in Halle', 'Brown Terror in Magdeburg', 'Nazi Murders in Lippe'. Scarcely an issue went by in those final two years without one and usually two, three or four,

---

[67] Ernst Hanfstängl: *Hitler – The Missing Years*, p. 76.
[68] Id., p. 47.
[69] Konrad Heiden, op. cit., p. 94.

brief dispatches reporting the blatant cold-blooded murder of political opponents by Hitler Party members ... What is missing from the grander explanations is what one sees on the ground, so to speak, the texture of daily terror apparent in the pages of the *Munich Post*, the systematic, step-by-step slaughter of Hitler's most capable political opponents, murdered by this party of political criminals".[70]

But Captain Ehrhardt, the autocratic commander of an elite Free Corps brigade, refused, just like Röhm, to give in to a man who in his eyes was an amateurish and pretentious, if not lunatic, ex-corporal. (At that time Adolf Hitler's name was in the ranks of his own people often mockingly abbreviated to "Ahi".) According to Höhne's sources, Ehrhardt not only withdrew his men from the SA, he turned against Hitler and his Party. "In close cooperation with Government circles and under nationalist cover, Captain Ehrhardt is preparing to form a [new] Free Corps; to judge from the manner in which it is being recruited and in view of Captain Ehrhardt's former attitude, its object must be to destroy the NSDAP". These doings will convince Hitler of the need of a bodyguard tied by oath directly to his person. He founded the "attack troop" *Stosstrupp Adolf Hitler*, which would be replaced later by the black Order of the Death's Head, the SS.

(Hitler will not forget what Ehrhardt had dared to do to him, nor that he had sided with von Kahr at the time of the Munich putsch in November 1923.[71] In the "Night of the Long Knives", in which Röhm together with the leaders of his SA power base were taken care of, "everywhere the SS robots were hunting down supposed enemies of the State ... Captain Ehrhardt, Hitler's reluctant ally in 1923, withdrew into the woods of his own estate, taking a couple of shotguns with him and, as soon as the Gestapo had left his house, got some friends to smuggle him across into Austria".[72] He escaped

---

[70]Ron Rosenbaum, op. cit., pp. 44, 45.
[71]Ernst Hanfstängl, op. cit., p. 93.
[72]Heinz Höhne, op. cit., pp. 80, 137.

with his life. Röhm and many others, including von Kahr, were not so lucky.)

"Fortunate Wolf"

"Hitler liked to be called 'Wolf' in his intimate circle", we read in Fest. "The name, he decided, was the primitive Germanic form of Adolf. It accorded, moreover, with his jungle image of the world and suggested the qualities of strength, aggressiveness and solitariness. He also used 'Wolf' as a pseudonym occasionally and later gave it to the sister who ran his household".[73] And Toland writes: "Hitler was living up to his own name, for Adolf was derived from the Teutonic word meaning 'fortunate wolf'".[74] (Another source says that "Adolf" means *Adelwolf*, noble wolf.) Could it be a coincidence that the H in Hitler's signature, with the nick in the horizontal bar, resembles the rune *Wolfsangel*?

Hitler used his pseudonym quite frequently. Everybody on the Obersalzberg knew him as *Herr Wolf* before it became clear that it was the famous politician Adolf Hitler who had purchased *Haus Wachenfeld*, probably with money from the Bechsteins, and who was rebuilding the house into what would become the famous villa *Berghof*. "Wolf" was also his usual pseudonym in Bayreuth, where to Winifred and Siegfried's children he was "Uncle Wolf". Some of his headquarters in the field were called *Wolfsschlucht* (Wolf's Gorge), *Wolfsschanze* (Wolf's Lair) and *Werwolf*. The town where the Volkswagen, designed by Hitler together with Ferdinand Porsche, was to be build was called Wolfsburg, and has retained the name to this day. And so on.

It was on Hitler's birthday, 20 April, in 1922 that one of his bodyguards, Christian Weber, presented an overjoyed Hitler with a German shepherd dog. (Hitler's best friend during the war had been

---

[73] Joachim Fest, op. cit., p. 157.
[74] John Toland, op. cit., p. 130.

a small English fox terrier, "Foxl". "The bastard who has stolen him doesn't know what he has done to me!" he would say one night in the Wolfsschanze.) The shepherd was christened "Wolf" after his new master and became Hitler's "constant companion ... He was faithful and devoted. The Führer took the dog always with him on his walks and also to the meetings."[75] The dog can be seen on some photos taken when Hitler was reviewing a parade or making an open air speech. He will be the first of a series of Hitler dogs, till the last one in the Berlin bunker, Blondi, will be used to try out the poison with which Hitler and Eva Braun are supposed to have ended their life.

Another constant companion of Hitler in the early years was his dog-whip. At a certain moment he seems to have had three whips! "Hanfstängl introduced Hitler to Frau Elsa Bruckmann, the wife of the publisher Hugo Bruckmann, a pan-German sympathizer and anti-Semite ... Hitler's ingratiating manners and social naivety brought out the mother instinct in her. Whether it was the wish to afford him some protection against his enemies that persuaded her to make him a present of one of the dog-whips he invariably carried around, is not clear. Oddly, his other dog-whip – the first he possessed – had been given to him by a rival patroness, Frau Helene Bechstein, while a third heavy whip, made from hippopotamus hide, which he later carried, was given to him by Frau Büchner, the landlady of the Platterhof, the hotel where he stayed on the Obersalzberg." (Ian Kershaw[76])

What may at first sight seem shallow details and anecdotes are indicative of an element that, as mentioned above, was inherent in Nazism, which took it as it were by mimicry from its supreme role model, the Führer: violence, terror, cruelty. Sebastian Haffner saw the top Nazis, whisperingly called *Goldfasane*, "gold pheasants" because of their showy, bemedalled uniforms, strut around with

---

[75] Anton Joachimsthaler, op. cit., p. 298.
[76] Ian Kershaw, op. cit., pp. 187-88.

their whips. "They had", he writes, "this revolting way of playing with a whip without ever having sat on a horse".[77] The first to follow Hitler's example in this was the half-mad pervert Julius Streicher.

It looked like a remarkable coincidence that so many of the top Nazis, actors in the great German drama, converged at the same time on the Munich scene. "Men, whose encounter would start a new political and philosophical structure, destined to promote a civilization completely different from ours, began to converge toward Munich ... All principal members of the future high governing strata of the Third Reich happened to be on the same stage".[78] It has struck many that not even a perceptive person would have been able, at the time of the rise of the movement, to pick them out from among the average members of German society. After all, Hess was an honoured war pilot, student and friend of Professor Haushofer and winner of the prize for the first flight around the Zugspitze; Streicher was a teacher; Rosenberg was an architect; Himmler was an agricultural engineer; Hanfstängl was a former Harvard student and art dealer; Gregor Strasser was a pharmacist; Frank was a lawyer; Goebbels was a doctor in Germanic languages; Göring, last ace pilot to command the Richthofen squadron, had been awarded the highest German military decoration, *Pour le mérite*... Joseph Serpico wrote in his book on the first Nuremberg trial: "It would be hard to pick out most of these men as war criminals from a gathering of Rotarians or accountants".[79]

But when you saw those people together, once they had made it, at "a peaceful, petty bourgeois coffee circle of Party comrades from places here and there in the country, in the company of the Chancellor of the great German people, then the subject of their conversations was: killing, insurrection, imprisonment, murder,

---

[77] Sebastian Haffner: *Germany: Jekyll & Hyde – 1939, Deutschland von innen betrachtet*, p. 56.
[78] André Brissaud: *Hitler et l'Ordre noir*, p. 65.
[79] Joseph Persico: *Nuremberg – Infamy on Trial*, p. 188.

robbery!"[80] Both Strasser brothers had belonged to that successful gang. In fact, Gregor was around 1930 seen by many as Hitler's rival for the leadership of the NSDAP. Otto will write when in exile: "Göring is a brutal egoist who cares nothing for Germany as long as he becomes something. Goebbels is a limping devil and basically two-faced. Röhm is a pig. This is the old guard of the Führer".[81] And Gregor said, shortly before he too would be murdered in "the night of the long knives": "From now on Germany is in the hands of an Austrian [Hitler] who is a congenial liar, a former officer [Göring] who is a pervert, and a clubfoot [Goebbels]. And I tell you the last is the worst of them all. This is Satan in human form".[82]

"The only thing they all had in common were their petty rivalries and jealousies", writes Hanfstängl, who as an old supporter, adviser and – he presumed – friend of Hitler thought he could continue to be frank with him once he had become Chancellor, but had to flee for his life. "Too many of us realized too late that the regeneration of the national life and economy was only part of the goal. Hitler and a majority of his followers really believed their anti-clerical, anti-Semitic, anti-Bolshevist, xenophobic catch-phrases and were prepared to keep the whole country in uproar in order to put them into practical effect."[83]

---

[80]Hermann Rauschning: *Gespräche mit Hitler*, p. 87.
[81]John Toland, op. cit., p. 381.
[82]Ibid.
[83]Ernst Hanfstängl, op. cit., p. 231.

5

SETTLING ACCOUNTS

I believe there are people who attract death, and Hitler certainly was one of them.

HENRIETTE VON SCHIRACH

Annus terribilis

After a series of bad years, 1923 was a terrible year for Germany. In retaliation for unsatisfactory "reparations", ie punitive payments agreed upon in the Treaty of Versailles, three French and Belgian divisions occupied the Ruhr, Germany's industrial heartland. The German Government responded with "passive resistance", stopping all production. Yet the industrialists and the workers had to be compensated in some way, and the Government began to print money, thereby causing galloping inflation. The victors of the Great War were now being paid with worthless money, but the consequences were catastrophic for the German population, in the first place for the middle classes, who lost all their savings.

Soon the "hyperinflation" took on nightmarish proportions. Stacks of banknotes were no longer counted but measured with a ruler. "It was cheaper to burn money than coal", writes Weiss.[1]

---

[1] John Weiss: *Ideology of Death*, p. 228.

Heiden uses the term "starving billionaires". One egg cost five million marks. "Practically speaking there was no money any more in Germany", says Haffner.[2] Thousands lost their jobs; there was a spate of angry strikes and riots in which shops in the towns and farms in the countryside were attacked by hordes of hungry people; swindlers, black marketers and usurers thrived. The middle classes, who had their own code of honour in imitation of the respected nobility, the military and state officialdom, were severely shaken in their convictions, and turned as a consequence toward the extreme right-wing parties with their promises of drastic action to make Germany healthy, decent and self-respecting again. The membership numbers of the NSDAP shot up.

The Communists, now directly controlled by Moscow (which soon will mean Stalin), judged that the moment had come for the "second revolution" in Germany: the Bolshevik take-over of the Socialist (Menshevik) revolution which, as the Weimar Republic, was still in power. "Indeed, in Thuringia and in Saxony, where also since September a Popular Front was in power, the radical Left – as had been decided by the Politburo of the Russian Communist Party – made preparations for the great armed revolt. Military command groups were organized with the collaboration of Soviet instructors and the first 'revolutionary centuries' of armed workers were formed after the example of the revolutionary guards in Petersburg. Their task was ... to spread the revolution that was to expand like a wildfire from the middle of the Reich, and to bring about a 'German October' in imitation of the Russian October."[3]

Germany was split into Left and Right, with the looming possibility of civil war. But the Left was itself fatally divided into Socialists and Communists. The reason that the civil war in Germany did *not* break out in the years immediately following the armistice was in fact the bitter enmity between the two leftist ideologies,

---

[2] Sebastian Haffner: *Anmerkungen zu Hitler*, p. 189.
[3] Ralph Reuth: *Hitler*, p. 146.

turned more fiercely against each other than against the Right. An ironical upshot of this situation was that the social-democratic government had to rely on the ultra-nationalist Army, the Reichswehr, to clamp down on the communist uprisings and keep itself in the saddle.

The social-democratic governments of Scheidemann and Stresemann, at times in coalition with the Liberals and Catholics of the centre, were capable and patriotic, dedicated not only to the improvement of the lot of the workers but also to the well-being of their country as a whole. But they had inherited an unmanageable situation, first in having to execute the clauses of the Treaty of Versailles and second in having to govern a nation on the brink of disaster – all the while being disdained and mocked by the rightist, reactionary, nationalist part of the population which considered itself the true Germany and the living incarnation of its values. This attitude of reactionary Germany, which may be called instinctive, towards the ideological values of Socialism and its representation of the fourth estate was a direct cause of the conditions that made Hitler possible, and will be exploited to the utmost by the man himself.

The general in command of the Reichswehr was Hans von Seeckt, a monocled officer of the Prussian school, very capable and very aware of his vital position and clout. Some counted him among the candidates for a rightist dictatorship. True, the German army had been reduced to 100 000 men, without a navy or air force. But there were the thousands of trained and fanatically nationalist men of the Free Corps and the state militias, which Seeckt himself cleverly incorporated into a "Black Reichswehr", often camouflaged as youth organizations or sports clubs. It was now Seeckt's job to put down the communist uprisings in Thuringia and Saxony, plus those in Hamburg, in the Ruhr and elsewhere. This does not seem to have been very difficult, maybe because he could count on the support of every non-communist German, as Communism, only six years after the Russian revolution, was still generally feared and abhorred.

A more serious problem for General von Seeckt, and for the government of the Weimar Republic, was posed by Bavaria, which was anything but communist. Bavaria was to all German reactionaries the bulwark of the nationalist spirit, and had, as we have seen, put its doors wide open for any activist rightist in distress or fugitive from justice. One should bear in mind that the German states still commanded a considerable degree of independence; the army and the police, for instance, were run by the state. Another important factor is that Catholic Bavaria was strongly separatist and involved in a battle for prestige with Protestant Prussia. Munich, "Athens on the Isar", was synonymous with culture, while Prussian Berlin stood for boorishness and aberration. "Since Bismarck had founded the Second German Reich, Bavaria had been little more than a provincial vassal and here opportunity was being offered for Munich to assume the leadership of Germany and take it away from the despised Prussians in Berlin."[4]

The tension between Bavaria and the federal Government increased when Chancellor Stresemann no longer tolerated the aggression against himself and the Republic in the Munich rightist press, especially in the *Völkische Beobachter*, and when the open Bavarian defiance of the law exceeded all tolerable bounds by giving custody to people like Ehrhardt and Klintzsch against whom there were warrants of arrest. When General Otto von Lossow, commander of the Reichswehr in Bavaria, refused to act on his instructions, the federal Minister of Defence deposed him. Both the State Government of Bavaria and the federal Government of Germany declared a state of emergency on the same day in September. The President of Bavaria nominated Otto von Kahr "State Commissioner" with dictatorial powers and General von Lossow was reinstated as head of the Bavarian Reichswehr. This was an act of mutiny: Bavaria was now in open defiance of the Weimar Republic.

---

[4]Ernst Hanfstängl: *Hitler – The Missing Years*, p. 98.

Taking into account the occupation of the Ruhr, which the French tried to make into a separate state apart from the German fatherland, the communist uprisings instigated by Moscow, the red hot tension between Bavaria and the central Government, and the catastrophic state of the finances and the economy with the resulting riots and unemployment, it is no wonder that Sebastian Haffner writes: "In the autumn of 1923 the German Reich was on the verge of political extinction".[5] Joachim Fest is of the same opinion: "The harassed [central] government might well see the events in Munich as the signal for total collapse".[6]

A putschist in tail coat

"The three vons", State Commissioner Gustav von Kahr, General von Lossow, commander of the Bavarian Reichswehr, and Colonel von Seisser, head of the state police, formed a triumvirate with practically unlimited power in Bavaria. As rightist reactionaries they did not hesitate to further intensify the confrontation with the Weimar Republic and declared Bavaria "a stronghold of threatened Germanhood". The Bavarian army had to swear an oath not to the constitutional central government but to the State. The triumvirate justified most of its rebellious actions as measures against the communist threat in adjacent Thuringia, but nobody doubted that they were planning another rightist coup against the Weimar Republic and that they were looking for support from nationalist circles anywhere in the country, even in Berlin. They were, however, not only separatists but also monarchists, who wanted to bring the Wittelsbach dynasty back on the Bavarian throne in the person of Crown Prince Rupprecht, as a field marshal the former commander of the Bavarian army during the war and still "enjoying an almost mystical respect". Rupprecht was now pulling all possible strings to

---

[5]Sebastian Haffner, op. cit., p. 189.
[6]Joachim Fest: *Hitler*, p. 174.

re-enter the royal palace in Munich which his father had hurriedly left in the middle of that November night in 1918.

There was no love lost between "the three vons" and Adolf Hitler. The ultra-rightist Hitler was, as a fanatical Pan-German, an arch-opponent of Bavarian separatism, with a deep resentment against royalty and nobility in general. The triumvirate, for its part, looked down on the Austrian ex-corporal who, in their eyes, was "a pretentious young man of obscure origin who seemed somewhat cracked".[7] Ernst Hanfstängl will bear witness to the fact that "Hitler's fight against this attitude [of disparagement] was to take him years".[8] Writers on Hitler's life usually mention some of his remarkable achievements, eg redeeming the economy, rebuilding the German army or the masterly strategy of the invasion into France; seldom, though, does one read about his fight against the social prejudices and obstacles during his climb to power. Yet it was this tenacity that made all the rest possible and that must have been rooted in an extremely powerful conviction, or inspiration, or vision, to take him where he ultimately arrived.

Kahr and his two acolytes did everything in their power to block Hitler's ambitions, prohibiting some Nazi manifestations or occasionally the publication of his paper, the *Völkische Beobachter*. "The brown phalanx", the SA, was expanding rapidly, as was the membership of the NSDAP, and rumours of a putsch were rife, still more so after Mussolini had become *Duce* of Italy as a consequence of the "March on Rome". Who in Germany knew in those days that this "march" was largely mythical? And who took into consideration that the social and political circumstances in Germany differed totally from those in Italy? One has only to cast an eye on the map of Germany and consider the geographical distance between Munich and Berlin, plus the fact that Seeckt's disciplined Reichswehr could easily halt whatever Bavarian phalanxes might move northwards, to

---

[7]Id., p. 184.
[8]Ernst Hanfstängl: op. cit., p. 98.

ask oneself how the triumvirate as well as Hitler could possibly dream of marching on Berlin. But troubled times hatch troubled schemes.

Besides, Hitler had painted himself into a corner. He had accepted and exploited the comparison with Benito Mussolini and allowed himself now generally to be called *Führer*, ie leader, *duce*, of the Nazis. (Soon this designation will become obligatory in the NSDAP, and former acquaintances who habitually addressed him as "Herr Hitler" will incur his wrath when continuing to do so.) The growing ranks of the SA, now mostly recruited among the unemployed, had to be fed and kept occupied. Many of them, although enjoying the comradeship and the intimidating swastika armbands and uniforms (if they had one), were no idealists: they were just hungry and penniless. They could not forever be kept marching and chanting in the streets or collecting money for the Party – while doing a little mischief on the side, for instance beating up an old Jew. They were looking forward to what was promised to them – power, food and money – and this not in the long term but as soon as possible.

"Hitler had already for some time become the hostage of his own propaganda, in which he himself had announced time and again that he would soon settle accounts with the 'November criminals'. If he did not risk the putsch now, he would be a boaster and vacillator in the eyes of his followers and sooner or later be overtaken by the dynamics of the situation." (Ralph Reuth[9]) "The storm troopers were impatiently pressing for action. Their restlessness had various causes. Many of them were professional soldiers, who after weeks of conspiratorial preparations were all keyed up for action. Some of the paramilitary organizations, which had been on battle alert for weeks, had taken part in the 'fall manoeuvres' of the [Bavarian] Reichswehr, but now all their funds had been used up. Hitler's treasury was also exhausted, and the men were going hungry." (Joachim Fest[10])

---

[9]Ralph Reuth, op. cit., p. 152.
[10]Joachim Fest, op. cit., p. 179.

The Hitler Putsch on 8 and 9 November 1923 was one of the worst prepared, most amateurish and even comical events (except for the shooting) in German history. Hitler and his cronies tried to hijack, on the evening of 8 November, a meeting in the Bürgerbräukeller organized by Kahr, Lossow and Seisser, fearing that the trio might beat him to the putsch and proclaim an independent Bavaria under king Rupprecht. From the start everything went wrong.

Hitler, at the head of the helmeted and armed Shock Troop Hitler, appeared in the overcrowded beer hall in tail coat, which made him look like a head waiter. (Nobody has found out where he got the idea of donning this original dress to conduct a coup.) Brandishing his pistol, he silenced the crowd with a shot into the ceiling. "The national revolution has begun!" he shouted. He announced that a new national government had been formed with himself at the helm and Ludendorff as chief of the army (an arrangement about which Ludendorff had not been consulted and which he will never forgive). Hitler forced the triumvirate to swear an oath of collaboration with him, which they broke as soon as he made the mistake of leaving them, going somewhere else where he was not needed. They fled from the beer hall, declared all initiatives of the Nazis illegal and started organizing the suppression of the putsch. After a long and indecisive night in which many more blunders were committed and many a litre jug of beer (at a billion marks apiece) emptied, the Nazis, on Ludendorff's initiative, started on a march towards the city centre around 11 am on 9 November.

"Most marchers wore ragged uniforms from old army stocks, combined with articles of civilian dress such as felt hats and shawls. One of the participants got the impression that he and his comrades looked 'like a defeated army that had not been doing battle'. Another asked himself if these shabby figures would actually make an impressive effect on the population. But who could have expected more? None of the participants had known beforehand that they were to execute a propaganda march through the city, and in the bygone night they had slept little and drunk much beer. Many suffered from a nasty hangover." (David Large[11])

Hitler marched in the front row, behind the flags and banners, with Ludendorff on his left and Scheubner-Richter on his right; also in the front row were Göring as head of the SA, Kriebel, commander of the Kampfbund, Rosenberg, and Hitler's bodyguard Ulrich Graf (butcher, wrestler and great brawler). Then there followed, in three columns side by side, the Shock Troop Hitler, the veteran Munich SA and the Bund Oberland, with behind them "the motley collection of men", all together some two to three thousand.

Having arrived at the Marienplatz, Munich's central square with the Gothic Townhall, Hitler proved again incapable of taking a decision and it was again Ludendorff, "in full regimentals", who continued marching, this time in the direction of the *Feldhernhalle*, a famous Renaissance monument near Odeon Square. But the narrow street the marchers engaged into was blocked by a cordon of state police. Nobody knows who fired the first shot. When the exchange of fire ended after thirty seconds – a long time under fire – fourteen of the Nazi marchers and four policemen lay dead. Killed by one of the first shots was Scheubner-Richter next to Hitler. Graf had thrown himself on his prostrate Führer and was hit no less than eleven times. (He survived.) This is one of the many occasions on which Hitler was protected by Destiny, or whatever one cares to call it. He escaped with a dislocated left shoulder to Hanfstängl's newly built villa in Uffing, in the countryside. There he tried to commit suicide, but was prevented from doing so by Hanfstängl's wife, the beautiful Helene, who wrestled the pistol from his hand.

The day he "fell on his face" or "fell from the tightrope", as he himself would say later, will remain a painful memory for Hitler throughout his life. It was also the day on which the learning phase in his political life came to an end. He would switch to completely different political tactics: the attainment of power by legal means.

---

[11]David Clay Large: *Hitlers München*, p. 236.

Historians are still writing that the November putsch was an improvised occurrence. Brigitte Hamann in her book on Hitler and Winifred Wagner, however, makes us think otherwise. Hitler visited *Haus Wahnfried* in Bayreuth for the first time on 1 October 1922, a month before the putsch. All present were touched by his solemn first contact with the place where the revered Richard Wagner had lived, worked, and lay buried. "It is certain that Hitler told the Wagners also about the planned putsch", asserts Hamann. "He had obviously planned his visit to Wahnfried with great care and went there at a time when he was already regarded as a special personality, even as the future 'saviour of Germany' who was awaited everywhere, and when he already occupied a leading position in the nationalist German associations. That he went there precisely at this moment, shortly before the putsch and the expected assumption of power, had the effect of something like a consecration. As religious people go on a pilgrimage before making an important decision, thus Hitler went to obtain the blessings of [Houston] Chamberlain and of the departed Master, Richard Wagner."[12] Rumours were abroad, plans were made, the tail coat was rented, and the whole affair turned into a resounding fiasco – which made Hitler a figure of national importance.

"Bolshevism from Moses to Lenin"

Where was Dietrich Eckart during the Hitler Putsch? John Toland spots him at the Bürgerbräukeller, just before the marchers left there, and near the Isartor, watching them pass by singing the "Storm Song" which he had written for the SA.[13] He was already gravely ill in those days and must have followed the column of the putschists in a car. He was arrested after the failed coup and imprisoned, first in Stadelheim prison, then with Hitler and the others in the fortress at Landsberg.

---

[12]Brigitte Hamann: *Winifred Wagner, oder Hitlers Bayreuth*, p. 84.
[13]John Toland: *Hitler*, pp. 229, 230.

An important document in the Hitler saga is the unfinished "dialogue" Eckart wrote a few months earlier, in April and May 1923: *Bolshevism from Moses to Lenin: A Dialogue between Adolf Hitler and me.* This text is not the rendering of a real dialogue but of a fictitious one, no doubt based – and herein lays its special value – on conversations which must have taken place between the two men. If these pages were pure invention, Eckart would never have given them to others to read and they would never have been published after his death, certainly not by the Nazi Hocheneichen-Verlag.

The German historian Ernst Nolte was the first to draw attention to this document, in 1961, and Margarete Plewnia's Eckart biography, in which the dialogue is comprehensively analysed and commented upon, appeared in 1970, but only recent authors begin to read it in earnest. Hitler's first steps on the political stage have been insufficiently studied. Not only is this astonishing gap in the Hitler biographies the cause of a lack of understanding, or of a wrong understanding of Hitler's mind, it allows also full play for the most extravagant imaginations.

Plewnia, from her point of view, shows how Hitler's anti-Semitism took shape "between the autumn of 1919 and the summer of 1920" under Eckart's influence, which can be traced in Hitler's speeches, preserved in the files of the Munich police. The effect of Eckart's brand of "metaphysical anti-Semitism", mentioned in a previous chapter, is incontestable, eg in the following passages: "We do not want to be emotional anti-Semites who seek to create the atmosphere of the pogrom: we are driven by the relentless resoluteness to expose the evil at its base and to eradicate it root and branch. To attain our goal any means will be justified, even if we have to make a pact with the devil". (6.4.1920) And: "We have to eliminate the poison [ie the Jewish spirit] outside and inside us when we want to become cured again." (17.4.1920)

Hitler's anti-Judaic ejaculations had become increasingly violent from the time of his propaganda pep-talks at Lechfeld and the Gemlich letter onwards. They will climax (for the time being) in a speech on 13 August 1920, less than a year after his entry in the Harrer and Drexler circle. The title of this speech was explicit: "Why are we Anti-Semites?" and Hitler gave a recital of his complete anti-Jewish repertoire. In the police protocol of the speech is noted the usual crescendo in the response of the audience: "laughter – applause – bravo and applause – tumultuous applause – long tumultuous applause …" Documents like this show, beyond any doubt, the preparedness of the German soil for the seeds sown by Hitler and his likes.

It is reasonable to assume that Eckart intended the "dialogue" as a lasting testimony to his mentorship of Hitler. One possible reason for putting everything down on paper was that his health was declining rapidly. Another reason may have been that Hitler remained no longer satisfied with Eckart's "metaphysical anti-Semitism" and turned to more tangible justifications of his mission. True, Eckart was a blazing Jew-baiter, preaching a purification of the German race from the Jewish Evil and the advent of a Führer who would lead the Germans toward their glorious future; but his way of reasoning and his philosophical categories were too abstract for Hitler's demagoguery. How could Hitler preach the elimination and extermination of the Jews while saying that their evil, the poison of a demonic race, was there in all of humanity, including every German in his audience? Darwinism, as interpreted by Chamberlain and Rosenberg, was much more straightforward and handier. Anti-Semitism, after all, is a matter of gut feelings, and any combination of simplistic arguments will do to justify it, even if very loosely stitched together. The assent of the audience was obtained by the power of speech, not by the reasoning behind it.

Still, so many terms (poison, parasite, bacillus) and concepts Hitler was using, and will keep using in the future, are there in the Eckart text, written in the form of a dialogue among equals not to offend the recently proclaimed Führer if he were to read it. There is the schizoid interpretation of the biblical narration about the Jews in Egypt: the Jews were not kept in bondage by the Egyptians, on the contrary the Jews did their usual subversive work in trying to overthrow the throne of the pharaoh. There is the assertion that it was the Christians, followers of Paul, the Jew of Tarsus, who undermined the Roman Empire and caused its downfall. (To Hitler – as to Wagner, Chamberlain, Rosenberg and most of the Nazis – Christ was not a Jew but an Aryan and an anti-Semite.) There is the fundamental Jewishness of the Catholic Church, for is their holy book not Jewish literature, and are many of their feasts and ceremonies not of Jewish origin? – this in direct contradiction to the anti-Semitism for which Christianity and the Catholic Church were primarily responsible. And there are of course the theories of the Jew Karl Marx, propagated to dominate the world and as such the inspiration of Lenin and his Judeo-Bolshevism.

One finds such convictions, which he had from Eckart, scattered through Hitler's conversations and nightly musings also in later years. And he will proclaim on several occasions that Nazism has to wage a fight against Bolshevism on the left and against Capitalism on the right because both are strategic instruments of the attempt by the Jews to bring the world under their control. Eckart worded this as follows in his *Dialogue*: "Against left *and* right stands our front. This is the cause of the strange fact that we are attacked from two sides which fight against each other. The Reds shout at us that we are reactionaries, and the reactionaries that we are Bolshevists. From both sides it is the Jew who blows the storm clouds toward us".[14]

When one reads such an accumulation of crankiness, one wonders how millions of people, belonging to the most cultured nation in the world (at least in their own eyes) could accept them as plain truth. And there was much more of the same alloy, eg the world ice theory, the theory of the hollow earth, and the official proclamation of an Aryan science in opposition to the Jewish science of Einstein and similar scatterbrains – not to forget the "scientific" murderous race theories.

---

[14] Margarete Plewnia: *Auf dem Weg zu Hitler*, p. 101.

The political, social and cultural fantasies of Hitler and his Nazis were bizarre, but the underlying fact, the base of the volkisch movement to which Nazism belonged, was a very important phenomenon on the European cultural scene: it was the refusal to accept the ideals of the Enlightenment, born of Reason, and the stubborn, instinctive resistance against them. It is in these ideals as a coherent whole that we find the target of the dark and spiteful aggression of all that was supposed to constitute the true, fundamental human values born from "the German soul" in an embellished past. Modernism, equated with enlightenment and progress, was to the fundamentalist volkisch reactionaries synonymous with materialism, capitalism, liberalism, internationalism, democracy, socialism, communism, Bolshevism, etc. Take any of these terms in the writings, speeches and conversations of Hitler and you will find them associated with "the Jew". The words "Jew" and "Jewish" could be used for anything Hitler and his people found unpleasant, inferior, unjust, inimical or criminal. Philosophically, however, they always related to the changing world in progress, of which the Enlightenment was the cause and justification. Nazism as a volkisch movement was part of the general European reaction, born out of disorientation, insecurity and fear, against the coming into being of a new world.

How does one become an anti-Semite? The concrete reason or occasion in Eckart's case is unknown, as it is in the case of many others. There was a germ in the air, a poison in the mental nourishment of that time which became virulent when the personal constitution proved receptive because of certain surroundings or a traumatic experience. The German mind – and not only the German – had become poisoned by what John Weiss calls an "ideology of death". And Eckart had read all the books. In his *Dialogue* there are references to Otto Hauser, Werner Sombart, Henry Ford, Gougenot des Mousseaux, Theodor Fritsch, Friedrich Delitzsch, etc., plus a number of periodicals, and Eckart had chewed all that for Hitler to digest.

There was also a new factor which played an important role since 1917: the Russian Revolution. Lenin, Trotsky, Bolshevism, a Republic of Councils, Bela Kun, Spartacists, red flags, the hammer and sickle, new leftist terms and slogans: it all became part of the popular awareness, and all of it was felt as threatening. The presence of these elements in Hitler's thought structures is the surest indication that they were formed in Munich, directly by Eckart through his writings and his frequent contacts with Hitler, indirectly by the Thule Society and its related circles animated by Sebottendorff. What remains to be explained is the power which "the man from nowhere" commanded to pull off the impossible, and which made that "there was no viable alternative to Hitler".[15]

RIP

Some students of Hitler's life and of Nazism, who know about the decisive role played by Dietrich Eckart, are of the opinion that Hitler more and more distanced himself from his mentor in the course of 1923. One sign, they say, is the fact that Eckart was replaced by Alfred Rosenberg as editor of the *Völkische Beobachter*. This argument is not convincing because Eckart's health problems had become very serious and because he was not the kind of steady worker to run the *Beobachter*, which had become a daily newspaper.

Another argument is the passage in Ernst Hanfstängl's autobiographical book *The Missing Years*, where he writes that Eckart told him one night in Berchtesgaden: "You know, Hanfstängl, something has gone completely wrong with Adolf. The man is developing an incurable case of *folie de grandeur*. Last week he was striding up and down in the courtyard here with that damned whip of his and shouting: 'I must enter Berlin like Christ the Temple of Jerusalem and scourge out the moneylenders', and more nonsense of that sort. I tell you, if he lets his Messiah complex run away with him, he will ruin us all".[16] Another symptom of a possible change

---

[15]Robert Gellately: *Backing Hitler*, p. 11.
[16]Ernst Hanfstängl, op. cit., p. 83.

in the Eckart-Hitler relation was Eckart's reflection to Hanfstängl: "I am fed up with this toy-soldier stuff of Hitler's. Heaven knows the Jews are behaving badly enough in Berlin and the Bolshevists are an even worse lot, but you cannot build a political party on the basis of prejudices alone. I am a writer and a poet and I am too old to go along with him any more".[17]

It is nevertheless demonstrable that Eckart went along with Adolf till the very end. When the NSDAP held its first *Parteitag*, on 27 and 28 January 1923 in Munich, Eckart stood in the place of honour, one pace behind Hitler, to review the parade marching through the snow. This was also the day on which the first SA standards were consecrated, all of them carrying the slogan *Deutschland erwache!* (Germany awake), a battle cry coined by Eckart as the last line of both stanzas of his "Storm Song". Plewnia reproduces a facsimile of this song written during a nocturnal session by the author in the guest book of the Bratwurstglöckl on 18 January 1923; Eckart has illustrated the song with a drawing of Hitler striking a martial pose as a flag-bearer, and both have signed the masterpiece.[18] On 20 April, Hitler's birthday, the *Beobachter* published a poem by Eckart with the title "Führer of Germany", announcing that that Führer had come: "Who want to see, can see! The Force is there, causing the night to flee!"[19]

When in April 1923 Eckart had to go into hiding because there was a warrant of arrest out against him for libel against President Ebert, he withdrew incognito into the mountains above Berchtesgaden. "Eckart's contact with the NSDAP was not interrupted during the period of his exile. Drexler, Amann, Weber, Esser and Hitler stayed with him as visitors."[20] Eckart returned to Munich when the warrant was withdrawn and spoke two times at

---

[17]Id., p. 81.
[18]Margarete Plewnia, op. cit., p. 86.
[19]Id., p. 90.
[20]Id., p. 91.

NSDAP meetings. During the November Putsch he met Hitler at the Bürgerbräukeller just before the march on the Feldhernhalle set off. After the putsch he tried for a while to keep the dispersed Nazi movement together, collaborating to this end with Rosenberg. But he too was arrested and wrote, in Stadelheim prison, a scathing poem on the Germans for deserting their Führer in his bid to save the fatherland: "Cowardly people! You despise anyone who faithfully cared for you! ... You are born for the yoke of the slaves and think of nothing but gorging yourselves!"[21] Surely, this last instance shows that the tie between Eckart and Hitler was still there. Plewnia also quotes the words of a friend of Eckart's, a certain Reid, who would have heard from Eckart's mouth in the summer of 1923: "When there is a man whom Destiny has chosen to save Germany, then that man is Adolf Hitler, and no other". And even after the November Putsch Eckart would have confided to Reid that "he continued to believe in Hitler, because he was under a Star".[22] But the strongest confirmation of the unbroken tie between the mentor and his disciple are the numerous ways in which the Führer honoured Eckart's memory once he had come to power, and the tears which came to his eyes whenever he remembered him. This was truly exceptional for a character like Hitler's, who never forgot or forgave the least personal slight.

Dietrich Eckart was dismissed from Landsberg prison because of serious heart trouble. Hanfstängl writes that he collapsed during an alarm exercise. He died in Berchtesgaden on 26 December. Towards the end of his life he is supposed to have said: "Follow Hitler. He will dance, but it is I who wrote the tune. We have given him the means to communicate with Them ... Do not mourn for me, for I will have influenced history more than any other German".[23] Historical or not, hyperbolical or not, these words contain a great deal of truth.

---

[21]Id., p. 112.
[22]Ibid.
[23]André Brissaud: *Hitler et l'Ordre noir*, p. 53.

Having been away from Germany for years, Sebottendorff seems not to have followed the events there attentively, and badly misread Hitler's character. He published *Before Hitler Came* a few months after the Nazi Chancellor had taken office. The title attracted attention, in the first place of the Bavarian political police. There is little doubt that Sebottendorff wrote the book to present Hitler with the bill of formerly rendered services, and that he thought he might claim his share in the success of the movement he had aided to launch. Soon after the Munich Republic of Councils, when the Thule had been at its most active and several of its members had been executed, he recalled, the society started on its downward slide and began to disintegrate. "Heavy inner struggles began which would mean the end of the Society. It had accomplished its goal; it had to disappear in order that new things could come about which stood already on the threshold. A few weeks after Sebottendorff's departure [he is writing in the third person], Adolf Hitler entered the rooms of the Thule, and he participated in the great propaganda days when under the leadership of Dannehl [Sebottendorff's successor] the whole of Munich was covered with leaflets and posters."[24]

This was not the kind of memories Hitler liked to be reminded of. "Hitler felt it as a personal offence when somebody, struck by the similarity of Hitler's thought with that of others, drew his attention to precursors or like-minded thinkers. Hitler wanted to have thought out everything by himself and without examples. He considered it a diminution of his greatness when one pointed out analogous ideas."[25]

Nor will he have liked the idea that it was Sebottendorff's disappearance which had made his appearance possible: "Sebottendorff had to sacrifice himself", writes Sebottendorff, "he had to go not to smother the frail plant" – of National Socialism, that is.[26] The former Master of Thule made matters worse by trying

---

[24]Id., p. 167.
[25]Hermann Rauschning: *Gespräche mit Hitler*, p. 212.
[26]Id., p. 170.

to relaunch the Society, perhaps envisioning a place of honour in the Third Reich for himself and his former adherents. "Today is fulfilled what those seven [executed members of Thule] and the Thule as a whole looked forward to ... We recognize the greatness and the merit of Adolf Hitler. He has created what we longed for; we gathered the elements, he led to the goal! ... It was to members of Thule that Hitler first came, and Thule members were the first who allied themselves with Hitler."[27] Another grave mistake by Sebottendorff was that he called on the anti-Semitic ex-Jesuit Berhard Stempfle to help resuscitate the Thule Society, for Stempfle, one of the readers and correctors of the *Mein Kampf* manuscript, had hurt Hitler, probably in the murky Geli Raubal affair, and would become another victim of the "Night of the Long Knives".

The reader may remember that Sebottendorff, after his arrest by the Gestapo, was saved by former Thule-Brother Rudolf Hess. "Almost all collaborators of Hitler [in the Munich years] had to do with the Thule Society in one way or another, if they were not members themselves", asserts Hermann Gilbhard.[28] The list of links between Hitler's NSDAP and the Thule Society is indeed significant. The DAP was founded by Thule-Brother Harrer and "guest" of Thule Drexler; the swastika was Thule's emblem; the *Völkische Beobachter* had been one of Thule's publications before it was purchased by the NSDAP; many members of Thule's Free Corps entered the SA ("the [Thule] Free Corps Oberland is the backbone of the present-day SA Hochland and anyway of the first SA units"[29]); there was, through Eckart, a direct connection between Thule's ideology of German nationalism and anti-Semitism and Hitler; and many Nazis once belonged to the Thule Society or its affiliated circles.

---

[27] Id., "Widmung".
[28] Hermann Gilbhard: *Die Thule-Gesellschaft*, p. 170.
[29] Rudolf von Sebottendorff, op. cit., p. 130.

"Rudolf von Sebottendorff's life after 1934 has remained a mystery in spite of all kinds of speculations and rumours", writes Gilbhard. "There are several unproved versions of his destiny, especially those originating in circles of the German secret service which were active in the Orient during the Second World War". Herbert Rittlinger, biographer of Rudolf von Sebottendorff, alleges "without producing any proof that Sebottendorff was pulled dead from the Bosporus on 9 May 1945, and concludes from this fact that the founder of the Thule committed suicide".[30] The date mentioned was V-E Day, the day the armistice with Germany was signed.

The November Putsch marked a turning point in Hitler's life as well as in the history of the Nazi movement. What had for the most part been Bavarian history would now become German and world history. This may therefore be the point to take leave of another of the men who made Hitler possible, in this case the one who actually discovered him: Karl Mayr. He had been promoted to major and left the Army in March 1920, when Hitler became a civilian (on 31 March) because his backer in the Army was no longer there. Reuth has it that Mayr was discharged dishonourably.[31] He does not mention the reason, but says that Mayr used to act on his own to a remarkable degree. It may be that the social-democratic authorities finally caught up with the machinations of the rightist officer.

Yet, most amazing is the fact that Mayr made a complete turnabout and became a leader in the German Socialist Party and its paramilitary corps, the *Reichsbanner* (not to be confused with Röhm's *Reichsflagge*), where a man with his capacities and experience was welcomed; he was also an editor of their journal for some time. When Röhm got in serious trouble because of his circle of homosexuals and some scandalous letters were published by the *Munich Post* in 1932, it was to Mayr that he turned for help. Heiden says that Röhm proposed to detach the SA from the Hitler Party and work towards a brotherly

---

[30] Hermann Gilbhard, op. cit.,, p. 173.
[31] Ralph Reuth, op. cit., p. 118.

collaboration of all uniformed workers. This is not improbable in the light of what we have learned before. Mayr's cynical but clairvoyant comment on this proposal was: "Would you like me to tell you the name of your future murderers?"[32] He meant Hitler and his henchmen, of course. And right he was.

When Hitler came to power, Mayr, like many others, fled the country into France. But his name was on Hitler's black list because of his betrayal of the cause – and possibly still more because of an anonymous article of his, later on published in the American review *Current History* under the title "I was Hitler's Boss – By a former Officer of the Reichswehr". It was in this article that Mayr compared the Austrian corporal in the first months after the Great War to "a worn out stray dog" who would accept a crust of bread from anyone who wanted to be his master, even from a Frenchmen or a Jew. Mayr was caught and handed over to the Germans. He died in the Buchenwald concentration camp on 9 February 1945.[33]

---

[32] Konrad Heiden, op. cit., p. 356.
[33] Anton Joachimsthaler: *Hitlers Weg begann in München 1913-1923*, p. 226.

6

MEIN KAMPF

Great liars are also great warlocks.

ADOLF HITLER

Germany subjected itself to a religion it did not know; it followed rites it did not understand; it exulted and died for a mysterium in which it was not initiated. Only 'the Führer' had real knowledge, no National-Socialist doubted that. And the Führer kept to himself what he did not want to share with others.

JOACHIM KÖHLER

The Landsberg retreat

The failure of the putsch came as a shattering blow to Hitler, in the first place because he felt covered with ridicule. On arrival in the prison at Landsberg he was given a spacious cell – some say more comfortable than his room in Munich at that time – vacated for him by Anton von Arco auf Valley, the assassin of Kurt Eisner. Hitler refused to eat for something like a fortnight. Afterwards several visitors claimed the honour of having talked their Führer into eating again, among them Anton Drexler, Hans Knirsch (a Czechoslovakian Nazi), the ever faithful and present Helene Bechstein, and Helene Hanfstängl, on whom Hitler seems to have had a crush.

From a local celebrity Hitler had become a national hero, and he was even occasionally mentioned in the foreign press, to announce his demise as a politician. "The *New York Times* printed his political obituary on the front page: 'The Munich putsch definitely eliminates Hitler and his National Socialist followers'".[1] Still, his foolhardy but courageous stunt had endeared him to many nationalists, especially in Munich, who felt nothing but contempt for verbose but impotent leaders of the kind of Kahr, Lossow and Seisser. "In Munich Hitler was still taken seriously. That Christmas a group of Schwabing artists in the movement celebrated the holiday season in the Blue Café with a living tableau, 'Adolf Hitler in prison'. The curtain rose on a cell. Snowflakes were falling outside a small barred window. A man sat at a desk, face buried in hands, and an invisible male chorus was singing 'Silent Night, Holy Night'. Then an angel placed an illuminated Christmas tree on the table. Slowly the man turned and revealed his face ... A half-sob went through the hall", so telling was the resemblance with Hitler of the actor on the stage.[2]

Hitler feared the trial for high treason, which opened on 26 February 1924, for two reasons. One was that he might be court-martialled, that consequently the trial would not be accessible to the public and that his means of defence would be limited. The other reason, and the most important one, was that he, as an Austrian citizen, would be extradited to his country of origin.* But his fears were allayed when he learned that he would appear before an ordinary, civil court and that the presiding judge, appointed by the Bavarian Minister of Justice Gürtner, was to be Georg Neithardt, "an ardent

---

[1] John Toland: *Hitler*, p. 246.
[2] Id., p. 250.
*The house where he was born, in Braunau-am-Inn, stood only a stone's throw away from the border with Germany, at that place the river Inn. It is a strange coincidence that Eva Braun, his future mistress and wife-of-one-day, passed some time of her youth in the opposite German village, Simbach-am-Inn, in a finishing school run by nuns. (See John Lukacs: *The Hitler of History*, p. 54, footnote, and Anna Maria Sigmund: *Die Frauen der Nazis*, p. 232.)

nationalist". Hitler saw at once that "the disaster of the bungled putsch could be converted into a demagogical triumph ... The defendants were Hitler, Ludendorff, Röhm, Frick, Pöhner [former police chief of Munich], Kriebel [commander of the Kampfbund] and four other participants [in the putsch], while Kahr, Lossow and Seisser appeared as witnesses".[3] This was a flagrant injustice and a compelling argument which Hitler would not fail to use, for "the three vons" too were guilty of insurrection against the legal government.

Hitler managed to use the trial as a prolonged act of theatrical propaganda. "All of this helped Hitler turn the trial to his own purposes. Still, one should not fail to mark the boldness with which Hitler faced the proceedings, even after so recent a defeat. He assumed responsibility for the whole sorry operation and thus contrived to justify his actions in the name of higher patriotic and historic duty".[4]

His powerful peroration, quoted in all Hitler biographies, still reverberates through history. "The army we have trained is growing from day to day, from hour to hour. At this very time I hold the proud hope that the hour will come when these wild bands will be formed into battalions, the battalions into regiments, the regiments into divisions ... that the old banners will wave on ahead, that reconciliation will be achieved before the eternal judgment seat of God which we are ready to face. Then from our bones and our graves will speak the voice of that court which alone is empowered to sit in judgment upon us all. For not you, gentlemen, will deliver judgment on us; that judgment will be pronounced by the eternal court of history ... I already know what verdict you will hand down. But that other court will ask us: did you or did you not commit high treason? That court will judge us ... as Germans who wanted the best for their people and their Fatherland, who were willing to

---

[3]Joachim Fest: *Hitler*, pp. 190-91.
[4]Id., p. 192.

fight and die. May you declare us guilty a thousand times: the goddess of the Eternal Court will smile and gently tear in two the brief of the State Prosecutor and the verdict of the court: for she acquits us".[5]

It was always hazardous to let Hitler speak because of the power with which his words were charged. Now he became a star. "The reading of the verdict was a real society event in Munich. The courtroom was crowded with spectators ready to applaud this troublemaker with so many friends in high places. The verdict once more laid stress on the 'pure patriotic motives and honourable intentions' of the defendant, but sentenced him to a minimum of five years in prison. However, he would become eligible for parole after six months. Ludendorff was acquitted. The law called for the deportation of any troublesome foreigner, but the court decided to waive this in the case of a man 'who thinks and feels in such German terms as Hitler'".[6] He would leave prison before the end of the year.

Events seemed to be timed in response to Hitler's deeds and needs. While he was in Landsberg prison the conditions in Germany took a turn for the better, so much so that the period from 1924 till 1929 would be called "the golden years" of the Weimar Republic. The two men responsible for steering their country on a more propitious course were Premier Gustav Stresemann and the "financial wizard" Hjalmar Schacht, who created a new monetary system – and who would play a similar, and equally important, role in the Third Reich. The Nazi Party, now without its strong-willed Führer, went adrift and split up in several factions. Hitler had foreseen this and let it happen, for it might come useful when he would take up the reins again and decide on an action plan of strict law and order – or something like it.

He put Alfred Rosenberg in charge of the NSDAP, aware how little appreciated this pale-faced intellectual was among his brown-

---
[5]Id., p. 193.
[6]Ibid.

shirted comrades. Drexler had not forgotten Adolf's disparaging conduct towards him, the founder of the Party, when shoving him aside in July 1920. "Drexler wanted to remodel the party along his own less revolutionary lines".[7] And then there was the Strasser faction, including a very ambitious and still very socialist-minded Dr Joseph Goebbels, which will promote the Nazi Party in northern Germany and remain the most serious challenge to Hitler till he took up the chancellorship. And there was pompous Erich Ludendorff who had slyly denied any responsibility for the putsch; who had been slighted by Hitler proclaiming himself head of state and the field marshal his commander-in-chief of the army; and who wanted now "to centre the control of the nationalist groups in his own hands and take advantage of Hitler's absence to neutralize him permanently".[8]

Hitler had a great time in Landsberg, his "university at state expense". He was honoured, even by the warden and the prison staff (most of whom converted to Nazism), as a king with his court of fellow Nazi-prisoners. He had plenty of free time without constantly having to make decisions, read books, received visitors, held his inevitable and dreaded endless monologues, and presided at the table. "The others waited behind their chairs until Hitler strode in, then someone called out 'Attention!' He stood at the head of the table until every man in turn came forward with his table-greeting".[9] "He received favoured treatment which included freedom to accept gifts of food from outside, and this again gave him a further hold over his warders ... He and Hess had not so much cells as a small suite of rooms forming an apartment. The place looked like a delicatessen store. You could have opened up a flower and fruit and a wine shop with all the stuff stacked there. People were sending

---

[7] Ernst Hanfstängl: *Hitler – The Missing Years*, p. 117.
[8] Id., p. 117.
[9] John Toland, op. cit., p. 263.

presents from all over Germany and Hitler had grown visibly fatter on the proceeds".[10]

Then came the day that he decided to write a book, which would become *Mein Kampf*, but which at first was titled *Four and a half years of struggle against lies, stupidity and cowardice*. "Without the time in prison *Mein Kampf* would not have existed", reflected Hitler later, "and I may say that, during that time, I reached conceptual clarity about many things which before I had propagated more from intuition."[11] Prison presented him with the occasion of prolonged introspection.

If one has not read the book, one should discard once and for all that idea that *Mein Kampf* is a kind of trivial, wacko oddity, written by an illiterate maniac. Certainly, it does not belong in the class of the belles-lettres, and it contains the most improbable ideas as well as "utter amorality", and lies, and sophistry in abundance, plus undisguised threats to Western civilization and disdain for the human being and human values in general – and much more of this sort. And there is that "curiously nasty, obscene odour" perceived by Joachim Fest as emanating from the book's pages. But behind all that there is a vision by which Adolf Hitler had been and would continue to be driven, which was unprecedented and revolutionary, and which aimed at a new world and a new man. "He who writes this sees himself in his prison cell like Johannes in his cave on Patmos and is in his solitude open for inspiration", writes Karin Wilhelm. "While writing Hitler too follows a voice which he hears inside himself in the act of writing, and meanwhile his eyes are clairvoyant".[12]

The first pages of *Mein Kampf* were dictated by Hitler to his chauffeur and co-prisoner Emil Maurice. Maurice noted down the dictates and Hitler had to type them afterwards with two fingers on a Remington portable. This changed when another participant

---

[10]Ernst Hanfstängl, op. cit., p. 114.
[11]*Monologe im Führerhauptquartier*, p. 262.
[12]Karin Wilhelm in *Der Nationalsozialismus als politische Religion*, p. 232.

in the putsch, Rudolf Hess, gave himself up to the police and joined his adored Führer in prison. Now Hess, who was a student of Karl Haushofer, professor of "geopolitics" at Munich University, typed the dictates directly on the machine and helped with suggestions and corrections. "There was a very close bond between the two during this period, and for the first time I heard them speak to each other on 'thou' terms, although later in public they did not", remembers Hanfstängl. The number of people Hitler ever addressed in the confidential manner can be counted on the fingers of one hand. "This was the period of Hess's greatest and lasting influence", according to Hanfstängl, who elaborates on "the emotional quality of the friendship that had developed with Hess".[13]

There may have been truth in Hanfstängl's impressions of the homoerotic, though not homosexual, relation between Hitler and his later deputy; homoeroticism is after all a common phenomenon among persons of the same sex sharing long-term experiences, and "male bonding" was widespread at the time of our story, when a more liberal sexuality was not even imaginable, and men's associations and groupings were rife in Germany. But there may have been another element in the Hitler-Hess connection which Hanfstängl did not perceive because there were no receptors for it in his awareness: the occult dimension. Hess was, after all, not only a Brother of Thule, he was also intensely interested in all kinds of occult phenomena, and so was Hitler.

Toland describes how the Hitler court at Landsberg was distinctly divided into two levels corresponding to two classes, the one of the inner circle around Hitler with their cells on the upper floor, the other comprising the "commoners" and lodged on the lower floor. There is no doubt that Hitler's Landsberg experience included a profound meditation on his life's mission and a reactivation of it, in which Hess, constantly close to him, seems to have played a part. This may have been the main reason of the intimacy between the

---

[13]Ernst Hanfstängl, op. cit., pp. 115, 123.

two men, and of the fact that Hess became Hitler's secretary and afterwards the second man in the Reich, although there was a unanimous opinion among the top Nazis that Hess was a poor politician and organizer. Behind his back fellow Nazis sometimes called him *Fräulein Anna*, Miss Anna, for he read poetry and listened to chamber music and was therefore held to be a sissy – although he had been a fighter pilot during the war and was always the first to jump into a beer hall fray or street brawl at the head of his SA unit. He was, moreover, the intermediary between his Führer and his teacher, Professor Karl Haushofer.

Hitler bares his mind

William Shirer, the American journalist who has followed "the rise and fall of the Third Reich" from nearby, writes: "It might be argued that had more non-Nazi Germans read [*Mein Kampf*] before 1933 and had the foreign statesmen of the world perused it carefully while there was still time, both Germany and the world might have been saved from catastrophe. For whatever other accusations can be made against Adolf Hitler, no one can accuse him of not putting down in writing exactly the kind of Germany he intended to make if he ever came to power and the kind of world he meant to create by armed German conquest. The blueprint of the Third Reich and, what is more, of the barbaric New Order which Hitler inflicted on conquered Europe in the triumphant years between 1939 and 1945 is set down in all its appalling crudity at great length and in detail between the covers of this revealing book".[14] We find Shirer's opinion confirmed by Christian von Krockow, at present a popular author in Germany: "Actually one has to be astonished: what was said in *Mein Kampf* was exactly what Hitler afterwards did, but people had not read or not taken seriously what was written there."[15] And

---

[14] William Shirer: *The Rise and Fall of the Third Reich*, p. 81.
[15] Christian von Krockow: *Hitler und seine Deutschen*, p. 98.

Christian Zentner states simply: "The politics of the Third Reich cannot be understood without *Mein Kampf*".[16]

Yet the book is often considered a nutty curiosity. And it is believed by many that nobody in Nazi Germany read it. Eberhard Jäckel, for instance, writes that *Mein Kampf* "was hardly read and still less understood".[17] Both parts of Jäckel's statement should be qualified. As to the first part: some ten million copies of *Mein Kampf* were printed till 1945; all couples were presented with a copy by the mayor as part of their marriage ceremony (many such copies are still gathering dust in German garrets); copies of the book were kept in all places where Nazidom was thriving; *Mein Kampf* was prescribed study material in all educational institutions, and the German youth had to learn by heart whole passages from it.

Moreover, the German media studded their propaganda with quotations from the Führer's book, which was revered as the Nazi bible. How literally one should take this is shown by the fact that a copy of *Mein Kampf* was to be present at the SS-ceremonies of baptism, initiation into the Order, marriage and death. We find another confirmation in the following articles of the National Reich Church: "... 14. The National Reich Church declares that to it, and therefore to the German nation, the Führer's *Mein Kampf* is the greatest of all documents. It not only contains the greatest but it embodies the purest and truest ethics for the present and future life of our nation ... 19. On the altars there must be nothing but *Mein Kampf* (to the German nation and therefore to God the most sacred book) and to the left of the altar a sword".[18] And there were of course Hitler's speeches, *Mein Kampf* in action, obligatorily listened to by every German in a non-solitary situation at the time of their delivery, and bellowed from specially installed loudspeakers in all public places. It may be supposed that few people read *Mein Kampf*

---

[16] Christian Zentner: *Adolf Hitlers 'Mein Kampf'*, p. 177.
[17] Eberhard Jäckel: *Hitlers Weltanschauung*, p. 135.
[18] William Shirer: *The Nightmare Years 1930-1940*, pp. 156-57.

from cover to cover, for it is heavy fare for any reader – and how many ever take up ideological literature anyway? But its most accessible ideas were spread, repeated and commented upon all the time and everywhere in Naziland, and served as the mental framework of the life and work of its citizens.

One can agree with the second part of the Jäckel statement, that *Mein Kampf* was not understood, if this lack of understanding, or misunderstanding, refers to Hitler's vision as a whole. On this point hardly any of the learned commentators, even with the advantage of present hindsight, are agreed – as little as the top Nazis around Hitler were agreed on it among themselves. This is the fundamental paradox of this book, which confers to it a special place in history. "Rarely and probably never in history has a ruler, before he came to power, put down in writing, as Adolf Hitler did, what he subsequently carried out", writes Jäckel, and he quotes Hans Gisevius: "If one reads *Mein Kampf* post facto, then one finds there everthing, really everything, what this man has done to the world".[19]

Others speak of "an unreal candour", which causes Zentner to label *Mein Kampf* a *Bekenntnisbuch*, a confession, which it was to the extent that Hitler in later years sometimes expressed regret of having written the book. Yet he gloated over the fact that most of his intimate thoughts were there for all to read, but – and this is the paradox – that hardly anybody understood or believed their meaning. One reason for the lack of understanding was that people in general are not capable of, or interested in, digesting theoretical, abstract thinking; another reason was that the book as a whole was the expression, albeit in a clumsy way, of a central vision in the author, the core of which he kept secret even from the people closest to him; and a third reason was that *Mein Kampf*, at the time it was written and read, aimed at the politically and ideologically impossible, and therefore not understandable, because incredible. If *Mein Kampf* is that important, then it is worth a closer look.

---

[19]Eberhard Jäckel, op. cit., p. 7.

Mortal enemy France

In the First World War the Germans were fighting on two fronts. This made the divided efforts of their armies indecisive, and the unending war caused ever greater suffering in the Fatherland. Because of this problematic situation the German power elite – the Army, the heavy industry and the banks – as one man supporting the military dictatorship of the duo Hindenburg-Ludendorff, did their utmost to bring about the downfall of the Russian empire. When Lenin came to power, it was thanks to the Germans – a fact conveniently forgotten by Hitler in his diatribes against Lenin and his "Judeo-Bolshevism". The Peace of Brest-Litovsk, concluded on 9 February 1918 with the Ukraine and on 3 March with Russia, looks like the finishing off and robbing the corpse of a defenceless enemy.

The German troops were immediately transported from the eastern to the western front. Operation Michael, the great battle for France, was launched on 21 March. The first German successes were overwhelming and their armies, four years after August 1914, threatened Paris again. But the Americans had entered the war and the Allies, stronger and better armed than ever before, beat "the Hun" back. In August Ludendorff realized that defeat was inevitable and suffered a nervous breakdown. Now he and Hindenburg manoeuvred to let the politicians solve the enormous problem in which the German nation had got itself involved. The Kaiser, according to the armistice conditions laid down by the Allies, had to go. Left to themselves, the politicians of the German Socialist Party, the SPD, almost by accident proclaimed Germany a republic.

Such was the background for a catastrophic sequel to the First World War. After three years of frustration the Germans, because of Brest-Litovsk, had been certain of imminent and triumphant victory ("until the very end military censors had allowed only reports of victories; even the Reichstag was left in the dark"[20]); their armies

---

[20] John Weiss: *Ideology of Death*, p. 211.

had not been defeated; therefore the signatories of the armistice and afterwards of the "dictated" Treaty of Versailles, in the first place Matthias Erzberger, had betrayed their country. Germany was not guilty of starting the war; it had lost the war because it had been betrayed by the Social-Democrats, communists and Jews within its own house; the nation must become strong and powerful again and take revenge. These were the inexhaustible themes of Adolf Hitler, who had been as shocked as the rest of the German nation by the November debacle. We find them in all his speeches as a beer hall tribune, and they make up a substantial part of *Mein Kampf*.

But Germany was living a complex lie, which served as the justification for its hurt but not eradicated pride and unabated ambitions, and of which the importance and the consequences cannot be overrated. "The legend of the stab in the back", the *Dolchstosslegende*, became widely accepted and was soon considered historical truth, which it remained for a generation and longer. Siegfried, the mythological hero, had slain a dragon and become invulnerable by bathing in its blood, except on one spot of his body. His wife Kriemhild found out that this spot was between his shoulder blades and foolishly told this to Hagen, who one day sneaked up behind Siegfried, plunged his dagger between his shoulders and killed him. Now, once again, "the fighting Siegfried [i.e. Germany] succumbed to the dagger plunged in his back [by the pacifist Social-Democrats and other 'Jews']", wrote Hitler in *Mein Kampf*.[21] This untruth, a lie called legend, launched by Hindenburg before a commission examining the cause of the German collapse, was reinforced and propagated by Ludendorff, and was still believed in after Hitler had done his damage. "It has poisoned, as nothing else, the internal political atmosphere of the Weimar Republic".[22]

The Treaty of Versailles, signed on 28 June 1919 in the Hall of Mirrors at the Versailles palace of Louis XIV, was another cause of

---

[21] Adolf Hitler: *Mein Kampf*, p. 510.
[22] Christian Zentner, op. cit., p. 192.

German and Hitlerian wrath, and the author of *Mein Kampf* used his choicest vocabulary for lashing out at it. Versailles was "a scandal and a disgrace, and the dictate signified an act of highway robbery against our people"; it was "an instrument of unrestricted oppression", "like a whip-lash on the [German] people", "an instrument of unlimited blackmail and shameful humiliation", showing "the sadist cruelty" of the dictators. "Each point of that Treaty should have been engraved on the minds and hearts of the German people and burned into them, until sixty million men and women would find their souls aflame with a feeling of rage and shame, and a torrent of fire would burst forth as from a furnace, and one common will would be forged from it, like a sword of steel. Then the people would join in the common cry: 'To arms again!'"[23]

Many authors still assert that the harsh terms of the Versailles Treaty were an immediate cause of Nazism and the Second World War. They might ponder for a while the words of Fest: "The terms in fact could stand comparison with the conditions Germany had imposed on Russia in the treaty of Brest-Litovsk and on Rumania in the Treaty of Bucharest".[24] Shirer gives some specifics concerning Brest-Litovsk, "a peace treaty which to a British historian, writing two decades after the passions had cooled, was a 'humiliation without precedent or equal in modern history'. It deprived Russia of a territory nearly as large as Austria-Hungary and Turkey combined, with 56,000,000 inhabitants, or 32 per cent of her whole population; a third of her railway mileage, 73 per cent of her total iron ore, 89 per cent of her total coal production; and more than 5000 factories and industrial plants".[25] But Brest-Litovsk is "the forgotten treaty", though it was not forgotten by Hitler who, as an army propagandist, wrote "a circular" and gave several talks on it, as he did later for the DAP. "I compared the two treaties [Versailles and Brest-Litovsk]

---

[23]Adolf Hitler, op. cit., pp. 386, 514, 515.
[24]Joachim Fest, op. cit., 82.
[25]William Shirer, op. cit., p. 57.

with one another, point by point, and showed how in truth the one treaty [Brest-Litovsk] was immensely humane, in contradiction to the inhuman barbarity of the other [Versailles]".[26]

In truth, the "war aims" (*Kriegsziele*) of the Germans, formulated by Chancellor Bethmann Hollweg in September 1914, after the war had started, and expanded by the Pan-Germans and the pressure group from the heavy German industry and the banks, were much more comprising and much more merciless than the dictate of Versailles. 1. Germany was to expand into a *Mitteleuropa* (a central European block) and exert political and commercial domination over France, Belgium, Holland, Danemark, Austria-Hungary, Poland, and eventually Italy, Sweden and Norway; 2. France would have to part with the coal and iron basins of Longwy-Briey and the Atlantic ports facing southern England; it would have to pay reparations "so high that it would not be able to finance its rearmament in the next fifteen to twenty years"; it would have to become permanently dependent commercially on Germany as a German *Exportland*; 3. Belgium would have to cede the region around Liege plus the port of Antwerp, at the time the busiest in Europe; commercially it would become a German province; 4. Some of the French colonies and most of the Belgian Congo would fall to Germany; 5. To the above should be added the necessary conquests which would give Germany access to the wheat fields and ore basins of Russia and to the oil fields in the Middle East, a war aim prefigured in the peacetime construction of the Berlin-Baghdad railway.[27]

This was the minimum programme the German leadership had in mind, to be carried out if they won the war; the conditions of the Peace of Brest-Litovsk were only part of it. One finds this programme seldom, if ever, mentioned in the history books meant for general consumption, although it illustrates with great clarity the

---

[26] Adolf Hitler, op. cit., p. 389.
[27] Fritz Fischer: *Griff nach der Weltmacht*, p. 93. See also Edouard Husson: *Comprendre Hitler et la Shoah*, ch. III, "*Les thèses de Fritz Fischer*".

objectives which caused on two occasions death and destruction on such a horrendous scale. Hitler kept these war aims in mind and executed them almost to the letter.

The historical awareness of Germany, and of the rest of the world, had to wait till 1961, the year Fritz Fischer published his *Griff nach der Weltmacht* (the bid for world power), to be reminded of the German intentions at the beginning of the twentieth century. And the Germans had to wait to be told by the same Hamburg historian, fifty-seven years and another world war after the fact, that in 1914 Germany "carried the decisive part of the historical responsibility for the outbreak of the general war",[28] and that article 231 of the Versailles Treaty, the "war guilt article" which stated this responsibility, was not unjustified. Fischer's bold but unpleasant revelations, sober in their wording and erudite in their justifications, caused an uproar which has not yet died down completely.

Humiliation of an undefeated nation, the stab in the back, victimisation by an inhuman treaty and the wrongful accusation of having started the war: this arsenal of injustices, misrepresentation and offended patriotic feelings provided abundant ammunition for Hitler's broadsides against "Germany's enemies", real or imagined, internal and international. (And exposing the whole lot as Jews always elicited consent from his audiences.) France, however, was his favourite target among the Allies. This country was "a victor which should not have been one", for it was unjust "that such a highly developed cultural people as the Germans had lost the war".[29] For Hitler France "was and would remain the implacable enemy of Germany", "the mortal enemy of the nation". "The French nation which is slowly dying out", he wrote, "not so much through depopulation as through the disappearance of the best elements in the race, can continue to play an important role in the world only

---

[28]Fritz Fischer, op. cit., p. 82.
[29]Klaus von See: *Barbar, Germane, Arier – Die Suche nach der Identität der Deutschen*, pp. 191, 193.

if Germany be destroyed. French policy may take a thousand detours on the march towards its fixed goal, but the destruction of Germany is the end which it always has in view as the fulfilment of the most profound yearning and ultimate intentions of the French".[30]

The fanatical racist in Hitler had been stung by the French stationing, in 1923, coloured Senegalese troops in the occupied Rhineland. This was to him a direct attack on the blood stock of Aryan Germany aiming at its racial degradation, and he would never forgive the French for the dastardly act. (In 1937 the children of these African soldiers and German woman were among the first to be sterilized in the eugenic scheme of the Third Reich.[31]) "As long as the eternal conflict between France and Germany is waged only in the form of a German defence against the French attack, that conflict can never be decided and from century to century Germany will lose one position after another ... Only when the Germans have taken all this fully into account will they cease from allowing the national will-to-life to wear itself out in merely passive defence; but they will rally together for a last decisive contest with France. And in this contest the essential objective of the German nation will be fought for. Only then will it be possible to put an end to the eternal Franco-German conflict which has hitherto proved sterile".[32]

In the evaluation of Hitler's actions, the war in Western Europe is nowadays often looked down upon as of secondary importance in comparison with the attempted conquest of Eastern Europe. Yet the putting down of France and its "civilization" by the Nordic Germans and their *Kultur* was a prime part of the German aspiration and of Hitler's personal ambitions. He, who had spent four years of his youth in the dust and mud of trenches dug in French soil, would one day reverse the armistice signed on 11 November 1918

---

[30] Adolf Hitler, op. cit., pp. 505, 542, 548-49.
[31] André Pichot: *La société pure – de Darwin à Hitler*, p. 15.
[32] Adolf Hitler, op. cit., p. 549.

in that train wagon in the forest of Compiègne, and ride one early morning in June 1940 as conqueror through the streets of Paris.

"The System"

The language Hitler used when he wrote or talked about the government of the Weimar Republic was even worse than the way he talked about the hated French. "November criminals", designating all Leftists and Jews allegedly responsible for the armistice and related events, was used by him on uncountable occasions and became a sort of political concept in Naziland. But there was much more, and better, also in *Mein Kampf*; for if the war with France had to be envisaged in the future, the struggle with the Left and their centrist partners in government was happening in the present; it had to be won before the power could be gained and the revenge against Germany's mortal enemy prepared.

Hitler called the government "the present Jewish-Democratic Reich, which has become a veritable curse for the German people"; they were "those ruffians of Jews who came into power in 1918 and were able to rob the nation of its arms"; they were "a gang of bandits".[33] "According to the laws that govern human history, it is inconceivable that the German people could resume the place they formerly held without retaliating on those who were both cause and occasion of the collapse that involved the ruin of our State. Before the judgment seat of posterity November 1918 will not be regarded as a simple rebellion but as high-treason against the country".[34]

"On the most miserable of pretexts these parliamentary party henchmen filched from the hands of the nation and threw away the weapons which were needed to maintain its existence and therewith defend the liberty and independence of our people". The Versailles Treaty abolished the German navy and air force, limited the army

---

[33]Id., pp. 469, 279, 288.
[34]Id., p. 280.

to 100,000 men and severely restricted its armament. "If the graves on the plains of Flanders were to open today the blood-stained accusers would arise, hundreds of thousands of our best German youth who were driven into the arms of death by those conscienceless parliamentary ruffians who were either wrongly educated for their task or only half-educated. Those youths and other millions of the killed and mutilated were lost to the Fatherland simply and solely in order that a few hundred deceivers of the people might carry out their political manoeuvres and their exactions or even treasonably pursue their doctrinaire theories".[35]

What actually happened in that fateful month of November 1918? We know that Ludendorff and Hindenburg realized that the war was lost, that Germany had to come to terms with its enemies, that therefore the Kaiser had to go – and that the Supreme War Lord and his Quarter-Master General managed to shift this whole burden to the ineffective and powerless government of which Max von Baden was the chancellor at that moment. Then "Prince Max bowed out, handing over the government to the moderate leader of the Social Democrats, Friedrich Ebert, a forty-year-old saddler and trade union leader.

"Like many other Social Democrats, Ebert favoured the establishment of a constitutional monarchy on the British pattern, but his hopes were scuppered by his deputy, Philipp Scheidemann, who proclaimed a republic almost accidentally. Scheidemann had rushed to the Reichstag to tell his colleagues of Ebert's appointment. Having done so, he was eating lunch in the restaurant when he was told that Karl Liebknecht, the leader of the extreme left Spartacus Party, was setting up camp in the Royal Palace, from where he intended to announce a soviet-style republic modelled on Lenin's Russia ... There was no time to lose. Leaving his meal, he strode out on to the small balcony outside the Reich library. The vast crowd cheered his appearance, then quietened as he began an off-the-cuff

---
[35]Id., p. 228.

speech ... Needing a rousing finish, he cried: "The rotten old monarchy has collapsed. Long live the new [government]! Long live the German Republic'! And so it was done, almost as an afterthought".[36]

The records are there to prove that Ebert the saddler and Scheidemann the journalist were men of goodwill who did their best to keep Germany afloat in stormy circumstances which were not of their making. The burden shoved unto their shoulders by the defeated and sneaky pin-helmeted warlords would have been too heavy for whomever. "Within Germany, the bitterness over the terms of the peace treaty increased the resentment against the republic, for it had proved incapable of sparing the country the distress and privations of this 'shameful dictated peace' ... To a growing number of Germans the very term 'republic' seemed synonymous with disgrace, dishonour, and powerlessness. The feeling persisted that the republic had been imposed on the Germans by deception and coercion, that it was something altogether alien to their nature. It is true that in spite of all its drawbacks it held a certain promise; but even in its few fortunate years its was 'unable to arouse either the loyalty or the political imagination of the people' ".[37]

The Versailles Treaty "was a peace that was no peace in the eyes of most Germans", writes Maurersberger. "All at once it had become clear, also to the last German in favour of reconciliation, that the European Allies of the USA did not want to negotiate, but that their only objective was to annihilate the political and economic power of Germany once and for all".[38] Matthias Erzberger, the minister who accepted to sign the Treaty of Versailles and thereby solve an otherwise insoluble situation, became the scapegoat. The nationalist press wrote: "It is on the majority wanting peace and their leader

---

[36] Anthony Read: *The Devil's Disciples – The Lives and Times of Hitler's Inner Circle*, p. 21.
[37] Joachim Fest, op. cit., p. 83.
[38] Volker Maurersberger, op. cit., pp. 95, 96.

Erzberger that rests the responsibility for the blood of the millions who died since the summer of 1917, for the thousands of millions marks which were lost to Germany and the culture of the world, and for the shameful peace under which the German people are now sighing".[39] Erzberger would be assassinated by members of Organization Consul; Ludendorff would be fêted in Weimar as "the volkisch king" and Hindenburg would be honoured as the *Ersatz Kaiser*, substitute emperor, and elected president in 1925.

"The Weimar Constitution was felt as something superimposed on Germany by the Western Powers – which would make Germany like the rest of Western culture – something alien to German racial and national tradition, making it cosmopolitan and rational, something which was foreign to its history".[40] This explains the term "the System", denigratingly used for the Weimar Constitution and its form of government, which were directly inspired by the ideals of the Enlightenment and therefore by Reason. The German rooted, traditional, volkisch, hierarchical sense of values and of belonging felt "the System", the political contract, as unnatural and therefore inimical. "The fear of the bourgeois class for democracy and social change was so intense that it decided against the Republic and in favour of a new authoritarian state"[41] – which was to be the Nazi state.

"Germany, awake!"

Dietrich Eckart's pithy exhortation, embroidered on all Party banners, was an important component of *Mein Kampf,* which was after all the announcement and the programme of the man who intended to lead a resurrected Germany towards its glorious future. Yet the real meaning of this exhortation was not its literal meaning; having

---

[39]Id., p. 114.
[40]Quoted in Hugo Friedrich: *Before the Deluge*, p. 324.
[41]Volker Maurersberger, op. cit., p. 87.

fought a war, mourned its dead, being shaken by revolts and obliged to fight for its daily sustenance, Germany had had no time to fall asleep. What the Eckart-Hitler slogan meant was that Germany must regain its place and power as the foremost nation of the world, that it must rebuild all means necessary to occupy its rightful place on the globe after having been humbled so shamefully by other nations. Pre-war slogans were still in use whenever national feelings welled up: *Heute Deutschland, morgen die ganze Welt!* (today Germany, tomorrow the whole world); *Den Deutschen gehört die Welt!* (the world belongs to the Germans); *Deutschland über alles in der Welt!* (Germany above all else in the world); and everybody still knew by heart songs like *Die Wacht am Rhein* (the guard on the Rhine). There were numerous nationalist and volkisch associations in the country and all published their literature, of which these songs and slogans contained the essential message in a nutshell.

At this phase of our story colonialism was at its zenith, the white race thought of itself as the finest fruit on the tree of evolution and its culture was the acme of the human mind. The Germanic peoples were convinced that they occupied the highest rung on the hierarchical ladder within the white race, and if they were not too sure of what "Germanic" meant they called themselves "Nordics", and if they were uncertain about that they were "Aryans". But all three terms were problematic. The word "Germanic" was of Latin origin, *germanus*, and may originally have meant nothing more than an amalgam of barbarians beyond the Rhine. This amalgam was complex, for even Hans Günther, the leading Nazi racial scientist, had to concede that the Germanic people consisted of Nordic, Alpine and Mediterranean elements. To these one should add the considerable part of the German population that was of Slavonic origin; for the original Prussians were a Slavonic tribe, and Germanic people had intermingled with Poles, Balts, Russians and many others during the centuries of their struggles and conquests on their eastern borders.

Some German racists, playing it safe, called themselves "Nordics" and included the Scandinavian and Icelandic peoples among the elect. Otherwise how to explain that the largest part of the "authentic" Germanic customs and traditions, so much admired by volkisch nostalgia and rendered visually famous by the costumes of the Wagnerian heroes and heroines, were in fact those of the Vikings, who were Scandinavians? And how to explain that most artefacts of the earliest "Germanic" times, many inscribed with runes, were found in Sweden?

Most problematical, however, was the term "Aryans", for "originally the Aryan question was a linguistic question. It appeared in 1776 when William Jones was struck by the resemblance between several languages: Sanskrit, Greek, Latin, German, etc. These languages were then brought together into one family, and their resemblance was accounted for by the fact that all of them derived from the same original language, which in 1813 was baptized 'Indo-European' by Thomas Young ... This original language was supposed to have been the language of a people which was also called 'Indo-European', and which was supposed to have lived in former times somewhere between central Asia and eastern Europe. (There were theories about many different locations, from India to northern Scandinavia.) This means that a language was made [illicitly] into a people, and that this people was made [illicitly] into a race".[42] The Aryan race existed only in the imagination of some scholarly racists, who released their pure-bred chimera into the fields of the imagination of a presumptuous Germany.

"Every manifestation of human culture, every product of art, science and technical skill which we see before our eyes today, is almost exclusively the product of the Aryan creative power", wrote Hitler in *Mein Kampf.* "This very fact justifies the conclusion that it was the Aryan alone who founded a superior type of humanity; therefore he represents the archetype of what we understand by the term MAN. He is the Prometheus of mankind, from whose shining

---

[42] André Pichot: *La société pure*, p. 395. See also Léon Poliakov: *Le mythe aryen.*

brow the divine spark of genius has at all times flashed forth, always kindling anew that fire which, in the form of knowledge, illuminated the dark night by drawing aside the veil of mystery and thus showing man how to rise and become master over all the other beings on the earth. Should he be forced to disappear, a profound darkness will descend on the earth; within a few thousand years human culture will vanish and the world will become a desert.

"If we divide mankind into three categories – founders of culture, bearers of culture and destroyers of culture – the Aryan alone can be considered as representing the first category ... It is the Aryan who has furnished the great building-stones and plans for the edifices of all human progress; only the way in which these plans have been executed is to be attributed to the qualities of each individual race".[43] The Aryan was "the standard-bearer of human progress". "It will be a greater honour to be a citizen of this Reich, even as a street-sweeper, than to be the king of a foreign state." [44] For the Aryan is "the highest image of the Lord",[45] and the Aryans are "a race destined to become master of all the other peoples and which will have at its disposal the means and resources of the whole world".[46] And Hitler said later in a speech to his youth at Ordensburg Sonthofen: "We want to take our Volk to the very first rank! Whether they like us, is of no interest to us, if only they respect us! Whether they hate us, is of no importance to us, if only they fear us!"[47] "They" were the others, the non-German humans on the levels below the Aryans, but also the Aryan Germans who misunderstood or withstood their Führer.

"Although much may be very questionable, the results of science cannot alter one important fact: that the 'meaning of world history',

---

[43] Adolf Hitler, op. cit., p. 243.
[44] Id., pp. 246, 368,
[45] Christian Zentner, op. cit., p. 161.
[46] Adolf Hitler, op. cit., p. 322.
[47] Henry Picker: *Hitlers Tischgespräche im Führerhauptquartier*, p. 704.

irradiating from the North, has spread over the whole earth, carried by a blue-eyed, blonde race, which in several cultural waves determined the cultural outlook of the world", averred Alfred Rosenberg, the official theorist of Nazi ideology, in his *Myth of the Twentieth Century*. The Nordic-racist Atlantis myth of the people with the blue eyes, blonde hair, pinkish skin, dolichocephalic and tall "reached a public of millions through Blavatsky for the Theosophists, Steiner for the Antroposophists, List and Lanz for the Ariosophists, and Rosenberg and Wirth [founder of the *SS-Ahnenerbe*] for the National-Socialists".[48]

How was the Germanic-Nordic-Aryan race held together and how did it propagate itself? Through the blood. "What makes a people or, to be more correct, a race is not language but blood".[49] In the veins of a pure race runs pure blood, or rather if pure blood runs in the veins of a race, this race is pure; the blood is the carrier of its life. For the racists the blood became a mystic concept, surviving from animistic times when humanity had no other idea of the way in which characteristics could be inherited. In matters of race, and therefore of basic existence, all depended on the purity or impurity of the blood. The existence of a people, of a Volk, could be degraded by mixing its pure blood with the putrid blood of degenerated races. This was one of the fundamental ideas of the volkisch movement, propagated in the literature of the Germanenorden and the Thule Society. "Keep your blood pure!" was one of their slogans, and Arthur Dinter's novel *The Sin against the Blood* was a bestseller in Germany during the inter-war period. As sexual contact was the only way of mixing blood with blood, one finds here the nexus with the widespread sexual and even pornographic character assassination of those intentional spoilers of the Aryan blood: the Jews.

"If nature does not wish that weaker individuals should mate with the stronger", one reads in *Mein Kampf*, "she wishes even less

---

[48]Franz Wegener: *Das Atlantidische Weltbild*, pp. 45, 61.
[49]Adolf Hitler, op. cit., p. 326.

that a superior race should intermingle with an inferior one; because in such a case all her efforts, throughout hundreds of thousands of years, to establish an evolutionary higher stage of being, may thus be rendered futile. History furnishes us with innumerable instances that prove this law. It shows, with a startling clarity, that whenever Aryans have mingled their blood with that of an inferior race the result has been a downfall of the people who were the standard-bearers of a higher culture ... In short, the results of miscegenation are always the following: (a) the level of the superior race becomes lowered; (b) physical and mental degeneration sets in, thus leading slowly but steadily towards a progressive drying up of the vital sap. The act which brings about such a development is a sin against the Eternal Creator. And as a sin this act will be avenged".[50]

"Racism and Darwinism are entering into a symbiosis in Hitler's *Mein Kampf*", writes Zentner.[51] The link is obvious: pure blood means a healthy, strong, superior race; mixing of the blood results in degeneration. The fittest, the purest of blood survive. But here racism drew an un-Darwinian conclusion: the fittest-purest also have the right, conferred by Nature or "the Lord", to dominate the others. Of course, their whole line of reasoning accorded with the inclusion of the human race into the animal kingdom, something which Linnaeus was the first to do and a theory which, if consequently applied, swept away in one go all humanistic, religious and spiritual values.

"The ideology which bases the state on the racial idea must finally succeed in bringing about a nobler era, in which men will no longer pay exclusive attention to breeding and rearing pedigree dogs and horses and cats, but will endeavour to improve the breed of the human race itself", teaches Hitler in *Mein Kampf*. According to this "veterinarian ideology", as one commentator calls it, "what is stronger must dominate and not mate with what is weaker, which would

---

[50]Id., pp. 239-40.
[51]Christian Zentner, op. cit., p. 160.

mean the sacrifice of its own higher nature". This is "a fundamental law – one may call it an iron law of nature". "The movement ought to educate its adherents to the principle that struggle must not be considered a necessary evil but something to be desired in itself".[52] "War is what is most natural, most common", said Hitler to Hermann Rauschning. "War is always. There is no beginning, there is no peace at the end. War is life".[53] "Nature knows no political borders. She puts the living beings on this planet and looks on at the free play of forces. Who has the strongest courage and industry obtains then, as her dearest child, the right of the lordship over all beings".[54] One Nazi leader summed it up: "National Socialism is applied biology".[55]

The leader and the masses

In *Mein Kampf* Hitler left no doubt as to who was going to lead the Aryans in their struggle for supremacy. Although the book was written at a time when still several candidate-dictators were around, and Hitler never names himself, one does not have to cogitate much before finding out whom he means for instance in the following lines: "It is a characteristic feature of all great reforms that in the beginning there is only one single protagonist to come forward on behalf of several millions of people. The final goal of a great reformation has often been the object of profound longing on the part of hundreds of thousands for many centuries before, until finally one of them comes forward as a herald to announce the will of that multitude and becomes the standard-bearer of the old yearning, which he now leads to a new realization in a new idea".[56]

---

[52] Adolf Hitler, op. cit., pp. 340, 239, 238, 294.
[53] Quoted in Christian von Krockow, op. cit., p. 240.
[54] In Christian Zentner, op. cit., p 159.
[55] Max Weinreich: *Hitler's Professors*, p. 34.
[56] Adolf Hitler, op. cit., p. 277.

To dominate the masses, Hitler-the-Leader had been gifted with the power of the spoken word and was very much aware of its potential; he had been able to test out "the superior oratorical art of a man who has the compelling character of an apostle" on audiences of all kinds, small and large. "The force which has ever and always set in motion great historical avalanches of religious and political movements is the magic power of the spoken word. The broad masses of a population are more amenable to the appeal of rhetoric than to any other force. All great movements are popular movements. They are the volcanic eruptions of human passions and emotions, stirred into activity by the ruthless Goddess of Distress or by the torch of the spoken word cast into the midst of the people. In no case have great movements been set afoot by the syrupy effusions of aesthetic litterateurs and drawing-room heroes. The doom of a nation can be averted only by a storm of glowing passion: but only those who are passionate themselves can arouse passion in others".[57] The passionately spoken word was, with the tenacity of his convictions and the influence which at times emanated from his presence, Hitler's trump card in his climb to power.

"The psyche of the broad masses is accessible only to what is strong and uncompromising. Like a woman whose inner sensibilities are not so much under the sway of abstract reasoning but are always subject to the influence of a vague emotional longing for the strength that completes her being, and who would rather bow to the strong man than dominate the weakling – in like manner the masses of the people prefer the ruler to the suppliant and are filled with a stronger sense of mental security by a teaching that brooks no rival than by a teaching which offers them a liberal choice. They have very little idea of how to make such a choice and thus they are prone to feel that they have been abandoned ... They are scarcely conscious that their freedom as human beings is impudently abused, and thus they have not the slightest suspicion of the intrinsic fallacy of the whole

---

[57]Id., pp. 395, 100.

doctrine. They see only the ruthless force and brutality of its determined utterances, to which they always submit".[58]

What is so unsettling about *Mein Kampf* is the barefaced disdain with which Hitler wrote about "the masses" who were, after all, his own audiences – who were the German people. This may have been the main reason why in later years he expressed regret about having written the book, for on so many pages was set down that the leader of the German masses, their adored Führer, would not hesitate to use and abuse them, indeed that it was his intention to do so. He should not have bothered, though; the atmosphere created in a limited way at the meetings and afterwards in a general way when the whole of Germany had become his theatre and audience, proved prohibitive to the use of the faculty of reason. Hitler could write freely about "millions of German imbeciles", "the dunder-headed multitude", "the vacillating crowd of human children", "the feebleness of their understanding and the quickness of their forgetting": they would applaud him frantically nonetheless. This proved that his insight in the psychology of the masses was right, whether he got it from Gustave Le Bon or Georges Sorel via Eckart, from reading *The Protocols of the Wise Men of Zion*, or from his own intuition and experience. Hitler, the theatre man, was a genius at mass psychology, which made him a genius at propaganda; and when he picked out Joseph Goebbels as his right-hand man in these fields, his intuition was proved correct once more.

We are now at the heart of the German tragedy. Hitler sought not only to dominate the masses: his objective from the first to the last was to use them. "The readiness to sacrifice one's personal work and, if necessary, even one's life for others shows its most highly developed form in the Aryan race. The greatness of the Aryan is not based on his intellectual powers, but rather on his willingness to devote all his faculties to the service of the community. Here the

---

[58] Id., p. 48.

instinct for self-preservation has reached its noblest form; for the Aryan willingly subordinates his own ego to the common weal and when necessity calls he will even sacrifice his own life to the community".[59] Being against the acquisitions of the Enlightenment, Nazism was against all forms of individualism. The total uniformization of Germany, the forests of stiffly raised arms, the clicking of boot heels, the endlessly pulsating roars of *Sieg Heil!* – all of that was an unmistakable warning which was not heeded. "What Hitler had in mind", writes Zentner, "was the inner unity of the nation, welded into a strictly organized marching column, prepared for self-sacrifice and ready at any time to execute any order of the National-Socialist leadership".[60] Hitler compared the unified masses which were the nation to a sword, his weapon to wage war. "War and destruction were essential to restore the shaky balance of the world: that was the morality and the metaphysics of his politics". (Fest[61]) He formulated these objectives quite openly: "To forge this sword is the task of the interior political leadership; to secure the forging and look for allies in the battle is the task of the exterior political leadership".[62]

"One should seriously doubt if Hitler has loved the Germans", ruminates Eberhard Jäckel.[63] "I know that I have to be a stern educator. I first have to create the Volk before I can think of solving the problems we as a nation are confronted with in the present time", said Hitler to Rauschning. "We have to be prepared for the toughest struggle which a people ever had to wage. It is only through such a test of the will that we can grow ready for the overlordship to which we are called. It will be my duty to wage this war without concern for the losses. The blood sacrifices will be enormous. Anyone

---

[59] Id., p. 249.
[60] Christian Zentner, op. cit., p. 103.
[61] Joachim Fest, op. cit., p. 209.
[62] Quoted in Christian Zentner, op. cit., p. 125.
[63] Eberhard Jäckel, op. cit., p. 138.

of us knows what total war means ... Towns will become ruins, noble buildings will disappear for ever. This time our sacred soil will not be spared. But I don't fear this. We will stand firm, we will not stop fighting. Germany will arise from these ruins more beautiful and greater than any country in the world, ever." [64]

Blind faith

Writing in *Mein Kampf* about his first contacts with the DAP in September 1919, Hitler says that, after long reflection, he came to the conclusion that "what had to be proclaimed here was a new ideology and not a new political slogan".[65] That this reflection was not a solitary exercise has become evident in the first chapters of our story. May it be reminded that, amazingly, he entered the circle of Harrer and Drexler with an ideology apparently ready to be put into practice, that he "wanted to found a party" of his own, and that his plans were to use the insignificant DAP to this end.

In 1924, when writing the first part of *Mein Kampf* in the prison at Landsberg, his dreams and visions had already been concretized to a considerable extent. True, the beginnings of Hitler's work seemed modest and the accomplishment of his ambitions questionable to most observers at the time, but not to Adolf Hitler himself. The effect the Landsberg retreat had on Hitler was that of a complete reassurance about his vocation and a total confidence in the execution of his mission. Discretion still prevented him from proclaiming himself Führer of the German nation, but in the pages of *Mein Kampf* he leaves no doubt as to who and what he was, without naming himself as such.

"Do you feel that Providence has called you to proclaim the Truth to the world? If so, then go and do it", Hitler wrote. "But you ought to have the courage to do it directly and not use some

---

[64]Hermann Rauschning: *Gespräche mit Hitler,* pp. 22, 265.
[65]Adolf Hitler, op. cit., p. 191.

political party as your mouthpiece, for in this way you shirk your vocation. ['Using a political party' here means using its programme without being able to proclaim an authentic, personal one.] In the place of something that now exists and is bad, put something else that is better and will last into the future". "Out of the army of millions who feel the truth of these [volkisch, nationalist and anti-Semitic] ideas, and even may understand them to some extent, one man must arise. This man must have the gift of being able to expound general ideas in a clear and definite form and, from the world of vague ideas shimmering before the mind of the masses, he must formulate principles that will be as clear-cut and firm as granite. He must fight for these principles as the only true ones, until a solid rock of common faith and common will emerges above the troubled waves of vagrant ideas. The general justification of such action is to be sought in the necessity for it and the individual will be justified by his success". There is no doubt which man the author had in mind. "Genius of an extraordinary stamp is not to be judged by normal standards whereby we judge other men".[66]

Hitler saw himself as a man of ideas and their practical executioner bundled into one: "When the abilities of theorist and organizer and leader are united in one person, then we have the rarest phenomenon on this earth. And it is that union which produces the great man". "Within long spans of human progress it may occasionally happen that the practical politician and the political philosopher are one. The more intimate this union, the greater will be the obstacles which the activity of the politician will have to encounter. Such a man does not labour for the purpose of satisfying demands that are obvious to every philistine, but he reaches out towards ends which can be understood only by the few. His life is torn asunder by hatred and love. The protest of the contemporaries, who do not understand the man, is in conflict with the recognition of posterity, for whom he also works ... The great protagonists [of history] are those who

---

[66]Id., pp. 108, 320, 375.

fight for their ideas and ideals despite the fact that they receive no recognition at the hands of their contemporaries. They are the men whose memories will be enshrined in the hearts of the future generations".[67] Hitler was already building a mausoleum for himself and reserving his place in the Walhalla of the great.

"One thing is certain", he declared, "our world is facing a great revolution".[68] According to Jäckel, "Hitler held himself for the prophet of a new world vision".[69] This is true but perhaps stated too mildly. In any case, Hitler himself repeatedly wrote that he stood for "a new and great idea", "a novel missionary idea". "Political parties are prone to enter compromises, but an ideology never does this. A political party is inclined to adjust its teachings with a view of meeting the teachings of its opponents, but an ideology proclaims its own infallibility. While the programme of the ordinary political party is nothing but the recipe for cooking up favourable results out of the next general elections, the programme of an ideology represents a declaration of war against an existing order of things, against present conditions, in short, against the established ideology".[70] In sum, Hitler had a new message for the world, a new ideology or *Weltanschauung* "pure and absolutely true", a new creed or gospel, a new Faith.

To give his vision a concrete shape in the world he needed an organized body of men who would execute his commands. Religious world-reformers call this a Church; Hitler will later call it "an Order", and even say "we too are a Church". In the beginning of his political career, however, he could not but call it a political party. "It is the task of such an organization to transmit a certain idea which originated in the brain of an individual to a multitude of people and to supervise the manner in which this idea is being put into practice". "From

---

[67]Id., pp. 474, 183.
[68]Id., p. 357.
[69]Eberhard Jäckel, op. cit., p. 13.
[70]Adolf Hitler, op. cit., p. 379-80.

general ideas a political programme must be constructed and a general ideology must receive the stamp of a definite political faith". "That is why the programme of the new movement [the NSDAP] was condensed into a few fundamental postulates, twenty-five in all. They are meant first of all to give the ordinary man a rough sketch of what the movement is aiming at. They are, so to say, a profession of faith which on the one hand is meant to win adherents to the movement and, on the other hand, to unite such adherents together in a covenant to which all have subscribed". "For the majority of our followers the essence of the movement will consist not so much in the letter of our theses as in the meaning which we attribute to them".[71] This last phrase should be read: "as in the meaning which *I* attribute to them".

Once the twenty-five articles of his creed had been formulated Hitler never allowed them to be changed, although some of them became irrelevant as the national-socialist movement marched on. Their literal meaning was not really important. The creed was like a shell, symbolical, dogmatic, to be learned by heart and professed by the mass of followers, while inside that shell or behind the dogma there lived and acted the spirit that knew — and which was Hitler's spirit. This explains why he kept his NSDAP separated so trenchantly from the volkisch movement, which professed for the most part some vaguely romantic and even sentimental notions, and which was a mass of motley trends from Wotanism to nudism. To Hitler, being volkisch was a pose or a game, if not a flight from reality; being a Hitlerite, on the contrary, was a matter of imminent worldwide revolution.

Hitler did not hesitate to pour ridicule on the volkisch movement, in which the Nazi movement had its roots and with which it was closely associated in the eyes of its own followers and of the general public. "Not less dangerous are those who run about as semi-volkists

---

[71]Id., pp. 290, 319, 382, 384.

formulating fantastic schemes which are mostly based on nothing else than a fixed idea which in itself might be right but which, because it is an isolated notion, is of no use whatsoever for the formation of a great homogeneous fighting association and could by no means serve as the basis of its organization ... At best they are sterile theorists but more frequently they are mischievous agitators of the public mind". One might ask where Hitler had come by his ideas and how mischievous *he* was. "They believe that they can mask their intellectual vanity, the futility of their efforts and their lack of ability, by sporting flowing beards and indulging in ancient German gestures".[72] The last sentence was aimed at such organizations like the Germanenorden and the disciples of Guido von List and Lanz von Liebenfels to whom, after all, Hitler was indebted, but from whom he now wanted to dissociate himself.

A militant movement

Hitler owed the successes of his NSDAP to his insight that, in the given post-war circumstances, no new party could make headway if it was not able to stand up to the other parties, the Socialists and especially the Communists, with brute force, for they ruled the streets and broke up any meeting or manifestation which was not to their liking. Humanity being what it is, Hitler was right in concluding from history that a revolutionary idea needs a revolutionary movement to make its physical appearance and growth possible in society.

He wrote: "Any ideology, though a thousand times right and supremely beneficial to humanity, will be of no practical service for the maintenance of a people as long as its principles have not yet become the rallying point of a militant movement ... If an abstract conception of a general nature is to serve as the basis of a future

---

[72] Id., p. 385.

development, then the first prerequisite is to form a clear understanding of the nature and scope of this conception. For only on such a basis can a movement be founded which will be able to draw the necessary fighting strength from the internal cohesion of its principles and convictions. From general ideas a political programme must be constructed and a general ideology must receive the stamp of a definite political faith". "We had declared one of our principles thus: 'We shall meet violence with violence in our own defence'. Naturally that principle disturbed the equanimity of the knights of the pen. They reproached us bitterly not only for what they called our crude worship of the cudgel but also because, according to them, we had no intellectual forces on our side. These charlatans did not think for a moment that a Demosthenes could be reduced to silence at a mass-meeting by fifty idiots who had come there to shout him down and use their fists against his supporters". "We, by our aggressive policy, are setting up a new ideology which we shall defend with indomitable devotion".[73]

'Faith' and 'devotion' are religious terms, used by Hitler freely and intentionally, for the new ideology of which he was the prophet was not a political programme to be realized by a political party and with political objectives: it was a fundamental and therefore religious creed, intended to use the German nation as an instrument for conquest of the world and the establishment of a new world order. Hitler as a human being may have been petty and in some ways ridiculous, but the vision which had taken hold of him was world-encompassing and did cause global upheaval. "Do you now understand the depth of our national-socialist movement?" he asked Hermann Rauschning after having lifted a tip of the veil. "Can there be something that is greater and more comprehensive? He who has understood National-Socialism as no more than a political movement doesn't know anything about it."[74]

---

[73]Id., pp. 319, 304, 317.
[74]Quoted in Peter Orzechowski: *Schwarze Magie – Braune Macht*, p. 187.

Hitler defended keeping his party programme unchanged by writing: "The function which dogma fulfils in religious belief is parallel to the function which party principles fulfil for a political party which is in the process of being built up ... A doctrine which forms a definite outlook on life cannot struggle and triumph by allowing the right of free interpretation of its general teaching, but only by defining that teaching in certain articles of faith that have to be accepted and incorporating it in a political organization". "The essentials of a teaching must never be looked for in external formulas, but always in its inner meaning. And this meaning is unchangeable".[75] The essentials of Hitler's teaching were indeed unchangeable – in his own head; so many of the people more or less close to him have testified to the fixity of his leading ideas, and to their secrecy. About his new gospel he wrote the following dreadful but revealing words: "A revolutionary conception of the world and human existence will always achieve decisive success when the new ideology has been taught to a whole people, or subsequently forced upon them if necessary, and when, on the other hand, the central organization, the movement itself, is in the hands of only those few men who are absolutely indispensable to form the nerve-centres of the coming State".[76] The man foresaw all essentials of his future reign of terror, and they were written there for all to read.

"Since the first day of our foundation we were resolved to secure the future of the movement by fighting our way forward in a spirit of blessed faith and ruthless determination", writes Hitler. "If the struggle on behalf of an ideology is not conducted by men of heroic spirit who are ready to sacrifice everything, within a short while it will become impossible to find real fighting followers who are ready to lay down their lives for the cause ... In order to secure the conditions that are necessary for success, everybody concerned must be made to understand that the new movement looks to posterity

---

[75] Adolf Hitler, op. cit., pp. 322-23, 383.
[76] Id., p. 476

for its honour and glory but that it has no recompense to offer to the present-day members". "It is always more difficult to fight successfully against faith than against knowledge. Love is less subject to change than respect. Hatred is more lasting than mere aversion. And the driving force which has brought about the most tremendous revolutions on this earth has never been a body of scientific teaching which has gained power over the mass, but always a devotion which has inspired them, and often a kind of hysteria which has urged them to action".[77]

In this connection Ralph Reuth quotes Goebbels: "Goebbels reflected once: 'What we want is according to the laws of science not attainable and not to be achieved. We know that. But we act nevertheless according to our thought because we believe in miracles, in the impossible and unattainable. To us, politics is the miracle of the impossible!'" And Reuth comments: "In this irrationality, in this metaphysics of blind faith lay the actual essence of National-Socialism as a political religion."[78] Because Hitler kept his most intimate thoughts a secret, "Germany subjected itself to a religion it did not know; it followed rites it did not understand; it exulted and died for a *mysterium* in which it was not initiated. Only 'the Führer' had real knowledge, no National-Socialist doubted that. And the Führer kept to himself what he did not want to share with others".[79]

"Hitler has shown his political abilities also by the fact that he always discussed his political plans in detail only within a certain circle, and let only very few have a glimpse of the interconnection between his ideas as a whole. Before he came to power, the main reason for this was that only very few of those lower middle class bourgeois, who were his closest backers, could stretch their minds wide enough not to recoil before new ideas which surpassed all boundaries of a 'reasonable' nationalism and socialism. Hitler was already suspect as

---

[77]Id., pp. 305, 99, 213.
[78]Ralph Reuth: *Hitler*, p. 185.
[79]Joachim Köhler: *Wagners Hitler*, pp. 8-9.

an illumined seer and fantast with the 'realists' in the party. That precisely the 'fantastic' ideas of Hitler would made it possible for him to go his peculiar way, which gave the lie to all sceptics, was in those days understandable only to a few". (Hermann Rauschning[80])

"Great master of the lie"

If the Aryan was "the Prometheus of mankind, from whose shining brow the divine spark of genius has at all times flashed forth", his antagonist was the Jew. "The Jew offers the most striking contrast to the Aryan", wrote Hitler. "There is probably no other people in the world who have so developed the instinct of self-preservation as the so-called 'chosen' people. The best proof of this statement is found in the simple fact that this race still exists. Where can another people be found that in the course of the last two thousand years has undergone so few changes in mental outlook and character as the Jewish people? ... What an infinitely tenacious will-to-live, to preserve one's kind, is demonstrated by that fact!"[81] In these words one may find why Fest writes that "[Hitler] admired the Jews ... Basically, he regarded them as something like negative supermen".[82]

However, on the globe there was place for only one chosen people, the Aryans. And if there was a rare touch of admiration for the Jews in Hitler's writings, it was covered over by the much stronger, all-pervading feeling of hate which Hitler entertained towards them from the very beginning of his political career till the time he dictated his political testament, a few hours before his death. "His expansionist dreams for Germany, his concern with the fate of Europe as well as issues of world domination, and his advocacy of a single leader principle all involved a global messianic touch. What is more, this universalist-missionary touch appeared not only two

---

[80]Hermann Rauschning, op. cit., p. 71.
[81]Adolf Hitler, op. cit., p. 251.
[82]Joachim Fest, op. cit., p. 533.

decades later but also before *Mein Kampf* was written ... It was part and parcel of a persistent ideological stance in which, with great grandiosity, Hitler placed himself in charge of the global battle that carried with it ultimate stakes. This had been the focus of his anti-Semitic worldview". (Jay Gonen[83])

It did not require a great effort from Hitler to find words for his hate of the Jews. Books like Theodor Fritsch's *Handbook of the Jewish Question* provided him with an inexhaustible stockpile of anti-Semitic libel through the centuries, and Eckart, who had used much of it in his magazine *In Plain German*, was an admired teacher. If the Aryan was the highest being in a human form, the Jew was the lowest; in fact, he was not even subhuman and his human shape was only a deceptive appearance. "The Jew wriggles his way in among the body of the nations and bores them hollow from inside", teaches *Mein Kampf*. He is "a parasite among nations", "a parasite, a sponger who, like a pernicious bacillus, spreads over wider and wider areas"; "he is a real leech who clings to the body of his unfortunate victims and cannot be removed".[84] The Jew is "a fission fungus of humanity", "a bacillus spreading tuberculosis of the races". He is a scavenger and "common prey attracts him". As he is human only in appearance, "his activities are not hampered by moral considerations of any kind"; typical of him is "the general brutality and rapacity of his nature".[85] This was the kind of language the Germans under the Nazi regime read daily in their newspapers and their youth imbibed in the schools. These were the notions imprinted on the minds of the Jew-exterminators.

"Jewry has always been a nation of a definite racial character and never differentiated merely by the fact of belonging to a certain religion".[86] However confidently stated, this was flagrantly untrue,

---

[83]Jay Gonen: *The Roots of Nazi Psychology – Hitler's Utopian Barbarism*, p. 22.
[84]Adolf Hitler, op. cit., pp. 538, 256, 255, 260.
[85]Id., p. 271.
[86]Id., p. 256.

for the heterogeneous composition of the Jewish people was well established. Yet, to conceive of the Jewish people as a race was necessary for the coherence of Hitler's theories about race and blood. "[The Jew] poisons the blood of others but preserves his own blood unadulterated ... The religious instruction of the Jews is principally a collection of instructions for maintaining the Jewish blood pure".[87] Therefore, what was at stake in the war between the Aryans and the Jews was nothing less than the life of humanity. "The Jew is the enemy of human existence. His ultimate aim is the breaking up of the nations, the intermingling and bastardization of the other peoples, the lowering of the level of the highest races and the lordship over the ensuing racial mixture through elimination of the peoples' intellectuals and their replacement with members of his own people ... If the Jew, with the help of his Marxist creed, is victorious over the peoples of this earth, then his crown will be the death-dance of the world; then this planet will again, just like millions of years ago, drift through the ether empty of human beings".[88]

"Though bubbling over with 'enlightenment', 'progress', 'liberty', 'humanity', etc. [the Jew's] first care was to preserve the racial integrity of his own people. He occasionally bestowed one of his fellow [female] members on an influential Christian, but the racial stock of his male descendants was always preserved fundamentally unmixed. He poisons the blood of others but preserves his own blood unadulterated".[89] It is typical of reactionaries and fundamentalists that they think they are the "decent", "healthy" people, whereas "the others" are degenerate and immoral. It is also typical to find behind the decent people's façade much filth and rottenness, a condition compared by a great Teacher to "whitewashed tombs". Hitler's obsession about "the black-haired Jewish youth", who "lies in wait for hours on end, satanically glaring at and spying

---

[87] Id., pp. 264, 257.
[88] Eberhard Jäckel, op. cit., p. 96.
[89] Adolf Hitler, op. cit., p. 264.

on the unsuspicious [Aryan] girl whom he plans to seduce, adulterating her blood",[90] is one example of the perversion at the bottom of his sick racism. Equally so was his obsession with syphilis, and his support for Julius Streicher's lewd anti-Semitism in the latter's magazine *Der Stürmer*.

In the first quote of the previous paragraph Hitler makes once again a direct attack on the spirit and the ideals of the Enlightenment and on "progress", *the* slogan of the nineteenth century. "To mask his tactics and fool his victims, [the Jew] talks of the equality of all men, no matter what their race or colour may be. And the simpletons begin to believe him ... During this phase of his progress the chief goal of the Jew was the victory of democracy, or rather the supreme hegemony of the parliamentary system, which embodies his concept of democracy. This institution agrees best with his purposes; for thus the personal element is eliminated and in its place we have the dunder-headed majority, inefficiency and, last but by no means least, knavery".[91] If one realizes the measure in which the social-democratic way of life has become the norm by which humanity is organizing its societies at present, and that many are even prepared to give their life for the freedom it provides, one may sense in which direction Hitler was working out his reactionary goals: social hierarchy (the 'Führer principle') instead of equality before the law, and ultimately an order in which the master race of the Germanic-Nordic-Aryans rules over the other races, the subjugated subhuman slaves. It may be noted in passing that "no Jew played a noteworthy role in the [French] Revolution nor in the philosophical revolution by which it was preceded".[92] On the contrary, leading writers like Voltaire were outspoken anti-Semites.

---

[90] Id., p. 273.
[91] Id., p. 265.
[92] Norman Cohn: *Histoire d'un mythe – La "conspiration juive" et les protocoles des sages de Sion*, p. 31. This is the French translation of *Warrant for Genocide*.

In his stance against the Enlightenment and progress, Hitler was as volkisch as could be and an exponent of the times in Germany. But he extended this oppositional attitude to everything deemed by him to be anti-German, which in point of fact meant opposed to Hitler and his new ideology. In this he followed his propagandist principle: to focus the whole attention of a movement, a mass or a people on a single opponent – who for Hitler was the Jew. Thus he created a thought-world of total paranoia, which he succeeded in developing into armed paranoia. Hitler's Germany, isolated in its 'parallel world', became one enormous and enormously destructive instrument of deathly delusion.

Hitler's apocalyptic view of the final global war between the deceitful and the true 'chosen people' was in certain of its aspects still indebted to Dietrich Eckart, who had conceived of a struggle between good (the Aryan side) and evil (the Jewish side) in humanity as a whole and in each of its members in particular. But Hitler had now recast these principles in the Darwinian-racist mould, stimulated, especially after Eckart's death, by Alfred Rosenberg, who "wielded a tremendous influence on Hitler" (Hanfstängl). From this man, steeped in the virulent Russian anti-Semitism of the turn of the century (which resulted in a massive exodus of East-European Jews), Hitler borrowed the reasonings to turn his 'intellectual anti-Semitism' into an 'exterminationist' anti-Semitism. Of this Eckart most probably would never have dared to dream despite his hardened prejudices; it may have been the cause of his suspicion that his pupil began to suffer from a serious case of *folie de grandeur*. The conviction that the Jews did not belong to the body of the German Volk, that they were obnoxious to it and therefore had to be eliminated from it, or at least confined and controlled within it, was current in Germany and propagated in violent slogans. People who drew the extreme conclusions from such propaganda are nonetheless generally supposed to have been few in number. Still the general feeling about the Jews would certainly facilitate the execution of what Hitler had in mind and what the executioners of his armed paranoia would be proud to implement.

The Protocols of the Wise Men of Zion

Alfred Rosenberg was born in Reval (Estonia) in 1893. He studied engineering and architecture till the outbreak of the Russian Revolution in 1917. Staunchly anti-communist and anti-Semitic, which meant one and the same to him, he fled Russia and landed, towards the end of 1918, in a Munich in upheaval. There he became part of the community of Russian refugees, many of whom had connections with the rightist extremists. It may have been *In Plain German* which led Rosenberg to Dietrich Eckart, who accepted him as his collaborator, although Rosenberg's first language was Russian and his German still very poor. And Eckart introduced him to Hitler. Rosenberg was strongly influenced by Houston Chamberlain's *The Foundations of the Nineteenth Century*, which had made its author the revered guru of the German nationalists, the favoured thinker of Emperor Wilhelm II and, as the husband of Winifred Wagner, resident master at House Wahnfried in Bayreuth. But a still stronger influence on Rosenberg was exerted by *The Protocols of the Wise Men of Zion*.

The *Protocols* pretended to provide a report of the instructions given by a mysterious Supreme Master to the heads of the twelve tribes of Israel at midnight on the Jewish churchyard in Prague. Their objective was Jewish supremacy over the whole world, their strategy a ruthless but surreptitious campaign against everything held sacred by the despised *goyim*, their ideology an unconditional materialism which would use the principles of the Enlightenment as its guidelines and ultimately result in the submission of a zombie-like humanity of slaves to the Jewish master race. The *Protocols* were a fake concocted by members of the Russian secret police in France to convince Tsar Nicholas II of the danger the Jews represented to his throne. It was one fake among many in a tradition of similar anti-Semitic writings, most probably written at the time of the Dreyfus Affair in France, which split that country into two, and of the first Zionist Congress held at Basel in 1897.[93]

---

[93]See Norman Cohn, op. cit., p. 106.

"The *Protocols* and the myth of the Jewish world conspiration were exploited by the Nazi propaganda in all its stages", writes Norman Cohn, "from the birth of the Party in 1919-20 until the collapse of the Third Reich in 1945. They were used successively to help the Party come to power, to justify its regime of terror, to justify the war, to justify the genocide, and finally to postpone the capitulation. The history of this myth, and of its utilization for various ends, reflects accurately the rise and fall of the Third Reich itself". According to Cohn, "One may not be mistaken when writing that, exception made for the Bible, the *Protocols* were around 1925 the most widely read book in the whole world".[94]

About the *Protocols* Hitler wrote in *Mein Kampf*: "How much the whole existence of [the Jewish] people is based on a permanent falsehood is proved in a unique way by *The Protocols of the Wise Men of Zion* ... What many Jews unconsciously wish to do is here clearly set forth. It is not necessary to ask out of what Jewish brain these revelations sprang; but what is of vital interest is that they disclose, with an almost terrifying precision, the mentality and methods of action characteristic of the Jewish people, and these writings expound in all their various directions the final aims towards which the Jews are striving. The study of real happenings, however, is the best way of judging the authenticity of those documents. If the historical developments which have taken place within the last few centuries be studied in the light of this book, we shall understand why the Jewish Press incessantly repudiates and denounces it. For the Jewish peril will be stamped out the moment the general public come into possession of this book and understand it".[95]

"Hitler, in the depth of his feeling, if not of his intelligence, was surely convinced of the Jewish world conspiracy", writes Konrad Heiden.[96] One finds this confirmed on several pages of *Mein Kampf*

---

[94] Id., p. 192, 166.
[95] Adolf Hitler, op. cit., p. 258.
[96] Konrad Heiden, op. cit., p. 456.

where Hitler writes about "the aspiration of the Jewish people to become the despots of the world".[97] A direct and sad refutation of a Jewish world conspiracy were the inner divisions among the Jews during the war, their lack of cooperation to receive their co-religionists who had to flee Germany, and the way so many allowed themselves to be led "like lambs to the slaughter". Cohn quotes the testimony after the war of SS-general Erich von dem Back-Zelewski, one of the notorious Jew-slayers: "Had the Jews only in the least been organized, millions of them could have been saved, but they were entirely taken by surprise".[98]

In his book on Hitler, one of the earliest biographies ever written and still in print, Konrad Heiden states repeatedly that the Nazi Führer imitated the methods described by the forgers of the Protocols. Heiden's assertion seems at first overblown and inspired by his hatred for Hitler and everything the Nazis stood for. But when one reads the *Protocols* again after having studied *Mein Kampf*, one finds analogies on practically every page. Hitler's aim was indeed world domination, and to this end he would exploit 'ruthlessly' (one of his favourite words) the foibles of the human condition, common to his own people as to all others, using exactly the same means and ploys as those recommended to the imaginary Wise Men of Zion.

A phrase which Hitler in *Mein Kampf* often applied to the Jews was 'great masters of the lie'. This expression had been often used by Eckart, who copied it from their admired philosopher Arthur Schopenhauer. The phrase is, in fact, perfectly applicable to Hitler himself. He had an instinct to sense and play on the weaknesses of human nature, of the mass as well as of the individual, and he had learned how to brashly mislead, distort and lie, something so obvious in *Mein Kampf* that it may be another reason why he regretted having written the book.

---

[97] Adolf Hitler, op. cit., p. 538.
[98] Norman Cohn, op. cit., p. 250.

"The common people are credulous of everything, whether because of their ignorance or their simple-mindedness", he wrote. "In the big lie there is always a force of credibility, because the broad masses of a nation are always more easily corrupted in the deeper strata of their emotional nature than consciously or voluntarily, and thus in the primitive simplicity of their minds they more readily fall victims to the big lie than to the small lie ..." Promises are made not to be kept, Treaties are signed to be betrayed. But Hitler's greatest lie was to the German people, whom he pretended to be his bride, 'Germania', and therefore the reason for his remaining single. He gave them employment, bread, radios and self-esteem – for some time – and lots of martial and theatrical hoopla, but he did not tell them that they were fattened to be eaten by Death.

"The great master of the lie", the great sophist, was Adolf Hitler, the persuader who distorted all terms and reasonings, but did so in a passionate and therefore convincing way which bypassed logical thought. If *Mein Kampf* has the nasty odour Fest writes about, it is because of its mendacious contents. This book is a true warning from history, but by most people who know of its existence it is unfortunately considered to be some sort of a curiosity.

What, in the final analysis, was the reason of Hitler's anti-Semitism? Ron Rosenbaun asked the question of Alan Bullock, who answered, after all the years he had spent on studying the dictator: "I don't know. Nobody knows. Nobody's even began".[99] "Hitler never suggested, not even with a single word, that he was planning the biggest autodafé [ie the Holocaust] in history", writes Köhler.[100] "In spite of all the details we know, the cause of Hitler's anti-Semitism is not completely explainable", opines Maser.[101] And yet, Hitler's intention to eradicate the Jews is written on every page of *Mein Kampf*; it was shouted by him from the rooftops and echoed

---

[99] Ron Rosenbaum: *Explaining Hitler*, p. 83.
[100] Joachim Köhler, op. cit., p. 410.
[101] Werner Maser: *Adolf Hitler*, p. 267.

from thousands of throats in classrooms, meetings and demonstrations, on radios in the homes and from loudspeakers in the streets, and it was printed in newspapers, magazines and a flood of books. But his bride Germania did not really believe it (nor did the rest of the world) – it was too horrendous to be true – or she preferred not to think about such disturbing things, or she kept her distance not wanting to think about her responsibility.

"For [the Jew] language is not an instrument for the expression of his inner thoughts but rather a means of cloaking them", Hitler wrote. "He will stop at nothing. His utterly low-down conduct is so appalling that one really cannot be surprised if in the imagination of our people the Jew is pictured as the incarnation of Satan and the symbol of evil". "As has so often happened, Germany is the chief pivot of this formidable struggle. If our people and our state should fall victims to these oppressors of the nations, lusting after blood and money, the whole earth would become the prey of that hydra. Should Germany be freed from its grasp, a great menace for the nations of the world would thereby be eliminated".[102]

Living space for the master race

"See to it that the strength of our nation does not rest on colonial foundations", wrote Hitler in *Mein Kampf*, "but on our own native territory in Europe. Never consider the Reich secure unless, for centuries to come, it is in a position to give every descendant of our race a piece of ground and soil that he can call his own. Never forget that the most sacred of all rights in this world is man's right to the earth which he wishes to cultivate for himself and that the holiest of all sacrifices is that of the blood poured out for it".[103] Hitler left no doubt where that piece of ground and soil was to be found. The conquest of 'the East', actually the territories belonging to Baltic,

---

[102] Adolf Hitler, op. cit., pp. 257, 272, 508.
[103] Adolf Hitler, op. cit., p. 541.

Slavonic and other peoples in eastern Europe, had been drawing the Germanic tribes for centuries, so much so that the *Drang nach Osten* (the impulse to move east) was, except for rare periods of friendly relations, something like a cyclic instinctive urge. Waves of Vikings rowed down the Dnieper from 'Gothland', mainly Sweden, to Kiev and Constantinople; the Teutonic Knights subjugated Prussia and the territories of what is now called Poland, the Balticum and the Ukraine; later, German settlers became landlords in these regions and their descendants were still living there, proud of their Germanic ancestry. (Stalin will send them to Siberia.)

Hitler formulated his *Lebensraum* (living space) theory for the first time clearly and in detail when writing *Mein Kampf*, whereas before he had used predominantly German resurgence and revenge against the French arch-enemy as the main themes of his speeches and propaganda. Yet, Russia, the East and Lebensraum had always been on his mind, and it could not have been otherwise after the fear of Communism caused by the 1917 October Revolution and its aftermath in Germany, a fear made worse by the spate of Red revolts within the country. Important centres of anti-Communism and anti-Semitism were the circles of Russian refugees in France and Germany. Most of these refugees belonged to the nobility and upper bourgeoisie, were therefore Right-wing and connected with Right-wing extremists in the host country. They were the people who carried *The Protocols of the Wise Men of Zion* in their luggage. Alfred Rosenberg was a typical example, and so was Erwin von Scheubner-Richter, who marched not without reason by Hitler's side in the Beer Hall Putsch and whose name might be much better known if he had not been killed.

"The drive for Lebensraum was never just a Nazi goal".[104] The conquest of the East had, in fact, always been a matter of Teutonic pride, arrogance and cupidity. The Catholic Teutonic Knights deemed themselves a superior breed compared with the barbaric, heathen

---

[104] John Weiss, op. cit., p. 211.

Pruss and similar vile peoples. (It is ironic that their Prussian descendants would proclaim themselves God's favourite people, carriers of the highest culture and by right – which right? – lords of humanity.) Fritz Fischer has shown how in more recent times Germany's "epochal turn against Russia" was initiated by Bethmann Hollweg in 1913. This happened, writes Fischer, after the Chancellor had been travelling through Russia in the previous year and seen with his own eyes, "in a kind of revelation", what enormous riches of human and natural resources were available there.

Once more the primal cause of this epochal turn was German arrogance, for at that time Germany had brought about its first *Wirtschaftswunder* (economic miracle). "Germany sees how its population is increasing day by day; its navy, industry and commerce are developing without comparison; it needs expansion, it has a claim to 'a place in the sun'", said the German Chancellor.[105] "A place in the sun" was one of the nationalist and pan-German slogans at the time. Was an expansion at the cost of other nations, and justified with 'scientific', pseudo-Darwinist arguments, really necessary for Germany? The enormous industrial and commercial growth around 1900 proved that it was not; and Christian von Krockow writes about the new *Wirtschaftswunder* after the Second World War: "On a drastically reduced national territory [Germany was broken up into two] one got nevertheless and at last the longed for *Lebensraum*, without having to use anything but personal industry".[106]

During his Landsberg retreat, Hitler's views had not changed fundamentally: the Germans were to become the masters of the earth; they would avenge on France the humiliation of the Treaty of Versailles (he entertained the same irrational hopes for an understanding with Great Britain as the German leadership before the Great War); the protagonist of the Aryan race, the Jew, had to be discarded in one way or another. But now Hitler dared to express

---

[105] Fritz Fischer: *Hitler war kein Betriebsunfall*, pp. 146 ff.
[106] Christian von Krockow, op. cit., p. 296.

what could only have drawn ridicule when he was still known as the Austrian corporal: Germany must conquer the world for the Aryan race, and they would begin where they had left off six centuries ago, in 'the East'. In Landsberg prison he had had the time to reflect, to meditate, to round off the vision of his mission. And he had been profoundly influenced by the opinions of Alfred Rosenberg and, through Rudolf Hess, by the geopolitical theories of Karl Haushofer. A few days after his release from Landsberg, Hitler was on a visit at the Hanfstängl home. "To my horror he spouted a still further distilled essence of all the nonsense that Hess and Rosenberg had been concocting", remembers Ernst Hanfstängl. "I am sure that this is the point at which his latest radical tendencies started to crystallize ... Hess had succeeded in pumping his head full of the Haushofer thesis ..."[107]

Karl Haushofer, born in 1869, was a cultured military man who had become a major-general in the First World War. Earlier, he had been appointed military attaché to the German Embassy in Japan. At that time he had undertaken many travels in India, Tibet, Manchuria, China and Korea which would have a lasting influence on him. He was appointed honorary professor of geopolitics at Munich University in 1924 and published shortly afterwards his handbook *Geopolitics of the Pacific Ocean*. A close friendship tied him to Rudolf Hess, who adulated Hitler and was one of the most enthusiastic Nazis. Haushofer, acquainted with Hitler since 1921, visited Hess several times in Landsberg prison, where he inevitably also met with Hitler, for Hess had a cell next to Hitler's on the upper floor and these cells gave out unto a common room.

There is no doubt among historians that Haushofer, through his confidant and mouthpiece Hess, played an important role in matters of Hitler's ideological outlook, more specifically his plans for the conquest of Lebensraum. What Haushofer's influence meant

---

[107] Ernst Hanfstängl, op. cit., pp. 120-21.

concretely is still under discussion. According to Martin Allen: "Basically, geopolitics was the theory, as promulgated by Haushofer, that in the future the world would be restructured into an age of great land-empires, dominated by 'the Heartland', an area 'invulnerable to sea-power in Central Europe and Asia'. This, Haushofer asserted, would revolutionize the world's balance of power, ushering in a new age of stability, peace and prosperity for all".[108]

One finds in the works of the commentators on Hitler's intentions conflicting versions of his plans of conquest. Some maps show Hitler's Greater German Reich occupying the middle part of Europe, from Scandinavia to Italy, but other maps extend the Reich up to the Urals. Both land masses are supposed to be the base, established by Hitler, for future German world conquest. "Any thought of world politics is ridiculous as long as one does not rule the Continent", Hitler is reported to have said in 1944.[109] Did he mean the European continent, or the land mass of which Europe is no more than a peninsula? He certainly stooped to having friendly relations with the Japanese, a coloured race of small stature, and declared them to be 'honorary Aryans' to further his plans in Asia and the Pacific Ocean, in this relying on Karl Haushofer as the chief intermediary. The plans for his lifetime, as the founder of the Third Reich which others would have to build up and complete, did not include colonies. Water was an element Hitler disliked, and Ernst Hanfstängl, who maintains he tried to convince Hitler of the capacities of the USA, writes: "He thought only in European terms."[110]

How did Hitler justify his demand for living space in *Mein Kampf*? The principle was unequivocal: "Only a sufficiently large space on this earth can assure the independent existence of a people". From this he deduced: "We, National-Socialists, must stick firmly to

---

[108]Martin Allen: *The Hitler/Hess Deception*, p. 9.
[109]*Monologe im Führerhauptquartier*, p. 110.
[110]Ernst Hanfstängl, op. cit., p. 121.

the aim that we have set for our foreign policy, namely that the German people must be assured of the territorial area which is necessary for it to exist on this earth. Only for such action as is undertaken to secure those ends can it be lawful in the eyes of God and our German posterity to allow the blood of our people to be shed again ...

"State frontiers are established by human beings and may be changed by human beings. The fact that a nation has acquired an enormous territorial area is no reason why it should hold that territory perpetually. At most, the possession of such territory is a proof of the strength of the conqueror and the weakness of those who submit to him. And in this strength alone lives the right to possession. If the German people are imprisoned within an impossible territorial area and for that reason are face to face with a miserable future, this is not by the command of Destiny, and the refusal to accept such a situation is by no means a violation of Destiny's laws. For just as no Higher Power has promised more territory to other nations than to the German, so it cannot be blamed for an unjust distribution of the soil. The soil on which we now live was not a gift bestowed by Heaven on our forefathers; they had to conquer it by risking their lives. So also in the future our people will not obtain territory, and therewith the means of existence, as a favour from any other people: they will have to win it by the power of a triumphant sword". [111]

Hitler drew of the Slavonic people a picture that was at the same time frightful and repulsive, and that would vindicate the barbaric invasion he seems to have envisioned even then. The main theme of his propaganda was that Germany had to be built up as a bulwark against the Danger from the East in its many shapes, that it was the knight in shining armour who would protect Europe and the values it stood for against the hordes from the Asian steppes (a metaphor already used by William II). The effects of this propaganda, developed and adapted by the SS, will attract thousands of idealistic young

---

[111] Adolf Hitler, op. cit., pp. 523, 531, 532.

Europeans to join the divisions of the Waffen-SS and sacrifice their lives on the Russian plains. What Hitler really had in mind, and what he wrote in 1928 in a never published so-called 'second book', was "the idea that this Europe was not to arise as the result of a federation, but by the racially strongest nations [none other than the Germanic, of course] subjugating the others ... National-Socialism will extend its revolution until the New Order has been achieved all through the world".[112]

"As things stand today, vast spaces still lie uncultivated all over the surface of the globe", wrote Hitler in *Mein Kampf*. "Those spaces are only waiting for the ploughshare. And it is quite certain that nature did not set those territories apart as the exclusive pastures of any one nation or race, to be held unutilized in reserve for the future. Such lands await the people who have the strength to acquire it and the diligence to cultivate it. Nature knows no political frontiers. She begins by establishing life on this globe and then watches the free play of forces. Those who show the greatest courage and industry are the children nearest to her heart and they will be granted the sovereign right of existence".[113]

"We put an end to the perpetual Germanic march towards the South and West of Europe and turn our eyes towards the lands of the East. We finally put a stop to the colonial and trade policy of pre-war times and pass over to the territorial policy of the future. When we speak of new territory in Europe today, we must principally think of Russia and the border states subject to her. Destiny itself seems to wish to point out the way for us here ... For the Russian State was not organized by the constructive political talent of the Slav element in Russia but was much more a marvellous exemplification of the capacity for state-building possessed by the Germanic element in a race of inferior worth ... For centuries Russia owned the source of its livelihood as a State to the Germanic nucleus

---

[112] Joachim Fest, op. cit., p. 688.
[113] Adolf Hitler, op. cit., p. 123.

of its governing classes. But this nucleus is now almost wholly broken up and abolished ... This colossal empire in the East is ripe for dissolution. And the end of the Jewish domination in Russia will also be the end of Russia as a state. We are chosen by Destiny to be the witnesses of a catastrophe which will afford the strongest confirmation of the nationalist theory of race".[114]

---

[114] Id., p. 533.

PART TWO
The roots of Nazism

7

SUPERIOR PEOPLE

War, then, and if needs must, war against everybody, to convince everybody and to win, that was what fate had willed. We were bursting with the consciousness that this was Germany's century, that history was holding her hand out over us; that after Spain, France, England, it was our turn to put our stamp on the world and be its leader; that the twentieth century was ours.
　　　　　　　THOMAS MANN'S NARRATOR IN *Doctor Faustus*

Hitler was no accident

How was all that possible: Hitler, Nazism, the Second World War, the Holocaust…? The major tragedy of the twentieth century has remained an unexplained mystery with a thousand explanations, justifications and refutations, especially among the people who started it all, the Germans. Were they not universally considered, before their nation plunged into its delirium, to be a people of *Denker und Dichter*, poets and thinkers, and perhaps still more essentially musicians? The previous chapters may have shown some force lines leading up to the tragedy (and we are not yet at the end of our story). But the historical concatenations are hardly known except to students of history, and Hitler is mostly represented in the popular mind as a devil or a clown, or both. The unusual dimensions of the movement he created, the admiration and enthusiasm he evoked, and the slaughter he caused, made some Germans explain away their guilt by positing that his apparition on the political stage and the subsequent global tragedy in which he starred were something out of the ordinary, irrational, and therefore an 'accident' of history.

Several knowledgeable people have pointed out that Hitler was *not* an accident. So for instance George Mosse, who wrote: "National Socialism was not an aberration; neither was it without historical foundation. It was, rather, the product of the interplay of economic, social and political forces on the one hand, and human perceptions, hopes and longing for the good life on the other. National Socialism was successful as a mass movement precisely because it was able to turn long-cherished myths and symbols to its own purpose".[1] Sebastian Haffner, who had to flee from Nazi Germany, wrote: "We overestimate Hitler's capacities enormously if we believe that he has been able to produce this mass [of supporters] in a span of twenty years from nothing. He must have found them ready. Hardly perceptible from outside, the raw material for the national-socialist leadership stratum must already have been available in such a way that it was only to be brought to the surface from the amorphous mass of German people".[2] And Joachim Fest observes: "Ultimately everything terminated in Hitler; he was by no means a 'German catastrophe', as the title of a well-known book asserted, but a product of German consistency".[3]

Among the first to use the word 'accident' in connection with Hitler seems to have been Thomas Mann, the great novelist, writing or addressing his radio messages from exile to the German people. He wrote in November 1939: "Hitler, wretched as he is, is no accident;

---

[1] George Mosse: *The Crisis of German Ideology*, p. viii.
[2] Sebastian Haffner: *Germany: Jekyll & Hyde*, p. 44.
[3] Joachim Fest: *Hitler*, p. 375.

he would never have been possible without the psychological preconditions which have to be sought much deeper than in inflation, unemployment, capitalistic speculation or political intrigue".[4] In John Weiss' *Ideology of Death* we find: "The two most popular intellectuals of late nineteenth-century Germany [Paul de Lagarde and Julius Langbehn] were indistinguishable from Nazi ideologists. Given this cultural fact, it is amazing how many still think that National Socialism had little intellectual connection with the German past ... The future leaders of Germany and their supporters were created long before 1914. It was never just Hitler and a few Nazis ... By 1914 significant numbers of upper- and lower-class conservatives welcomed the ideas we call Nazi ideology, and they did so even though Germany had not suffered the traumas of a lost war, inflation, or depression. Hitler's themes were well known before he ever spoke ..."[5]

It was also Thomas Mann who in 1934 pointed out the influence of Luther on the Nazi movement in general and Hitler in particular: "No, Hitler is no accident, no inexplicable misfortune, no derailment. From him 'light' reflects on Luther, and one has to recognise the latter to a large degree in the former. Hitler is a true German phenomenon".[6] Another writer in exile, Hans Habe, expressed the same idea in one of his novels: "Everything has started with Luther ... Luther is the inventor of National Socialism. The textbooks of National Socialism are no more than copies of the Wittenberg Theses ... Luther's Church is already the 'German Church' – and therefore no church any longer. The spreading of the Lutheran teaching started with a terrible war, and since then there has been no end to the splitting up of the world into two. Luther invented a church for one nation and he tried to hire the Lord God for his people. In all wars since then one finds the Lutheran germ – also in the [First]

---

[4]Thomas Mann: *Deutschland und die Deutschen – Essays 1938-1945*, p. 83.
[5]John Weiss: *Ideology of Death*, p. 139, 142, 154-55, 234.
[6]In Günter Scholdt: *Autoren über Hitler*, p. 434.

World War. The arrogant simplicity of Protestantism has gifted the German people with the delusion of their being the chosen people".[7]

"National Socialism is the fulfilment of what the Germans call their 'being'", wrote Joseph Roth. "A direct path leads from Luther by way of Frederick II, Bismarck, William II and Ludendorff to Hitler and Rosenberg ... As to me, I can, with all respect for the Protestants, not see any difference between Luther's writings, for example those to the German nobles, and the writings of Mister Rosenberg. [Luther's] ninety-five theses accord exactly with [Rosenberg's] *Myth of the Twentieth Century*. A straight line leads from the famous inkpot, with which Luther is said to have had a go at the devil, to the equally famous 'scrap of paper' [Hitler's disdainful designation of the neutrality treaty with Belgium]. Who cannot see already in Luther's betrayal of the peasants, the princes and the Jews an early example of the betrayal by the Prussian-Protestant officers of their Church and the world as a whole, is no more than a naïve fool".[8]

Superior people

There were even before Luther marks of a German road that would eventually lead to Hitler. An anonymous publicist, called "the Revolutionary of the Upper Rhine", wrote the *Book of a Hundred Chapters* in 1510, at a time that European thought, stirred up by the revolution of the Renaissance, was in total turmoil. (Luther would pin his ninety-five theses on the door of a church at Wittenberg in 1517.) This elderly fanatic, writes Norman Cohn, "was thoroughly familiar with the enormous mass of medieval apocalyptic literature and drew freely from it".[9] He wrote in German

---

[7] Ibid.
[8] Id., p. 435.
[9] Norman Cohn: *The Pursuit of the Millennium*, p. 119. The following quotations are from the same chapter.

for Germans what was "a communication from the Almighty, conveyed by the Archangel Michael".

The message of the Revolutionary of the Upper Rhine was that the Emperor Frederick Barbarossa, asleep in the Kyffhäuser mountain, would wake up, appear on a white horse and lead "a new chivalry" to establish a reign, or Reich, of a thousand years. This would happen through massacre and terror in a crusade "to smash Babylon in the name of God". Those to be massacred would be "the rich, well-fed, loose-living clergy", the chief enemy, who must be annihilated. "'Go on hitting them', cries [Frederick] the Messiah to his army, 'from the Pope right down to the little clerics. Kill every one of them!' He foresees that 2300 clerics will be killed each day for four and a half years." Others to be slain are the money-lenders, rich merchants, overcharging shopkeepers, unscrupulous lawyers. Then will start the reign of the common people in "abundance of bread and barley and wine and oil at a low price ... All property shall become one common property; then there will indeed be one shepherd and one sheepfold". These were the common expectations of the Middle Ages, a time of misery unimaginable, when the poor were at the mercy of illness, pest and famine, and of the greedy clerical and secular hierarchy pressing down upon them.

"But", writes Cohn, "in one respect the Revolutionary of the Upper Rhine was truly original: nobody before him had combined such devotion to the principle of commercial or public ownership with such megalomaniac nationalism. This man was convinced that in the remote past the Germans had in reality 'lived together like brothers on the earth', holding all things in common. The destruction of that happy order had been the work first of the Romans and then of the Church of Rome ... The Old Testament was dismissed as valueless; for from the time of the creation onwards it was not the Jews but the Germans who were the Chosen People. Adam and all his descendants down to Japheth [one of the three sons of Noah], including all the Patriarchs, were Germans speaking German ... It was Japheth and his kin who first came to Europe, bringing their language [ie German] with them. They had chosen to settle in Alsace [then a German principality], the heart of Europe, and the capital of the Empire which they founded was at Trier".

This amazing load of nonsense is not only typical of a feverish late-medieval brain: all its elements, and lots more, can be found in German writings throughout the following centuries. One finds much of it in *Mein Kampf* and still more in the Nazi publications, especially those of the SS. But the Revolutionary of the Upper Rhine had more to say. He defined for the first time the European "North-South divide" which will play such an important part in the German world vision. "Very different was the history of the Latin peoples. These wretched breeds were not descended from Japheth and were not numbered amongst the original inhabitants of Europe. Their homeland was in Asia Minor, where they had been defeated in battle by the warriors of Trier and whence they had been brought to act as serfs of their conquerors. The French – a peculiarly detestable lot – ought therefore by rights to be a subject people, ruled by the Germans. As for the Italians, they were descended from serfs who had been banished over the Alps ... Roman law, the Papacy, the French, the Republic of Venice [in 1510 still flourishing] were so many aspects of an immense, age-old conspiracy against the German way of life ... Emperor Frederick would restore Germany to the position of supremacy which God intended for her ... The future Empire was indeed to be nothing less than a quasi-religious community of the German spirit. This is what the Revolutionary had in mind when he cried, jubilantly: 'The Germans once held the whole world in their hands and they will do so again, and with more power than ever'".

Norman Cohn comments: "In these fantasies the crude nationalism of a half-educated intellectual erupted into the tradition of popular eschatology. The result is almost uncannily similar to the fantasies which were the core of National-Socialist 'ideology'. One has only to turn back to the tracts of such pundits as Rosenberg and Darré to be immediately struck by the resemblance. There is the same belief in a primitive German culture in which the divine will was once realized and which throughout history has been the source of all good – which was later undermined by a conspiracy of capitalists, inferior, non-Germanic peoples and the Church of Rome – and which must now be restored by a new aristocracy, of humble birth but truly German in soul, under a God-sent saviour who is at once a political leader and a new Christ. It is all there – and so were the offensives in West and East – the terror wielded both as an instrument of policy and for its own sake – the biggest massacres in history – in fact everything except the final consummation of the world-empire which, in Hitler's words, was to last a thousand years".[10]

The quest for world domination

"The Germans once held the whole world in their hands and they will do so again, and with more power than ever", wrote that exalted anonymous German in 1510. Similar feelings were given vent to in the following centuries (as we will see below), not in reference to the *Book of a Hundred Chapters,* which was discovered late in the nineteenth century, but expressing what had become a fixed emotional component of the German character. As Germany was a patchwork of principalities for centuries, also when constituting the basis of the Holy Roman Reich, and became a nation in the true sense only in 1871, there must have been some underlying ideological foundation for the feeling of 'Germanness', of belonging to a German *Volk*. It was this special sense of belonging which made them sing, long before they raised their right arm to Hitler: "Today Germany belongs to us, tomorrow the whole world", and shout slogans like *"Am deutschen Wesen wird die Welt genesen"*, meaning that the rest of the world would regain its health if it shared in the German being.

The rest of the world could only become healthy on condition that all submitted to the Germans and polished their boots. Léon

---
[10]Id., p. 125.

Poliakov calls this "the megalomaniac German delirium", which would lead to "the Nazis' dead-bringing delusion of being the masters of the world" (Rüdiger Sünner). "The German patriotism was the weakest point in the Germany of the pre-Hitler period", writes Sebastian Haffner in 1939, "the spot where the toxin of National-Socialism could infiltrate. And that is still now the only point on which the Nazis and many civilized Germans agree".[11] In this quotation everything depends on the meaning of the word 'patriotism', which can be no other, considering Germany's fragmented past, than 'volkisch ego' or, for the sake of convenience, 'national ego', in its numerous variants from 'self-awareness' up to 'feeling of superiority'. From the time of the Renaissance onward the Germans developed a chronically inflated or inflamed ego, which would in the end blind them to reality. This national ego was the main cause of the Hitler phenomenon and the disasters following in its wake. It made the Germans rally around their Leader; it made them go out and spill their blood for a Greater Germany to which the world would have to bow; it made them feel the true Chosen People, entitled and even missioned, to exterminate the false pretenders, the Jews.

This development is rather surprising if one has a look at the history of the German master race. As a Volk they were a battered people for centuries, moving, in the words of HR Trevor-Roper, "from disaster to disaster". The Thirty Years' War (1618-1648), actually a series of wars between the Catholic, Lutheran and Calvinist religions, but exploited by all participants to further their material interests, was fought mainly on German soil by mercenary armies. It was so devastating that at its end all German principalities lay in ruins and one third (in some places more than one half) of the population had fallen victim to the war. Some say that Germany never recovered from this scourge. The patchwork of principalities and 'free cities' was perpetuated by the Peace of Westphalia (1648) which concluded

---

[11]Sebastian Haffner, op. cit., p. 130.

the war; their particularities and rivalries, which Hitler tried hard to efface, live mutedly on to this day.

"The very real difference that separated Germany from the West" (Mosse) was caused by the political and cultural isolation resulting from the Thirty Years' War. Germany as a whole did not participate in the philosophical movement of renewal which is called the 'Enlightenment', although some of its thinkers and princes were open to it and even contributed to it; the body of the people remained stuck in its 'sacred' traditions, mainly superstitions deeply rooted in the dark ages. Even if the names of the old gods were practically forgotten, a certain mentality from olden times survived, especially in the countryside, and Christianity was, on the more popular level, no more than a set of additional superstitions added to the ancient beliefs. The German tribes, Christianized by force, had been 'badly baptized'. Even Hitler will compare the Christian culture in Germany to a veneer covering a world of ancient fears and impulses still very much alive. These were the hidden realities Romanticism fell back on, as did, in its wake, the volkisch movement which built up an imaginary world fed by deep instincts. "National Socialism was a volkisch movement", states George Mosse. "Yet Hitler would never have succeeded in demonstrating the political effectiveness of the volkisch world vision had this perception of reality not already been shared by a great many Germans".[12]

Hitler's global ambitions

Several authors have expressed their doubt as to Hitler's intentions to conquer the globe and make the Germans, literally, masters of the world. They interpret his sayings and writings as a claim to a place among the prominent world powers of that day, more specifically France, Great Britain and the USA. His claim would have been similar to the German demand for "a place in the sun", the slogan

---
[12]George Mosse, op. cit., p. 50.

of the great industrial and commercial nation Germany had become around the year 1900. Such opinions fail to perceive Hitler's real intentions behind some of his sayings. Just as there was a time that he could not yet proclaim his ambition to become the dictator of Germany, so there was a time that he could not yet openly formulate his global ambitions, quite simply because the Germans in general, and his most faithful supporters in particular, would not have understood them, might have failed to follow him in such a dizzying adventure, and would have put his mission in jeopardy.

"It is certainly true that Hitler improvised in accordance with the measure of his political power", writes Ralph Giordano. "All the same it is an indisputable fact that his last aim in foreign politics lay not in the East, but that it had global dimensions. The way leading to it was not traced out in every single detail, but the guidelines for the permanent struggle of the 'movement', to be waged over centuries, were laid down. Hitler saw himself as the founder of a new world epoch in which the German claims at absolute world mastery would be realized ... The will to absolute dominion is inextricably bound up with the phenomenon Hitler. At the high tide of his victories, Hitler laid claim to the hegemony over Europe, and further on to Germany's position as master of the world, which was to be its future task".[13]

There is no other conclusion from Hitler's words possible if one admits that they contain any truth at all. The Germans, as Aryans, were the foremost race on earth, being the "highest image of the Lord", fountainhead of all culture and everything worthwhile in the history of humanity, and they were the Chosen People. If the false pretenders to the title of Chosen People were the Jews, if the ultimate aim of the Jews was world dominion, as documented in *The Protocols of the Wise Men of Zion*, and if Hitler's Aryans had to exterminate them "to do the work of the Lord" and found the Kingdom of God as the Thousand Year's Reich, then the stage of

---

[13]Ralph Giordano: *When Hitler den Krieg gewonnen hätte*, p. 74.

this eschatological event could be no other than the whole earth. To put this in doubt is to efface the perspectives of Hitler's messianic vision, and a diminution of his vision leaves no place for an explanation of the worldwide historical tragedy which was its consequence.

But let us open *Mein Kampf* once again and see what the author himself had to say. "We all feel that in the distant future man may be faced with problems which can be solved only by a superior race of human beings, a race destined to become master of all the other peoples and which will have at its disposal the means and resources of the whole world ... We, National Socialists, must stick firmly to the aim that we have set for our foreign policy, namely that the German people must be assured the territorial territory which is necessary for it to exist on this earth. And only for such action as is undertaken to secure those ends can it be lawful in the eyes of God and our German posterity to allow the blood of our people to be shed once again. Before God, because we are sent into this world with the commission to struggle for our daily bread, as creatures to whom noting is donated and who must be able to win and hold their position as lords of the earth only through their own intelligence and courage."[14] We recall that it would be "a greater honour to be a citizen of this Reich, even as a street-sweeper, than to be the king of a foreign state".

Mein Kampf was written in 1924-25, at a time when Hitler had to make a new start in order to give shape to his dreams and world dominion which was an envisaged but still vague aim. How, then, did Hitler speak when he held the reins of power? For instance thus, to an assembly of deputies from the *Länder*, the federal states: "[What I have told you] is not about equality with others but about power over others ... In all these conquered countries it will be your task to play the leading role in the name of the German people ...' As the Jews were able to become the all-encompassing world power from their diaspora, so will we today, as the true people of God,

---

[14] Adolf Hitler: *Mein Kampf,* pp. 322, 526, 531.

from our dispersion throughout the world become the omnipresent power, the master people of the Earth".[15]

Walter Darré, Hitler's minister of agriculture and prominent SS-ideologist, said in a speech given in the Führer's presence: "Instead of a horizontal levelling of the European tribes, a vertical one has to be introduced. What this means is that a German elite is called to become the masters in Europe and ultimately in the world ... What has to be done is the conscious reintroduction of an order of classes, or rather of a hierarchical order. This will, however, no longer be possible on such a small territory like Germany, but only on the whole continent, in the whole universe".[16] Be it noted that in Hitler's *Ordensburgen,* the highest Nazi elite schools, young people were trained to become the future governors of the conquered nations. Hardy Krüger, later starring in *Hatari!* and *The Wild Geese,* was one of the students. He remembers: "I took it for granted at the time that, after the final victory, I would become the governor of Moscow, at least ... The teachers and educators needed nine years to hammer all that nonsense of German world dominion and superiority into my head." Others were looking forward to similar posts in Siberia and Chicago.[17]

What spoke more than words of Hitler's visions and intentions were the cities and buildings Hitler planned with his architects, one of whom, Albert Speer, was for years his closest confidant in such matters. In his biography of the young architect who would become the Reich's minister of armaments and who directed a work force of twelve million, mostly non-German slave labourers, Fest writes: "That domed hall", a prominent feature in Germania, as Berlin was to be renamed, "was 'worth more than three victorious wars'", Hitler observed on another occasion, returning to his fixation about the psychological power of great works of architecture to overwhelm.

---

[15] Hermann Rauschning: *Gespräche mit Hitler,* pp. 138-39.
[16] Id., p. 39.
[17] Johannes Leeb (ed.): *Wir waren Hitlers Eliteschüler,* pp. 63, 67, 17.

He dreamt of addressing the nations of the Greater Germanic Empire from the Führer gallery and of imposing laws on a humiliated world. Similarly, the Triumphal Arch would 'finally and for ever drive out the pernicious idea from the people's minds that Germany had lost the [First] World War', he proclaimed. Upon entering the Führer's palace everyone was to 'have the feeling that he was visiting the master of the world'. Psychological reflections of this kind combined with Hitler's fantasies of omnipotence were similarly at work when, standing in front of the model in the early spring of 1939, he pointed to the top of the dome: 'The eagle should no longer stand above the swastika here', he said to Speer: 'To crown the greatest building in the world the eagle must stand above the globe'."[18]

Speer himself wrote about Hitler's "strategic concept of achieving domination of the world step by step".[19] In this, Hitler was very much aware that to himself he could accord no more than the founder's role of one who launched a new *Weltanschauung* and to whom the concrete foundations of the Greater German Reich, incorporating this new world vision or religion, were to be the monuments he planned in proportions becoming of the world's masters. From 1937 onwards Hitler had hypochondriac fears about his health and constantly drove his architects on to speed up the execution of his plans; he wanted 'Germania' to be terminated by 1950. It may have been the same fear about his life span which made him commit the decisive blunder of exacting too big an effort from the German people in a series of invasions, most of all the one taking on Russia.

Speer writes in his memoirs: "These monuments were an assertion of his claim to world dominion long before he dared to voice any such intention even to his closest associates ... I found Hitler's excitement rising whenever I could show him that at least in size we had 'beaten' the other great buildings of history. To be sure, he

---

[18] Joachim Fest: *Speer – The Final Verdict*, p. 76.
[19] Albert Speer: *Spandau – The Secret Diaries*, p. 50.

never gave vent to these heady feelings. He was sparing in his use of high-sounding words to me. Possibly at such moments he actually felt a certain awe; but it was directed toward himself and toward his own greatness, which he himself had willed and projected into eternity ... Hitler one day abruptly stopped me on the stairs to his apartment, let his entourage go on ahead, and said: 'We will create a great empire. All the Germanic peoples will be included in it. It will begin in Norway and extend to northern Italy. I myself must carry this out. If only I keep my health'. That was still a relatively restrained formulation. In the spring of 1937 Hitler visited me at my Berlin showrooms. We stood alone in front of the nearly seven-foot high model of the stadium for four hundred thousand people ... We talked about the Olympic Games, and I pointed out, as I had done several times before, that my athletic field did not have the prescribed Olympic proportions. Without any change of tone, as if it were a matter settled beyond the possibility of discussion, Hitler observed: "No matter. In 1940 the Olympic Games will take place in Tokyo. But thereafter they will take place in Germany for all time to come, in this stadium. And then *we* will determine the measurements of the athletic field'".[20]

And Speer continues: "Hitler wanted a huge meeting hall, a domed structure into which St Peter's Cathedral in Rome would have fitted several times over. The diameter of the dome was to be eight hundred twenty-five feet. Beneath it, in an area of approximately four hundred and ten thousand feet, there would be room for more than a hundred and fifty thousand persons to assemble standing ... The station was to surpass New York's Grand Central Station in size ... The idea was that when visitors, as well as ordinary travellers, stepped out of the station they would be overwhelmed, or rather stunned, by the urban scene and thus by the power of the Reich".[21] Fest quotes Hitler's words, spoken in

---

[20] Albert Speer: *Inside the Third Reich*, pp. 115-16.
[21] Id., pp. 121, 198-99.

1937: "Because we believe in the eternity of this Reich, its works must also be eternal ones, that is ... not conceived for the year 1940 and not for the year 2000; rather they must tower like the cathedrals of our past into the millennia of the future". "In 1938 he conceived the plan of converting Berlin into a world capital", comments Fest, "comparable only to ancient Egypt, Babylon, or Rome".[22]

Renaissance and Reformation

Whereas the so-called Revolutionary of the Upper Rhine thought and wrote in the tradition of the medieval eccentrics, the Renaissance scholars formed a network all over Europe, sharing their erudition, discoveries and enthusiasm for "the new learning". They were, in a way, the first Europeans. But such were those turbulent times that the universality of their learning found itself obliged in each case to chose sides, religiously or politically, and that some paid with their lives for the refusal to bow to any particularism. It was still a time of dungeons, gallows and pyres. The Christian age which we call the Middle Ages was coming to an end; the age that followed, subdivided by the historians in various periods, is not over yet. The Renaissance rediscovered the courage and art of thinking for oneself in the way the ancient Greeks and Romans had done, but this was a very suspect exercise in the eyes of the powers-that-be. They did not like questions because they did not like being put into question.

The movement called 'Renaissance' was much more complex than commonly realised. Nowadays it is superficially associated with the art of geniuses like Leonardo da Vinci, Michelangelo and Raphael, and with humanist scholars like Erasmus of Rotterdam. The art of the Renaissance was of course a most important aspect of the new way of looking at the world. A certain form of art always crowns a great cultural period. Yet it is little known that another current in the movement was the rediscovery of hermetism and magic, as

---
[22]Joachim Fest: *Hitler,* p. 527.

shown in Frances Yates' essay *Giordano Bruno and the Hermetic Tradition* and some of her other publications. She writes: "It cannot, I think, be sufficiently emphasized that these two Renaissance experiences [the intellectual and the magical] are of an entirely different order, using different sources in a different way, and making their appeal to different sides of the human mind".[23] Marcello Ficino, who translated Plato, and Giovanni Pico della Mirandola were not only erudite classicists, they were also magicians, as was Giordano Bruno, who was burned for it at the stake in the year 1600. On the contrary, Desiderius Erasmus, Thomas More and John Colet, among many others, were literary humanists. Pico made the difference clear when he wrote to a friend: "We have lived illustrious and to posterity shall live, not in the school of the grammarians and teaching places of young minds, but in the company of the philosophers, conclaves of the sages, where the questions of debate are not concerning the mother of Andromache or the sons of Niobe and such light trifles, but of things human and divine".[24] However, magic and occultism, although wellsprings of modern thinking and science, would remain an undercurrent in European culture and never reach the maturity they once obtained in Egypt and India. The intellectuals, 'the grammarians', would win the day and develop the 'natural philosophy' we call science.

There was also a third component in the Renaissance movement, the 'emotional'. In Thucydides, Demosthenes and Pericles, as in Caesar, Cicero and Tacitus, the Renaissance men rediscovered the pride and glory of belonging, of patriotism, of 'the general weal', of the heartening inspiration of tradition and the past of the body of which every citizen was a part, which was a greater ego to him and for which he was required to give his life in times of peril. The medieval society had been a caste-hierarchy in which a person had his fixed place and only a handful at the top did the thinking and

---

[23] Frances Yates: *Giordano Bruno and the Hermetic Tradition*, p. 159.
[24] Id., p. 162.

made the decisions. Now the Renaissance and Reformation, examining the ways of antiquity, rediscovered the value of the individual and his faculty of thinking for himself. It would not take long before a monk at Wittenberg claimed the right for himself and for all individuals to think freely, even if he had to stand up against the highest authority. And together with the need of self-examination arose the need of a definition of the general body to which the self belonged: patriotism became part of the consciousness.

The complete edition of Tacitus' *Germania* was published in 1510. "A codex containing Tacitus' *Germania* had survived the Middle Ages in a monastery at Herzfeld and had been taken to Italy in the fifteenth century. The effect of the discovery of this manuscript on the image the Germans would form of themselves can hardly be overestimated, for the way in which the humanists interpreted Tacitus remained a steady reference even in the twentieth century." [25] *Germania* was written in 98 CE. In this book Tacitus (c.56-c.120) composed a few sentences which would remain the pride of the Germans forever, the source of their patriotic imaginings, and the cause of much detriment. "The Germans themselves, I am inclined to think", wrote Tacitus, "are natives of the soil and extremely little affected by immigration or friendly intercourse with other peoples ... For myself I accept the view that the peoples of Germany have never been tainted by intermarriage with other peoples, and stand out as a nation peculiar, pure and unique in its kind. Hence the physical type, if one may generalize at all about so vast a population, is everywhere the same – wild, blue eyes, reddish hair and huge frames that excel only in violent effort".[26] This text would become the principal document to justify the German claim to racial purity and superiority. Neither the obvious distance in time and space from which Tacitus wrote nor the conjectural phrasing of the sentences

---

[25] Julia Zernack in: *Völkische Religion und Krisen der Moderne* (Stefanie Schnurbein and Julius Ulbricht ed.), p. 228.
[26] In Jonathan Glover: *Humanity – A Moral History of the Twentieth Century*, p. 319.

would deter even some of the best German brains from accepting Tacitus' statement as the word of God. "Each one of the German humanists developed the theme of German greatness in his own way, and they were vying among themselves as to the variety and originality of their arguments."[27]

As we saw, Tacitus wrote that the Germans had *caeruli oculi, rutilae comae,* blue eyes, reddish hair, and that they had 'huge frames'. These characteristics, together with a dolichocephalic skull, would become, especially from the last decennia of the nineteenth century onwards, the famous standard image of the racially pure German, 'the Blond Bestie' and the ideal SS-man. How misleading Tacitus assertion in this matter was, as in others which were not of his own experience, was discovered not so long ago. *Caeruli oculi, rutilae comae,* scholars found out, was a 'topos' used by classical authors to impress their readers with the curiousness of the barbarian people they were writing about; in other words, it was a historiographers' cliché. The Greek historian Herodotus applied the same cliché to the Scythes, and Pliny the Roman used identical words to depict the Singhalese in Ceylon! In this way myths are born, perilous myths when they are held to be the truth by armed fanatics.

One of the great German Renaissance men was the adventurous knight Ulrich von Hutten (1488-1523), patriot, satirist and supporter of Luther's cause. He made the historical figure of Arminius, the Cheruscian, into 'a real cult figure' of German nationalism and Nazism as the German who had stood up to the Romans and dealt them, in the year 9 CE, a deadly blow in the Teutoburg Forest. Arminius, Germanized into 'Hermann', "came from a [tribal] princely family and was educated at the Emperor's court in Rome". He was a typical example of the assimilation of their conquered peoples by the Romans. Arminius even became a tribune of the Roman army, a rank equivalent to lieutenant-general, and fought, like many others, against the people from whom he originated, commanding German

---

[27]Id., p. 123.

auxiliaries. He was therefore awarded, as the first German, Roman citizenship and knighted. The reason why he turned against Rome is unclear. He became the head of a conspiracy, led three of Rome's crack legions under Varus into a trap and annihilated them. This was the heaviest defeat the Roman legions ever suffered and the reason that their conquest halted at the Rhine.[28]

The embellished story of Arminius, who was later murdered by his own people, became one of the main features in the German nationalist myth, built up from the Renaissance onwards. It became an argument in the establishment in the North-South divide which would give the Germans the feeling that they were different from the rest of the world, that they, the people in the middle, were surrounded and threatened, and that they had to stand up to the other nations. The humanists were the first to create "the Germany-Rome antithesis" (von See), which reached a climax in Luther. The Germans now felt themselves different from the Roman-Latin-Welsch peoples; Protestants would fight Catholics, *Kultur* would confront *Zivilisation*. Eventually the Germans would declare themselves the embodiment of the Spirit, some of them even affirming that they were the sole people with a soul. The Roman-Latin-Welsh, together with the coloured and all other kinds of peoples, were on the contrary 'materialists', not much more than material beings in an animal-like state, *Untermenschen*, i.e. subhumans, or lower humans, or half-humans, and even non-humans although human in appearance (such as the Jews).

The German stage was set for Martin Luther (1483-1546). "It fell to Luther to amplify considerably the rise of a nationalism which fused with the Reformation and gave to Lutheranism its specifically German hue."[29] Luther had travelled to Rome and seen there with his own eyes the abominations around the Chair of the 'Antichrist'. He had also felt deeply offended by the superior and disdainful

---

[28] See Herbert Rosendorfer: *Deutsche Geschichte – Ein Versuch*, pp. 30 ff.
[29] Léon Poliakov: *Le mythe aryen*, p. 125.

attitude of the Southerners towards the backward Germans: "No nation is more despised than the German nation! Italy calls us animals, France and England mock at us; all the others do likewise." "A certain German paranoia" (Poliakov) was building up and would be finally compensated by the conviction of being a special, superior kind of humans. In psychological language: an inferiority complex was compensated and turned into a complex of superiority.

Luther also made the German mother tongue into an honoured, well-sounding and malleable means of expression. "I thank God for being able to hear and find my God in the German language, for neither you nor me would ever have been able to find him in Latin, Greek or Hebrew." "German was promoted to the fourth holy language, more admirable than any other and comparable only to the Hebrew spoken before the confusion of Babel, the language of Adam."[30] Luther was not the only German in those days to think that Adam and Eve conversed in their language.

"What we see converging from German humanism is a clearly defined German romanticism", writes Paul Joachimsen, who points to the analogy with the Romantic Movement around 1810. The concept of a German nation took shape. "This concept, while extending back to the German beginnings in time, led to the elaboration of a certain ideal of the German character."[31] What in the eyes of others was German backwardness or inferiority, not to say barbarism, was taken up by the Germans and transformed, by means of a romantic interpretation of the past, into a source of pride and self-assertion. Just as Hermann the Cheruscian had defied the Roman colossus, just so was the German Volk, with its unadulterated strength, ready again to take on the racially weakened, feminine, over-civilised Roman-Latin-Welsh peoples, and on any others who dared to challenge it.

---

[30] Id., p. 127.
[31] Id., p. 128.

Romanticism (1770-1840)

The three trends we distinguished in the Renaissance continued to dominate the cultural and intellectual life in Europe – and do so even today, quite simply because they are elementary aspects of the human make-up. This consists of an emotional, a mental and a spiritual part, in whatever way they are mixed and expressed. To these three elements should be added the material domain of the human personality, which is its basis on this Earth, and which in most cases remains its principal interest. Intellect and emotion went on affirming themselves in the centuries following the Renaissance, more often in discordance than in harmony. (In Europe the magical, occult, semi-spiritual side of existence would remain in the background, although it was always present behind the other two elements of the triad.) Bearing this in mind, it is no simplification to state that the Romantic Movement throughout Europe was a reaction against the preponderant role Reason played in 'the Age of Reason', as the century of the Enlightenment was called (in German *Aufklärung*, in French *les Lumières*).

German Romanticism presented the world with some of the greatest novelists, poets, philosophers and musicians: the literary men Herder, Goethe, Schiller, Novalis, Heine, Hölderlin; the philosophers Fichte, Schlegel, Hegel, all of them having to define themselves against Kant, paragon of the Aufklärung; and musicians of the stature of Mozart, Beethoven, Schubert and Schumann, who even today delight so many hearts with an art incomparably refined, profound and sublime.

The Age of Reason, especially in its French representatives, the *philosophes* Rousseau, Voltaire, Diderot, d'Alembert, d'Holbach, de la Mettrie, and others, dominated the European scene, making French the common language of the nobility, the intellectuals and the international relations between countries. It was the time that Voltaire stayed at the court of the Prussian King Frederick II, and Diderot held long conversations with Catherine II of Russia, emphasising his words with forceful taps on her thigh. But Reason was a newcomer on this scene, in the sense that previously, in the Middle Ages, it had been no more than 'the handmaid of faith', whereas now it showed pretences to the throne of absolute ruler. True, Reason, after its long sleep since the heydays of classical Greece and Rome, had to regain its freedom to make the human personality, stunted without it, complete. But such fundamental changes or reorientations in the human condition do not come about easily; like all important changes in history they provoke resistance and often passionate enmity. The existential and ideological growth of humanity was mostly fought out on the battlefield (and so was its spiritual growth).

The role of the emotions or life-forces in humanity can be followed, in their dialectical battle with reason, from the Middle Ages through the Renaissance into the Romantic period. The importance of all this for our story is that this development leads directly to the volkisch movement, Fascism in general and Nazism in particular. Passions clashed with the effort to render humanity reasonable; nature was extolled against the modern city, farming and the corporate system against industrialisation, the traditional past against change and progress. The Volk, embodiment of a living soul, was put against the individual and individualisation – and if the individual genius was so highly considered by the Romantics, it was because he or she was the channel through which the soul of the Volk could communicate with God, or with the World Soul, or with the universal Spirit. The greatest genius was to be the Leader of the Volk, the Great One sent to do great deeds. Such were some of the themes which later also dominated the mind of the many thousands involved in volkisch, nationalist and pan-German organisations.

The great hero of the romantic period was Napoléon Bonaparte, much admired and not less hated, riding through Europe at the head of his armies and implementing the ideals of the French Revolution, which were the ideals of the Enlightenment. "Napoleon burst upon the Germans like a hurricane. He dissolved the Holy Roman Empire, replacing hundreds of separate sovereignties with thirty-eight;

outraging clergy, he abolished ecclesiastical states, church courts, tithes (titles?), monasteries and convents, and seized church property. Nobles fumed as he abolished their feudal states, feudal dues and tax exemptions, broke up large estates, and cut their power over their peasants. Decreeing equality before the law, Napoleon opened public office to the middle class, guaranteed private property, established modern economic laws and institutions, and built public works, roads, canals, and bridges. He created secular public schools to spread the ideals of the revolution. Most shocking of all, he not only destroyed the ghettos, he gave Jews freedom of worship and the right to own land and practice trades."[32]

All this happened at the time of dominance of the French culture and its vehicle, the French language. The political and cultural reaction against this 'Welsh' imperialism grew vehement and became an important step in the evolution of the German self-consciousness. "The German wave of liberation against the French conqueror and ruler by force, Napoleon I, definitively awakened the national awareness in the German people. It awakened such a plenitude of national enthusiasm, force and longing ... that whole future generations would be nurtured by its inheritance."[33]

It is rather puzzling that some of the foremost mouthpieces of this heightened German national awareness were the philosophers, discoursing from their influential positions at the universities. Puzzling this is because as a whole they formed the school of 'German Idealism', which attained some of the most elevated and abstract thinking in the history of philosophy, and is therefore often compared with the Socrates-Plato-Aristotle period in classical Athens. Nonetheless, figures of the format of Fichte, Schlegel and Hegel were so much embedded in the German awakening that, in one way or another, they managed to regard their idea of Germany as the culmination of world history and world culture. "With the significant

---

[32] John Weiss, op. cit., p. 64.
[33] Dietrich Bronder: *Bevor Hitler kam*, p. 102.

exception of Slavs and Jews, Fichte [1762-1814] believed all Europeans to be related by blood. But the Germans were the only people who retained their ancient spirit undistorted by foreign influences. While the French adopted a Latin language, Germans kept their original tongue, retaining the spiritual qualities as 'the original race'. Still close to the ways of their tribal warrior-ancestors, they were free of Latin, French and Jewish individualism, obsession with property, and the crass pursuit of material well-being. We alone, Fichte said, still feel as did the ancient Germanic tribes: duties and rights are derived from subordination to the common will. Only Germans are fit for the new era of social cooperation and collective moral idealism."[34] This anti-individualistic thinking will lead directly to the bonding of the volkisch youth organizations and the Nazi slogan *Du bist nichts, dein Volk ist alles:* you are nothing, your people is everything.

But Fichte went still further when in his *Addresses to the German Nation* (1807-08) he proclaimed: "It is you Germans who, of all peoples, possess most clearly the germ of human perfectibility, and to whom belongs the leadership in the development of mankind ... There is no alternative: if you sink, then mankind sinks with you, without any hope of resurrection."[35] "Fichte and other Romantics radicalized the Christian apocalyptic", writes Michael Ley, "the salvation of humanity is no longer the task of God but of Man, in whom God incarnates himself. The new bringers of salvation and redeemers of the world are the Germans ... The Germans will build a worldwide empire of the spirit ... The Jews incorporate the Antichrist, who must be subjugated ... To protect oneself from the Jews Fichte proposes either to cut their heads off or to send them into the Promised Land."[36]

---

[34]John Weiss, op. cit., p. 72.
[35]Id., p. 73.
[36]Michael Ley in *Der Nationalsozialismus als politische Religion*, Michael Ley and Julius Schoeps ed., p. 19.

According to Friedrich Hegel (1770-1831) the sense of history consists in the working out of the Idea of the Spirit, unfolding itself in phases. For there is a World Spirit which incarnates itself in world history, thereby aiming at a cosmic salvation. The dominant people in the ongoing phase of world history were, taught Hegel, the Germans. "The other peoples have no rights against the absolute right of the Germans to be the carriers of the present phase of the development of the World Spirit", and the other peoples "do not count any longer in world history". To the Germans fell the mission once entrusted by God to the Jews. On the shoulders of the Germans rested therefore the salvation of the world. And (once again) the freedom of the individual lay in the voluntary submission to the State, which was to be revered as something divine in an earthly form. Such a kind of thinking, comments Ley, "means factually the incorporation of the individuals in the state and encourages any kind of totalitarianism."[37]

These are a few examples of a school of thought which has deeply influenced German thinking by positing the superiority of the German people and its mission for the salvation of humankind, the insignificance of the individual and the all-importance of the State. These ideas can be found, sometimes verbatim, in the volkisch publications, in those of the Pan-Germans and in the literature of the Nazis. In fact, several anthologies of sayings by the romantic and idealist thinkers were published in the later part of the nineteenth and the first half of the twentieth century. Some such anthologies, for instance Treitschke's *Handbuch des Judentums*, sold in enormous numbers and were reprinted till the end of the Third Reich.

What the nationalist literature did not promulgate were the visionary predictions of a Romantic like Heinrich Heine (1797-1856), who was a Jew. "Christianity – and this is its nicest merit – has somewhat softened the crude German fighting spirit but could not eradicate it, and when the taming Talisman, the Cross, falls to

---

[37] Id., p. 153.

pieces, then the savagery of the old fighters will erupt again, the senseless rage of the berserker, of which the Nordic poets sang and spoke so much. That talisman is now corroded and the day will come when it will collapse. Then old stony gods will arise and rub the dust of millennia from their eyes, and Thor with his gigantic hammer will jump up at last and smash the gothic cathedrals ...

"And when the time comes when you hear the cracking of a thunder as it has never cracked before in the history of the world, know: the German thunder has finally struck its aim. At this terrible noise the eagles will drop from the sky and the lions in the farthest deserts of Africa will draw their tails between their legs and crawl into their royal dens. A play will be enacted in Germany compared to which the French revolution was but an innocent idyll. And that time shall come."[38]

List and Lanz

We have met Guido von List and Jörg Lanz von Liebenfels in the first chapters of our story. We recall that these Austrian mythic visionaries were widely read and exerted a direct influence on the Germanenorden, of which the Thule Society was a chapter. Both saw the Germanic race as a people of god-men who temporarily had forgotten their divine origin, but who would, in the near future, regain their status of world-dominators, using the other races as their slaves. "For his descriptions of the millennium [List] tended to make use of mythological materials drawn from medieval German apocalyptic, Norse legends, and modern theosophy in order to convey its fantastic nature. He related the medieval tale of Emperor Frederick Barbarossa who lay sleeping inside the Kyffhäuser mountain. Once he awakened, Barbarossa would unleash a wave of Teutonic fury across the world prior to the establishment of German hegemony. This tale owed its inspiration to a complex of medieval millenarian

---
[38]Ibid.

hopes which had originally crystallized around the Hohenstauffen emperors."[39] (Hitler will call the invasion of Russia 'Operation Barbarossa'.)

List also gave voice to a strong, profound expectation in the German people of the coming of a Saviour, a *Herzog* who would raise the people from their age-old misery and conduct them at last into their glorious future. This need of an all-powerful master was an important feature in the psychological make-up of the Germans long before the strong man became the paragon of Fascism in many European nations. The *Führer* (i.e. leader) was longed and prayed for; he was expected before he took shape in Adolf Hitler. It was not the least of Hitler's intuitions that he knew exactly how to take on the part and act in a way to which the German masses subconsciously responded with religious fervour. "The cry for a leader", writes Günter Scholdt, "arose from the searing wish for somebody who would provide meaning in a secularized time, which apparently burdened the individual with an excess of individual responsibility and made him feel lonely".[40] And he quotes Bruno Brehm: "This is a dream dreamt by all peoples: when princes and lords, learned men and priests no longer know how to go on because the laws no longer obtain, the faith is troubled and the people confused; then appears, called by no one and longed for by all, from the despairing crowd a simple man to save them. The people see this man, feel that he has come at the very last moment, recognize themselves in him and suddenly know what they want".[41]

"As early as 1891, List had discovered a verse of the *Voluspa* which invoked an awesome and benevolent messianic figure:

A wealthy man joins the circle of counsellors,
A Strong One from Above ends the factions,

---

[39] Nicholas Goodrick-Clarke: *The Occult Roots of Nazism*, p. 87.
[40] Günter Scholdt: *Autoren über Hitler*, p. 45.
[41] Id., p. 33.

He settles everything with fair decisions,
Whatever he ordains shall endure for ever.

This 'Strong One from Above' became a stock phrase in all of List's subsequent references to the millennium. An ostensibly superhuman individual would end all human factions and confusion with the establishment of an eternal order. This divine dictator possessed particular appeal for those who lamented the uncertain nature of the industrial society. List eagerly anticipated the advent of this leader, whose monolithic world of certainties would fulfil the socio-political conditions of his national millennium."[42]

"'The Unconquerable' was that heroic prince supposedly already prophesied by the ancient Germanic Edda. List considered it his life's task to prepare this 'Strong One from Above' and the Germanic world domination", writes Brigitte Hamann. "The longed for Germanic people's leader, 'the Strong One from Above', would, according to List, rule as a god-man and be subject to no law. This heroic prince would be recognizable by the fact that he would be victorious in every battle. 'The Strong One from Above' would always be right. For List saw him attuned to the forces of Nature ... He could make no mistakes. To him the 'final victory' was assured." And Hamann reproduces a facsimile from one of List's books in which he says: "I offer with this work the highest and holiest that has been offered for long centuries: the proclamation of the Ario-Germanic dawn of the morning of the gods – the Strong One from Above is coming again!"[43]

Lanz von Liebenfels, List's disciple and friend, was not less outspoken. "Germany could no longer allow 'the apish louts [the subhuman, animal-like Chandalas] to fleece the world', since the entire planet was her natural colony with a farm for every bold soldier and, in accordance with the hierarchical principle of racial purity, a country estate for every officer.

---

[42]Nicholas Goodrick-Clarke, op. cit., p. 88.
[43]Brigitte Hamann: *Hitlers Wien*, pp. 304 ff.

"An apocalyptic battle would be released upon the corrupt and resistant world, in order to attain this racist millennium. Lanz's words echoed List's own prophecy of the First World War: 'Amid the jubilation of the liberated god-men we would conquer the whole planet ... the fire should be raked until sparks fly from the barrels of German battleships and flashes start from German cannon ... and order is created among the quarrelsome Udumu-band [of subhumans]'. This envisaged order was a pan-German racist and hierarchical paradise, which included gnostic hierophants, a new caste of warriors and a world revolution to establish eternal German hegemony.

"This apocalypse fused several German intellectual traditions into a millenarian vision of the new fatherland. The bards and sages of early Romanticism marched with the princes and soldiers of pre-industrial conservatism into a religious paradise, defined by such [Lanzian] neo-gnostic symbols as the Holy Grail, the electron and the Church of the Holy Spirit. Its attainment was conditional upon the total subjugation of the inferiors."[44]

A place in the sun

Germany as a coherent nation was born in 1871, strangely enough in the Hall of Mirrors of Louis XIV's palace at Versailles. Its formation was the result of the political talent and unrelenting efforts of one man, Otto von Bismarck, who became its first chancellor. The emperor of the new nation was the Hohenzollern William I, king of Prussia, who thus became the *primus inter pares* of no less than eighteen German princes, including four kings, all continuing to wield the sceptre in their hereditary principalities. Prussia became not only the heartland of the new nation, to which it would impart its autocratic and militaristic peculiarities, it also accounted for something like two thirds of the total territory, comprising most of the Rhineland.

---

[44]Nicholas Goodrick-Clarke, op. cit., p. 98.

A profound change took place in the new Germany, clearly discernible in the last decade of the nineteenth century: the transition from an agrarian country into an industrial state. Sebastian Haffner writes: "Germany had already to a great extent become an individual state under Bismarck [who was Chancellor until 1894], but it was in the Wilhelmian period [ie under William II] that the industry developed as it did in no other land except far away America".[45] The statistics provided for instance in Fritz Fischer's *Krieg der Illusionen* are impressive. Germany in those years beat its neighbours in practically every field. It became the leading nation in the chemical, electrical and optical industries, backed up by the powerful banks. It planned and began building the Berlin-Baghdad Railway, aimed directly at the ever more important oil fields in the Middle East and at the heart of the British colonial empire, while securing a strong foothold in Turkey, on the southern threshold of Russia. It intended to challenge Great Britain also on the seas.

In step with "the enormous German economic upswing" (Fischer) grew its hardly less considerable self-esteem, which might also be called Prussian arrogance or conceit. Haffner says that "an excessive feeling of power" developed at that time. "The nation's mood of conscious power could absorb unlimited bombast", writes Barbara Tuchman sarcastically. "Germans knew themselves to be the strongest military power on earth, the most efficient merchants, the busiest bankers, penetrating every continent, financing the Turks, flinging out a railroad from Berlin to Baghdad, gaining the trade of Latin America, challenging the sea power of Great Britain, and in the realm of the intellect systematically organizing, under the concept of *Wissenschaft*, every branch of human knowledge. They were deserving and capable of mastery of the world. Rule by the best must be fulfilled. By this time Nietzsche, as Brandes wrote in 1909, held 'undisputed sway' over the minds of his countrymen. What they lacked and hungered for was the world's acknowledgment of their

---

[45]Sebastian Haffner: *Von Bismarck zu Hitler*, p. 90.

mastery. So long as it was denied, frustration grew and with it the desire to compel acknowledgment by the sword."[46]

The slogan of those years was that Germany, latecomer among the dominant European nations, wanted its own "place in the sun" – but then a rather ample one. Its industry consumed vast amounts of iron ore and coal, of which it had only limited reserves; therefore its industrialists and military planners cast a greedy eye on the iron ore mines and coal fields in Belgium and northern France. The myth of the lack of 'living space', launched at that time of a rapid population increase (and actually contradicted by the success of its industry and economy), initiated the first ideas of a conquest of spaces in Russia, sparsely populated by backward, inferior people. Germany should become at the very least the dominant nation in Central Europe, not only economically but also politically and culturally. "Since Bismarck's departure a kind of big power awareness had manifested itself. Many Germans of the Wilhelmian time, including members from all social classes, saw suddenly a great national vision, a national goal: we become a world power, we spread over the whole world – Germany on top of the world!" All this led to an unbridled pride, reflects Haffner, but unfortunately also to "a bombastic, excessively self-conscious, self-loving attitude".[47]

The members of 'all social classes', as Haffner would have it, belonged mainly to the middle class on the traditional, conservative right. They were the nurturing ground of the fanatically Rightist university students at the feet of nationalist and anti-Semitic professors like Treitschke; and they constituted the reading public of authors like Lagarde, Langbehn, Bernhardi and Spengler who edged Germany on along its predestined glorious path of world hegemony. One finds the diverse trends represented by those authors merged in the writings of a curious figure, Houston Chamberlain (1855-1927), especially in his hugely successful book *The Foundations of the Nineteenth Century*, published in 1899. Chamberlain was the

---

[46] Barbara Tuchman: *The Proud Tower*, p. 331.
[47] Sebastian Haffner, op. cit., pp. 88-89.

son of an English admiral and cousin of the statesman Neville Chamberlain; he was educated in France, became a qualified biologist, and chose Germany as his second fatherland. He wrote (sometimes in trance) in German, and married Eva, the daughter of Richard Wagner, thereby becoming the master of *Haus Wahnfried* in Bayreuth, where the composer had spent the last years of his life and were he lay buried. Georges Mosse calls Chamberlain "the most influential of racial theorists", and Joseph Goebbels praised him as "the father of our thought".

"If from now on [the Germans abroad] remain closely bound to Germany, consciously, openly and proudly German", wrote Chamberlain, "then the world conquest will mature with astonishing rapidity. To mention but one example: why should Germany have to conquer Australia? How would this conquest be begun? How would it be executed? But once even ten per cent of the inhabitants of that continent are conscious Germans, they will constitute nine tenths of the intelligence and education, and consequently provide the guiding mind". Konrad Heiden, who quotes these words, comments: "Chamberlain writes 'Australia', because the vigilant military censorship forbade the intended 'South America' or plain 'America'. Inspired by the mania of perfection, he foresaw a perfect Germany that would create a perfect world".

And Heiden quotes Chamberlain again: "Once Germany has achieved the power – and we may confidently expect her to achieve it – she must immediately begin to carry out a scientific policy of genius. Augustus undertook a systematic transformation of the world, and Germany must do the same ... Equipped with offensive and defensive weapons, organized as firmly and flawlessly as the Army, superior to all in art, science, technology, industry, commerce, finance, in every field, in short, teacher, helmsman and pioneer of the world, every man at his post, every man giving his utmost for the holy cause – thus Germany, emanating efficiency, will conquer the world by inner superiority".[48] Race was for Chamberlain "the

---

[48]Konrad Heiden: *The Fuehrer*, p. 194.

dominant principle of history. He saw the German race as the only one capable of creating culture and rising up, since the third century, from the 'chaos of peoples' caused by the Roman Empire and the Catholic Church. To this race belonged the future if it could free itself from the anti-Germanic elements, in the first place from the Jews. Of all Germanic peoples it was specifically the Germans who were called to rule the world. If they did not succeed in this, they were condemned to perish".[49]

Emperor William II was one of Chamberlain's readers, considered him his intellectual advisor and even mentor, decorated him with the Iron Cross, a war medal, and decreed that a copy of *Foundations* should be present in every Prussian library. As late as 1922 the emperor would write in his memoirs: "Germanhood in its glory was first explained and preached to the enthused German people by Chamberlain".[50]

Another admirer paying homage to Houston Chamberlain was Adolf Hitler when in 1923, a few weeks before his Beer Hall Putsch, he visited *Haus Wahnfried* for the first time. "It is clear that Hitler had carefully planned his visit to *Wahnfried*", writes Brigitte Hamann, "which happened at a moment when he was already considered someone special, even the generally hoped for future 'saviour of Germany' ... That he went there at that very moment, shortly before the Putsch and the expected breakthrough to power, took on the air of a sort of consecration. As religious believers go on a pilgrimage before making an important decision, so Hitler went to obtain the blessings of Chamberlain and of the deceased master, Richard Wagner".[51]

By then Chamberlain was a bedridden man who could only hold Hitler's hand and mumble some hardly understandable words. But afterwards he still managed to write a letter to Hitler in which he

---

[49]Fritz Fischer: *Krieg der Illusionen*, p. 66.
[50]Klaus von See: *Barbar, Germane, Arier*, p. 292.
[51]Brigitte Hamann: *Winifred Wagner, oder Hitlers Bayreuth*, p. 84.

thanked God for having been able to meet, at the end of his life, the redeemer of Germany. "That in the hour of her deepest need Germany gives birth to a Hitler proves her vitality ... May God protect you!"[52] Siegfried Wagner was equally impressed by Hitler's first visit: "Hitler is a wonderful man, the real soul of the German people. He must succeed."[53]

"Hitler appears as the specifically radical representative of a concept of German world hegemony that can be traced back to the late Bismarck period. As early as the turn of the century, it had condensed into specific war aims, and after the failed attempt of 1914-18 a fresh attempt was made to carry it out, with new and greater resolution, in the Second World War. An imperialistic drive nearly a century old culminated in Hitler." (Joachim Fest[54])

The First World War

"The tension of the present time must result in a discharge", wrote Helmuth von Moltke, chief of the German general staff, a few weeks before the First World War began. When the explosion finally occurred, in August 1914, it was greeted in all concerned countries with jubilation, caused by an instantaneous inflation of the national egos. The Archbishop of Cambrai proclaimed in a pastoral letter: "The French soldiers feel more or less strongly and clearly that they are soldiers of Christ and Mary, defenders of the Faith, and that dying in the French way means dying in the Christian way. It is Christ who loves the French".[55] And the English poet Rupert Brooke wrote on the occasion: "Now, God be thanked who has matched us with His hour ..."

Nowhere was the enthusiasm greater than in Germany, convinced that, by way of a lightning-quick war, God was clearing its long-

---

[52] Quoted in William Shirer: *The Rise and Fall of the Third Reich*, p. 109.
[53] Brigitte Hamann, op. cit., p. 85.
[54] Joachim Fest, op. cit., p. 616.
[55] Fritz Fischer: *Hitler war kein Betriebsunfall*, p. 186.

deserved and promised place among the peoples. Fritz Fischer quotes Max Lenz, his predecessor on the chair of history at Hamburg University, who wrote in the first days of the war: "Our youth, jubilant as if they went to a feast, submit themselves to the trial by ordeal of the battles. In our people the spirit of Siegfried has arisen in which the principal characteristics of all true religiosity are present: humility, loyalty, obedience, a sense of duty to the extreme, and the strength of our faith in the victory of a just cause … We will be victorious because we have to be victorious, for God cannot abandon his people".[56]

The military men were not the only promoters of the war; they were strongly supported, not to say pushed, by the great industrialists and by the Pan-Germans – in fact by the whole block of nationalist reactionaries. They were also supported by the Protestant Church, which since the times of its founder, Martin Luther, had always been a nationalist Church. This Church, addressing the faithful every Sunday from the pulpit, was a very influential voice in the concert of opinions, which was already essentially nationalistic and inimical to the rest of an inferior but threatening world.

"In those days hundreds of war sermons were published as testimonies to the German spirit and faith", writes Fischer. "There one reads time and again that persevering will be possible only if 'the spirit of 1914' remains alive. Together with these ideas there was the conviction that the Germans were the chosen people. In sermons without number the Germans were presented as God's people because God had entrusted them with the task of lifting up the world, by means of this war, to a higher cultural level. The reasoning follows that God has proposed to them to become victorious and powerful also on the material level; they have to accept this proposal because God's intention is the well-being of the German people".[57] And Fischer quotes the words spoken at a ceremony in honour of William II: "If anywhere

---

[56]Id., pp. 187-88.
[57]Id., p. 191.

in history, then it is in our history that the divine providence is palpably present. God has come to meet us, it is God's will that acts in world history. Being one with our history means being one with God". Which goes to show that Hegel's way of seeing things was very much alive. "The German people are frequently mentioned as the instrument of God", writes Fischer. "One often reads: we believe in the task our people have to accomplish for the world".[58]

As shown in the previous pages, the acme the German national ego reached in August 1914 was prepared throughout the preceding century, not as a vague sentiment but in clearly articulated thought and formulation. A time bomb had started ticking in the young, ambitious German nation. There were threats that it would explode on several occasions in the first years of the twentieth century, for instance at the time of the Morocco crises and the wars in the Balkan. When in the end a handful of prominent Germans in sensitive political and military positions decided, somehow to their own perplexity, to do the decisive deed, the nation exulted.

Sharing in the exultation on the *Odeonsplatz* in Munich was a twenty-five year old painter of watercolours who had been rejected as unfit by the Austrian army, but who now volunteered to sacrifice his life for Germany in a Bavarian regiment. In Adolf Hitler's later speeches and writings one can trace all the thoughts touched upon above, but fitted into his own peculiar frame of mind. The more one studies the two World Wars, the more one is intrigued by the parallels between the first and the second: the drive for world hegemony in Germany, the intended conquests in Belgium and France, the unfulfilled hope of an agreement with Great Britain, the plans for a colonisation of Russia, the two-front-war feared and nevertheless engaged into, the pretence of being the leading, superior people in the world ... The First World War and the Second World War were actually two episodes of one and the same war.

---

[58] Id., p. 192.

8

LONG SKULLS AND BROAD SKULLS

> *We will never be brutal or heartless when it isn't necessary. We Germans, the only people in the world with a decent attitude towards animals, will also have a decent attitude towards these human animals.*
>
> HEINRICH HIMMLER

The white man's pride

We have met the noble Aryan – the 'Prometheus of mankind', 'standard-bearer of human progress' and 'highest image of the Lord' – when leafing through Hitler's *Mein Kampf*. We recall that the discovery of an Aryan root language was made around 1800, in that fecund period of literary Romanticism and philosophical Idealism, and that this discovery went hand in hand with a keen interest in Indian culture and religion. The hypothesis of a language common to great parts of Europe and Asia was erroneously extended to the existence of an Aryan people which spoke that language and of which the best among the surviving human tribes descended.

All these complex intellectual exercises took place against the background of expanding colonialism, when a few West European nations were venturing all over the globe, encountered little resistance from peoples who looked so different, felt themselves to be their rightful conquerors and appropriated their possessions. This they did in the name of their racial superiority, their culture and their one true God. What is now called racism was for those West-Europeans at that time a normal component in their way of perceiving the world, based on the supposedly incontestable fact that some people (with white skins) were stronger, more intelligent and inventive, and more religious than other people (mostly with coloured skins). "What today we find abominably racist in the writings of Gobineau, Darwin, Haeckel, Büchner, Vogt, Gumplowicz, etc. ... was then the prevalent opinion, common to the point that hardly anybody thought of criticizing it, either on the left or on the right", writes André Pichot[1] Dietrich Bronder is therefore right in reminding us that racism as such "did not actually originate in Germany, that it started in France and England", but that the dimensions racism took in Germany resulted eventually "in such terrible political consequences".[2]

Some sayings from that time will illustrate Bronder's point. The Scottish philosopher David Hume 'inclined to presume', in 1754, that generally speaking "all other races of human beings were naturally inferior to the white race". The other races had never developed a civilised nation or prominent individuals in any field. Even among the most barbarous white people, like the ancient Germans, something outstanding could be found. Such a constant and uniform difference between whites and non-whites "could not have existed if nature had not made an original distinction between the human races". The German professor Christoph Meiners wrote that only the white peoples, especially the Celts, "possessed true courage, the love of freedom, and the other passions and virtues of great souls". The 'black and ugly people' were characterised by a deplorable absence of virtues and the presence of some horrible vices.

---

[1] André Pichot: *La société pure – de Darwin à Hitler*, p. 386.
[2] Dietrich Bronder, op. cit., p. 291.

"What would the world be without the Europeans?" asked Johan-Christian Fabricius, a disciple of the Swedish botanist Linnaeus (1707-78). The European, called by Destiny to the hegemony over a world which he alone can enlighten with his intelligence and subjugate by his valour, is the human being par excellence and the head of the human race; the others, a vile mixture of barbarians, are by way of speaking no more than its embryo. Charles White, a surgeon in Manchester, was of much the same opinion, for he wrote in 1799: "Climbing up the ladder, we arrive at last at the white European who, being the furthest removed from the animal creation, can therefore be considered the most beautiful product of the human race". Nobody would dare to cast doubt upon the superiority of his intellectual powers. Where else but in the European could one find such a well-shaped head, such a large brain, where such a straight stature and noble gait? "In which other region of the globe shall one find that exquisite blush spreading on the countenance of the beautiful European women, cynosures of modesty and delicate feelings?"[3]

Europe dominated the world, saw the world through its own eyes and felt as dominators do. By its own history it measured the history of all others; its scientific and cultural acquisitions – and they were many – were to be infused gradually and cautiously into other peoples; its economic exploitation was the legitimate reward of its efforts; its God was the true God, and the idols of the heathen had to be broken. It would take a long time before this 'Eurocentrism' would be put into question, before the rest of the world would awake from its temporal sleep, reassert its values and powers, and retake possession of its rightful material and cultural property. This process is still ongoing.

The Aryan myth was one of the consequences of the Eurocentric manner of perceiving the world. To have been the cradle of the Aryans was soon denied the brown-skinned, idolatrous Indians and the uncultured Iranians; the birthplace of the Aryans shifted

---

[3] In Léon Poliakov: *Le mythe aryen*, pp. 195, 220, 223, 225.

successively to South, Central and finally North Europe, where the northern part of Germany and the south of Sweden became 'the womb of the peoples'. Of course, nobody knew what actually had happened there as recently as two or three hundred years before Christ. This left the gates wide open for all kinds of speculations about Hyperborean, Thulean and Atlantidian origins.

The Nazi mythology was an extreme outcome of the European myths as construed by the feelings of superiority of the white people. Some haughty feelings in those myths were tempered by the Christian faith and morals, and by the ideals of the Enlightenment. Romantic and volkisch Germany, however, sought to renew its vitality through contact with its pre-Christian origins, through re-rooting itself in the powers of its old gods. It would take the fancies about being *Herrenmenschen* literally, and when it thought it had, under Hitler, built up the necessary military capability, try to turn them into reality.

Social Darwinism

Racism found itself justified by Darwin's theory of evolution published in 1859 under the title *The Origin of Species by Means of Natural Selection*. The racism deduced from Darwin's revolutionary view of nature was that all life is a continuous struggle for existence in which the fittest (strongest, cleverest) win the upper hand and survive, and that their position has to be defended against constant challenge. Thought through, Darwinism declared nature to be the playground not of Life but of Death; in the words of a French biologist: "Life is the totality of functions which resist death".

The racial egoism of the time, however, took a positive view of Darwinism as a daring, manly, quasi aristocratic attitude towards life. "To understand the obsession with war in Darwinian sociology, one has to know to what extent and in which way Darwinism influenced biology towards the end of the nineteenth century."[4] As Poliakov

---

[4] André Pichot, op. cit., p. 61.

mentions: "Max Nordau noted already in 1889 that Darwinism was becoming the supreme authority of the militarists in all European countries: 'Since the theory of evolution has been promulgated they can cover their natural barbarism with the name of Darwin and give free play to their bloodthirsty instincts as their being the last word of science' ... The gospels of power were preached above all in imperial Germany and in the Anglo-Saxon countries. In the latter too 'Social Darwinism' was easily combined with the Germanic-Aryan idea, also called 'theory of the Teutonic origins'".[5] In fact, some biologists, and not only those of Anglo-Saxon origin, put the British side by side with the Germans, if not above them, at the top of the tree of humanity.

Darwinism was taken for granted as solid science – which it was not. André Pichot, a French epistemologist and historian of the ideas underlying science, shows in his essay *La société pure – de Darwin à Hitler* that Darwin's evolutionary theory, based on his observations of nature, did not have a scientific leg to stand on. The reasoning supporting the theory was borrowed, he says, from British sociologists and economists, especially from Adam Smith, Thomas Malthus and Francis Galton. *How* the species evolved, which was the process of the changes and the mechanism of the mutations within the cell, Darwin simply could not know.

"His *Origin of Species* dates from 1859, and Darwinism took more than fifty years to work itself out, finding its definitive formulation only in the years 1900-15, after the rediscovery of the laws of Mendel and the beginnings of genetics. Before 1900, lacking a theory of heredity worth its name, and lacking a theory of variation (a mutation was then considered an exceptional perturbation without importance), Darwinism was a badly confirmed and formless theory. The only point on which there was a real agreement and some constancy was natural selection ... Between 1900 and 1915 genetics gradually comes into its own ... and agrees well with Darwinism ...

---

[5] Léon Poliakov, op. cit., pp. 390-91.

Thanks to this, Darwinism takes on a form which is somewhat more convincing and scientific. This is the form it has kept until now and which owns, all in all, rather little to Darwin himself."[6]

Darwin's theory of evolution, contrary to what is often thought, became an instant success and "the idea of applying Darwinism to society and politics was immediate". "As soon as *The Origin of Species* had been published, perceptive thinkers understood that not only the ideas about history and the evolution of the human societies but even the bases of morals and politics could no longer be as they had been before ... Darwin, by formulating the principle of the struggle for existence and selection, did not only revolutionize biology and natural philosophy: he transformed political science. Possessing this principle enabled to get hold of the laws of life and death of a nation, laws which had escaped the speculation of philosophers", wrote Vacher de Lapouge.[7] The application of Darwinism to society and politics, to which Darwin himself might not have agreed, is called 'Social Darwinism'.

According to Social Darwinism the human being is no longer created directly by God: it did and does belong to the animal kingdom and is the result of a long evolution. The human being is a higher animal, but still an animal. Linnaeus had been the first, in 1751, to determine the three kingdoms of nature: mineral, vegetable and animal; he classified man in the animal kingdom, in the order of primates, together with the apes. This idea was extremely controversial in a world still dominated by the Christian religion, and some biologists proposed a fourth kingdom reserved specifically for man. It was not Darwin but Lamarck who, in 1809, following the way shown by Linnaeus, made man descend from the ape. Darwin, shocked by the logical implications of his scheme of nature, did not write upon this subject in his *Origin* but waited till the publication of *The Descent of Man*, in 1871, when the animal origin of man had already

---

[6]André Pichot, op. cit., pp. 186-87.
[7]Id., p. 70.

been extrapolated from his thesis and become accepted knowledge among the general public.

The strife, no longer of individuals but of groups of humans – tribes, classes, races, nations – became now a 'scientifically founded' and justified phenomenon, easy to accept because history had little else to show. Just as the fittest individual won the upper hand over the weaker one, so the stronger group of individuals would and should conquer the weaker group. This 'law of nature' was universally applicable; not to follow it, for instance by letting the weaker compassionately survive and even procreate, would mean tampering with the order of nature, whether or not created by a God. (Eugenics – and ultimately the eradication of a people that was supposed to be harmful, like the Jews – was therefore a development in the logical order of things.) Such reasoning left no longer any possibility open for an upward evolution beyond animal man, into a future where the human being might rise above his animal characteristics. In a materialistic era Social Darwinism, however ramshackle the scaffolding of the science supporting it, won the day. It is still very much alive in some of its variants, eg. socio-biology, and even recent philosophers and sociologists felt the inclination to submerge the individual into the mass, asserting that the individual is nothing but a cell in a social organism. (Yet, it is never social organisms which put together philosophical or scientific theories, or which write books.)

"Racism and Darwinism enter into a symbiosis in Hitler's *Mein Kampf*", writes Christian Zentner.[8] Some of the sources of Hitler's book are now familiar to us, and we know that it became gospel truth in Nazi Germany, where it moulded the thinking of millions through political propaganda, education and the media. Moreover, its fundamental Social Darwinism struck a chord with contemporary German thought. The following sayings of Hitler will speak for themselves.

---

[8]Christian Zentner: *Adolf Hitlers "Mein Kampf"*, p. 160.

In *Mein Kampf* he writes: "Nobody can doubt that this world will one day be the scene of dreadful struggles for existence on the part of mankind. In the end the instinct of self-preservation alone will triumph. Before its consuming fire the so-called humanitarianism, which connotes only a mixture of fatuous timidity and self-conceit, will melt away as under the March sunshine. Man has become great through perpetual struggle. In perpetual peace his greatness must decline".[9] At the end of *Hitler's Table Talk*, Henry Picker has included a secret speech by Hitler, delivered in May 1942 to 10 000 young lieutenants, 'his military successors', to whom he said: "A deeply meaningful sentence by a great military philosopher [Clausewitz] says that struggle, which means war, is the father of all things. He who has a look at nature, seeing who she actually is, will find that these words apply to all living beings and to all that happens, not only on this earth but far beyond it. The whole universe seems to be dominated by this thought alone: that an eternal selection takes place in which the stronger keeps the right to remain alive and the weaker succumbs. Therefore some say that Nature is cruel and without mercy, but others will understand that Nature, in so doing, only obeys an iron law of logic." This was the lesson Hitler had learned, and which he worded rather civilly in one of his nightly monologues: "One must not take pity on people who are marked by destiny to perish ... One must in no way take pity on whoever lacks the necessary hardness in life".[10]

"Life is cruel", reflected Hitler, deep in the night reclining in a comfortable chair at his eastern field-headquarters. "To become, to be and to stop being: everything always means to kill. All that is born must die, whether because of illness, accident or war, it is all the same. Yet those who have been struck down by the war can find solace in the fact that their sacrifice has been made for the future of their people." For he reasoned as follows: "If some reproach me

---

[9]Adolf Hitler: *Mein Kampf*, p. 124.
[10]Henry Picker: *Hitlers Tischgespräche im Führerhauptquartier*, pp. 707, 261.

that one hundred thousand or two hundred thousand people have died because I wage this war, then I can answer them: because of what I have done until now the German nation has increased by more than two and a half million people. If I demand ten percent of them to be sacrificed, then I have given them ninety percent. I hope that in another ten years there will be ten to fifteen million Germans more in the world – men or women, I don't care: I create the necessary conditions for life."[11] "War is what is most natural, most common. War is always, war is everywhere. There is no beginning to it, there is no peace, ever. War is life. War is in every contest, war is the primeval state", said Hitler to Hermann Rauschning. And also: "Nature is cruel, that's why we may be so too."[12]

And yet Hitler did not believe in Darwin's theory of evolution. In the composite arrangement of his mind the most irrational and contradictory ideas existed side by side (as they did in the ideology called 'Nazism'); he accepted the practical interpretations of Darwin's vulgarisers, but not the theory as such. For if Darwin had it right, all human beings originated from a common ancestor; how then could one justify the existence of superior and inferior people? In addition, Darwin had never said that natural selection would lead to a race of superior people; according to Darwin the mass of living beings was quite undifferentiated, and to be the fittest on a certain occasion did not imply any permanence of that status. Furthermore, Darwin's theory applied only to individuals; its extension to social bodies was not of his doing and constituted in fact a distortion of the original theory.

In 1942, after having gone through 'a book about the origins of the human races', Hitler therefore said: "From where do we get the right to believe that man has not been what he is today from his very beginnings? The study of nature teaches us that in the kingdoms

---

[11]*Adolf Hitler: Monologe im Führerhauptquartier 1941-1944*, Werner Jochman ed., pp. 143, 66, 67, 58.
[12]Hermann Rauschning, op. cit., pp. 12, 129.

of plants and animals changes and developments occur, but we find nowhere within a species a change as big as the jump man must have made if he had to develop from the ape-like state to his present state".[13] Ultimately he found a satisfactory explanation in the bizarre 'World Ice Theory' of Hans Hörbiger, which held that the universe resulted from a battle between fire and ice, that the solar system was created by the explosion of a big cosmic body, and that the geological periods were to be explained by the crashes of successive moons upon our planet Earth.

Treitschke, Fritsch, Haeckel

It was to be expected that the self-affirmation of the Germans would reach high peaks at times when the material and racial feelings were singularly stimulated. Two such occasions were the foundation of the German nation in 1871 and the take-off of its industry and economy in the Wilhelmian period before the Great War.

The foremost nationalist representative of the first of these periods was *Herr Professor* Heinrich von Treitschke (1834-96). "He was active before the unification, but his influence was especially notable during the last decades of the century ... Standing before packed audiences, Treitschke eloquently proclaimed his faith in a German morality and his deep feeling for the Volk. A note of militancy pervaded his lectures [at the University of Berlin], as if he were attempting to transcend his deafness and in his lectures accomplish the feats of courage denied him on the battlefield."[14]

"Heinrich von Treitschke's career mirrors the increasing racism and reaction of the universities", writes John Weiss. "The favourite of the Prussian establishment, he was appointed royal historiographer by the Kaiser, and no middle-class household was complete without his famous *German History of the Nineteenth Century* [in five volumes

---

[13] *Hitlers Tischgespräche im Führerhauptquartier*, p. 127.
[14] George Mosse: *The Crisis of German Ideology*, p. 200.

and unfinished] ... Idol of the German Student Federation, Treitschke gave scholarly sanction to establishment prejudices. For two decades his public lectures at the University of Berlin were attended by the highest-ranking members of the government and the military, his classes crammed with their sons and future schoolteachers, who, while their opposite numbers in France taught the virtues of republicanism, taught those of autocracy ... His strident voice harshened by near deafness, Treitschke ranted like a demagogue, praised imperialism, denounced the Jews, and raged against democracy and socialism. Civilians, he insisted, should have no say over the sacred army budget; thank the God of Battles there had been no universal suffrage when Prussia unified Germany."

Here were created or consolidated the elements of the German mind: Prussian nationalism and racism, autarchy, militarism, respect for the social hierarchical pyramid, unconditional obedience and a sense of duty; they would buttress the national ambitions and make belligerency part of the air the Germans breathed. This spirit was so pervading that even the Left gave in to it in 1914 and again in 1933. It was this spirit which would render democratic republicanism impossible, quite simply because the democratic principles were foreign and therefore incomprehensible to it. "Why give the vote to readers of a daily press that encouraged every ignoramus to utter opinions on matters best left to a few? Universal elementary education created discontent. If it must be, appoint retired non-commissioned officers as teachers to instil the right values. For Treitschke, socialism was the treason of the Jews, feminism the illegitimate offspring of Jewish socialism and Hebrew females. Violating nature, feminism also threatened the sources of Prussian greatness, the patriarchal family and the warrior ethic. As the Nazis would insist, the woman's role was one of childbearer for the race, nurse to the warrior, symbol of the gentler sentiments.

"Treitschke even criticized Bismarck for not completing the holy task of uniting all Germans in an imperial *Weltmacht* (world power). A people with the power to conquer and absorb weak states had a divine mandate to do so. 'Brave peoples expand, cowardly peoples perish.' Treitschke looked forward to the day when a German fleet would sail up the Thames and a German army occupy London ... If Austria and Russia fought, Germany must support Austria [as it would do in 1914 and by so doing unleash the war], for it was the racial duty of Germans to rule over 'inferior' Slavs. In politics, all was force. War united the race and fostered the heroic; peace mutilated the personality and brought the domination of vulgar commerce. Might did not make right: it *was* right. Treitschke said, as Hitler would say: 'History is nothing other than the eternal struggle of race against race'." John Weiss calls the *Herr Professor* "the crude voice of the barracks writ large".

"The enormous popularity of Treitschke's harsh simplicities illustrates how racism enabled so many upper-class Germans to reduce social and moral complexities to racial differences and take seriously those who later, in the midst of social upheavals, preached racial revolution and war. Treitschke's writings were revived by the radical right in the 1920's, and he was one of the very few nineteenth-century writers to win a place in the official Nazi pantheon of required reading. Quotations from Treitschke were included in the small books of readings carried into battle by German soldiers during World War II."[15]

During the second great spasm of German nationalism and racism in the Wilhelmian period, Theodor Fritsch was another powerful figure. He also acted through politics, yet he preferred the more hidden ways, which is why we met him earlier in our story as the founder of the *Germanenorden*. In all cases German racism was practically identical with anti-Semitism, for the Jews were the main foreign organism, often compared to a germ or a virus, in the living body of the Volk. (Compared to the numbers and the economical and cultural influence of the Jews, the Gypsies were hardly of any importance – if the murder of half a million of them can be said to be of little importance.)

---

[15]John Weiss: *Ideology of Death*, pp. 132 ff.

Fritsch, called by some "probably the most important racist and anti-Semite before Hitler", was a very capable and prolific organizer. We remember that he launched the periodical *Der Hammer*, from which resulted the local Hammer Societies, which were unified in 1908 in the *Reichshammerbund*. To counteract the presumed secret activities of the Jews, who wanted to bring the whole world under their power, Fritsch founded the equally secret Germanenorden as a sister organisation of the Reichshammerbund – and the Germanenorden became the parent organisation of the Thule Society, which introduced us in our early chapters to the lively but murky political world of post-war Munich.

Treitschke and Fritsch were not the only racists of their time, by far. The response they found proves that they were more symptoms than initiators of a mentality which cannot be called otherwise than 'common'. Nor did this mentality belong only to historical and literary brains: one of the most powerful racist dynamo's in Germany before the First World War was the *Alldeutsche Verein*, the Pan-Germans. They never numbered more than four thousand, but they were a kind of nationalist freemasonry to which only the most influential and high-ranked personalities had access. The historian Karl Lamprecht, advisor to Chancellor Bethmann Hollweg, was a Pan-German, as were the sociologist Max Weber, still studied today, Gustav Stresemann, the future foreign minister, Ludwig Schemann, publisher of Chamberlain's works, and many politicians, industrialists and bankers.

Sebottendorff called the Pan-Germans "the most important volkisch association of the pre-war period". Had he written today, he would probably have used the term 'pressure group'. "The development of the Pan-German Association is an example of the coming together of nationalist, volkisch and anti-Semitic circles through the gradual integration of racist thought and anti-Semitism justified by racism in the nationalist and imperialist policies." (Hermann Gilbhard[16]) Besides being squarely racist, the Pan-Germans

---

[16] Hermann Gilbhard: *Die Thule-Gesellschaft*, p. 39.

stood chiefly for the integration of all Germans into one Greater German Empire or Reich, and for the hegemony by this Reich over other nations within its sphere of influence. The German 'war aims' were their brainchildren, adopted by the politicians and by the Hindenburg-Ludendorff tandem. We have seen that these war aims were actually realized in the East in February 1917, when Russia signed the Treaty of Brest-Litovsk, and that they came very close to being realised in the West before the tide of the war definitively turned.

Another Pan-German was the zoologist Ernst Haeckel (1834-1919). Nowadays his name is seldom printed outside Germany, but during his lifetime he was *the* teacher to the German nation of the life sciences, and translations of his works appeared in many languages. Of *Die Welträtsel*, the riddles of the world, published in 1889, 400,000 copies were printed up to 1933. Haeckel was one of the first adherents of Darwinism, which he popularised in his writings. He was also an important scientist in his own right, and a many-sided one, for his research touched fields outside zoology and biology. As his basic outlook on life he conceived a kind of mystical pantheism, postulating that the organic and inorganic realms were ruled by the same physical laws. This led him to pioneering research in the border region between matter and life, and he was the first to surmise that the cell played an important role in matters of inheritance, although science had not yet invented the technical means to explore this field.

Of direct importance to our story were Haeckel's theories about race, more specifically the way in which he thought the human being was related to the primates and the hierarchical order he surmised within the species *homo sapiens*. In Haeckel and in all his contemporaries, though they spoke with great authority and were believed with respectful amazement because of their astonishing revelations, 'science' consisted mainly of cultural, political, and especially racial prejudices. "[Haeckel's] criteria are among the most vague. They relate to the nature of the hair, the colour of the skin, the form of the skull and a number of biological characteristics [afterwards to be applied by the racial researchers of the *SS-Ahnenerbe*], but added to these are also all kinds of other considerations, intellectual, linguistic, social, etc. Haeckel's classification is a taxonomic fantasy."[17]

Haeckel found that humanity consisted of thirty-six races, divided into twelve species. He drew a human ancestral tree in which all of them fitted hierarchically. It will surprise no one that the Indo-Germans came out on top of the tree. What *is* surprising is that, when drawing the genealogy of the Indo-Germans, Haeckel placed the Anglo-Saxons next to the High-Germans (*Hoch-Deutsche*), apparently a degree more developed than the Low-Germans and the Dutch. The Negro tribes were hardly different from the 'man-apes'. Like most of his contemporaries, Haeckel found a considerably greater 'psychic' difference between the higher and the lower humans than between the lower humans and the apes.

"Haeckel and other authors like him would evidently have had a tough time explaining the degree of biological evolution according to which they classified the races, but the problem did not even come to their mind", writes Pichot. "In fact, they hierarchized civilization and transposed this hierarchy into the biological domain because they gave to the civilizations a hereditary basis: the superiority of the Germans and the Anglo-Saxons in Haeckel is manifestly inspired by the greater progress of the industrial revolution in these peoples. Nevertheless, however fictitious the evolutionary degree may have been as a criterion of the hierarchization of the races, it worked perfectly within the social-Darwinian ideology of the time, and it supported its inherent racism by giving it a semblance of scientific justification."[18]

Another surprise of Haeckel's tree of humanity is that he, though a prominent Pan-German, put the Semites on a nearly identical level with the Indo-Germans. If the Jews were hated and feared, it was in

---

[17] André Pichot, op. cit., p. 326.
[18] Id., p. 332.

part because they were secretly admired (also by Hitler) for their surviving qualities and purity as a race, and for their intelligence. The characteristics of the Jews, stereotyped by Christianity in general, were ingrained, 'programmed' in the thinking modes of the people; yet it was during Haeckel's lifetime that such thought attitudes would become virulent and aggressive because German nationalism and racism became virulent and aggressive. Even Treitschke wanted to give the Jews a chance to integrate into the nation, by converting to Christianity, before he became a militant anti-Semite and coined the slogan "The Jews are our misfortune", which would resound through the coming generations. Ernst Haeckel seems never to have gone that far.

Gobineau and Vacher de Lapouge

At the beginning of every history of modern racism, in Germany as in the whole of Europe, one finds the name of the French aristocrat Joseph de Gobineau (1816-82). Some even call him "the father of racial theory". His fame is based chiefly on his *Essai sur l'inégalité des races humaines,* (essay on the inequality of the human races) published in four volumes in the years 1853-55. This major work met with little success for several decades. "Not until 1894 [ie after Gobineau's death] was there a concerted attempt to introduce Gobineau's ideas into Germany", writes George Mosse. "In that year, Ludwig Schemann founded the Gobineau Society to honour his name and revive his theories both in Germany and France. The French branch received little support and never really flourished. It was not really popular in Germany either, but there it received the wholehearted support of the Richard Wagner circle, of which Schemann was a member. In addition, Schemann, active on the board of the Pan-Germans, was able to obtain the support of this significant conservative group for the cause of racial theory. In the end, his assertion proved correct: 'Only Germany can be the receptacle for Gobineau and his ideas'."[19]

---

[19] George Mosse, op. cit., p. 91.

The sequence of events as sketched here by Mosse has to be somewhat adjusted. According to Cosima Wagner, Gobineau, a very cultured and widely-travelled man, had obtained access into the circle around her husband, Richard Wagner, and had found compensation in the composer's 'enthusiastic response' for the general neglect of his racial theory. "It was thanks to Wagner that the Frenchman became the inspirational source of the future pure Aryan state. But it was soon forgotten that behind Gobineau's popularity, as well as behind the popularity of Chamberlain, stood the Master of Bayreuth."[20] According to Joachim Köhler, Schemann's Gobineau Society was started with the blessings of Cosima, one of whose friends was Heinrich Class, chairman of the Pan-German League, of which Schemann was a member. So we meet once more, at the end of several converging lines, the Bayreuth Circle, which seems actually to have been a most active secret society for the promotion of nationalism and racism, and the well-heeled, influential, omnipresent Pan-Germans, who in their turn supported the Germanenorden. These were the three power centres without whose support, nothing of much importance could happen on the nationalist-racist scene in Germany. They directed the events – visible like the Kapp-Putsch and invisible like many underhand dealings and 'physical eliminations' – which led straight to Adolf Hitler, whom they thought would execute their designs and be the puppet dancing on their strings.

What did they find that was so special in Gobineau, whose name today hardly rings a bell? He was the first to explain that race was the determining factor in the evolution and composition of mankind; he taught that the mixing of pure with impure blood was the cause of race deterioration; and his reasonings pointed back to the existence of an original master race with uncontaminated blood. What suited the volkisch-minded Germans of the aforementioned societies also was that Gobineau was a through and through reactionary and anti-modernist. He was, moreover, a highly cultured writer who could

---

[20]Joachim Köhler: *Wagners Hitler*, p. 166.

muster a wealth of arguments and historical facts to confer an appearance of veracity to his theses. And his theories preceded those of Darwin, for the four volumes of his *Essay on the Inequality of Human Races* were written before the publication of *The Origin of Species*.

Yet, "Gobineau was not a biologist but a literary man of the nineteenth century, and his work [the *Essay*] contains not exactly what its title announces".[21] He was "a diplomat of inferior rank who wrote novels and essays" and who acquired a permanent place in French literature with works like *The Pleiades, Tales of Asia, History of the Persians* and *The Renaissance*. "His *Essay* has in common with Darwin's *Origin* that it is much more often mentioned than actually read ... Gobineau's racism really has not much to do with the biological notion of race. His inspiration is not so much taxonomy as a certain social order, and even an order of the world modelled on the principle of the Indian castes. This racism should therefore be seen in the context of the Aryan myth, which also relates to India."[22] The white race, with its highly developed civilisation, is evidently superior to the others; it is even the only truly civilised race. The black race is hardly capable of becoming civilised, and the yellow race has a place somewhere in between.

The nobleman Gobineau was a devout Catholic, shocked by the turn things were taking because of the French Revolution, the titanic actions of Napoleon and the industrial revolution. He, like so many others still deeply rooted in the *ancient régime*, felt like a fish out of water in a century which ideals had become secular and centred on the well-being and progress of humanity. Therefore Gobineau was a pessimist through and through, and, like the Catholic Church at the time, 'terribly reactionary and retrograde'.

Taking all this into account, Gobineau could never agree with Darwin. As a Catholic he had to stick to the biblical story of the

---

[21] André Pichot, op. cit., p. 24.
[22] Id., p. 308.

creation of man and could not try to provide a scientific explanation. He had no justification for the existence of a superior race, or races, for if all human beings originated from Adam and Eve, and some of them were of pure blood, then where might the others come from, the un-pure contaminators?

There was no doubt in the minds of Gobineau and many of his disoriented contemporaries that the world was sliding towards its doom. It should be kept in mind what a traumatic series of events the French Revolution had been for the *ancien régime*, in the first place for the nobility and the clergy, and how firmly they were still anchored in the religious, social and cultural structures of the Middle Ages. The new rationalist philosophers no longer had faith in the Word of God and some of them put it outright into question or even ridiculed it. A world based on such principles of theistic, atheistic or materialistic modernism could only lead to perdition. To take an anti-modernist stance was a matter of life and death for the likes of Gobineau. And deeply felt convictions of the kind he and many others nurtured always find the intellectual, philosophical and 'scientific' arguments with which to attire their essential nudity.

That humanity will 'devolve' into a uniform miscellany of animal-like imbeciles and finally die out was, according to Gobineau, certain. What then about the German *Herrenmenschen* and the future glories of the Third Reich – the aspirations of a country in which a French count was honoured as a pioneer of racist thought? Honoured perhaps, but probably little studied. People's movements thrive on slogans, and the thinking with which political parties justify their programmes and actions consists of little more than some elementary ideas, formulated in a few thoughts knitted together and not seldom contradictory. Although man is a rational being, thinking for himself is felt to be a burden, and it is astonishing to what extent even people who are trained, professional thinkers parrot the thoughts of others. The general trend of Gobineau's world-view was diametrically opposite to the world-view of the Nazis, but they would nevertheless refer to him appreciatively in their racist writings.

Hitler was a 'practical thinker', in the sense that he picked out what fitted into his peculiar mental framework and memorised it, with the purpose of having those thoughts at his disposal when he needed them. He did this quite systematically and defended his way of acquiring this kind of knowledge in *Mein Kampf*. That he had heard of Gobineau is undeniable when one reads the following passage in *Mein Kampf*: "When men have lost their natural instincts and ignore the obligations imposed on them by nature, then there is no hope that nature will correct the loss that has been caused, until recognition of the lost instincts has been restored. Then the task of bringing back what has been lost will have to be accomplished. But there is serious danger that those who have once become blind in this respects will continue more and more to break down racial barriers and finally lose the last remnant of what is best in them. What then remains is nothing but a uniform mishmash, which seems to be the dream of our fine Utopians. [Here Hitler has a go at the democrats and socialists.] But that mishmash would soon banish all ideals from the world. Certainly a great herd could thus be formed. One can breed a herd of animals; but from a mixture of this kind men such as have created and founded civilizations would not be produced. The mission of humanity might then be considered at an end".[23]

The most dangerous contamination in Hitler's eyes was, of course, the Jew. ("He poisons the blood of others but preserves his own blood unadulterated.") In the following paragraph of *Mein Kampf*, one of the most often quoted, one again hears an unmistakable echo from Gobineau: "If with the help of his Marxist faith the Jew is victorious against the peoples of this world, then his crown will be a dance of death of humanity and this planet, empty of human beings, will again wander through space for millions of years. Eternal Nature avenges inexorably the trespassing of her laws. This is why I believe that today I act in conformity with the intention of the

---

[23] Adolf Hitler, op. cit., pp. 336-37.

almighty Creator: in acting against the Jews I fight for the work of the Lord".[24]

A name often read in connection with Gobineau's is that of Vacher de Lapouge. Strange to say, Georges Vacher de Lapouge (1854-1936) too was a Frenchman, a count, and not a qualified scientist. Mosse writes that 'he was widely admired in Germany', which is true. According to Bronder he was a 'professor at the University of Montpellier', which is not true: he was assistant-librarian at the university of Montpellier and in later years, librarian at Rennes and Poitiers. He had actually studied law, but never practised either as a barrister or as a magistrate. He preferred to read books, acquired an enormous erudition and a steadily growing fame as 'free lecturer', and became the author of essays like *The Social Selections* (1896), *The Fundamental Law of Anthroposociology* (1897) and *The Aryan – His special role* (1899).

Like Haeckel and Gobineau, Vacher de Lapouge was convinced that race was the determining factor in the development of humanity and the relations between the human groupings. He too conceived a hierarchy of the human races and, of course, put the Aryans on top. We know now that all this racial 'science' was actually the result of a very time-embedded and 'Eurocentric' vision of the global relations in an era of colonialism. Yet Vacher de Lapouge surprises us by elevating not the Germans but the Anglo-Saxons to the top of the human ladder as 'the most Aryan people in the world': "The British Isles are almost the only place to show us the physical type and the quite robust character of the first inhabitants of Europe." Pichot writes: "In those days, the Aryan theories tended as much, if not more, towards the Anglo-Saxon mania as towards the German barbarians". And he quotes Vacher de Lapouge: "The superiority of the Yankee [of Aryan stock], the Englishman, the Dutchman and the Scandiavian over the Frenchman, the Italian, the Spaniard and

---

[24] Christian Zentner, op. cit., p. 29.

the South American is not only the consequence of the superiority of the race but also of the blood".[25]

"The great future of the British Isles is the result of the fortunate fact that brachycephalics have never set foot there", reveals Vacher. For it was he who drew the attention of the racial scientists to the distinction between people with a narrow, longish skull, the dolichocephalics, and people with a round skull, the brachycephalics – another of those zany racial specifications which have led to piles of learned nonsense and much injustice and suffering in the racists' victims. "The main characteristic of the thought [of Vacher de Lapouge] is an obsession with the shape of the skull: he studied the dolichocephalic or brachycephalic character of all imaginable populations and in every possible manner. One of the most comical examples was the relation between the shape of the skull and the use of the bicycle, evaluated according to the taxes paid by the various populations." Vacher's conclusion was that longish skulls showed more interest for the new invention which the bicycle was at the time, and that round skulls remained immune to it, as well as to all other forms of progress. "Vacher de Lapouge is an extremely heterogeneous author, now lucid and prophetic, then again completely ridiculous. The least mistaken evaluation of him is that his works provide a fairly successful caricature of the socio-biological ideas of his time", concludes Pichot.

What Vacher also shared with Gobineau was 'an absolute pessimism', for he was convinced that 'the final catastrophe' and 'the annihilation of the species' were unavoidable. He wrote: "An analysis of the social selections leads ultimately to absolutely pessimistic conclusions. The future does not belong to the fittest, but in the best case to the mediocre. The benefits of the natural selection change, as civilization develops, into scourges setting upon humanity ... Civilization shifts ceaselessly. It has now reached the west and north-west of Europe, and we feel at present that the life of Europe

---

[25] André Pichot, op. cit., pp. 24, 353, 349.

is coming to a standstill and that the days of our world are numbered. [Oswald Spengler was already conceiving his *Decline of the West*.] There is no race which can withstand the inevitable decay ... This is the last stage. It will last as long as the active elements of the race will last, and it will end when only the passive elements remain, however blond and dolichocephalic they may be. Humanity is in ferment. It has reached the threshold of a long period of convulsions beyond which the beginning of the decline can be perceived. The sum of knowledge and material means will increase into an ever greater accumulation, but man will stop growing in valour, and the shining future dreamed by utopians for generations yet to come will be lived only by mediocrities, fathers of still lesser mediocrities".[26]

Chamberlain and Rosenberg

"It is probably no exaggeration to say, as I have heard more than one follower of Hitler say, that Chamberlain was the spiritual founder of the Third Reich."[27] With whatever proviso one quotes these words of the experienced journalist who was William Shirer, it is a fact that the influence of the Englishman Houston Chamberlain penetrated profoundly into Hitler Germany, where his *Foundations of the Nineteenth Century* was 'a tremendous success'.

"By 1900 there were several rival racial theories," writes George Mosse. "Most of them had grown with the refinement of the anthropological criteria and had incorporated elements of the 'survival of the fittest' axiom of Social Darwinism. They were correspondingly more optimistic about the direction history was taking. Instead of concentrating on the inevitability of racial contamination and the consequent decline of civilization, these theorists looked toward a developing race that would save Western culture and stamp it with its own uniqueness. Of these, Houston Stewart Chamberlain was

---

[26]Id., pp. 45-46.
[27] William Shirer, op. cit., p. 103.

the most important. Unlike Gobineau, Chamberlain analyzed the totality of civilization, not because he was concerned with its decline, but, on the contrary, because he yearned for a better, more beautiful racial future."

As we have seen before, Chamberlain was a qualified biologist "fascinated by plant pathology, and he might well have become a scientist had it not been for his health. Instead, he fused his scientific training with a mystical love of nature and a Social Darwinism which was so typical of much radical thought. This transformation from scientist to radical racist was catalyzed by his encounter with the work of Richard Wagner ... He provided the New Romanticism [volkisch and therefore racist] with a scientific base and thus lent the tone and the goals of science to his racial theories".[28] This is a risky undertaking in which usually either science or mysticism loses out, or both.

According to Chamberlain, "on the one hand there was a German science which determined, with the utmost accuracy, that which existed empirically; on the other hand, there was a German religion which bestowed infinite vistas upon the German soul. In terms of importance the religion took priority, since it alone could fathom the true essence of things. As it also functioned in the realm of ideas, it served to keep science within its proper limits, and at the same time appropriated empirical evidence in support of itself. Through their inner selves, which were enveloped in a mystical Germanism, Chamberlain asserted, men could determine the meaning of the external world."[29] This will lead straight to the official proclamation by the Nazis, Nobel Prize winners among them, of a true 'German science' as opposed to a false 'Jewish science' of which the world-famous Albert Einstein was the epitome. That this kind of irrationalities, or plain idiocies, did not prevent German engineers to produce an astonishing range of new inventions shows that the engineer does not

---

[28] George Mosse, op. cit., pp. 93, 94.
[29] Id., p. 94.

need an ideological support of his work. It was 'German science', though, which accepted the 'world ice theory' and the 'hollow earth theory' – and the theory of the superiority of the Aryan race. Nazism was fanatical irrationalism, armed by technological engineering.

Houston Chamberlain was an admirer of Gobineau although, contrary to the Frenchman's pessimism, he proposed a gloriously positive outlook. Like many of his contemporaries, including Nietzsche, Chamberlain had a problem with the descent of the human from the primates, which did not prevent him to accept Social Darwinism, "so typical of much radical thought". Radicals do tend to deem themselves superior to others. Chamberlain found convincing support for his view in animal breeding. A race was in fact a soul seeking to incarnate, to acquire a material form dependent on the blood. Therefore a race could be improved, purified, even created by breeding from "a favourable mixture of blood".[30] In this way Chamberlain evaded the thorny problem of the origin of the existing races, also of the Aryan or Teutonic ones. A race was to be made by breeding – a view which Hitler will adopt.

Chamberlain was a visionary, no doubt, a kind of rational racial mystic. (Shirer tells us that, when writing the *Foundations*, "Chamberlain was again possessed by one of his 'demons'.") Races are spiritual entities which have to be served by the individuals whose material bodies are the cells of the organism that is the race, and who are all of one blood. From this followed that the racial egoism could not accept the general humanitarian and internationalist ideals of the Enlightenment. What also followed was that the organism of the own race was sacred, a direct expression of the will of God, or the Universal Spirit, or Nature. It should therefore be kept in a state of purity, synonymous with purity of the blood, and must repel or expel anything foreign to it and contaminating it.

"In regard to race, Chamberlain used a scientific base to prove its absolute nature, its totality, which encompassed both internal and

---

[30]See Klaus von See, op. cit., p. 292.

external appearances. At the end of the nineteenth century, he wrote, no scholar could ignore the fact that skull measurements and the external appearance of the brain decisively influenced the conceptions of aesthetic form that lay within. After all, went the analogy, a building was characterized by the materials used in its construction; they provided the outward form and expressed the 'ideas' inherent in the erection." And Mosse goes on to tell how one Dr Burger-Villingen constructed an instrument, called a plastometer, with which he measured the 'geography of the human face and thus the cast of a person's soul'. Of course, it was the Germans who were the noblest race existing on earth, the saviours of the world and the creators and carriers of the supreme Western culture.

"The Aryan was distinguished by a physical form that typified the Germanic ideal of beauty; the Jew was his very opposite. Symbolically, only to be too deeply believed later on, the two represented the polarization of God and the devil ... God was, so to speak, embodied in the German race, and the devil in the Jewish race. These were held to be the two pure races – and between flourished the 'chaos of peoples', bastard mixtures of various races."[31] And Shirer writes: "Chamberlain claimed that the Teutons and the Jews were the only pure races left in the West." Was he, then, not an anti-Semite? "The Jews", he says, "are not inferior to the Teuton, merely different. They have their own grandeur; they realize the sacred duty of man to guard the purity of the race. And yet as he proceeds to analyze the Jews, he slips into the very vulgar anti-Semitism which he condemns in others and which leads, in the end, to the obscenities of Julius Streicher's caricatures of the Jews in Hitler's time. Indeed a good deal of the 'philosophical' basis of Nazi anti-Semitism stems from this chapter [on the Jews in the *Foundations*]."[32] It seems to have been impossible to be a German racist without being an anti-Semite.

---

[31] George Mosse, op. cit., pp. 94 ff. passim.
[32] William Shirer, op. cit., p. 107.

But what about Jesus Christ? Although they had been 'badly baptized', the Germans considered themselves a Christian nation, in a way the only *real* Christians, as proclaimed to the world by Martin Luther. Was Christ, the founder of their faith, not a Jew? Chamberlain contended that he was not. At the time Christ walked upon the earth Galilee was inhabited by non-Jewish tribes. Christ had "a large proportion of non-Semitic blood", and: "Whoever claimed that Jesus was a Jew was either being stupid or telling a lie."[33] This irrefutable argument was duly repeated after Chamberlain by countless German Christians, while he himself was only repeating what Richard Wagner had said on the subject, who in his turn may have referred to Schopenhauer and Fichte. The Germans were not only the purest Aryans, they were the foremost in every field, also the religious, and 'much more devout Christians than other peoples'.

Hitler too believed that Christ was not a Jew. "Christ was an Aryan", he said in one of his monologues, "but Paul abused his teaching to mobilize the dark forces and to organize a proto-Bolshevism".[34] How far speculations of this sort can be spun out is shown by the following quotation from *The German Christ*, a book by Max Brewer, published in 1907. "It is known that precisely around the time of the birth of Christ large armies from Schleswig-Holstein had appeared in northern Italy, whose blood, despite their defeat, will not have mixed with the Romans completely. Since the time of Caesar, the exchange of blood between Rome and the lands along the lower Rhine had become very intense. It is said that Pilate's bodyguard consisted of soldiers from Lower Germany. In any case, shortly before the birth of Christ German blood had again been instrumental in Galilee. Everything Christ says about reincarnation seems to be inspired by the bodily reincarnated blood."[35]

---

[33]Ibid.
[34]*Monologe im Führerhauptquartier*, p. 150.
[35]Stefanie von Schnurbein and Justus Ulbricht (ed.): *Völkische Religion und Krisen der Moderne*, p. 176.

Alfred Rosenberg (1893-1946), the German Balt who had fled the conflagration of the Russian Revolution and been introduced to Hitler by Dietrich Eckart, was another admirer of Houston Chamberlain. The pale, zealotic intellectual Rosenberg fitted badly in the rude and crude entourage of Adolf Hitler, was loved by none and hated by many, and was in later years ridiculed even by the Führer himself. During the early years in Munich, however, his influence on Hitler was more important than is now generally appreciated. "Hitler was deeply under the spell of Rosenberg", testifies Ernst Hanfstängl, who calls him "Hitler's most dangerous mentor".[36] It was the resentful Rosenberg who sharpened Hitler's ideas about the lowly character of the Russians, who first drew his attention towards the wide-open Russian spaces available for the taker, and who systematically equated Bolshevism with Judaism.

It was also Rosenberg, a member of the Thule Society, who acted as the most anti-Semitic promoter of *The Protocols of the Wise Men of Zion*, as well in his contributions to the *Völkische Beobachter*, the Nazi newspaper of which he succeeded Eckart as the editor in 1923, as in his other prolific writings, eg., *The Protocols of the Wise Men of Zion and Jewish World Politics*. Though Hitler spoke sometimes scathingly of him in private, officially he remained regardful of Rosenberg's intellectual contribution to the formation of National Socialism, and called him "a man of whose integrity of personal intention I am absolutely convinced".[37] He appointed Rosenberg general supervisor of National-Socialist ideology for the whole Reich and would later nominate him governor-general of the Eastern Occupied Territories.

Rosenberg's prestige rested, besides on his supposed closeness to Hitler, mainly upon a thick book he published in 1930, *The Myth of the Twentieth Century*. The title evokes at once Chamberlain's *Foundations of the Nineteenth Century*, and Rosenberg did indeed

---

[36] Ernst Hanfstängl: *Hitler – The Missing Years*, pp. 41, 269.
[37] Geoffrey Stoakes: *Hitler and the Quest for World Dominion*, p. 77.

intend his book to be a sequel. "Rosenberg sold his seven hundred page *Myth* in editions of hundreds of thousands", writes Albert Speer. "The public regarded the book as the standard text for party ideology, but Hitler in those teatime conversations bluntly called it 'stuff nobody can understand', written by 'a narrow-minded Baltic German who thinks in horribly complicated terms'." Indeed, Rosenberg was still tougher reading fare than *Mein Kampf*, and Hitler "expressed wonderment that such a book could ever have attained such sales".[38]

Rosenberg's fundamental theses were not all that difficult to understand and resemble closely many of the ideas we have met with above. He too saw the development of humanity and the history of the world as the history of races in conflict, even on a wider scale than drawn by his predecessors. For him too the Aryan-Nordic-Germanic people were superior to all others and deserving of the others' homage and submission. Northern Europe was, again, 'the cradle of humanity', 'the centre of creation' and the origin of all cultures worth the name, an origin which went back to Atlantis.

The Nordic race had spread over the world in three phases or waves. – One wonders once more at the 'Eurocentric' vision of these instructors. – First there had been the Indo-Germans who, fanning out everywhere (no longer from India or the Near East, but from the north of Europe), had started the classical cultures; then there had been the migrations of the Germanic tribes, who laid the foundations of all European nations; thirdly, there was 'the colonization of modern times', intended to encompass the whole globe.[39]

Race was sacred, the Nordic race that is, and a direct expression of the Creator; it should be made into a religion. The holy land was not Palestine, but Germany. Rosenberg bolstered the dualism of a world divided into Nordic people and Semites, more particularly

---

[38] Albert Speer: *Inside the Third Reich*, p. 150.
[39] Klaus von See: *Barbar, Germane, Arier*, p. 308.

Jews. As such, he deepened the 'North-South divide', all the same extending the south eastwards, for his hate of the Russia that had made him an expatriate never abated. The Nordics had been the masters of the world in former times and would become so again in the near future; their opponents were the Jews, the Christians and the Bolsheviks, three faces of the same enemy. For Christianity was the brainchild of the Jew Paul of Tarsus and had propagated a morality of compassion and love for one's neighbour in order to weaken the nations and make them the Jews' easy prey. And Bolshevism was preaching internationalism and universal brotherhood of the proletariat, which went straight against the competitive theory of the races. Were not Jews to be found in the vanguard of every socialist or communist revolution?

These racist themes have become increasingly familiar to us, but now they were part of the doctrine of National Socialism. From 1933 onwards they would be the official doctrine of the Nazi state, and it would be Hitler's intention to implement them as soon and fully as possible. He would try to cement them during his lifetime into the foundations of a Reich that would last a thousand years.

Hitler's racism

Hitler wrote in *Mein Kampf:* "It would be futile to attempt to discuss the question as to what race or races were the original standard-bearers of human culture and were thereby the real founders of all that we understand by the word 'humanity'. It is much simpler to deal with this question in so far as it relates to the present time. Here the answer is simple and clear. Every manifestation of human culture, every product of art, science and technical skill which we see before our eyes today, is almost exclusively the product of the Aryan creative power".[40] For, as we know, the Aryan was 'the Prometheus of mankind'. All the same, this is an intriguing statement

---

[40] Adolf Hitler, op. cit., pp. 242-43.

by Hitler, the supreme racist: if one could not discuss what race or races were 'the original standard-bearers of human culture', how could he maintain that those standard bearers were the Aryans? Was this then nothing to him but a blunt political assertion, a pseudo-scientific fancy without any foundation?

"I know of course as well as all those pedantic intellectuals that in the scientific sense race does not exist," said Hitler one day to Hermann Rauschning. "But being a politician, I need a concept which allows me to dissolve the order which until now was resting on historical interconnections, and to enforce a totally new, anti-historical order, providing it with an intellectual support ... I have to free the world from its historical past. The nations are the manifest forces of our history. Therefore I have to re-melt the nations into a higher order if I want to remove the chaotic residues of a historical past which has become absurd, and to this end the concept of race is useful for me. It dissolves what is old and creates the possibility of new connections. It was with the concept of the nation that France took its great revolution across its borders. It is with the concept of race that National Socialism will conduct its revolution, which will lead to a new order in the world."[41] Here again Hitler sees race as an abstraction, a 'concept', without any necessary foundation in reality, but to be used as a tool to build a new world-order out of the remnants of the nations. Who were those 'pedantic intellectuals' whom Rauschning did not name? They may have been the linguists who pointed out the wrongful reasoning which extended the discovery of a common Aryan language to the factual existence of an Aryan race.

Hitler was, unbeknownst even to his closest paladins, cherishing a dream of world domination, of which the concrete foundations had to be ensured during the few years of his life. To this end he had been sent among the German people, unconsciously prepared by their history as the Volk which was to serve as his instrument.

---

[41]Hermann Rauschning, op. cit., pp. 218-19.

As he was placed in this situation, he had to accept, to a certain extent, the volkisch myths which the Germans had adopted as their past and the justification of their existence. But Hitler, although he himself was dreaming great dreams, understood perfectly well how unreal and in a way childish such legends and myths were. He could not bluntly reject them, for his own movement considered itself fundamentally a volkisch movement, and if he bared his inmost thoughts, he would have been taken for a madman. Moreover, an individual cannot all by himself create a new myth and turn it into a movement within the short lifetime of a human being.

This explains why Hitler was so ambivalent in his appreciation of volkisch matters, which, on the one hand, he had to encourage while on the other, he often ridiculed them in private and even condemned some of their implications publicly. "It was not without good reason that, when we laid down a clearly defined programme for the new movement, we excluded the word 'volkisch' from it. The concept underlying the term 'volkisch' cannot serve as the base of the movement, because it is too indefinite in its application", he wrote politely in *Mein Kampf*. "The word 'volkisch' does not express any clearly specified idea." Then, less cautiously: "Not less dangerous are those who run about as semi-folklorists formulating fantastic schemes [at that time there were many such men in Germany, and Hitler was one of them], which are mostly based on nothing else than a fixed idea which in itself might be right but which, because it is an isolated notion, is of no use whatsoever for the formation of a great homogeneous fighting association and could by no means serve as the basis of its organization."[42] For this was what Hitler wanted to forge the German people into: a well-organised, well-equipped and fully brainwashed weapon for the execution of his vision.

The volkisch leader in National-Socialist Germany was Heinrich Himmler. Himmler saw his SS, the exemplars and at the same time

---

[42] Adolf Hitler, op. cit., pp. 303, 318, 385.

guardians of the Volk, as an embodiment of the volkisch ideals of his youth and hoped to found one day an SS state based on these ideals. Hitler knew exactly how to manipulate Himmler, yet he often made him the butt of his sarcasm, for instance in a conversation with Speer. "Why do we call the whole world's attention to the fact that we have no past? It isn't enough that the Romans were erecting great buildings when our forefathers were still living in mud huts; now Himmler is starting to dig up these villages of mud huts and enthusing over every potsherd and stone axe he finds. All we prove by that is that we were still throwing stone hatchets and crouching around open fires when Greece and Rome had already reached the highest stage of culture. We really should do our best to keep quiet about this past. Instead Himmler makes a great fuss about it all. The present-day Romans must be having a laugh at these relegations."[43] Laugh they did, the Romans, Mussolini loudest of them all.

Hitler knew perfectly well that the knowledge of the 'pedantic intellectuals' about the German tribes and races of the past did not go back much farther than one or two centuries before what is now called 'the common era', and that incessant contacts and intermingling with other races had taken place before and after that time. The largest territory of such racial blending was the ever shifting border region with the Slavs, where the Teutonic Knights had spearheaded the Germanic colonisation and Christianisation.

The Prussians, practically identical with the modern German nation, were originally a Slavonic tribe, the Pruss. "Roaming along the coast of the Baltic Sea amidst furious slaughters, the Teutonic Knights seized Prussian lands and virtually exterminated the indigenous people. Building castles, forts and towns, they converted the remaining natives to Christianity, reduced them to serfdom and made themselves lords of the land."[44] "Half of the German Reich was established on what originally had been Slavonic territory",

---

[43] Albert Speer: *Inside the Third Reich*, p. 148.
[44] John Weiss: *Ideology of Death*, p. 33.

writes Christian von Krockow, "and what finally became the German nation arose from a mixture of Germanic and Slavonic tribes".[45] In a conversation with Rauschning, Hitler talked about the danger for the German people of containing a too high percentage of Slavonic elements. This would alter the character of the people, he said. "We have already too much Slavonic blood in our veins. Doesn't it strike you how many people in important positions in the Germany of today are having a Slavonic name?"[46]

The appearance of Hitler himself, as of most Germans, hardly agreed with the Aryan norm. Many tribes from the West and the East had traversed the Austrian Waldviertel, the region where he came from, and one of his grandfathers remains unknown. He was acidly mocked in the pre-1933 leftist press for his 'emphatically non-Aryan appearance', especially his fleshy nose.[47] The inanity of the Aryan myth in the Third Reich was glaringly demonstrated by the physical appearance of its top leaders: Göring was fat and a drug addict; Goebbels was stunted, big-headed and club-footed; Himmler had a mongoloid face; Hess had bushy dark eyebrows and buckteeth; Borman was stocky and round-skulled. In Hitler himself one will look in vain for the blond hair, tall and forceful stature, and the longish skull, although some say he had blue eyes. There were countless jokes abroad about the non-Aryan features of the Nazi leadership, and many jokers ended up in a concentration camp.

In practice *Volk* was identified with *Rasse*, and Hitler will direct his propaganda towards a definition of both to fit within the framework of his intentions without bothering the volkisch romantics too much. "A race is what we have to become – at least consciously" is one of his pithiest formulations, reported by Henry Picker in the *Table Talk*.[48] We note again that Hitler omits to take the past of the

---

[45] Christian von Krockow: *Hitler und seine Deutschen*, p. 85.
[46] Hermann Rauschning, op. cit., p. 128.
[47] See the chapter in Ron Rosenbaum's *Explaining Hitler:* "Fritz Gehrlich and the Trial of Hitler's Nose".
[48] *Hitlers Tischgespräche im Führerhauptquartier*, p. 694.

glorious Aryan-Nordic-Germanic race into account. What, then, were they according to Hitler, the contemporary Germans, pride and fulcrum of humanity? The answer may surprise: they were an 'adulterated' people. "Our volkisch stock has been so much adulterated by the mixture of alien elements that, in its fight for power, Jewry can make use of the more or less 'cosmopolitan' circles which exist among us, inspired by the pacifist and international ideologies." Hitler, as we know, had notions of Gobineau: "The adulteration of the blood and racial deterioration conditioned thereby are the only causes that account for the decline of ancient civilizations; for it is never by war that peoples are ruined, but by the loss of their powers of resistance, which are exclusively a characteristic of pure racial blood ... The Aryan neglected to maintain his own racial stock unmixed and therewith lost the right to live in the paradise which he himself had created."

The Germans, just like any other race in the world, had neglected to keep their blood pure. "Unfortunately the German national being is not based on a uniform racial type. The process of welding the original elements together has not gone so far as to warrant us in saying that a new race has emerged. On the contrary, the poison which has invaded the body of the Volk, especially since the Thirty Year's War, has destroyed the uniform constitution not only of our blood but also of our national soul. The open frontiers of our native country, the association with non-German foreign elements in the territories that lie along our frontiers, and especially the strong influx of the blood into the interior of the Reich itself, have prevented any complete assimilation of those various elements, because the influx has continued steadily. Out of this melting-pot a new race arose. The heterogeneous continue to exist side by side ... Beside the Nordic type we find the East-European type, beside the Eastern there is the Dinaric, the Western type intermingling with both, and hybrids among them all."

In due course this situation would lead, as it would for the peoples all over the world, to a complete mongrelisation, and ultimately to the extinction of humanity as pictured by Gobineau. Yet the Germans – who would have expected otherwise? – were an exception, which Hitler explains as follows: "Though on the one hand it may be a drawback that our racial elements were not welded together, so that no homogeneous body of the Volk could develop, on the other hand it was fortunate that, since at least a part of our best blood was thus kept pure, its racial quality was not debased." He explains nowhere how this miracle happened. "A benefit which results from the fact that there was no all-round assimilation is to be seen in that even now we have large groups of German Nordic people within our national organization, and that their blood has not been mixed with the blood of other races."[49] These sentences would become the tenets of the Nazi state and are no more than a fictitious justification of a pseudo-historical process, concocted to demonstrate the primacy of the Germans as a race, a Volk, a nation.

But if the possibility to regenerate the German race still existed, how much time would this take? In *Mein Kampf* Hitler paints a rather grim picture of such an eventual regeneration, which was the main goal of the National-Socialist movement, as all its other targets depended upon it. "Look at the ravages from which our people are suffering daily as a result of being contaminated with Jewish blood. Bear in mind the fact that this poisonous contamination can be eliminated from the national body only after centuries, or perhaps never [!] Think further of how the process of racial decomposition is debasing and in some cases even destroying the fundamental Aryan qualities of our German people, so that our cultural creativeness as a nation is gradually becoming impotent and we are running the danger, at least in our great cities, of falling to the level where Southern Italy is today. This pestilential adulteration of the blood, of which hundreds of thousands of our people take no account, is systematically practised by the Jew today."

---

[49] Adolf Hitler, op. cit., pp. 508, 248, 332, 333.

Hitler also wrote the following, which may be taken as a summing up of his basic ideas on the subject of race: "Therewith we may lay down the following principle as valid: every racial mixture leads of necessity sooner or later to the downfall of the mongrel product, provided the higher racial stratum of this cross-breed has not retained within itself some sort of racial homogeneity. The danger to the mongrels [which is what the Germans had become at the time these words were written] ceases only when this higher stratum, which has maintained certain standards of homogeneous breeding, ceases to be true to its pedigree and intermingles with mongrels. This principle is the source of a slow but constant regeneration whereby all the poison which has invaded the racial body is gradually eliminated so long as there still remains a fundamental stock of pure racial elements which resists further cross-breeding ... There is only one right that is sacrosanct and this right is at the same time a most sacred duty. This right and obligation are: that the purity of the racial blood should be guarded, so that the best types of human beings may be preserved, and that thus we should render possible a more noble development of humanity itself ... The State should consecrate [matrimony] as an institution which is called upon to produce creatures made in the likeness of the Lord and not create monsters that are a mixture of man and ape."[50]

"Even if it were proved that there never has existed an Aryan race in the past, we want that there be one in the future. This is what matters for men of action."[51] These are not words of Adolf Hitler but of Houston Chamberlain, and they illustrate once more how certain force lines in the thought of the German people converge in Hitler. However abstract, dry or dull the above quotations from *Mein Kampf* may appear: it is these words which would be elaborated into the racial doctrine of the Nazi state, formulated in the directives of the SS, justify the teachings and experiments of the Nazis' racial

---

[50]Id., pp. 459, 460, 336, 337.
[51]Klaus von See, op. cit., p. 292.

pseudo-science, and in the end result in the piles of corpses bulldozed into mass graves at Buchenwald and so many other places of unprecedented horror. Reasonably speaking Hitler's convictions were balderdash, but they were made effective by a people's neurotic pride, and lethal by its submission to a 'genius' who proved to be an archangel of Death.

9

THE VOLKISCH MOVEMENT

Politics consist less of rationality than of myths and mythologies.
                                                    MICHEL WINOCK

We must constantly bear in mind that it was precisely these fantasies that were taken seriously.
                                                    GEORGE MOSSE

We have met the word 'volkisch' time and again and found that it is directly related to, if not synonymous with, terms like race, people and nation. John Weiss says that 'volkist', his Anglicisation of *völkisch*, "is a term derived from [the German] *Volk*, or people,* but indicating a tribal unity of blood, unmodified by ideas of a common humanity. Religious in the intensity of their beliefs, volkists had no real equivalent in other Western nations".[1]

---

*The common origin of *Volk* and the English words 'folk' or 'folks', 'folklore', 'folk tale', 'folk music', etc. is significant.
[1]John Weiss: *Ideology of Death*, p. 108.

The Volkisch movement forms an important part of George Mosse's seminal essay *The Crisis of German Ideology*, in which he writes: "*Volk* is a much more comprehensive term than 'people', for to German thinkers ever since the birth of German romanticism in the late eighteenth century *Volk* signified the union of a group of people with a transcendental 'essence'. This 'essence' might be called 'nature' or 'cosmos' or 'mythos', but in each instance it was fused to man's innermost nature and represented the source of his creativity, his depth of feeling, his individuality and his unity with other members of the *Volk*. The essential element here is the linking of the human soul with its natural surroundings, with the 'essence' of nature."[2]

Hermann Gilbhard sees it like this: "At the core of the volkisch idea is the thought that the *Volk*, as the supreme entity, stands above the state, that it precedes the state and surpasses it. In a way, only the *Volk*, in opposition to the state and to society, is considered sacred. The concept *völkisch*, which after 1918 became a widespread political slogan, is defined in the Brockhaus [an authoritative German dictionary] as 'Germanization of the word 'national' in the sense of a kind of nationalism which is based on the idea of race and therefore decidedly anti-Semitic'."[3]

What a *Volk* generally has in common is its language, also held by many linguistic researchers as well as volkisch believers to be the sacred 'mother tongue' and even capable, if not of creating it, at least of binding a *Volk* together. Most of the German literary men and philosophers mentioned in previous chapters have pronounced panegyrics on their language, some even declaring it to have been the language of Adam. Hitler stated in *Mein Kampf*: "What makes a people or, to be more correct, a race, is not language but blood". Nonetheless, the Greater German Reich was intended to encompass all German- and Germanic-speaking peoples, whether Dutch, Flemish, Scandinavian, Alsatian, Swiss, Polish, Czech, or whichever. As we

---

[2]George Mosse: *The Crisis of German Ideology*, p. 4.
[3]Hermann Gilbhard: *Die Thule-Gesellschaft*, p. 35.

have seen, race, and still more blood, was practically indefinable, and so therefore was *Volk*. But language, the mother tongue, was very much definable and in fact the criterion of determining who belonged to the German *Volk*.

Throughout his career Hitler did a lot of juggling with the words *Volk*, race, state and nation, using them according to his mood and inspiration. "The word *volkisch* does not express any clearly specified idea", we read in *Mein Kampf*. It is 'a vague concept' which 'everybody interprets in his own way'. We know, however, that he could not do without the volkisch multitude from which he had to recruit his own people and of which the concepts were so closely associated with Germany's past and future, and with its greatness as a people and a nation. Therefore we find a few pages further on in *Mein Kampf*: "The volkisch concept of the world is in profound accord with Nature's will because it restores the free play of the forces which will lead the race through stages of sustained reciprocal education towards a higher type, until finally the best portion of mankind will possess the earth and will be free to work in every domain all over the world and even reach spheres that lie outside the earth [?] We all feel that in the distant future man may be faced with problems which can be solved only by a superior race of human beings, a race destined to become master of all the other peoples and which will have at its disposal the means and resources of the whole world".

"Contrary to Himmler, Hitler was sparing with esoteric and mythological speculations in public", writes Rüdiger Sünner. "This is rather an indication of his tactical skill than of his vision of the world, which was anything but rational ... His occasional digs at Himmler's Germanic cult or at volkisch-occult organizations make clear that he did condemn the unearthliness of such groupings but not the ideas underlying them. Besides, Hitler was extremely discreet in matters of personal belief, and he always knew how to adapt his words to the opinions of his audience. When probing deeper into them, however, one discerns behind his ideology a supporting base of mythology without which his so often extolled mission of the Aryans would not be comprehensible. In this, together with apocalyptic Christian elements which we find sometimes in his sayings, legends, sagas and symbols relating to the Nordic myths played an important role".[4]

For sure, Hitler had always been fascinated by the sagas and legends about the German past, even during his drab years in Vienna, as we know from August Kubizek. Perhaps the most formative element of his vision and his mission was the mythological world created by Richard Wagner. Considering the contradictions between his rejection of the volkisch lore and the importance some of it had for him, we cannot but conclude that at the bottom of both contradictory attitudes there lay something else but fundamental which he did not speak out – about which 'he was extremely discreet', as Sünner says – and which was of crucial importance to understand him. We will have to return to this later. For the time being, we have to remain satisfied with Mosse's conclusion that, for Hitler, "the volkisch thinkers did not respond to 'real' developments in the manner of political commentators. In fact, the nature of their ideas tended to detach them from real events rather than compel them to take new developments into consideration ... It was the genius of Adolf Hitler to wed the volkisch flight from reality to political discipline and efficient political organization".[5]

Volkisch romanticism

The importance of the Volkisch movement can be deduced from its diversity, by which it adapted itself to all aspects of German life, and from the number of its adherents. This was a popular movement in the real sense of the word. It found much of its justification in the enduring appraisal of the literature of the great romanticists Herder,

---

[4]Rüdiger Sünner: *Schwarze Sonne*, p. 54.
[5]Georges Mosse, op. cit., p. 9.

Goethe, Schiller, Novalis and others. A supposedly glorious past, the communication with that past in the sanctuaries of nature and at the sites of the prehistoric monuments, a contact with the deepest individual soul fusing with the soul of the Volk, and an experience of the forces of nature, which were the forces of gods thought to have been long dead and forgotten but in fact still very much alive – these main romanticist themes were now revived and felt to be more important than ever. The reason was the increasingly intense confrontation with the modern, urban way of living in the West. The German 'new romanticism' corresponded exactly with the great European period of intellectual upheaval and innovation which started around 1880.

"Besides the orders founded by List and Lanz, dozens of other volkisch-esoteric groups shot up from the soil which began to fill the intellectual and religious vacuum ... with a kind of secret underground movement", writes Sünner. "Next to the Neo-Germanics appear also free religious movements, associations of vegetarians, nudists and Heimat-lovers along with theosophical and anthropological circles. The *Wandervögel* [migratory birds, sometimes translated as 'birds of passage'] too belong to this large mass of people in search of meaning. In them a gradual development takes place from beginnings in romanticism and a mysticism of nature to an ever stronger ideological polarization, till in the end their members enter practically without friction into the youth movements of the National-Socialist regime ... Dozens of such organizations are founded with names which most often already tell the way they intend to follow". Sünner gives a few examples: Midgard Fraternity [in Nordic mythology 'Midgard' is the garden at the centre of the world], Young Germans, Goths, Order of Young Germans, Nordic Tribe, League of Loyalty for an Uplifting Life, Friends of the Light, Vikings, Eagle and Falcon, Storm Bird, etc.[6]

---

[6]Rüdiger Sünner, op. cit., p. 23.

All these groups of very dedicated and mostly young people – National Socialism too has been characterised as a youth movement – turned their back on the present and sought meaning and solace in the past. There were similar movements in other countries, but not on this scale or with this intensity. Most amazingly, Germany, at a time of an unheard-of economic and material expansion, turned inwardly away from a modern, progressive world with which it could not identify and to which it felt superior. Considering the dimension of this singular movement by an entire nation, soon to be equipped with the most advanced means for peace and war, a confrontation with its rival nations was practically inevitable – and would occur in the summer of 1914. Indeed, "the turning back towards the past is the political programme of all nationalists; they see in the revival of myth their political future". (Michael Ley[7]) After all we have seen in the last chapters there can be no doubt that Germany identified itself as a nation with the future of the world, which it had to rule and lead on the right path – something which could only come about after a series of armed conflicts.

Considerations of this kind make Michael Burleigh quip that Germany was "going boldly into the future in search of an imaginary past".[8] Volker Mauersberger, narrating the surrender to the Nazis of Weimar – as the town of Goethe, Schiller and Nietzsche a symbol of German culture – quotes a historian who said that the Volkisch movement, culminating in Nazism, was "the reconstruction of a past which was resplendently gilded in the collective memory of the Germans".[9] It is an amazing fact that so many learned and highly cultured intellectuals, expressing the spirit of a Volk, could turn a mostly fictional past into a sequence of manifestations of paradise upon earth, although they had the historical sources demonstrating

---

[7] Michael Ley: *Apokalypse und Moderne*, p. 38.
[8] Michael Burleigh: *The Third Reich – A New History*, p. 50.
[9] Volker Mauersberger: *Hitler in Weimar*, p. 98.

the contrary at their disposal. To the insecure and fearful human species the future is a constant threat and the present a problem that is never solved, while the past becomes more and more embellished, 'gilded', the farther it drops away.

"O what a delightful time the Middle Ages were, when everything was learned under the guidance of masters", mused Paul de Lagarde[10] — when knights in shining armour lived in draughty, crowded castles and died of the most common illnesses because there was no known cure, and when the major part of the population lived the miserable existence of serfs. Greatly admired by the German youth were the orders of fighting monks, especially the Knights Templar and the Teutonic Knights, because they put their lives unconditionally at the service of an ideal. It is typical for the admirers of olden times to fancy themselves in the most glamorous roles, where they never have to smell the stench of rottenness, suffering and death.

Another much sung period was that of the Vikings, who were not Germans but Danes, Norwegians and Swedes. Bands of marauding adventurers in their long boats, they were allotted by their volkisch-minded admirers the role of conquerors and dispensers of culture. It is true that, in spite of themselves, History knew how to use their bold spirit of enterprise. It were Vikings who, having become the French-speaking Normans, won the Battle of Hastings in 1066; who, as settlers in southern Italy, participated in the First Crusade under King Bohemund; who descended the great Russian rivers and traded at Kiev; who even became the palace guard of the emperor at Constantinople.

"The German, in his historic reality, is hardly more than a fiction", states Klaus von See.[11] In how far were the Nibelungs Germanic? Brunehild was 'Norse', probably Icelandic; Siegfried came from Xanten, in the present-day Netherlands; the good king Gunther and

---

[10] In George Mosse, op. cit., p. 35.
[11] Klaus von See: *Barbar, Germane, Arier*, p. 29.

his knights were Burgundians; and Kriemhild married Attila the Hun. Nevertheless, the *Nibelungen Treue*, the legendary loyalty of the Nibelungs, would become the highest praised of German virtues, and Himmler had it embroidered on the sleeves of his SS: *Meine Ehre heisst Treue*, loyalty is what honour means to me – loyalty to the death.

Following the sources of the main German myths backward in time, we arrive at Arminius the Cheruscian, the illustrious Hermann, slayer of three Roman legions in the year 9 CE and later murdered by people of his own tribe. The volkisch attitude towards the Romans remained ambivalent, for the Romans, inheritors of the Greek culture, had been undoubtedly a civilised people; but they were 'southerners' who had intended to conquer the Germans, which would have cut the latter from their racial roots and bastardized them. To quote Fichte: "If the Romans had succeeded in subjugating the German people too, and to annihilate them as a nation [which they were not], then the whole further development of humanity would have taken a different, probably less pleasant direction".[12] Moreover, had not the Romans allowed Jewish Christianity to erode their strength from within, a neglect which would lead to the dissolution of their empire?

More securely appreciated than the Romans were the ancient Greeks, not only because they had never confronted the Germanic tribes but also because their culture was evidently of a higher order than the Roman civilisation, which had borrowed so much from them and still remained practical and square. The Greeks, as well as the Romans, had been of Germanic stock. Indeed, the simplest logical reasoning showed you that, if all higher culture was originally due to the Aryans, cultured peoples like the Greeks and the Romans must have been of Aryan blood, and Aryan meant the same as Germanic. Hitler, borrowing from the volkisch tradition when it suited him or when he did not know better, was of the same opinion. "By the Greeks he meant the Dorians. Naturally his view was affected

---

[12] In Michael Ley, op. cit., p. 35.

by the theory, fostered by the scientists of his period, that the Dorian tribe which migrated into Greece from the north had been of Germanic origin and that, therefore, its culture had not belonged to the Mediterranean world."[13] "When one asks who were our forefathers, we must always point back to the Greeks", Hitler said.[14]

Everything belonging to this exalted but fictitious past shared in the volkisch adulation. The runes, used from the second century CE till the end of the Middle Ages, and brought back into the focus of volkisch attention by Guido von List, were widely studied as symbols and sacred signs of power. Most (in)famous would become the double *sig* rune which the SS wore on the lapels of their uniforms, while their honorific ring, designed by the magician Weisthor, a friend of Himmler, was also inscripted with runic signs. "Prehistorians generally accepted that the runes had possessed a symbolism over and above their phonetic value and use in writing, so that they were accordingly used for divination, the casting of lots, magical invocations, and the preparation of amulets and charms."[15] To the followers of the volkisch movement, the runes became a sacred, quasi initiatory alphabet.

This sacral character was assigned to anything which had survived from ancient times or which was assumed to have any connection with those times. Former holy shrines, like the Extern Rocks, became places of pilgrimage and improvised neo-pagan rites. "You wander through the expanses of the German heath, where loneliness is most deeply felt, and you stand there fascinated by the remains of the mighty burial sites of your forefathers. Suddenly you hear whispered words, uttered in silent earnest, about your fathers, o German! These words keep resounding in your memory and you understand them, the silent language of life long past but eternally renewed ... Names and pictures resurface from history and from the realm of

---

[13] Albert Speer: *Inside the Third Reich*, p. 151.
[14] *Monologe im Führerhauptquartier*, pp. 214, 232.
[15] Nicholas Goodrick-Clarke: *The Occult Roots of Nazism*, p. 157.

legend, and you envision again their deepest meaning!" Sünner quotes these words from one of the volkisch periodicals, *Nordland*.

"Such thoughts were often found in books and reviews of the Third Reich", continues Sünner. "Their aim was to replace gradually the Christian prayers and visits to the church by a new creed and 'Germanic places of worship'. Especially the SS re-evaluated the megalithic burial sites as 'sanctuaries of stone' and 'houses of eternity' ... The people of six thousand years ago, said the SS review *Das Schwarze Korps*, had piled blocks weighing many tonnes one upon another 'to tell their descendants in times to come about their distant era before history and the greatness of their people. The eternal succession, passed on by the blood from father to son of the same Nordic leadership from millennium to millennium, found in these ancient family tombs – for this is what they were, the colossal megalithic structures in the North – its most meaningful symbolical expression. Born from the soil, built with material provided by Nature and with a gigantic combination of human strength, these structures of eternity are meant to survive millennia without number and to inform us about the dawn of history, when for the first time generations of leaders emerged and began to guide the people'".

And Sünner concludes: "Today we know very little about the so-called 'megalithic culture' whose dolmen, stone circles and burial hills have been erected everywhere in Europe since circa 4000 BCE; they seem to tell of a religion which must have had command, before the Egyptian pyramids, of considerable technical and astronomical knowledge. To this culture belong not only Stonehenge in England and Newgrange in Ireland, but also similar megalithic constructions in Portugal, Spain and the island of Malta. Whether they originated in north-western Europe and spread from there towards the east, or vice versa, remains controversial among the experts ... These stone relicts have hardly any connection with the early history of the Germanic tribes or with the Germans".[16]

---

[16] Rüdiger Sünner, op. cit., pp. 67-69.

Back to nature

Nature was the temple of God where, in ever varying beauty, harmony and grandeur, one could communicate with Him and contact one's inmost soul. Nature was timeless and allowed one to transcend time. In nature everything was the visible expression of the life-forces; there one could come to rest from the frenzy and artificiality of the oppressive human conglomerates which were the modern towns and cities. Romanticism had been one big hymn to nature, conciliating man with suffering and death, and it was to nature that 'the new romanticism', refusing to yield to modern life, turned back. "Many of our generation sought such contact with nature", wrote Albert Speer, the son of a stiffly conventional upper middle-class family. "This was not merely a romantic protest against the narrowness of middle-class life. We were also escaping from the demands of a world growing increasingly complicated. We felt that the world around us was out of balance. In nature, in the mountains and the river valleys, the harmony of creation could still be felt. The more virginal the mountains, the lovelier the river valleys, the more they drew us."[17]

Joachim Fest, the biographer of Speer as well as of Hitler, comments: "His love of nature was even more formative, and probably also more typical [than his love for the great romanticist literature]. The mountain tours that he made with his future wife in those years and paddling in a canoe were, he later said, a form of 'bliss'. This euphoria was inspired by the simple life in mountain huts and boat houses, the hours of silent harmony and being deeply moved by nature. The world was far away. Up on those heights there were unforgettable moments when he experienced pity for the 'wretched people' below the cloud banks who were subjected to the narrowness, the noise and the bustle of the city. This was the side of 'the war youth generation' that shunned reality ... This rejection of reality

---

[17]Albert Speer, op. cit., p. 39.

was not an individual impulse but a widespread mood of the day".[18]

The nineteenth century had been the century of the bourgeoisie. The ideals of the American and French revolutions had never gained the spontaneous adherence of the religious creed they had replaced. The result was a dry, conventional morality, of which the norms were constantly breeched by the vital urges in the human being. (It was on such soil that Freud's perceptions arose.) The youth, fresh before the future, suffered from the hollowness behind the factitious façade of the bourgeois world, in Germany more than anywhere else, because there the militaristic hierarchisation of society lend a touch of the grotesque to bourgeois everyday life.

"The beginning of the youth organizations is still idyllic and partly carried by the real utopian and emancipationist spirit", writes Sünner. "They profit from the general crisis in which the family, the school and the Church are involved. The family ties form no longer a close unity which would be able to provide a seeking youth with aims and values. The younger ones long for enthusiasm, tests of courage and overwhelming experiences with which neither pastor nor teacher can provide them. It is in this no man's land that student unions and other groups appear in which the restless and experience-hungry youth come together. The *Wandervogel* is founded in 1904; its groupings will become the main reception centre of all such expectations and longings, and they will expand fast. 'Trekking should teach us to see and to envision' is one of the points in their programme. The intense common experience of the landscape, culture, usages and traditions of the land of one's fathers is at the centre of their excursions. They build tent camps and fires, prepare their meals together and sleep under the starry sky. Old-German feasts are brought to life again."[19]

---

[18]Joachim Fest: *Speer – The Final Verdict*, p. 21.
[19]Rüdiger Sünner, op. cit., p. 24.

Fest sees the youth movement as a specifically German tradition, despairing of modernity. "Filled with terror the youth identified the dictates of the hour with the crisis into which their familiar world had plunged, and combined their reaction with the 'world role' they assigned to their country, although it had only just been united and attained power. That role consisted in the specifically German mission to preserve 'culture' against the destructive assault of 'civilization'. The country's defeat and the disgrace inflicted upon it merely intensified the pain of what was happening, lending it universal significance."[20] Around the year 1900 this way of experiencing the world had already produced "a vanguard of associations and groupings, the most notable of which were the life-reforming groups which sprang up everywhere". Vegetarianism became fashionable, as did naturopathy and the propagation of all kinds of 'natural' diets. Nudism was practiced with abandon, and so were astrology and the other symbolical arts, stimulated by the teachings of theosophy, ariosophy and anthroposophy. Spiritism will become widely practiced after the Great War, when the countless bereaved ones sought communication across the material confines with their fallen husbands, brothers and sons. This was 'New Age' *avant la lettre*, but as varied as in the nineteen-sixties and taken up with no less conviction.

"They rebelled against the bourgeois world and all that went with it: the neuroses and the high-flown banality, the hypocrisy and the sham, the operatic German myths and the indoor palm. They wanted to replace them with simplicity, love of nature, dedication and the values they engendered. These categories in themselves reveal how far removed from reality those who subscribed to these new beginnings were. None of the rebellious demands they made of their world contained a feasible model of society. It often seemed that they did not so much intend to change the state of affairs they all

---

[20]Joachim Fest, op. cit., p. 22.

deplored as just to vent their anger at it ... 'Swayed by youthful passion and mindless', is how Speer characterized himself, looking back on those years. But the description applied to his generation as a whole, and any 'bliss', no matter how deeply felt, merely amounted to empty self-satisfaction."[21]

"There were already many youth organizations of this kind before the First World War", Bronder too points out, "protesting against the satisfaction and the bourgeois mentality of their world, the end of which was greeted with jubilation in 1914. From the 'German Youth' originated the movement of the *Wandervogel*, many of whose best elements would later join National-Socialism ... Their ideology was based on the 'blood and soil' motto, hate against all civilization and liberalism, humanism and pacifism, social democracy and Bolshevism, as well as against Judaism." After 1918 the youth movement became dominated by the "volkisch-anti-Semitic-pan-German" thought, says Bronder; the social-democratic Weimar Republic did no longer seem worthwhile to be defended, and they wanted to replace its humanitarian stance with values like communal life, egalitarianism, authority, obedience, and the 'leadership principle', the notorious *Führerprinzip*, which will become the backbone of Nazism.

Most members of the volkisch youth associations enlisted as volunteers for the front and created 'the Langemarck Myth' of unconditional obedience to any command and the sacrifice of one's life for the nation. (Langemarck is the name of a small place in Flanders where a bloody First World War battle was fought.) "Individuality was replaced by the collective, the separate group integrated into the 'tribe', common maintenance chores were called 'service', and all activities went accompanied by shouted orders, drum rolls, fanfares and militant soldiers' and Landsknechts' songs. Life in the Hitler Youth, the German Army and the SS presented

---
[21] Ibid.

their recruits with very little they had not already known in one or other of their youth organizations."²²

Whose soul was linked more closely with 'the essence of nature' than that of the son of the soil, the countryman, the farmer, the peasant? To the volkisch eye the peasant was the original and true German, guardian of the knowledge of yore, in permanent contact and exchange with the forces of nature. The praise of the peasant is sung in many pages of Oswald Spengler's *Untergang des Abendlandes (The Decline of the West)*, a book that like few others mirrors the aspirations and desperations of the period in Germany which occupies us. The peasant, by living and working the way he does, 'becomes a plant himself', writes Spengler. He has his roots in the soil he tills. "The soul of the human discovers a soul in the landscape; a new tie of existence with the earth, a new way of feeling manifests itself. Inimical nature turns into a friend. The earth becomes Mother Earth. Between sowing and growing, harvest and death a deeply felt relation is revealed. A new devotion addresses itself in a chtonic cult to the fertile soil, which grows together with the human being."²³

Spengler's book, written during the war and published in 1918, made a general impact on the masses of young people who wanted to find their bearings after the horrors of Langemarck, Paschendaele, Ypres and *Le chemin des dames* – together with those who had wanted to join their brothers in sacrifice on the battlefield, but who had been too young and were now without prospects in a time of unemployment and overall turmoil. To go and live as farmers on the land was the dream of many of the toughest members of the Free Corps. They went fighting in Poland and the Baltic lands not only to push the Bolsheviks back but also to find there a plot of land for them to till and spend the rest of their days in peace. This will remain an important factor in the German ambition of conquering the fertile lands of Russia, and Hitler will describe in detail the

---

²²Dietrich Bronder: *Bevor Hitler kam*, pp. 216 ff.
²³Oswald Spengler: *Der Untergang des Abendlandes*, p. 660.

fortified farms he intended to build there for his warrior-farmers, lords over a population of Slavonic slaves.

Heinrich Himmler was one of those who kept the dream of the volkisch farmer alive, after having tried in vain to join the Army at the end of the war and to march under the flag of one of the Free Corps. Himmler became a member of the *Artamanen*,* a volkisch league founded in 1924 by young men and women whose ideal it was to live on the land and till it with all their dedication and strength in the manner they supposed their forefathers had done in olden times. "This association was already known to me through their publications at the time I was still in prison, and I have given it the best of myself. It was an association of young, volkisch-conscious people, boys and girls, from the youth movements of all nationalist-minded political parties, who wanted to return to a natural way of living on the land, far from the unhealthy, confusing and superficial life in the towns, especially in the cities. They despised alcohol and nicotine – in fact all that is harmful to a healthy development of the spirit and the body. Guided by these principles, they wanted a complete return to the soil from which their forbears had come, to the fount of life of the German people, to the healthy way of living of the peasant."[24]

The man who wrote these words, shortly before being executed by hanging, was Rudolf Höss, the former commandant of Auschwitz. Many prominent Nazis and SS-chiefs had passed through the volkisch

---

Artamanen should not be confused with *Armanen*, Guido von List's name for the supermen who, throughout history, kept the primeval Germanic tradition alive and of whom a few were incarnated as high priests even now. The Artamanen were founded in 1924 by Willibald Henschel as "an exponent of racial hygiene, whose aim was to renew the Germanic race" (Peter Padfield, *Himmler*, p. 37). The meaning of the name is explained in different ways, but according to Padfield "expressed an attitude which saw cities as sinks of decadence and the land as the real source of strength of a people". At one time Himmler was a regional leader of the Artamanen in Bavaria.

[24] Rudolf Höss: *Kommandant in Auschwitz*, pp. 76-77.

and disciplined life of the Artamanen, for instance Walter Darré, leading SS-ideologist and Hitler's Minister of Agriculture, and Martin Bormann, after Hess' flight to Great Britain as Hitler's private secretary one of the most powerful and dangerous men in the Third Reich. Bormann's wife Gerda, a fanatical Nazi, wrote: "He [her husband] divided all the people in three groups: peasants, rooted in the soil, nomads roaming through the steppes, and parasites living from trade and commerce. The representatives of the peasants, rooted in the soil, are we [the Germans], the Japanese and the Chinese. Only the people who are rooted in the soil have real culture; they know that they have to protect the heritage of their forefathers, and that their labour will bear fruit for their children and grandchildren. Their whole being turns around the concepts of seed and harvest".[25] It may be assumed that people talking like this were admiring the countryman from the comfortable position of not being one – of not being duty-bound year-in year-out to labour on the soil and care for the animals on the farm, day after unforgiving day from early morning till late at night.

If the country was good, the city was bad; a harvest was nature's gift from the land, a city was man's product from the mind; 'culture' was related to the land and healthy, 'civilization' was an artefact of man's brain, rootless, and symptomatic of decline. This dualism is again abundantly expounded by Spengler in his utterly negative book. (For Spengler, as for Gobineau, humanity had no purpose.) "The colossus of stone that is the metropolis stands at the end of the lifetime of every culture", he wrote. "This mass of stone contains the exalted symbolism of the death of what finally 'has been'." Cities are mind, nothing but mind, without contact with the soil, with the life-giving womb of nature. "Man becomes 'mind', free and similar to the nomads, but more narrow and cold. 'Mind' is the specific urban form of the apprehending awareness. All art, all religion and

---

[25] Anna Maria Sigmund: *Die Frauen der Nazis II*, p. 37.

science become gradually mental, foreign to the land, incomprehensible to the earth-bound peasants. Civilization is the onset of the menopause of a people. The age-old roots of being are withered in the stone masses of their cities. The free mind looks like a flame which rises into the air in splendour and slowly evaporates."[26]

Once more we meet with a thinker who condemns thinking as a symptom of decadence and would like to dispense with it, in order to return to a peasant-like existence free from the burden of reflection. Texts like this one by Spengler bear witness to the neurosis the German people were suffering from. A nation which was technologically the most advanced in the world was expressing doubt as to modernity and progress, and dreaming of going back to embellished values of a past which had never existed. But the powers responsible for and profiting from Germany's first economic *Wirtschaftswunder* will not allow its industry and economy to stop in their tracks; on the contrary, they will bundle their strength to make their nation ever more prosperous and domineering over the rest of the world. But they will put their superior position at the service of what was essentially the volkisch vision, taking pride in their difference from a materialistic, hollow modernism, and feeling convinced that they stood above everybody else as a race, a culture and a nation.

A German religion

The 'North-South divide', in fact a confrontation of the Germans and their *Kultur* with the humanist West-European spirit, was the expression of an attitude induced by a very old streak in the subconscious memory of the German people. It was fundamentally the same divide which had opposed the Roman civilisation against the barbarian world of the Germanic tribes, who afterwards, in wave

---

[26] Oswald Spengler, op. cit., p. 664.

after wave, had poured over Europe in the first centuries of the Christian era. The Roman civilisation had been felt as an imposition of a way of life which was foreign to the Germanic nature and soul. Still more so was felt the Christianisation which Romanised rulers had imposed on the 'pagans' by force; for if the Roman empire had sought to integrate the conquered peoples, the Catholic Church allowed for no compromise, and conversion was often a matter of life and death. (Charlemagne, 'slaughterer of the Saxons', had thousands of them killed for resisting baptism.) One German author puts it as follows: the Catholic Church was always considered "a foreign presence within the spirit of the Germanic people".[27] The response with which Luther met in 1517 was much more than instant enthusiasm: the Germans had been ready for a long time "to recapture the fortress stolen by Christianity".

To be sure, the Christianisation of the heathen tribes had been a crude crusade. "Like it or not, this is what our sources tell us over and again: demonstration of the power of the Christian God meant conversion. Miracles, wonders, exorcisms, temple-scorching and shrine-smashing were in themselves acts of evangelization", writes Richard Fletcher in his *Conversion of Europe*.[28] It had to be demonstrated to the barbarians that the Christian God was more powerful than their gods. The Christian God could command the weather, restore health, win battles and provide his worshippers with wealth and healthy offspring. The holy places of the pagans, whether natural sites or constructions erected by human hands, were to be destroyed and Christian churches built in their stead. (The cathedral of Chartres, the Notre-Dame in Paris, the Dom in Cologne and St Paul's Cathedral in London were constructed on former sites of pagan temples.) The gods of the pagans were all declared to be demons. "The demons also persuaded men to build

---

[27] Moritz Bassler and Hildegard Châtellier (ed.): *Mystique, mysticisme et modernité en Allemagne autour de 1900*, p. 172.
[28] Richard Fletcher: *The Conversion of Europe*, p. 45.

their temples, to place there images or statues of wicked men and to set up altars to them, on which they might pour out the blood not only of animals but even of men. Besides, many demons, expelled from heaven, also preside either in the sea or in rivers or springs or forests; men ignorant of God also worship these as gods and sacrifice to them", wrote Martin, bishop of Braga.

Yet, to change one's religion is a complicated long-term process. The instruction of the pagans in the articles of the creed was less than rudimentary, and the belief in the gods who had since times immemorial presided over their destiny lived on in secret. Ordinary religion is in the first place, a matter of instinctive fear; if you fall short of your religious obligations the gods will punish you, make you or your kin ill, confuse your brain, lure you into a trap, strike you with cowardice in battle, have you killed or make you die in your bed and refuse you entrance into the heaven of the warriors, Walhalla. The Christian God had to prove that he was able to protect against such misfortunes, and if the newly converted remained unconvinced, they returned to their old gods, often clandestinely. "The Christian God is a god of the churches. The churches are his castles. Every seven days the people have to show up and he holds a speech to his faithful. Then they return into the indifferent field of everyday life. They still gibe for a while or mock for a while what the foreign god has told them; soon it is forgotten. They bring back the old gods from their hiding places, the wise old woman and the shepherd who knows the good old magic formulas. And they work according to the ten commandments of the Lord of their forefathers."[29]

"The piety of the countryman in the present day is older than Christianity. His gods are older than any higher religion", wrote Spengler.[30] Hitler too considered Christianity no more than a thin layer of veneer on a massive substance of old traditions and beliefs.

---

[29] Stefanie von Schnurbein and Justus Ulbricht (ed.): *Völkische Religion und Krisen der Moderne*, p. 170.
[30] Oswald Spengler, op. cit., p. 669.

Romanticism had directed the attention back to nature and to the powers the Germans had venerated for many centuries before being burdened with Christianity. Now the 'new romanticism', with a treasure of newly translated sagas and legends and new, visionary interpretations at its disposal – Guido von List's foremost among them – upgraded what formerly had been inspired literature to the status of sacredness. For the volkisch movement it was "unbearable that their Nordic race had borrowed the god of another race, the Semites, and held on to him. Each people has its own God, they asserted, thinking of Nietzsche who once had stated that 'the Nordic races should be embarrassed not to have produced a single own god in two thousand years'".[31]

The authentic need of the volkisch Germans was for a personal, direct experience of the own soul and of God. This presupposed 'a religion without dogmas' which should be *gottesunmittelbar*, without any intermediary to God. A Church always posits itself as the intermediary between the faithful and the Deity, even condemning as blasphemy the effort to approach or experience God directly. 'Religion' is therefore the teaching of a Church summarised in the articles of a creed which has to be accepted; 'spirituality' is the personal, direct approach of God through the soul or through the higher reaches of consciousness. All true mystics have followed one or other path of spirituality, although many of them were forced by their Church to bow to authority.

Martin Luther's popular appeal lay in his claim that every individual had the right to approach God directly – 'every man is his own priest' – but he could not prevent that this originally spiritual way also hardened into a Church, which broke up into a manifold of Churches, all based on some individual experience or other. That Luther was not a solitary phenomenon but the epitome of a German tradition is shown by the writings of Eberlin of

---

[31] Dietrich Bronder, op. cit., p. 219.

Günsburg, whom Léon Poliakov calls "the most popular Lutheran propagandist of the years 1520-30". "The ancient Germans, according to this former Franciscan, were 'good and pious Allemans', Christian people in the true sense of the word. They had long ago been turned away from the straight path by missionaries from Rome, who preached to them an adulterated and 'circumcised' gospel. This is how 'the German people were fraudulently diverted from the [real] Christian faith to the papist law, from plenitude to misery, from truth to lie, from virility to femininity'. But Luther and von Hutten, sent by God, brought back the German people to the straight way. 'It now pleases God to have the real Christian faith spread throughout the world by the German nation', of which they will be capable thanks to their exceptional qualities."[32]

A key-figure in this movement towards a genuine spirituality was Eugen Diederichs (1867-1930), the publisher, we remember, of the *Sammlung Thule*, the series of translations of old Nordic sagas and legends. Not only did Diederichs provide the Volkish movement with translations of the original texts, he was a real power centre for the spreading of a German mysticism adapted to the new times and going back to the in Europe unparalleled tradition of mystics like Hadewych, Meister Eckhart and Angelus Silesius. He recognized that the Protestant theologians after Luther's death were 'shallow quarrellers' who nipped Luther's inspiration in the bud. "I have the strong feeling that I have to steer my publishing house in the direction of a deepened religion without dogmas, and that the coming period will produce the people needed for this purpose", he wrote.[33]

What the youth wanted was 'the God in one's own heart', 'Christ in us'. "The human being obtains its own salvation: this is the new religion", Diederichs wrote. It was only natural that they turned towards Meister Eckhart (c 1260-1328), the great German mystic whose words remain as fresh today as they were seven hundred

---

[32]Léon Poliakov: *Le mythe aryen*, p. 133.
[33]Moritz Bassler and Hildegard Châtellier (ed.), op. cit., p. 169.

years ago. If in the Christian West there is one example of the purest and highest mysticism, it is this experience of a Dominican Prior and Master of the Sorbonne who broke through all prescriptions and all dogmas of the Catholic creed, and through all religious conventions, to meet and become *That* in him. 'That' could no longer be called 'God', for That was all and all was That, including the dissolved I of the mystic experiencer, whose words sounded so revolutionary because they originated from the Source. "It cannot be stressed with sufficient emphasis that Meister Eckhart means more for the Protestants in the future development of a German religion than Luther", wrote Diederichs. "Despite the past four hundred years everything is still to be done: the Reformation is still in its beginning".[34]

No doubt, around the year 1900 there was a sincere aspiration and an opportunity to start an authentic spiritual movement in Germany. Unfortunately, here too the fundamental German ego distorted the purest intentions and made them subservient to the general mentality of the nation. The religious leaders whom Diederichs expected did not show up, and he himself proved in the end not to be immune to the influence of the Pied Piper bearing the crooked cross. The Germans were the superior people – also in matters of religion and spirituality. "Christianity shows itself of such a strong *vis formativa* [power of formation] in no other Volk as in the Germans. Badly handicapped by the presence of a materialist science and held down by the claws of the unsocial people of the Jews, still at the bottom of the German heart the Christian spirit has remained as vivid as in the Middle Ages. At least, it fights nowhere so forcefully against the adverse forces as in Germany. There is no other Volk that has realized 'the fruits of the Kingdom of God' in more beautiful ways than the Germans, and no other Volk that tries in the same measure to produce still more such fruits

---

[34] Id., p. 170.

… If one becomes aware of this highest harmony between the Germans and the Christian spirit, as shown so convincingly in the course of history, does one not have the right to apply to the Germans the words of Christ that other people [than the Jews] will once occupy a chosen position? All the rich fruits which the Christian spirit has borne among the Germans show that Christ's heart itself is German, that it contains the sap of their sap, the blood of their blood."[35] "We must declare ourselves [ie the Nazis] the only true Christians", wrote Joseph Goebbels in his diary.[36]

Nobody was more convinced that the Reformation had remained unfinished than Arthur Dinter, founder in 1927 of a "Fighting League for the Completion of the Reformation". One looks in vain for his name in the *Enzyklopädie des Nationalsozialismus* (1997) although Dinter played a significant role in the formative years of Nazism.[37] He would even claim to be a precursor of Nazism and not hesitate to assert this for all to hear. A militant anti-Semite, he had held one of the very first Jew-baiting speeches as early as 1914, at the Zirkus Busch in Berlin, to a crowd of five thousand. He befriended Dietrich Eckart in Munich and Julius Streicher in Nuremberg, and corresponded from 1916 till 1921 extensively with Houston Chamberlain, whose *Foundations* he considered a revelation.

Dinter had been an officer in the First World War, an experience which hardened his anti-Semitism into fanaticism. Seriously wounded, he was discharged from military service. He now wanted to propagate Chamberlain's ideas in the form of a novel. *The Sin against the Blood* was written in 1917, published in 1921, and became 'a phenomenal best-seller'. The novel "depicts a rich Jew who violates an innocent Aryan girl, polluting her blood. A volkist, Dinter believed that intercourse with a Jew destroyed the capacity of Aryan women to

---

[35] Max Brewer in Stefanie von Schnurbein and Justus Ulbricht (ed.), op. cit., p. 177.
[36] Joseph Goebbels: *Tagebücher*, p. 1049.
[37] The author is indebted for the information in these pages to Martin Sobieroj: *Der Stern des Abgrundes* (manuscript), pp. 139 ff.

reproduce anything but racially polluted offspring",[38] a theme which will be repeated ad nauseam by Julius Streicher.

Dinter became acquainted with Hitler through Eckart and Streicher. At one time he greeted the moustachioed ex-corporal as "the Führer by God's grace, sent by heaven to the German people". He would become *Gauleiter*, i.e. regional leader, of Thuringia, the German federal state which became a hotbed of National-Socialism after having been a centre of revolutionary communist activity, and perhaps in reaction to it. Dinter, now famous for his vicious hatred of the Jews, was also elected a member of the Thuringian parliament at Weimar. In 1928 he was the chief organizer of the first National-Socialist 'Day of the Party' where the Nazis, under the stony gaze of Goethe and Schiller, showed their intentions uninhibitedly and the savage way they were to go about them.[39] It was on this 'Day of the Party' that Hitler, after the debacle of the November Putsch in 1923 and his imprisonment, took the reins of the Party again in his own hand and put an end to the factional squabbles.

Dinter, however, was very much his own man, even when boasting about his early convictions and his closeness to Hitler. Deep within himself he could not accept that Adolf Hitler was the one and only God-sent Führer, for had he himself not been an anti-Semite long before the Austrian even had become interested in such notions, and had he not seen Hitler come to the fore among equals, even among mentally superior people who had acted as his promoters and mentors?

When Ludendorff was still a serious nationalist candidate for the leadership of Germany, Dinter had demanded at a public function that all present would swear to bring the social-democratic government down (this was an act of high treason), and that they stand as one man behind Erich Ludendorff. Now that Hitler was strengthening his grip upon the Party again, it must have become clear to Dinter in which direction the Führer had chosen to go and

---
[38] John Weiss, op. cit., p. 250.
[39] See Volker Mauersberger: *Hitler in Weimar*, pp. 222 ff.

how he distanced himself from everybody else, also from those who had marched by his side.

Dinter would have none of this and protested openly. He resigned as Gauleiter at the end of 1927. In August of the following year he demanded that the Party should constitute a commission with the power to control Hitler, and was consequently excluded from the Party. A few months later he wrote: "Only the blind, uncritical admirers of Hitler or people who do not want to see the truth can doubt as yet that the Hitler Party is a party of Jesuits who, under the volkisch banner, are doing the business of Rome". Dinter certainly knew that he was putting his life at risk, for so many had disappeared for far less, but he was not to be intimidated.

Now his zealous Christian side, the complement of his hatred of the Jews, came to the fore. He founded the *Geistchristliche Religionsgemeinschaft*, which may be translated as 'Religious Community of Christian Intellectuals'. In 1930 he called Hitler 'a sentimental dreamer and babbler'. The future of the nationalist-volkisch movement was not "in the hands of Hitler or of paramilitary organizations; the future lies with the German youth movement, the young, Spartan groups who are the bearers of destiny and the mortal enemies of the Western mentality"; and Dinter names as their examples Ernst Jünger, Otto Strasser and Ernst Niekisch. Otto Strasser was the brother of Gregor Strasser and a principled socialist, even as a member of the Nazi Party, who had caused Hitler a lot of trouble and ultimately broke with him. To put him up as an example sufficed to have Dinter casually executed by the SA or SS.

But Dinter went still further: a faction of National-Socialists, disillusioned by the not so nice happenings within their Party, pressed him to start a protestant Nazi movement as 'the conscience of the volkisch freedom movement'. The result was the foundation of the *Dinter-Bund*, on 9 November 1932. Hitler would become Chancellor of Germany less than three months later and start at once to cut down everybody who had ever dared to withstand him. Dinter, since long ejected from the NSDAP, was forbidden any public form of activity. That after such a spectacular rebellion against Hitler he was not sent to a concentration camp or simply murdered is a riddle for which we may suggest a solution later on. He died in 1948, seventy-two years of age.

A revived Christianity, a pseudo-German Christianity or a genuine German religion: it was all the same *quatsch*, the same nonsense to Hitler, who had something totally different in mind but who kept such thoughts to himself for the time being. Once, when the subject of religion came up, he said to Hermann Rauschning: "Let Fascism [he meant Mussolini] make its peace with the Church. I will do so too. Why not? It will not prevent me from extirpating Christianity in Germany root and branch ... The Old Testament or the New, or only the words of Jesus, as Houston Stewart Chamberlain prefers: all that is nothing but the same Jewish swindle. It is all the same and it does not set us free. A German Church, a German Christianity is rubbish. One is either Christian or German. One cannot be both. You may eliminate the epileptic Paul from Christianity. Others have done so before us. You may turn Jesus into a noble human being and deny his divinity and his role as an intermediary. Some people have done so in former and more recent times ... All that is no use, you cannot get rid of the mentality, which is what really matters. We want free people who know that God is within them and who feel Him there."[40]

The light of Apollo, the frenzy of Wotan

We had a look at some of the ideas which became ever more articulated in 'the new romanticism' that was the Volkisch movement. We met with a new German history favouring heroes whose actions and ideals seemed worthy of imitation; there was the Motherland with its natural beauty and the places where ancestors had dwelt; and there were the ancient gods, still alive among the people nearest to

---
[40]Hermann Rauschning: *Gespräche mit Hitler*, p. 103.

the soil – the gods who were revered and whose powers vibrated once more in the ranks of a youth who opened their hearts to them. The ways to approach these supernatural beings were not logical theorems and mathematical equations, but the fascinating mysteries of occultism, 'sciences' based on experience, and wisdom.

"The irrationality of these cults, as well as the anti-rationalistic romanticism then in vogue, made an astonishing number of men receptive to equally, and at times more, outlandish theories of national heritage, race and religion", writes George Mosse. "Occultism, in fact, became essential to another aspect of volkisch thought. For some thinkers it provided a link between the present and the past; it was a bridge that spanned a thousand years of neglect. The past, which Christianity had done its best to destroy, could be recovered and applied to the present needs of the Volk through occultism. Occultism was the chalice that quenched their thirst, and at the same time made irrelevant anything that historical scholarship might do to show events in an entirely different light".[41]

Nicholas Goodrick-Clarke, in his *Occult Roots of Nazism*, interprets the flourishing of occultism at the time as follows: "The wide range and confusing variety of racist occultism during the years of the Republic and the Third Reich might tempt one to dismiss the phenomenon as a crankish outgrowth of a larger occult movement in German society during a troubled period in history. While it is undeniably true that these astrologers, rune magicians and Edda mystics were occultists, to leave the matter there is to fail to understand the basic ideological and political motive of this special kind of occultism. All these thinkers were united in a profound reaction to the contemporary world. They perceived the German Republic as vulgar, corrupt, and the symbol of defeat. As cultural pessimists they lifted their eyes from the frustrations and disappointments of the present to behold a vision of high Aryan culture in a fabulous prehistoric past. Astrology, the myth of the

---

[41] George Mosse: *The Crisis of German Ideology*, pp. 72-73.

Edda and the runes, whether mysteriously whispered or cut as strange magical characters, all represented a marvellous link with that golden age. They were all the promissory tokens of a new era, in which magic, mystical vision and world-power would be restored to all true-born Germans."[42]

While to its practitioners occultism was a method, based on wisdom, to find out the laws of nature and to use them to certain ends, the pagan rites of power were almost exclusively put at the service of the barbarian urges of self-aggrandisement and the physical force to dominate others, gain honour in battle, a place in the heaven of the warriors, and, on the side, grab the property of others. The Catholic Church thought it had eradicated the cult of the 'demons', but now it found to its amazement that, suddenly, the demons seemed to be immortal and were reasserting their power with renewed vigour, writes Rüdiger Sünner in his chapter on the 'Neo-pagan Outburst around the Turn of the Century'.

"German utopianism in the nineteenth and early twentieth centuries almost always meant a return to pre-Christian, pagan spirituality in some form", declares Richard Noll. "Goethe exemplified this trend in the romantic movement by suggesting replacing the fairy tale of Christ-worship with sun worship. The romantic revival of the Greek gods in Germany also led to utopian visions of a Hellenic Germany, based on the best, most rational and most aesthetically superior Apollonian aspects of ancient Greek culture. In the 1870s, Nietzsche and Wagner unleashed a stream of utopian fantasies that reversed these notions with their appeal to a return of an irrational, organic, Dionysian community of oneness of will and expression".[43] Apollo and sun worship, and a Dionysian frenzy of possession: both trends were present in the Volkisch movement.

Sünner summarises an article in the volkisch periodical *Die Sonne* (the sun) to illustrate the hankering for light and warmth in the

---

[42] Nicholas Goodrick-Clarke: *The Occult Roots of Nazism*, pp. 162-63.
[43] Richard Noll: *The Jung Cult – Origins of a Charismatic Movement*, p. 260.

Germany of that period. "The metaphor of the rising sun and the onset of spring were used to express the unease with the present time and the hope for a fundamental change. In the German world something was falling apart, something was withering, and something new was coming up. The gods worshipped until recently, viz. capitalism and socialism, had become morally bankrupt." The pure 'pleasure principle' had left the people cold, and there was an urge in all social classes and circles to become free of any form of intellectualism and to enter into a direct experience. The people felt civilization as something cold and dark.[44] "There has hardly been another period in history when there was so much talk of 'light' and 'sun' as in the period under consideration", Sünner writes. "One really got drunk on these words, like hungry and freezing people who, in a gloomy dungeon, are longing for light and warmth."

"The lightning-shaped SS-rune was interpreted as a symbol of 'sun' and 'illumination', and Himmler declared Hitler to be 'one of the greatest Beings of Light', destined by 'the karma of Germanhood' to wage 'the battle against the [Slavonic] East'. Alfred Rosenberg, chief ideologist of the NSDAP, spoke of 'the victory of the Nordic-Apollonian light principle' at countless places where the fallen heroes were honoured and 'eternal flames' were burning. Reviews were called *The Path of Light* or *The Sun,* and an age-old 'site of the solar cult' was supposed to have existed at every real or hypothetical Germanic sanctuary. There was an almost obsessive thirsting for the power of the radiant celestial body, and the hope of rebirth in its rays after the alleged humiliations …

"The Nazis considered themselves the only rightful heirs of a hoary solar religion which must have originated in the North, because only the people there had experienced the return of the vernal sun as a special revelation. Proof of this were the swastikas and other spiral-shaped symbols, found on rocks and cult objects as early as the Bronze Age; they were without much ado interpreted as symbols

---

[44] Rüdiger Sünner: *Schwarze Sonne*, p. 16.

of an 'altaric' solar cult ... The Hitler Youth began to celebrate the solar solstices already in 1933, and similar celebrations were organized from 1935 onwards in all regional subdivisions of the Party, sometimes in big stadiums filled with 100 000 people. According to SS-Führer Reinhard Heydrich they believed, in this way, to draw from the same power source as their forefathers had done thousands of years ago. In the summer of 1935 there was even a 'Reich solar solstice' in which eight thousand fires were lit simultaneously along the Bay of Lübeck. In the winter of the same year chains of fires started from a big fire on the Brocken [Heath] in central Germany and ran in six rays to the borders of the nation, thus creating an imaginary solar wheel as big as the Reich ...

> In the darkness of the world the Aryans brought the light.
> The great illumination came from the North ...
> Longer lasting and older than Rome, longer lasting and older is Germany."[45]

The Artamanen also celebrated the solar solstices. "One wears the folkloric dresses and organizes dances and symbolic plays under old trees. Here too the solar celebrations are the most important feasts to bring the youth into contact with the soul of the forebears." Sünner quotes a description of such a feast from *The Book of the Wandervögel*: "They assembled in silence around the pile of wood. The tarred torch is lit. 'Arise, o flame!' Not a word is heard when the last sounds of the song fade away. One man steps forward from the circle and speaks, turned towards the fire, of the true liberation, of the purifying blaze of the new ideals ... Who does not know that this youth hides the intensity of their feelings under an outwardly boisterous joy does not understand why, after the harangue and the song, a circle of apparent madmen dances around the fire ... When

---

[45] Id., pp. 80-82, passim.

the pile of burning wood collapses all jump over the embers, as if they wanted to show that burning by the fire cannot frighten them."[46]

The fabricated myth of the German past, of a Volk whose origins and therefore its very existence were arguable, had to fill the vacuum left by the rejection of Christianity and the disillusionment of the Enlightenment. The pathetic effort at imagining to be the superior people rested fundamentally on nothing. What Noll called the German 'utopianism' was often a hysterical overreaction against the angst of nihilism. This explains the German fascination with *Götterdämmerung,* the twilight of the gods and the catastrophic end of a world – with the Nietzschean act of self-affirmation in a world without an essential meaning.

"It was in keeping with their divorce from reality that the idea of a 'soldierly existence' was based not on the real experiences of the war but upon vainglorious illusions; not upon dirt, disgust and the fear of death, but upon that myth of the front-line soldier with which the older generation compensated for defeat. The first steps towards a contempt for life developed by the Wandervögel, the battlefield romanticism with 'mounds of dead', the transfiguration of striking and stabbing and throttling, the whole aestheticization of violent death culminating in the intoxication of grandiose disasters, now underwent unlimited extension in an ignorantly blissful shudder before the Nibelungen and the Last of the Goths, before the Lost Warrior Bands of the Middle Ages, before Langemarck, Koltschak and the samurai ideal … All this was not merely the expression of a historicizing hero-worship but also a symptom of a deep-rooted tendency of German educational tradition to prepare the young for death rather than life. Rarely did the character of the Bündische Jugend, in its mixture of commonplace metaphysics, ego-assertion and pseudo-military spirit, find for itself a more apt formula than

---

[46] Id., pp. 27, 24.

in the 'German trinity' proclaimed by one of its members: 'God, myself and my weapons'." (Joachim Fest[47])

One of the works of art most popular with the volkisch movement was Albrecht Dürers engraving 'The Knight, Death and the Devil', of which an imitation in the form of a cartouche hung behind Hitler's desk at his new Chancellery in Berlin.[48] The medieval knight, flanked by Death on one side and by the Devil on the other, is riding through a nightmare world towards his end, ready for to wage the battle without a stake. "The German people are inclined to believe in the moral superiority of dark and hard ideas over ideas that are clearer and gentler. This agrees with their deeper disposition for the tragic side of life and the necessity of evil in the world", wrote Thomas Mann, the author of *Doktor Faustus*.[49]

As the volkisch protest movement against the modern world turned towards nature and the old gods, it was inevitable that the darker, vitalistic forces of life would seek an outlet through this youth. The youth associations were almost exclusively close bondings of groups of men; women had no access to these *Männerbünde* and were disdainfully relegated to the conventions and duties of the bourgeois world. If Greece stood as an example here, it was Sparta, not Athens. Their songs were martial ones, often those of the former *Landsknechte*, the drifting mercenaries who, like the Free Corps, obeyed only their captain, as long as he fed and paid them, and were in spite of their religious superstitions also nihilists marching on between Death and the Devil. The ultimate ideal of the volkisch youth was sacrifice, the sacrifice of life to Death, unconditionally accepted in total obedience to the command of the leader, the *Führer*. The expectation of a Great Leader, 'a Strong One from Above', to lead them into a future as glorious as the imagined past, was common at that time. But if the future nevertheless would turn

---

[47]Joachim Fest: *The Face of the Third Reich*, pp. 340-41.
[48]See Frederic Spotts: *Hitler and the Power of Aesthetics*, p. 365.
[49]Thomas Mann: *Deutschland und die Deutschen*, p. 100.

out to be another *Götterdämmerung*, so be it, they were ready to lay down their life with dignity.

These were the realities as the volkisch youth saw them; they led straight to Nazism. 'National Socialism was a volkisch movement', states Mosse in the very first pages of his thorough study of the movement. We know about Hitler's reservations on this point and will draw our conclusions later. It was part of Hitler's remarkable intuition, however, to use the volkisch aspects of Nazism to the utmost. The same volkisch youth who had been marching and chanting in the Wandervogel and its numerous sister organizations, was now marching and chanting at the NSDAP rallies, but integrated (*gleichgeschaltet*) into the Nazi moloch and proudly wearing their carefully designed uniforms.

The testimony of Denis de Rougemont, written in 1936 after having participated in a mass rally of the NSDAP, is often quoted: "I had thought to assist at a mass demonstration, at a political rally. But they celebrate their cult!" He goes on to describe how he was physically affected, not to say crushed, by the force of the religious belief of the 40,000 present there, bawling out in unison their faith in the Führer and Germany. The French ambassador, André François-Poncet, present at one of the *Reichstage* at Nuremberg, writes in a similar vein: "Still more astonishing and actually indescribable is the atmosphere of collective enthusiasm in which this old town is bathing, the extraordinary drunkenness which has overtaken hundreds of thousands of men and women, the romantic fever, the mystic ecstasy, the kind of sacred delirium by which they are possessed".[50] Heine's prediction was coming true. Thor was swinging his hammer again.

The German youth, around their camp fires, during their treks and their ceremonies of initiation and dedication at sacred sites, was listening to seductive voices which also whispered to them in their dreams and impelled them to spend their energy, blindly, for the

---

[50] André François-Poncet: *Souvenirs d'une ambassade à Berlin*, p. 268.

great Cause assigned to them by the charismatic Führer, that 'Being of Light'. For these young men Wotan, whom others called Odin, was present again – he, the one-eyed god with the green hat, who leads the wild hunt of dead riders seen in times of upheaval, when storms are wailing or the moon makes the nights ominous. 'Wotan' is from the same root as 'Wut', which means rage or fury.

"We have to become the berserkers of our inner being and our faith", wrote Goebbels in his diary, and: "We are the berserkers of the new German idea".[51] Spengler, at the end of his famous book, had pointed in a similar direction: "The race pushes itself once more to the fore, pure and irresistible ... From now on a destiny of heroes in the style of ancient times is possible again".[52] And René Alleau quotes the Austrian author Otto Höfler who wrote: "The most honored god of the German tribes was the lord of demonic possession ... Wotan is the savage god of possession, the divine master of the ecstatic *Männerbünde*, the unpredictable god of war and tempest, of the runes and the dead, of rage and sorcery, of masks and human sacrifices".[53]

The 'ecstasy', the possession by the vital forces of a god or an animal, was not a matter of escape, as nowadays sought in drugs, but of 'a cultic identification' of the individual and communal existence. When a person opens himself to such powers, he leaves his normal personality behind and "accepts the obligations of the community of the dead-but-immortals". This experience, with its relations to Germanic prehistory, can be understood only in the Third Reich, writes Klaus von See. National-Socialism was a movement, an existentially and ecstatically 'moved movement'. And he shows how during the Nazi period the word 'fanatic' is no longer defined as 'passionately zealous' but as 'filled with an idea, enthusiastic'.[54]

---

[51] Joseph Goebbels: *Tagebücher*, pp. 142, 158.
[52] Oswald Spengler: *Der Untergang des Abendlandes*, p. 1102.
[53] René Alleau: *Hitler et les sociétés secrètes*, p. 174.
[54] Klaus von See, op. cit., p. 229, passim.

This brings us straight back to Hitler who in *Mein Kampf* repeatedly pressed for a 'fanatical' faith in the National-Socialist movement, and who used *fanatisch* as a key-word in many speeches. No true Nazi who did not have the *Glaube*, the faith; no true Nazi who was not fanatical. To turn Germans into fanatics was an essential part of the education and training in the Reich, as it was of the propaganda-cum-brainwashing directed by Joseph Goebbels. The effort succeeded wonderfully well, alas, thanks to the volkisch preparation briefly related above. What counted was instinct, not intellectual reasoning or 'causalities', as Spengler names them. This falling back on animal instincts may also provide a clue to the cruelty with which so many Germans, citizens of one of the foremost civilised nations, treated and killed their victims.

It is an essential point in the understanding of Hitler that, while founding the Reich of a Thousand Years, he lived constantly under the shadow of the possibility of a new *Götterdämmerung*, which he consciously did try to bring down upon Germany when it was evident that his Thousand Year Reich would be stillborn. Supposing he had succeeded in building his Reich, which would have been its supporting ideology, the ground, the meaning of it all? Hitler had something in mind which he never expressed directly and which remains to be discovered. It was definitely not the volkisch dream of a return to imaginary olden times. But neither did he intend to build a Reich on 'scientific-methodological' foundations. His mindset was far too unscientific, not to say irrational, and his inspiration, as shown by his actions and realizations, was religious, occult, or, as many have maintained, demonic. Hitler "claimed to serve not the emancipation but the redemption of mankind", writes Fest. If this is true, the question is legitimate: redemption in the name of what or of which god?

About the ritualistic events of the *Reichstage* at Nuremberg, Speer wrote: "When I saw Hitler virtually canonizing the ritual in this manner, I realized for the first time that the phrase [a Reich of a thousand years] was intended literally. I had long thought that all these formations, processions and dedications were part of a clever propagandistic revue. Now I finally understood that for Hitler they were almost like rites of the founding of a church ... It now seemed to me that he was deliberately giving up the smaller claim to the status of a celebrated popular hero in order to gain the far greater status of founder of a religion".[55] There were mass rituals, initiations, the swearing of sacred oaths, the magical transmission of the power contained in the *Blutfahne,* the banner sanctified by the blood of the Nazi martyrs fallen in the November 1923 Putsch in Munich; there were torches, and fires, and long silences, and music, and songs, and the rhythmic sound of many men marching. "'Party' is a wrong concept. I would prefer to say 'order' ... Don't you see that our Party has to be something similar: an order, the hierarchic ordering of a secular priesthood ... I will tell you a secret: I am founding an order ..." This, Hitler confided to Hermann Rauschning, lifted a tip of the veil over his inmost thought.

What kind of religion was it which Hitler wanted to launch? 'The Order of the Death's Head', the SS, may suggest an answer. Many of Himmler's hobbyhorses were not to Hitler's taste, but the fundamental ideas behind this order of 'black knights' were doubtlessly approved if not prescribed or inspired by him. Their ideals were exactly the same as those of the volkisch youth organisations: loyalty, sacrifice, heroism, the pride of being the superior race, unconditional obedience unto death. They were the elite legions of Death wearing the death's head on their caps and conditioned 'to give and take death' without questioning and without giving in to one's feelings. The effects of the *furor teutonicus,* the Teutonic furor or 'ecstasy', can still be seen in the documentaries filmed at mass rallies of the Nazis, bellowing their mantra's; they can also be read from places where the SS celebrated its cult of barbarian revenge, for instance the ruins of Oradour-sur-Glane and the wasteland where

---

[55] Albert Speer: *Spandau – The Secret Diaries,* p. 262.

once Lidice stood; but among the most unbelievable consequences of that pagan frenzy are the piles of emaciated corpses found where the Order of the Death's Head had implemented to the letter the regulations of their faith.

"Mass demonstrations on the grand scale not only reinforce the will of the individual but they draw him still closer to the movement and help to create an esprit de corps ... [The individual] is gripped by the force of mass-suggestion which comes from the excitement and enthusiasm of three or four thousand other men in whose midst he finds himself. If the manifest success and the consensus of thousands confirm the truth and justice of the new teaching and for the first time raise doubt in his mind as to the truth of the opinions held by him up to now, then he submits himself to the fascination of what we call mass-suggestion. The will, the yearning and indeed the strength of thousands of people are in each individual. A man who enters such a meeting in doubt and hesitation leaves it inwardly fortified; he has become a member of a community." Hitler wrote this in 1926, in the second part of the book known as *Mein Kampf*, where one also finds: "I was now able to feel and understand how easily the man in the street succumbs to the hypnotic magic of such a grandiose piece of theatrical presentation".[56]

About the impressionability of the German 'man in the street', Pfeffer von Salomon, one-time commander of the SA, had this to say: "The sight of a large body of disciplined men, inwardly and outwardly alike, whose militancy can be plainly seen or sensed, makes the most profound impression upon every German and speaks to his heart in a more convincing and persuasive language than writing, oratory or logic ever can." These words are quoted in Fest's biography of Hitler, of whom we read there the following words: "We [the Germans] have another value: our fighting spirit. It is there, only buried under a pile of foreign theories and doctrines. A great

---

[56]Adolf Hitler, op. cit., pp. 398, 408.

and powerful party goes to a lot of trouble to prove the opposite, until suddenly an ordinary military band comes along and plays. Then the straggler awakes from his dreamy state and joins their columns. That's the way it is today. Our people only have to be shown this better course – and you'll see, they'll start marching".[57]

In defiance of reason

The rejection of reason as the guiding light of man, of the revolutionary changes the Enlightenment had brought about, and of the new world and the civilisation it attempted to realise, are characteristic of all trends within the Volkisch movement. The volkisch experience derived in a straight line from the great romanticist period which had declared that reason was an usurper of the authentic life experience, and that tradition, the racial roots and the soul of the Volk were the true sustenance on which that Volk should thrive. Sünner describes the general mood as follows: "The people felt civilization as something cold and dark ... One heard of fatigue, coldness, decadence and darkness, of aversion for a rational world in which the traditional religion neither had any stamina left for new spiritual impulses".[58]

Again there are some passages in Spengler's *Decline of the West* worth mentioning if only because of the resonance this book had in Germany, also on people who were not markedly volkisch or Nazis. (The Nazis tried to win over Spengler to their cause, for at first he had greeted their rise with enthusiasm; when he openly professed his growing disillusion, he was allowed to withdraw in silence till his death, in 1936.) "The French Revolution", wrote Spengler, "is no more than a result of rationalism. The Western races carry the dynastic sense in their blood, which is the reason why they loathe the mind. For a dynasty represents history, she *is* the incarnated

---

[57]In Joachim Fest: *Hitler*, pp. 244, 256.
[58]Rüdiger Sünner: *Schwarze Sonne*, p. 16.

history of a country, while mind is located outside time and is a-historical ... The common rights of men, freedom and equality are literature and abstraction, not facts."

We remember Spengler's hymnal praise of the peasant and his abomination of the city, 'made of stone and making everything into stone'. The city is the sure sign that mind has triumphed over life, that culture has been converted into civilisation and that the end of civilisation is near. "Instead of a world: a city, a spot, in which all life of large countries concentrates while the rest withers. Instead of a healthy Volk, grown one with the soil: a new nomad, a parasite, the inhabitant of the city, pragmatic man, without tradition, drifting in a formless, fluctuating mass, without religion, brainy, impotent, with a deep-seated repulsion against the peasantry – which means a decisive step towards the inorganic, towards the End."[59] Hitler too will rail against the city, but only occasionally, for instance when in *Mein Kampf* he tried to get the proletariat on his hand, "those decent working people ... who could not and did not grasp the downright infamy of the doctrine taught by the socialist agitators".[60] It was of course the cities and towns who formed the basis of his movement – Munich, the 'capital of the movement', Dinter's Weimar, Streicher's Nuremberg, Winifred Wagner's Bayreuth, Goebbels' Berlin – and on the streets of which the Nazis did battle with the Reds, those 'decent, misguided working people'.

Klaus von See relates the saying of a classical Roman author that the Germanic tribes, at home in the woods, evaded the towns 'as if they were tombs wrapped in nets', and that they considered the walls of a town as 'ramparts of servitude'. The aversion to the town and everything it stood for must have been a deep-seated trait of the German psyche to have remained so pronounced at the time Germany was the foremost industrial nation in the world and worked

---

[59] Oswald Spengler: *Der Untergang des Abendlandes*, p. 778.
[60] Adolf Hitler: *Mein Kampf*, p. 50.

hard to make everybody else recognise this. It is a curious paradox that, while battleships and Zeppelins were being built, the German dreamt of a life-giving traditional 'culture' in opposition to the detestable life-taking modern 'civilization'; that while the Berlin-Baghdad Railway was being constructed he suffered from *Kulturpessimismus*; that, while the whole world was using his precision instruments, paints and chemicals, he felt himself 'uncomfortable with civilization'. Here surely a psychological anomaly was festering which before long could reach a critical state, for the Germans did not see the split in their national personality as a threat to their country's health but as a source of strength.

"[Germany's] neurotic relationship with the modern world narrowed its view and made it primitive; it was always the German fields, the German forest or glistening snow-capped peaks that were played off against the urban scene, the philistine existence of peasants was played off against metropolitan civilization, the cult of Wotan against the conveyor belt, the ways of the Northmen against present-day social structures. It was with a false inwardness that it meditated upon essentials behind shuttered windows: the plough, the sword, and then in the evening happiness under the linden tree."[61]

That Joachim Fest, who wrote this, was not exaggerating one jot may be shown by a paragraph from the German author Ernst Wiechert, written in 1949 (four years *after* the Second World War): "It has appeared to seers and interpreters of the present time and history that Western man of the last two hundred years has been committing the most disastrous sin of them all: the sin of the intellect. The intellect has left behind the grace of the Middle Ages and the ancient times in order to be like God. It has left the magical soil in which rest the primitive ones ... It has enthroned the *ratio* which lives in the conscious mind and only in the conscious mind, and for which the unconscious is a stupidity and a source of irritation.

---

[61] Joachim Fest: *The Face of the Third Reich*, p. 386.

As to me, however, I am certain that they, the 'unconscious' ones, will remain as the last ones, when the purple mantle of the 'clear-minded', those who 'know', will slide from their shoulders as a worn-out piece of cloth. Those who shall remain will be the seers, the true artists, the true believers, and the children. They are the ones who will bring their works to the surface from the dark depths of the soil where no intelligence can reach, no mathematical or chemical formula, no philosophical theory, no human questioning".[62]

This mentality, the essence of the Volkisch movement, is strongly denounced by Joachim Fest: "National Socialism laid bare phenomena of which the movement itself was in turn only a symptom: the most consistent expression in the field of political power groupings of a multiplicity of pseudo-religious longings, a need for fundamental certainty, intellectual discontent, and impulses to escape from practical intellectual activity into the more hospitable semi-darkness of substitute metaphysical realms. These motivations in turn were permeated by the longing of the intellectual, isolated in the world of his letters, for solidarity with the masses, for a share in their unthinking vitality and closeness to nature, but also in their force and historical effectiveness as expressed in the myth of the national community. Fundamentally National Socialism represented a politically organized contempt for the mind ...

"Its hostility to reason was intellectual, just as it was essentially a movement of failed intellectuals who had lost their faith in reason. It was intellectuals above all who made possible that intellectual façade without which, in a scientific age, it is impossible to win over the petty-bourgeois masses: even the denial of reason must be represented in intellectual terms ...

"Such corrupting cultural and ethical criteria were the outcome of a long process reaching back far into the nineteenth century, in the course of which the mind turned away from itself in the name

---

[62] In Ralf Schnell: *Dichtung in finsteren Zeiten – Literatur und Faschismus*, p. 176.

of a philosophy of life, of the will to power, of rough dynamic vitality, and continually renounced the European rationalist tradition. Generations of philosophers, historians, sociologists and psychologists had a hand in bringing the 'mind as the adversary of the soul' [this is the title of an influential book by Ludwig Klages] into disrepute and replacing it by intuition, blood, instinct, to which it gave a status that inevitably raised stupidity to the level of an authority and produced a moral indigence, a 'defeatism of humanity' such as had never been seen before ...

"This vehement anti-enlightenment, fed by romantic impulses, was a phenomenon common to the whole of Europe; names like Carlyle, Sorel and Bergson underline this and at the same time indicate some of the main lines along which this reversal in the history of ideas moved. But nowhere did this critique of reason so fully expand into a 'destruction of reason', nowhere was it carried out with such a vengeful thoroughness as in Germany."[63] These insights were formulated in 1963 and they retain their validity.

Let us now listen to what Hitler himself had to say to Rauschning on the subject. "We stand at the end of the era of the intellect". "The mind, glorifying itself, has become an illusion of life. Our [National Socialist] revolution is not only political and social: we stand before an enormous change in the moral concepts and the intellectual orientation of the people. It is only now, with our movement, that the middle period, the Middle Ages, are brought to a conclusion. We put an end to a wrong path taken by humanity. The tables of Mount Sinai have lost their validity ... A new era of a magical interpretation of the world is commencing, an interpretation by the will, not by knowledge.

"It is only in an upsurge of feeling and in action that one comes into contact with the true being of the world. I don't like Goethe, but I am inclined to overlook a lot of him for one thing he has said:

---

[63]Joachim Fest, op. cit., pp. 377 ff.

'In the beginning was the deed'. Only the man of action becomes conscious of the true being of the world. Man abuses his intellect. It is not the seat of a special human dignity: it is no more than an expedient in the struggle for life. Man is there to do things. It is only as a being in action that he fulfils his national destiny. Contemplative natures, retrospective like all religious people, are dead beings who miss out on the meaning of life. Precisely the Germans, who have spent so much time floating in thoughts and dreams, had to rediscover the truth that only action and unending movement can give meaning to life."[64]

A path apart

Putting together the glimpses of German history which we could catch in our story about the roads that led to Hitler, we detect a certain outline, useful for the interpretation of the whole. The first contact of the Germanic tribes with the rest of the continent on which they lived was their confrontation with Rome. After having migrated over practically the whole European continent and part of North Africa, a second confrontation with Rome and its civilisation took place about the acceptance of the Christian faith. Germanic tribes which had occupied Roman territory found little difficulty to convert, as exemplified in the story of Clodowech, alias Clovis, if only to consolidate their conquests or raise their status. (Many of them would become founders of the feudal family trees, later branching out into the blue-blooded and very Christian nobility.) They were actually the driving force behind the evangelisation of the still pagan tribes who lived on the original pagan lands. Many Germans will find difficulty in forgiving Charlemagne, a Germanic king, for the slaughter of thousands of recalcitrant Saxons, and Himmler will have to issue an order compelling his SS to do so, after Hitler's example.

---

[64]Hermann Rauschning, op. cit. pp. 210-11.

We saw that German nationalism awoke as part of the 'romantic' trend of the Renaissance, its most powerful voice being that of Martin Luther. Around this time, the awareness of a difference between the Roman-Latin-Welsh south and the Aryan-Nordic-Germanic north was mooted for the first time. "Luther detested the urban and humanistic culture of the Renaissance, which was a threat to the simple peasant piety he admired ... Luther was the only religious reformer to identify himself narrowly with nationalism. In his most important work, an 'Address to the Nobility of the German Nation', he announced that he spoke only to and for Germans, demanding that German princes control ecclesiastical matters and throw off the subversive influence of Rome. He would often be cited later by German philosophers, politicians and theologians who interpreted the Reformation as the first great expression of the Germanic soul, rejecting Catholic Christianity as Latin, un-German and cosmopolitan, a threat to the Teutonic people second only to international Jewry."[65] Luther's attitude and the enthusiastic response it encountered resulted in the fact that, as Albert Speer noted, "fundamentally the Renaissance skirted Germany when it spread from Italy to France and England. Perhaps one of the roots of Hitler's successes may be traced to this failure on Germany's part to participate in humanistic culture".[66]

In the series of religious wars following Luther's reformation, the terrible Thirty Years' War devastated the lands we call Germany and left them backward and exhausted for centuries to come. One of the consequences was that Germany remained a patchwork of principalities at a time that elsewhere in Europe the unifying idea of the 'nation' began to take shape, mainly because of the innovative ideas put forward by the thinkers of the Enlightenment. "While in England and France the concept of the nation and the state had a

---

[65] John Weiss: *Ideology of Death*, p. 29.
[66] Albert Speer: *Spandau – The Secret Diaries*, p. 151.

rational-humanistic foundation, going back to Calvin on the one hand and the Enlightenment on the other, in Germany the concept of state and Volk was made into a sacred myth by the Romantic movement. The rejection of the Enlightenment and the mythicization of the Volk are the specific factors which led in Germany to a separate development [*Sonderentwicklung*] of which the consequences should not be underestimated".[67]

The first effects of the specifically German idea of a nationalism based on race and Volk came about as a reaction to the stormy conquests of Napoleon and his imposition of the guiding principles of the French Revolution. The Germans fell back on what they considered their true origins, the rural, and the military temperament of their elders, thus creating the Prussian spirit and the Prussian state. "East Prussia, forged out of the bloodied and Christianized territories of the Teutonic Knights, never lost its feudal character ... Prussian military and autocratic values were sanctified among the German elites and eventually the middle classes as well. Once again German history deviated from that of the liberal West."[68] Prussia will be the core of the Bismarck state, the first political entity which may be called 'German' in the full meaning of the word.

The innate German sense of duty and zest for work brought about the first *Wirtschaftswunder*, managed by a caucus of politicians, industrialists, bankers and military men, and demanding for Germany 'a place in the sun' among the nations who looked down upon it as a newcomer. Inwardly, Germany was now divided into three: a group with the Pan-German League as its mouthpiece and which aimed at becoming a world power; the Volkisch movement which turned its back on the modern world and its industrialism, and which created a self-enclosed imaginary world of medieval and primitive fantasies; and the sombre masses of the fourth estate, the proletariat, increasingly to be reckoned with and felt as a threat by

---

[67] Michael Ley, op. cit., p. 68.
[68] John Weiss, op. cit., p. 35.

the established social classes. These parts of the German body politic overlapped; they were also, in times of crisis, tied into temporary unity by the feeling of belonging to a superior people with a special mission in and for the world. For the Germans, writes Haffner, were 'an ambitious people'.

Their sense of superiority was egged on by the unexpected and therefore staggering defeat of 1918, the fictitious 'stab in the back', and the feeling of injustice caused by several articles in the Treaty of Versailles. Revenge became the common motive as a means of self-affirmation, drawing its strength from the specific Germanic character and values. That the Germans were special, a Volk apart, capable of justifying its claims as leaders of the world's destiny, would be proven – that, or nothing. The despicable Weimar Republic was a miscarriage of the Enlightenment fathered by the victorious Allies. Once a Leader was found to bundle and direct the energies of the Volk, it would put its inmost powers into effect, realise its ideals and, at last, create a world worthy of its existence.

George Mosse writes about "the very real difference that separated Germany from the West", and which is often called *Sonderweg*, meaning 'path apart'. "Was Germany unique in Europe?" he asks. "Other nations had movements similar to the New Romanticism. Barrès and Maurras in France also called for an internal renewal of their nation, a transformation that would entail both a metaphysical religious conviction and political action. But this impetus never penetrated as deeply as in Germany, nor did it lead to the same end. It is important to clarify this once again, since German historians, of late, have been happy to point out parallels with other Western nations. Yet, even though these may have shared certain elements with the New Romanticism, the chemistry of the German movement was quite different. In Germany, the romantic, volkisch ideology established a frame of reference which reached deeper into the nation."[69]

---

[69]George Mosse, op. cit., pp. 50, 66.

Germany felt itself possessing true values and not modern mental constructs, a divine soul and not only an arbitrary mind, strength rooted in an ever-present authenticity and not the weakening morality of an alien Judaic creed, and pure blood that was not degraded. It felt itself as the chosen people and not a false pretender, as the heroes of the future against the impotent people of a civilisation in decline. Having suffered much in its history, it had arrived on the world scene at a late hour, but it staked its claim to a worthy place, in fact to the prominent place which was its due and destiny. Rival powers were encircling it, intending to throttle its industrial life lines and the nourishment of its people. Undefeated on the battlefield, Germany would stand up again stronger than ever, and reach at last its ultimate fulfilment in a Third Reich. What was foreseen in the plan of God would be accomplished by the works of man.

10

THE JEWISH QUESTION

> *It is indispensable for us to undermine all faith, to tear out of the minds of the goyim the very principle of Godhead and the spirit, and to put in its place arithmetical calculations and material needs ... The King of the Jews will be the real Pope of the Universe, the patriarch of an international Church ...*
> THE PROTOCOLS OF THE WISE MEN OF ZION

The Jewish stereotype

In the previous chapters we had glimpses of the anti-Jewish aspect of the Volkisch movement, because both were inseparable: being volkisch meant being racist, at least to some degree, and in Germany racism was practically synonymous with anti-Semitism. It was the aim of the Volkisch movement to restore the health of the body of the Volk; this could only be done if all elements alien to this body, acting as enfeebling parasites or illness-causing germs, were discarded from it. Such an eliminatory attitude, caused by the inherent egoism of all closely bounded groupings, societies and nations, has been the common stance throughout history. In most of Europe the Jews became the suspects and victims of the Christians, who forgot that when the Christian movement was still young they themselves, for almost identical reasons, had been persecuted by the Romans, thrown to the lions, or crucified and lit as torches by Emperor Nero.

"Anti-Semitism became the chief vehicle for the diffusion of the volkisch movement", writes George Mosse. "Those who were attracted primarily by anti-Semitism had no difficulty in accepting the basic volkisch ideas, and those already in the movement took readily to the precepts of anti-Semitic racism ... The anti-Semitism embraced by Hitler was not just an opportunistic device, but a deeply felt conviction strengthened by the whole volkisch outlook. And even though it was part of a spiritual disposition and an attitude toward life that was founded on belief in an irrational cosmology, life forces and nature mysticism (and consequently could have been derided as the outlook of a mentally deranged person), it was real nonetheless".[1] If this is correct, it should be added that Hitler's anti-Semitism was a radicalised version of the most aggressive volkisch variations of anti-Semitism which covered the whole spectrum, from respectful coexistence to the views of outright elimination in whatever way. It remains nevertheless a subject of discussion that anyone but Hitler ever thought of doing away with the Jews physically.

The Volkisch movement, especially through its youth organisations, became a gigantic instrument to propagate anti-Judaism in Germany; the mentality it stood for, imprinted on the minds of a great part of the German youth, will contribute in a substantial measure to the background which rendered the Holocaust possible. One propaganda technique, borrowed from the popular lore, is to make the 'other', whether enemy or just 'not one of us', into a stereotype. The volkisch stereotype of the Jew would afterwards be taken over by the propaganda machine of the Third Reich. "The Jew lacked a soul, all virtues, and the capacity for ethical behaviour for the reason that Judaism was a fossilized legalism. What a striking contrast this made with the German soul, steeped as it was in communion with the

---

[1] George Mosse: *The Crisis of German Ideology*, pp. 133, 298.

cosmos, the recipient of nature's mysteries, striving to relate itself to the glorious deeds of its ancestors, and rooted in nature, the soil and the landscape ...

"Slowly the stereotype took its effect. On the ethical and religious fronts, it was asked whether, if the Jew lacked a proper soul, he could be classed as human. On the economic and social front it was asserted that Jews had consorted in diabolical intrigues to seize power in order to dominate the Gentile world ... In a whole series of novels Jewish characters lacked all human qualities and met miserable fates, victims of their egoistical power drives. The objectification of the Jew as evil by means of his inner drives was reinforced by an emphasis on his outward appearance. Race, after all, was a total criterion. The physical properties of the Jew were accordingly contrasted with the Germanic ideal of beauty; a contorted figure resting on short legs, a greedy and sensual corpulence, and, of course, 'the Jewish nose', were unfavourably compared with the aesthetically proportioned figure of the Nordic man. To be sure, such stereotypes had been in existence since the sixteenth and seventeenth centuries, but they were not as critical then. The Jew at that early date was still pictured as a comic, though grotesque, figure. In the image presented by the volkisch thought, he became a menace; he held the Germans in actual bondage.

"The racial stereotype attributed so many grotesque qualities to the Jew that he was in essence dehumanized", concludes Mosse.[2] Dehumanisation is the necessary condition for the superior man to activate and justify his feelings of superiority towards other humans or the rest of humanity as a whole. The 'others' are then no longer human beings but a kind of lowly, despicable and expendable things, which can be treated at will and even done away with without psychological qualms. (Franz Stangl, former commandant of the Treblinka extermination camp, called the arriving trainloads

---

[2] Id., pp. 129, 140, 143.

of Jews 'cargo'.*) It is one of the wondrous capabilities of the human being to be able to reduce his fellow creatures to things, even to nothings.

'Cargo'

The literature about Nazism is abundant with instances of such absurdity – if 'absurdity' is the right word. For instance, Anna Maria Sigmund, in her biographies of prominent Nazi women, quotes the father of Gerda Bormann as saying: "The Jew is not a human being. He is an element of decay. Just as the fission fungus chooses rotten wood to settle and destroys its tissue, just so the Jew has found the occasion to insinuate himself into the German Volk and do his mischief when, weakened by the loss of blood in the Thirty Years' War, it began to degenerate". Walter Buch, the father in question and chairman of the NSDAP committee of inquiry into internal Party irregularities, 'never tired of preaching this to his children'. Another example provided by the same author: medical doctors at the Dachau concentration camp performed a series of experiments testing the reactions of human beings to rapid changes in air pressure at high altitudes. "For a short time experiments with animals had been carried out. But these were in contravention of the National-Socialist laws for the protection of animals and had to be stopped on the personal intervention of Reich Marshall Göring, the 'Supreme Master of the Hunt'. This opened the way for experiments with human beings."[3]

---

*Gitta Sereny interviewed Stangl in 1971, shortly before his death. "So you don't feel they were human beings?" – "Cargo", he said tonelessly. "They were cargo." – "When do you think you began to think of them as cargo? ..." – "I think it started the day I first saw the *Totenlager* [camp of the dead] in Treblinka. I remember Wirth standing there, next to the pits full of blue-black corpses. It had nothing to do with humanity – it couldn't have; it was a mass of rotting flesh." (Gitta Sereny: *Into that Darkness*, p. 201)
[3] Anna Maria Sigmund: *Die Frauen der Nazis II*, pp. 10, 274.

Hitler, another animal lover, said in one of his monologues when expressing his aversion to hunting: "I can swear that never in my life I hurt a little hare". And Himmler boasted in one of his speeches to his black Captains of Death that the Germans were "the only people in the world who had a decent attitude towards animals". They would therefore also adopt a decent attitude towards the Russian 'human animals', about whom he had just said: "If during the construction of an anti-tank ditch ten thousand Russian women do or don't collapse from exhaustion, it only interests me in so far as the ditch is got ready for Germany ... That other peoples live in prosperity or perish with hunger interests me only in so far as we need them as slaves for our culture, otherwise it does not interest me".[4]

Eugen Fischer, a Nazi doctor who worked mainly with children, wrote in 1939: "When a people wants, somehow or other, to preserve its own nature, it must reject alien racial elements, and when these have already insinuated themselves, it must suppress them and eliminate them. The Jew is such an alien and, therefore, when he wants to insinuate himself, he must be warded off. This is self-defence. In saying this, I do not characterize every Jew as inferior, as Negroes are, and I do not underestimate the greatest enemy with whom we have to fight. But I reject Jewry with every means in my power, and without reserve, in order to safeguard the hereditary endowment of my people". When Fritz Klein, another Nazi doctor, involved in the euthanasia programme, was asked how he had been able to reconcile his doctor's oath with his activities in Auschwitz, he answered: "Of course I am a doctor and I want to preserve life. And out of respect for human life I would remove a gangrenous appendix from a diseased body. The Jew is the gangrenous appendix in the body of mankind".[5]

---

[4]Norbert and Stephan Lebert: *Denn Du trägst meinen Namen*, p. 46.
[5]Jonathan Glover: *Humanity – A Moral History of the Twentieth Century*, pp. 324, 325.

"The Jew too is a human being, nobody has ever doubted this", said a sarcastic Joseph Goebbels. "But the flea is also an animal, though not a pleasant one. And as the flea is not a pleasant animal, we don't have the duty to ourselves and to our conscience to care for it and to protect it, and to make it prosper in order to let it sting and torture us, but to make it harmless".[6] And Heinrich Himmler, again, reminded his troops in 1942: "From a biological standpoint [the Jew] seems completely normal. He has hands and feet and a sort of brain. He has eyes and a mouth. But, in fact, he is a completely different creature, a horror. He only looks human, with a face similar to a human face, but his mind, his soul is lower than that of an animal. A terrible chaos runs rampant in this creature, an awful urge of destruction, primitive desires and unparalleled evil. He is a sub-human and nothing else".[7]

Along with the shaping of the Jewish stereotype the old vicious rumours were revived about the stealing of consecrated hosts, the poisoning of wells and springs, and the abduction and murder of Christian children. "In Germany, France and the Austrian Empire the ritual-murder legend was far from dead. It was revived periodically, especially encouraged by intellectuals, and grew to a popular clamour that took on the proportions of a movement. In the Austrian Empire alone there were no less than twelve trials for ritual murder between 1867 and 1914. ... To the public at large, the trials and the sensationalism that surrounded them demonstrated the Jewish conspiracy against the Gentiles."[8] These hateful notions of the Jews were so vivid in the memory of the German people that in Munich, 'Athens on the Isar', Rudolf von Sebottendorff could threaten the commissioner of police that he might unleash a pogrom by grabbing a Jew and dragging him through the streets on the accusation of having stolen a consecrated host.[9]

---

[6]Dieter Wunderlich: *Göring und Goebbels*, p. 47.
[7]Guido Knopp: *Hitlers Helfer*, p. 186.
[8]George Mosse, op. cit., p. 130.
[9]Rudolf von Sebottendorff: *Bevor Hitler kam*, p. 92.

The Jew was ugly, dirty, stank with the *foetor judaicus* (which, some said, disappeared the moment he was baptized), and was a sexual pervert. The fear that the pure Aryan race would be contaminated by the Jews through sexual intercourse became an obsession. Lanz von Liebenfels had published pictures of buxom naked women, pure-blooded but weak and lustful, who were being sexually assaulted by ape-like monsters. Hitler had written in *Mein Kampf* about the black-haired Jewish young man who lay in wait for hours to disgrace the unsuspecting Aryan girl with his blood and steal her from her Volk; and in his early speeches he kept hammering on this theme, and spoke of the pimps, 'merchants of young girls', who were all Jews, without exception. The Jew was presented as a threat to German 'decency' and to the effort at restoring the purity of the race. Race was a matter of breeding; breeding meant sexual contact; sex awakened basic instincts, often as base as basic. *Der Stürmer*, the widely read magazine launched by whip-flaunting Julius Streicher bears testimony to this. But Hitler appreciated its pseudo-pornographic contents and supported Streicher, the Nazi chief of Nuremberg, as long as possible. There is little doubt that this dark sexual component of Nazism, directed against the Jews, enforced the cruelty of the way in which they were treated.

One of the chief traits of the Jewish stereotype, current to this day, is its relation to money. The Jew as a banker, pawnbroker, usurer and miser has become proverbial in several European languages. "The stock exchange jobber, the corpulent banker, these were the stereotypes of the Jew that were widely accepted and disseminated through popular literature. The stock exchange in particular became the symbol of the nightmarish capitalism that had been foisted upon the Germans by the Jews. It came to represent the hub of their control system, and it was there, early volkisch thinkers proclaimed, that the world revolution to oust the alien money lords would emanate ... But popular anti-Semitic propaganda was to go one better: it fused the images of Jewish hunger for money with the lust for Aryan women. The resulting image widely used as propaganda pictured a fat Jewish banker caressing a blond woman on his knee."[10]

In his *Histoire de l'antisémitisme,* Léon Poliakov shows how the handling of money became, in the course of European history, the only occupation left to the Jews, and their lifeline. This was why their attitude towards money grew into "a sacral attitude, source of all life. Little by little each step and each action in the daily life of the Jew were subject to the payment of a tax: he had to pay taxes for coming and going, for buying and selling, for having the right of communal prayer, for marrying, for the child that is born, even for the dead who were taken to the cemetery. Without money the Jewish collective was inevitably doomed to disappear ... It is in this sense, and in this sense only, that it may seem to a superficial observer that the Jews have been the prime agents of the 'capitalist mentality'". Poliakov also remarks that, far from being Rothschilds all of them, "the great majority of the Jews were small money lenders or dealers in second hand cloth, who earned their bread as circumstances permitted and lived in insecurity and misery without end".[11]

'Without Christianity no anti-Semitism'

The popular anti-Semitic mentality, in the rest of Europe as well as in Germany, was the result of a historic process which went back all the way to the life and death of Jesus Christ, and which was closely connected with Christianity. The attitude of Europe, where Christianity became the chief element of the culture, rested on the assumption that the Jews had refused to accept Christ as the Messiah and that they had killed him. This was written in the New Testament, revered as holy scripture and therefore indubitable truth. In *The Origin of Satan,* Elaine Pagels shows how the authors of the four

---

[10] Georges Mosse, op. cit., p. 142.
[11] Léon Poliakov: *Histoire de l'antisémitisme I,* pp. 321, 320.

canonical Gospels – Mark, Luke, Matthew and John – gradually grew more inimical towards the Jews. In this they followed the footsteps of Paul of Tarsus, himself a Jew who had converted to Christianity, and who would transform the Judaic sect of the followers of Christ into a potentially universal ('catholic') religion no longer bound to a particular people and its religious beliefs and customs.

Pagels demonstrates how the Gospel authors, who wrote one to two generations after the facts they claim to report, exempt step by step the Romans from the guilt of Christ's execution by shoving the responsibility onto the shoulders of the Jews. The stern Roman governor, Pilate, "grows more and more mellow from gospel to gospel ... The more removed from history, the more sympathetic a character he becomes". In historical fact, Pilate seems to have been as ruthless an office holder as any other Roman governor or proconsul. "Mark's benign portrait increases the culpability of the Jewish leaders and supports the contention that Jews, not Romans, were the primary force behind Jesus' crucifixion." Pilate washed his hands, according to Matthew, to indicate his innocence of bloodshed, and at that moment "the Jewish leaders as well as 'the whole nation' acknowledged collective responsibility and invoked what turned out to be a curse upon themselves and their progeny: 'His blood be upon us and upon our children!'".[12]

Judas Iscariot, who betrayed Jesus to the Jewish authorities and will be regarded as the typical representative of the Jewish people, was according to the Gospel writers possessed by the Devil before committing his loathsome deed. Before long, this diabolic possession will be transferred to the Jewish people as a whole. "When Judas isn't singled out for his Jewishness in the New Testament (all the disciples were at least nominally Jewish), the identification was made official by papal pronouncement as early as the fifth century ... Unofficially, elements of the Judas story in the Gospels have lent themselves –

---

[12] Elaine Pagels: *The Origin of Satan*, p. 33, 2.

or helped create – the most pernicious stereotypes of the Jews: his treachery was mercenary (he sold Jesus to the authorities for thirty pieces of silver), he was a greedy embezzler (in the Gospel of John he's filching from the disciples' funds for the poor), and, above all, he was a dishonest, deceitful traitor, a smiling villain who kissed Jesus on the mouth while stabbing him in the back. Indeed, one can hear incendiary anti-Semitic echoes of the Judas story in the stab-in-the-back accusation Hitler manipulated to convince the German public that the heroic German army had not lost the First World War but had been betrayed, stabbed in the back, by treacherous Jews and Jewish-paid politicians on the home front."[13]

"For nearly two thousand years", writes Pagels, "many Christians have taken for granted that Jews killed Jesus, that the Romans were merely their reluctant agents, and that this implicates not only the perpetrators but (as Matthew insists) all their progeny in evil. Throughout the centuries, countless Christians listening to the gospels absorbed, along with the quite contrary sayings of Jesus, the association between the forces of evil and Jesus' Jewish enemies. Whether illiterate or sophisticated, those who heard the gospel stories, or saw them illustrated in their churches, generally assumed both their historical accuracy and their religious validity ... And because Christians as they read the gospels have characteristically identified themselves with the disciples, for some two thousand years they have also identified their opponents, whether Jews, pagans, or heretics, with forces of evil, and so with Satan".[14]

This is thoughtfully worded. Hyam Maccoby, 'an Oxford-educated literature scholar turned historian of religion', puts the same conclusion much more bluntly in a conversation with Ron Rosenbaum: "Christians say the Holocaust is part of the evil of humanity. It isn't the evil of humanity. It's the evil of Christendom ... Hitler was brought up to hate the Jews, particularly to hate the

---

[13] Ron Rosenbaum: *Explaining Hitler*, p. 324.
[14] Id., pp. xx, xxiii.

Jews as the people of the Devil. He lost his Christian faith, but he retained the hatred of the Jews as the people of the Devil ... I don't blame Germany for the Holocaust; I blame Christendom for the Holocaust".[15]

The anti-Judaic standpoint arrived at by the Gospel authors was soon taken over and confirmed by the so-called Fathers of the Church, who turned it into Church doctrine, obligatorily accepted in the centuries to come. Origen (ca 185 - ca 254) wrote: "We can therefore assert with the utmost confidence that the Jews will not regain their former position, for they have committed the most heinous crime by hatching the complot against the Saviour of humanity ... It is in consequence necessary that the city where Jesus suffered be destroyed from top to bottom, that the Jew be chased from his home, and that others [i.e. the Christians] be called by God to the blessed election". Gregory of Nyssa, around the same time, preached in the true Christian spirit: "Murderers of the Lord, assassins of the prophets, rebels against and haters of God, they distort the Law, resist the grace and reject the faith of their fathers. Collaborators of the devil, race of vipers, informers, slanderers, with obscured brains, pharisaic yeast, sanhedrin of demons, accursed, despicable, stoners, enemies of all that is beautiful ..." And from John Chrysostom's golden mouth (the meaning of 'chrysostom') flowed this eloquence: "Brothel and theatre, the synagogue is also a cave of robbers and a den of wild animals ... Living for their belly, their mouth always gaping, the Jews do not behave better than swine and billy goats in their lewd baseness and their excessive gluttony ..."[16]

The crusades and the Black Death

The Jews remained relatively unmolested – throughout their amazing history they were never secure – till the calling of the first crusade

---

[15]Ron Rosenbaum, op. cit., ch. 18, passim.
[16]Id., pp. 32-33.

by Urban II in 1095. Taken by a sudden fervour, thousands of the most destitute people in Western Christendom left the little they possessed, if anything, and followed preachers like Peter the Hermit in the hope of finding lasting happiness, or a full stomach, beyond the forests which formed the horizon of their small and ignorant world. These hordes, fanatical in their ignorance and therefore dangerous, acted independently of the organised crusade of the princes and knights, and robbed and killed for their survival. It seems a rumour started circulating that duke Godfrey of Bouillon, one of the leaders of the crusade, had sworn to revenge the death of Christ in the blood of the Jews. "There was no shortage of preachers to incite at massacring the Jews without waiting for the confrontation with the Saracens." The reasoning was simple: hadn't the Jews killed the Son of God? Wasn't the Antichrist to be born from them? Why march toward the Orient to kill the Saracens and leave this devil's brood behind unharmed? The first Jews were murdered at Rouen, in the North-West of France, and the Judaic communities in that region sent warnings to their brothers in Germany, for the 'crusaders' were expected to follow the Rhine upstream into central Europe. "But the communities in the Rhine Valley, well settled, prosperous and having acquired a special statute, did not heed the warning."[17] This they would regret.

The first German victims were slaughtered in Speyer; then followed Worms, Mainz, and several villages where Jews had sought refuge. The chief instigator of the killings was a German count, Emicho von Leisingen, 'a noble of low repute and a brigand' according to some, 'a very noble and mighty man' say others. "The bishop of Würzburg collected butchered Jews. Fingers. Thumbs. Feet. Hands. Severed heads. He anointed these bloody pieces with oil and buried them in his garden since it is the nature of a man to perform his office. Count Emicho's Jerusalemfarers marched along the Rhine to

---

[17] Pierre Barret and Jean-Noël Gargand: *Si je t'oublie Jérusalem*, pp. 80 ff.

Cologne. Here, as elsewhere, Israelites scattered, disguised themselves. Some who were caught and refused to acknowledge 'the light of the world' were slain, their synagogues wrecked, burnt."[18] And the hordes marched on, singing of Jerusalem with many a rapturous 'hallelujah', robbing and destroying, and leaving behind a trail of Jewish blood in Metz, Trier, Regensburg, Bamberg, Prague, Nitra ...

Rather than letting themselves be baptised, which would have saved their lives, the German Jews first killed those who were near and dear to them, and then committed suicide. "This one killed his younger brother, that one his parents, wife and children. All accepted wholeheartedly the divine verdict [of their death]; recommending their souls to the Eternal, they cried out: "Hear, o Israel, the Eternal is our God, the Eternal is One!" Poliakov considers the slaughter by the crusaders 'a capital moment' in the history of the Jews. In the course of that summer of 1096, he writes, the tradition was born of a heroical and total refusal adopted as the attitude towards a majority by a minority ready to give their lives "to sanctify the Name" – a tradition which will serve as an example to future generations.[19]

Henceforth the Jews were fair game for any mob, gullible and excitable, looking for a scapegoat and for loot. "More animal-like than the animals themselves / Are all the Jews, there is no doubt. / One hates them much, and I hate them ... / And God hates them / And everybody must hate them", wrote a chronicler. The Jews were now to wear a distinctive sign – a yellow patch, the Star of David, or, as in Germany, a yellow conical hat – as prescribed by the IVth Lateran Council in 1215. "In the countries where the Christians are not distinguishable from the Jews and the Saracens by their dress, relations have taken place between Christians and Jewish or Saracen women, or vice versa. In order that such enormities may no longer

---

[18] Evan Connell: *Deus lo volt – A Chronicle of the Crusades*, p. 12.
[19] Léon Poliakov, op. cit., pp. 243, 245.

be excused as having been committed by mistake, it is decided that from now onwards the Jews of both genders will distinguish themselves from the other people by their dress, as has moreover been prescribed by Moses."[20]

Poliakov tells of one of the worst pogroms in the small German town of Röttingen where the Jews, in 1298, were suddenly accused of desecrating a host. One Rindfleisch led a mob against them and they were killed and burnt to the last person. But Rindfleisch did not stop there, for this 'butcher of the Jews', as he became known, led his troupe of Jew-baiters from place to place, attacking and slaying the Jews wherever he found them, except when they consented to be baptised. The killer wave ran through Franconia and Bavaria, making tens of thousands of victims. "What is new in this case is that for the first time a crime allegedly committed by one or a few Jews was held to be the responsibility of *all* the Jews in the country ... We can say in our modern language that it was (exception made for the excesses of the crusaders) the first case of 'genocide' of the Jews in Christian Europe." [21]

The next phase in our ever darker tale was caused by the Black Death, which ravaged Europe for three years, from 1347 till 1350, and exterminated at least a third of its population. Many historians have been of the opinion that this was one of the lowest points ever known in the continuity of history, in a century which one historian calls 'the Devil's century'. "In the cities they became ill in their thousands and nearly all died for lack of care and assistance. In the morning one found their corpses before the doorstep of the houses where they had died during the night ... It came to the point that one did not care more about a person who died than one does nowadays about the lowliest animal", wrote Giovanni Boccaccio. But questions began to be asked: why this scourge, and how had

---

[20]Id., pp. 252, 260.
[21]Id., pp. 283-84.

it come about? Was it sent by God or by Satan? Didn't everybody know who were the agents of Satan on earth? The scapegoats were found – the Jews! – and they would remain cast in this role for many centuries.

At Strasbourg two thousand Jews were burnt in their own cemetery and their possessions were distributed among the citizens. Colmar followed, and Worms, Oppenheim, Frankfurt, Erfurt, Cologne, Hannover ... Then the flagellants appeared upon the scene, bands of organised fanatics who went in procession from place to place and beat themselves in public with whips and spiked thongs till their flesh was torn from their bones. They invoked God's pity for this miserable world and preached general repentance, for the end was near. And as the end meant first the coming of the Antichrist, his accomplices, the Jews, were declared outside the law and often massacred after the flagellants had performed their pious acts.

"From the second half of the fourteenth century onwards", writes Poliakov, "the hatred against the Jews reached such an intensity that we can unreservedly fix at that time the crystallization of anti-Semitism in its classical form, which later led to the statement of Erasmus: 'If it is the sign of a good Christian to hate the Jews, then we are all good Christians' ... Even if the Jew is no longer present in some places [the Jews were banished from Spain, France and England], the people invent him, and the less a Christian population runs into Jews in its daily life, the more it is haunted by their image, about which it is told by its literature, at whom it stares in its churches, and whom it finds caricatured in its children's games and miracle plays ... The Jews will be despised in France and England no less than in Germany and Italy. The intensity of the feelings towards them seems to depend on the substratum on which rests the national culture, and to be more accentuated in the Germanic than in the Latin countries. In this way everything leads up to Germany becoming the predominant country of anti-Semitism."[22]

---

[22]Id., p. 303.

Luther, the anti-Semite

Then came the Reformation with the towering personality of Martin Luther, who threw his long shadow ahead in German history. In a previous chapter we have seen him as the precursor of nationalism; here now we will have a look at his influence on the sentiment which is inseparable from nationalism, namely racism, in this case mainly manifesting as anti-Semitism. "It is true that, right at the beginning, the Jews welcomed the Reformation, because it divided their enemies", writes Paul Johnson. "It is true also that Luther, in particular, turned to the Jews for support of his new construing of the Bible and his rejection of papal claims. In his 1523 pamphlet, *On the Fact that Christ was born a Jew*, he argued that there was now no reason at all why they should not embrace Christ, and foolishly looked forward to a voluntary mass conversion. When the Jews retorted that the Talmud conveyed an even better understanding of the Bible than his own, and reciprocated the invitation to convert, Luther first attacked them for their obstinacy, then in 1543 turned on them in fury. His pamphlet *On the Jews and their Lies*, published in Wittenberg, may be termed the first work of modern anti-Semitism, and a giant step forward on the road to the Holocaust."[23]

Luther's anti-Semitism grew into an obsession, as did everything which he thought justified his cause, and he became "the poison spitting author of strident anti-Semitic works", a whole series of them. He wrote for instance: "O, how the Jews love the Book Esther, which agrees so well with their bloodthirsty, revengeful, murderous greed and hope. The sun will never shine on a more bloodthirsty and revengeful people, which therefore thinks that it is the people of God and that it has to murder and strangle the heathen".[24] Or: "Cursed *goy* [ie non-Jew] that I am, I cannot understand how the Jews manage to be so skilful, unless I think that

---

[23]Paul Johnson: *A History of the Jews*, p. 242.
[24]Dietrich Bronder: *Bevor Hitler kam*, p. 352.

when Judas Iscariot hanged himself, his guts burst and emptied. Perhaps the Jews sent their servants with plates of silver and pots of gold to gather up Judas' piss with the other treasures, and then they ate and drank his offal, and thereby acquired eyes so piercing that they discovered in the Scriptures commentaries that neither Matthew nor Isaiah himself found there, not to mention the rest of the cursed *goyim*".[25]

"What shall we, Christians, do with this depraved, damned people of the Jews?" asked Luther. He had the answer ready: their schools and synagogues were to be burnt; their houses were to be flattened; all their prayer books and Talmuds were to be confiscated, for they were full of idolatry, lies, malediction and calumny; their rabbis should be forbidden to teach, on punishment of death; the Jews should be forbidden to walk freely in the streets; their usury should be forbidden and all their valuables in gold and silver taken from them; the young and strong Jews of both sexes should be forced to work in the sweat of their brows; they should compensate for all the money fleeced from the Germans, and be expelled from the country ...[26] Several authors who mention this programme proposed by Luther remind their readers that it was exactly what Hitler, who called Luther 'that powerful enemy of the Jews', would implement – adding a point of his own which for others had remained unthinkable, at least to such an extent. "The historical connection of the Lutheran anti-Judaism with the National-Socialist anti-Semitism is clear for all to see."[27]

"Luther was a racist pure and simple", states John Weiss, "not at all bothered that his hatred of the Jews denied the power of Christ to redeem all humanity. To him the Jew was simply not human. As the Protestant 'German Christians' of the Nazi movement would

---

[25] John Weiss: *Ideology of Death*, p. 23.
[26] Dietrich Bronder, op., cit., p. 352.
[27] Michael Ley: *Apokalypse und Moderne*, p. 153.

later claim: the blood of the Jew was beyond redemption."²⁸ "A line of anti-Semitic descent from Martin Luther to Adolf Hitler is easy to draw. Both Luther and Hitler were obsessed by a demonologized universe inhabited by Jews. 'Know, Christian', wrote Luther, 'that next to the devil thou hast no enemy more cruel, more venomous and violent than a true Jew.' Hitler himself, in that early dialogue with Dietrich Eckart, asserted that the later, anti-Semitic Luther was the genuine one. Luther's protective authority was invoked by the Nazis when they came to power, and his anti-Semitic writings enjoyed a revival of popularity. To be sure, the similarities of Luther's anti-Jewish exhortations with modern racial anti-Semitism and even with Hitler's racial policies are not merely coincidental. They all derive from a common historic tradition of Jew-hatred." (Lucy Dawidowicz[29])

Luther, with all his talents but also with his obvious flaws, seems to have been the embodiment of the German national character. Sebastian Haffner finds that 'he almost personifies the German character', and Thomas Mann calls him 'a gigantic incarnation of the German being'. There was in him the refinement, broad interest and great learning of the Renaissance; his inspired use of the written and spoken word practically created the German language anew; he had a feeling for music and liked to play within the circle of his family. There was the recognition of the use of reason, the refusal to accept what was felt to be erroneous, and the preparedness to stand up for the autonomy of reason within the individual domain. There was also the spiritual impulse, born from the soul and claiming the right of an unhampered individual development. In contradiction with all this there was in the same person coarseness, no doubt in accordance with the popular mentality of the time, but too often debasing itself to the boorish and scatological. The world of 'this Germanic prophet

---

[28]John Weiss, op. cit., p. 24.
[29]Lucy Dawidowicz: *The War against the Jews 1933-45*, p. 50.

of a Nordic religion' (Mosse) was filled more with the pestering presence of the Devil than with the consolation of the grace of God. And Luther's few lilies of pure spirituality flowered on a compost heap of psychological conflict and desperation. The Germany which responded to the call of Adolf Hitler will suffer from similar internal contradictions, and it will be torn apart by them.

A less prejudiced attitude

How, then, did the next stage in Europe's history, the Enlightenment, treat the Jews? Its principle was a radical questioning of all certainties and dogmas formerly held to be unquestionable. The field of questioning was broadened constantly by discoveries of new lands and peoples, and the religious and political dogmas had already suffered a severe shaking in the atrocious wars of religion among supposedly civilised countries. Moreover, science had changed the way men looked at the cosmos and, in consequence, the idea they made of its Maker. Copernicus had long been accepted, Galileo had discovered new heavenly bodies, and Newton's laws suggested a universe hardly compatible with the Biblical stories of creation. And scholars like Richard Simon had shown that the Bible, when philologically examined like any other literary document, proved to be a much less consistent document than could be expected of the Word of God.

England, the country of origin of the Enlightenment, was the exemplar of tolerance. Names like John Toland, John Locke and David Hume, willing to draw the last consequences of the enlightening but fallible human reason, are an ornament to its culture. In France there was Pierre Bayle (1647-1706), 'the great apostle of tolerance', who in still very intolerant times had to flee to Holland, the continental haven of intellectual freedom at that time. His *Historical Dictionary*, composed in Rotterdam, 'remains one of the most devastating indictments ever of the shameful behaviour and the mental confusion of men', while his *Treaty on Tolerance* set the tone for a less prejudiced attitude.

But then there is the case of that other *philosophe*, as the thinkers of the Enlightenment were called, Jean-Marie Arouet, alias Voltaire. Strange to say, this man, who was one of the prominent champions of the new ideals of liberty, equality and fraternity, was also 'a vicious anti-Semite' (Weiss). The many barbs against the Jews in his *Philosophical Dictionary* are there for all to read, eg. 'the Jews, our teachers and our enemies, whom we believe and detest', or: "The Jews thus treat history and ancient fables as their old-clothes-men threat their worn garments: they turn them and sell them for new at the highest possible price". Etc.[30] The English editor and translator of the *Dictionary* tries to defend his author: "This sort of thing is common form in Voltaire, and the legend of his anti-Semitism has persisted ... He did not dislike the Jews on 'racial grounds', but only because they were the people of the Old Testament and the precursors of Christianity" – which looks like a curious reason for his dislike.[31]

"I therefore ask, gentlemen, for the Protestant French as for all non-Catholics of the Kingdom, what you demand for yourselves: freedom, the equality of rights. I ask this also for that people torn from Asia, always on the move, always outlawed, always persecuted during more then eighteen centuries, which would take up our ways and customs if it were incorporated into us by our laws, and to which we do not have to reproach its morals, since they are the result of our own barbarism and of the humiliation to which we have condemned it unjustly!"[32] Thus resounded the voice of a deputy in the French National Assembly during the Revolution. The Jews, not without wrangling, were legally emancipated on 27 September 1791. Napoleon based his *Napoleonic Code* (1804) on the principle that all citizens were equal before the law and implemented it in the lands he conquered, breaking with the tradition of ages and giving their peoples a first taste of equality in freedom. Like all new beverages

---

[30]Voltaire: *Philosophical Dictionary*, pp. 16, 19.
[31]Id., p. 16 (footnote).
[32]Id., p. 107.

it tasted strange and some rejected it. The ideals of the French Revolution pervaded the minds and the political practice only gradually, in the advancing and retiring waves of the nineteenth century revolutions with repercussions in all European countries. Hitler and Nazism, arisen on a soil which remained inimical to these ideals, attempted the ultimate effort to counteract and annul them.

'The Jews are our misfortune'

"A Jew remains a Jew, in Germany or any other country. We can never change this race, even by centuries of residence among other people", says the *Handbook of the Hitler Youth,* published in 1937.[33] This statement, a point of doctrine for Hitler's young, rash and ready heroes, is a logical absurdity when put within the framework of their own beliefs. Isn't race a matter of blood, and isn't blood always changed, for better or worse, by mixing with other kinds of blood? If such a change were not possible, how could the Germanic race be purified by a gradual upgrading of its blood, a process which Hitler and Himmler wanted to bring about? Or how could Germans 'sin against the blood' through sexual intercourse with the depraved race of the Jews or with other subhumans?

Fichte was 'the philosopher of the German war of national liberation against Napoleon', in which quality we have met him before. His famous *Addresses to the German Nation* (1808) were delivered while French troops still occupied Berlin. In these addresses he said as one of the very first that, if Germany went down, the rest of the world would go down with it. "Called the father of German nationalism, Fichte has also been called the father of modern German anti-Semitism. His celebration of German nationalism was matched by his denigration of the Jews. In 1793 he had argued against German emancipation, characterizing the Jews as a state within a state that

---

[33] John Weiss, op. cit., p. 97.

would undermine the German nation. Jewish ideas were as obnoxious as French ideas. The only way in which he could concede giving rights to the Jews, he said, would be 'to cut off all their heads in one night, and to set new ones on their shoulders, which should contain not a single Jewish idea'."[34]

Lucy Dawidowicz sees the Jewish emancipation progressing from Napoleon onwards in cycles, closely connected with the heightening waves of nationalist feelings and German self-assertion. Every gain of freedom by the Jews was paralleled by a more intense and outspoken anti-Semitic reaction. "The stronger the longing for national unity, the more burning became the preoccupation with the Jewish question", George Mosse too observes. One important focus of such a cycle was of course the unification of Germany by Otto von Bismarck in 1871. From that date onwards the open attacks on the Jews will no longer be felt to be a general matter of opinion or racial theory, but a necessary defence of the well-being of the nation. The seriousness of this defence was directly proportional to the seriousness of the Germans' idea about their value as a Volk and the vocation of this Volk in the world. The Jewish 'foreign body', though a minority of one percent, was considered highly obnoxious to the health of the Volk – and came very convenient as a scapegoat for all the problems of a country which was deeply divided and under severe psychological stress.

Onto the Jews was projected everything reactionary Germany did not want to be, or pretended it did not want to be, or could not be, or actually *was* without wanting to be. The Jews were associated with a modern world in the making, while reactionary Germany persisted in looking inward, which was a good thing, but also backward, which was not. That it developed simultaneously into the foremost industrial nation in the world made it more schizophrenic, and the Jew still more guilty. And that the Jews were intelligent and some of them highly visible, did not help either.

---

[34] Lucy Dawidowicz, op. cit., p. 54.

A few quotes from the literature will have to do. They are intended to suggest the anti-Jewish atmosphere of a period in the German past when anti-Semitism became an organized movement in a structured, even if psychologically afflicted, society. Paul de Lagarde, a leading authority in Oriental studies who then became 'the volkisch patron saint of the anti-Semitic movement', published his *German Essays* in 1878. He had become convinced that the Jews of his own day "had lost all true connections with the ancient Hebrews; they were fossilized, a living example of the spirit run dry. Pharisaic fundamentalism was now the essence of Judaism, based as it was on the literal observance of the laws. Since such a sterile religious attitude was incompatible with a vital mysticism, it could never fuse with the living and developing Germanic religion. By the same token, the Jews could never be Germans ... Lagarde attributed conspiratorial motives to contemporary Jewry. The lack of true religion meant a turning toward evil, a substitution of materialistic desires for inward faith.

"Lagarde seems to have believed that the Jews practised ritual murder and he even declared that the Talmud and its prescriptions rendered the Jews a powerful weapon in the unavoidable power struggle. The Jewish question was therefore not to be met with tolerance. Instead it was reducible to a mortal contest: either the Jewish or the 'true' German way of life must prevail in the end ... The Jew became the incarnation of evil. Any humaneness Lagarde possibly possessed was eventually obscured by his call for the extermination of the Jews like bacilli"[35] – a simile which was to enjoy a long life. Be it once more remembered that these kinds of texts were published or quoted from not only by the Nazis, but also by all anti-Semitic organisations, and that pre-Nazi Germany was flooded with them.

The 'Anti-Semitic League', the first organisation to bear an explicit anti-Semitic name, was launched in 1879. Eugen Dühring, philosopher

---

[35] George Mosse, op. cit., p. 38.

and economist, published *The Jewish Question as a Racial, Moral and Cultural Question* in 1880, claiming that he was the first in Germany to consider this 'question' in racial terms. "Dühring looked upon the Jews as a 'counter-race' separated from all humanity, whom neither conversion nor assimilation could affect because their basic nature was evil and unchangeable. He shared the Wagnerian thesis that Christianity was a product of 'Hebraic Orientalism', and that those who clung to the 'entire' Christian tradition could not truly oppose Judaism or defend the 'Nordic tradition'."[36] "Only the Nordic gods could help the German people to victory, for only the Nordic religion was able to combat Jewish infiltration. According to Dühring the battle lines were drawn between the forces of Jewish materialism and Old Germanism. With their inherent racial strength the Germans would triumph over the alien intruders. In this manner, the formulations of the volkisch thought began to be used as weapons in a widespread German anti-Semitism."[37]

"1880 was a watershed year", writes Dawidowicz, "the start of a torrent of anti-Semitism that did not abate for nearly twenty years. It was as if all the quiet streams of prejudice conjoined in a massive flow of anti-Semitic hate, inundating the whole country. It began at the end of 1879, when Heinrich von Treitschke, National Liberal and prestigious professor of history at the University of Berlin, started a series of articles on the Jewish question in the *Preussische Jahrbücher*, which he edited. 'Even in circles of the most highly educated, among men who would reject with disgust any ideas of ecclesiastical intolerance or national arrogance, there resounds as if from one mouth: *Die Juden sind unser Unglück!* (the Jews are our misfortune) – the phrase was to ring down through the next German generations. Heinrich Class, a leading anti-Semite [and Chairman of the Pan-Germans] one generation later, wrote that 'the phrase became a part of my body and soul when I was twenty years old; it essentially

---

[36]Lucy Dawidowicz, op. cit., p. 68.
[37]George Mosse, op. cit., p. 131.

influenced my later political work'. Issued in pamphlet form, Treitschke's articles gave reinforcement and professional authoritativeness to the anti-Semitic movement. Treitschke spoke, the anti-Semites said, 'for thousands, perhaps millions of his countrymen'".[38] Poliakov calls Treitschke *le maître à penser* of the German nationalist youth, which is how he became known to us in an earlier chapter.

It should in fairness be mentioned that Treitschke's anti-Jewish writings caused a wave of disagreement. His foremost opponent in this was the great Latinist Theodor Mommsen, who warned that Treitschke had rendered anti-Semitism respectable and that it would lead to a conflict without mercy. "Till the end of his days Mommsen gave the best of his powers to a struggle against German chauvinism and racism, against 'those nationalist idiots who want to replace the universal Adam with a German Adam, and bestow him with all the splendours of the human spirit'". Directly or indirectly, these discussions became part of the common ideas and "anti-Semitism was integrated in the bourgeois way of life; anti-Semitic movements and parties multiplied; international conferences were called (Dresden 1882, Chemnitz 1883); numerous student organizations decided to exclude the Jews ..."[39]

Theodor Fritsch, who played an important part in our story as the founder of the *Hammerbund* and the *Germanenorden*, became "a linchpin in the anti-Semitic movement, holding it together as a political organizer, publisher and author from its early political stirrings in the 1880's until Hitler's accession to power". (Fritsch died in 1933.) George Mosse writes about him: "The racial stereotype attributed so many grotesque qualities to the Jews that he was in essence dehumanized. Fritsch's work again demonstrates this ominous development, for in his *Fireballs* (1881) he explicitly denied human

---

[38]Lucy Dawidowicz, op. cit., p. 65.
[39]Léon Poliakov, op. cit., p. 277.

status to the Jews. Here he claimed that God had created the Jew as a buffer between man and ape. The Nazis assimilated this thought in their own propaganda when, in 1931, one of their speakers asserted that non-Nordic man occupied an intermediary position between Nordic man and the animal world. The non-Nordic man was not a whole man, for he still shared traits with the apes."[40]

The Austrian *Antisemitenbund* was founded in 1889, in a country which was even more anti-Semitic than Germany, and where figures like Georg von Schönerer and Karl Lueger made a lasting impression on 'Adi'. The next year saw the birth of the German *Antisemitische Volkspartei*, which received 48,000 votes, but three years later 260,000. "In fact, anti-Semitism became the chief vehicle of the diffusion of the volkisch movement. Those who were attracted primarily by anti-Semitism had no difficulty in accepting the basic volkisch ideas, and those already in the movement took readily to the precepts of anti-Semitic racism."[41]

In 1890 Hermann Ahlwardt published *The Desperate Struggle between the Aryan Peoples and Judaism*. "Ahlwardt stated that a people who rid itself of the Jews freed itself for the material development of the Volk, and thereby rose toward dominion over the world. For him, as for the romantic advocates of the Volk, Jewry was the Mephistopheles of world history. In dealing with the Jews, Christian mercy was decidedly out of place ... Was this a plea for violence? Certainly! But, when it came to concrete proposals to effect such measures, he displayed an ambivalence which was, as yet, typical. When he drew up an actual programme, Ahlwardt could only advocate the imposition of stringent restrictions upon Jews, a decree proclaiming them foreigners on German soil and excluding them from all areas of German life and culture. He also proposed that eventually all Jews be deported from Europe and their surplus

---

[40] Georges Mosse, op. cit., p. 143
[41] Id., p. 133.

capital retained by the German nation. Curiously, this was almost exactly the same as the National Socialist programme for dealing with the Jews ...

"Ahlwardts's programme broadly foreshadowed that of the Nazis, for they also reflected an ambivalence. On the one hand, there were the fanatics who asserted that the 'final solution' must bring about a correct correspondence between ideology and action and that the deportation of the Jews to distant places only evaded the issue. On the other hand, there were those functionaries and leaders in the party who wanted to encourage Jewish emigration at all costs ... The ultimate consequences of a glorification of merciless cruelty within volkisch ideology, and the Nazi extension of it, finally engulfed the minds of Germany's leaders. Extermination became the literal fact, not just a rhetorical device to arouse human passions."[42]

These examples leave little doubt about the general thrust of anti-Semitism in Germany at the end of the nineteenth century. The book that capped it all was the much admired 'racist bible', *The Foundations of the Nineteenth Century*, Houston Chamberlain's blockbuster, published in 1899. "Convinced that all great creations stemmed from Teutonic blood, he believed the only flaw of the ancient tribes was their failure to destroy all peoples within their reach. We must correct this error, he insisted, and also breed for superior human types, as dictated by Darwinism. However stern the measures necessary, Aryan blood must be purified, liberating its martial spirit and creative power.

"The Jew was the most powerful foe. Other races were merely inferior, but Jews, the unnatural result of accidental crossbreeding in the ancient Middle East, through millennia of inbreeding had created a uniquely evil racial force ... The Jews knew Germany was the last obstacle; elsewhere they had subverted civilization through the intellectual Judaization of Enlightenment ideas, ideas denying

---

[42] Id., pp. 138-39.

the reality of race, preaching cosmopolitanism, and denying blood loyalties. If purged, however, the race of Luther could not fail in the struggle with the race of money changers. Chamberlain, darling of conservative intellectuals, envisioned the future as Hitler would do: a racial battle to the death against Jewry."[43]

In this context the racist extremism of most German university professors, secondary teachers and their students has to be mentioned. It explains, among other things, why whole batches of young men volunteered enthusiastically for the First World War, why the Nazis found such easy access to the universities, and why a 'Germanic science' could be defined in opposition to a 'Jewish science'. "There was nothing comparable in [other] Western nations. From 1890 to 1914 the generation that would support the Nazis found the superiority of Germanic racial stock a textbook cliché. Countless memoirs of German and Austrian Jews tell of harassment received from public school teachers, petty classroom tyrants enforcing the discipline of the barracks, spiritual warriors for the Germanic soul. Although millions of Germans supported liberalism and socialism, their ideas were not to be found in the schools. Jewish teachers might have contradicted stereotypes, but of some eight thousand teaching appointments from 1875 to 1895, about forty went to Jews. Prussia never had more than twelve [Jewish] secondary school teachers."[44]

Most of the *Burschenschaften*, the traditional student societies, introduced 'the Aryan paragraph', a clause in their charters which excluded Jews from membership. Consequently 'the exclusive and famous duelling fraternities' too refused to admit Jews, as 'they had no honour to defend'. The curious tradition of duelling among students was upheld to bear testimony to their virility. No student was truly a man without a scar in his face telling anyone in his later

---

[43] John Weiss, op. cit., p. 136.
[44] Id., p. 130.

life of his courage in the face of possible death. (Duellists died only, and exceptionally, by accident.) "Brotherhoods such as the Apollo, each with its own *Gasthaus* or beer-cellar, distinctive coloured cap and ribbons and duelling matches against rival fraternities, were the focus of student social life; they were at the same time initiation into manhood. The duelling was not so much a test of skill as an ordeal to be withstood without flinching, the sewing up afterwards a trial of self-mastery. Beer was drunk in the same spirit until it leaked from every flushed pore while songs of 'knights and giants, of chivalry and wine and honour' were roared out."[45]

By this path, we arrive again at the powerful nationalist and anti-Semitic organisations, in part secret, which were the Pan-Germans, the Germanenorden and the more informal but very influential Bayreuth circle, three high roads to Hitler. From 1920 onwards *The Protocols of the Wise Men of Zion* will exert their influence in the background; the traces of their poison are detectable on each and every occasion when anti-Semitism was involved. Their influence is made plain by the following entry in Joseph Goebbels' diary, written as late as 13 May 1943: "I study once more in detail the Zionist Protocols. Until now I had always encountered the opinion that they were not useful for actual propaganda. Now I find, while reading them, that we can use them very well. The Zionist Protocols are today as modern as on the day they were published for the first time. At midday I talk with the Führer on this subject. The Führer is of the opinion that the Zionist Protocols can claim absolute authenticity".[46]

This rough outline of the intensifying anti-Semitism before the First World War would remain incomplete without drawing the attention to one of the most potent inductors of the anti-Jewish sentiment, Richard Wagner (1813-83). His influence as a composer was enormous, not only in Germany but everywhere in Europe, especially in France. But, as so often happens, the everyday personality

---

[45] Peter Padfield: *Himmler – Reichsführer-SS*, p. 40.
[46] Joseph Goebbels: *Tagebücher V*, p. 1932.

of the artist did not always fit with the greatness of his creations. The exceptional quality of the best of Wagner's visionary music remains beyond dispute. (Léon Poliakov calls him "that medium of the nineteenth century".) His character, on the contrary, was often egotistical in the extreme, violent, vindictive, and on occasion plain nasty.

He succeeded single handed in giving life and colour to the German national myth by recreating the legend of the Nibelungs and evoking in soul-stirring music the world of the Nordic gods, their powers, and their ultimate *Götterdämmerung*. He also played a crucial role in the integration of the myths of Christianity into the vision which confirmed the German people in their role as carriers of the destiny of mankind. *Parsifal*, 'the sacred masterpiece of Bayreuth', upon which Wagner meditated for a quarter of a century and which would become his apotheosis, was generally recognised as a symbolic play of the purity of the blood, Germany's Holy Grail. Wagner too turned Christ into a German superhero, and Bayreuth into 'the national sanctuary of the volkisch revival movement' (Köhler).

This symbiosis of the Nordic and the Christian religions, so typical for the Germany of that time, is a most amazing feat of intellectual inconsistency, confusion or schizophrenia. "The supreme god of the Germans [Wotan] did not necessarily have to make way for the God of the Christians", wrote Wagner, "he could even be perfectly identified with him. It was sufficient to strip him of the superficial attributes which the various peoples, in accordance with their character, land and climate, had ascribed to him ... This primitive, unique and national god, from whom the races originated, was not in the least abandoned and forgotten; for in him was found, as it was in Christ, son of God, the decisive analogy that he too had died and been mourned and revenged, as we now are revenging Christ on the Jews. The faith and adherence were more easily transferred to Christ because in him people recognized the primitive god."[47]

---

[47] Léon Poliakov, op. cit., p. 241.

"The Wagnerian heroes and the Wagnerian music have animated the German armies from 1914 till 1918, still more in their hours of misfortune and sacrifice than in their hours of triumph."[48] This is even more true of the German armies in the Second World War, for they fought under the command of a Wagnerian, Adolf Hitler, who had seen to it that they grew up with Wagner's music in their ears at every important public or political manifestation. Hitler had made Wagner into the official composer of the Third Reich; living composers, like Richard Strauss, only moved in Wagner's shadow. The reason was that Wagner and his music had played such an important role in Hitler's own life. From his years in Linz onwards, he had eaten and drunk Wagner, seen his operas an astonishing number of times and read every published word of him.

He knew Wagner's music by heart, as is testified by many witnesses, and could whistle it faultlessly. A few measures of Wagner sufficed to calm him down in any circumstances and made him behave as if entranced. "This music affected him physically", wrote Ernst Hanfstängl, "it had become part of Hitler's being."[49] And Hitler himself said one day: "When I hear Wagner, it is as if I hear the rhythms of the world in its beginnings".[50] Hitler never hid what he owned to Wagner and he thanked him by taking Bayreuth and Wagner's legacy under his special protection – as told by Brigitte Hamann in her *Winifred Wagner, oder Hitlers Bayreuth.*

Wagner's art helped spreading his anti-Semitism, which intensified over the years to the point where he declared: "I hold the Jewish race to be the born enemy of pure humanity and everything noble in it. It is certain that it is running us Germans to the ground, and I am perhaps the last German who knows how to hold himself upright in the face of Judaism, which already rules everything".[51]

---

[48]Ibid.
[49]Ernst Hanfstängl: *Hitler – The Missing Years*, p. 49.
[50]*Monologe im Führerhauptquartier*, p. 234.
[51]In Robert Wistrich: *Hitler and the Holocaust*, p. 1.

From him is also: "That the human race would perish, would not be a pity; but that it would perish because of the Jews would be an ignominy".[52] Joachim Köhler puts it trenchantly: "Nobody will take from [Wagner] the merit of having been the first in German history to contribute with his writings to the advent of the 'disappearance' of the Jews".[53]

Assimilation

When having read all this, it may come as a surprise how intimately the Jews felt integrated in Germany. Walter Rathenau, the epitome of the German Jew, declared: "I am a German of Jewish descent. My people is the German people, my fatherland is Germany, my religion that Germanic faith which is above all religions."[54] Professor Heinz Moral committed suicide after being dismissed from his university post for racial reasons; in a letter to the dean of faculty he had written: "I am a Jew and have never made a secret of it, but my entire outlook is German, and I have always been proud to be a German whose religion is Jewish." According to Günter Rohrmoser "an equally successful symbiosis was achieved in no other Western country as it was between the Jews and the Germans. It is one of the most incomprehensible and also really tragic occurrences that this Holocaust has happened precisely in the country in which such a close and fruitful intellectual and philosophical symbiosis was realized as between Jews and Germans."[55] And Christian von Krockow writes: "In hardly any other country have the Jews felt themselves so national as in Germany, and nowhere have they provided such an important cultural contribution."[56]

---

[52] Léon Poliakov, op. cit., p. 247.
[53] Joachim Köhler: *Wagners Hitler*, p. 92.
[54] Otto Friedrich: *Before the Deluge*, p. 113.
[55] Günter Rohrmoser: *Deutschlands Tragödie – Der geistige Weg in den Nationalsozialismus*, p. 74.
[56] Christian von Krockow: *Hitler und seine Deutschen*, p. 90.

Viktor Klemperer, a Jewish professor of French literature, wrote in 1939 in his diary: "Until 1933 and for at least a good century before that, the German Jews were entirely German and nothing else. Proof: the thousands and thousands of half- and quarter-Jews etc. Jews and 'persons of Jewish descent', which is proof that Germans and Jews lived and worked together without friction in all spheres of German life. The anti-Semitism which was always present is not at all proof to the contrary, because the friction between Jews and 'Aryans' was not half so great as, for example, that between Protestants and Catholics, or between employers and employees, or between East Prussians, for example, and southern Bavarians, or Rhinelanders and Berliners. The German Jews were a part of the German nation, as the French Jews were part of the French nation, etc. They played their part within the life of Germany, by no means as a burden on the whole. Their role was rarely that of the worker, still less of the agricultural labourer. They were, and remain (even though now they no longer wish to remain so), Germans, in the main intellectuals and educated people."[57]

It is a fact that the Jews, 'a highly diverse community', were closely involved in the German life. The degree to which they were 'assimilated' or 'integrated' is corroborated by the difficulty of trying to extricate them again. Wagner, Hitler, Rosenberg and Heydrich were themselves suspected of having Jewish blood in their veins (Hitler's case remains pending, probably forever); Emil Maurice, Albrecht Haushofer, Erhard Milch and other prominent people in Naziland were part Jewish. Emile Maurice, Hitler's chauffeur, lover of his niece Geli Raubal, notorious street brawler in the SA and co-founder of the SS, had to be declared a 'honorary Aryan' by his boss, the only member of the SS ever to enjoy the privilege.[58]

---

[57]Viktor Klemperer: *Tagebücher 1937-1939*, pp. 132-33. This translation in Robert Wistrich: *Hitler and the Holocaust*, p. 49.
[58]See Anna Maria Sigmund: *Des Führers bester Freund*.

Besides, what does it actually mean to be half, or a quarter, or an eight, or a sixteenth Jewish – or of any other race? Where is that fraction located in a person? It is only in recent years that scientists can *try* to find it in the genes, together with so many other traces of a physical inheritance which soon fades into the mists of the past. The Germanic tribes had on countless occasions mixed with other peoples, as was of course known to all anthropologists. The problem with the Jews was that they had kept their religious identity as a people and that their religion demanded a separate existence, while generally speaking people were not yet ready to mix with others on their home turf. The Nazis, Hitler in the first place, always contended that their racial cleansing was not a matter of religion but of purification 'of the blood'; yet the proofs of a person belonging to the Jewish race were in most cases religious registers and other documents, also concerning the ancestry of Jews who had converted to Protestantism or Catholicism, or who had become a-religious.

The Jewish menace

"Numerically, the Jews remained a tiny minority, never more than about one percent of the population. Those few, however, tended to congregate in Berlin. The 50 families of 1671 grew to a population of 3322 in 1800, to 92,000 in 1900, to a peak of 173,000 in 1925 (about six times the 29,000 in Frankfurt, Germany's second-largest Jewish community)." Even during this increase, Berlin's Jews never numbered more than five percent of the city's population, but they managed to acquire some very visible positions of power and prestige. They were enormously influential in commerce, dominating the giant Deutsche, Dresdner and Darmstädter banks, and huge department stores like Wertheim, Tietz and Kaufhaus Israel. The most important newspaper groups were owned by Jews, and, to a very considerable extent, the spectacular culture of Berlin in the 1920s; the culture dominated by personalities like Max Reinhardt and Bruno Walter and Albert Einstein, was a Jewish culture. "To the

Jews, this was naturally a matter of pride, and more than one Jewish chronicler has pointed out that one quarter of all the Nobel Prizes won by Germans in the first third of this century were won by German Jews. [Twenty Jewish Nobel Prize winners will emigrate after 1933.] To many gentiles, however, even those who vehemently deny the accusation of anti-Semitism, this flowering of Jewish life represented the triumph of an alien and vaguely threatening force."[59]

When reading about Nazism and the Holocaust, it is rather unexpected to find that the Jewish people, its character and its activities in the present as in bygone times are rarely dealt within the general literature. Many books and chapters of books endeavour to analyse and explain the Holocaust, or at least give due consideration to the monstrous event, but its victims remain practically unknown to the common reader. Even Joachim Fest, most insightful where Hitler's character and the war are concerned, hardly touches this subject. Only a few recent writers like Michael Burleigh and John Weiss make the effort to find out who the German Jews actually were, how they lived, and, most important, in how far the accusations of their torturers and executioners were justified.

Were the Jewish people really one coherent, monolithic body, striving to fulfil its destiny as a race? Was it to this end that the Jews gathered the world's money in their hands, and that they tried to crown Reason as the new God of humanity, thereby intending to loosen and destroy all established values? This was what Hitler asserted. He also said that Socialism and Communism, children of the Enlightenment, were clearly agencies, as were capitalism and so-called 'progress', meant to engulf the existing world, break it up and wash it to its doom. The Jews had worked themselves to the top in order to take over German society and turn it into one of their global colonies. Having brought about the First World War, they did not risk their skin at the front but exploited the war situation for their profit and advancement. Ultimately, they would attempt to

---

[59] Otto Friedrich. op. cit., pp. 110-11.

dominate the world and establish their rule as the Chosen People. Then the Antichrist would mount his throne and cause the world's destruction.

'The Jew'

"'The Jew' was invariably referred to in Nazi discourse as a type to which *all* Jews conformed, whether western or eastern, men or women, secular or religious, assimilated or unassimilated, bourgeois or proletarian. Even baptised Jews were irrevocably tainted in Nazi ideology by the stigma of degenerate blood. Jews as a 'counter-race' were perceived as the polar opposite to the German 'Aryans', being inherently destructive, parasitical, and agents of decomposition."[60] We find this statement by Robert Wistrich confirmed by Léon Poliakov, who writes: "'Jews' and 'Judaism' – and this cannot be repeated too often – were only words, covering very diverse matters of which the status of being non-Christians may have been the only common denominator".[61]

By far the greatest numbers of German Jews were North and East European Ashkenazim, very different in their beliefs and lifestyle from the Sephardim, of Portuguese and Spanish origin and who lived mainly in Southern Europe. The Jewish community in Germany was further divided into orthodox Jews, following the prescriptions of their faith to the letter, and less strict or sceptical believers; then there were the apostate Jews who had converted to Protestantism or Catholicism, and who were baptised; and there were the atheist Jews, who no longer believed in a God of any kind, or maybe in the abstract God of Spinoza or of the Enlightenment's deism. Another dividing line among the Jews ran between the 'assimilationists' and the separatists, the latter being mostly orthodox, and was caused by differences in attitude towards a desired or despised integration into

---

[60]Robert Wistrich, op. cit., pp. 110-11.
[61]Léon Poliakov, op. cit., p. 42.

the society of the *goyim*. And there were, as relative newcomers, the Zionists, for whom leaving the European host countries and going back to Jerusalem was the only solution to the Jewish question.

The political choice of the Jews, now legally free citizens of the German nation, was inevitably influenced by the tribulations in their past. Not only did the reactionary German right disagree with their emancipation, many Rightist organisations frowned at Jewish membership and more and more of them inserted 'the Aryan paragraph' into their statutes. The majority of Jews who participated in the political process were therefore found among the liberal parties at the centre of the political spectrum, while some no longer confessing activists moved to the Left and joined the socialists and the communists. This choice was also influenced by another differentiation within the Jewish community between rich, well-to-do and poor. There were only a few Rothschilds, Rathenaus, Ballins and Wittgensteins, but many peddlers and pawn-brokers, with in between the respectable middle class of lawyers, doctors, journalists and clerks.

The most eye-catching difference in the German Jewish population was that between the 'assimilated' Jews and the *Ostjuden*, Jews who had recently arrived from the East. The majority of the German Jews felt at home in Germany and considered the country their fatherland. Not only had they fully adapted to the culture of the Gentiles and did they feel comfortable in it, they actually loved Germany, were proud of being Germans, and would not hesitate to give their lives for the country. They married Germans and could in most cases not be told from them, for the caricatural stereotype did not often agree with the real people.

The *Ostjuden*, however, were of a different kind. They were refugees from Eastern Europe, mainly from Russia, and belonged to orthodox, socially backward communities. They were "frequently unemployed and disoriented by the post-war upheavals and revolutions in Eastern Europe. Moreover, they were cultural outsiders and an easy target for xenophobic accusations of economic parasitism.

In the Weimar Republic they were approximately one fifth of the Jewish population. The more assimilated and established members of German Jewry tended to believe that the revival of anti-Semitism was directed primarily or even exclusively against the Ostjuden, but this turned out to be a tragic self-deception".[62] In fact, the integrated Jews detested the Ostjuden, who, in their black kaftans, with their unkempt beards, large hats and weird hairdo, were so highly visible, and who therefore put into question the security which the integrated Jews thought they had obtained.

The stream of Ashkenazi Jews from the East towards Austria, Germany and, in their tens of thousands, towards the USA, had started moving because of a wave of pogroms in Russia in the wake of the 1903 events in Kichinev. Kichinev was the capital of Bessarabia and forty-five percent Jewish. The inimical feelings against the Jews climaxed, as usual, in the Holy Week before Easter, when in many places the murderers of Christ were even forbidden to appear in public. Though there were unmistakable signs of an imminent eruption of anti-Semitism, the authorities took no preventive measures, which enforced the populace in their belief that the Tsar himself wanted it. Jews were killed, many more were wounded, and their houses were ransacked. What the Russian authorities had not foreseen was the international outcry caused by this pogrom in 'primitive, barbarian Russia', where the belief that 'the Judeans cut the throat of the Russian child and drink its blood' was still widespread. When pondering the number of Jews killed in the Russian pogroms at that time – 47, or 110, or 810 ... – Poliakov has the reflection: "It is hard to repress a nostalgic thought about a past when the massacre of 810 Jews prompted a universal condemnation",[63] when after the Holocaust the habit of reading and writing the numbers of thousands, tens of thousands and even millions made our souls callous.

---

[62] Robert Wistrich, op. cit., p. 33.
[63] Léon Poliakov: *Histoire de l'antisémitisme II*, p. 347.

A Jewish race?

Has there ever been a pure race which might be called Jewish? The historical data are dubious, according to André Pichot, to whom we turn once more for our information. At the time of Vacher de Lapouge and Ernst Haeckel, when in Darwin's footsteps the first trees of humanity were drawn up, the Jews sometimes came out on top on the same level as the Aryans, although, as we have seen, many of those trees were the result of a fertile imagination and cultural prejudice, not of facts gained by a scientific method. Pichot calls such constructs of the imagination a *roman*, literally a novel, which is a story based on the imaginative quality of the intellect.

"It was difficult to characterize a Jewish race, even if Haeckel admitted in the 1860s the existence of such a race", writes Pichot. What *did* exist were, in Eastern Europe, communities of Jews who separated themselves from the rest of the population and who, by marrying among themselves, bred 'characteristic genetic groups', by the later racist scientists wrongly defined as determinants of a race. As a matter of fact, the Jews 'had been mixed for many centuries with the other European populations', and were certainly 'well integrated' into German society.

Vacher de Lapouge did not believe in the existence of a Jewish race. "In sum, the Jews are not a race but a nationality, of which the primary common characteristics are the religion and a special psychology, due to a small number of Canaanite infiltrations. In reality, Israel is outspread over the nations, and even weighs heavily upon them, but there is no Israelite race in the anthropological sense of the word ... The persecution of them, which has little by little raised its head everywhere, has slowly eliminated the elements which were not sufficiently homogenous; what remains of the assumed ubiquity of the Jews is nothing but one more example, and a curious one, of social selection." The community of people called 'the Jews' was therefore based on 'psychic convergence' and not on the physiological or taxonomic facts. To be a Jew, according to Vacher de Lapouge, was to belong to a group with the 'Jewish mentality', which was the result of religion and tradition.

Pichot concludes: "The notion of race – whether Jewish or any other – has never had the essentialist aspect with which the historians have endowed it." This means that the notion of 'race' has never been based on scientific fact. It was precisely because the notion of race lacked a strict definition that it was possible to designate the Jews as a race, "although there were no clearly defined biological criteria in their case. Was this quasi-race of the Jews held to be an inferior race? Not really. It was rather 'unwanted'. Vacher de Lapouge, however anti-Semitic, does not qualify the Jews as an inferior race; he rather holds them up as a kind of model for the establishment of a new aristocracy by natural or eugenic means." Here Pichot quotes from Hitler's dictates to Bormann, on one of his very last days at the bunker in Berlin, saying that the Jew is fundamentally a stranger, and that the Jewish race is foremost a community of the mind, shaped by a common destiny through all the persecutions they had to suffer in the course of the centuries.[64] There are several indications of Hitler's grudging admiration for the Jews, because of their spirit of resilience as a people and their remarkable intellect. But this secret admiration too will add fuel to his burning, obsessive hatred of them.

Money

It is an amazing fact that in Germany the medieval guild system was still very much in use in the first decades of the twentieth century for anybody who wanted to learn and practice a craft. Emil Maurice, for instance, Hitler's part-Jewish chauffeur whom his boss made into a 'honorary Aryan', earned his living first as an apprentice watch repairer, then as a watch repairer in his own shop and finally as a

---

[64] Id., pp. 404, 403.

master watch maker, from whom Hitler sometimes ordered the gold watches which he wanted to gift on certain occasions.[65]

The continuation of this medieval practice in an apparently modernised society is symptomatic for many of the themes we have met with in the last chapters. Medieval attitudes had remained part of the reactionary German mentality of the middle classes, causing them to remain behind the times in the quickly developing industrial modernisation which determined the life of the lower social classes. With the respectful attitude towards the traditional craft went an attitude towards money, equally old-fashioned, feeling threatened by notions of capital and interest, and expressed in theories like that of Gottfried Feder, who wanted the world to return to a kind of barter economy. The Jews were closely associated with modern capitalism. They were even suspected of dominating and manipulating capitalism worldwide. And if there was one commodity they were practically synonymous with, it was money.

Yet, the Jews have not always been 'money people'. "In Egypt and the Near East, they were mostly agricultural colonizers; elsewhere they were mostly represented in great numbers in the crafts of that period, especially as weavers and dyers, professions which in some regions they almost monopolized; but one found them also as goldsmiths, glass blowers, and as producers of bronze and iron." Paul of Tarsus was a tent maker, and Baruch Spinoza polished lenses for a living. "Some were simple labourers, others lived from commerce or the liberal arts. Still, as the historian J. Juster rightly underlines, 'no pagan author has typified them as merchants; one encounters nowhere the identification of Judaism with trade, which a few centuries later will become commonplace'.

"Still other Jews were much appreciated professional soldiers, fighting or mounting guard on the frontiers of the [Roman] empire. There were also Jewish administrators, sometimes of a very high

---

[65] See Anna Maria Sigmund, op. cit.

rank; in the imperial hierarchy there were Jewish knights and senators, Jewish legates and even Jewish praetors. To this one could add that the Jews of the diaspora adopted as a rule the language as well as the dress of the province where they lived, and that from the linguistic and cultural standpoints they were 'assimilated', even Hellenizing or Latinizing their names. From all of this one may conclude that they did not seem to suffer from a special animosity, and that nothing except their cult made them conspicuous in the mosaic of peoples which constituted the population of the Roman Empire."[66]

The association of the Jews with money seems to have been the result of the Christians associating them with Judas Iscariot and his thirty pieces of silver. "During the early Christian centuries the myth of the Jews as an avaricious race of parasites added force to that of the Jews as deicides. As Roman influence waned and Christian clergy gained power, they successfully restricted the activities of Jews, creating the basis for endless calumnies about the alleged Jewish attraction to dishonest practices in petty commerce, second-hand trade, and money-lending, as well as complaints that the Jews refused to assimilate and preferred parasitic and non-productive commercial activities in order to dominate local and international trade and harm honest Christians ... The attack against the Jews for their supposed unwillingness to do productive work became one of the first of many self-fulfilling prophecies common in the history of Christian attitudes. For the accumulated hostility of Christians in the early centuries restricted Jews to such activities, keeping them, with rare exceptions, in the lowest, least profitable and most despised branches of commerce until the late eighteenth century." (John Weiss[67])

Jewish traders entered Europe 'in the footsteps of the Roman legions', whom they provided with the trivial luxuries or curiosities which brought some diversion in the tough life of those professional

---

[66] Léon Poliakov: *Histoire de l'antisémitisme I*, pp. 16-17.
[67] John Weiss, op. cit., pp. 9-10.

soldiers. "Jewish settlers first came to Europe as international merchants bringing the much desired products of the advanced civilizations of the Middle East, China, India and Spain. Small and flourishing communities of Jews were soon established along the great European trade routes and in urban centres. By the ninth century the Jews of Europe enjoyed their greatest success as international merchants and traders; the words Jew and merchant were virtually synonymous. Along with Greeks, Syrians and Italians – Christians all – Jews were the advance agents of a society yet to come ... Down to our own time, the wealth of some highly visible members of the Jewish community has generated a righteous anger not directed at rich Christian merchants."[68]

As the situation of the Jews became more precarious and they were, to use a modern expression, more discriminated against in medieval society, few options remained open to them. "Banned from other professions, Jewish merchants in Europe remained in commerce, and for them as for other merchants money lending was convenient because they possessed liquid capital. Jews never dominated money lending, their tiny numbers alone prevented that; but they did predominate in some areas, especially where loans to peasants were refused by Christian businessmen with more profitable options ... The bulk of money lending in Europe was in fact carried on by wealthy clerical and monastic institutions [the Knights Templar among them] along with secular officials and groups such as the Lombards, Venetians, Syrians and Greeks – Christians all. The Vatican itself was known for its sophisticated credit practices." It may be remembered that Judaism, Christianity and Islam all condemned money lending as a sin. "Some complaints accused Christians of charging higher rates than Jews, for usury was a problem even where no Jews lived."[69] From that time onwards the complaints against the Jews became more or less standardized, inventing or exaggerating

---

[68] Id., pp. 10-11.
[69] Id., pp. 14, 53.

Jewish misdeeds and closing the eyes to Christian misconduct, especially in money matters.

To the Jews, as their history had taught them, money was a lifeline and consequently acquired an aura of sacredness. This is not the same as saying that it was the exclusive focus of their existence, or that they were a supremely coordinated global power which decided on all financial transactions and therefore determined the fate of humanity. The Jews were human beings all right, with the virtues and shortcomings of human beings. Yet most of the communal characteristics they showed in a country like Germany had been forced upon them in the past; and a coordinated global power they have never been, in spite of their far-reaching communal relations, one of the reasons being simply that, as an intellectual people, they were far too individualistic and therefore diverse. "In spite of the myths of the anti-Semites", concludes John Weiss, "the German economy would not have been significantly different had there never been a German Jewish community". And: "The Jews were not and never have been a menace to Germany, except in anti-Semitic mythology".[70]

Intelligence

"Intelligence is the mortal sin of the Jews", said one Friedrich Gentz. The Jews were indeed thought to be an intelligent sort of people, and they were hated and feared for it. Hitler himself wrote in *Mein Kampf*: "The intellectual faculties of the Jews have been trained through thousands of years. Today the Jew is looked upon as especially 'clever', and in a certain sense he has been so throughout the ages. His intellectual powers, however, are not the result of an inner evolution but rather have been shaped by the object lessons which the Jew has received from others ... Since the Jew never had

---

[70] John Weiss, op. cit., pp. 317, 384.

a civilization of his own, he has always been furnished by others with a basis for his intellectual work. His intellect has always developed by the use of those cultural achievements which he has found ready-to-hand around him".

It was part of the stereotype of the Jew that his mind was dry, sterile, incapable of creation, and that he was a parasite or a vampire of the life-force and creativity of others. "The Jewish intellect will never be constructive but always destructive", wrote Hitler. "In the course of a few years [the Jew] endeavours to exterminate all those who represent the national intelligence. And by thus depriving the peoples of their natural intellectual leaders, he fits them for their fate as slaves under a lasting despotism"[71] – which was exactly what he himself and others of his ilk, like Stalin and Pol Pot, were going to do.

In his *History of Anti-Semitism,* Léon Poliakov writes: "One has been able to state that the history of the Jews commences in 586 BC in Babylonia [where the two remaining tribes of Judea were taken into slavery] ... It is there that the unfailing faithfulness to Zion was born and that the last remnants of idolatry were extirpated; it was there that the Pentateuch was redacted in its definitive form; and it was especially there that the exiles drew the consequences from their history, that they managed to give a meaning to their tribulations and permanence to this meaning, and that they developed their particular historical memory of being Jews".

In Babylonia most of the Jews were farmers. Studying that period "one discovers how highly manual labour was esteemed by the sages of Israel; it was then the predominant occupation and placed well above commerce". It was in Babylonia that the Talmud was codified in its definitive form, and if there is one point in the Talmud on which everybody agrees, stresses Poliakov, "it is the absolute primacy of study. As one text says in a very expressive way: 'The whole world

---

[71]Adolf Hitler: *Mein Kampf,* pp. 251-52, 254, 274.

lives by the breath of the scholars'. Elsewhere it is assured that, day by day, only the sight of the savants and the students can turn the divine anger away from the world. From those times onwards, Jewish instruction was obligatory, free of charge and general".[72]

Many centuries later, when for the Jews 'the indispensable money' had become "that precious commodity without which it was impossible to affirm oneself in a hostile and loathsome world", "the inner world of study constituted a not less indispensable counterweight. Through the ages the rabbis had placed the study of the Law above earthly possessions, but these prescriptions had never before been followed with such intense ardour. The way the Jews in Germany and in the North of France plunged into the Talmud was really frenetic; they analyzed it day and night in the synagogues, without even laying down to rest. One text says: it is good to kill oneself by studying. Thus originated that famous Jewish ambiguity which caused money to become overestimated, as without money one ran the risk of death and expulsion – while, being overestimated, money became also an object of contempt and the first place was given to other values". In this way was developed the intelligence and the high culture of "the people that has been reading for a thousand years". "The rabbis taught incessantly that nothing was more admirable than study, and that to help poor children obtain instruction was the most pious act imaginable, surpassing even the building of a synagogue."[73]

Once the Jews had become emancipated and were (relatively) free to lead their lives within the host society, their intellectual capacities became apparent, especially at the institutions for higher education. "The proportion of Jewish undergraduates was high", writes John Weiss about the last decades of the nineteenth century. "For every 100,000 males of each denomination in Prussia, 33 Catholics, 58 Protestants and 519 Jews became university students.

---

[72]Léon Poliakov, op. cit., pp. 35, 38, 275-76.
[73]Id., p. 329.

In 1885 one student in every eight in Berlin was Jewish, though Jews comprised less than 1 percent of the population. The figures were even more lopsided in Vienna. In part it was a natural reaction to discrimination. Upper-class students had connections and lower-middle-class Germans could rise by ability, but Jewish males had to cultivate professional skills if they were to avoid discrimination: higher education meant liberation ... Law and medicine were the favourite studies of Jews because careers in these professions avoided institutional discrimination, but this meant competition with Germans unable to count on family connections, fearful of becoming an academic proletariat. Consequently they were among the most extreme racists in Austria as well as Germany, highly overrepresented in the Nazi elite. In western societies university attendance tended to lessen racism and conservatism; in Germany emphasizing one's racial uniqueness and identifying with the ruling class advanced one's career ..."

No wonder that Jews were generally associated with the Enlightenment, the high tide of Reason and the intellect in Europe, even if they had had *nothing* to do with the formulation of the ideas of the *philosophes*. On the contrary, as has been mentioned, some *philosophes*, eg Voltaire and d'Alembert, were caustically anti-Semitic. But it was the Enlightenment which had prepared the French Revolution and the emancipation of the Jews, and in the *Napoleonic Code* they had acquired an equal status with all others, something Napoleon implemented in the countries he conquered. From then onwards the Jews were identified with 'the French spirit' and would remain so, even when later on they were vehemently opposed by the nationalist and Catholic right in France itself, and when French deism and atheism were strongly condemned by the orthodox Jews. Most of the assimilated Jews, however, saw in the ideals of liberty and equality a gateway to freedom, an opportunity never offered to their people before. They were to be found among the liberals at the centre of the political spectrum, and some, more progressive or revolutionary, joined the ranks of the Socialists and Communists.

Socialists and Communists

Although 'socialist' was a component of the name of the National-Socialist Party, the word meant to Hitler something quite different from its ordinary significance; it was included into the Party name mainly to attract the workers, as had been the initial purpose of the Thule Society when it set Anton Drexler and Karl Harrer on their way. A juggler with words and concepts, Hitler's idea of 'true democracy', which he also called 'German democracy', was a hierarchical society organised according to the Führer principle – which was of course no democracy at all, but rather the opposite. Likewise, 'socialism' did not mean to him the rise of the fourth estate in its struggle against the bourgeois society for a just distribution of the common weal, but a functional integration into the body of the Volk or nation, cancelling out any notion of individualism.

Actually Hitler – supreme leader, genius and artist – had a profound disdain for the workers, except when he tried to lure them into the ranks of his Party, or when he needed their effort to prepare Germany for war. After all, the workers were part of the despised 'dunder-headed mass'. Authentic socialists, like the young Joseph Goebbels and the Strasser Brothers, will soon be confronted with Hitler's real feelings about socialism, as will the Socialist and Communist Parties and the trade unions barely weeks after he had become the master in the country.

Socialism as well as communism (and capitalism!) were creations of the Jews to dominate the world, and they were therefore to be opposed by the right-thinking with all their might. "My socialism is something different from Marxism", Hitler said to Hermann Rauschning. "My socialism is not a class struggle, but order. Who thinks of socialism as revolt and demagoguery of the masses is not a National-Socialist. Revolution is not a spectacle by the masses. Revolution is hard work. The mass sees only the steps after they have been undertaken; but it surpasses their knowledge – and it should surpass it – what an immense amount of labour has to be done before a new step forward can be made ... National-Socialism is what Marxism could have been if it had separated itself from the absurd, artificial connection with a democratic order."[74]

Konrad Heiden, a closely involved observer of the events we are describing, writes in his biography of Hitler: "The relatively high percentage of Jews in the leadership of the Socialist Parties on the European continent cannot be denied. The intellectual of the bourgeois era had not yet discovered the workers, and if the workers wanted to have leaders with university education, often only the Jewish intellectual remained – the type which might have liked to become a judge or Government official, but in Germany, Austria or Russia simply could not. Yet, though many Socialist leaders are Jews, only few Jews are Socialist leaders. To call the mass of modern Jewry Socialist, let alone revolutionary, is a bad propaganda joke. The imaginary Jew portrayed in *The Protocols of the Wise Men of Zion* ostensibly wants to bend the nations to his will by revolutionary mass uprisings; the real Jewish Socialist of France, Germany and Italy, however, is an intellectual who had to rebel against his own Jewish family and his own social class before he could come to the workers ...

"The Jewish socialist, as a rule, has abandoned the religion of his fathers, and consequently is a strong believer in the religion of human rights; this type, idealistic and impractical even in the choice of his own career, was often unequal to the test of practical politics and was pushed aside by more robust, more worldly, less sentimental leaders arising from the non-Jewish masses. A historic example of this change in the top Socialist leadership occurred in Soviet Russia between 1926 and 1937, when the largely Jewish leaders of the revolutionary period (Trosky, Zinoviev, Kamenev) were bloodily shoved aside by a dominantly non-Jewish class (Stalin, Voroshilov, etc.)."[75]

---

[74] Hermann Rauschning: *Gespräche mit Hitler*, pp. 164, 175.
[75] Konrad Heiden: *The Fuehrer*, p. 58.

In Germany and Austria 'hundreds of thousands' of the higher classes believed in 'the threat of Judeo-bolshevism', especially because their new governments after the First World War 'were run by socialists, always assumed to be a Jewish front', according to John Weiss.[76] First and foremost, however, there was the fear of revolution as a backlash of the Bolshevik Revolution in Russia, about which the most horrible rumours were circulating, many of them not unfounded. Moreover, the Bolshevik leaders had declared that their revolution was a world revolution, and that Germany was an immediate aim. After all, Germany had for a long time been singled out by the Marxists as the ideal country to unleash the proletarian revolution, while none of them had thought it would happen in backward, agrarian Russia.

"Bolshevik propaganda heralded the imminent conquest of Germany by the united strength of the international proletariat; this would be the decisive step on the road to world revolution. The obscure activities of Soviet agents, the continual unrest, the Soviet revolution in Bavaria, the Ruhr uprising of 1920, the revolts in Central Germany during the following year, the risings in Hamburg and later in Saxony and Thuringia, were all too consistent with the Soviet regime's threat of permanent revolution."[77] (What Fest does not mention here is the uprising of the Spartacists led by Karl Liebknecht and Rosa Luxemburg in Berlin, maybe because they were not guided directly by Moscow.) "This threat dominated Hitler's speeches of the early years", writes Fest. Given the continuous unrest in Germany, and the direct, painful experience of it in Munich, Hitler had no difficulty in stirring up his audiences, the more so as he dished up his oratory with a spicy anti-Semitic sauce.

What were the facts about the Jews leading the socialist and communist movements and revolutions? "Inflamed by a flood of pamphlets highlighting the Russian Jews among the Bolshevik

---

[76] John Weiss, op. cit., p. 214.
[77] Joachim Fest: *Hitler*, p. 92.

leadership, the public did not know that only some 7 percent were of Jewish origin, though Jews composed some 12 percent of the populations from which Bolshevik leaders were drawn ... From 1900 to 1920 more Russian Jews fled the country than ever chose revolution. In 1920 the highest proportion of minority peoples in the Bolshevik leadership were in fact Russians of German origin; Jews, Georgians and Armenians came next. The information fit no racial stereotype ... The vast majority of politically active Jews favoured the Mensheviks [moderate socialists], who rejected Bolshevik dictatorship and worked for a democratic Russia. The German Social Democrats, including the most radical, Rosa Luxemburg, also feared Bolshevik success. Only during the civil war in the Soviet Union, when the choice was either Lenin or the tsarists, did large numbers of young Jews choose the Bolsheviks – and they were atheists, a requirement for joining." (John Weiss[78]) The total number of Jews murdered by the tsarists in the Ukraine between 1918 and 1920 was more than 60,000.

The Socialist Republic and the Workers' Councils immediately after the war in Munich were very visibly lead by Jews, most of them foreigners in the city and for years to come used as bogeymen in the Nazi propaganda. The messy situation these Leftist amateurs created, and the misdeeds they committed, will remain an inexhaustible stock of oratorical ammunition for Hitler, who of course never mentioned that among the mourners of the Jew Kurt Eisner, and wearing a red armband, there had been himself.

Taking all this into consideration, it is rather ironical that the Jew Karl Marx, a favourite target of Hitler's anti-Judeo-Bolshevik rhetoric, was a life-long anti-Semite – a fact for which he is rarely remembered. "Karl Marx, the prototype of the supposed Jewish labour leader, came from a baptized Christian family, and his own relation with Judaism can only be characterized as anti-Semitism; for

---

[78] John Weiss, op. cit., pp. 214-15.

under Jews he understood the sharply anti-Socialist, yes, anti-political Jewish masses of Western Europe, whom as a good Socialist he coldly despised."[79] In 1843 Marx wrote a pamphlet, *The Jewish Question*, in which his attacks on the Jews were as poisonous as those of Hitler. "What was the basis of the Jewish religion? The practical need, egoism ... Money is the jealous god of Israel, before whom no other god must remain ... The bill of exchange, *that* is the true god of the Jews ... The Law without foundation or reason of the Jews is no more than a religious caricature of morality ... The social emancipation of the Jews means the emancipation of the society of Judaism ..." Etc. Léon Poliakov remarks dryly: "It may be noted that he applied the adjective 'Jewish' only to others, never to himself".[80]

Front soldiers

No historical context gives a more telling idea of the Jewish dilemma than the extreme situation created by the outbreak of the First World War. The anti-Jewish feeling followed the culminating curve of frantic German nationalism. It was nevertheless at this time that the Jews as a community gave irrefutable proof of their love for Germany to the point of sacrificing their lives for the country. In the midst of all arguments for and against them, and in view of all they had and will have to suffer, their contribution to the First World War remains a monument to what could have been, if the irrational and egocentric attitude of the Germans as a Volk had not been whipped up and given free rein by their Führer.

"When World War I began, the Jews expressed their sense of German nationalism by swarming into the army with an ardour as lemming-like as that of the gentiles. Some 100,000 Jews (one out of every six, including the women and children) entered the German Army. Of these, 80,000 served in frontline trenches, 35,000 were

---

[79]Konrad Heiden, op. cit., p. 58.
[80]Léon Poliakov: *Histoire de l'antisémitisme II*, pp. 233-34.

decorated for bravery, and 12,000 were killed. 'The Jews were pathologically patriotic', says Rabbi Prinz. 'My father served in the war, and my grandfather was wounded in 1866, in the war against the Austrians. He was enormously proud of that' ... The Jewish population in Germany was only one half of one percent. The Jewish deaths in the war were three percent'."[81]

In spite of this, the contribution of the Jews to the German national effort was not appreciated; on the contrary, suspicion against them increased. "Because they fought on all sides and yet were still considered one people, the Jews were in the greatest danger. Allied publicists accused them of betraying their liberal principles to fight for autocracy; German publicists accused them of secretly favouring the Allies because they were liberals. In fact, Jewish communities supported the war efforts of their separate nations ... German Jews hoped their sacrifice in war would convince all of their patriotism, and indeed, in the name of national unity, German anti-Semitism was muted at first", writes John Weiss.

However: "Soon German racism surpassed even pre-war intensity, encouraged by the German army. When Jews were accused of slacking, the general staff requested the Ministry of War to conduct a count of Jews at the front. The results were never made public, for they showed that the proportion of Jews who fell in battle was the same as in the German urban population and only slightly less than the population in general; peasants suffered the most. Adjusted to reflect the numbers of those with educational and professional skills needed for tasks behind the lines, there were more Jewish casualties than should have been expected. And almost half the German Jews who served were decorated. In an army famous for treating Jewish soldiers with contempt, the medals must have been doubly earned. Anti-Semitism was so strong at the front that German Jewish officers were often amazed when their orders were obeyed."[82] (The officer

---

[81] Otto Friedrich, op. cit., p. 110.
[82] John Weiss, op. cit., p. 207.

who recommended Corporal Hitler for the Iron Cross 1st Class was Jewish.)

The Marburg professor of philosophy Hermann Cohen wrote in 1916: "As Germans we want to be Jews, and as Jews Germans", and he thought he saw how in the perspective of history Germans and Jews would fuse into unity. "It was from this angle", writes Dietrich Bronder, "that the Jews *as German soldiers* have affirmed themselves on all occasions, even in Hitler's armies, and that they were second to none of their non-Jewish comrades, even when they were grossly offended as in a slanderous pamphlet distributed in the streets of Berlin in 1919 and which said: 'They stare you in the face everywhere, but in the trenches nowhere!'"

"When in the First World War an anti-Semitic newspaper printed a provocation, promising an award of 1000 marks to whomever could name a Jewish mother with three sons who had been in the trenches, if only for three weeks, Rabbi Freund-Hannover named twenty mothers of his community alone who fulfilled the condition, and he could name families with seven or eight sons at the front", writes Dietrich Bronder. Then he mentions the participation of the Jews in past German wars, and the high honours awarded to them. In the First World War, 35,000 Jews were decorated, of whom 1000 with the Iron Cross 1st Class and 17 000 with the Iron Cross 2nd Class; 23,000 were promoted, 2000 to the rank of officer. Ten thousand Jews entered the army as volunteers. The National Association of Jewish Front Soldiers', founded in 1919, counted 35,000 members. "In October 1933, when Hitler already had gathered all power in his hands, they still wanted 'in true military discipline to stand with their German fatherland to the last', but were dissolved in 1939. In 1941 Jews were forbidden to wear their war medals. From 1942 onwards no exceptions were made any more for former participants in the First World War – they too were sent to Theresienstadt and Auschwitz."[83]

---

[83] Dietrich Bronder: *Bevor Hitler kam*, pp. 343-44 (emphasis in the text).

World conspiration

One of the prevalent accusations against 'international Jewry' was that the Jews were plotting a conspiracy to dominate and exploit the world, and that they were using the liberal and capitalist Rightist movements as well as the socialist and communist Leftist movements to achieve their aim as 'the Chosen People' to whom their God had promised the world. It may be noted that the Jews were not the only ones saddled with this design, and that the arguments against the others were much better founded in reality. Bolshevism, for one, openly proclaimed its intention to promote the proletarian world revolution; the grasp for global power by the former USSR was to become one of the main features in the history of the twentieth century. And it has for many centuries been the purpose behind the policies of the Catholic Church to establish itself as the Universal Church which it pretends to be. Moreover, as narrated in a previous chapter, it was the objective of Adolf Hitler himself to conquer the globe for the Aryan master race, and it was this objective which resulted into his opposition to the alleged global aspirations of the Jews, propagated by malicious pamphlets like *The Protocols of the Wise Man of Zion* but never substantiated. "The thesis of a Jewish world conspiration, of a centrally directed, racially determined and systematically executed world conquest [by the Jews] is so absurd that only a narrowed, diseased mind and a consequently calcified psyche could perceive such obvious fabrication of the imagination as reality." (Christian Zentner[84])

In Germany the Jews were "few enough to be helpless and numerous enough to be held up as a menace", in the words of Justice Jackson, president of the Nuremberg Military Tribunal in 1946. There are countless documents telling of the sadistic power trip of the brown storm-troopers and the Hitler Youth, who could humiliate and beat up any Jew, and destroy his property, without as much as

---

[84]Christian Zentner: *Adolf Hitlers "Mein Kampf"*, p. 158.

a gesture of resistance, and who became hardened by this practice to do worse. It remains a startling fact that Jewish crowds of hundreds or thousands allowed themselves to be led 'as sheep to the slaughter'. Raul Hilberg gives the following explanation: "In exile the Jews had always been in a minority; they had always been in danger; but they had learned that they could avert danger and survive destruction by placating and appeasing their enemies. This was a two thousand-year-old lesson. The Jews could not make the switch [when their leadership realized] that the modern machine-like destruction process would engulf European Jewry".[85] "The simple truth remained that the Jews as a group were weak, vulnerable, and at no time had harboured any aggressive designs against Germany", writes Robert Wistrich.[86]

Léon Poliakov, looking for the causes of such acquiescence, finds them already in the Middle Ages when, after the slaughter by the crusaders at Worms, Mainz, and many other places, "martyrdom became what one could call an institution ... Each new victim of Christian furor was a combatant fallen to sanctify the Name; one often bestowed on him the title of 'kadosh' (saint), which is a kind of canonisation ... In particular the sacrifice of the children, killed by their own parents [to prevent them from being slain or baptized by the Christians] is seen in the light of the sacrifice Abraham was willing to perform, and the story of the patriarch and his son became, under the title 'akeda' (Isaac's sacrifice) the symbol of the Jewish martyrology."[87]

Nonetheless, "the common cliché that Jews did not resist their persecutors and simply went 'like sheep to the slaughter' is neither an accurate nor a fair description ... When presented as a blanket criticism, it overlooks the extraordinary lengths to which the Nazis went in disguising the genocidal intent of their policy toward the Jews. The perpetrators deliberately encouraged false hopes and the

---

[85] In Robert Wistrich: *Hitler and the Holocaust*, p. 59.
[86] Id., p. 72.
[87] Léon Poliakov: *Histoire de l'antisémitisme I*, pp. 278, 275.

illusion that compliance and work might be the salvation of Jewry", writes Wistrich.

And he continues: "The slogan of 'sheep to the slaughter' also overlooks the fact that the notion of total physical extermination was not only unprecedented but must have seemed to most Jews (and Gentiles) like the product of a diseased imagination. It underestimates the state of sheer exhaustion and demoralization in which the ghettoized Jews found themselves and the degree to which they were isolated and cut off from the outside world. It ignores the intimidating effects of collective punishment as practiced by the Nazis whenever they were faced with even the most trivial and minor acts of defiance. The knowledge that the Germans would exact terrible reprisals was a serious disincentive all over Europe to any armed resistance. There were relatively few efforts at revolt, for example, by the many well-trained Allied soldiers and the hundreds of thousands of Russian prisoners of war in German camps, though they were watched over by a fairly small number of guards. Charges of passivity have rarely been made against them. Yet Western prisoners were not subjected to the unrelenting dehumanization that was the common fate of the Jews in the ghettos and the Nazi camps.

"The Jewish population, to a much greater extent than any other, had the terrifying experience of being hunted down like wild animals. To make matters worse, they found themselves – at least in Eastern Europe – in a generally hostile and anti-Semitic environment. Even in the event of escape, Jewish men were still marked by circumcision, often easily identified by their beards and facial features or else by their distinctive garb. Despite these great obstacles, Jews did subsequently rebel in the ghettos of Warsaw and Bialystok, in the death camps of Treblinka, Sobibor and Auschwitz, and took up arms with the partisans wherever they succeeded in escaping their tormentors."[88] Armed revolts broke out 'in at least twenty ghettos in Eastern Europe'. Best known is the uprising in the Warsaw ghetto,

---

[88]Robert Wistrich, op. cit., pp. 79-80.

from 19 April until 5 May 1943, where in terrible circumstances about a thousand Jewish fighters, armed with light firearms, grenades and Molotov cocktails, confronted the three thousand elite soldiers of SS-General Stroop, equipped with heavy machine guns, howitzers, armoured vehicles and artillery, eventually backed-up by tanks and bombers.

The decisive counter-argument against the allegation of a Jewish attempt at world domination, however, is the unwillingness of the supposedly Jewish-friendly governments to let in the Jewish refugees from Germany after the Hitler take-over. "The Jewish world power did not show itself very powerful", notes Konrad Heiden.[89] And Robert Wistrich has the following comment: "Even American Jewry, though by 1939 the richest, largest and strongest Jewish community in the world, was still far from being the organized, vigorous, disciplined, cohesive lobby of the post-war era, able to influence the foreign policy of the US government. On the contrary, it was so lacking in unity or self-confidence and seemingly so cowed by the rise in American anti-Semitism during the depression years that it was unable to seriously challenge the draconian immigration restrictions that helped to seal the fate of European Jewry. Much the same could be said of the smaller Jewish community in Great Britain, even though a few individual Jews did achieve prominence in British life during the interwar years".[90]

The question why the Jews, as a people with a revealed religion, were marked with such a contorted and tragic destiny remains, to the non-Jewish observer, unanswered.

War and extermination

"Concerning the Jews, Hitler will never change", wrote Ambassador François-Poncet in his memoirs. "He told me one day that, to his

---

[89] Konrad Heiden, op. cit., p. 458.
[90] Robert Wistrich, op. cit., p. 23.

mind, the Jewish problem should be solved by putting all the Jews in the universe on an island, Madagascar for instance. Actually, the only satisfying solution according to him would be to exterminate all of them, for they are the enemies of the Aryan race, responsible for all the evil of which Germany and the world have to suffer. In fact, it is this hidden thought of total extermination which inspires his conduct and that of his Party."[91] The British historian Ian Kershaw confirms the words of the French ambassador: "For Hitler, whatever the tactical considerations, the aim of destroying the Jews – his central political idea since 1919 – remained unaltered. He revealed his approach to a meeting of party District Leaders at the end of April 1937, in immediate juxtaposition to comments on the Jews: 'I don't straight away want violently to demand an opponent to fight. I don't say "fight" because I want to fight. Instead I say: "I want to destroy you!" And now let skill help me to manoeuvre you so far into the corner that you can't strike a blow. And then you get the stab into the heart'".[92]

There is unanimity among the students of Hitler's life that his hatred of the Jews and his intention to do away with them remained unaltered from 1919 until his death. When the day before his suicide he went into a separate room with one of his secretaries, Traudl Junge, and announced that he was going to dictate his political testament, Junge expected to hear revelations nobody had heard before. "Now at last comes what we have been awaiting for days: the explanation of all what has happened, a confession, even a confession of guilt, or perhaps a justification. In this last document of the Reich of a Thousand Years should be written the truth, admitted by a man who had nothing to lose anymore. But my expectation remained unfulfilled. Detached, almost mechanically, the Führer utters declarations which I, the German people and the whole world know already."[93] In the last sentence of this testament

---

[91] André François-Poncet: *Souvenirs d'une ambassade à Berlin*, p. 120.
[92] Ian Kershaw: *Hitler – 1889-1936 Hubris*, p. 573.
[93] Traudl Junge: *Bis zur letzten Stunde*, p. 202.

Hitler obliged the leadership of the nation, newly appointed by him, to "a strict implementation of the racial laws and to a merciless resistance against the poisoner of all peoples, international Jewry".

In his letter to Adolf Gemlich on the subject of the Jews, and written at the request of Captain Mayr in 1919, twenty-five years earlier, Hitler had already insisted upon the necessity of 'the removal of the Jews'. As we have seen in the first chapters of this book, Hitler's hatred of the Jews seems to have been a phenomenon with a sudden origin in which his mentor Dietrich Eckart was involved and for which he was possibly responsible. It can hardly have been a coincidence that the Austrian corporal without a future contacted the German Workers' Party, founded as an initiative of the Thule Society, in the days his military superior asked him respectfully to write a letter on the Jewish problem for the enlightenment of a fellow army propagandist.

The line of Hitler's anti-Semitic development can clearly be followed in his daily tutoring by Eckart, 'the spiritual godfather of Nazism' (Wistrich); in his study and memorization of the anti-Semitic literature, of which Fritsch's *Antisemiten-Katechismus* alone provided him with 650 pages of quotations; in his conversations with Alfred Rosenberg, propagator of *The Protocols of the Wise Men of Zion* and theorist of anti-Semitism. Less than a year after the Gemlich letter, Hitler delivered his speech "Why are we anti-Semites?" presenting his enthusiastically responding Munich audience with an outline of his anti-Semitism which will not be changed for the rest of his life – except that 'the final solution' still remained unspoken, though probably not unimagined. The cosmic dimensions of the necessary confrontation between Aryans and Jews were present behind all he said or wrote on the subject, and they were formulated in *Mein Kampf*. "Should the Jew, with the aid of his Marxist creed, triumph over the people of this world, his crown will be the funeral wreath of mankind, and this planet will once again follow its orbit through the ether without any human life on its surface, as it did millions of years ago. And so I believe today that I am acting in accordance with the will of the Almighty Creator: in standing guard against the Jew I am defending the handiwork of the Lord."[94]

As Chancellor of the Reich, Hitler knew how to talk peace and became known, in Germany and abroad, as 'the Chancellor of Peace', although he had been preparing for war from his first day in office. Likewise, he knew how to restrain his vituperations against the Jews, and even to keep silent about them for a while, when the political situation required him to do so during the chaotic period and the series of successive elections before his 'legal' access to power. But no sooner had the goal been reached or he started executing his programme, beginning with point number one: his war against the Jews.

First there was the boycott of the Jewish shops, only a few weeks after the *Machtergreifung*, the acquisition of power; then, gradually, there was the smothering of the Jewish community within German society. Step by step the Jews became non-persons, outlaws, worse than pariahs, still allowed to stay alive, but barely. The Germans, who liked to joke that 'the soup is never eaten as hot as it is served', now found out that their Führer and his brown-shirts had meant what they said, but it was too late to protest. The Nuremberg Laws put the seal on what had been announced as the fate of the Jews from the birth of National-Socialism, and what was now being pushed inexorably towards its fulfilment.

On 30 January 1939, the solemnly commemorated anniversary of the *Machtergreifung*, Hitler pronounced the words against the Jews which Lucy Dawidowicz characterises as 'a declaration of war', but which were actually a death sentence, the 'war' against the Jews having been declared years earlier. By this time Hitler had decided to invade Western Europe, and he realised that military action was the ideal cover to solve the Jewish problem through physical extermination. "I have often been a prophet in my life", he said, "and

---

[94] Adolf Hitler: *Mein Kampf,* p. 66.

I was often laughed at. At the time of my struggle to obtain the power, it was in the first place the Jewish people which greeted with laughter my prophecies that, one day in Germany, I would assume the leadership of the state and simultaneously of the whole *Volk*, and that then I would, among other things, bring the Jewish problem to a solution. I think that the hilarious laughter of the Jews has meanwhile stuck in their throats. Today I will be a prophet once again: if the international finance-Jewry in and outside Europe would succeed in plunging the peoples into war once more, then the outcome will not be the Bolshevization of the earth and consequently the victory of Jewry, but the annihilation of the Jewish race in Europe."

The acclamation greeting this direct threat, and preserved on film, was deafening. Who in that crowd at the Kroll Opera, or listening under the loudspeakers in the streets of towns and villages, or sitting at home near their *Volksempfänger*, the cheap popular radio set specially built to spread the Nazi propaganda – who thought of the mendacious distortions in these few sentences? True, thinking about fundamentals was no longer what one did in Germany, or what was even permitted. No Jews had taken the rise of National-Socialism as a laughing matter, even if they had kept hoping that things would turn out better than expected and reasoned the danger away; no Jews had wanted war; and Bolshevism was not identical with Judaism.

Hitler's idea that the waging of war was to be combined with 'the final solution' of the Jews has been pointed out by Lucy Dawidowicz, who found that time after time, when Hitler reminded his audiences of the threat enunciated on 30 January 1939, he mistakenly put it on 30 September 1939, the date of his invasion of Poland and the beginning of the Second World War. The war was to serve as camouflage for the execution of the secret and humanely unthinkable plan. 'Extermination' was a term habitually used by the Nazis and by many other Germans, but it was hardly ever taken seriously. The Jews were objects of suspicion, scorn, ridicule, and on occasion of physical attack, but the outspoken intention of murdering any of them, not to say all of them, seems not to have been around – which does not mean that 'the ideology of death' in Germany has not considerably contributed to its becoming reality. "The Final Solution grew out of a matrix formed by traditional anti-Semitism, the paranoid delusions that seized Germany after the First World War, and the emergence of Hitler and the National Socialist movement. Without Hitler, the charismatic political leader who believed he had a mission to annihilate the Jews, the Final Solution would not have occurred. Without that assertive and enduring tradition of anti-Semitism by which the Germans sought self-definition, Hitler would not have had the fecund soil in which to grow his organization and to spread its propaganda ...

"Anti-Semitism was the core of Hitler's system of beliefs and the central motivation for his policies. He believed himself to be the saviour who would bring redemption to the German people through the annihilation of the Jews, that people who embodied, in his eyes, the Satanic hosts. When he spoke or wrote about his 'holy mission', he used words associated with chiliastic prophecy (not only in the millennial concept literally rendered as the 'Thousand Year Reich'), like 'consecration', 'salvation', 'redemption', 'resurrection', 'God's will'. The murder of the Jews, in his fantasies, was commanded by divine providence, and he was the chosen instrument for that task."[95]

The unwritten order

"The grand design [of the annihilation of the Jews] was in Hitler's head", writes Dawidowicz. "He did not spell it out in concrete strategy. Nothing was written down. (On 29 April 1937 he advised NSDAP leaders: 'Everything that can be discussed orally should *never* be put in writing, never!') He even elevated his tactics of

---

[95] Lucy Dawidowicz: *The War against the Jews 1933-45*, p. 208.

secrecy into a strategic principle: as few people as possible to know as little as possible as late as possible."[96]

"On the basis of the structure of the system of authority [in Hitler Germany], one can with certainty accept that an operation so extensive and demanding such great resources in personnel and materiel, as did the murder of millions of people in all parts of Europe, was only possible with the consent of the man at the top, where all threads came together", writes Peter Longerich in his book *Der ungeschriebene Befehl* (the unwritten order) about the direct responsibility of Hitler. He asserts that this responsibility can be proven by examining Hitler's many utterances and talks to generals, groups of people belonging to the regime, and personal conversations. It was Hitler's aim, says Longerich, never to give direct instructions, but to create 'a certain climate' in which the executive organs of the regime would know that any radicalisation of the politics against the Jews was authorized by the highest representative of the regime. On top of this, "Hitler gave confidentially direct oral orders with which he started particular operations of the systematic mass murder of the Jews".[97]

This is carefully worded by Longerich and supported by many persons involved in the historical process. Albert Speer said: "Nothing of any magnitude could conceivably happen, not only without [Hitler's] knowledge, but without his orders", and he repeated Rudolf Hess' words: "Hitler reserved all his important decisions for himself".[98] Kershaw quotes Heinrich Himmler as saying: "I do nothing that the Führer doesn't know about".[99] Christa Schroeder, one of Hitler's secretaries, exclaimed during an interview after the war: "Of course Hitler knew! Not only knew, it was all his ideas, his orders!"

---

[96] Id., p. 202.
[97] Peter Longerich: *Der ungeschriebene Befehl – Hitler und der Weg zur "Endlösung"*, pp. 185-86.
[98] Gitta Sereny: *Albert Speer: His Battle with Truth*, pp. 7, 100.
[99] Ian Kershaw, op. cit., p. 248.

And she described how shocked Himmler had looked after he had apparently received *the* order from Hitler.[100] "When he did not give specific orders or instructions", writes Robert Gellately, "his ideas, hate-filled speeches and wishes inspired police, justice and SS-cadres all along the line".[101]

What was the cause of Hitler's obsession with the Jews, who 'inhabited Hitler's mind'? "I don't know. Nobody knows. Nobody's even began", said Alan Bullock in desperation after many years of study.[102] Werner Maser confesses: "The cause of Hitler's anti-Semitism, despite the knowledge of so many details, is not completely explainable",[103] which is a historians' understatement. And Joachim Fest puts it as follows: "We can probably no longer plumb the cause of this ever-growing hatred [of the Jews], which lasted literally to the last hour of Hitler's life". "He admired the Jews", says Fest. "Their racial exclusiveness and purity seemed to him no less admirable than their sense of being a chosen people, their implacability and intelligence. Basically, he regarded them as something akin to negative supermen. Even Germanic nations of relatively pure racial strains were, he declared in his table talk, inferior to the Jews: if 5000 Jews were transferred to Sweden, within a short time they would occupy all the leading positions".[104]

The mystery of the cause of Hitler's hatred of the Jews must have been closely connected with 'his vision of the apocalyptic conflict between the Aryans and the Jews', which we have briefly examined when leafing through *Mein Kampf*. "It was his own Manichean version of the conflict between good and evil, between God and the Devil, Christ and the Antichrist." If there is a solution

---

[100] Gitta Sereny, op. cit., p. 248.
[101] Robert Gellately: *Backing Hitler*, p. 7.
[102] Ron Rosenbaum: *Explaining Hitler*, p. 83.
[103] Werner Maser: *Adolf Hitler – Legende, Mythos, Wirklichkeit*, p. 267.
[104] Joachim Fest, op. cit., pp. 39, 533.

of this mystery, it should be looked for in the occurrences at the time of Hitler's 'turnabout' when, in 1919, and under the influence of Captain Mayr and Dietrich Eckart, he suddenly turned out to be an expert in anti-Semitism, and a personality interesting enough to be pushed into a position from where he could give shape to his mission and his message, and go out to conquer Germany. This would explain how the end lay in the beginning: why, regarding the Jews, he still was when dictating his testament what he had become during that summer in Munich.

"The ideology, the blueprint of his leadership, was at the same time accessible to everybody and yet secret." Trevor-Roper had a similar impression when he wrote about "those walls which the Führer has erected around his convictions, and behind which he allows nobody to see. Can it be that there is really nothing there – only the gigantic obstinacy of a deluded spirit, sacrificing all to its self-worshipping Ego?"[105] (Would this then be the solution to the riddle: that the greatest and most tragic event in human history was caused by a 'self-worshipping Ego'?) John Lukacs finds Hitler "a very secretive man, perhaps not less secretive than Stalin", and he quotes him as having said: "You will never be able to discover my thoughts and intentions".[106] "The higher one was, the less one knew", confided Speer to Gitta Sereny.[107] Speer's words might be illustrated with passages from Goebbels diaries, showing that even the proud propaganda-tsar of the Reich was informed about some important events only post factum.

"Hitler has never revealed the secret of his mission", writes Joachim Köhler in *Hitlers Wagner*, p. 21. "The core of his message was not decoded (p. 22) ... The struggle against the Jews was indeed Hitler's totally personal and therefore not further explainable or discussable basic conviction (p. 98) ... He knew that he could not

---

[105] HR Trevor-Roper: *The Last Days of Hitler*, pp. 179-80.
[106] John Lukacs: *The Hitler of History*, pp. 47, 130 footnote.
[107] Gitta Sereny: *The German Trauma*, p. 280.

be attacked as a politician because he kept his objectives hidden in a mystic darkness ... Hitler showed himself indefinable and has remained so till today (p. 193) ... What were the contents of Hitler's inner truth, nobody knew ... Hitler was not a politician who had to work out a programme and to justify his actions to the people, but the saviour of an esoteric cult, who had set himself the task of liberating the world from the Jews ... In actual fact, the Germans did not have to know anything, they only must have faith (pp. 334-35) ... He clearly held a secret in which he believed with 'granite' infallibility (p. 336) ... 'When we eradicate this plague [i.e. the Jews]', Hitler had prophesied during the march on Moscow, 'we shall accomplish something for humanity of which our men at the front cannot have an idea as yet'. This also meant that those men killed and died without knowing why. And the people around him cheered without knowing why. They became excited when Hitler told them what was at stake and believed in his infallibility because he demanded this belief from them. As his successes seemed to justify his actions, his intentions justified all the means. (p. 337) ... Hitler never gave away, not even with a single word, that he was planning the biggest auto-da-fé in the history of mankind (p. 410)."

11

THE GERMAN ASPIRATION

> Once in a Golden Age we merged with all,
> For aeons now the crowd has shunned our call.
> We are the Rose: the young and fervent heart,
> The Cross: to suffer proudly is our part.
>
> STEFAN GEORGE

The search for meaning

The analysis in the previous chapters of the German mentality which lead directly to Hitler would not be complete without paying attention to the sincere longing behind even the most delirious extremes of national egoism, the historical and cultural fancies, and the aversion to everything 'modernity' stood for. In the end the perverted fancies gained the upper hand, which was tragic when one considers the high cultural and spiritual values in Germany's past which were also there in the decades of its ordeal, but which were stifled by forces which we have seen darkening and which we still have to identify.

In his book *Hitler: The Führer and the People*, JP Stern has titled one of the chapters which leads up to the Third Reich 'A Society

Longing for Transcendence'. There he writes: "What the Germans now seek is a religious solution – religious in the sense of being total and absolute and an object of faith rather than of prudential thinking. Since they are seeking a single, 'total' thing, their 'idealism' appears wholly incompatible with material satisfactions. What they are looking for is in fact not a solution but a salvation – not however as an alternative to and an unworldly substitute for material concerns and demands, but as the subsuming and validation of such demands".[1]

"The search for 'a third way', as an alternative to capitalism or Marxism, occupied much of German thought during the Weimar Republic", writes George Mosse. "Even earlier, toward the end of the post-unification period [i.e. the years preceding the First World War], men had raised similar questions – in a more theoretical manner, but just as seriously. Indeed, the search for a viable 'third way' was an integral part of the volkisch concern ... Disenchanted with the world as they found it, German thinkers attempted to find some way to raise the Volk above its temporal restrictions. They were determined to liberate it from the shackles of a materialistic civilization imposed by a state that callously disregarded the essentially spiritual needs of the Volk. The postwar era thrust the 'third-way' alternative again into the foreground ... Everywhere in Europe, Fascism was based upon the urge toward a 'third way', and volkisch thought here intersected with the mainstream of an international movement ... Whatever the alternative presented by the advocates of the 'third way', the underlying basis was always metaphysical. During the 1920's, intellectuals continued to view the coming German revolution primarily in spiritual terms ...

"Möller van den Bruck, in his famous work *The Third Reich* (1923), which he first called *The Third Way*, considered Germany to be a 'new nation', as distinguished from the overripe 'old nations' of the West, a nation with a mission. It was a country of the future

---

[1] JP Stern: *Hitler – The Führer and the People*, p. 79.

that had not yet developed its inherent peculiarities and greatness. What it had lacked until now, a shortcoming that accounted for the failure of the recent past [the defeat in 1918], van den Bruck declared, was a chiliastic ideal. The 'new' Germany, he asserted, had to be fired by the idea of the Germanic past and of Germany's potential future greatness; it had to revive and make operative in a new age the traditions of medieval messianism. Contemporary materialism, contemporary society and science, had to be discarded and the German soul must take wing and follow the unrestrained course of the *Geist* ... Van den Bruck was advocating a truly spiritual revolution."[2]

"To the liberal and peace-loving bourgeois, the product of European rationalism, the Fascists ... oppose the cult of the feelings, of emotivity, of violence, duty and sacrifice, of the heroic virtues", writes Zeev Sternhell. "Fascism develops to the full and applies to the realities of the postwar new ethics which had originated on the eve of the war: the yearning to serve, the cult of power, of commanding and obeying, of a collective faith and abnegation. Fascism means adventure and also, as in Sorel, 'the deed and nothing but the deed' ... But what in the first decade of the [twentieth] century was nothing more than a theoretical aspect of Social Darwinism became after the war, to the generation which had survived the trenches, a concrete experience and a standard of behaviour. The former combatants considered themselves the bearers of a spiritual mission: they wanted to transmit their unique experience to the whole of society and imprint upon it the heroic virtues of the warrior, namely discipline, sacrifice, self-denial and comradeship."[3]

If one lets the character traits enumerated by Sternhell overlap, the result is a kind of robot photo of the ideal character of the average German at the time under our consideration, especially the need for order, discipline and obedience, and the dedication to

---

[2] George Mosse: *The Crisis of German Ideology*, pp. 280-82, passim.
[3] Id., pp. 551-52.

loyalty and sacrifice. "The nation had a deeply rooted instinct for rules and discipline", writes Fest, "it wanted the world orderly or it did not want the world at all ... The German mind accords universal respect to the categories of order, discipline and self-restraint ... Hitler was able to play on such attitudes and use them to further his plans for dominion. Thus he created the cult of obedience to the Führer or staged those military-like demonstrations whose precise geometry offered protection against the chaos so feared by all and sundry".[4]

"We had been rendered susceptible to such ideas from our youth on", writes Albert Speer in self-defence. "We had derived our principles from the *Obrigkeitsstaat*, the authoritarian though not totalitarian state of Imperial Germany. Moreover, we had learned those principles in wartime, when the state's authoritarian character had been further intensified. Perhaps the background had prepared us like soldiers for the kind of thinking we encountered once again in Hitler's system. Tight public order was in our blood; the liberalism of the Weimar Republic seemed to us by comparison lax, dubious, and in no way desirable."[5]

"Many of [the Nazis], moreover, came from homes whose patterns were based on the rigid mores of the cadet schools. Hitler profited greatly from the peculiarities of an authoritarian educational system."[6] The patriotic, rigidly authoritarian German teachers had sent 'the Langemarck Youth' into the trenches of the First World War; the same kind of teachers, seconded by martinet fathers, are to be found in practically every biography of Germans in the Second World War, be they Hitler, Bormann, Speer, Goebbels, or whoever. This was "a nation literally schooled to admire such traits ... the obedience to authority was intrinsic to the German character before and during Hitler's time". The Prussian tradition of *Kadavergehorsam*, obedience

---

[4]Joachim Fest: *Hitler*, pp. 148, 378.
[5]Albert Speer: *Inside the Third Reich*, p. 68.
[6]Joachim Fest, op. cit., p. 284.

as of a corpse, was still very much alive, as was the saying of the drill sergeants: "We leave thinking to the horses, they have bigger heads".

Where could a youth, endowed with or stiffened by such traits, turn to when it refused to accept the ways of worn out religious dogmatism as well as of a modern world it did not understand and dreaded? What could satisfy their longing for order, obedience and sacrifice, and most of all for a cause which would give meaning to life and death? Arminius' Cheruscians and other Germanic tribes of yore had nothing to offer that could be called 'spiritual', and the Greeks, admired as creators of culture and the arts, had no tradition which exceeded the arbitrariness of a world as depicted by Homer or Sophocles' tragic human destinies. However, true spirituality, fulfilling all the requirements, could be found where the great Romantics had looked for it and where 'the new romanticism' followed in their tracks: in the (idealised) Middle Ages. The monastic orders, more specifically the military monastic orders, peopled the dreams of a youth riding in trains and working in a chemical laboratory, a bank, or a watchmaker's shop.

On most crossroads in the imagination of a Germany thinking in the volkisch way we meet with the Knights Templar or the Teutonic Knights. Lanz von Liebenfels had started dreaming of becoming a Templar at the age of twelve and would found the New Order of the Templars, taking vows to fight for the final victory of the blond Aryans over the subhuman Chandalas. The poet Stefan George, who "appointed himself custodian of Germany's spiritual and cultural future", assembled around him an elite circle of young men who had not only to be esoteric initiates but also mystic warriors, "soldiers of the spirit engaged in a spiritual crusade. In this respect, they were heir to the knights in his poem entitled 'Templars', although George meant by the term something very different from the Ariosophist New Templars of Lanz von Liebenfels".[7] Himmler's organisation of his 'Black Order' is often said to have been inspired by the Order

---

[7] Michael Baigent and Richard Leigh: *Secret Germany*, p. 259.

of the Templars or of the Jesuits, who, after all, were the Catholic Church's warriors to fight the Reformation. And Hitler himself confided to Rauschning: "I shall tell you a secret: I am founding an order." The top elite schools of "his" youth were the three *Ordensburgen* at Krössinsee, Sonthofen and Vogelsang. Even the ordinary Hitler Youth, obligatorily joined by all young Germans from the age of six, had to live up to the ideals of a military order, and took pride in it.

The backbone of the whole self-denying attitude in Germany was, of course, Prussian. Discipline, respect for the military rank, pride in the uniform, clicking of the heels, energetic saluting, shouting of orders and a ruthless training were as common in the twentieth century as they had been at the time of Frederick II. What for most 'new romanticists' had been an exercise of the imagination turned into dire reality in the First World War. The ideals of total obedience, unconditional discipline and self-sacrifice became a matter of daily practice. The surviving generation will be indelibly imprinted with these ideals. The Templar and Teutonic Knight were replaced by Dürer's Knight riding between the Devil and Death towards an unknown destiny. His sky was the sky of nihilism, adorned with the clouds of any ideal or empty. The undefeated German soldiers marched home and joined a Free Corps, where they kept on marching side by side with youngsters who regretted having been born to late for the war. These soldiers of fortune, these *Landsknechte*, had lost their ideals while keeping up the routine, and served as an example to the generation of 'the birds of passage'. And none will know better how to fill up the emptiness in their heart and exploit their readiness to serve than Adolf Hitler. He will use them to build up *his* New Templar Order to defend 'the Holy Grail of the pure blood'.

The 1880 watershed

At this point we have to direct our attention once more to the important change in the European cultural landscape which took place around 1880, and which announced the global upheavals of the twentieth century. The importance of those years – called by one German author *Zeitbruch 1880*, a break or dividing line in the times, something like the great moments of change which Karl Jaspers called *Achsenzeiten*, axis times – is not yet generally recognized in official history. "A wild pain is felt in this time and the suffering is no longer bearable. The call for a saviour is common and the crucified are everywhere. Is this a great dying that has come into the world? It is possible that we have reached the end, the death of an exhausted humanity, and that these are nothing but the last convulsions. It is also possible that we are at the beginning, at the birth of a new humanity."[8] The questioning of the Renaissance and the reign of the intellect in the Age of Reason had undermined the age-old Christian tradition and tried to install the foundations of a new future. The certainties of the past had decayed, but Reason could not tell what the new future would be.

George Mosse wrote, as we have seen above, that 'the search for a viable 'third way' was an integral part of the volkisch concern', and that this 'third way' was 'an alternative to capitalism and Marxism'. For once we have to disagree with him. The third way the volkisch movement was looking for, and with them all those who suffered the pain of the insecurity in the period 1880-1914, was not an alternative to capitalism and Marxism: it was an alternative on the one hand, to the lost certainties of the Christian past and, on the other hand, to the fear of an unknown 'modern' future, including capitalism as well as Marxism – as well as the steamrolling industrialisation and urbanisation which crushed all accepted and familiar traditions. If there is one thing the ignorant and vulnerable human beings abhor, it is change.

Dissatisfied, not to say disillusioned, with the temporary tyranny of Reason, which in Germany had anyway been treated with suspicion,

---

[8] Hermann Bahr quoted in Michael Ley and Julius Schoeps (ed.): *Der Nationalsozialismus als politische Religion*, p. 209.

the volkisch and like-minded people were looking for teachings and practices which could satisfy the needs of the *whole* person. Man does not live by bread alone, and neither does he live by the intellect alone. In him there are the realms of the life-forces, impulses and feelings; there is the physical body with its hunger, its need of movement, sexual satisfaction and health; and there is the soul at the centre of the being, the place where one feels connected with the soul of the Volk, with nature, and with God. The traditional, dogmatic answers did not any longer satisfy a generation which, after all, had come alive to the questions and criticisms of the Renaissance and Enlightenment thinkers — not to forget the stance taken by Martin Luther of the individual's right to turn towards God directly and be saved by his personal faith, without the interference of a religious institution.

HP Blavatsky's Theosophy, founded in 1875, had the effect of a revelation and spread from America to Europe and India in no time. (The first German section was started as early as 1884.) Here at last, as noted in a previous chapter, was a teaching which involved the whole person, which taught that God was within and could be contacted and even realised there, and which put an end to the fear of eternal damnation. Theosophy offered a practical spiritual programme, provided an explanation of humanity's past, related to identical views in other religions, and even had space for the theories and discoveries of science.

"Theosophy swept Europe with an impetus and energy comparable to that of Wagner or Nietzsche. Wagner may have created a religion of his own, but few people at the time would explicitly have acknowledged it to be such. Theosophy, on the other hand, did announce itself as a full-fledged organized religion – or rather as the definitive and supreme synthesis of all religions, the universal and all-encompassing ultra-religion of the future. It thus posed a challenge and a threat to existing faiths that generated considerable alarm. With its declared foundations in what purported to be 'esoteric Buddhism', its hierarchy of 'secret masters' and its all-embracing scope, Theosophy offered a complex framework that incorporated all other creeds within itself."[9]

Together with Theosophy re-emerged occultism, the exploration of realities which are not accessible to our ordinary senses. Because the human being has been constituted complex and diverse, occultism has always been its natural, prime fascination, along with religion. The practice of both is in fact one and the same – a Church which condemns occultism will use magical formulas to change bread and wine into the body and the blood of its God – and it is only in the 'great' religions that both are separated. If one defines spirituality as the essence of religion, as authentic religion without dogma, one can even maintain that all spirituality is of necessity occult, although all occultism is not necessarily spiritual.

Occultism has always been part of the European culture, but it was often driven underground because the impatient European temperament never allowed it to reach maturity. ("Most Western occultism is long on text and short on practice – contrary to forms of occultism found in the East, which rely on strict discipline, rigorous mental and physical exercises, and the constant supervision of a teacher or 'guru'." Peter Levenda[10]) Paradoxically, the Age of Reason was also one of the most active occult periods. "No historical period is so rich in successful spiritists, magicians, charlatans, etc., as the period which is commonly classified under the labels of enlightenment and reason ... Since the Enlightenment the shadow sides of the reason exert an unprecedented fascination; they are, apparently, the inevitable counterbalance to the pronounced rationality of the bourgeois period."[11] Now, in the years following 1880, the fault line between two worlds, the occult aspects of existence came to the fore again.

This actually seems a 'normal' development when put against the background of those years. Heinrich Hertz produced electromagnetic

---

[9] Michael Baigent and Richard Leigh, op. cit., p. 247.
[10] Peter Levenda: *Unholy Alliance*, p. 44.
[11] Thomas Freller: *Cagliostro – Die dunkle Seite der Aufklärung*, p. 74.

waves, Wilhelm Röntgen discovered the X-rays, Giuglielmo Marconi sent the first messages on invisible waves, and Henri Becquerel, followed by Marie and Pierre Curie, discovered the first elements which radiated in the dark without apparent reason. At a time when renowned scientists proclaimed that science had reached its limits and only a few gaps remained to be filled up, physics broke through the barriers of tridimensionality into the realms of relativity and quantum mechanics. Friedrich Nietzsche wrote almost simultaneously his works about the 'will to power' and the 'superman', aiming at a 'transvaluation of all values'. His work and that of his admirer Henri Bergson, who thought out the philosophy of the stream of consciousness and the *élan vital*, would lead the human reflection from the fortress of positivism unto new paths of vitalism and to Sigmund Freud. In 1880 Impressionism had reached its zenith and was already splitting up into other, no less amazing or disturbing schools of art. In its footsteps followed the literary symbolism of Baudelaire, Rimbaud, Verlaine, Mallarmé and Valéry, now venerated as god-like statues at the gates of all modernist writing.

"It may be pure accident or arbitrary selection", writes Eric Hobsbawm in *The Age of Empire 1875-1914*, "that Planck's quantum theory, the rediscovery of Mendel, Husserl's *Logische Untersuchungen*, Freud's *Interpretation of Dreams* and Cézanne's *Still Life with Onions* can all be dated 1900 ... but the coincidence of dramatic innovation in several fields remains striking". Then, a few pages further he writes casually: "We are apt to overlook the vogue for occultism, necromancy, magic, parapsychology (which preoccupied some leading British intellectuals) and various versions of eastern mysticism and religiosity, which swept along the fringes of western culture".[12] We, his readers, are not apt to overlook a sweeping 'vogue' which was part of the still unnamed revolution at a fault line in history which would cause the devastating earthquake of the First World War.

---

[12] Eric Hobsbawm: *The Age of Empire 1875-1914*, pp. 256, 262.

Things visible and invisible

It is a symptom of the confusion in the Western 'consensus mentality', supposedly materialistic and scientific, that occultism remains a subject of suspicion while millions accept the occult ceremonies of their Churches without questioning them, and while thousands of the social elite are practising Freemasons. The same suspicious attitude prevails among academic historians. "I have studied history and psychology at the University of Munich and became years later a doctor in philosophy", writes Peter Orzechowski. "In the course of these studies it has become clear to me that history, as a simple presentation of the facts, cannot explain the historical events. This is especially true as far as the history of the Third Reich is concerned ... There is a wealth of quotations which show that Hitler conceived National Socialism as a religion. Until now no historian has drawn serious conclusions from this fact. The National Socialist religion appeared too abstruse to the analytical, scientific intelligence for it to be worthy of an examination. This religion seemed to be rooted too deeply in the occult for a historian to be able to study it without becoming himself suspect of occultism to his colleagues."[13]

"Irrationalism in its multifarious manifestations belongs to the fundamental facts of all societies, also the most 'advanced'", writes Detlev Rose. "The liberal-enlightened idea of human thought and action solely guided by the intellect is nothing more than wishful thinking. Who does not want to accept that thought conceptions, world views and impulses to act are also determined by irrational forces, fails to recognise an elementary part of the realities of life."[14] Nicholas Goodrick-Clarke, in his unanimously appreciated *The Occult Roots of Nazism*, formulates the same opinion more prudently as follows: "For historians trained exclusively in the evaluation of concrete events, causes, and rational purposes, this netherworld of

---

[13] Peter Orzechowski: *Schwarze Magie – Braune Macht*, pp. 14, 11.
[14] Detlev Rose: *Die Thule-Gesellschaft*, p. 9.

fantasy may seem delusive. They would argue that politics and historical change are driven only by real material interests. However, fantasies can achieve a causal status once they have been institutionalized in beliefs, values, and social groups. Fantasies are also an important symptom of impending cultural changes and political action."[15]

All depends on what one considers the 'fantasies' which can achieve a causal status to be. One might legitimately ask if, excepting the physical activities of Nature, there has been and is anything else but 'fantasies' determining the acts of humans. What, in the present times, is not recognised as 'scientific fact' may be classified as 'fantasy'. If so, the whole of humanity in the whole of its known history before the last two centuries, roughly speaking, lived in a world of fantasy, and one wonders how it managed to finally reach the era of scientific realism, which is the era in which we are living. Amazingly, this is also the era in which Christmas Father has become an international figure; Olympic flames are lit again; people continue taking part in magical Church ceremonies; millions mourn a jet-setting British princess; film stars are venerated as saints after their death; and libraries are written by scientifically qualified materialistic scholars on Jung and Freud – while the killing for reasons of fantasy continues unabated. A striking example of the selectiveness of historic writing, in this case by the person at the centre of the Nazi event, is what now is commonly called the 'near-death experience' of Albert Speer, Hitler's architect, 'favourite minister and one of his possible successors'.

In January 1944 Speer was hospitalised for a serious knee and lung infection. The time was not opportune for him because Göring, always covetous of more power, had been intriguing against him, using the sinister Martin Bormann to bring Speer in disfavour with Hitler. The medical institution where Speer's condition had grown

---

[15]Nicholas Goodrick-Clarke: *The Occult Roots of Nazism*, p. 1.

critical was a state-of-the-art Party hospital at Hochenlychen, near Berlin, run by Dr Karl Gebhardt. This was an SS-Gruppenführer and the personal physician of Himmler, who, according to Speer, had directed Gebhardt to eliminate him. In *Inside the Third Reich* Speer writes: "The doctors prepared my wife for the worst. But in contrast to this pessimism, I myself was feeling a remarkable euphoria. The little room expanded into a magnificent hall. A plain wardrobe I had been staring at for three weeks turned into a richly carved display piece, inlaid with rare woods. Hovering between living and dying, I had a sense of well-being such as I had only rarely experienced."[16]

In Speer's conversations with Gitta Sereny, however, we read what *really* happened: he, the very ambitious, very materialistic and very matter-of-fact architect, powerful minister and top Nazi, had had a near-death experience! As Sereny reports that conversation: "'I have never been so happy in my life', [Speer] said. He was 'above' he said, looking down at himself in bed. 'I saw everything very clearly. The doctors and nurses hovering, and [his wife] Margret, looking sort of soft and slim, her face small and pale ... What Professor Koch and the nurses were doing', Speer continued, 'looked like a silent dance to me. The room was so beautiful' ... He smiled at the memory. 'I was not alone; there were many figures, all in white and light grey and there was music ... And then somebody said, "Not yet"'. And I realized they meant I had to go back and I said I didn't want to. But I was told I had to – it was not yet my time. What I felt then was not something I know how to describe. It wasn't just sadness, or disappointment – it was a long feeling of loss ... To this day I think that I felt things in those hours which the man I know myself to be cannot feel, or see, or say. I tell you one thing: I've never been afraid of death since. I'm certain it will be wonderful."

Then why hadn't he written all this in his memoirs? Speer's answer: "Well, I was supposed to be that super-rational man, you

---

[16] Albert Speer: *Inside the Third Reich*, p. 448.

know, writing a definitive book on this terrible history of our time. What do you think readers would have said if in the middle of that book I had suddenly written that I am sure, sure to this day, that I died that night and came back to life? Can you imagine the fun the critics would have had with that?"[17] This is how and why crucial experiences are omitted from 'official' history, which is like a layer of hardened ashes on the red-hot magma of reality.

As we have seen, the human being, in the non-materialistic view, is per definition occult because it is mostly constituted of occult, to the ordinary senses imperceptible parts, and because therefore most of its activities and experiences – thoughts, feelings, impulses, dreams – are 'occult'. That occultism has so often been abused by frauds and mountebanks does not invalidate this viewpoint. Not only is the individual life for the most part an occult occurrence, the foundations of the scientific-materialistic world too are steeped in occultism. The magic component of the Renaissance has been mentioned. The inspiration of Descartes' philosophical re-evaluation of the bases of Western knowledge was revealed to him in three dreams. August Comte, the theorist of positivism, launched a new religion of humanity. Nietzsche's thinking, however this-worldly in its intention, started from and returned to a-material suppositions. And theoretical physics in the last one hundred years has been leading up to 'the matter myth'.

In the preceding paragraph we have skipped Isaac Newton. As the result of a 1936 auction at Sotheby's in London "scholars were enabled, for the first time, to assess the magnitude and scale of Newton's Hermetic interests", write Michael Baigent and Richard Leigh. "It came as a startling revelation. The first commentator to publish the hitherto suppressed work was John Maynard Keynes, who concluded that Newton's 'deepest instincts were occult, esoteric, semantic ...' According to Keynes: 'Newton was not the first of the age of reason. He was the last of the magicians' ... In the words of

---

[17]Gitta Sereny: *Albert Speer: His Battle with Truth*, pp. 416-17, passim.

a subsequent commentator: 'It may safely be said that Newton's alchemical thoughts were so securely established on their basic foundations that he never came to deny their general validity, and in a sense the whole of his career after 1675 may be seen as one long attempt to integrate alchemy and the mechanical philosophy'".[18]

Nicholas Goodrick-Clarke entitles the second chapter of *The Roots of Nazism*: "The modern German occult revival 1880-1910". There he writes about that period: "Occult science tended to stress man's intimate and meaningful relationship with the cosmos in terms of 'revealed' correspondences between the microcosm and macrocosm, and strove to counter materialist science, with its emphasis upon tangible and measurable phenomena and its neglect of invisible qualities respecting the spirit and the emotions. These new 'metaphysical' sciences gave individuals a holistic view of themselves and the world in which they lived. This view conferred both a sense of participation in a total meaningful order and, through divination, a means of planning one's affairs in accordance with this order".[19]

Goodrick-Clarke sketches the rapid spreading of Theosophy in Germany and mentions the publication in Leipzig of a twelve-volume book series, *Library of Esoteric Writings*, in 1898-1900, and in 1894-96 of a thirty-volume book series, *Theosophical Writings*, in Weimar. In 1906 a Theosophical Publishing House was established in Leipzig, under the imprint of which 'a wave of occult magazines' appeared. From his survey Goodrick-Clarke is able to deduce that the German occult publishing activity reached another peak between the years 1906 and 1912. It was the flourishing of the German occult movement which would influence the German speaking (and dominant) population in Austria. "The impetus came largely form Germany, and both List and Lanz drew their knowledge of theosophy from German sources ... Theosophy in Vienna after 1900 appears

---

[18]Michael Baigent and Richard Leigh: *The Elixir and the Stone*, pp. 253-54, passim.
[19]Nicholas Goodrick-Clarke, op. cit., p. 29.

to be a quasi-intellectual sectarian religious doctrine of German importation, current among persons wavering in their religious orthodoxy but who were inclined to a religious perspective."[20] We know that the Austrians List and Lanz would pay back their debt to Germany a thousandfold and directly inspire the Germanenorden and Nazism.

The tragic events of the First World War, like all great crises, produced a new wave of occult interest. The post-war period was a time in which, as Ulrich Linse formulates it, "many nervously disposed people occupied themselves with occult and mystical things, and showed themselves exceptionally receptive to suggestive influences. It is well known that just after the war a great number of hypnotists, magnetizers, telepaths, and whatever else they might call themselves, performed in public and presented their 'mystical' and healing powers in well-organized shows".[21] The crisis atmosphere in Germany in that period of defeat and humiliation, Right and Left wing revolutions and surreal hyperinflation, lasted for years. It was the time of the stigmatized Therese Neumann, the spiritist Weissenberg Church and the famous magician and show man Hanussen. In 1925, German Freemasonry reached its absolute maximum with 82,194 Brothers in 632 loges.[22] Nazism too was part of this search for new, different and potent, not to say miraculous, values.

"Saviours appeared everywhere", remembers Sebastian Haffner, "people with long hair and hair shirts, declaring that they had been sent by God to save the world. The most successful in Berlin was a certain Häusser, who used posters and mass meetings and had many followers. His Munich counterpart, according to the press, was a certain Hitler who, however, differed from his Berlin rival by the exciting coarseness of his speeches, which reached new levels of vulgarity in the extravagance of their threats and their unconcealed

---

[20] Id., p. 30.
[21] Ulrich Linse: *Geisterseher und Wunderwirker*, p. 119.
[22] Helmut Neuberger: *Winkelmass und Hakenkreuz*, p. 51.

sadism. While Hitler wanted to bring about the millennium by a massacre of all the Jews, there was a certain Lamberty in Thuringia who wanted to do it by folk dancing, singing and frolicking. Each saviour had a style of his own. No one and nothing was surprising; surprise had become a long-forgotten sensation."[23]

"The German mind contains a strong 'irrational' component", writes Jochen Kirchhoff, "which feels itself superior to the West-European rationalism ... From the viewpoint of this mind the Cartesian *clarté* appears to be flat, superficial ... The German spirit has this brooding inclination towards the 'far-off' and abysmal realm of being. This corresponds with the German fascination for things spiritual, esoteric, supra-sensual, occult, and for magic and secret societies of any kind ... In the German philosophy there is always a part of mysticism, an element of Meister Eckhart and Jakob Böhme ... West-Europeans feel inclined to situate 'German irrationalism' next to demonism, to relatedness with death, and to sense behind all that a relapse into the Middle Ages, into 'diutisc' barbarism ... This relates to the layer of 'the day before yesterday' in the German mentality, the 'age-old neurotic base', the 'secret relation of the German nature with the demonical', as Thomas Mann puts it, who sees in this one of the roots of National Socialism ..."[24]

The living and the dead

The years we are looking back to were also those of a high tide of spiritism, then together with astrology the most practiced form of occultism. Spiritism in its many varieties has been, since times immemorial, a way of contacting the invisible worlds and the beings that are supposed to populate them; it plays an important role in the world's myths and legends. Nowadays spiritism is called 'channelling', which is essentially the same occult practice.

---

[23] Sebastian Haffner: *Defying Hitler*, p. 53.
[24] Jochen Kirchhoff: *Nietzsche, Hitler und die Deutschen*, p. 49.

The denigrating ways in which some people at present look down on contacts with the dead ignore the seriousness of the spiritist movement, which conquered America and Europe about a century ago. This movement originated in the USA, with the poltergeist experiences of the Fox Sisters in 1848, and developed rapidly into a craze which contributed to the preparation of the soil for the seeds of the Theosophical Society, planted by Blavatsky and Olcott in 1875. It is worth a moment of reflection that the Enlightenment as well as spiritism and Theosophy emerged in Anglo-Saxon countries, generally known for their realism and pragmatism. (The Americans commonly use the term 'spiritualism'; we will use the term 'spiritism', not to cause confusion with the practice of spirituality.)

Spiritism was considered no less than a new religion by its adherents. "The question of the continuation of life and the hope that death at the end is actually not the end are too deeply anchored in the human being not to try to respond to them."[25] "It is for the most part people thirsting for instruction and enlightenment who gather in what one might call a 'circle'. The official way of the [Christian] Churches and their regular sermon on Sunday, which the mass of those present lets passively go over their heads without actually listening to it, does not satisfy them any longer. Their living spirit demands more nourishment than that."[26] As such, spiritism is clearly part of the pulling out of the medieval roots and the transition toward new times.

"In the 1860s and 1870s numerous progressive spiritist groupings began to hold their own gatherings on Sundays, as an alternative to the Christian religious services. They consisted of lectures, prayers and sermons, held by trance mediums, and community singing for which there even were spiritist song books. One did not hesitate to call these spiritist organizations 'churches'. Still, the faith which was

---

[25] In Moritz Bassler and Hildegard Châtellier (ed.): *Mystique, mysticisme et modernité en Allemagne autour de 1900*, p. 95.
[26] Id., p. 96.

propagated there had to be free of dogmas and revealed truths, and be entirely founded on verifiable and commonly understandable natural phenomena."[27] The medium replaced the priest. "Spiritism gave especially the educated the exciting feeling to be present at the crossing of the frontiers between the revealed Christian creed and the empirical knowledge of the material sciences. In this sense, Spiritism was an avant-garde science in the era of the belief in progress. After the discovery of electricity, telegraphy and X-rays, the concept of concrete matter had begun to dissolve; it now seemed more than plausible that the realm of the supersensory too would no longer remain closed to empirical research. One was on the way to a 'transcendental science of spiritism'."[28]

What answers had spiritism to offer, especially concerning the problem of our own death and the death of those near and dear to us, and therefore about the meaning of life? "The answer of spiritism was that our dear ones lived on in 'summerland', continuing there the development of their souls, and that they also were invisibly present among us in individuals, took an active part in our lives, and that contact with them was possible at any time. In this way the individual personality as well as the community of family and friends remained in existence beyond death. In a kind of revolt against the prevailing ideas about death and immortality spiritism therefore propagated an interpretation of death according to which there was no reason to mourn, because it did not mean an extinction of the personality and the ties with others."[29]

It is a fact that spiritism saw itself as scientific, or at least as part of the research that would lead to a new science in which the extra-material would have its legitimate share and even could be seen as the foundation in which the material was embedded. Scientists of renown were interested in spiritism, such as the astronomer Camille

---

[27] Ulrich Linse, op. cit., p. 62.
[28] Moritz Bassler and Hildegard Châtellier (ed.), op. cit., p. 104.
[29] Ulrich Linse, op. cit., p. 15.

Flammarion, the physiologist Charles Richet, the psychologist Jean Piaget and the chemist and physicist William Crookes (as were the writers Victor Hugo and Arthur Conan Doyle). A main point consisted in establishing the immortality of the soul and of reincarnation, no longer as articles of faith but experimentally. "Occultism", stated the German researcher Carl du Prel, "is nothing but as yet unknown natural science. It will be proved by the natural science of the future".

The natural environment of the spiritist 'séance', or sitting, was the restricted circle, generally dominated by a medium. There were speaking mediums, giving voice to a spirit through their mouth, writing mediums, who lent their hand to a spirit to write a message or who made tables or other objects communicate the message by means of an agreed upon code, and their were mediums who healed, painted, played or composed music, and even danced. These mediums were mostly women, 'admired priestesses'. "Spiritism was, at least partially, a feminist religion. As is known, the new creed was founded by the Fox Sisters in the USA. Even if most of its theorists were men – Andrew Davies, Allan Kardec, Aleksander Aksakov and others – the greatest number of trance mediums were women. They dominated the circles."[30] Therefore spiritism played an important role in the first stages of the feminist revolt, one of the principal changes in recent times. Ulrich Linse is reminded, by the women who functioned as the priestesses of the new 'Churches', of the prophetesses in the apocalyptic movements of the past. In 1871 Arthur Rimbaud wrote: "When the endless servitude of the woman will be come to an end, when she will live for herself and by herself ... she will be a poet, she too!" By 'poet', Rimbaud meant the highest condition a human being can attain. "The woman will discover matters that are still unknown!"[31]

---

[30]Moritz Bassler and Hildegard Châtellier (ed.), op. cit., p. 106.
[31]Arthur Rimbaud: *Oeuvres complètes*, p. 272.

Linse also points to "the obvious relation of the art of the modern avant-garde with occultism". True, inspired art is, after all, occultism and as such a permanent stumbling block in the dogmatic universalisation of positivist science. Where does art originate? Where do the poet and the painter see, and where does the composer hear? If the soul is an illusion and the mind an epiphenomenon of matter, then there is no place for the artistic inspiration and no possible explanation of it. The greatest creations of humanity are then something like matter gone mad.

In her essay on the influence of spiritism on Vasili Kandinsky (1866-1944), Marion Ackermann shows how deeply this founder of abstract painting was influenced by the occult movements in the world around him, especially in Munich. "The thesis that there is a fourth dimension of space, since 1870 supported by several theories and discussed in popular scientific publications, had deeply penetrated the public consciousness around the year 1900, as had the connection of the fourth dimension with the spirit world ... The concept of the fourth dimension influenced the artists already in the years before the First World War. The cubists, futurists, rayonists and suprematists believed in their ability to make the fourth dimension visible."[32]

The 'new age' phenomenon around 1900 was as varied as the wave which shocked the world from the mid-1960s onwards. It was, as indicated before, closely connected with the various trends of the volkisch movement. Theosophy and spiritism, and occultism in general, often prospered in the same milieus as vegetarianism, reform centres, wholism, homeo- and naturopathy, magnetic healing, 'back to nature' movements, nudism and orientalism. One will find substantial traces of all this in Nazism.

Occultism in general developed in parallel with the industrialisation of Germany, so much so that "in almost no other

---

[32] Marion Ackermann: "Ueberlegungen zum Einfluss des Spiritismus auf Kandinsky", in *Mystique, mysticisme, etc.*, p. 190.

country there were so many miracles performed, so many ghosts conjured, so many illnesses cured and so many horoscopes read as in Germany up to the Third Reich". The spiritists themselves came in different flavours: New Psychologists, plain Occultists, Animists, Spiritualists of the Anglo-Saxon school, Davisians, Allan-Kardecians, Psychists, Theosophists, Neo-Occultists and Xenologists, among others, and not to forget the Christian spiritists. "All looked jealously towards France", remarks Linse, "where all spiritists seemed to be united, at least in appearance, as followers of Allan Kardec". Kardec (1804-69) said he had his name from the Gallic druid who he had been two thousand years ago. His real name was Hippolyte Rivail; he wrote the *Book of the Spirits* in 1857, which was reprinted again and again, and started publishing the 'Spiritual Review' the next year. Soon the number of his followers ran into several millions and he was called 'the pope of spiritism'.

The chief centres of spiritism in Germany were Berlin, Leipzig, with its very active spiritist publishing house *Verlag O. Mutze*, and above all Munich – more specifically that colourful part of the city called Schwabing, where in the streets walked practically all celebrities and eccentrics of the time. The poets Rainer Maria Rilke and Stefan George, the novelist Thomas Mann, the Russian communist leader Leon Trotsky, the artists of *Der blaue Reiter,* the group to which Kandinsky belonged, and so many more – all could be met in the Türkenstrasse or Schellingstrasse, on the Odeonplatz or in the neighbourhood of the university. Not to forget the personages populating the first chapters of this book.

Rudolf Hess tried out practically all occult fads. His Master at the Thule Society was the occultist and renowned astrologist Rudolf von Sebottendorff. The Thule Society itself was a chapter of the Germanenorden, of which many members and one of the founders, Philipp Stauff, were spiritists. The Thule Society was, moreover, a secret organisation, founded officially to study and spread the volkisch, nationalist and occult sciences. David Clay Large writes that 'magic rituals' were intended to bring present-day Nordic people into contact with the dead ancestors in order to find out their secrets, which would enable the Germans of the twentieth century to found a new master race.[33] Like Dr Gutberlet with his 'astral pendulum', many birds of occult plumage must have visited Thule's seat, the hotel *Vier Jahreszeiten* in the Maximilianstrasse.

Heinrich Himmler is known to have practised spiritism. His biographer, Peter Padfield, mentions that Himmler read a book, *Der Spiritismus,* around 1923 and that this book, according to his diary, "allowed him for the first time really to believe in spiritism".[34] As Peter Levenda has it: "It was within the great dining hall with its round table [in the Wewelsburg] that Himmler and his inner Court of Twelve [Ober]gruppenführers would engage in mystic communication with the realm of the dead Teutons and perform other spiritist exercises".[35] And Heinz Höhne writes in his book on the SS: "Himmler was continually entering into contact with the great men of the past. He believed he had the power to call up spirits and hold regular meetings with them, though only, as he told Kersten, with the spirits of men who had been dead for hundreds of years. When he was half-asleep, Himmler used to say, the spirit of King Heinrich ['the Fowler', 875-936] would appear and give him valuable advice; [Himmler] often began with the words: 'In this case King Heinrich would have acted as follows'. He became so obsessed with his hero that he gradually came to regard himself as the reincarnation of the King".

When the Nazis came to power, they forbade all forms of occultism, and many of its practitioners were thrown into concentration camps. Himmler said to the astrologer Wilhelm Wulff, who towards the end of the war was asked to work for him: "I am sorry that I had to have you imprisoned, but I simply had to put a stop [no doubt on Hitler's orders] to the public practice of

---

[33]David Clay Large: *Hitlers München*, p. 110.
[34]Peter Padfield: *Himmler*, p. 71.
[35]Peter Levenda: *Unholy Alliance*, p. 176.

astrology ... In the National Socialist state astrology must remain a *privilegium singulorum* [privilege of the few]. It is not for the broad masses ... We base our attitude on the fact that astrology, as a universalist doctrine, is diametrically opposed to our own philosophical view of the world ... A doctrine which is meant to apply in equal measure to Negroes, Indians, Chinese *and* Aryans is in crass opposition to our conception of the racial soul."[36]

Waiting for Godot

The coming of the Great Man who would redress the German Volk in its hour of humiliation and inner confusion, and lead it to glory, was an essential part of the German aspiration. "It was a time of prophets", writes George Mosse, "of poetic seers; it was a time when only a charismatic seer seemed capable of ending the malaise of the intellectuals. Thus the intelligentsia looked to a heroic leader for release." Once again "the most vivid image of this leader" was exemplified by Dürer's knight, who "in the forbidding company of death and the devil, but tranquil and full of hope, rides toward the Holy Grail of Germany's future".[37]

We know about 'the Strong One from Above', a term Guido von List had borrowed from the Voluspa Edda and which became popular in volkisch-oriented milieus. The coming Strong One was generally associated with the legend of Frederick Barbarossa, who lay asleep in the Kyffhäuser mountain and would wake up in Germany's destined hour. "The Strong One from Above became a stock phrase in all List's subsequent references to the millennium. An ostensibly superhuman individual would end all human factions and confusion with the establishment of an eternal order. This divine dictator possessed particular appeal for those who lamented the uncertain nature of the industrial society. List eagerly anticipated the advent

---

[36]Wilhelm Wulff: *Zodiac and Swastika*, pp. 110-12, passim.
[37]George Mosse: *The Crisis of German Ideology*, p. 206.

of this leader, whose monolithic world of certainties would fulfil the socio-political conditions of his national millennium."[38]

"Many people in the post-war years were yearning for a Führer who would be hard and at the same time clever, who would establish order, impose discipline on the people, put a stop to the multi-party system, take the reins of the leadership in his own hands and know how to keep them there", writes Sebastian Haffner, adding: "Hitler was indeed the fulfilment of the dreams of many Germans."[39]

The Leader for whom the Germans were waiting did not yet have a face. Heinrich Class, the chairman of the Pan-Germans, had already written a chapter entitled 'Waiting for the Leader' in his influential book *If I Were the Emperor*, published shortly before the war. There he wrote that an elite troop of eager combatants stood at the ready "to follow a decided leader with enthusiasm. But he keeps us waiting!" Yet he admonishes his readers: "Patience! Patience! He will not stay away much longer ... The leader, when he appears, will be amazed how many loyal followers he has and how these valuable, selfless men stand by him. Are there people who have not yet heard the call of the leader? Then it must reverberate still louder, so that it may not remain unheard any longer!"[40]

"The whole of Germany waits only for one man." (Karl Schworm) To most this man was *not* Adolf Hitler, and he was to many either the deposed Emperor William II, or one of the princes who had abdicated in November 1918. The Bavarian coup in November 1923 prepared by 'the three vons', representing the constitutional government, and which Hitler tried to hijack, was intended to restore the monarchy and put Crown Prince Ruprecht on the throne. Class himself was a candidate for the dictatorial leadership of the nation, as were Hugenberg and von Seeckt, although the most serious candidate, especially in the years 1924-25 when Hitler remained

---

[38] Nicholas Goodrick-Clarke, op. cit., p. 88.
[39] Sebastian Haffner: *Von Bismarck zu Hitler*, p. 220.
[40] Dietrich Bronder: *Bevor Hitler kam*, p. 128.

sidelined, was Erich Ludendorff, pushed on by his ambitious wife-to-be, Mathilde von Kemnitz. To all of them an imperial restoration was the chief aim. Even the Berlin 'Club of the Barons', who practically put Hitler in the saddle, hoped to be able to bring William back from Holland in due time, and it was because of this expectation that Paul von Beneckendorff und von Hindenburg was called the 'Ersatz Kaiser', which might be translated as 'emperor-ad-interim'. Hitler, then, was one among many men of destiny, at times well-nigh forgotten or written off, and always underestimated.

When at the beginning of 1920 Rudolf Hess heard Hitler speak for the first time, he was carried away. He would smilingly stare into the void and murmur *"der Mann! der Mann!"* (the man, the man). His wife would later say: "He was like a new person, alive, radiating, no longer silent and depressed. Something totally new, something tremendous must have happened to him". Shortly afterwards a wealthy South American endowed a prize at Munich University for a thesis entitled "What must the man be like who will lead Germany back to its greatness?". To Hess the expected Leader was no longer unknown, he had a face and a name: Adolf Hitler. He had heard 'the man' with the thundering, mesmerizing voice; he had talked with him and knew that this was 'the Strong One from Above'.

Hess participated in the competition and won. Among other things he wrote: "For the sake of national salvation the dictator does not shun to use the weapons of his enemy, demagogy, slogans, street parades, etc. Where all authority has vanished, only a man of the people can establish authority. This was shown in the case of Mussolini. The deeper the dictator was originally rooted in the broad masses, the better he understands how to treat them psychologically, the less the workers will distrust him, the more supporters he will win among these most energetic ranks of the people. He himself has nothing in common with the mass; like every great man, he is all personality ... When necessity commands, he does not shrink before bloodshed. Great questions are always decided by blood and iron. And the question at stake is: shall we rise again or be destroyed ...

In order to reach his goal, he is prepared to trample on his closest friends ... The law-giver proceeds with terrible hardness ... One day we shall have our new, Greater Germany, embracing all those who are of German blood ..."[41]

The man who actually proclaimed Hitler 'the Führer' was Dietrich Eckart. After having become acquainted with Hitler, he published on 5 December 1919 in his magazine *In Plain German* a poem entitled *Geduld* (patience). In this poem he stated that the unknown, expected Leader was to some people not unknown anymore, although he was still "a nameless one, whom everybody feels but none has seen". He bade his time, "the hero on whom we build". Patience, patience, 'he' was there and would soon make himself known. Significantly, Eckart would publish this poem a second time on 25 August 1921 in the *Völkischer Beobachter*, the NSDAP paper of which he was the editor, after Hitler had demanded and been assigned dictatorial powers in the Party thanks to the intervention of Eckart.

Heinrich Himmler would later say: "[Hitler] came to us in our deepest need, when there was no longer a future for the German people. He belongs to the great Beings of Light who always arise among the Germans when they find themselves in the deepest physical, mental and spiritual need. Goethe was such a being in the realm of the mind and Bismarck in the political field, but the Führer is such a being in all fields: political, cultural and military. He is predestined by the karma of Germanhood to wage the war against the East in order to save the Germanhood in the world. One of the greatest Beings of Light has found its incarnation in him".[42] Himmler had the term 'Being of Light' from Houston Chamberlain, who had proclaimed Hitler to be such a being after meeting him in 1923.

Another of the Führer's paladins, Joseph Goebbels, the propaganda minister, described his Leader still on 31 December 1944 as follows: "He is the greatest among the personalities who are

---

[41]Konrad Heiden: *The Fuehrer*, pp. 84-85.
[42]Peter Orzechowski, op. cit., p. 171.

making history today, and he stands far ahead of them in the prevision of things to come. [By then the Russians were already deep in Germany and their Allies stood on its Western border.] He surpasses them not only in genius and political instinct, but also in knowledge, character and will power ... He passes his days and a great part of his sleepless nights in the circle of his closer and closest collaborators, but stands nevertheless, even among them, in the icy loneliness of the genius, soaring triumphantly above all and everything. Never a word of falsehood or baseness crosses his lips. *He is Truth itself.* One only has to be in his vicinity to feel physically how much power he irradiates, how strong he is and how much strength he communicates to others. From him *an uninterrupted flow of faith* and emphatic will power carries us to greatness".[43]

These are expressions of the full-blown Führer myth. A Great Man had once more been given to Germany at a time of direst need and was leading the Volk to its destined glory as masters of the world. This great man was a genius, seer, hero and modern dragon slayer, achiever of age-old dreams, prophet, and the mystic saviour of the Volk in possession of magic powers for the consummation of his mission. "Words of the Führer replace the prayers, the National Socialist morning drill replaces the mass. The picture of the Führer with the swastika replaces Christ on his cross. Instead of the Old and New Testament there is *Mein Kampf* and *The Myth of the Twentieth Century*; instead of processions there are marches with the swastika as mystic symbol; instead of the Christian caritas as a private initiative there is the state-organized *Winterhilfe* [assistance to poor people, especially in winter] as 'Church of the deed'. The 'divine mission' of the Führer seems to have been more than a gimmick for the supernatural glorification of the regime and the unbridled expansion of its power, for there are unmistakable indications that Hitler took himself for the Messiah."[44]

---

[43] Id., p. 174 (emphases in the text).
[44] Günter Scholdt: *Autoren über Hitler*, p. 115.

Hitler was considered the intermediary between the Volk and God, writes Scholdt. "Solemnly he strides/in silence through his brown army/as a priest who blesses/the germinating seeds". However, Hitler was much more than the high priest of Germany: he was the Saviour sent by God, the instrument and executor of the divine intervention. "The Führer commands: it is God's will." A poem addressed to Hitler's (late) mother has the line: "It is the Saviour you have borne for our people".[45] Altars with Hitler as the deity could be seen in many homes; people whose hand he had touched did not wash it for weeks and were treated as saints in their villages; pilgrims to the Obersalzberg treasured a pebble on which his foot had stood; roses, streets, squares, church bells, villages and children were named or re-named after him, and the Chancellery in Berlin had often to intervene in order to separate the reverential from the ridiculous.

Hitler himself stimulated the crescendo of his popularity into adulation, veneration and deification. "Especially in speeches to his old followers, after a period of silence in memory of the dead, he frequently fell into a tone of total rapture; in strange phrases he held a kind of mystic communion until the searchlights were lowered to strike the middle of the arena and flags, uniforms, and band instruments flashed red, silver and gold. 'I have always felt', he cried in 1937, 'that a man, as long as life is given to him, ought to yearn for those with whom he shaped his life. For what would my life be without all of you! That you found me long ago and that you believed in me has given our lives a new meaning, posed a new task. That I have found you is what has made my life and my struggle possible!'

"A year before he had cried to the same assemblage: 'At this hour do we not again feel the miracle that has brought us together! Long ago you heard the voice of a man, and it struck your hearts, it

---

[45] See id., pp. 114 ff.

awakened you and you followed this voice. You followed it for years without so much as having seen him whose voice it was; you heard only a voice, and you followed. When we meet here we are all filled with the wondrousness of this coming together. Not every one of you can see me, and I cannot see every one of you. But I feel you and you feel me! It is faith in our nation that has made us small people great, that has made us poor people rich, that has made us vacillating, dispirited, anxious people brave and courageous; that has made us who had gone astray able to see, and that has joined us together.'"[46]

And so it came to happen that little German children prayed, kneeling by the side of their beds: "I fold my hands and bow my head/and think of Adolf Hitler/who gives us work and bread/and saves us from every need". The star in the top of the Christmas tree was replaced by an illumined swastika. And the most intimate of the Christmas songs was nazified into: "Silent night, holy night/All are asleep, but one stands guard/Adolf Hitler over Germany's fate /He leads us to greatness, glory and happiness."[47]

A new human being

In the insecurity and confusion caused by the vortex of change, the longing for a meaning which would make life worthwhile was accompanied by a feeling that a new world, a new golden age was in the making. At the 'historical juncture', the *Zeitbruch* around 1880, the idea, not to say the need, of a new human being can be found everywhere in the expectations of thinkers, poets and artists receptive to the ambience of the times. The anticipation of a higher being with the capacities to create new values and a new world is one of the most striking signs of a fundamental change in the times.

---

[46]Joachim Fest, op. cit., pp. 514-15.
[47]Peter Orzechowski, op. cit., p. 173.

The most perspicacious interpreter of this time-hinge period in which he was living, was Friedrich Nietzsche (1844-1900). So insightful were many of his perceptions that they would remain sources of inspiration for many philosophers throughout the twentieth century and up to the present day. When reading some of his exegetes, one is surprised by the extent to which Nietzsche's personality is seen as detached from the Germany in which he had grown up – the background outlined in the previous chapters of our story. This is, needless to say, in direct contradiction with one of the pillars of the Nietzschean thinking: 'perspectivism', which states that any event and any being is determined by and dependent on the circumstances in which it comes about, that it is shaped by the flow of time or history in which it exists.

In Nietzsche's writing we find, therefore, the main themes of the volkisch thought, some of them confirmed, others rebuked. His famous saying that 'God is dead' means – this is often misunderstood – that the image of the *Christian* God has lost its general acceptance in the West. It means, as Nietzsche writes in *The Gay Science*, "that the belief in the Christian God has ceased to be believable". This, according to Nietzsche, who wrote that book in 1882, is 'the greatest recent event'. He considered "the Christian conception of God one of the most corrupt conceptions of God arrived at on earth", mainly because it turned the fulfilment of life away from the earth toward a fictional hereafter. The death of the Christian God is for Nietzsche "the cardinal event of modern history and of the contemporary world, the ghost that looms behind his every important thought".[48] What this pronouncement meant fundamentally was that the European Middle Ages, with their Christian civilisation, were coming to an end.

As a thinker and critic of the formerly established but now disintegrating values, religious and moral, Nietzsche could not

---

[48] JP Stern: *Nietzsche*, p. 92.

disregard the Enlightenment which claimed the superiority of reason. In general, he had the highest regard for the *philosophes*, knowing from his own experience what it took to formulate an unarticulated perception and to fight for one's convictions on the battlefields of the mind. "Every smallest step in the field of free thinking, and of the personally formed life, has ever been fought for at the cost of mental and physical tortures." He himself suffered continuously from migraines, bad eyesight and *paralysis progressiva*. "Change has required its innumerable martyrs ... Nothing has been bought more dearly than that little bit of human reason and sense of freedom that is now the basis of our pride."[49] Nietzsche also gave special importance to France and its 'cultural superiority over Europe', as opposed to what he called the German backwardness, heaviness and shallowness.

What Nietzsche could not accept was the monopoly or autocracy of reason. He sharply and repeatedly attacked Socrates, according to him the thinker responsible for the reverence assigned to the mind in European civilisation. He called autonomous thought a deadly illness, and opposed to Apollo, the god of light and clarity, the wholeness and wholesomeness of Dionysus and the frenzied Dionysian experience. Socratic thought, said Nietzsche, was the source of Christian morality, in other words of the weakness and degradation at the roots of the Christian civilisation, and responsible for its degradation and certain extinction. (Oswald Spengler, author of *The Decline of the West*, has been called 'Nietzsche's monkey'.) As the pathfinder of a new way Nietzsche thought of himself as an incarnation of the god Dionysus come to fight the shadow left by the dead Christian God, and as Zarathustra come to bring the new 'evangel' of the superman.

As Nietzsche saw it, the mind was part of a whole consisting of the life-forces, bundled in a 'will to power'. In this he made the disastrous mistake – for mind *and* life *and* matter are part of a

---

[49] In Walter Kaufmann: *Nietzsche – Philosopher, Psychologist, Antichrist*, p. 245.

greater, encompassing whole – which exalted him into the patron saint of the Vitalist movements, including Fascism in general and Nazism in particular. As JP Stern has it, according to Nietzsche "life cannot be defined: to define it would be to subordinate it to reason, its servant. This logical conundrum turned out to have most disreputable consequences. It was handed down to Nietzsche from Schopenhauer, and from Nietzsche to Alfred Rosenberg, to Ernst Jünger in the twenties, Gottfried Benn in the early thirties, and a host of other influential German authors".[50]

Nietzsche had a profound disdain for the masses, one of the new social phenomena of the times. It seems that he never thought beyond the rise of the bourgeoisie, 'the third estate' which carried the Enlightenment and the French Revolution, and was therefore hindered by a blind spot to mark the rise of the fourth estate, the proletariat. Socialism, Marxism and their masses remained beyond his ken. He was an out-and-out individualist who saw in self-mastery, the effort of 'self-overcoming', the means of growth into a higher being. This was the manner in which the world, as a perfected aesthetic phenomenon, would become totally satisfactory. "Attacking the fashionable idea of progress, he argued that 'the goal of humanity' must lie 'in its highest specimens', and these may occur, and recur, in every age."[51] For a vision in the Swiss mountains of Engadin had revealed to him that all things happen again eternally, in exactly the same fashion, and this filled him, strangely, with a kind of mystic exaltation. The value of Nietzsche, however, does not lie in the consistency of his philosophical system, which he never intended and even wholeheartedly despised, but in the depth of his insights which continue reverberating to this day.

"All creatures hitherto have created something beyond themselves: and do you want to be the ebb of this great tide, and return to the animals rather than overcome man? What is the ape to men? A

---

[50]JP Stern, op. cit., p. 69.
[51]Id., p. 108.

laughing-stock or a painful embarrassment. And just so shall man be to the superman."[52] No doubt, Nietzsche knew Darwin; Walter Kaufmann even mentions that the young Nietzsche "was aroused from his dogmatic [Protestant] slumber by Darwin". Yet, although Nietzsche accepted the possibility of transcending a given natural state, he was 'consistently hostile' to Darwinism because it was a theory of chance, numbers and pure matter, which left no place for his staunch individualism, for the effort of self-overcoming and the will to power. "The single man alone is the bestower of values ... The only absolute imperative a man should obey is that of his inward potential: whatever it is given to a man to become, *that* should indicate the direction, and be the goal, of his intense striving, his will."[53] Nietzschean evolution, in the human species at least, was a matter of individuals striving for greatness, not of races struggling for a momentary superiority on earth.

Another important tie of Nietzsche with the period in which he lived was his relationship with Richard Wagner. "His identity was so bound up with Wagner that it might collapse if they separated", writes Carl Pletsch.[54] When Wagner died, Nietzsche wrote in a letter: "Wagner was by far the fullest man I have ever known". His music "seeped into the being of its listeners and transformed them from within. Nothing in the history of music was so daring in composition and so seeringly accurate and dangerously effective in conveying the power and nature of the human *Machtgefühl* [feeling of power]. Wagner's music was an extraordinary elemental embodiment of will." (Lesley Chamberlain[55])

All the same, Nietzsche broke with Wagner when the latter became too *reichsdeutsch*, too much accepted, and enjoying the acceptance, by the German nationalist and conservative elite, which

---

[52] In Philip Novak, op. cit., p. 135.
[53] JP Stern, op. cit., pp. 71, 77.
[54] Carl Pletsch: *Young Nietzsche – Becoming a Genius*, p. 197.
[55] Lesley Chamberlain: *Nietzsche in Turin – An Intimate Biography*, p. 52.

was riding on its wave of pride and superiority after the victory over France in 1871 and the foundation of the German nation. "'German' has become an argument, *Deutschland, Deutschland über alles* a principle; the Teutons represent the 'moral world-order'", wrote Nietzsche indignantly. "There is now a historiography that is *reichsdeutsch*; there is even, I fear, an anti-Semitic one ... and Herr von Treitschke is not ashamed."[56] Wagner's, and therefore Bayreuth's, virulent anti-Semitism was another element inimical to Nietzsche's feelings, who was convinced that a mixture of races would be beneficial to humanity, and proud to be an anti-anti-Semite.

It was against this background that Nietzsche's idea of the superman took shape. It is worth noting that commentators from Walter Kaufmann onwards have become aware that 'superman' is not the correct, and in fact a misleading, translation of *Uebermensch*. A 'superman' could be something like an aggrandisement of existing man, while *Uebermensch* clearly suggests a being *beyond* existing man, not inflated, but on a higher level and different. Kaufmann and others use the term 'overman', which is the literal translation of *Uebermensch*; Philip Novak, also annoyed with the word 'superman', still uses it, but along with 'higher man'.* Awareness of these nuances may prevent misunderstandings of a word, idea and ideal which, in the wake of Nietzsche's fame, will appear in practically all contemporary writings at the time of the dizzying turn the world was taking into – maybe – a very different and better future.

"The superman is the future of the world" stated Nietzsche. "I teach you the superman", said his Zarathustra. "Man is something that should be overcome ... Man is a rope fastened between animal and superman – a rope over an abyss ... This is the great noontide:

---

[56]Walter Kaufmann, op. cit., p. 163.

*When writing about personalities and the cultural life of bygone times, the problem of 'gender specific language' is unavoidable, and a satisfying adaptation of the terminology and the texts is practically unfeasible. This may hurt present sensibilities and is regretted.

when man stands at the middle of his course between animal and superman ... All gods are dead; now we want the superman to live". And in *On the Genealogy of Morals*, he wrote: "This man of the future, who will redeem us not only from the hitherto reigning ideal but also from that which was bound to grow out of it, the great nausea, the will to nothingness, nihilism; this bell-stroke of noon and of the great decision that liberates the will again and restores its goal to the earth and his hope to man, this Antichrist and anti-nihilist; this victor over God and nothingness: *he must come one day*."[57]

What kind of being would Nietzsche's superman be? Stern has composed an outline of his character from *Also sprach Zarathustra*: "The superman is open towards the world and its vicissitudes; trusts in others and in chance; in him the cardinal vices of lust, greed for power and egoism are transformed into positive values; and he is in love with the earth, with his own fate, with his own life, and ready to sacrifice that life for life as lived by those who are open to the world and its vicissitudes ... Based on the premise of a Godless world, the superman embodies the enhancement of man's untrammelled will to power under the quasi-religious dispensation of 'the eternal recurrence of the same'".[58] Alas, all this does not tell us much. It is difficult, if not impossible, to envision a being higher than oneself. An approximation may be found in the way in which humans have imagined their gods and other supernatural beings to be. Nietzsche himself projected on to or within himself a being at times like Zarathustra, and in his ultimate crisis like what he supposed to be the god Dionysus. But trying to overpass the mind is a dangerous wager for human beings and must, for those who persevere, end in a consciousness as reported by the great yogis – or, if things go wrong, in madness.

---

[57]Emphasis in the text.
[58]JP Stern, op. cit., p. 104.

As Nietzsche's ideal of the superman reflected the intuition and yearning of the time, and as Germany was ever more powerfully impelled to national as well as cultural superiority, it was inevitable that the superman would be hijacked by the nationalist movement and be understood to be a Darwinistic Aryan. This was completely incongruous with Nietzsche's thought. But it was not difficult to choose many of his sharper sayings and, omitting the context, put them at the service of the volkisch convictions.

The main culprit in this art of thought laundering was Nietzsche's sister Elisabeth. In 1885 she married, to Nietzsche's indignation, the militant anti-Semite Bernhard Förster and followed him to found a Teutonic colony in Paraguay, *Nueva Germania*. The aim of this colony, one of the many utopian communes of the time, was to preserve at least a handful of German Aryans from miscegenation, in order that the race might survive in some of its purest specimens and eventually be renewed by them. The colony soon succumbed to internal troubles, but some descendants still survive in the original location. In 1934 Elisabeth would receive the Chancellor of the German Reich, Adolf Hitler, at the Nietzsche Archives in Weimar with a flashy right arm salute, and create the occasion for a photo session of Hitler with the bust of Friedrich Nietzsche, symbolising the philosophical tradition of Nazism.

Nietzsche's superman was not the only new human being expected by Germans. There was also, for instance, the 'Ario-Germanic god-man' of Guido von List. This god-man was supposed to be the present-day successor of a long line of 'heirs of the sun-king' going back all the way to Atlantis: the Armanen. The Atlantidians were supposed to have been a divine race. The line of carriers of their secret knowledge and powers had never been interrupted and was surfacing again today. They would be instrumental in creating the future, for List "saw as the culminating point of the universal development the Ario-Germanic god-man".[59]

---

[59]Franz Wegener: *Das Atlantidische Weltbild*, p. 68.

Nicholas Goodrick-Clarke writes: "The myth of an occult elite is not new in European ideology. It has been a perennial theme of post-Enlightenment occultism, which attempts to restore the certainties and security of religious orthodoxy within a sectarian context ... The hidden elite confers an unaccountable authority upon the visible representatives of the cult. The imaginary priest-kings of the past similarly endorsed List's claims to secret knowledge and special authority. At the same time, the putative existence of a modern *Armanenschaft* suggested to believers that the golden age might be soon restored, and that Germany and Austria would be united in a theocratic pan-German realm, wherein non-German interests would play no part. Within thirty-five years this vision was instituted as the foreign policy of the Third Reich."[60]

The well-read Dietrich Eckart was familiar with List's publications, a fact which we find confirmed in Ralph Reuth's Hitler biography, and communicated this knowledge, along with much more, to his Austrian pupil. There is also the testimony of a Munich librarian that Hitler borrowed List's books, and Brigitte Hamann mentions several occasions on which he used Listian language.[61] Intriguing, moreover, is the following fact: "In Hitler's partially surviving personal library, there is a book by Tagore on nationalism with a handwritten dedication on the occasion of his 1921 birthday: 'To Mr Adolf Hitler, my dear Armanist Brother, B. Steininger'. Babette Steininger has been identified as an early member of the Nazi Party in Munich". And Hamann cogitates: "This could be an indication that Hitler had contacts with a secret organization connected with List", adding: "The word 'Armanist' could also be meant generally, to stress Hitler's high rank within the 'Germanic' hierarchy."[62]

The 'Aryan god-man' of Jörg Lanz von Liebenfels resembles in the main List's superhuman ideal. We remember Lanz's depiction of

---

[60]Id., pp. 64, 65.
[61]Brigitte Hamann: *Hitlers Wien*, p. 299.
[62]Id., p. 300.

the conquest of the globe by this superior being. "Through the trampling down and eradication of the primitives and the subhumans, the higher, heroic race arises from the tomb of racial mixture and degeneration, and climbs up to godmanhood, to immortality and divinity in root and race", wrote Lanz. "Then the blond, high bred gods walk on the earth: the races are separated again, the obstacles are eliminated. Then there is heaven on earth. And the blonds know whom to thank for that heaven: gods and goddesses with the sun in their hair and heaven in their eyes, eternally healthy and eternally young shall praise the Great Mother who suffered all for them."[63] We saw in an earlier chapter that Lanz imagined a future order which re-assembled the SS much more than what List expected, including a holocaust of the subhumans.

Another announcer of the superman was the novelist Karl May, Hitler's favourite author. In Hamann we find that May, then seventy years of age and famous, gave a talk in Vienna on 22 March 1912 with the title: "Up toward the Reign of the Noble-man", if this is how *Edelmensch* should be translated. The auditorium which could hold three thousand was full up to the last seat. May, a Protestant Christian, was fascinated by the East, occultism and magical powers. "A real great writer could not have been greeted more tumultuously and enthusiastically", a reporter wrote. "May has always been striving towards the heights, towards a free spirited kingdom of the noble-man. He calls himself alternately a soul, a drop of water in the ocean, and especially a spiritual aviator … The most remarkable in his discourse is the seriousness, the pathetically real enthusiasm which has something of religious enthusiasm." Karl May had given shape to his idea of the superman in Old Shatterhand, the embodiment of German superiority in action, and in Winnetou, the Apache, who was the 'masterpiece' of a German professor and emigrant, Klekih-petra. Young Hitler, then wayward and poor in a Viennese men's

---

[63]Wilfried Daim: *Der Mann, der Hitler die Ideen gab*, pp. 210-11.

hostel, was present at May's talk and was 'immeasurably enthusiastic', according to an anonymous witness.⁶⁴

Schwabing

"The part of Munich called Schwabing is at that time a hotbed of the most different groups. Theosophists, mystics, Gnostics, Taoists, Mazdaists, Buddhists, Neo-Buddhists, Zionists, nihilists, trade-unionists, Bolsheviks and pacifists: all are searching for an explanation of the historical occurrences and looking for disciples", writes Peter Orzechowski, who omits a few – anthroposophists, spiritists, black magicians – as it is impossible to remember them all.⁶⁵ Besides, Orzechowski enumerates only philosophical, religious and occult groups, while in Schwabing these were intermingling with writers, poets and artists, among whom were some of the very greatest then alive. This colourful mixture of all expressions and explorations of the human spirit has lead many commentators on that period to stick the label 'bohemian' on Schwabing, which is as misleading as calling Dietrich Eckart a comical, half-crazed poet. For sure, the whole fauna of the bohemian scene was present at Schwabing, but the place, like Montmartre and Ascona, was one of the cultural centres of Europe were the future was prepared and the remnants of the past put to the test.

These were "good times for religion, good times for prophets, gurus and saviours who claim being able to bring order in the chaos by simple truths".⁶⁶ Such types were also present in Schwabing, for instance Rudolf Pannwitz, whose book *German Teaching* was intended as a prophecy and a charter for the religion of a new Europe. He was 'a prophet of the Hyperboreans' who filled more than four hundred pages with admonitions, commands and

---

⁶⁴Brigitte Hamann, op. cit., pp. 546-47.
⁶⁵Peter Orzechowski, op. cit., p. 38.
⁶⁶Stefan Breuer: *Aesthetischer Fundamentalismus – Stefan George und der deutsche Antimodernismus*, p. 12.

exhortations, all of them beginning with 'the Spirit of your God speaks as follows', and whose new religion would contain the knowledge and love of all past and present religions. And there was Ludwig Derleth, 'the Prophet of Schwabing', who wanted to clean up and reform the Church, and found a new theocracy in which he himself would hold the highest office. He wanted to reactivate a militant and heroic Christianity and to revive the original Christian values in a degraded world. His Christian elite troops, living under the vows of poverty, chastity and obedience, would follow the example of the Sufi order of the Assassins, of the Knights Templar and of the Jesuits, and wage a holy war against the mob, the democratic ways of the modern world, the nation state, the market economy, and a Christian Church which had torn itself from its roots. Conquest of Europe, subjugation of the world and the foundation of a global dictatorship would be the ultimate objectives of Derleth's legions.[67]

And there was also 'The Cosmic Circle', often called 'the Cosmics' or 'the Enormous', a small but qualitatively significant group. The Cosmics, according to David Clay Large, wanted to rejuvenate a calcified and too much intellectually shaped modern world through a renaissance of paganism. Their common points, however much they may have differed on others, were again the rejection of industrial modernity, liberal rationalism, parliamentarian democracy and orthodox Christianity. They had an inclination toward mysticism and occultism. They wanted to gain access to higher states of consciousness by penetrating into the hidden, dark parts of the human personality, following as their guides Friedrich Nietzsche, Sigmund Freud, Carl Jung and Johann Bachofen. Those who mastered such perilous paths would become a new kind of supermen. The efforts of the Cosmics, writes Large, showed "a fascinating mixture of unconditional absolutism, hunger for great solutions, hero worship and readiness for sacrifice in the name of a fundamental purification

---

[67]Id., pp. 120 ff.

and salvation". When Thomas Mann looked back half a century later on his brief contact with them, he located the roots of the German catastrophe in these milieus of an all-absorbing feeling of superiority.[68]

Spiritist séances were common practice in Schwabing. When studying that period through some of its representatives 'it is possible to sense that very special climate', namely "a vivid religious interest but very critical towards the teaching of the established Churches, and seeking for an alternative transcendence of mystical and occult inspiration", writes Hildegard Châtellier. In her study of the Munich poet Hanns von Gumppenberg, who wrote a play called *The Spiritists* as early as 1885, and who faithfully noted down the instructions of his spirit guide Geben, she finds once more the awareness of a new turn to take, together with the will to overcome the pure rationalism inherited from the Enlightenment and to go beyond the traditional religious forms. What counts is the unity of all that exists. "God is pure spirit; but as matter exists, his creation demands the perfection of God." The unity of all existence implies also "a continuity between all forms of life; the world, in this manner, represents a hierarchical system consisting of many tiers, and there is an uninterrupted concatenation of the spirits, the human beings, the animals, the plants, and matter. Life does not end with death, for after death the soul continues its evolution in a succession of supra-terrestrial worlds. The earth and humanity are part of the cosmic whole".[69]

The dictations Gumppenberg received from his spirit mentor seem almost classical in their genre. The spiritist séances in the Cosmic Circle were much more violent, bordering on the demoniac and sometimes overstepping these borders. This does not mean that the Cosmics were crazy nitwits. Karl Wolfskehl was a renowned professor of German literature at Munich and Heidelberg (where Joseph Goebbels was one of his admirers); Alfred Schuler was a

---

[68] David Clay Large, op. cit., pp. 57, 66.
[69] Hildegard Châtellier: *Entre religion et philosophie: approches du spiritisme chez Hanns von Gumppenberg*, in: *Mystique, mysticisme, etc.*, pp. 115 ff.

propagator of Nietzschean ideas, flavoured according to his own recipe, and an habitué at the Bruckmann salon, frequented by Rilke and other celebrities (and soon by Adolf Hitler); and Ludwig Klages would write *The Mind as the Opponent of the Soul,* a book of lasting interest (and he would join the Nazis). And for a while, during his stay in Munich, there was Stefan George, whose contact with the Cosmics nearly proved fatal.

Schuler, involved in black magic, was always in search of spiritist mediums, who, he imagined, would effect a new breakthrough of the cosmic powers which had been repressed by patriarchal, mammonist and rationalist forces. To this end, he tried to force into collaboration the soul of Stefan George, then already reputed as a poet, during a 'Roman' feast in which all the participants would dress up and endeavour to act like Romans. The feast took place in Schuler's house and soon turned into a spiritist séance, during which George grew more and more excited and showed all signs of becoming possessed. He would confess afterwards that he had been suffering for a long time from the consequences of 'the poisoned magic of that nightly session'. George managed to distance himself from the Cosmics and founded his own group, 'The George Circle'.

'A devil or a god'

About this circle, Peter Aschheim writes: "The *Georgekreis* was a circle of disciples and initiates, a sect without formal or obligatory statutes, but which was completely centred upon its master. Although small changes kept taking place in the inner circle, the number of members of this 'secret Germany' never exceeded forty. In spite of this small number the circle became an example of a cultural elite and had an enormous influence on the anti-establishment poetry, literary science and historical writing".[70] This circle displayed indeed

---

[70]Steven Aschheim: *Nietzsche und die Deutschen – Karriere eines Kults*, p. 72.

all the characteristics of a sect or a cult. The first contact with it was felt to be a decisive turnabout in life, a new birth. The choice of the disciples depended exclusively on the master, who acted in all respects as the guru. There were initiation tests and the admission was sealed with a holy oath. And the selected few were given a new name by the master, who alone knew who actually belonged to the circle and who did not.

The centre of all that was Stefan George (1868-1933), a generally appreciated poet whose fame in those days surpassed that of Rainer Maria Rilke. "It has been said that all young Germans of the 1920s were influenced by Stefan George, whether or not they had ever heard his name or read a single line he had written."[71]

> From his words, spoken unobtrusively low,
> A domination emanates and a seduction;
> The empty air he makes to circle and enclose you,
> And he can kill without having to touch.[72]

George was indeed considered a god by some, a devil by others. One person "confessed having experienced for the first time in George's presence what the divine actually is", another "had the impression of a terrible, demonic, earth and world perturbing force of nature".[73] "While regarded as the greatest German-language poet of the age ... he was also revered as a prophet and a magus, a magisterial 'guru' and oracle presiding over an elite hand-picked cadre of intellectual and cultural initiates who 'stood in awe of him' as one might of a high priest. In Berlin, Munich and Heidelberg he held court to a small circle of the brightest, most imaginative and dynamic young men in Germany – the hope, as he saw them, of the country's future. From this cenacle, he issued his often arcane and

---
[71] Otto Friedrich: *Before the Deluge*, p. 226.
[72] Hugo von Hofmannsthal, in Stefan Breur, op. cit., p. 25.
[73] Ibid.

enigmatic pronouncements, and published the cryptic verse that became a cultural beacon to a generation."[74]

George Mosse sketches Stefan George as follows: "He seriously believed in his role as a poet-seer, as a herald of change. To him it seemed that poetry was the most suitable vehicle for describing the tragic conditions of the times, which, he thought, could be alleviated only through the strength and determination of a leader. Poetry struck at the heart of the matter and was, at the same time, impartial and uncommitted to any particular political solution. Above all, a poet was not limited by the seeming fatalism of materialistic, historicist or realistic considerations. He was above them. He was in direct touch with the pulse of the nation. In this framework it was logical that the poet should stride forth as the new prophet".[75]

In the George circle there was no place for women, it was a *Männerbund,* exclusive male territory. For this reason and his sanctification of a boy, Maximin, George and his disciples were suspected of homosexuality, although some students of his life deny the accusation. Such male bonding was a 'normal' part of the personalities of the circle, all deeply embedded in the contemporary environment, as was their reaction against modernity, intellectuality and the democracy of the masses. Another typical, darkly foreboding element of the George cult were "the fantasies of omnipotence and the death wishes which played such an important part among the Georgeans". Considering the number of suicides and of untimely deaths in the circle "one is almost inclined to speak of a death urge" among them.[76] In those days, the Knights Templar and the Hospitallers rode between Death and the Devil side by side with the knight etched by Dürer.

"George concentrated on defining the need for an elite leadership – which did not preclude the emergence of a single leader. Instead of

---

[74] Michael Baigent and Richard Leigh: *Secret Germany*, pp. 110-11.
[75] George Mosse, op. cit., p. 209.
[76] Id., p. 68.

the image of the single knight George promoted the concept of the 'order', such as the Knights Templar of the Crusades. The eschatological urge was strong in him, for he sincerely believed that solutions would eventually be found. The coming century was to be the age of the elite, not of the masses. It would be an era in which great personalities would impress their image, creativity, and accomplishments upon the face of society and culture. George saw these new personalities as representing both godliness and manliness and possessing extraordinary powers of will ... Among his disciples, all with dispositions similar to his own, was the core of the elite." (George Mosse[77]) They embodied the true soul of Germany. He called this true soul *'das geheime Deutschland'*, secret Germany.

Claus von Stauffenberg

Times of extremes often produce remarkable personalities trying to bridge the extremes. In our story Stefan George would be no more than one of the exceptional Germans above the masses of average people if from his circle there had not issued Claus Schenck von Stauffenberg (1907-1944), the driving force behind the attempt on Hitler's life on 22 July 1944. "I had the greatest poet of the age as my master", said Stauffenberg proudly. His inspiration for a daring undertaking, which he knew could cost him his life, were George's ideals, and after the attempt had misfired and Stauffenberg was put up against a wall, his last words echoing within that courtyard on the Bendlerstrasse were: *"Es lebe das geheime Deutschland"*, long live Secret Germany – a Germany of greatness, not of murder, destruction and death.

Claus von Stauffenberg met George in 1924, a year after his two brothers had been accepted into the circle. "This meeting and the relationship that developed were to be among the most influential

---
[77]George Mosse, op. cit., pp. 210, 211.

experiences of his youth, and – occurring at a formative age – were to shape his development, his attitudes, his values, his entire *Weltanschauung* from then on."[78] Claus had all the characteristics of the ideal George disciple: he was an aristocrat, very much conscious of this status; he was tall and good-looking, resembling the fine medieval statue *The Bamberger Reiter*, the Knight of Bamberg, in the cathedral of this town; he was intelligent and talented; and he had an extraordinary will power.

To George and his disciples, poetry was more than a noble passtime; it was a way of fullest existence and a means of knowledge and power. "The poet should not replace the political Leader but prepare him", wrote Wolfskehl, a member of the George Circle. "He should tune the German soul to the global will, revealed through him; he should provide her with the grace of her second wedding and prepare her for the break of dawn when the youth of the new fatherland feels its ardent unity amidst the clanging of their formerly deep buried weapons." "The poet as leader": in this slogan was manifested not so much the claim of the George circle to exert political leadership as the mission which would consist in leading the Leader.[79]

George's disciples "were to be the custodians of Germany's future, an exclusive and elite cadre meticulously nurtured and honed for the task of leadership. The training and refinement of this cadre was something George regarded as a mission, a sacred duty, a discharging of his own personal responsibility to Germany – and, beyond Germany, to humanity as a whole, to the life of the spirit, to the cosmos and whatever gods or governing principles presided over it".[80]

They also had to be mystical warriors, soldiers of the spirit engaged on a spiritual crusade. In this respect they were heirs to the knights in George's poem *'Templars'* (from which the motto of our present chapter is chosen) – of course not those of Lanz von

---

[78]Michael Baigent and Richard Leigh, op. cit., p. 110.
[79]Stefan Breuer, op. cit., p. 225.
[80]Baigent and Leigh, op. cit., p. 274.

Liebenfels' Order of the New Templars, but the medieval high-minded, spiritual warriors ready to sacrifice everything for their ideals and the protection of others. "The latter-day 'Templars' George gathered around him comprised for him an unique kind of nobility and aristocracy of the spirit, not unlike that extolled a few years earlier by Nietzsche and a few years later by DH Lawrence ... It was for this nobility, for the sources of their inspiration and for what they were expected to achieve, that the words 'Secret Germany' were first employed ... George, unlike Nietzsche, did not choose to be alone; it was the heart of his method to build a secret empire for the sake of the new Reich to come ... It was an elitist programme pushed to the very limits of elitism; the secret Germany was a club to which new members were elected and for which they were trained, one by one."[81]

Claus von Stauffenberg chose to serve his fatherland in the armed forces. One of his subordinates remembered later: "I was extraordinarily impressed by Stauffenberg's personality. He seemed to me the ideal of an officer ... He was a man possessed of natural authority". He was also "universally recognized as the single most brilliant and promising young officer in the entire Wehrmacht ... One of his colleagues observed: 'What surprised me was the manner in which those who surpassed him in rank recognized his natural superiority and yielded to it'. In view of one of his commanders, he was 'the only German staff officer of genius'. Heinz Guderian, the mastermind of German armoured warfare and architect of its panzer formations and the Blitzkrieg, was soon to put Stauffenberg's name forward as most likely candidate for Chief of the General Staff".[82]

Then Adolf Hitler became Chancellor of Germany. "George had always decreed that politics were alien to art – and, by extension, inimical to the life of the spirit and to the very essence of humanity itself. His attitude towards the Nazis, however, sometimes appeared

---

[81]Id., pp. 260-61, passim.
[82]Id., pp. 4-5, passim.

inconsistent, and this allowed a few members of his circle to support them ... Ultimately, George was hostile to the new regime ... George's sometimes equivocal disapproval did not deter the Nazis from hailing him as a spiritual precursor and trying to co-opt him, much as they did Nietzsche."[83]

Resurgence and greatness of a new German Reich, leading to a new world and a new man; the fulfilment of the Führer expectation; the redress of alleged injustices by the morally and culturally inferior victors of 1918; ostentation of strength and will power; rituals and music which made the German innards vibrate – National Socialism had everything to allure national, conservative and traditional Germany, including the idealists, who were much more influenced by all these notions than they themselves realized. Hitler masterly conducted his revolutionary movement to exploit these elements in the mentality of the German population, and few escaped the spell of the music of this Pied Piper.

"Thus a generation of young men and women could be duped with a readiness that now appears both inexplicable and culpable. Yet had not Nazism evolved as it did, and culminated in the horrors that have seared themselves into our collective consciousness, its appeal would have been considerable today, not just to louts and skinheads, but to the literate, the thoughtful, the well-educated, the artistically inclined ... A number of the future conspirators ... found elements in National Socialism they felt they could endorse. So, too, could certain members of Stefan George's circle." Claus von Stauffenberg would say: "Hitler is capable of putting into words certain basic and genuine ideas which could lead to a spiritual revival. As a result both the idealistic and the high-minded might indirectly be attracted to him." According to one of his friends, Stauffenberg "was stirred by the magnetism this man was able to generate, and by his vehemence which made what seemed impossible in a stagnant

---

[83] Id., p. 130.

world suddenly appear feasible ... [Stauffenberg] had initially been quite impressed by Hitler's accomplishments ... By the time I met Stauffenberg, however, he had already become thoroughly alarmed over what was taking place".[84]

The falling of the scales from his eyes happened gradually. The iron-fisted totalitarianism, the vulgar and systematic suppression of the Jews, the never ceasing flood of blatant propaganda, the black side of Hitler and his paladins, the arrogance and ruthlessness of the SS, the atmosphere of suspicion and fear – it all looked more and more ominous to those who managed to keep their head an inch above the water. Revealing steps in their growing awareness were 'the beheading of the SA' in what is called 'the Night of the Long Knives' in 1934, and in 1938 what Nazi humour called the *Kristallnacht*, the night of shattering crystal, but what was in fact the biggest pogrom in German history. Stauffenberg was 'mortified'.

In 1941, Stauffenberg was horribly wounded in Africa when a P-40 strafed his staff car. "He was found half-conscious beside his overturned, burnt out and shell-pocked vehicle. His injuries were appalling. His left eye had been hit by a bullet, his right seriously damaged as well. His right forearm and hand had been virtually shot away, as had two fingers on his left. One knee was badly wounded and his back and legs were pitted with shrapnel ... While the surgeons laboured over him, he adamantly refused all pain-killing drugs, all soporifics, anaesthetics and sedatives. Even the Gestapo report speaks admiringly of the great will-power with which he embarked on his recovery ... To an uncle who visited him at the hospital he confided that his survival had not been coincidental; his life, mutilated though it might now be, had been spared for some specific purpose, some ordained design."[85]

Stauffenberg reached the conclusion that Hitler had to die, this in spite of his own moral principles, his code of honour and the oath

---

[84] Id., pp. 136-37, passim.
[85] Id., pp. 6-7, passim.

of allegiance to Hitler he had sworn as an officer. There was no longer an alternative. "I know that he who acts will go down in German history as a traitor; but he who can and does not will be a traitor to his conscience. If I did not act to stop this senseless killing, I should never be able to face the war's widows and orphans." For now it was no longer a matter of the killing of a hundred persons whom Hitler disliked, or of a thousand Jews caught at random, but of hundreds of thousands of German soldiers, people of other nations, and of the systematic genocide of the Jews. In Stauffenberg's position as a staff officer he could not but know about this, even if he did not know all of it. "Stauffenberg was the acknowledged leader of the conspiracy, the figure to whom everyone turned for guiding force and strength of resolve."

General Henning von Tresckow, one of the chief conspirators, is reported to have said: "The assassination must be attempted at all costs. Even if it should not succeed, an attempt to seize power in Berlin must be undertaken. What matters now is no longer the practical purpose of the coup, but to prove to the world and for the records of history that the men of the resistance movement dared to take this decisive step. Compared to this objective, nothing else is of consequence".[86] Who wanted to stand up to Hitler had to put his life on the line, there was no other way since he had been handed the power on 30 January 1933. Even one week before that day Hitler could have been pushed into the dustbin of history; from that day onward the fate of Germany was sealed.

How many attempts have there been on Hitler's life? Will Berthold has published a book about *Die 42 Attentate auf Adolf Hitler*, others say there have been more than forty-six. The fact is that Hitler survived all of them, often in the most incredible way as if he was forewarned or protected. The Stauffenberg attempt on 20 July 1944 affected him worse than officially acknowledged, and from that day onward his health will decline rapidly. After meeting with him,

---

[86]Id., pp. 33, 35, 39.

Goebbels noted in his diary that Hitler "was firmly decided to set a bloody example", and that in the weeks since the coup "he had been almost exclusively occupied with planning his revenge".[87] It was on Hitler's orders that the surviving conspirators, including a field-marshal and several high-ranking generals, were hanged with piano strings instead of ropes, thus being slowly strangled, and that the proceedings were filmed so that he could watch and enjoy them at his villa on the Obersalzberg. The killing of other conspirators, accomplices, suspected accomplices and relatives continued until the very moment of the Armistice; the reprisals took more than 5000 lives.

Not only Goebbels propaganda machine but also public opinion in general condemned the attempt unanimously. Tresckow, like Stauffenberg, had foreseen this reaction and said on the day after the attempt's failure: "Now they will all fall upon us and cover us with abuse. But I am convinced, now more than ever, that we have done the right thing. I believe Hitler to be the arch enemy not only of Germany, but indeed of the entire world ... A man's moral worth is established only at the point where he is prepared to give his life for his convictions ... Just as God once promised Abraham that he would spare Sodom if only ten just men could be found in the city, I also have reason to hope that, for our sake, he will not destroy Germany." "According to some accounts", write Michael Baigent and Richard Leigh, "[Major-General Henning von] Tresckow walked from his headquarters to the front line and there shot himself. According to others, he simply strode out amid an artillery barrage into the no-man's-land between German and Russian lines."[88]

Afterwards the conspirators have been accused time and again of betraying their fatherland in its hour of need, and of not honouring their soldier's oath, sworn on Adolf Hitler by name. It is seldom mentioned that such an oath had never before been sworn on a

---

[87]Joseph Goebbels: *Tagebücher V*, pp. 2084, 2106.
[88]Baigent and Leigh, op. cit., pp. 64, 60.

particular person, and that it was sworn under duress, in circumstances hastily set up the day after President von Hindenburg's death and in which no man could refuse to swear without paying dearly for his refusal. Nor is it remembered that Hitler himself had written in *Mein Kampf*: "A State is entitled to demand respect and protection for its authority only when such authority is administered in accordance with the interests of the nation, or at least not in a manner detrimental to those interests. The authority of the State can never be an end in itself, for, if that were so, any kind of tyranny would be inviolable and sacred. If a government uses the instruments of power in its hands for the purposes of leading a people to ruin, then rebellion is not only the right but also the duty of every individual citizen. The question of whether and when such a situation exists cannot be answered by theoretical dissertations but only by the exercise of force, and it is success that decides the issue."[89] Finally, there is the question of the weight of an oath against the monstrous acts of inhumanity of which the man on which it was sworn, and the regime built up and directed by him, were guilty.

"The nine months between 20 July 1944 and the end of the war in Europe were to witness an appalling loss of life ... Altogether they took more lives than the previous four years and eleven months of conflict. This statistic offers some gauge of the stakes involved in Stauffenberg's conspiracy. Had Hitler died on 20 July 1944, the total casualties of the Second World War would have been halved." (Baigent and Leigh[90])

A higher and a lower choice

The German aspiration for a new and total spiritual experience was spontaneous and sincere. The existing religions had always promised a fulfilment of all expectations in another world, but human intuition

---

[89] Adolf Hitler: *Mein Kampf*, p. 91.
[90] Baigent and Leigh, op. cit., p. 66.

knew that, if God was something more than a simulacrum residing above the clouds, then the earth and the life of the human being must have a meaning. These were bewildering times of change, in which a new world and a new, higher human being were expected. The Enlightenment had asked all the questions, but it had given very few dependable answers. The tectonic plates of the religious and philosophical certainties were felt to be moving; the results were a series of earthquakes – one revolution after another, then one war after another – and a feeling of instability, disorientation and fear. The familiar structures of a hierarchical society had crumbled and previously unknown social phenomena – especially the human masses – had arisen and were felt as primitive and threatening, in a modern world which uprooted people and assembled them in urban agglomerates, provoking close, direct and often baffling relationships.

The "revival of the mystic spirit around the turn of the century [1900]" longed for something neither the Churches nor the philosophers had been able to provide: a sense of total fulfilment of the external and internal life, something authentic, not imported from other cultures and certainly not imposed. The Catholic Church had always been "a foreign body to the sensibility of the Germanic people, and this had created an often expressed aversion against the Paulinian-Augustinian Christianity of the father-god Jehova". A Nazi author put it as follows: "Germany did not need oriental symbols, and in a land which had generated a religion like the German mysticism around 1300, the belief in a jealous Yahweh-god was felt as hypocritical and as an obsession."[91]

"A resolute rejection of the Jewish transcendental speculation, together with the severing of the link between the German mind and the theology of revelation" was the need at a time that the last great episode in the history of global Christianity, Protestantism, came to an end. In this context a new religion was expected to be

---

[91] *Mystique, mysticisme, etc.*, p. 172.

"a religion without Jewishness, without intermediaries, without dualism: a German religion of deepest inwardness". This was to be found in Meister Eckhart and the mystics of the Rhineland and Flanders, who constitute a unique, fascinating Western phenomenon. "There can be no doubt that our possibility to escape from the present circumstances, distorted at their origin, and to obtain a religion which is adapted to our actual way of seeing the world, can only be sought in the direction of the way as gone by Eckart."[92]

Meister Eckart (1260-1328) was a Dominican monk, though not the medieval monk as one might picture him in one's imagination: living in seclusion and looking all the time upwards in contemplation of God. He was widely travelled, became a Master of Theology at the Sorbonne in Paris – even a *magister actu regens*, "an exceptional honour at the time which put him on a par with Thomas Aquinas" – and he was invested with some of the highest offices within his order. Eckart's example was Albert the Great, another towering figure of the Middle Ages, and he was an exponent of a mystic peak which, in its broadest context, produced luminaries like Hadewych and Dietrich von Freiburg. His experience, expressed not only in Latin but also in his High-German mother tongue, is so direct, pure and complete that it joins the experience of the great Eastern mystics.

It is an amazing fact that a Dominican Prior and instructor could preach that God was to be found in the heart; that He was not a mental concept but a direct, overwhelming and unutterable experience; that the 'spark' of the soul was the Divine itself, and that one who lived in it fully *was* the Divine, in space and time and beyond it; that in the Divine all opposites fused together and disappeared in the great unity; that the Divine was everything in the manifestation, but that it was also completely itself without the manifestation. The learned Master of Theology must have taken his arduously studied texts seriously and gone, with his insight, beyond them into the experience, while simultaneously remaining the realist

---

[92]Id., p. 173.

who found God's presence in all things and was active in the most diverse ways.[93] His person narrowly escaped condemnation as a heretic, but some of his mystic assertions did not.

Meister Eckart became part of "the longing for the supposedly integral culture of the Middle Ages ... The endeavour of the Old Romantics was much learning and a universal humanity, and they animated their knowledge because they tried not only to think out their ideals but also to live them. The same road will be taken by the New Romantics [mainly the volkisch movement], going back to the spontaneity, originality, artistry and joy of living of the people at the time of Paracelsus and Dürer." (Justus Ulbricht[94]) A leading promoter of this movement was the publisher Eugen Diederichs, the key figure whom we have met when discussing the revival of the Germanic myths and legends, and a new, German religion. Diederichs, though, never meant to remain stuck in the past, but tried to contribute the utmost for a greater future.

He wrote in a letter: "Do not believe that I consider the new Romanticism as the goal of all development ... But why would it not be a part of the development of the present man? Together with mysticism, that is ... Our Protestantism would be very different from what it is now if the theologians after Luther's death had not been such quarrelsome blockheads ... I have the strong feeling that, with my publishing house, I have to steer toward a deepened religion without dogmas, and that the forthcoming period will most probably produce the men needed for this. Tolstoy, Eugen Schmitt and Emerson are for me the first steps in this direction. Also Meister Eckhart."[95] As Ulbricht tells us, the shaken and confused intellectuals around 1900 looked for the presence of God in their own heart, something which in their cultural space they could only find in the

---

[93]See Alain de Libera: *La mystique rhénane*.
[94]Justus Ulbricht: *Die Rückkehr der Mystiker im Verlagsprogramm von E. Diederichs*, in *Mystique, mysticisme, etc.*, pp. 165 ff.
[95]Id., p. 169.

mystics like Meister Eckhart, Heinrich Seuse and Johannes Tauler. "The renaissance of mysticism around 1900 belongs therefore to the history of the religion of the German intellectuals and their idea of self-redemption. 'The human being redeems itself: this is the new religion', is written already in 1892 in a notebook of the young bookseller Diederichs, whose reading of Nietzsche had obviously not remained without consequences. One also perceives in him the suffering because of the 'death of God' which, all the same, was seen by his generation as an opportunity for religious emancipation ...

"Some ten years after the start of his activities toward a new religion, Diederichs summarized, in a prospectus for 'Books for a religious development', his efforts made for the liberation of the religious forces from calcification through the history process and the transmitted fixed Church forms, to bring them again in direct contact with present-day life ... In the same prospectus one reads moreover: "It should be stressed emphatically that Meister Eckhart means *more* than Luther for Protestantism in the future development of a German religion." Diederichs will also write: "In spite of the last 400 years [since Luther's reformation], everything is still to be done."[96] This evaluation encompassed more than Protestantism: it expressed the general feeling of bankruptcy of the established religions, and the longing for a new world and a new man which at last would be the justification and the wholly satisfying fulfilment of God's creation of life on earth.

That Germany did not need "oriental religious symbols and the belief in a jealous Yahweh-god" was a quote from Alfred Rosenberg's *Myth of the Twentieth Century*. The reader will remember that Rosenberg was the official chief-ideologist and inspector of ideology in the Nazi Reich. (Unofficially, but most effectively, it was Adolf Hitler who held this job and who supervised the inspector.) As we have seen, what Germany needed according to Rosenberg was "a

---

[96]Id., p. 170.

religion without Jewishness, without intermediaries, without dualism: a German religion of the deepest inwardness. And Meister Eckart was its initiator."*

The disturbing word in this quotation is the word 'German'. Meister Eckhart was no doubt of German origin, although the Germany of 1300 was very different from what is meant by the word today. But could he, a leading member of the international order of the Dominicans, Master of the Parisian Sorbonne, and above all a Roman Catholic Christian, be appropriately called a *German* mystic? Seen from another angle: could his integral realization of the Divine be restricted and fitted into a German framework? The great medieval mystic too was now being *gleichgeschaltet*, integrated into the pseudo-culture of the Nazi moloch. "In the German mystic there appears for the first time in history and fully consciously – although in the garments of his time – the new, the reborn German man."[97]

Even Eugen Diederichs let himself be enticed by the Nazi ideals and promises of a greater future, and shortly before his death he gave talks for Rosenberg's *Kampfbund für deutsche Kultur*. Nazism was horrendous in its outcome, but it was also tragic at the time of its inception and growth as a movement. Whatever its inner contents, whatever the Hitlerism at the core of Nazism, the movement was a touchstone and upshot of the times, not only in Germany but in the Western world. Dogmatic religion in general had obviously failed; the painful yearning was for 'a true religion', for a spirituality which involved the whole being in this life, on this earth, proving at last worthy of a total dedication, a total self-sacrifice, in the experience of which faith would gradually turn into living Truth.

---

*Several top Nazis had their favourite mystic. For Rosenberg it was Eckhart, for Dietrich Eckart it had been Tauler, and Himmler is said to have always had a copy of the *Bhagavad Gita* in his pocket. As the remainders of Hitler's personal library show, he was fascinated by Christ.

[97]Id., p. 176.

This was the aspiration behind apparently queer sects like George's 'Secret Germany', as it was the intuition behind Nietzsche's supermen who would be the 'children of the noon'. In the Germany of our story the possibility of a choice was present: either to surpass the prevailing human condition in a (difficult) effort towards a greater tomorrow, or (with less effort) to turn back towards the past, towards the old gods, even when representatives of the purest possibilities, like Meister Eckhart, had to be incorporated into this pantheon of the past. Carrying the destiny of the world and having to choose in pressing circumstances, Germany made the easier choice.

PART THREE
Hitler and his God

12

THE VISION OF ADOLF HITLER

> *National Socialism was a religion and Hitler was its Christ.*
> JOHN TOLAND

Nazism

"There was actually no ideology as such, no coherent, compact theory which could be called National Socialism. Even central concepts like 'race' or 'Nordic' were defined in quite differing and loose ways, or not at all," writes the former Heidelberg Professor Klaus von See.[1] Heinz Höhne, historian of the SS, sees the National Socialist programme in the same way: "Hardly an article of the NSDAP creed was undisputed by its members".[2] Hans Frank, in the early years Hitler's lawyer and later a high Nazi dignitary, stated that "fundamentally there were as many National Socialisms as there were leaders". And Ralph Reuth calls the Nazi movement "a hotchpotch of various ideological trends".[3] Sayings like these might have surprised the Party's rank and file, who lived not by bread alone

---

[1] Klaus von See: *Barbar, Germane, Arier*, p. 210.
[2] Heinz Höhne: *The Order of the Death's Head*, p. 67.
[3] Ralph Reuth: *Hitler*, p. 198.

but by the slogans which were inculcated into their brains, but they seem very credible to us now that we have acquired an idea of the varied background from which National Socialism emerged.

In National Socialism there was a Christian current represented by figures like Dietrich Eckart, an admirer of the mystic Johannes Tauler, Arthur Dinter, who wanted to bring the Reformation to a successful end, and Joseph Goebbels, the Catholic who projected his apocalyptic expectations on Hitler and his Third Reich. There was a pronounced tendency towards occultism in Rudolf von Sebottendorff, Master of the Thule Society, and Eckart and Rudolf Hess, both members of this Society; in Otto Rahn, the SS-man with a mission to find the Holy Grail; and in Heinrich Himmler and his *Ahnenerbe* (ancestral heritage), who relied for several years on the assistance of the Austrian seer Karl Maria Wiligut, alias Weisthor. Himmler made the SS into a combatant occult order.

There was a socialist tendency represented by the brothers Gregor and Otto Strasser, by Goebbels (till Hitler turned his mind), and by a considerable faction of leading SA-men, including Hugo Stennes, who will risk an open revolt against Hitler in Berlin, and also including the chief of the SA, Ernst Röhm, who will stubbornly hold on to his demand that Hitler launches a 'second revolution', more or less socialist. There was an outspoken volkisch vein mainly via the Artamanen, to whom had belonged Himmler, Walther Darré, minister of agriculture, Rudolf Höss, commandant of Auschwitz, and Martin Bormann, Hitler's scheming assistant. And there was even a strong oriental influence through Paul de Lagarde, an orientalist precursor, Sebottendorff, renowned astrologer and closely connected with the Turkish aspects of occultism and sufism, Karl Haushofer and his son Albrecht, well acquainted with its religions and its spirituality, Hess, significantly born in the Egyptian city of Alexandria, an occult crossroads between East and West, and Himmler, with his interest in yoga and the *Bhagavad Gita*. This short list of names which have become familiar to us in the course of our story and which represent various sections of the German population, could be extended endlessly when following the ramifications and the diversity of Nazi interests, many of which were intertwined or overlapped.

The basics of National Socialism may be summarised as follows. The corner stone of the rather ramshackle ideological construction is the idea of the racial superiority of the Aryan-Nordic-Germanic people. Theoretically speaking, the Aryan was, in Hitler's words, 'the Prometheus of mankind'; practically speaking the Germans were the *Herrenmenschen*, a people above all others, worthy of lording it over them and being served by them. We have seen numerous examples of this fundamental and outspoken conviction in the previous chapters, more specifically in the one entitled 'Superior People'. Every form of Fascism is a profession of exalted nationalism. In Germany the sense of superiority and of national Ego, imbibed with the mother's milk, took on extraordinary proportions. From it resulted all the rest.

The backbone of National Socialism was the *Führerprinzip*, the leadership principle. This did not relate only to *the* Führer, Adolf Hitler, but also to the pyramid of all his underlings, from the heads of the *Gaue*, or provinces, over the leaders of the districts, localities and sub-localities, to those responsible for the neighbourhoods. It was Hitler's declared intention to equate the Party with the State, and vice versa. As he said in a speech to one of his *Ordensburgen*, the highest Party schools: "Our democracy [sic] is built on the idea, firstly, that in every leadership position the responsibility has to be carried not by somebody elected from below, but by somebody selected from above, and this all the way down to the lowest rank; secondly, these persons have an undisputed authority downwards and an absolute accountability upwards ... What we have in this way is the principle of absolute obedience and absolute authority".[4] Quite absolute and absolutistic indeed. This totalitarian system Hitler called 'true democracy', in his opinion infinitely superior to the

---

[4] Peter Orzechowski: *Schwarze Magie – Braune Macht*, p. 191.

despicable political system commonly called as such, based on the masses and on vote counting.

However, at the top of the pyramid, and invisibly present everywhere else, there was *the* Führer, fervently awaited and, now that he had manifested himself as Leader of the German Volk, venerated as the messiah who would redress all injustices and lead them into a new golden age. "Hitler and his propaganda officials were fully aware that the Führer concept was the slogan which responded to the longing of the Germans to be led." Children in the kindergartens sang a little song which went: "We believe in the Führer/We live for our Führer/We die for our Führer/Till we be heroes". And the first oath, solemnly sworn by ten year olds, went as follows: "In the presence of the Blood Banner, which represents our Führer, I swear that I shall dedicate all my force and all my strength to the saviour of our country, Adolf Hitler. I am willing and ready to give my life for him, so help me God. One Volk, one Reich, one Führer!"[5]

The third basic principle of National Socialism was *Gleichschaltung,* a term best translated by 'integration' – integration into the body of the nazified Volk, that is. The existing order of society had to disappear, as had the existing structure of the German state. At that time, Germany still consisted of no less than seventeen federal parts, which were states in their own right and possessed state prerogatives. In a matter of months Hitler effaced these remnants of the feudal age and replaced them with a structured totalitarian system in which ultimately everybody would become uniform and wear uniform. Hitler's idea of 'true democracy' turned out to be the rigidly structured hierarchy of the army, in which the insignia on the uniform mattered, not the person inside it. As a Nazi poet sang, they were becoming 'the fist of the Führer'. Only the insight gained by analyzing the German 'refusal to think' can make us, people of this postmodern age, understand not only that 'democracy was surrendered

---

[5] Id., p. 192.

without a fight' (Kershaw) and that "seldom a nation surrendered as readily all its rights and liberties" (Friedrichs), but also that the loss of democracy was 'very widely' felt as 'a redemption and a liberation' (Haffner).

The fourth principle of National Socialism concerned the relations with the world outside Germany, in the first place the settling of accounts with France. Most of Hitler's hottest propaganda in the years of the budding Nazi movement was quite simply an expression of the general feelings among the population about the war defeat, the false mythification of the causes of this defeat, and the humiliation of being forced to accept the Treaty of Versailles. The germ of Germany's superiority complex had been the early feeling of inferiority of a backward medieval country towards 'the South' and its cultural riches. Its hatred had focused more and more upon neighbouring France, especially when France became the culturally dominant nation in Europe whose language replaced Latin as the European *lingua franca*. Napoleon conquered and abolished the Holy Roman Empire of the German Nation in 1806. The shock of his presence and drastic reforms was, as we have seen, the direct incentive to Germany's revival.

Hitler, if he meant anything at all, had to avenge Versailles; his carefully staged signing by a humiliated France of the armistice at Compiègne, in June 1940, carried him to the pinnacle of his prestige and power. Now he had to realise the rest of the pan-German 'war aims', create 'a place in the sun' for Germany and conquer the 'living space' which would provide his people of *Herrenmenschen* with their rightful possessions and resources. Justifications for such immoral Darwinist actions, be they theories, treaties or conquests, did not really matter. Whether erecting 'a wall against communism' or signing a non-aggression pact with the same communists: the people would accept anything as long as they felt that it was for their glory and betterment.

This brings us to the fifth and last principle of National Socialism: anti-Semitism. John Weiss called the prevailing anti-Jewish atmosphere in Germany its 'ideology of death'; Daniel Goldhagen caused an uproar with his 1996 book on 'eliminationist anti-Semitism in modern Germany'. Both books were a necessary and very late reflection on the German responsibility for the Holocaust, as were the vehement reactions and comments following in their wake. Throughout our story we have seen the growth of the irrational anti-Jewish sentiment. There are numerous records of *pro*-Jewish gestures by German Aryans, but it is undeniable that the general atmosphere was inimical towards the Jews.

There is no doubt that Hitler did not have to push much to make a National Socialist kick a Jew, and harassing those 'other' people was a lot of fun for a member of the Hitler Youth, as retaliation was out of the question. National Socialism wanted to discard the Jews from German society. Hitler wanted to eradicate them physically, sooner or later, from the body of humanity. Did a National Socialist realize this? Almost certainly not, although he could have guessed it if he had attentively read what his Führer had written, or if he had carefully listened to what his Führer shouted from the rooftops. But even if a 'brownshirt' had known it, he would have repressed the thought. Thus he helped directly or indirectly to execute his Führer's orders, and in so doing participated in the slaughter.

Hitlerism

The NSDAP programme, at the beginning of 1920 hastily concocted by Hitler and Anton Drexler, lost much of its actuality as the movement evolved, especially the more or less cranky articles concerning the state finances and the economy. Still Hitler refused to change one iota of the programme – except the point concerning the powers of the Party Führer, who in the original version remained under the control of a senior committee, but whose power of course had to become absolute once Hitler was accorded dictatorial powers.

"Hitler's 'Catholic' streak seldom emerges so clearly as in his respect for rigid, immutable formulas. All that really matters is a political creed, he would say, 'that is what the whole world revolves around'. And he would add that 'no matter how idiotic' a programme was, 'people would believe in it because of the firmness with which it is advocated'. In fact Hitler declared the old party programme, in spite of its obvious weaknesses, 'unalterable'. The outmoded, archaic features of the programme transformed it from an object of discussion to one of veneration. Moreover, its purpose was not to answer questions or define aims but to attract attention. Clarification would mean division, Hitler said. Faith was all. Once he had insisted on the identity of Führer and idea, the principle of the infallible, immutable Führer was equally established. One of his adherents put it in a nutshell: 'Our programme can be expressed in two words: Adolf Hitler'."[6]

Hitler was the man who walked by himself. "Nothing is more misleading than to speak in the same breath about Hitler and such potentates like Goebbels, Göring, Ribbentrop and Himmler, and to consider Hitler as *primus inter pares* [first among equals], as sometimes happens. He is a phenomenon apart, a force which walks independently from the Party chiefs, who are put in their positions by him, whom he uses, and who are in no way capable to act independently from him."[7]

"We knew only the very least about him", admits Rauschning. "His most intimate Party comrades had no idea of what he was planning, of what he intended to lay at least as the foundations".[8] We have seen that even Speer and Goebbels remained in the dark, not only about the big picture but about crucial decisions. "Never in my life have I met a person who so seldom revealed his feelings", testifies Speer, "and if he did so, who instantly locked them away again. During my time in Spandau [prison, after the war] I talked with Hess about this peculiarity of Hitler's. Both of us agreed that there had been moments when we felt we had come close to him.

---

[6]Joachim Fest: *Hitler*, pp. 240-41.
[7]Sebastian Haffner: *Germany: Jekyll & Hyde*, p. 41.
[8]Hermann Rauschning: *Gespräche mit Hitler*, p. 229.

But we were invariably disillusioned. If either of us ventured a slightly more personal tone, Hitler promptly put up an unbreakable wall."[9]

Speer also asserts that Hitler put up a different act in different circumstances, adapting himself to the people present. In connection with the 'table talk' at the Rastenburg headquarters, Speer warns: "Hitler tended to falsify himself when he sat at the table in the Führer's headquarters. I was always struck by the choiceness with which he would express himself in a group of officers and other cultivated persons, sometimes to the extent of using a distinctly stilted style. This was a different Hitler from the one I knew in the private circle; again, he must have been altogether different in the company of Gauleiters and other Party functionaries, when he relapsed into the jargon of the period of struggle and comradeship".[10]

Nazism is generally considered to have been a form of Fascism, after the First World War symptomatic in almost every developed nation on the globe. This is only partially true and in its most superficial features: the greatness of the nation, the integration of the whole nation into one body, its hierarchisation and uniformisation, and the heroic posturing towards its neighbours. All fascisms also had their 'leader' – Führer, Duce, Caudillo, Netaji, or with whatever word 'leader' was translated. Specific to Nazism, however, was the special character of its leader and the fact that the movement was *identified* with him, in a way even Italian Fascism and Mussolini could not be compared with. "Nothing is more misleading than to call Hitler a fascist", writes Sebastian Haffner in his *Anmerkungen zu Hitler* (notes on Hitler), "his nationalism was everything except a fascism".[11]

"National Socialism was fundamentally and from the very start 'Hitlerism', and Hitler himself was, seen in this way, the first convinced

---

[9]Albert Speer: *Inside the Third Reich*, p. 156.
[10]Albert Speer: *Spandau – The Secret Diaries*, p. 345.
[11]Sebastian Haffner: *Anmerkungen zu Hitler*, p. 71.

'Hitlerite'", writes Jochen Kirchhoff. He repeats Gottfried Benn's question: did Hitler create the movement or did the movement create him? The answer of all knowledgeable people is unanimous: "There was and is no National Socialism without Hitler. Both are identical".[12] If Hitler was Germany, as Rudolf Hess cried out in front of the brown battalions at Nuremberg, then he was a fortiori National Socialism. Therefore Fest can quote prominent Nazis as stating not only that "Hitler was the most radical Nazi of all", but even that he was 'the only Nazi' – just as Nietzsche said that Christ had been the only Christian. It was this way of seeing which allowed Konrad Heiden to entitle a chapter of his early Hitler biography 'Hitler versus National Socialism', in which 'National Socialism' stood for the common view of fascism, while Hitler and Hitlerism were something different altogether, and much more extreme.

There are many testimonies to the fact that "Hitler's plans and war aims never changed", as Speer puts it. Fest writes about "the tenaciously pursued vision in the background", and says that "the structure of [Hitler's] thinking was such that he understood every phenomenon merely as a further argument for ideas fixed long ago", which revealed "the continuity in Hitler's thought".[13] Hitler began his public life at the age of thirty, and wrote in *Mein Kampf:* "When a man has reached his thirtieth year he has still a great deal to learn. That is obvious. But henceforward what he learns will principally be an amplification of his basic ideas; it will be fitted in with them organically so as to fill up the framework of that fundamental *Weltanschauung* which he already possesses".[14]

The 'amplification' in Hitler's ideas is easy to follow. He started in Munich, under Eckart's guidance, with the adamant conviction that the Germans were the *Herrenmenschen*; that he was the one come to lead them towards the fulfilment of their Volkhood and

---

[12]Helmut Heiber in Peter Orzechowski, op. cit., p. 190.
[13]Joachim Fest, op. cit., pp. 8, 390.
[14]Adolf Hitler: *Mein Kampf,* p. 68.

their highest aims; and that the Jews were the enemies of this fulfilment. The practical aspects of this task coincided for the most part with the political aspirations of that time. In the prison at Landsberg, and most probably under the influence of Rosenberg, Hess and Haushofer, the scope of Hitler's aims widened. He now became the missioned Leader who had to conquer a firm and durable foothold in Europe for the Aryan race, and to ready his Aryan legions for world conquest. Then, as Chancellor of the Reich, he capitalised on the political situation to secure the foundations of the Aryan world empire, and to execute what until then had been unthinkable, the genocide of the Jews.

Hermann Rauschning* has already been quoted elsewhere as saying that Hitler could not proclaim his great, basic ideas openly from the start. He had at first to stick to the 'fascist', i.e. 'national' and 'socialist', programme which the recruits of the movement could understand and accept. Because of his demagogic style and his Führer mentality Hitler was already considered by the realists among the Nazis 'a clairvoyant and fantast', even without the proclamation of his global ambitions. Only his quasi-miraculous internal and external successes as Chancellor will heat up the expectations to a point where the German Messiah could publicly formulate any ambition,

---

*Hermann Rauschning (1887-1982) is an important source of Hitler's confidential sayings during the years 1932-34. He was a rich landowner and a cultured man who had become the National Socialist president of the Senate of Danzig, then a 'free city' under the protection of the League of Nations. Rauschning's written memoirs of a few conversations with Hitler and of thoughts he heard Hitler express have been attacked by such authors as Theodor Schieder in 1972 and Wolfgang Hänel in 1983. Ian Kershaw states peremptorily in his preface to his Hitler biography that *Hitler Speaks*, ie the *Gespräche mit Hitler* from which we quote, is "a work now regarded to have so little authenticity that it is best to disregard it altogether". It may therefore be appropriate to point out here that Rauschning's testimony was highly regarded by Hugh Trevor-Roper and Alan Bullock as well as by the respected German historian Günter Moltmann. The younger generation of German historians – Giordano, Köhler, Kirchhoff, Reuth, Hesemann, and others – refers to Rauschining not only without reservations, but with outright appreciation.

however grandiose, and order its execution. What, then, were the differences between Nazism and Hitlerism?

Pure Hitlerism was the creation of the SS as a personal bodyguard within the SA. At the appropriate moment, after the SA had been beheaded in 'the Night of the Long Knives', the SS would become independent and directly responsible to Hitler alone. The Black Knights were intended to be the embodiment of Hitler's racial ideal, and functioned like a religious order, 'the Order of the Death's Head'. Apart from and feared by all other National Socialist organisations, and acting as a ruthless police force only accountable to the supreme chief, they grew practically into a state within the state, and would after the successful completion of the war enjoy the status of supermen as the highest racial nobility among the Aryans.

However arrogant the Nazi attitude was towards Germany's opponents, real and fictional, the average National Socialist could hardly take Hitler's claims for 'living space' in Eastern Europe seriously. The obvious reason was that such living space could not be acquired, given the system of European alliances and the presence of 'arch enemy France' on its Western border, without a war on two fronts, doomed to be fatal for the fatherland. Hitler launched nonetheless 'Operation Barbarossa', the military plan for the invasion of Russia, immediately after his triumphant Blitzkrieg in the West, and sent General Jodl to inform the highest staff officers that preparations had to be made accordingly. John Toland relates the consternation of these experienced officers in his popular Hitler biography. "A chorus of protests erupted. This was the two front war which had defeated Germany in the First World War. And why this sudden change after the [non-aggression] Pact with Moscow?" But Jodl cut short the debate. "Gentlemen", he said, "this is not a question for discussion but a decision of the Führer".[15] Hitler reigned supreme and alone.

---

[15] John Toland: *Adolf Hitler*, p. 855.

National Socialism in the mind of its adherents meant in the first place an internal revolution which would give them stability and order instead of chaos, employment instead of joblessness and desperation, and bread instead of hunger and poverty. True, a national feeling of superiority was part of the German character, and to avenge the Versailles Treaty was one of the main items on the National Socialist agenda, but it was secondary to the internal redress. World conquest and a final struggle with international Jewry were no more than fantastic ideas in the mind of 'Adolf', used to excite his audiences when he was somewhat carried away. "That these fantastic ideas of Hitler would allow him to go forward on his exceptional path and give the lie to all sceptics, was at the time clear to only a very few."[16]

There can be no doubt that 'the final solution' was in Hitler's mind from the beginning of his career and remained always present, even when circumstances forced him to agree for a while with the Madagascar plan or with the emigration of the German and Austrian Jews. The ultimate settlement of accounts between the false and the true Chosen People was, in Hitler's vision, inevitable. The growth of the National Socialist movement, the regained prosperity of Germany, and the industrialisation and regimentation of the German people never had any other aim than the war of the Aryans to conquer the world, which in Hitler's mind was only possible by slaying the enemy, 'international Jewry'. "Of what Hitler's inner truth consisted, nobody knew", writes Joachim Köhler, but the apocalyptic battle with the Jews was certainly part of it. "He clearly kept a secret in which he believed with 'granite' infallibility ... Hitler has never revealed with a single word that he was planning the biggest autodafé in history,"[17] writes Jochen Kirchhoff. And he concludes: "What many thought to be National Socialism was only a façade or masquerade".[18] It was fare for the disdained masses.

---

[16] Hermann Rauschning, op. cit., p. 71.
[17] Joachim Köhler: *Wagners Hitler*, pp. 334, 336, 410.
[18] Jochen Kirchhoff, op. cit., p. 54.

The Messiah

Hitler reportedly said in one of his monologues: "*Ich bin auf Grund höherer Gewalt da*".[19] '*Höhere Gewalt*' means an act of God, and Hitler's words may be translated as "I am here through an act of God", something he declared directly or indirectly in many ways throughout his career. Instead of 'God' he often used the word *Vorsehung*, Providence, for instance when he said: "When my life comes to an end, then the Work too must be finished, entrusted to me by Providence, or whatever you want to call it".[20] Ernst Hanfstängl, at one time Hitler's constant companion, heard this word often from his mouth. "A professional 'Knight of the Holy Grail'", said Hanfstängl later, "Hitler was convinced that all his actions were guided only by the common weal. His faith in his own destiny let not doubt him for a moment that Providence had called him for a mission. Consequently, everything that did not agree with the way he saw things must be bad and reprehensible, or the work of a satanical opponent".[21]

After he had become Germany's idol, Hitler could overlook his life and assert: "In spite of a totally inimical environment, I have chosen my way in my inner self and I have followed it, unknown and nameless, up to the final success. Often declared dead and always wished dead, in the end I have nonetheless been victorious ". When bullying like a gangster boss the Austrian Chancellor von Schussnigg during his fateful visit to the Obersalzberg in February 1938, shortly before the Anschluss, Hitler shouted: "I have a historic mission, and this historic mission I will fulfil because Providence has destined me to do so ... He who is not with me will be crushed ... I have chosen the most difficult road that any German ever took;

---

[19]*Monologe im Führerhauptquartier*, p. 303.
[20]Peter Orzechowski, op. cit., p. 182.
[21]Id., p. 182.

I have made the greatest achievement in the history of Germany, greater than that of any other German!"[22]

During an open air speech before a massive audience at Würzburg, in 1937, Hitler declared: "However weak each single man finally is in his being and actions before almighty Providence and Its will, he will become immeasurably strong the moment he acts in accordance with this Providence. Then a force pours down into him, which is the hallmark of all great personalities the world has known. And when I look back on the five years we have behind us, then I think that I may say: 'This was not the work of men alone!' If Providence had not guided us, then sometimes I would not have found all those tangled roads. Nobody can make the history of a people or of the world when he does not have the blessings of Providence on his intentions and abilities".[23]

Secretary Traudl Junge narrates how in 1943 she asked Hitler why he had not married. His first reason was the usual one: that he would not have been able to be a good family man. Then, to Junge's consternation, he added that he did not want children, because "the offspring of geniuses mostly has a tough time in the world. One expects from them the same greatness as that of their famous fathers and does not forgive them for being average. Besides, most of them become cretins". "This was the first expression, to be taken seriously, of a personal delusion of grandeur which I heard from Hitler's mouth", remembers Junge. "Until now I sometimes had had the impression that Hitler was megalomanical in his ideas and in his fanaticism, but his own person had never been involved. What he mostly said was: 'I am an instrument of destiny and have to follow my way, on which I have been put by divine Providence'."[24] The young woman must not yet have been part of Hitler's intimate circle at the Rastenburg headquarters when he said: "I feel at ease

---

[22] William Shirer: *The Rise and Fall of the Third Reich*, p. 326.
[23] Peter Orzechowski, op. cit., p. 181.
[24] Traudl Junge: *Bis zur letzten Stunde*, p. 121.

in the historical company to which I will belong if there is an Olympus. In the one I shall enter, there will be all the most brilliant minds of all times".[25]

"Hitler was never interested in establishing a mere tyranny", writes Fest. "Sheer greed for power will not suffice as an explanation for his personality and energy. Unquestionably, power, the virtually unrestricted use of it, with no necessity to account to anyone – that kind of power meant a great deal to him. But he was at no time satisfied with it alone. The restlessness with which he conquered, extended and applied that power, and finally used it up, is evidence of how little he was born to be a mere tyrant. He was fixated upon his mission of defending Europe and the Aryan race from deadly menace, and to this end he wanted to create an empire that would last ...

"In the introductory passages of his speeches he again and again evoked the myth of 'the man from the people', the days when he had been 'an unknown frontline soldier in the First World War', 'a man without a name, without money, without influence, without a following', but summoned by Providence. He liked to introduce himself as 'the lonely wanderer out of nothingness'. Thus he liked to have resplendent uniforms around him, for they pointed to the simplicity of his own costume. His air of unassuming austerity and soberness, together with his unwedded state and his withdrawn life, could be splendidly fused in the public mind into the image of a great, solitary man bearing the burden of his election by destiny, marked by the mystery of self-sacrifice."[26]

An entry in Goebbels' diary mentions that Hitler told him, in the awareness of being missioned: "I will not die too early or too late".[27] Yet, he became ever more obsessed with the shortness of time allotted to him for the execution of his task. "A letter of his written

---

[25] *Monologe im Führerhauptquartier*, p. 303.
[26] Joachim Fest, op. cit., p. 417, 521.
[27] Joseph Goebbels: *Tagebücher*, p. 409.

in July 1928 makes the point that he is now thirty-nine years old, so that 'even at best' he has 'barely twenty years available' for his 'tremendous task'. The thought of premature death incessantly tormented him. 'Time is pressing', he said in February 1934, and continued: 'I do not have long enough to live ... I must lay the foundation on which others can build after me. I will not live long enough to see it completed'. He also feared assassination; some 'criminal or idiot' might eliminate him and thus prevent the accomplishment of his mission."[28]

"We knew only the very least about him", writes Rauschning. "Even his most intimate party comrades had no idea of what he had in mind and of what he had to lay at least the foundations. A terrible nervous fear of no longer being able to reach the goal was pushing him forward at times."[29] Werner Maser confirms this and documents how the hypochondriac streak in Hitler's character became still more pronounced from 1937 onwards. The factors of his age and for the most part imaginary health problems, which he entrusted to the care of the unlikable Dr Morell, doubtlessly played a crucial role in his decisions to go to war, each time as soon as possible.

Claus-Ekkehard Bärsch states straightaway: "The model for Adolf Hitler is Christ",[30] and John Toland asserts that "National Socialism was a religion and Hitler was its Christ".[31] This is much more than a simile. Hitler took his role of saviour "with the utmost seriousness", writes Joachim Fest, and attached a special significance to the fact that he had begun his public life at the age of thirty, as Christ had done. "We are admittedly small in number", he said in the early years of the movement. "But once another man stood up in Galilee, and today his teaching rules the whole world." "Hitler presented himself as the Messiah, who as a warrior, filled with the fanatical faith in

---

[28] Joachim Fest, op. cit., p. 535.
[29] Hermann Rauschning, op. cit., pp. 190, 229.
[30] Claus-Ekkehard Bärsch: *Der junge Goebbels*, p. 111.
[31] John Toland, op. cit., p. 294.

the righteousness of his ideas, goes his predestined way", concurs Michael Rissmann. And Hitler said that one day would be written on his tomb: "A man who never capitulated, who never gave up, who never made compromises, who knew only one goal and the way toward it, who had a great faith named 'Germany'". The work "which Christ had begun, without being able to finish it, he, Hitler, would accomplish."

It came as a surprise that in the remainders of Hitler's considerable library were found a great deal of books on occultism and religion. Timothy Ryback examined the part of the collection which is now kept in the Library of Congress in an article in *The Atlantic Monthly*. These books, which survived the looting and chaos during the last days of the war in Europe, were discovered in the spring of 1945, in a salt mine near Berchtesgaden, by soldiers of the American 101st Airborne Division (to which E Company of *Band of Brothers* belonged). Ryback writes: "I found a Hitler I had not anticipated: a man with a sustained interest in spirituality. Among the piles of Nazi tripe ... are more than 130 books on religious and spiritual subjects, ranging from Occidental occultism to Eastern mysticism to the teachings of Jesus Christ ... Also included were a German translation of Stanley Jones's 1931 best seller, *The Christ of the Mount;* and a 500-page work on the life and teachings of Jesus, published in 1935 under the title *The Son: The Evangelical Sources and Pronouncements of Jesus of Nazareth in Their Original Form and With the Jewish Influences.* Some volumes date from the early 1920s, when Hitler was an obscure rabble-rouser on the fringe of Munich political life, others from his last years, when he dominated Europe."[32]

In some of his books Hitler had made "underlines, question marks, exclamation points and marginal strikes", for instance in the works of Fichte, presented to him by the celebrated film maker Leni Riefenstahl. "As I traced the pencilled notations, I realized that

---

[32] Timothy W. Ryback: "Hitler's Forgotten Library", in *The Atlantic Monthly*, May 2003.

Hitler was seeking a path to the divine that led to just one place. Fichte asked: 'Where did Jesus derive the power that has held his followers for all eternity?' Hitler drew a dense line beneath the answer: 'Through his absolute identification with God'. At another point Hitler highlighted a brief but revealing paragraph: 'God and I are One. Expressed simply in two identical sentences – His life is mine; my life is his. My work is his work, and his work my work'."[33]

"The propaganda which transformed Hitler into a saviour was not meant for recruitment pure and simple, it was not cold calculation. The propaganda made by Goebbels, Hess, Streicher and Strasser expresses what Hitler believed of himself. Hitler really saw Jesus Christ as his precursor," writes Peter Orzechowski. And he quotes Hitler's words from a speech made during the high tide of Nazism: "Today, my German Volk, I ask from you: come and stand with your faith behind me. Be henceforth the source of my strength and my faith. Do not forget: he who does abandon himself in this world shall never be abandoned by the Almighty! ... I have taught you how to have faith, now give me your faith!"[34]

"A new system of values based on brutality and violence" was of course not what Christ had brought to the world, it was the opposite. What Hitler admired in Christ was not his essential message, the inner path of the soul, however much he may have been fascinated by it, but his greatness and fame, still alive among millions, and his key role as the initiator of a new world at a decisive turning point of the times. What also intrigued him was that Christ was directly inspired by God, that he was the missioned 'Son of God' to execute a task which Hitler indubitably saw as on a par with his own.

"Providence has predestined me to be the greatest liberator of humanity", Hitler said to Rauschning. "I liberate man from the coercion of a mind which becomes a goal in itself, from the foul and humiliating pangs of a chimera called 'conscience' and 'morality', and

---

[33]Id., pp. 13, 14.
[34]Peter Orzechowski, op. cit., p. 176, 180.

from the demands of a liberty and personal independence of which anyway only a very few are capable ... To the Christian teaching of the nothingness and insignificance of the human individual soul and personal responsibility, I oppose with icy clarity the liberating teaching of the nothingness and insignificance of the individual and his development within the concrete immortality of the nation. In place of dogma and the representative suffering and death of a divine saviour comes the representative life and action of the new Führer and lawgiver, who releases the mass of the believers from the burden of the free decision."[35]

These are crucial quotes which put Hitler's mission, as he understood it, in focus. Hitler had been sent, and was constantly guided, to change the conscience and morality of man into something like the opposite of Christianity; where humanity made an effort to become step by step more conscious and individualised, Hitler saw the human individual as nothing more than a cell in a body, an ant in a nest. The perspectives this opens reveal something of the real dimension of the evil to be discovered behind all the destruction and slaughter caused by this German Messiah.

What he said to Speer, when planning his gigantic buildings, cannot be taken literally enough: "I tell you, Speer, these buildings are more important than anything else. You must do everything you can to complete them in my lifetime. Only if I have spoken in them and governed from them will they have the consecration they are going to need for my successors".[36] "He frequently spoke of his tomb as exerting a political influence upon the nation that must not be underestimated", says Speer. And he reminisces elsewhere about the gigantic hall to be built in Berlin, the one topped with an eagle

---

[35] Hermann Rauschning, op. cit., pp. 212, 83. Those who are familiar with George Steiner's novel *The Portage to San Cristobal of A.H.* (1981), in which an aged Hitler, caught by Israeli Nazi hunters in South America, pronounces his own defence, will find in these paragraphs one of the main sources of the arguments.
[36] Albert Speer: *Spandau – The Secret Diaries*, p. 16.

carrying the globe in his talons: "The hall was essentially a place of worship. The idea was that over the course of centuries, by tradition and venerability, it would acquire an importance similar to that St. Peter's in Rome has for Catholic Christendom."[37]

When one surveys the landscape of Hitler's mind as we have been discovering it up to this point in our story, a big divide seems to run straight through it. On the one side is everything which represents the 'mystic' Hitler: the visionary who saw the world as an apocalyptic clash between two Chosen Peoples, who pronounced that the time for this decisive confrontation and the birth of a new world for a new man was now, and who was convinced that the main protagonist in that drama of worldwide dimensions was he himself, chosen or sent by Providence. Hitler was able, thanks to his special powers, to communicate this vision to his German audiences, preconditioned by a long-standing conviction of their inherent superiority and by their expectation of a Leader who would give them their rightful place under the sun.

On the other side of the gap in Hitler's mindscape we find the most banal and incoherent thoughts, which seemed to belong to another, far inferior being. "I know nothing about the hereafter, and am honest enough to say so ... Mind and soul return surely into the big common reservoir, just like the body. In this way we serve as the nourishing element for the foundation from which new life arises. I don't have to break my head about the how and why. The essence of the soul we will never find out ... Somewhere we have our place in the scale of the world ... Somewhere everything results in an awareness of the helplessness of the human being in relation with the eternal law of Nature – that the whole redemption of the human being lies in the fact that he tries to understand the divine Providence and does not believe that he is capable of revolt against the Law. When man thus complies humbly with the laws, then it is

---

[37] Albert Speer: *Inside the Third Reich*, p. 222.

wonderful ... An Omnipotence which creates the worlds has assigned its tasks to every single being. Everything happens the way it has to happen ... If I want to believe in a divine commandment, it can only be the commandment to preserve the race ..."[38]

This, in a nutshell, seems to have been the Hitlerian metaphysics, at least in the later period of his life. The trend as a whole seems quite agnostic and in contradiction with his personal belief in divine guidance and Providence. It is prudent to recall Speer's warning that Hitler adapted his words to his audiences. The fundamental difference between the two ways of seeing and speaking seems to reside in the fact that the visionary Hitler was an inspired man, while the philosophising Hitler was a rather pedestrian thinker who had gathered his thoughts by the roadside.

The rickety thought structure of the pedestrian Hitler rested on some curious supports. He believed in the 'hollow earth theory', according to which the earth is a bubble in an infinity of rock. He believed in the 'world ice theory' of Hans Hörbiger, rejected even by high-ranking researchers of the SS-Ahnenerbe, but imposed upon them by Himmler because the Führer accepted it. He thought that the ancient Greek tribes were Germanic and that the Roman legionaries were vegetarians. He believed that Christ was an Aryan and a proto-anti-Semite. The fictitious world of Winnetou and Old Shatterhand kept influencing his decisions till the end. And he staunchly insisted on an Aryan science in opposition to the false international, Jewish science. "There is indeed a Nordic and National Socialist science which has to be in opposition to the liberal-Judaic. The latter no longer performs its function but is in the process of eliminating itself".[39]

---

[38] *Monologen im Führerhauptquartier*, pp. 135, 151, 135, 158, 149.
[39] Hermann Rauschning, op. cit., p. 210.

Faith

What held together this fantastic, paranormal world of Hitler, which was more and more becoming the world in which lived the whole German nation, was *faith* and the *will power* which faith generates. Hitler squarely stated that 'faith was all'. Faith in Aryanhood and in Germany's greatness was the primary condition for all those who belonged to the volkisch movement and indeed for reactionary Germany as a whole. The Führer had become identified with the Volk, and faith in Germany became faith in Hitler. "Hitler was not a politician who based himself on a programme and who had to justify his actions to the people, but the redemptive figure of an exoteric cult whose aim was to liberate the world from the Jews ... Strictly speaking the Germans did not need to know anything. They only had to have faith."[40]

"I have taught you how to have faith: now give me your faith!" Hitler shouted. And he said on another occasion: "When one day in future centuries History, no longer influenced by the pros and cons of a controversial time, will critically examine these years of the National Socialist emergence, then she cannot but conclude that what happened was a wonderful victory of faith against the elements of the supposed realistically possible".[41] The last, emotional occasion on which Speer met Hitler in the Führerbunker, when Hitler knew that the man who once had been his 'unrequited love' did everything possible to counteract his 'Nero order' to destroy Germany, he asked: "Do you still hope for a successful continuance of the war or is your faith shattered?" "Once again Hitler reduced his demand to a formal profession of faith that would be binding upon me", writes Speer. "If you could at least hope that we have not lost!" said Hitler, while the continuous Russian bombardment made the bunker shake. "You must certainly be able to hope, that would be enough

---

[40] Joachim Köhler, op. cit., p. 355.
[41] Peter Orzechowski, op. cit., p. 179.

to satisfy me." And Speer's reply was, after a few hours of inner struggle: "*Mein Führer*, I stand unreservedly behind you". Hitler's eyes filled with tears, writes Speer. [42]

Only faith could work the miracle for which the Führer was sent into this world as the absolute 'Strong One from Above', the 'Being of Light'. His mission gave him the right to use the Volk as his instrument and to sacrifice it if necessary, as it gave him the right to exterminate 'ruthlessly' anyone who thwarted his objectives or stood on the opposing side in the final struggle.

These very common truths were confirmed by Hitler time and again. He fumed against the military men who knew the meaning of the words 'discipline' and 'obedience' but not of 'faith', as the former were military virtues and the latter a religious one. Where the generals saw their military operations as a matter of planning and efficiency, Hitler saw them as exercises in faith, infallible if the faith was entire. No one could ever live up to his expectations except by dying in the Hitler faith, and in the end he will roar in his bunker that *all* have betrayed him for lack of faith. The thousands and thousands of improvised crosses or helmets on a rifle butt in the snow-covered Russian steppes, the green lands of the Champagne and the grey, desolate fields of Germany were planted above the bodies of soldiers who had betrayed him, the Führer, by their lack of faith.

A new world

The influence of Oswald Spengler and his *Decline of the West* was widespread, and the Nazi intellectuals did their best to make him openly chose their side. Their attempt was not very logical considering Spengler's pessimistic view of the destiny of the West and of humanity as a whole, while the Nazis foresaw a golden future for the Aryan

---

[42] Albert Speer, *Inside the Third Reich*, pp. 604, 607.

race. Hitler was quite aware of this incongruity and did not hesitate to put things straight after having given, as the new Chancellor of the nation, an audience to Spengler in Bayreuth. "I am not a supporter of Oswald Spengler! I don't believe in the decline of the West. On the contrary, I consider it my task, conferred upon me by Providence, to contribute to its prevention." For he, Hitler, was convinced that "the old Aryan culture, under the leadership of Nordic man, would experience a rebirth". Moreover, Spengler made himself unpopular in Bayreuth because of his critical remarks about Richard Wagner, and was there henceforth referred to only as 'the Decline'.[43]

Hitler thought of himself as the prophet of 'an entirely new *Weltanschauung*', a word which may be translated as 'world vision' or 'ideology'. Comparing his world vision with the prevailing one in Europe, he wrote in *Mein Kampf*: "A philosophy of life which is inspired by an infernal spirit of intolerance [the 'Jewish' Enlightenment doctrine of liberty, equality and fraternity!] can only be set aside by a doctrine that is advanced in an equally ardent spirit [i.e. his own] and fought for with as determined a will, and which is itself a new idea, pure and absolutely true ... Political parties are prone to enter compromises, but an ideology never does this. A political party is inclined to adjust its teachings with a view to meeting those of its opponents, but an ideology proclaims its own infallibility ... While the programme of the ordinary political party is nothing but the recipe for cooking up favourable results out of the next general elections, the programme of an ideology represents a declaration of war against an existing order of things, against present conditions, in short, against the established ideology."[44]

It was the task of a political organised ideology, in contrast with an ordinary political party, "to transmit a certain idea which originated in the head of one individual [Adolf Hitler by name] to a multitude of people and to supervise the manner in which this idea is being

---

[43] Brigitte Hamann: *Winifred Wagner, oder Hitlers Bayreuth*, p. 258.
[44] Adolf Hitler: *Mein Kampf*, pp. 379, 380.

put into practice ... The greatness of every powerful organization which embodies a creative idea lies in the spirit of religious devotion and intolerance with which it stands out against all others, because it has an ardent faith in its own right ... The future of a movement is determined by the devotion, and even intolerance, with which its members fight for their cause. They must feel convinced that their cause alone is just, and they must carry it through to success, as against other similar organizations in the same field."[45] For "an ideology is intolerant and cannot be satisfied with the role of being 'a party among others'; it exacts peremptorily its own, exclusive and total recognition together with the complete adaptation of public life in accordance with its way of seeing things. Neither can it tolerate a survival of the institutions of the previous situation."[46]

Here the standpoint and intentions of Hitler's National Socialism were fully spelled out in black and white; from this line Hitler never wavered. He steadfastly refused to compromise with any other organisation, however Rightist or volkisch, a standpoint he sometimes had to fight out with his closest supporters when the NSDAP was still small in numbers. Hitler was the prophet of a new ideology based on faith which implied, to his mind, the overthrow of all existing ideologies and faiths, and which would create a new world. The rank and file of the NSDAP perceived only the external shell of Hitler's Messianic world view; rare exceptions had an inkling of the more profound meaning; and nobody knew the core of Hitler's vision, for he kept it locked within himself.

It will be abundantly clear from the preceding parts of our story that Hitler's vision, whatever its core, was anti-Christian and anti-Enlightenment. In the world which he envisioned the words 'love', 'soul', 'individualisation', 'equality', 'freedom', 'socialism', 'internationalism', 'liberalism', etc. were frequently used, but in a rhetorical way and always meaning something different from their

---

[45]Id., pp. 290, 294, 293.
[46]In Christian Zentner: *Adolf Hitler's 'Mein Kampf'*, p. 46.

common significance. What Hitler wanted to create was a Spartan totalitarianism (quite similar to Stalin's handiwork), with people who would be smiling, healthy, fanatical and soulless robots, totally integrated into the common body of the Volk and disdaining individual dignity as a kind of psychological leprosy.

We remember that Hitler wrote in *Mein Kampf* that the greatness of the (fictional) Aryan consisted in "his willingness to put all his abilities in the service of the community". In this Aryan the instinct of self-preservation had reached its noblest form, "since he willingly subordinates his own ego to the life of the community and, if the hour demands, even sacrifices it". That the German nation had to be subjected to a rigid regimentation was established in Hitler's mind from the very beginning. "I know that I have to be a strict educator", he said to Rauschning. "I first must create the Volk", which was to become the Führer's sword. "We have to be cruel (*grausam*)", he said. "We must again [as in the primitive past?] be able to be cruel with a good conscience. Only in this way can we eradicate the soft-heartedness and the sentimental philisterhood, the 'cosiness' and the bourgeois pettiness from our Volk. We have no time left for nice feelings. We have to force our people to greatness if it has to fulfil its historical task."[47]

"Together with the construction of tanks, cannon and airplanes the people in 'the community of the Volk' too were militarized. The dictator intended to wage the war for the living space with convinced National Socialists ... The Germans were being re-educated. The Führer dictatorship did not stop at the front door. Its tentacles reached out to the whole family and the inmost thought of the individual. In Hitler's words, there should not remain 'any free space in which the individual belongs to himself'. The process of total penetration took place almost unnoticed. Its main instrument was the [omnipresent] Party." (Guido Knopp[48]) For Hitler had written

---

[47] Id., p. 22.
[48] Guido Knopp: *Hitler – Eine Bilanz*, p. 201.

in *Mein Kampf* that the state was 'a means to an end', and that the end lay "in the preservation and advancement of a community of physically and psychically homogeneous creatures".[49]

"*A revolutionary conception of the world and human existence* will achieve decisive success only when the new world vision has been taught to a whole people, or subsequently *forced upon them if necessary*, and when, on the other hand, the control organization, the movement itself, is in the hands of only those few men who are absolutely indispensable to form the nerve centres of the coming state."[50] Henry Picker, the secret annotator (on Bormann's instigation) of Hitler's table talk, writes: "The NSDAP had de facto a complete control of every citizen ... With his uniformization of the whole nation Hitler had almost formed a new type of man who put the will above the intellect, and toughness and faith above the natural feelings". The daily life of the nation was "put under Prussian military discipline, the 'community of the people' was transformed into 'a battle-ready fighting community' in which every male from his youth to an advanced age was carrying weapons".[51] "The sacrifice of the individual existence is necessary in order to assure the conservation of the race", Hitler wrote, and later said the same in a less civil way: "The life of the individual should not be given such high value. A fly lays a million eggs, they all die. But flies survive".[52] Burleigh calls this "an unfeeling form of neo-barbarism", which may be an understatement.

Soon after the Hitler take-over their country became hermetically closed for the German people. This had to happen if Hitler's 'strict education' was to be effective, in other words if the propaganda, methodically planned to reorder the contents of the German brain, was to reach every individual in every corner of the Reich. Hitler

---

[49] Jay Gonen: *The Roots of Nazi Psychology*, p. 143.
[50] Adolf Hitler, op. cit., p. 476 (emphases added).
[51] Henry Picker: *Hitlers Tischgespräche im Führerhauptquartier*, pp. 289, 25, 36.
[52] Frederic Spotts: *Hitler and the Power of Aesthetics*, p. 119.

had written a whole chapter on propaganda in *Mein Kampf*, camouflaging it under the title 'War Propaganda', where he says: "I soon came to realize that the right use of propaganda was an asset in itself and that this art was practically unknown to our bourgeois parties". Ominous words at a time that the radio medium came into itself. "In the big lie there is always a certain force of credibility",[53] he wrote, thus stating his basic truth of the lie and giving his game away. But he should not have bothered. It is one of the object lessons of Hitlerian history and its aftermath how compelling the art of the brazen lie was in gathering the nation behind its Führer.

For sure, Hitler did not invent all this; some of this psychological knowledge of the human being belonged to ancient or common wisdom, other insights were found in contemporary French authors. Hitler, though, acquired a clear idea of the psychological mechanisms and their effectiveness, and by means of them he would recreate the daily reality of a Germany which became an island of total irrationality in a semi-rational world. "Propaganda demands the most skilled brains that can be found", he wrote. When Joseph Goebbels appeared within his field of vision Hitler somehow sensed his abilities at once, although the little doctor still thought of himself as a 'socialist' who wanted to expel the reactionary Hitler from the Party.

Joseph Goebbels, appointed cultural czar of the Third Reich and working under Hitler's close supervision, excelled in the comparatively new techniques of propaganda. His basic concept was plain and unencumbered by moral qualms: "The propaganda which produces the desired results is good and all other propaganda is bad".[54] According to William Shirer, who experienced the Third Reich from nearby, Goebbels "completely isolated the world the Germans lived in".[55] And Robert Gellately writes: "Hitler's Germany became a

---

[53]Adolf Hitler, op. cit., p. 198.
[54]Otto Friedrichs: *Before the Deluge*, p. 206.
[55]William Shirer: *The Nightmare Years 1930-1940*, p. 422.

modern mass society, in which there were not only millions of newspaper readers and regular consumers of the news at the movies but radio itself became enormously popular. Once radio overcame the mistake of spending too much time on obvious political messages, its attractions proved almost irresistible. Radio was listened to at home as well as in public places like restaurants and even at work. German broadcasters recognized that they had to provide the right mix of entertainment, news, and specials such as a Hitler speech".[56]

"In matters of propaganda our party comrades are the undisputed masters", wrote Goebbels.[57] The source of their inspiration, and this from the very beginning, was none other than Hitler himself. He had realised the importance of propaganda; he had organised the first public marches and ceremonies, which would be imitated and elaborated upon in the following years; he had chosen the symbols, slogans and uniforms with an impressive effectiveness; he had built up the omnipresent party pyramid; and he had detected the slumbering propagandistic talents of Dr Goebbels. Hitler's visionary shaping of the National Socialist movement was one of his great achievements. "At the end of 1926 the party set up a speakers' school to give its followers the techniques and information needed for effective public speaking. By the end of 1932 this school had, according to its records, trained some 6000 speakers,"[58] who spread the word, evening after evening, in the smallest and most remote hamlets of the country. This too was Hitler's initiative.

'National Socialism is a religion'

It was the future propaganda-tsar Goebbels who wrote in 1928: "National Socialism is a religion. Only the religious inspiration, which shatters the old, outmoded formulas and creates new ones, is still

---

[56] Robert Gellately: *Backing Hitler*, p. 185.
[57] Joseph Goebbels, op. cit., Vol. II, p. 626.
[58] Joachim Fest, op. cit., p. 252.

missing. What we lack is a ritual. The time must come that National Socialism becomes the state religion of the Germans. My Party is my Church, and I believe that I serve my Lord in the best possible way when I execute his will and free my suppressed people from the chains of slavery".[59] The younger generation of historians has no longer any difficulty in accepting Nazism as an ersatz-, pseudo- or semi-religion, or as a religion pure and simple, which it certainly was for those who responded to the call of the Führer-Messiah. "I call Hitler's world vision and consequently National Socialism a religion",[60] states Orzechowski; Bärsch writes that National Socialism "was not one or other ideology, but essentially a religion";[61] and Klaus Vondung sees as the decisive factor in National Socialism that it consisted of 'an independent religion'.[62]

The Nazis had their own yearly cycle of hallowed rites. Every one of these occasions developed its own regimented rituals, with forests of flags and banners, ambience-creating music, torches and fires, and was held at the most suggestive moment of the day or night. The great were praised, the dead commemorated and the living transformed into initiates in the mystic mysteries of the fatherland and of the holy blood flowing in their veins. And there were the ceremonies of initiation into the party organisations, the army and the SS, always including an oath on Adolf Hitler personally, represented by the Blood Banner, the sacred banner magically containing and able to impart the presence and force of the Führer.

The crowning festivity of the year was the Party Rally, held in Nuremberg in the month of September. It lasted a whole week and delegations of party organisations everywhere in Germany participated. In 1938 Hitler declared: "Several of the [ritual] acts have by now reached their definitive form". "Up to this point",

---

[59]Joseph Goebbels, op. cit., Vol. I, p. 327.
[60]Peter Orzechowski, op. cit., p. 187.
[61]Claus-Ekkehard Bärsch, op. cit., p. 279.
[62]In Günter Scholdt: *Autoren über Hitler*, p. 117.

writes Speer, "I had taken the phrase *Das Tausendjährige Reich* [the Reich of a Thousand Years] as purely theoretical, a mere claim to establishing something that would last more than a single lifetime. But when I saw Hitler virtually canonizing the ritual in this manner, I realized for the first time that the phrase was intended literally. I had long thought that all these formations, processions and dedications were part of a clever propagandistic revue. Now I finally understood that for Hitler they were almost like rites of the founding of a church ... It now seems to me more likely that he was deliberately giving up the smaller claim to the status of a celebrated popular hero in order to gain the far greater status of founder of a religion."[63]

For countless Germans, especially Protestants, the Hitler religion coexisted with their belief in Christ. For many others Hitler replaced Christ. Altars to him were built in the homes, daily adorned with fresh flowers and prayed for. Letters were written to "my dear, fantastic, almost improbable Führer" by women 'immeasurably surrendered' to him in "a madness of unimaginable happiness". Photos of the letter writers were sent "together with the totality of my life". Hands touched by the Führer were not washed for weeks, a pebble on which his boot had stepped became a relic, a woman at whom he had smiled was treated like a saint in her village. "While you liberated the Sudetenland, I knitted these stockings for you. Now we have both reached our goal, you a big one, I a small one", a teacher wrote to Hitler. "He does not speak, something speaks through him ... An essential characteristic of his is the absolute virility ... He is full of an immense kind-heartedness, a boundless faith, a total modesty about his person, but also a limitless pride of his people and what has been accomplished, and a noble hope in what will be accomplished ..."[64]

---

[63] Albert Speer: *Spandau – The Secret Diaries*, p. 262.
[64] Beatrice and Helmut Heiber: *Die Rückseite des Hakenkreuzes*, pp. 71, 151, 163, 42.

Hitler's true objectives, even though quite explicitly stated by him, were so fantastic that they were understood only metaphorically – at least by the first generation of Nazis, for the second generation of Hitler Youth, SS-men and young army officers towards the end of the war was already sufficiently fanaticised to take his words literally. All Hitler's efforts were focused on fighting the wars necessary to establish the foundations of the Aryan world empire, and the Germans of that time did not realise that their use consisted in bringing this about and serve as the required canon fodder. Hitler, though, had warned them early on: "If the struggle on behalf of the world vision is not conducted by men of heroic spirit who are ready to sacrifice everything, within a short while it will become impossible to find real fighting followers who are ready to lay down their lives for the cause ... In order to secure the conditions that are necessary for success, everybody concerned must be made to understand *that the new movement looks to posterity for its honour and glory but that it has no recompense to offer to the present-day members.*"[65]

"Hitler never left his people in doubt that war was to come", testifies Rauschning. "We must be prepared for the toughest war which a people ever had to wage," Hitler said. "Only by this test of the will can we mature for the sovereignty to which we are called. It will be my duty to fight this war without considerations for losses. The blood sacrifices will be appalling."[66] He was prepared "to justify the blood sacrifice of a whole generation of the German youth", if necessary surpassing the losses in the First World War, for he had "the right to send the youth to their death". When the day came that he would order war, he could not be withheld by "the thought of the ten million young men whom he would send to their death".[67]

We know about Hitler's contempt for the German people from the time we examined the main themes of *Mein Kampf*. (Goebbels

---

[65] Id., p. 99 (emphasis added).
[66] Hermann Rauschning, op. cit., p. 215.
[67] Id., pp. 42, 16, 79.

disdain for 'the human canaille' was not less.) Already during the battle of Stalingrad he said: "In this too I am cold as ice: if the German Volk is not ready to fight for its self-preservation, very good, then it must vanish".[68] This attitude of Hitler will take on monstrous proportions towards the end. "If the German people are no longer so strong and ready for sacrifice that they will stake their own blood on their existence, they deserve to pass away and be annihilated by another, stronger power ... If this is the case I would not shed a tear for the German people."[69] And to Albert Speer he said: "If the German nation is now defeated in this struggle, it has been too weak. That will mean it has not withstood the test of history and was destined for nothing but doom."[70]

The man became ever more cynical. "The less the population has to lose, the more fanatically it will fight", he said to Speer in connection with the bombings. "If the German people are incapable of appreciating me, I'll fight this war alone!" he exclaimed, in the safety of his bunker moving phantom armies about in imaginary positions with broad sweeps of his hand. Finally, when the allied fronts moved unstoppably forward towards the centre of Germany, Hitler issued the orders for his scorched earth policy. "No German was to inhabit territory occupied by the enemy", writes Speer. The entire population of the threatened areas was to be forcibly evacuated and all that remained behind destroyed. When his attention was drawn to the lack of transport for hundreds of thousands of people in the middle of the winter, he barked: "Let them walk!" and added to Keitel: "We can no longer afford to concern ourselves with the population".[71]

"If the war is lost", he said to Speer, "the people will be lost also. It is not necessary to worry about what the German people will need

---

[68] *Monologe im Führerhauptquartier*, p. 239.
[69] Joachim Fest, op. cit., p. 655.
[70] Albert Speer: *Inside the Third Reich*, p. 529.
[71] Id., pp. 585, 586.

for elemental survival. On the contrary, it is best for us to destroy even these things. For the nation has proved to be the weaker, and the future belongs solely to the stronger eastern nation [he meant the USSR]. In any case only those who are inferior will remain after this struggle, for the good have already been killed."[72] The Messiah had not failed the Chosen People, his people had failed and betrayed him, all of them.

A new man

Hitler was convinced that humanity had the potential of transformation into a higher species. According to him "man was subject to an enormous change. In the course of the millennia a transformative process, literally speaking, took place in him". Thus reports Rauschning, who asserts: "For Hitler was much more than a politician: he was the prophet of a new humanity".

And Rauschning reports the following amazing words of Hitler: "Creation is not finished, at least not where the human being is concerned. The human being stands, from the biological point of view, clearly at a turning point. A new kind of human being becomes discernible ... This causes the old human species, as we have known it until now, to become inexorably decadent ... All the creative power will be concentrated in the new human species. Both species will quickly separate and develop into opposite directions. The one will sink below humanity, the other will rise above the present humanity. I might call the former 'god-man' and the latter 'mass animal' ... Yes, man is something that has to be overcome. Nietzsche knew already something about this in his own way ... Man becomes God, this is what it all means in simple words. Man is the becoming God ..." And it was here that he spoke the oft-quoted words: "He who understands National Socialism only as a political movement

---

[72] Id., p. 588.

knows practically nothing about it. It is more than a religion: it is the will to create a new humanity."[73]

We remember that in the decennia around 1900 the idea of 'a new man' was put forward by thinkers of the most diverse tendencies. The longing for a more satisfactory human existence arose not only because of dissatisfaction with the present state of the human condition and a nostalgia for the past; man was now also seen by many as a transitory being which was carried forward by the tide of general change, and which would transform itself or be transformed by Nature or Providence into a higher being. Marxism had its theory of economic processes which would produce such a new being; Nietzsche's 'superman' became a cliché; Freud had his ideal of a being conscious of the hidden depths within itself and socially adapted or adjusted; Jung proposed techniques to identify with the archetypal godhead within; List and May foresaw the re-appearance of the *Edelmensch*; George taught the development of the more refined human capacities into a kind of amalgam of a super-poet and a Greek god. It is therefore no wonder that we find the expectation of 'the new man' in the diary of young Goebbels. "*Heil* and *Sieg* to the new man! ... We must descend into the deepest depths if we want to create the new man ... I am in search of the new Reich and the new man ..."[74]

Ernst Jünger too had perceived a new man, for in one of his books about the First World War he wrote: "The spirit of the battle with modern war materiel and in the trenches, fought more ruthlessly, mercilessly and savagely than any other battle in the past, produced men whom the world had never seen before ... These were new conquerors, natures of steel, adapted to battle in its most abhorrent form ... When I observe them, the insight lights up in me: this is the new man".[75] Jünger was personally admired and his writings were

---

[73] Hermann Rauschning, op. cit., pp. 231-32.
[74] Joseph Goebbels, op. cit., pp. I 95, 138, 162.
[75] In Christian von Krockow: *Hitler und seine Deutschen*, p. 38.

widely read. Especially his war reminiscences *In Stahlgewittern* (in storms of steel), the bible of the Free Corps, was a very popular book, read by those who had been battered in such storms and by those who regretted having been too young to be there.

When Hitler exclaims that the new man exists, he describes him with the characteristics of Jünger's *Frontschweine* (literally 'front pigs', a popular German designation of the trench soldiers). "The new man lives among us. He is here!" Hitler shouted triumphantly. "Are you satisfied now? I tell you a secret: I have seen the new man, fearless and terrible. He startled me!" It is puzzling who this superman, 'living among us', may have been. Most probably it was Hitler's image in the mirror, for 'among us' there was no place for somebody superior to the Führer. John Toland writes that he "came to regard himself as a man of destiny, superior to any other human being whose genius and will power would conquer any enemy. Mesmerized by his political and military victories, he explained to one Nazi commander that he was the first and only mortal who had emerged into 'a superhuman state'. His nature was 'more godlike than human', and therefore as the first of the new race of supermen he was 'bound by none of the conventions of human morality 'and stood above the law'."[76]

Freedom of all moral restrictions was an integral element of the gospel Hitler had come to preach among the Aryans. "We will free ourselves from all humane and scientific prejudices. Therefore I will have propagated, in the schools for Junkers which I will found and where all future members of our master state will be educated, the gospel of the free man – of the man who is master of life and death, of fear and superstition, and who has learned to control his body, muscles and nerves ... yet who also stands above the temptations of the mind and of a so-called free science."[77]

---

[76]John Toland, op. cit., pp. 884-85.
[77]Hermann Rauschning, op. cit., p. 47.

Hitler's new man would live according to and in harmony with his instincts; he would be a natural, 'spontaneous' being. "One must feel diffident about one's mind and conscience, and confident about one's instincts. We must regain a new naivety ... Providence has predestined me to be the greatest liberator of humanity."[78] What he wanted humanity to be liberated from, as we have seen, was the predominance of the mind, the torture of its conscience and moral sense, and the need of individual freedom and personal independence. All indications are that the Hitlerian superman was a fully conditioned barbarian, integrated into a barbarian Volk which considered itself the lord and master of all other peoples.

"It is with the youth that I commence my great educational project", said Hitler. "We, the older people, are used up. Yes, we are already old. We are tainted to the core. We don't have any unflawed instincts anymore. We are cowardly, we are sentimental. We carry in our blood the burden of a humiliating past and the dull memory of servitude and a cringing existence. But my glorious young ones – is there a more beautiful youth in the whole world? Have a look at these young men and boys! What a material! With them I can build a new world!"[79]

"My pedagogic principles are tough", continued Hitler. "The weak parts must be hammered away. In my *Ordensburgen* a youth will grow up that will startle the world. I want a violent, authoritarian, fearless, pitiless youth ... They must be able to stand pain. They may not have anything weak or soft. The free, magnificent beast of prey must again flash from their eyes. I want my youth strong and beautiful. I will have it built up through all kinds of physical exercises. I want an athletic youth – this first and foremost. In this way I eradicate the millennia of human domestication, and I obtain the pure, noble stuff of Nature. Thus will I be able to create the new.

---

[78]Id., pp. 211, 212.
[79]Id., p. 237.

"I want no intellectual education. With knowledge I spoil the youth. I would prefer to let them learn only what they spontaneously pick up in their games. But they have to learn self-mastery. They must learn to overcome the fear of death by means of the most severe tests. This is the stage of the heroic youth. From it will develop the stage of the free man, of the man who is the centre and norm of the world, of creative man, of the god-man. In my *Ordensburgen* there will be present the cultic example of the harmonious, self-mastering god-man, and he will prepare the youth for the next stage of virile maturity." "But here Hitler cut himself short", writes Rauschning, "as he could not elaborate on this. There were further stages of which he was not allowed to speak, not even he. Moreover, he thought he would communicate this as his secret when he was no more alive. Something very important was then to happen, a staggering revelation. To complete his mission, he was to have died a sacrificial death".[80]

"What Hitler had in mind", writes Christian Zentner, "was the inner unity of the nation, welded together into a marching column, organized with an iron hand, prepared for any joyful sacrifice, and ready at any time to execute any order of the National Socialist leadership".[81] "Hitler's education of the youth was all-embracing", remarks Henry Picker in his comments on the 'table talk', and he quotes Hitler's words which should be included in any anthology of totalitarianism: "These boys join our organization at the age of ten and get a breath of fresh air for the first time, then, four years later, they move from the Jungvolk to the Hitler Youth and there we keep them for another four years. And then we are even less prepared to give them back into the hands of those who create class and status barriers, rather we take them immediately into the SA or into the SS ... and so on. And if they are there for eighteen months

---

[80] Id., pp. 236-38.
[81] Christian Zentner, op. cit., p. 103.

or two years and have still not become real National Socialists, then they go into the Labour Service and are polished there for six or seven months, and all of this under a single symbol, the German spade. And if, after six or seven months, there are still remnants of class consciousness or pride in status, then the Wehrmacht will take over the further treatment for two years, and when they return after two or four years then, to prevent them from slipping back into old habits once again, we take them immediately into the SA, SS etc. and they will not be free again for the rest of their lives."[82]

"Hitler was prepared to write off the older generation, remarking in November 1933 that 'when an opponent says "I will not come over to your side", I calmly say "Your child belongs to us already ... You will pass on, but your descendants stand already in the new camp. In a short time they will know nothing but this new community"' ... A pluralistic youth culture was replaced by the monolithic Hitler Youth and League of German Maidens for fourteen- to eighteen-year-olds, and the German Young People and the League of Young Girls for the ten to fourteens."[83] By the end of 1938 the Hitler Youth numbered more than seven and a half million; in March of the next year it became the only authorised youth organisation in the Reich.

When a member had served his years in the Hitler Youth, he was in fact a fully trained military man. "While training in shooting and manoeuvre exercises was extended to all young men, the defence training of the Hitler Youth was expanded into special units. In 1938 the Naval Hitler Youth numbered 50,000, the Motorized Hitler Youth 90,000, the Air Force units 74,000, the model-airplane clubs of the German Youth 73,000, the Communications Hitler Youth 29,000."[84] Their idols would be the fighter pilots Galland, Mölders

---

[82]This translation in Michael Burleigh: *The Third Reich – A New History*, p. 215.
[83]Michael Burleigh, op. cit., p. 235.
[84]Joachim Fest, op. cit., p. 350.

and Marseille, and 'the Desert Fox' Erwin Rommel, the most popular soldier of the regime. This completely nazified and fanaticised 'second generation' – "I see the enthusiasm in their eyes when they speak of the Führer" – became awesome soldiers at the front, for instance as the tank division *Hitler Jugend* in Normandy and at Bastogne where, as diarist Goebbels notes, they performed 'miracles of heroism'. These very young soldiers, many of them still looking like children, were also the ones who defended the last bridgeheads on the Havel, in the suburbs of Berlin, an episode retold in Berhard Wicki's film *Die letzte Brücke* (the last bridge). And a small unit of them lined up in front of a stooped and limping Hitler, when for the last time he came out of his bunker to decorate them for bravery. By that time the dream of Hitler's *Ordensburgen*, the citadels of the Order, was bombarded into rubble and smoke.

The Order of the Death's Head

"I am going to tell you a secret", said Hitler to Hermann Rauschning somewhere in 1933, "I am founding an Order".[85] The idea of 'a small circle of real initiates' was not unknown among those close to Hitler, remembers Rauschning, for Alfred Rosenberg had already talked to him about it confidentially after having given a talk at the Marienburg, the central seat of the Teutonic Order. Actually the idea had nothing extraordinary, for whenever in history a really novel and compelling world vision appears, an almost automatic process of segregation takes place between its exoteric form, adapted to the mass, and its esoteric essence, destined for a select few."

This corresponded in the main to the way Hitler saw his movement. Firstly, there was the mass of the members for whom he wanted to keep the original Party programme forever unchanged like the dogmas of a Church; they would be kept going by their

---

[85] Hermann Rauschning, op. cit., p. 233.

unreflecting faith in the Party and its Führer. And there were the comrades who had stood at Hitler's side during the years of struggle, *die alten Kämpfer*, and who were now the lower Führers in the Party pyramid, the 'little Hitlers' as they were sometimes called. "Hitler knew that these men could not be won for a higher flight of the ideas. They were political toughs, hardened in the down-wearing struggle of every day. Their thought did not reach beyond the once accepted principles of National Socialism." Hitler knew their strengths and their weaknesses very well, and rewarded their loyalty by satisfying their ambitions and greed.

Only when this generation had died out could, secondly, 'a secular nation of priests' take shape, the first wave of "a new religion of humanity, the creation of a new human species". Hitler realised that this would be possible only after the decisive war of world conquest 'which was to come unavoidably'. National Socialism, or rather Hitlerism, was still in its infancy. "He touched repeatedly upon these topics in his conversations. And one felt, hidden behind his apparent resignation, the searing impatience to reach his proper stage: that of the creative statesman and lawgiver, of the exemplary artist and builder of cities, of the prophet and founder of a new religion."[86]

"'Party' is a wrong concept. I would prefer to say 'Order'", said Hitler.[87] What he had in mind was an organisation like the one worked out by Freemasonry, based on the example of the medieval guilds. "They formed a kind of priestly nobility. They set themselves apart by adopting special customs. They developed a secret teaching which is not so much a simple verbal creed as the gradual revelation of a higher insight by means of symbols and secret rites." The 'danger and greatness' of Freemasonry lay in its hierarchic organisation and the teaching through symbols and rituals which appeal to the imagination 'without the intervention of the intellect'. This was

---

[86]Id., p. 236, passim.
[87]Id., p. 187.

what fascinated Hitler and what he intended to emulate. "Don't you see that our Party must be something similar: an Order, the hierarchic ordering of a secular priesthood?" he asked Rausching. "But this means of course that there cannot be something similar on the other side. Either we are there, or there are the Freemasons, or the Church, but never two simultaneously. They are exclusive, something the Catholic Church has plainly understood, at least where Freemasonry is concerned [by excommunicating it]. Now we are the strongest and we will get rid of both others, the Freemasons *and* the Church."[88] In the case of the Church he had to tread carefully, for Christianity was deeply ingrained in the thought and customs of the German people, but there cannot be any doubt about his ultimate intentions. Freemasonry, on the contrary, was harmless and defenceless, and forbidden as soon as he came to power.

Hitler's obsession of having to found an Order was given a concrete shape in the SS, the Order of the Death's Head. The SS was founded at a time when Hitler, for strategic reasons, had to let the SA be included in a *Kampfbund*, a fighting association, along with other rightist paramilitary units. The SS was *his*: his personal bodyguard, sworn in on his name and loyal to him alone. Here was an elite created without any concessions, and this elite would be a new aristocracy of the Aryan blood, embodying the Hitlerian ideals to the fullest.

At first the SS was no more than some insignificant small units, in most cases unpaid, who accompanied Hitler as his bodyguard and would protect him with their life. But this changed in 1929, when Hitler appointed Heinrich Himmler as their commander. "Hitherto the SS had been no more than an organization", writes Heinz Höhne, "now it was to become an Order. Himmler had discovered from history an example on which he proposed to model his Order: the Jesuits ... In the Jesuits Himmler had found what he regarded as

---

[88]Id., pp. 226-27, passim.

the central feature of any Order's mentality: the doctrine of [unconditional] obedience and the cult of organization".[89]

"To have made from this handful of men [280 in 1929] the strongest ideological army ever, is [Himmler's] merit", said Hitler. "Little by little I have found in my SS the army against which I never had a complaint. There has never been a reason to expose them. It is Himmler who created their stature. From a small group of loosely connected men he has built a leadership apparatus. He is so to say the volkisch Ignatius of Loyola in the good sense."[90] "The SS organization was built up by Himmler on the principles of the Order of the Jesuits", writes Walter Schellenberg, himself an SS-general. "The service statutes and spiritual exercises preached by Ignatius of Loyola formed a pattern which Himmler assiduously tried to copy. Absolute obedience was the supreme rule; each and every order had to be accepted without question."[91] This explains why Himmler was sometimes called 'the black Jesuit' or 'the Grand Inquisitor', for safety's sake behind his back.

Equivalent to the rule of unconditional obedience was the purity of the blood. "The discovery of any drop of non-Aryan blood in SS veins invariably excited Himmler. From 1 June 1935, every SS commander from the rank of regimental sergeant-major upwards had to show proof that neither he nor his wife had Jewish ancestors; from 1 October 1935 the requirement was extended to include quartermaster-sergeants and sergeant-majors, and shortly thereafter every SS man. Everyone had to be able to produce an 'Aryan' family tree going back in the case of officers and officer cadets to 1750 and in the case of other ranks to 1800."[92] Moreover, the physical condition of a candidate had to be perfect. "The old Waffen-SS, the legion of pre-war National Socialist supermen, rejected every recruit with the slightest physical imperfection, even a single dental filling."[93]

---

[89] Heinz Höhne: *The Order of the Death's Head*, p. 163.
[90] *Monologe im Führerhauptquartier*, p. 169.
[91] Walter Schellenberg: *The Labyrinth*, p. 15.
[92] Heinz Höhne, op. cit., p. 162.
[93] Max Hastings: *Das Reich*, p. 26.

"Like monks and priests, or Communist Party members, there was a lengthy noviciate or candidate-membership, involving ideological instruction, labour and military service, and the acquisition of sporting prowess ... Arcane initiation rites heightened the solemnity of being admitted to a privileged caste, a sort of secular priesthood. The midnight oath-swearing ceremony was apparently evocative, according to one eyewitness: 'Tears came to my eyes when, by the light of torches, thousands of voices repeated the oath in chorus. It was like a prayer'. There was a bastardized catechism, in which the questions and responses included: 'Why do we believe in Germany and the Führer?' 'Because we believe in God, we believe in Germany which He created in His world, and in the Führer, Adolf Hitler, whom He has sent us.' Like all sects and totalitarian organizations, the SS recognized no departures and no separate private sphere. The individual was in for life." (Michael Burleigh[94]) "I don't doubt for a moment – many don't understand this at present – that in one hundred years the whole German leadership will come from the SS", said Hitler in one of his monologues.

We remember that Hitler had a rather low opinion of the racial purity of the Germans. After centuries of degeneration "a race is what we still have to become", he said and estimated that the racial re-generation would take something like a hundred years. It was one of the functions of the SS in the Germanic-Nordic-Aryan nation to constitute a base, or an ambulant blood bank, which would render the regeneration possible. The documents of racial purity, demanded from every SS man and his marriage partner, were one step in this direction. Another step was the gathering of the best blood from all the Germanic peoples and their descendants (Flemings, Dutch, Scandinavian, Swiss, even French) into the SS. The Waffen-SS divisions *Panzerdivision Nederland* and *Grenadierdivision Landstorm Nederland* were Dutch, the *Grenadierdivision Langemarck*

---

[94]Michael Burleigh, op. cit., p. 194.

was Flemish, the *Grenadierdivision der SS Charlemagne* was French. (Waffen-SS divisions of Slavonic people were formed only when the military situation became critical and the conditions of entering the SS were considerably lowered.) Another step of heightening the degree of purity of the German blood was the kidnapping in the occupied territories of thousands of Aryan-looking children, who were then raised with families in Germany. In the chapter 'Stolen Children' of her book *The German Trauma*, Gitta Sereny writes that these children numbered 'possibly a quarter of a million', most of them East European.

The SS men in their 'dashing and elegant' black uniforms were very status conscious and conditioned to be so. At the bottom of the pyramid of the Nazi state there were the ordinary people, Jews and Gypsies not included; above them ranked the National Socialist Party members; then came the uniformed members of the SA; and on top stood the SS, looking down on everybody else, also on the SA from which they had originated, but who in their eyes remained a farrago of brainless street brawlers. The very *crème de la crème* of the SS were the *Leibstandarte Adolf Hitler,* Hitler's pretorian guard, commanded by Sepp Dietrich; they were the closest an Aryan could resemble 'the image of the Lord', and they peopled the dreams of the League of German Maidens and the nightmares of non-Nazis.

Himmler stimulated the elitist character of the SS – "in the SS one found the better type of people", writes Schellenberg – by trying to allure as many members of the German nobility as possible, and by recruiting educated young men. In the higher SS ranks the number of officers with a university education, especially lawyers, economists and physicians, was considerable. They ran the SS as drilled technocrats, which explains the cancer-like growth of the Order within the body of the Third Reich. On this aspect of the SS, Burleigh remarks: "Historians have made much of the fact that many of them were lawyers or economists, two-thirds of whom had higher education and a third doctorates; less is predictably made of the truth that a doctorate sometimes merely betokens an assiduous mindlessness, signifying nothing about the wider personality. For, ironically enough, the universities were precisely the places in Germany which fostered an elite form of anti-Semitism, whose radicalism was ill disguised within a carapace of 'scientific objectivity' towards the 'Jewish Question'. Now these former student radicals had the chance to implement what they had so often talked of in their exclusive circles".[95]

It is now generally accepted that the SS was, in Peter Lebenda's words, "a fully constituted cult ... Himmler's dream was to create out of the SS a new religion." "Church marriages were prohibited for SS members, whose vows were solemnified in the SS's own ceremonies. Since spouses were subjected to exhaustive racial vetting, they were being co-opted into the emergent elite, with their fecundity being monitored through the unlikely medium of gifts of SS kitsch for the birth of each child. Children of SS men underwent an alternative form of baptism, with the seventh child being eligible for having Himmler as godfather. The centrepiece of the ceremony was a portrait of Hitler; instead of clergy there were SS men bearing standards with the swastika and the legend 'Germany awake' ... All of this is entirely in keeping with the well-documented habits of sects and other totalitarian organizations in shaping the individual member's whole environment."[96]

The standard black SS uniform (they also had a greyish or *feldgrau* one for everyday activities), with the twin Sig rune and the death's head on the cap, was feared by the German population no less than in the occupied countries, for everybody knew that it stood for ruthless Nazi-extremism, torture and death. "I know that there are many who fall ill when they see this black uniform", a gratified Himmler said in a speech to his commanders. "We understand this and don't expect that we will be loved by many people."[97] They had

---

[95] Ibid.
[96] Michael Burleigh, op. cit., p. 194.
[97] Id., p. 192.

their own ceremonies for birth, marriage and death, at which the local SS commander functioned as the priest; they had their own terminology for the ranks within the Order; and they had their own justice, for a member of the SS could not be called to account by anybody outside the Order, not even by the military tribunals. They lived in the conviction that they were the highest and noblest living beings on earth whose rightful task it was to rule the globe, as the descendants of the former Nordic master race, which was now regaining its rights and its spiritual powers, residing in or resulting from the purity of their blood.

Himmler stimulated these pretences to superhumanity in every way he could. One of his close consultants, with whom he had for some years a most cordial friendship, was an Austrian seer, Karl Maria Wiligut aka Weisthor, "the last descendant of a long line of German sages, the Uiligotis of the Asa-Uana-Sippe, which dated back to a remote prehistoric era".[98] Impressed by the proven veracity of some of Wiligut's visions, Himmler made him a full colonel in the SS and put him to work in the SS research centres concerned with the glorious olden times of the Germanic-Nordic-Aryans. It was Wiligut who designed the death's head ring, awarded by Himmler, as master of the Order, only to some of his highest-ranking and most deserving myrmidons, and it was Wiligut who convinced the Reichsführer-SS of the significance and the value for his Order of the Wewelsburg near the town of Paderborn.

This old and dilapidated castle was soon renovated by the inmates of a makeshift concentration camp, for it was to become "an SS-order castle comparable to the Marienburg of the medieval Teutonic Knights"; in other words, it was to become the "Vatican" of the Order of the Death's Head. That Himmler took this very seriously is shown by surviving plans for a huge complex of buildings, destined to be the Order's world centre and focused on the Wewelsburg.

---

[98]Nicholas Goodrick-Clarke: *The Occult Roots of Nazism*, p. 179.

Several authors remind us, moreover, that after the Nazi wars of conquest, the SS would reside in its own state, more or less covering the former territory of Burgundy – not the present-day vineyard region in France but the old land of the Burgundians, from Southern Germany all the way down to the Mediterranean. The symbolical meaning of this choice may be found in the fact that the Nibelungs were Burgundians, and that the primary SS slogan, embroidered on the sleeve of their uniforms, was *Meine Ehre heisst Treue*, faithfulness is my honour, inspired by the Nibelungs' legendary fealty, the *Nibelungen Treue*.

The freedom with which Himmler and his henchmen could act out their fantasies of past, present and future greatness is amazing; it demonstrates the extent to which Nazi Germany had become an island of irrationalism. Himmler could publicly proclaim that he was an incarnation of the medieval German emperor Henry the Fowler and, as the highlight of a grandiose ceremony, communicate with the Fowler's spirit in the tomb where his remains had been laid to rest with military honours. Or he could authorise and finance, in 1938-39, the Ernst Schäfer expedition to Tibet, where he suspected that traces of the first, godlike Aryans might be found. Similar expeditions were also sent to Iceland and Antarctica, and more were planned to the Far East and to Tiahuanaco, the old Inca city in the Andes, but cancelled because of the war.

If we put all this together, and remember that Hitler already in *Mein Kampf* took his distance from the bearded, impotent volkisch dreamers, then we must conclude that the Hitler-Himmler relation was ambiguous. Not, as far as known, from the side of 'the faithful Henry', although the inner tension may have influenced his ambiguous attitude at the time of the Stauffenberg attempt on Hitler's life and his decision towards the end of the war to negotiate with the Swedes. For he, Himmler, top policeman of the Reich, must surely have been aware of some of Hitler's barbs at his expense. For instance, Speer writes that Hitler had little sympathy with Himmler in his mythologizing of the SS. "What nonsense!" exclaimed Hitler.

"Here we have at last reached an age that has left all mysticism behind it, and now he wants to start all over again. We might just as well have stayed with the Church. At least it had tradition. To think that I may some day be turned into an SS saint! Can you imagine it? I would turn over in my grave." Then follows the passage where Hitler says that "the Romans were creating great buildings when our forefathers were still living in mud huts", and the question why the whole world's attention should be called to this fact.[99]

But the relation was more complex than that. Himmler had forged his SS into an essential instrument of the Reich, subservient only to the Führer and animated by the Führer's ideology and, most important, by faith. For the time being nothing of all this could be touched or altered, especially as it had grown under Hitler's own inspiration and supervision. "I am doing nothing that the Führer does not know about", said Himmler, who clicked his heels even when Hitler spoke to him on the telephone. There is every ground to believe him, at least till the time that the final collapse of the Reich seemed imminent.

We have therefore to disagree with the authors who would have us understand that Hitler distanced himself from some of Himmler's projects, for instance the Wewelsburg. For Rüdiger Sünner mentions that Hitler signed, on 2 July 1940, a "decree by the Führer and Chancellor of the Reich concerning building works in the region of the Wewelsburg", and that he thereby gave the Chief of the SS a free hand for all these plans. Höhne writes that Hitler "never appeared in the Wewelsburg", but this is contradicted by a photo in Lebenda's *Unholy Alliance*, showing Hitler and Himmler together in the hall of an old castle, with the caption: "Hitler and Himmler in the Wewelsburg".

In fact, the Order of the Death's Head was one of Hitler's most authentic creations, with Heinrich Himmler as his instrument. The SS was "the chosen elite who held the decision about life and death

---

[99] Albert Speer: *Inside the Third Reich*, p. 147.

in their hands".¹⁰⁰ Once more Ernst Jünger had set the tone: "Our work is to kill, and it is our duty to do our work well". The SS were trained to become the unfeeling, automatically obedient robots, or angels, or devils, of death. Theirs was 'an unfeeling form of neo-barbarism', ready at any moment 'to give and take death' (*den Tod zu geben und zu nehmen*). No, the symbol of the death's head on their caps, rings, weapons and tanks was not 'death-fixated kitsch', it expressed, together with the colour of their uniforms, exactly what it stood for. "Most of you will know what it means when one hundred corpses are laying there in a row, or five hundred, or a thousand. To have stood this and to have remained *decent* – not taking into account exceptions of human weakness – this has made us hard. This is a never written and never to be written *glorious page* of our history."¹⁰¹ Thus spoke Himmler to his commanders, and the emphases are his.

Reading about the Second World War in Europe, one finds that where there were Germans and death, there was the SS man. Doing evil made him feel stronger, more superhuman. Hans Hüftig had been the former commandant of the Buchenwald concentration camp – on the Ettersberg near Weimar, where Goethe once walked. To an interviewer he told in 1986, from his comfortable retirement: "Today it seems so cruel, inhuman and immoral. It did not seem immoral to me then: I knew very well what I was going to do in the SS. We all knew. It was something in the soul, not in the mind. We all knew what we were going to do in the SS. When it comes down to it, it is a very simple story. I was a Nazi."¹⁰²

---

[100] Christian von Krockow, op. cit., p. 245.
[101] Id., p. 246.
[102] John Weiss: *Ideology of Death*, p. 341.

13

Medium

The spirit is always more important than the external force which incarnates it.

Adolf Hitler

"I have thought and thought about it", Albert Speer said to Gitta Sereny, "and you know, even if all the people who had been close to Hitler during one or another period of his life were alive and available for questioning by the many historians and psychologists who have tried to come to grips with Hitler's personality, I cannot think of a single person who could have explained it".[1] And HR Trevor-Roper quotes Speer as saying: "The whole demonic figure of the man can never be explained simply as the product of these events [Second World War and the aftermath for Germany]. They could just as easily have found expression in a national leader of mediocre stature. For Hitler was one of those inexplicable historical phenomena which emerge at rare intervals among mankind. His person determined the fate of the nation. He alone placed it, and kept it, upon the path which has lead to this dreadful ending. The nation

---

[1] Gitta Sereny: *Albert Speer – His Battle with Truth*, p. 361.

was spellbound by him as a people has rarely been in the whole of history."[2]

Walter Langer, in his 1943 report for the Office of Strategic Services, expressed his puzzlement about the person of Adolf Hitler in equally candid terms: "If we scan the tremendous qualities of material and information that have been accumulated on Hitler, we find little that is helpful in explaining why he is what he is ... No matter how long we study the available material, we can find no rational explanation of his present conduct. The material is descriptive and tells us a great deal about how he behaves under varying circumstances, what he thinks and feels about various subjects, but it does not tell us why."[3]

Hitler was on the one hand 'the lonely wanderer out of nothingness', as he liked to introduce himself, while on the other hand he was a man 'summoned by Providence'. "Throughout his life, wherever he went, Adolf Hitler was always a mysterious stranger", writes Ron Rosenbaum.[4] Werner Maser has the same impression: "Hitler cannot be explained either by his social origin or by his education and early environment".[5] Speer, the man who had been so close to him, said also: "Hitler in a sense gave the impression of being a total stranger. He really came from another world. That was why, whenever he appeared on the scene in the course of the war, he always seemed so bizarre."[6]

All those who were able to observe Hitler for some time from nearby are agreed on what Konrad Heiden calls 'the sharp division in his personality'. There was what one might describe as 'the outward shell' of the perceptible person covering 'an empty core' (Speer), 'a hollow individuality' (Fest), 'the emptiness of the private person'

---

[2] HR Trevor-Roper: *The Last Days of Hitler*, p. 89.
[3] Walter Langer: *The Mind of Adolf Hitler*, p. 141.
[4] Ron Rosenbaum: *Explaining Hitler*, p. 6.
[5] Werner Maser: *Adolf Hitler – Legende, Mythos, Wirklichkeit*, p. 284.
[6] Albert Speer: *Spandau – The Secret Diaries*, p. 19.

(Kershaw). Fest also writes about "the resistance, still widespread today, to accepting such an inexpressible commonplace figure as Hitler as the man behind events of such extraordinary magnitude".[7] His outward appearance was often ridiculed by those who did not see a god in him. He was 'the great Adolf with the small moustache', 'terribly pale', a man smaller than the average German with 'his train conductor's cap' pulled deep over his eyes, "a weakish, mollusc-like being, pasty, cheesy, feminine, not the warrior but the hairdresser type".[8] "How shall one reconcile the gravity, the catastrophic magnitude of the events with the vulgar mediocrity of the individual who initiated them?" asks Rosenbaum.[9]

But oftentimes Hitler's vulgar mediocrity made place for a power from inside, or from behind, or from above, which transformed him into an irresistible 'charismatic' being. "Suddenly, in the midst of a conversation, Hitler's face grows tense as with an inner vision", writes Heiden from experience. "These are the moments in which the humanly repulsive falls away from him and the unfathomable is intensified until it becomes truly terrible. His eyes peer into the distance as though he were reading or gazing at something which no one else sees ... When suddenly this man, who has been awkwardly standing around, now and then muttering a remark that by no means dominates the conversation, is seized with determination and begins to speak, filling the room with his voice, suppressing interruptions or contradictions by his domineering manner, spreading cold shivers among those present by the savagery of his declarations, lifting every subject of conversation into the light of history, and interpreting it so that even trifles have their origin in greatness – then the listener is filled with awe and feels that a new phenomenon has entered the room. This thundering demon was not there before; this is not the same timid man with the contracted shoulders. He

---

[7] Joachim Fest: *The Face of the Third Reich*, p. 106.
[8] Günter Scholdt: *Autoren über Hitler*, p. 206.
[9] Ron Rosenbaum, op. cit., p. 295.

is capable of this transformation in a personal interview as well as when facing an audience of half a million."[10]

The same phenomenon normally took place when Hitler gave his speeches. Fest describes the care and the expertise with which he staged the whole event himself, making the evening build up to the highest possible tension in expectation of him. "He ruled out introductory speeches or greetings that could only distract the audience from his person. For a few moments he would linger before the platform, mechanically shaking hands, mute, absent-minded, eyes flickering restively, but ready like a medium to be imbued and carried aloft by the strength that was already there, latent, in the shouting of the masses. The first words were dropped mutedly, gropingly, into the breathless silence; they were often preceded by a pause that seemed to become utterly unbearable, while the speaker collected himself. The beginning was monotonous, trivial, usually lingering on the legend of his rise ... This formal beginning prolonged the suspense once more, into the very speech itself. But it also allowed him to sense the mood and to adjust to it. A catcall might abruptly inspire him to take a fighting tone until the first eagerly awaited applause surged up. For that was what gave him contact, what intoxicated him, and 'after about fifteen minutes', a contemporary observer commented, 'there takes place what can only be described in the primitive old figure of speech: the spirit enters into him'."[11]

"When the transformation takes place in his personality all his views, sentiments and values are also transformed. The result is that as 'Führer' he can make statements with great conviction that flatly contradict what 'Hitler' said a few minutes earlier. He can grapple with the most important problems and in a few minutes reduce them to extremely simple terms; he can map out campaigns, be the supreme

---

[10]Konrad Heiden: *Hitler*, p. 299.
[11]Joachim Fest: *Hitler*, pp. 326-27.

judge, deal with diplomats, ignore all ethical and moral principles, order executions or the destruction of cities without the slightest hesitation. And he can be in the best of humour while he is doing it. All of this would have been completely impossible for 'Hitler'." (Langer[12])

Ernst Hanfstängl, one of Hitler's closest confidants during his climb to power, recalls: "He had this chameleon-like gift of reflecting the wishes of the masses, and somehow their message was transmitted to him on a wavelength which was not that of speech, but some other set of vibrations into which he could tune himself. This may have been one of the reasons for his complete contempt for foreign languages and the necessity of learning and understanding them. He would talk to a foreigner, using an interpreter for the words, but his mediumistic gifts seemed to work just as well with a Hottentot or a Hindu."

"His characteristics were those of a medium," writes Hanfstängl, "who absorbed and gave expression, by induction and osmosis, to the fears, ambitions and emotions of the whole German nation ... He could sprawl for hours like a crocodile dozing in the Nile mud or a spider immobile in the centre of its web. He would chew his nails, look boredly into space and sometimes whistle. But as soon as some person of interest ... joined his company, you could almost see him mobilizing his internal machinery. The asdic pings of inquiry would go out and within a short time he had a clear image of the wavelength and secret yearnings and emotions of his partner. The pendulum of conversation would start to beat faster, and the person would be hypnotized into believing that there lay in Hitler immense depths of sympathy and understanding. He had the most formidable powers of persuasion of any man or woman I have ever met, and it was almost impossible to avoid being enveloped by him."[13]

---

[12] Walter Langer, op. cit., pp. 130-31.
[13] Ernst Hanfstängl, op. cit., pp. 267, 265-66.

Rauschning too compares Hitler to a medium. "Mediums are mostly ordinary, insignificant beings, but suddenly they acquire powers which lift them high above the norms of everyday life. These powers are not part of their actual personality: they are guests from another order of being. The medium is being possessed by them, but he himself remains untouched and unaltered by them. It is undeniable that such forces are passing through Hitler, truly demonic forces which use Hitler, the human person, only as an instrument. The ordinary linking up with the extraordinary – this is what gives the contact with Hitler such an unbearably ambiguous effect."[14] There was that 'magic power of greatness' emanating from a 'human nullity', 'a creature who as a man is smaller than you and I'.[15]

Magnetism

"Hitler's secretary Christa Schroeder, having observed him for fifteen years, concluded that he possessed 'the gift of a rare magnetic power to reach people', 'a sixth sense and a clairvoyant intuition'. He could 'in some mysterious way foretell the subconscious reactions of the masses and in some inexplicable manner mesmerize his interlocutors'. He possessed, she said, 'the receptivity of a medium and at the same time the magnetism of a hypnotist'."[16] Schroeder's statement is confirmed by numerous testimonies. The historian Hugh Trevor-Roper, for instance, mentions 'that compelling enchantment of Hitler'; the annotator of the 'table talk' writes about *that remarkable magnetic fluid which he emanated with such mastery* and emphasizes his words; Ernst Hanfstängl is struck by 'the extraordinary magnetism of his personality'; and Walter Langer too wonders at 'the magnetic quality' of the subject of his inquiry.

---

[14]Hermann Rauschning: *Gespräche mit Hitler*, pp. 274-75.
[15]Konrad Heiden, op. cit., p. 299.
[16]Frederic Spotts: *Hitler and the Power of Aesthetics*, p. 45.

In his Hitler biography, Fest writes: "[Hitler] possessed 'the most terrifying persuasiveness'. Along with this he had the power of exerting a hypnotic effect upon his interlocutor. The leadership of the party, the gauleiters and Old Fighters who had shoved their way to the top alongside him, undoubtedly were 'a band of eccentrics and egotists all going in different directions', and certainly were not servile in the traditional sense. The same is true for at least a part of the officers' corps. Nevertheless, Hitler imposed his will on them as he pleased. And he did so not only at the height of his power but equally well before, when he was a marginal figure on the political Right, and at the end, when he was only the burned-out husk of a once mighty man."[17]

"They were all under his spell", Speer said of Hitler's chief henchmen. "They obeyed him blindly, with no will of their own – whatever the medical term of this phenomenon may be".[18] And Sereny quotes Speer as saying: "One thing is certain: every one who worked closely with him for a long time was exceptionally dependent on him. However powerful they were in their own domain, close to him they became small and timid".[19] We saw how Himmler jumped to attention, clicking his heels, when Hitler phoned him. Goebbels 'was cowed by Hitler's magnetic powers'. Göring said to Hjalmar Schacht: "I try so hard, but every time I stand before the Führer, my heart drops into the seat of my pants".[20]

Schacht himself, 'the great economic and financial wizard', never left a conversation with Hitler without being deeply impressed and experiencing a feeling of re-invigoration", writes Rauschning. "He always felt revitalized, and the grand perspectives drawn by Hitler gave a renewed meaning to his efforts ... When even the cleverest of all economic leaders felt this way, how could I have felt otherwise?"

---

[17] Joachim Fest, op. cit., p. 519.
[18] Joachim Fest: *The Face of the Third Reich*, pp. 312-13.
[19] Gitta Sereny, op. cit., pp. 136-37.
[20] Id., p. 137.

For Rauschning too had to confess: "I often had the occasion to examine myself and I admit having come, time and again, under his spell, which afterwards I had to fight off like a spell of hypnotism".[21] Speer uses the expression 'when Hitler took possession of me' and writes in his Spandau diary: "The complicated feeling of being bound to him persists to the present day", in November 1949.[22]

The Hitler effect was equally strong on military officers, all of them trained in the curt Prussian way. Even the gallant Rommel came under Hitler's influence every time he met him. "Hitler emanated a magnetic, perhaps hypnotic power", he wrote to his wife.[23] Walter Blomberg, a Nazi general and for a time Minister of Defence, "used to say that a cordial handshake of the Führer's could cure him of his colds".[24] A former officer on the Eastern front, interviewed by Kempowski for his book *Haben Sie Hitler gesehen?* (did you see Hitler?), remembers: "When the nonsensical Führer orders continued to come, our division commander said: 'I am going to give this man a piece of my mind'. I still see him standing in the ravine in which our staff buses were parked. But when he came back [from his meeting with Hitler] he said: 'The Führer is right'."[25]

Admiral Dönitz called Hitler "a being from whom flows an influence and who has an enormous suggestive power". "The usually cool technocrat Karl Dönitz became mesmerized in Hitler's presence. After a few days he admitted to fleeing the Führer's headquarters in order to regain his independence of mind."[26] In March 1945, when the Russians were threatening Danzig, Gauleiter Forster "walked through my office, in complete despair at what was happening", recalls one of Hitler's secretaries. "He revealed to me that 1100 Russian tanks were closing in on Danzig, that the Wehrmacht had

---

[21] Hermann Rauschning, op. cit., pp. 178, 275.
[22] Albert Speer, op. cit., p. 144.
[23] Guido Knopp: *Hitlers Krieger*, p. 30.
[24] Joachim Fest: *Hitler*, p. 453.
[25] Walter Kempowski: *Haben Sie Hitler gesehen?* pp. 188-89.
[26] Joseph Serpico: *Nuremberg*, p. 29.

no more than four Tiger tanks to oppose them, and that they didn't even have any petrol. Forster was determined not to hide his view of things and to represent to Hitler the entire disastrous reality of the situation. 'You can rely on it, I will tell him everything, even at the risk of his throwing me out'. How great was my surprise when he came out of his interview with Hitler a totally changed man. 'The Führer has promised me new divisions for Danzig', he said. Seeing my sceptical smile, he added: 'Of course, I wouldn't know where he can find them. But he has told me he will save Danzig, and so the matter is beyond any doubt' ... Undoubtedly it was Hitler's fatal suggestive power that had worked upon him."[27]

These men were capable and powerful warlords, commanding the best trained and equipped armies and clusters of armies in the world. Hitler's initial successes raised them for a while to the zenith of their mastery and self-satisfaction. Yet, that in the presence of Hitler they became as obedient as his shepherd dog is a fact, intriguing and unexplained. Ulrich de Maizière, a general staff officer, testified: "A difficult to describe demonic power emanated from Hitler, and few were able not to fall under his spell. It was an influence which affected all soldiers in the same way and which is difficult to understand if one has not experienced it oneself". Young officers at the front, whom Hitler had called and who were decided to report to him how catastrophic the situation at the front was, left his headquarters saying: "This is a terrific man." The supreme commander of the *Heeresgruppe Mitte* [the middle one of the three army groups invading Russia and initially aimed at Moscow], Field Marshal von Kluge, had disagreed with Hitler on the phone using very harsh words. He was called to the Führer headquarters, where all responsible persons told him he must make clear to Hitler how bad the situation at the front was. After an hour Kluge came out from the conference room and said: "Hitler is right. I will try again."[28]

---

[27]JP Stern: *Hitler – The Führer and the People*, p. 52.
[28]Id., p. 245.

"I was not the only one to succumb to Hitler's strange fascination", writes Speer. "So did statesmen of importance, men like Hindenburg, Simon [British Foreign Secretary], Lloyd George [British statesman], Mussolini, and many others".[29] Famous among those others were the American aviator Charles Lindbergh; the Duke of Windsor, who could have caused serious complications if he had remained on the throne as Edward VIII; the Swedish explorer Sven Hedin; and Unity Mitford, daughter of Lord Redesdale, who had a crush on Hitler, loved to parade in Munich as a Nazi, and tried to commit suicide there in the English Garden when war erupted between her country and Germany. It should be mentioned however that Hitler's 'magnetism' had its effect not only on individuals but also on audiences and crowds of thousands, which he was able to bring to an ecstatic frenzy, and on the German nation as a whole. "The Führer has charged the entire nation as if it were a storage battery", noted Goebbels in his diary; and Trevor-Roper writes: "It was a spell wherewith the whole German people had been bewitched".[30]

George Ball, who was one of the interrogators of the Nazi bonzes under trial at Nuremberg, said to Speer: "From the point of most of us, what is most baffling of all is the constant references to the charisma or mystique or particular charm of Hitler. From the point of view of anyone in my country, or I think in Great Britain, who had the experience of seeing motion pictures of Hitler or of hearing him on the radio, and of reading the things he wrote, it was totally incomprehensible. How could anyone find a particular charm in this man? How do you explain it? This is the ultimate mystery, I think, as far as we are concerned."

"It is only explicable", Speer replied, "if you agree that there are human beings who have a kind of magnetism or hypnotic quality.

---

[29] lbert Speer, op. cit., p. 188.
[30] HR Trevor-Roper, op. cit., p. 171.

You try to evade this influence, get away from its effect, but you are in their ... you are ... you depend on him". According to Sereny, Speer wanted to translate the word *hörig*, which literally means 'enslaved' or 'in bondage', but did not find the English equivalent. "Ball suggested that perhaps just the effect of power could explain charisma, and Speer agreed that power exerted its own mystique. But he said that what had always puzzled him was how Hitler's effect on his environment had functioned just as effectively before 1933, when there was [political] defeat upon defeat and crisis upon crisis and yet he succeeded, almost entirely by force of personality. " 'It is a mystery', Speer said. 'But the fact is that it is impossible to explain Germany before 1933, and from 1933 to 1945, without Hitler. He was the centre of it all and always remained the centre'."[31]

Hugh Trevor-Roper, serving as a military intelligence officer, had been the first to examine a mass of authentic documents in order to write his report *The Last Days of Hitler*. Although in the course of time he had become Regius Professor of Modern History at Oxford, he had in the middle 1990s the courage to admit to Ron Rosenbaum: "Hitler certainly had an extraordinary power. It didn't work on everybody: it didn't work – to put it crudely – on the aristocrats or people who were sensitive to the vulgarity of his behaviour or surroundings. But when he wanted to mesmerize, he did have the wherewithal". "In the course of his research", Rosenbaum comments, "Trevor-Roper was surprised at the extent to which the Hitler spell still held sway even after ignominious defeat".[32]

"What Trevor-Roper sought to do in *The Last Days* was to describe the spell as an inescapable fact of any account of Hitler's life", continues Rosenbaum. "He does not try to explain it so much as evoke it. And yet by invoking it so eloquently, he came to be accused of perpetrating, indeed of falling under, the spell, of giving

---

[31] Gitta Sereny, op. cit., p. 137.
[32] Ron Rosenbaum, op. cit., p. 65.

it, giving the Hitler myth, a posthumous life."[33] In *The Last Days of Hitler*, one of the first, most famous and influential post-war Hitler books, Trevor-Roper states outright: "The power of the Führer was a magic power".[34] Similarly, in *The Face of the Third Reich* Fest writes: "... The character of Hitler's compulsive power over men's minds can only be understood in religious terms".[35] – How could there ever be an understanding of Hitler without an explanation of his powers? But, also, which established historian would take the risk to use religious terms or concepts for the explanation of a historical phenomenon?

Blue eyes

Hitler's hypnotic effect on certain individuals 'must be accepted as a fact', writes Konrad Heiden.[36] "It was a magnetic fluid he was using", asserts one of Kempowski's eyewitnesses. "The people were fascinated. It was a kind of hypnosis ... no independent judgment was possible anymore ... Nowadays there's nobody who still believes this."[37] It is indeed noteworthy that there is a fundamental difference between the testimonies of the direct witnesses and the reflections of the people in later years who know about Hitler only from hearsay or from reading about him. Guido Knopp, aware of this difference, reminds us: "Numerous are the contemporary witnesses who report that Hitler effectively must have had a hypnotic power at his command to impose his will on others, also in the private sphere."[38]

Laurence Rees gives the example of one Fridolin von Spaun, remembering an encounter with Hitler at a Party dinner. "Suddenly

---

[33]Ibid.
[34]HR Trevor-Roper, op. cit., p. 202.
[35]Joachim Fest: *The Face of the Third Reich*, p. 446.
[36]Konrad Heiden, op. cit., p. 292.
[37]Walter Kempowski, op. cit., p. 71.
[38]Guido Knopp, *Hitler – Eine Bilanz*, p. 149.

I noticed Hitler's eyes resting on me. So I looked up. And that was one of the most curious moments in my life. He didn't look at me suspiciously, but I felt that he was searching me somehow ... It was hard for me to sustain this look for so long. But I thought: 'I mustn't avert my eyes, or he may think I've something to hide'. And then something happened which only psychologists can judge. The gaze, which at first rested completely on me, suddenly went straight through me into the unknown distance. It was so unusual. And the long gaze which he had given me convinced me completely that he was a man with honourable intentions. Most people nowadays would not believe this. They'd say I am getting old and childish, but that's untrue. He was a wonderful phenomenon."

"Hitler had a similar effect on many others", writes Rees, and he mentions the experience of a fourteen-year-old girl who was allowed to shake Hitler's hand. "He came. Everything got quiet. And we were so excited, I felt my heart up here in my throat. And when he came to me I nearly forgot to give him my hand; I just looked at him and I saw good eyes. And in my heart I promised him: 'I always will be faithful to you because you are a good man'. That was in a dream-like time. And later I kept my promise."[39]

"It was the eyes that dominated the otherwise common face", writes William Shirer. "They were hypnotic. Piercing. Penetrating. As far as I could tell they were light blue, but the colour was not the thing you noticed. What hit you at once was their power. They stared at you. They stared through you. They seemed to immobilize the person on whom they were directed, frightening some and fascinating others, especially women, but dominating them in any case ... All through the days at Nuremberg I would observe hardened Party leaders, who had spent years in the company of Hitler, freeze as he paused to talk to one or the other of them, hypnotized by his penetrating glare. I thought at first that only Germans reacted

---

[39]Laurence Rees, op. cit., pp. 29, 89.

in this manner. But one day at a reception for foreign diplomats I noticed one envoy after another apparently succumbing to the famous eyes."[40]

A colonel who accompanied General von Kluge to meet Hitler before the war remembers how Hitler shook the hand of everybody present: "It was impressive. He had very big, deep blue, very dark blue eyes, the kind of eyes Frederick the Great too must have had. With his dark blue eyes he looked at the people, and they were so to speak hypnotized, like a frog by a snake ..."[41] Deep blue? Dark blue? The colour of Hitler's eyes according to the impressions of witnesses covers a scale from 'watery grey' and 'cold fish eyes' over 'dull grey' (François-Poncet) to the colonel's 'deep blue', 'bright blue' and Goebbels' 'marvellous blue – like stars'.

Even in the last days of Hitler's existence and that of his Reich, "the fascination of the eyes, which had bewitched so many seemingly sober men – which had exhausted Speer, and baffled Rauschning, and seduced Stumpfegger, and convinced an industrialist that [Hitler] had direct telepathic communication with the Almighty – had not deserted them. It was useless for his enemies to complain that they were really repellent. 'They are neither deep nor blue', protested Rauschning; 'his look is staring or dead, and lacks the brilliance and sparkle of genuine animation'; nevertheless, in spite of his explanations and evasions, Rauschning had to admit, what Speer freely confesses and thousands of less critical Germans (and not only Germans) too eloquently witness, that Hitler had the eyes of a hypnotist which seduced the wits and affections of all who yielded to their power. Even his doctors, and the most critical of them, admit the fascination of those dull, blue-grey eyes which compensated for all the coarseness in his other features ..." (HR Trevor-roper[42])

---

[40] Williamn Shirer: *The Nightmare Years*, p. 129.
[41] Walter Kempowski, op. cit., p. 138.
[42] HR Trevor-Roper, op. cit., p. 116.

"When the man looked at you, it went straight through you", said a teacher to Kempowski. "He looked every single person in the eye", said another teacher.[43] Hans Frühwirt had been chosen by his co-workers to participate in a parade before the Führer and was 'mighty proud of it'. "When we marched past Hitler and turned our heads towards him, something strange happened: I had the impression that Hitler looked me personally straight into the eyes. When I think of it, I still feel the shivers running down my spine. That moment moved me to the core. And all my comrades told me afterwards that they had had exactly the same experience."[44] Was Hitler himself aware of this? In one of his monologues he complained: "What is most strenuous is having to stand there for hours during a march-past. It already happened a couple of times that I felt dizzy. One has no idea how painful it is having to stand there for so long without bending the knees. I need protection from the sun. Last time I already made the greeting with the outstretched arm more tolerable". And then he added: "But I am used – for all those men turn their heads towards me – to look every one in the eyes."[45]

One such occasion, paid little attention in the literature although it happened at one of the crucial points in Hitler's career, requires a short historical introduction. The SA was the National Socialist Party's army, but it became also more and more the Party's burden, especially when its ranks swelled to nearly half a million after the crash of 1929 with the subsequent unemployment (three million unemployed in 1931, to culminate at six to seven million). What most of the SA expected from the NSDAP was jobs and bread, the basic socialist demands, in contradiction to Hitler's 'socialism' which meant something like the self-sacrifice and integration of the whole nation into one regimented body. The National Socialist Party therefore remained ideologically divided between its political and military wing.

---

[43]Walter Kempowski, op. cit., pp. 60, 152.
[44]Guido Knopp, op. cit., p. 90.
[45]*Monologe im Führerhauptquartier*, p. 225.

Moreover, several of the NSDAP leaders had started as convinced 'classical' socialists, interpreting the second adjective in the Party's name as a programme and a promise. Goebbels was one of them, as was his first NSDAP boss, Gregor Strasser, and still more Gregor's brother Otto. When Hitler increasingly sought support from the captains of German industry, needing their money, the socialist element in the Party accused him of becoming bourgeois and betraying the Party programme; they even went so far as to demand his resignation. This inner tension would be resolved only in 1934 by the murderously surgical Night of the Long Knives.

One occasion on which the conflict came into the open was the Stennes Revolt in 1930-31. Hugo Stennes was the regional SA chief in Berlin, where Goebbels was the gauleiter. In the German capital the National Socialist discord was still aggravated by the disdain of the 'cultured' North Germans for the 'boorish', beer-drinking and sausage-eating Bavarians, including the clique around Hitler in Munich. When Hitler held on to his gradual, legal way of coming to power, and the SA in North Germany demanded the instant socialist revolution, a rebellion erupted. The SA attacked the Party headquarters and the offices of the Party organ, Goebbels' *Der Angriff*, and Hitler was requested to step down as Party leader. Hitler won the direct confrontation thanks to his decisiveness and the support of the SS who, faithful to their oath, stood as one man behind him. (The rise of the SS in the Third Reich dates from this crisis.) Stennes and the rebellious SA commanders were replaced by loyal Hitlerites. The day would come that Stennes too had to run for his life. (He ran as far as China, where he became the commander of Chiang Kai-shek's bodyguard.)

Then, on 16 April 1931 Hitler held a roll call of the SA in the Berlin Sports Palace. Present there was the still unknown Albert Speer. "Silently we stood, hour after hour. Then Hitler arrived with a small retinue. From a great distance I heard the groups of those who had lined up being reported to him. But instead of going to the speaker's platform, as we all expected him to do, Hitler entered the ranks of the uniformed men. A breathless silence ensued. Then he began pacing off the columns. In that vast bowl, only those few footsteps could be heard. It went on for hours. At last he came to my row. His eyes were fixed rigidly upon the squadron; he seemed to want to take a vow from each man by his look. When he came to me, I had the feeling that a pair of staring eyes had taken possession of me for an immeasurable period of time. One element that impressed me was the fact that Hitler had the courage to walk without protection through the ranks of these SA men who had rebelled against him only days before. In vain I try to explain to myself today how Hitler could exert this psychological power for hours on end."[46]

The following two stanzas are from a volume of poems written by anonymous members of the Austrian Hitler Youth. "Even when a thousand people stand before you,/each one feels your gaze for himself/and thinks this must be the great moment for him,/and you will look deep into his soul ... For nobody has left you empty-handed/even if the ray from your eyes touched him only once;/we know that in each case you make us feel:/'I am with you – and you belong to me'."[47]

'A little guy yelled himself into a fit'

"The force which has ever and always set in motion great historical avalanches of religious and political movements is the magic power of the spoken word", wrote Hitler in *Mein Kampf*. "The broad masses of a population are more amenable to the appeal of rhetoric than any other force. All great movements are popular movements. They are the volcanic eruptions of human passions and emotions, stirred into activity by the ruthless Goddess of Distress or by the torch of the spoken word cast into the midst of the people."

---

[46] Albert Speer, op. cit., pp. 85-86.
[47] Günter Scholdt, op. cit., p. 101.

Who, then, was the ideal promulgator of the spoken word? "Among a hundred men who call themselves orators today there are scarcely ten who are capable of speaking with effect before an audience of street-sweepers, locksmiths and navvies, and expound the same subject with equal effect tomorrow before an audience of university professors and students. Among a thousand public speakers there may be only one who can speak before a composite audience of locksmiths and professors in the same hall, in such a way that his statements can be fully comprehended by each group while at the same time he effectively influences both and awakens enthusiasm, on the one side as well as on the other, to hearty applause."[48] This one in a thousand was Hitler himself, of course, and however boastful his claim, it was not untrue, as we know from witnesses who had heard him talk to professors and locksmiths, and to both kinds of people in the same audience.

"Even his greatest opponents concede that Hitler is the greatest orator that Germany has ever known. This is a great concession in view of the fact that the qualities of his voice are far from pleasant – many, in fact, find it distinctly unpleasant. It has a rasping quality that often breaks into a shrill falsetto when he becomes aroused. Nor is it his diction that makes him a great orator. In the early days this was particularly bad. It was a mixture of High German with an Austrian dialect. Nor was it the structure of his speeches that made him a great orator. On the whole, his speeches were sinfully long, badly structured, and very repetitious. Some of them are positively painful to read, but, nevertheless, when he delivered them they had an extraordinary effect upon his audiences."[49]

Hitler had a refined feeling of his public, with whom he was able to enter into a kind of occult communication. Even an implacable opponent like Otto Strasser had to concede: "This man, like a sensitive membrane, has found the way, thanks to an intuition which

---

[48] Adolf Hitler: *Mein Kampf*, pp. 100, 287.
[49] Walter Langer, op. cit., pp. 44-45.

could not be replaced by intellectual capacities, to become the mouthpiece of the most secret desires, the darkest instincts, the suffering and the inner restiveness of a people ... I have been asked so often what is the secret of Hitler's extraordinary talent as an orator. I cannot explain it in any other way than by saying that it is an indefinable intuition which provides him with the infallible diagnosis of the dissatisfaction from which his audiences are suffering. When he tries to underpin his speeches with learned theories, he hardly rises above a poor average. But when he throws away all crutches, when he storms ahead and speaks out what the spirit inspires into him, then he changes straight away into one of the greatest orators of the century."[50]

"This fiery oratory was something new to the Germans and particularly to the slow-tongued, lower-class Bavarians. In Munich his shouting and gesturing were a spectacle men paid to see. It was not his fiery oratory, however, that won the crowds to his cause. This was certainly something new, but far more important was the seriousness with which his words were spoken", writes Langer. He quotes Kurt Lüdecke: "Every one of his words comes out charged with a powerful current of energy; at times it seems as if they are torn from the very heart of the man, causing him indescribable anguish." And then Langer quotes Otto Strasser again: "Hitler's tongue was like a lash that whipped up the emotions of his audience. And somehow he always managed to say what the majority of the audience were already thinking but could not verbalize. When the audience began to respond, it affected him in return. Before long, due to this reciprocal relationship, he and his audience became intoxicated with the emotional appeal of his oratory."[51]

Another talent of Hitler's was that of the showman 'with a great sense of the dramatic', inborn in him and developed through his love and close contact with the theatre during the several hundreds of

---

[50] Ralf Georg Reuth: *Hitler*, p. 122.
[51] Walter Langer, op. cit., pp. 47, 48.

opera performances he had seen. August Kubizek, the only close friend Hitler had in Linz and Vienna, writes: "Hitler found a natural joy in the theatre and had a passion for it ... There is no doubt that my friend Adolf was talented as an orator from his earliest youth. He liked to speak and did so all the time ... He surely possessed great theatrical talent which, together with his oratorical talent, he knew how to use admirably".[52] Kershaw calls Hitler 'a consummate actor'; Fest asserts that 'fundamentally he was a theatrical person' who had the feeling that he was always acting on a stage; and Hitler, only half in jest, proclaimed: "I am the greatest actor in Europe", verily keeping everybody spellbound by his performance.

It was this sense for the theatrical effect which made Hitler one of the foremost stage directors, although he is seldom appreciated as such. (See eg. Frederic Spotts recent study: *Hitler and the Power of Aesthetics*.) What lives on in the memory and the nightmares of humanity as the outward pageantry of Nazism – the symbols, the uniforms, the rituals and mass manifestations – was all his doing. "Each detail was tremendously important to Hitler. Even in the festivals with their vast blocks of humanity he personally checked seemingly trivial points. He approved every scene, every movement, as he did the selection of flags and flowers. Significantly, Hitler's talents as a theatrical director reached their summit when the object of celebration was death ... He also had a distinct preference for nocturnal backdrops. Torches, pyres or flaming wheels were continually kindled. Though such rituals were supposed to be highly positive and inspirational, in fact they struck another note, stirring apocalyptic associations and awakening a fear of universal conflagration or doom, including each individual's own."[53]

Hitler saw himself as a tamer and leader of masses, a tribune in the literal sense. He despised but needed the masses, for they embodied

---

[52] August Kubizek: *Adolf Hitler, mein Jugendfreund*, pp. 80, 29, 30.
[53] Joachim Fest: *Hitler*, pp. 512-13.

his movement. "The mass has a simple thought and experiential scheme", he said. "What she cannot fit within [this scheme] makes her insecure. I can only dominate her if I take her laws of life into account. I have been reproached for the fact that I fanaticized the mass, that I arouse her into ecstasy. Clever heads are of the opinion that the mass should be calmed down and kept in dull apathy. No, gentlemen, exactly the contrary is true! I can only lead the mass when I awake her from her apathy. Only the fanaticized mass can be manipulated ... I have fanaticized the mass to turn her into an instrument of my politics. I have awakened the mass. I have lifted her above herself, I have given her a meaning and a function. I have been reproached of stirring up the lower instincts of the mass, but what I do is something different. When I present her with intellectual arguments, she does not understand me. When, however, I rouse in her the corresponding sensations, then she follows the simple commands which I give her. In a mass manifestation thinking is switched off. And as this is the condition I need, I see to it that everybody is sent to the manifestations where they become a part of the mass, whether they want it or not, the intellectuals and bourgeois together with the workers. I mix the people. I address them as a mass."[54]

"No doubt there was a deeper meaning to Hitler's frequent comparison of the masses to a woman. And we need only look at the corresponding pages in *Mein Kampf*, at the wholly erotic fervour that the idea and the image of the masses aroused in him, to see what he sought and found as he stood on the platform high above the masses filling the arena – his masses. Solitary, unable to make contact, he more and more craved such collective unions. In a revealing turn of phrase (if we may believe the source) he once called the masses 'his only bride'. His oratorical discharges were largely instinctual, and his audience, unnerved by prolonged distress and reduced to a

---

[54]Hermann Rauschning, op. cit., pp. 198-99.

few elemental needs, reacted on the same instinctual wave length. The sound recordings of the period clearly convey the peculiarly obscene, copulatory character of those mass meetings ... The writer René Schickele once spoke of Hitler's speeches as being 'like sex murders'. And many other contemporary observers have tried to describe the sensually charged liquescence of these demonstrations in the language of diabolism." (Joachim Fest[55])

The historian Karl Alexander von Müller had been one of the lecturers when candidate army propagandist Corporal Adolf Hitler attended the initiatory course at Munich University in 1919. He had followed Hitler's rise and sometimes met him in the Beckmann and Bechstein salons. In January 1923 he heard him speak in public for the first time. "How many public meetings had I already attended in this hall [of the Löwenbrau]. But neither during the war nor during the Revolution had I ever felt such a white-hot wave of mass excitement blast in my face the moment I entered ... Para-military maintainers of the order, a forest of glaring red banners with a black swastika, military and revolutionary elements, nationalist and socialist elements. In the audience mostly the struggling middle class in all its sections. For hours continual, booming march music; for hours short speeches by subordinates. When will *he* come? Has anything happened to hold him up? Nobody can describe the feverish state of suspense building up within this atmosphere. Suddenly movement at the entrance of the hall. Shouted commands. The speaker on the platform breaks off in the middle of a sentence. All leap to their feet, shouting *Heil!* And through the howling masses and the waving banners he comes with his retinue, he for whom all have been waiting. He strides rapidly up to the platform, right arm raised rigidly. He passed quite close by me, and I saw that this was a different person from the man I had met now and then in private houses."[56]

---

[55]Joachim Fest, op. cit., pp. 323-24.
[56]Anton Joachimsthaler: *Hitlers Weg begann in München 1913-1923*, p. 306.

The effect of Hitler the orator was like a bolt of lightning, striking the masses and many of the intellectuals mixed up with them. They had come to hear him out of curiosity and left totally convinced, converted, ready to dedicate their lives to that sweating man with the little moustache and the drooping forelock. After hearing Hitler for the first time Rudolf Hess sat smilingly staring into space, murmuring: "The Man! The Man!" Speer writes about Hitler's 'hypnotic power', his 'hypnotic persuasion', his 'magnetic force' which had "reached out to me the first time I heard him and had not thereafter released me". A substantial volume could be filled with such instant conversions. Kurt Lüdecke, for one, confesses: "Presently my critical faculty was swept away. I do not know how to describe the emotion that overwhelmed me as I heard this man. His words were like a scourge. When he spoke of the disgrace of Germany, I felt ready to jump on any enemy. His appeal to German manhood was like a call to arms, the gospel he preached the sacred truth. He seemed another Luther. I forgot everything but the man. Then, glancing around, I saw that this magnetism was holding these thousands as one ... The intense will of the man, the passion of his sincerity seemed to flow from him into me. I experienced an exaltation that could be likened to a religious experience".[57]

And there is the testimony of Leni Riefenstahl, the renowned film maker and photographer, who died recently at the age of 101. She went to hear Hitler for the first time in 1932. To Gitta Sereny she confided: "I noticed how emotional people became when they spoke for or against Hitler, so I got interested and I went to hear him. Well, it was like being struck by lightning".[58] Elsewhere she described that moment as follows: "That very same instant I had an apocalyptic vision that I was never able to forget. It seemed as if the earth's surface were spreading out in front of me, like a hemisphere that suddenly splits apart in the middle, spewing out an enormous

---

[57] Fritz Redlich: *Hitler – Diagnosis of a Destructive Prophet*, p. 52.
[58] Gitta Sereny: *The German Trauma*, p. 240.

jet of water so powerful that it touched the sky and shook the earth. I felt as if I were paralyzed. Although there was a great deal in this speech that I didn't understand, I was still fascinated and I sensed that the audience was in bondage to this man."[59]

In his autobiographical novel *Michael*, Doctor Joseph Goebbels recounted his moment of illumination. "I go, no, I am impelled to go to the rostrum. There I stand for a long time and look this One in the face. This is not an orator. This is a prophet! Sweat pours down from his forehead. In the greyish, pale visage sparkle the eyes like two brilliant stars. His fists are clenched. Word after word and sentence after sentence thunder forth as on Judgment Day. I know no longer what I am doing. It is as if I have lost my senses ... The man looks down at me for a moment. The gaze of his blue eyes hits me like a ray of fire ... Now I know where my road is leading, the road of maturity. I don't hear anything anymore. I am as it were intoxicated ... I put my hand into the warm, pulsating hand of a man. That was a vow for life. And my eyes sank deep into two big, blue stars."[60]

'Near-ultimate evil'

"During the post-war trials of the International Military Tribunal at Nuremberg, material relating to the influence of esoteric thought on National Socialism and the Nazi hierarchy was deliberately suppressed, and has been lost to the record", write Michael Baigent and Richard Leigh. "According to one of the British prosecutors, the late Airey Neave, large bodies of existing evidence were too bizarre to be admitted; they would have permitted too many high-ranking Nazi Party members to plead insanity and thereby escape retribution on grounds of diminished responsibility ... So flagrant an eruption of the irrational as the Third Reich represented was uncomfortable,

---

[59] Fritz Redlich, op. cit., p. 79.
[60] Claus Ekkehard Bärsch: *Der junge Goebbels*, pp. 186-87.

disturbing and potentially dangerous. For the world to be made aware of the sheer potency of the irrational, on so awesome a collective level, would have been to open a Pandora's Box of incipient ills for the future. And it would have been profoundly unsettling, for citizens of both the Western democracies and the Soviet Union, to confront too blatantly what precisely they had been up against ...

"In consequence, for a generation of post-war historians and commentators, the role of esotericism in the rise of Nazi-Germany was never accorded the attention it deserved. Instead of being assessed and explored as what it was, the religious dimension of National Socialism was nervously dismissed by such facile formulations as 'mass madness', 'mass hysteria' and 'mass hypnosis', and then subordinated to theories of economics, sociology and so-called political science. A few novelists attempted to address the matter honestly". Baigent and Leigh mention by name Thomas Mann, Hermann Broch, Michel Tournier and George Steiner. "But historians chose deliberately to ignore the entire issue for more than twenty years. When it was finally acknowledged, it was acknowledged by 'fringe' historians, who, with dubious 'facts' and luridly spurious theories, swung the pendulum wildly in the opposite direction."[61]

Günter Scholdt, who wrote a voluminous book about authors who were Hitler's contemporaries, is impressed by the number of them who saw an 'abysmal evil' in his person and his actions, and who used words like 'Satan', 'demon' and 'demonic' to characterise him. To mention a few: Konrad Heiden writes about 'the abysmal force' that was in Hitler, 'the demon, disguised as an unknown soldier from the Vienna lodging-house'. Emil Fackenheim, a 'theologian of the Holocaust', calls Hitler's reign 'a radical evil', 'an eruption of demonism in history'. To William Shirer, Hitler was 'a person of undoubted, if evil, genius', 'possessed of a demonic personality', 'the demonic dictator'.

---

[61]Michael Baigent and Richard Leigh: *Secret Germany*, pp. 240-41.

In an interview with Ron Rosenbaum, Alan Bullock exclaimed: "If *he* isn't evil, who is? ... If he isn't evil, then the word has no meaning." To Yehuda Bauer, "widely regarded as the most authoritative historian of the holocaust", Hitler represents 'near-ultimate evil'. Sebastian Haffner calls Hitler 'a truly evil man' and writes about 'the enormous evil in him'. Ambassador François-Poncet is of the opinion that Hitler was 'a man driven to the extreme by a demon'. The historian Milton Himmelfarb says: "I don't think that Hitler was a statesman. I don't think that Hitler was an accidental agent. I think he was an evil man, an evil genius". In Gitta Sereny we find: "Hitler's evil, I believe, went far even beyond this madness", by which she means the Holocaust. And Trevor-Roper too writes about 'that demonic character', 'that demonic and disastrous genius'.

Then there are also the persons who have a direct experience to tell. Admiral Karl Dönitz said: "Hitler was a demon". General Franz Halder stated: "I never found genius in him, only the diabolical". SS-general Walter Schellenberg wrote in his memoirs: "Hitler was ruled by the demonic forces driving him ..." Ulrich de Maizière, general staff officer: "From Hitler emanated a demonic influence which is hard to describe, but against which few people could protect themselves". Hjalmar Schacht, who made Nazi Germany's economic recovery possible, professed after the war: "Hitler was a genius, but an evil genius". And so on.

The list of the human instruments of 'the evil genius' at the top is long, although most have remained anonymous to the public or had names which faded in the public memory. There were not only Hermann Göring, Heinrich Himmler, Joseph Goebbels and Martin Bormann. There was Reinhard Heydrich, the epitome of 'the Blond Beast', whose name may still evoke some vague associations, as may the names of Rudolf Höss, commandant of Auschwitz, Adolf Eichmann and Amon Göth, the camp commandant in *Schindler's List*. But who knows the name of Theodor Eicke, the commandant of Dachau who founded the *SS-Totenköpfe*, the camp guards, and invented the inhuman regimen of the concentration camps? Or

Odilo Globocnik, amiably called 'Globus' by Himmler and charged by him with building the extermination camps in Poland? Or Hans Kammler, 'technocrat of annihilation' and commandant of that suburb of hell which was *Mittelkampf Dora*, where the V-2s were built? Or the commanders of the *Einsatzgruppen* in Russia – Walter Ohlendorff, Arthur Nebe, Friedrich Jeckeln ... — who performed such an effective job of slaughtering Jews and non-Jews alike in their tens of thousands?

Evil unexplained

In the preface to his Hitler biography, Ian Kershaw writes peremptorily: "To call Hitler evil may well be true and morally satisfying. But it explains nothing".[62] This statement throws some light on the confusion about the meaning of evil in modern Western civilisation. Kershaw, an established historian, seems to feel obliged to follow the latest and for a while dominating trend among the historians of his time which leans heavily on the French philosophic school of structuralism, in some of its variants known as functionalism. Structuralism integrates the individual personality into the underlying structures of the historical event, to the point of disappearance of the individual. The interweaving strands of the structure determine the event, including the individuals who are part of it, in the same way as the structures of the human body determine the individual cells and types of cells. The final conclusion is then that there is nothing to explain, that things are what they are.

Philosophical fashions come and go like other fashions, looking much less impressive when left deflated by the wayside than when floating, like colourful balloons, on the air currents of the moment. Carl Gustav Jung's explanation of Hitler, some sixty years before Kershaw's, was a very different one. "Hitler belongs in the category

---

[62] Ian Kershaw: *Hitler – 1889-1936 Hubris*, p. xvii.

of the truly mystic medicine men. Hitler's power is not political, it is magic", he said. According to Jung, Hitler's secret was that he allowed himself to be moved by his own unconscious. He was like a man who listens intently to whispered suggestions from a mysterious voice and "then *acts upon them*. In our case, even if occasionally our unconscious does reach us through our dreams, we have too much rationality, too much cerebrum to obey it – but Hitler listens and obeys. The true leader is always *led*".[63]

Are so many testimonies by honest and intelligent witnesses to be disbelieved because they do not fit within the framework of post factum theories with 'too much cerebrum', or because the current philosophical and religious interpretations of the world have no room for them? "Hitler abandoned himself to forces which pulled him along – forces of dark and destructive violence", writes Rauschning. "When he still thought that he had the free choice to decide, he already had surrendered to a kind of magic which one might call, on safe grounds and not only as a metaphor, demonic magic. And instead of a man who, while step by step climbing upwards, got rid of the dregs of a dark past and became more free and purified, one saw a being that became more and more possessed, at every step more tied down, subservient, powerless, the prey of forces which held him in their grip and did not let go of him anymore ... He chose the easier way; he let himself slide down; he abandoned himself to powers who pulled him into the pit."[64]

Another cultured and close observer of Hitler was the French ambassador André François-Poncet. He titles the last chapter of his ambassadorial memoirs '*Hitler, le possédé*', (Hitler, a man possessed). François-Poncet too describes the contrast between the Hitler in the 'neutral' mode and the same man when 'exalted'. "At the beginning of the conversation it was as if he did not listen or understand; he remained indifferent and as it were amorphous. What one saw was

---

[63] In John Toland: *Adolf Hitler*, p. 282 (emphasis in the text).
[64] Hermann Rauschning, op. cit., pp. 202-03.

a man absorbed for hours in a strange contemplation ... Then, all at once, as if a button had been pushed, he launched into an impetuous speech, speaking at a high pitch, passionately, furiously. His arguments succeeded one another, faster, more numerous, strident, expelled by a raw voice with rolling r's ... He shouted, he thundered as if he were addressing a crowd of thousands. It was the orator who had awoken, the great orator in the Latin tradition, the tribune ... And suddenly the flow stopped. Hitler became silent; he seemed exhausted; it looked as if he had emptied his batteries; he fell again in a kind of distraction and became inert." François-Poncet also writes that people of Hitler's entourage were talking about his crises "which went from devastating force to the plaintive sighs of a wounded animal ... What is certain is that he was not normal. He was a morbid man, almost demented, a personage from Dostoyevsky, one of the 'possessed'".[65]

Hermann Rauschning also writes, in the controversial last chapter of his *Talks with Hitler*: 'This man was not normal'. To Rauschning also somebody 'from Hitler's closest entourage' had told about his crises. "During the night he awakes with spasms of screaming. He shouts for help. Sitting on the edge of his bed he looks as if he were paralyzed. He is in the grip of a panic which makes him tremble so violently that the bed shakes. He utters confused and incomprehensible words. He gasps for breath as if he were going to choke. The same person narrated to me", recalls Rauschning, "a scene which I would not believe if it did not come from this source. Hitler was standing in the room, swaying, looking around in bewilderment. 'It's him! It's him! He has come here!' he groaned. His lips were blue. Sweat dripped from his face. Suddenly he started pronouncing numbers without any meaning, then unrelated words and snippets of sentences ... Then he stood still again, his lips moving. He was rubbed dry and given something to drink. But

---

[65] André François-Poncet: *Souvenirs d'une ambassade à Berlin*, pp. 351-52.

suddenly he yelled: 'There! There! In the corner! Who stands there?' He stamped on the floor and raged in the way he uses to. We showed him that there was nothing unusual there and he grew gradually quiet. Afterwards he slept for many hours. And then he was again bearable for some time."[66]

The novelist Joseph Roth wrote in his diary: "People have not yet understood, not even today, that National Socialism is not a political but an infernal movement. It cannot change its intentions because from the first only *one* intention was instilled into it according to the unfathomable will of the Eternal: the intention to destroy. The man [i.e. Hitler] is one of the hundred thousand tails of Satan, the scourges of God. Every word from his mouth is spoken by the tongue of Lucifer personally. That the metaphysical thinkers have not yet understood this, even today, but remain caught, imprisoned, limited, confined and incarcerated within the cheap traditional concepts of a rationalistically politicizing world, this is abundant proof of a Christian un-Christian tepidity. A Christian who does not feel the Devil can hardly understand God."[67]

In November 1941 the German troops advanced up to less than fifty kilometres from Moscow, the suburbs of which some of them could see through their binoculars, but temperatures of minus 30° Celsius and a complete breakdown of the maintenance of the troops brought the advance to a standstill. Moscow would never be taken. This failure, together with Hitler's baffling declaration of war with the United States of America, on 11 December, marked the turning point of the war in Europe. A frustrated Hitler blamed the turn of events on his generals, accusing them of a lack of faith – *Glaube* – in Nazism and its Führer, and took upon himself the responsibility of supreme commander of the German armed forces. The official communiqué by which the people were informed of this decision mentioned "the will and sense of responsibility, together with *an*

---

[66]Hermann Rauschning, op. cit., pp. 272-73.
[67]In Günter Scholdt, op. cit., p. 188.

inner vocation, which had induced the statesman Adolf Hitler to be his own warlord", and the intention of Hitler 'to reserve for himself all essential military decisions' in which he would *'follow his intuitions'*.

Thomas Mann, in exile in the USA, used the communiqué immediately for one of his radio broadcasts to Germany. He said about Hitler: "The monster, torn apart by his evil doings, went to Berchtesgaden to recuperate and there, in the reinvigorating mountain air, soon recovered the faith in his mission; he was quickly cured from his madness. Time and again the communiqué mentions his intuitions, his inner voices, his secret invocations; his neurologists have not been able to prevent this. Something equally romantic has not been seen since the Maid of Orléans ..."[68] This polemic outburst was not solely the fruit of Mann's imagination, for even in those days Hitler's sudden withdrawals to his villa 'Berghof' on the Obersalzberg and his reliance on his intuition and inner inspirations were known to many.

There is no doubt that Hitler's decisions, at least at the most important moments, were dictated by what commentators call his 'intuition', 'voice' or 'voices', 'sixth sense', or 'inspiration', depending on their view of things. He himself said to Rauschning: "No matter what you do: if it is not ripe, you won't be able to do it. That's what I, as an artist, know very well. And I know it also as a statesman. [If something is not ripe] the only thing one can do is remain patient, postpone, reconsider, postpone again. That goes then on working in the subconscious. It matures. Sometimes it fades away. If I don't have the inner, unmistakable certitude 'this is the solution, this is how it should be', I don't act. Even when the whole Party shouts at me 'do something!' I do nothing. I wait, whatever happens. *But when the voice speaks*, then I know 'this is it, it is time to act'."[69]

---

[68] Thomas Mann: *Deutschland und die Deutschen*, pp. 367-68 (emphasis added), 172-74.
[69] Hermann Rauschning, op. cit., p. 170 (emphasis added).

Walter Langer gathered the following information from his sources: "Although Hitler tries to present himself as a very decisive individual who never hesitates when he is confronted by a difficult situation, he is usually far from it. It is at just these times that his procrastination becomes most marked. At such times it is almost impossible to get him to take action on anything. He stays very much by himself and is frequently almost inaccessible to his immediate staff. He often becomes depressed, is in bad humour, talks little, and prefers to read a book, look at movies, or play with architectural models. According to the Dutch report his hesitation to act is not due to divergent views among his advisers. At such time he seldom pays very much attention to them and prefers not to discuss the matter …

"On some occasions he has been known to leave Berlin without a word and go to Berchtesgaden, where he spends his time walking in the mountains entirely by himself … It is during these periods of inactivity that Hitler is waiting for his 'inner voice' to guide him. He does not think the problem through in a normal way but waits until the solution is presented to him … As soon as he has the solution to a problem his mood changes very radically. He is again the Führer … 'He is very cheerful, jokes all the time and does not give anybody an opportunity to speak, while he himself makes fun of everybody.' This mood lasts throughout the period when necessary work has to be done. As soon as the requisite orders have been given to put the plan into execution, however, Hitler seems to lose interest in it. He becomes perfectly calm, occupies himself with other matters, and sleeps unusually long hours."[70]

Once the voice had been heard and the decision taken, it was unalterable and nobody could change, influence or even question it. This applied to particular decisions as well as to the inspiration at the origin of Hitler's 'mission'. "It seems to me that Hitler's plans

---

[70]Walter Langer, op. cit., p. 72.

and aims never changed." (Speer) "One cannot overlook the remarkable degree of consistency between Hitler's declared aims in the 1920s and the course of Nazi policy after 1933." (Geoffrey Stoakes) "From the very start of his political activity ... he could alter only the variations on the central themes but could not change the basic messages." (Stanley Gonen) Hanfstängl writes about 'the extraordinary tenacity of his ideas', JP Stern about his 'unusual consistency of purpose', and Kershaw about "his idée fixes which, in the principal points, remained unchanged up to his death in 1945".

On the mountain

The place of preference where Hitler went to receive his inspirations was his villa on a mountain in the Bavarian Alps, the Obersalzberg, just above Berchtesgaden and very near to Salzburg.* Hitler had discovered Berchtesgaden in 1922 through – whom else? – Dietrich Eckart, who went there in hiding when he was wanted by the authorities for libellous writings in his anti-Semitic magazine *In Plain German*. Hitler too began taking to this wonderful region, dominated by the Watzmann and the Untersberg. (The fact that Berchtesgaden is practically on the Austrian border may have played a part in Hitler's appreciation; for during his climb to power he might have to flee before the German law at any moment. He became a German citizen only in 1932.) In 1925 he bought *Haus Wachenfeld*, supposedly with money from the Bechsteins, and rechristened it *Berghof*. "Prior to 1939 [and on several occasions afterwards] the turning points, the 'world-shocking decisions', were taken at Hitler's mountain retreat at Obersalzberg in the Bavarian Alps."[71]

---

*Salz means 'salt'. This mountainous region has been known for its salt mines since prehistoric times, and it was in these mines that the Nazis hid many art treasures of their booty. The name 'Hitler', also spelled 'Hiedler' or 'Hüttler' by his forebears, means *Salz-Hütter*, i.e. 'guardian of the salt'. (*Tischgespräche*, p. 13)
[71]Richard Overy: *Interrogations*, p. 105.

"He meditated there", writes François-Poncet, perhaps the only foreign dignitary, excepting Mussolini, for whom Hitler developed a liking. It was on the Obersalzberg, *auf dem Berg* (on the mountain) as his mountain retreat was referred to in Hitler's entourage, that he received the French ambassador on his last visit. Yet the meeting did not take place at the Berghof but at the *Kehlsteinhaus*, within walking distance of the villa. The Kehlsteinhaus was built for Hitler on the initiative and under the supervision of Martin Bormann, and the construction cost the life of many slave labourers. For the structure was built on top of the Kehlstein peak and could be reached only by a lift in a shaft of 110 metres, hewn out in the rock. The view through the large bay windows was breathtaking.

"On all sides the eye plunges, as it would from an airplane in flight, into an immense mountain panorama", relates François-Poncet. "At the foot of the semi-circular mountain range one perceives Salzburg and the surrounding villages, dominated as far as the eye can see by a horizon of mountain peaks, with forests and green meadows on their flanks. Close to the house, which seems suspended in the air, a steep wall of rock rises almost vertically. The whole, bathing in the twilight of an autumn day, is grandiose, primitive, almost hallucinatory. The visitor asks himself whether he is awake or dreaming. He would like to know where he happens to be standing. In the castle of Montsalvat, where the knights of the Graal were living ...?" This lyrical association with the knights of the Grail obtains a more concrete significance if one knows that, in one of his monologues, Hitler reminisces about François-Poncet's perfect German and his last visit 'at the *Gralsburg*', the Caste of the Gral, by which he meant the Kehlsteinhaus.

From the Berghof, Hitler had a splendid view of the Untersberg where, as legend has it, Charlemagne is sleeping till one day he will awake and do battle with the Antichrist to make a new Golden Age possible – or, if you prefer, to lead the German people to their glory. "There he sat", remembers Speer, "with his view of the Untersberg where, according to legend, the Emperor Charlemagne still sleeps, but will one day rise to restore the past glory of the German Empire. Hitler naturally appropriated the legend for himself. 'You see the Untersberg over there: it is no accident that I have my residence opposite it!' ... Hitler's stays 'on the mountain' provided him, as he often stressed, with the inner calm and assurance for his surprising decisions. He also composed his most important speeches there ... He let the content of his speeches or his thoughts ripen during these weeks of apparent idling until all what had accumulated poured out like a stream bursting its bounds upon followers and negotiators".[72]

"It is not only because of the beautiful landscape that I go on the mountain", said Hitler. "There the imagination becomes more active. I leave the trifles and trivialities behind me and can then discern what is best, what is the right thing to do, and what will succeed ... During the night I often gaze for hours from my bedroom at the mountains. Then things become clear ... For me the Obersalzberg has become something very special ... Yes, I have a close tie with this mountain ..."[73]

"Here, above the world, out of reach, thrones the German Führer", writes Rauschning. "It is his *Adlerhorst* (eagle's nest). Here he confronts eternity. Here he determines the course of his century ... Here, where nobody disturbs him, in his crystal house in the mountains, he promulgates his commands, like a god in the clouds. Here the information he needs has to be brought to him. From here he wants to reign ... He also loves the lonely walks. The mountain forests intoxicate him. These promenades are his sacred gestures, his prayer. He eyes the passing clouds, he listens to the mist dripping from the spruce trees. He hears voices. I have met him in this state. Then he recognizes nobody. He wants to be alone. There are times that he shuns people."[74]

---

[72] Albert Speer, op. cit., pp. 137, 139.
[73] *Monologe im Führerhauptquartier*, pp. 167, 204, 207.
[74] Hermann Rauschning, op. cit., pp. 246, 267, 277.

Rienzi

Normally one does not become a medium, one is born with the disposition. Are there any indications of occult occurrences in Hitler's life prior to the period to which the testimonies refer? One such event is well known in the literature, but never followed up in its far-reaching consequences. At the age of sixteen Hitler saw in Linz for the first time, and in the company of his friend August Kubizek, Wagner's opera *Rienzi*. Kubizek has related Hitler's reaction to this experience in detail. What renders it especially important is that Kubizek's narration was afterwards confirmed by Hitler himself.

Wagner's *Rienzi* is based on the life of Cola di Rienzo (1313-54), the tribune who wanted to restore the glory of a corrupt and decadent Rome at the time that the Popes were residing in Avignon. Born in a humble family, Cola di Rienzo, in 1347, took up the gauntlet with the noble families who were de facto rulers of the city and oppressed the lower classes. Cola's dream was the revival of the dignity and power of the former capital of the world. His ideal of a 'sacred' and unified Italy bordered on the sublime, for he seems to have wanted to initiate the third period in humanity's history, the Realm of the Spirit, as envisioned by Joachim of Fiore. At first the populace followed Rienzi (as he became known), who saw himself as a tribune like the leaders of the people in ancient Rome had been and consciously behaved like one. But when he began perorating about his higher speculations, beyond the improvement of their daily life, the popular classes abandoned him. Ultimately they revolted against him, at the instigation of the nobles, and killed the tribune, whom Wagner lets die in a vast conflagration.

Young Adolf seems to have felt, unexpectedly and forcefully, that his own destiny was prefigured in the events on the stage, carried by Wagner's intensely evocative music. There was the idealistic man from nowhere; there was a crisis situation caused and exploited by despicable people; and there was the heroic protest and revolutionary action of a people's tribune whose intention it was to usher in a new era. The dramatic betrayal by his people and the final conflagration will most probably have been felt as no more than a theatrical climax, although Hitler kept the possibility of a *Weltenbrand*, a world conflagration, in mind even in the 1930s; but Wagner's opera libretto proved to be prophetical.

"It was the most impressive moment which I have known with my friend", writes Kubizek. "When I think back to my friendship with Adolf Hitler in my youth, what has remained most strongly and clearly in my memory are not his monologues and neither his political ideas, but that nightly hour on the Freinberg", where Hitler had "a visionary revelation of the way he was to follow". After they had seen *Rienzi* and were shaken by the tragic end of the hero, they left the opera house in silence. "It was now midnight, but my friend, serious and withdrawn, both hands deep in the pockets of his overcoat, continued walking down the street and out of the town." They walked up to the top of a hill, the Freinberg. There "Adolf stood in front of me. He grasped both my hands and pressed them in his. This was a gesture which I had not yet known of him. The pressure of his hands told me how deeply his was moved. The words did not flow from his mouth as easily as usual, they rather burst forth from it, raw and hoarse ...

"Gradually he freed himself by talking ... It was as if another I spoke through him, by which he was touched as strongly as I was. It was in no way as when one says from a glib orator that he becomes intoxicated with his own words. On the contrary! I rather had the impression that he himself underwent with amazement what burst forth from him with elementary force ... He was in an ecstatic state, a state of total rapture, in which he transposed what he had experienced in *Rienzi* into a formidable vision on another level, his own ... The impression received from the opera was only the outward occasion forcing him to speak. As an accumulated flood breaks through a bursting dam, so the words broke forth from him. In magnificent, compelling images he disclosed to me his future and that of his people ... He spoke about an assignment which he would receive from the people, to lead it from servitude up to the heights of freedom ... He spoke about a special mission which would be conferred on him." Many years would have to pass, wrote Kubizek, before he understood what that moment under the dark sky of a November night had meant for his friend. When they walked down from the hill into the town, the bells struck three. But Hitler turned around and started walking back towards the hill. "I want to be alone", he said — and never mentioned the experience again.

Till July 1939, 'before the war started', when Hitler was the world-renowned all-powerful German Führer and Chancellor, Kubizek, though an accomplished musician, had never done better than becoming the secretary of a small municipality. Hitler now had the pride and joy of inviting his rediscovered friend to the *Festspiele* in the Bayreuth of their venerated Wagner, where he reigned as the supreme protector and benefactor. In one of their conversations Kubizek reminded Hitler of that moment on the Freinberg, supposing that, after all he had gone through and the vastness of his task, he would have forgotten it. "But I noticed as soon as I said the first words that he remembered that moment precisely, in every detail ... I was also present when Adolf Hitler narrated to Mrs [Winifred] Wagner, whose guests we were, the occurrence which had taken place after the performance of *Rienzi* at Linz. Thus I found my own memory confirmed twice. And I have never been able to forget the words with which Hitler concluded his narration to Mrs Wagner. He said gravely: 'That was when it began'."[75]

The very reliable Brigitte Hamann writes: "Hitler found it later of importance to be known as the incarnation of Rienzi".[76] He was often called 'the Tribune', especially during the Munich period; and the not less reliable Ralph Reuth mentions that he was called 'the Tribune' by his co-prisoners at Landsberg "with reference to Wagner's

---

[75]August Kubizek: *Adolf Hitler, mein Jugendfreund*, pp. 111 ff. passim.
[76]Brigitte Hamann: *Hitlers Wien*, p. 40.

Rienzi".⁷⁷ This opera, Wagner's first, was hardly ever performed; we may therefore suppose that Hitler had confided to one of his followers what he would tell later to Winifred Wagner. The Party Rally in Nuremberg will each year open with the *Rienzi* overture, which Köhler calls 'the quasi official Reich overture' and 'a musical summary of Hitler's ideological programme', while Serpico calls it 'the unofficial hymn of the Third Reich'. "In the Third Reich the music of Wagner occupied a dominating position, because it was so eminently tuned to the Nazi myths and served as their ideal background."⁷⁸

And hereby goes a story. In the spring of 1938, Robert Ley, the *Reichsführer* of the German Workers' Front, asked Hitler why it was always Wagner's music which had to open the Party Rallies when there were so many excellent living composers in Germany, eager to express the National Socialist worldview in their music. Hitler was sceptical but fixed a date to hear the submitted compositions. The day before the audition, however, he asked that after the other works the Rienzi overture would also be played. And so it happened. "I must admit", wrote Speer years later in Spandau prison, "that the familiar sublimity of [the Rienzi overture], which hitherto regularly had opened the Party Rallies, came across like a revelation."

Hitler's words to Ley on that occasion have been passed down: "You know, Ley, it isn't by chance that I have the Party Rallies open with the overture to *Rienzi*. It's not just a musical question. At the age of twenty-four this man, an innkeeper's son, persuaded the Roman people to drive out the corrupt Senate by reminding them of the magnificent past of the Roman Empire. Listening to this blessed music as a young man in the theatre at Linz, I had the vision that I too must someday succeed in uniting the German Empire and making it great once more."⁷⁹ But the day came, in April 1945, that

---

⁷⁷Ralph Reuth: *Hitler*, p. 171.
⁷⁸Anna Maria Sigmund: *Die Frauen der Nazis II*, p. 252.
⁷⁹Albert Speer: *Spandau*, p. 88.

Kubizek was once more reminded of 'the primal scene of Hitler's career' on the Freinberg. "When in those terrible days of April 1945 I followed deeply shaken the battle for the Reich Chancellery which ended the world conflagration [the Second World War], I could not help thinking of the final scene in *Rienzi*, when the Tribune perishes in the flames of the burning capitol."[80]

Convergences

We are now arriving at a point in our story where some major lines of its development must be recalled in order to show their convergence. At its very beginning the discrepancy was demonstrated between the insignificant 'man of nowhere', Adolf Hitler, and the top position he attained among the German speaking peoples, an achievement resembling the fantastic transformations in fairy tales and myths, but in this case a fact of history. This discrepancy in Hitler's life between a nobody at one time and a man who put the world afire at another is what Ron Rosenbaum and other students of the Hitler phenomenon call 'the gap'. One of its aspects is "the abyss between the small-time film-noir grifter, the mountebank criminal the *Munich Post* reporters knew, and the magnitude of the horror Hitler created when he came to power in Berlin".[81] How this came to be is still an enigma even to the most prominent historians.

The first important episode in the rise of Adolf Hitler is what we have called the 'turnabout' and others the 'transformation' or 'turning point'. This mysterious change in the person of Hitler can be situated in the summer months of 1919, between the day Captain Karl Mayr said nonchalantly: "Oh, that's Hitler of the List Regiment", and the day he requested the corporal most respectfully to explain the Jewish problem to another army propagandist. There something

---

[80] August Kubizek, op. cit., p. 291.
[81] Ron Rosenbaum, op. cit., p. 77.

must have happened that led to the introduction of the Austrian corporal to the small and secret political offshoot of the Thule organisation, the DAP, and to the astonishing fact that Hitler entered politics fully prepared to use the irrelevant political circle as the springboard for a mass movement based on a revolutionary new world view. He entered the DAP with a prepared mind, the intention to hijack it, and the awareness that his entrance on the political scene was "a decision that would be for good, with no turning back".

How came that Hitler, who was not an anti-Semite in May 1919, at least not an outspoken one, became a militant Jew-baiter in the following months, as is evident from reactions to his pep talks as an army propagandist and from the Gemlich letter, written on 16 September? How had Hitler constructed the pillars of his world view: that the Aryan Germans were the world's master race, that he was the missioned one to lead them into a new and glorious age, and that the Jews were the enemy in this apocalyptic undertaking? All authorities are agreed on the fact that Hitler's convictions remained unchanged from the very beginning and that he had 'an unusual consistency of purpose' (JP Stern). Normally the acquisition of a new personal paradigm, or mental make-up, does not come about all at once, yet in Hitler's case it seems to have been quite sudden.

Hitler saw himself as the missioned one, the carrier of a new revolutionary world view of which he had to be the only and therefore absolute executor, being the only one who knew the secret mission in full – this in contradiction with one of the historian's myths about his life that, at first, he was only the 'drummer' drawing the crowds for a new historical act. As was shown in one of the first stages of our story, it is true that sometimes he designated himself as such, but only as a ploy or not to look ridiculous in circumstances which did not yet allow a full disclosure of his intentions. But *he* was the man who had been initiated in the secret of things to come, *he* was the chosen hero of the mission, and next to him there was no place for any other. This he showed as soon as there was a chance, and that chance came in July 1921 when he made the bold move of submitting his resignation from the DAP, thereby confronting the other leaders with the dilemma either to fade away into insignificance or to surrender to him 'the sole responsibility' of the Party.

The man who discovered the real Hitler was Dietrich Eckart. We find his presence at every important point in Hitler's career until Eckart's death in the last days of 1923. Eckart literally made Hitler, an expression which cannot be too strong if we consider the exceptional honours rendered by the Führer to his 'fatherly friend'. Eckart was indeed Hitler's 'godfather', i.e. his discoverer, initiator and protector, as such persons are known in freemasonry and other secret organizations. His influence must have been at least this important, for otherwise it is unthinkable that Hitler would have used his name as the organ-point with which *Mein Kampf* ends.

Eckart, albeit a staunch individualist, was also an exemplary person of his time. He was after all a poet, playwright and prolific publicist with an active social life. He was a militant nationalist, acquainted with dozens of important people not only in Munich but also in Berlin and elsewhere. He was, moreover, a vocal anti-Semite, familiar with the literature on this subject and contributing to it in his turn. And he was closely related with the Thule Society, which meant with the powerful Germanenorden and the Pan-Germans.

We now know the atmosphere in which these secret organisations functioned and played a determining role in opposition to the leftist half of the German population. Even in the political field their actions were everywhere a matter of secrecy and covert plotting, always of power politics and sometimes of murder. This, however, was only the surface of a world rife with religious expectation and steeped in occultism. (The Germanenorden saw itself as the answer to the clandestine bodies and schemes fomented by the world conspiracy of 'the Elders of Zion'.) If the German aspiration is clearly discernible in Dietrich Eckart, so is the 'occult' way in which he tutored his pupil Adolf Hitler. 'Occult' here means not only 'hidden'; it refers literally to the practice of the occult sciences.

The testimonies of Hitler's occult powers are written in history, however much academic historians try to overlook them. In his *Hitler and Stalin – Parallel Lives*, Alan Bullock writes: "In the copy of Napoleon's *Thoughts* found in his library, Stalin had marked the passage: 'It was precisely that evening in Lodi that I came to believe in myself as an unusual person and became consumed with the ambition to do great things that until then had been but a fantasy!' Neither Stalin, however, nor Hitler ever pinpointed a similar moment of revelation".[82] This, as we saw a few pages ago, is patently untrue as far as Hitler is concerned. August Kubizek has recorded such a moment after he and his friend Adi had seen a performance of Wagner's *Rienzi* for the first time. Not less important as a confirmation of that moment is Hitler's narrating it to Winifred Wagner – "That was when it began!" – as deemed worth mentioning by Brigitte Hamann (2002), Anna Maria Sigmund (2000) and Ralph Reuth (2003). Indeed, many historians of the younger generation are much more disposed than their immediate predecessors to take the *whole* historical evidence into consideration, including the facts which are not directly transparent to the reigning consensus mentality.

There is another occasion of an experience similar to the Rienzi revelation and also exactly pinpointable, namely when Hitler as a patient at the military hospital in Pasewalk was told by the local pastor that the German Emperor had abdicated and that Germany had lost the war. Hitler has written no less than three pages about this occurrence in *Mein Kampf*. "As for myself, I broke down completely when the old gentleman [ie the pastor] tried to resume his story by informing us that we must now end this long war, because the war was lost, he said, and we were at the mercy of the victor ... It was impossible for me to stay and listen any longer. Darkness surrounded me as I staggered and stumbled back to my ward and buried my aching head between the pillow and the blankets.

---

[82] Alan Bullock: *Hitler and Stalin – Parallel Lives*, p. 376.

I had not cried since the day that I stood beside my mother's grave ... The following days were terrible to bear, and the nights still worse ... During those nights my hatred increased, hatred for the organizers of this dastardly crime". Hitler means the German members of the government who, under the direction of 'the Jews', had accepted to sign the armistice. "During the following days my own fate became clear to me ... There is no such thing as coming to an understanding with the Jews. It must be the hard and fast 'either-or'. For my part I then decided that I would take up political work."[83]

The Pasewalk experience* was as important for Hitler as the revelation of his destiny on the Freinberg some thirteen years earlier, and in a way its corroboration ("my own fate became clear to me"). Hitler's narration indicates that in Pasewalk he went through a profound existential crisis. "Hitler was abruptly delivered from his misery, as he lay in despair on his cot, by a 'supernatural vision'", writes John Toland.[84] According to Ron Rosenbaum he experienced "some kind of transformative vision or hallucination. It was a life-changing moment of metamorphosis ... Hitler conceived the mission and the myth that would bring him to power fifteen years later."

---

[83] Adolf Hitler, op. cit., pp. 176 ff., passim.
*It is sometimes contended that Hitler was cured by a hypnotic suggestion, and that the revelation of his destiny was put into him in the same way. A sensationalist book about how a Dr Edmund Forster thus created Hitler has been written by David Lewis and published in 2003 as *The Man Who Invented Hitler*. This book is based on a novel by Ernst Weiss, and all links with the facts behind the story are very thin and in most cases nothing more than suppositions. Besides, one must have a poor idea of what it took Hitler to become Hitler and to start the fateful realisation of his ideas to think that the whole, enormously complex tragedy could be based on a single posthypnotic suggestion. In 2004, Bernard Horstmann published *Hitler in Pasewalk – Die Hypnose und ihre Folgen* (the hypnosis and its consequences), in which he tells exactly the same story as Lewis without mentioning the latter's book among the bibliographical sources.
[84] John Toland, op. cit., p. xviii.

Rosenbaum also mentions that Hitler "heard 'voices', or [had] a providential vision from on high", and that "Hitler himself claimed he received a visionary impetus to redeem Germany from Jews and Bolsheviks".[85]

In Walter Langer's report for the Office of Strategic Studies we find: "It was while he was in the hospital [at Pasewalk], suffering from hysterical blindness and mutism, that [Hitler] had the vision that he would liberate the Germans from their bondage and make Germany great. It was this vision that set him on his present political career and that had such a determining influence on the course of the world events. More than anything else it was this vision that convinced him that he was chosen by Providence and that he had a great mission to perform. This is probably the most outstanding characteristic of Hitler's mature personality, and it is this that guides him 'with the precision of a sleepwalker'". Langer quotes moreover the following words of Hitler from an interview which appeared in the *Pariser Tageszeitung* on 23 January 1940: "When I was confined to bed [at Pasewalk], the idea came to me that I would liberate Germany, that I would make it great. I knew immediately that it would be realized".[86] All this in spite of Hitler being a lonely nonentity in those days.

Although Hitler apparently did not tell the whole truth about what Haffner calls 'his experience of awakening' in Pasewalk, he never made a secret of it, no more than he made a secret of his experience on the Freinberg in Linz. Both experiences are similar and in a way complementary. What seems to have been added in the Pasewalk vision was the identification of the Jews as the enemy of his world-transforming task. All three main pillars of his world view were now revealed to him: the redemption of Germany, his leading role in it, and the opposition of the Jews in all their disguises. It is an intentional distortion of Hitler's to state that it was at Pasewalk

---

[85]Ron Rosenbaum, op. cit., pp. xiv, xxxvi.
[86]Walter Langer, op. cit., pp. 159, 33.

that he decided 'to take up political work', for this happened in the summer of next year in Munich. By writing thus, he may have wanted to camouflage the facts that the decision had not been his, or not entirely his, or that it was taken in circumstances which he did not want to be known.

The Pasewalk and Freinberg experiences, just like most decisive moments in Hitler's life, remain rather hot to handle for people whose mind-frame leaves no room for 'supernatural' or extra-material phenomena. In Kershaw's monumental Hitler biography, for instance, we read: "Hitler referred to his Pasewalk experience on a number of occasions in the early 1920s. There were even embellishments to the story which was to appear in *Mein Kampf*. He told a variety of associates that as he lay blinded in Pasewalk he received a type of vision, message, or inspiration to liberate the German people and make Germany great again. This highly unlikely, purported quasi-religious experience was part of the mystification of his own person which Hitler encouraged as a key component of the Führer myth that was already embryonically present among many of his followers in the two years leading to the putsch attempt".[87] Statements of this sort explain nothing. A professional and much respected historian like Alan Bullock deserves our appreciation for changing the basis of his understanding of Hitler, for admitting that he does not know of any definitive explanation of the man, and for even candidly confiding to Ron Rosenbaum: "I think the mystics have something to say in the question".[88]

It is unreasonable to qualify as irrelevant or fanciful what Hitler himself said repeatedly about some of his fundamental experiences, the more so as his attestations, whether direct or indirect, provide illuminating pointers to the facts. And it is unreasonable to wave away countless testimonies by reliable and intelligent witnesses of

---

[87] Ian Kershaw, op. cit., p. 103.
[88] Ron Rosenbaum, op. cit., p. 92.

the way they perceived Hitler, on the grounds that a certain kind of consensus holds such experiences to be unreliable, unfounded or even untrue without having anything better to propose.

The occurrences in Linz and Pasewalk were mediumistic experiences. The reality of these occurrences is proven by the subsequent historical events – which shows that they were anything but illusory or hallucinatory. *This* was what Hitler fundamentally believed, what was behind his amazing actions, and the full scope of which he kept secret in his heart. Captain Mayr may have had some knowledge or suspicion of it. Dietrich Eckart must have shared in the secret when he took Hitler under his wing and, together with Mayr, launched him on his career with so much care, dedication and conviction. There is truth in Eckart's often reported saying, historical or apocryphal, that he had composed the tune to which Hitler was dancing. It explains why Hitler could enter the political scene with a full-fledged programme; why he took a decision from which he could not back out (he could not evade his revealed destiny); why he could not stand anybody above him or next to him; and why he never deviated from the path once taken.

A medium is a person with the capacity to open himself to the intervention of an immaterial being. When the being becomes active through the medium, the latter can be said to be possessed by it. We have seen several instances of the manner in which the insignificant Hitler suddenly became the inspired, irresistible orator. There was also the lowly Hitler who became the almighty Führer of the Germans, with the aspiration to rule the world. Such an idea may seem crazy, but it was certainly there and terribly effectual. And there was the bohemian, work-shy Hitler who was capable of quasi superhuman bursts of energy when spurred on by his inspiration. As there was the Hitler who could 'mesmerize' and possess people, or who waited for 'the voice' to speak before taking his major decisions.

A voice does not exist in an isolated state, it is always the voice of someone, of some entity. Hitler said that he had received his mission from Providence, that it was Providence which guided his steps, and that only could happen to him what Providence wanted or allowed to happen. His confidence in his guidance was absolute; as we have seen, once the voice had spoken his decision was inalterable, even in the face of apparent impossibility. He took pride in being a *Vabanque Spieler*, a gambler, a runner of risks, knowing that his guidance would not desert him – which it did not up to a certain point. His career was the illustrious confirmation of the correctness of his inspiration, taken by many for authentic genius, 'the greatest genius in history' (Goebbels). On the one hand, there was the pedestrian Hitler who believed in the world ice theory and the Aryanhood of Christ, on the other there was the inspired man who dreamed great dreams, confronted one crisis after another and solved or conquered it, rising from anonymity in the barracks to be the adored German Messiah for whom nothing was impossible, "however often and how close he came to failing" (Bullock).

The word one encounters time and again when the power emanating from Hitler is discussed, is 'charisma', usually with a reference to Max Weber (1864-1920). Weber defined charisma as "the quality of a personality held to be out of the ordinary (and originally thought to have magical sources, both in the case of prophets and men who are wise in healing or in law, the leaders of the hunt or heroes in war), on account of which the person is evaluated as being gifted with supernatural or superhuman or at least specifically out of the ordinary powers not accessible to everybody, and hence as a 'leader'".[89] However, in most cases when the word 'charisma' is used, even with reference to this definition, its spirit as formulated by Weber is not. 'Charisma', generally, is no more than a handy label used by academic authors to designate the upper limit of their conception of a person with an emanation of power, an upper limit beyond which they are not willing to go. If for Weber terms like 'magical sources', 'supernatural' and 'superhuman' had some meaning,

---

[89] Stephen Turner (ed.): *The Cambridge Companion to Weber*, p. 94.

they mean nothing for the present-day users of his charisma concept. Weber had an openness which most established historians do not have today. 'Charisma' has to say it all without saying anything.

When looking for the roots of Nazism we have come to the conclusion that the Western world view is defective. Its components are the remnants of a fundamentalist Judeo-Christian doctrine, illogically mixed with the tenet of materialism that "all is matter because there cannot be anything else than matter". The scientific view rules in one compartment of the modern mind, which does not find any inconvenience in coexisting, in another compartment, with a dogmatic creed and often with the most bizarre superstitions – just like in Adolf Hitler's mind. Is there, then, a frame of mind, or a world view, or a coherent system of encompassing experience according to which the complexity of Hitler's personality would be explainable?

"Hitler is a sort of a mystic. He says he is guided by an inner voice. He goes into silence in his villa and waits for the voice. Whatever the voice says he will carry out. He is possessed by some supernormal Power and it is from this Power that the voice, as he calls it, comes. Have you noticed how people who at one time were inimical to him come into contact with him and leave as his admirers? It is the sign of that Power. It is from this Power that he has constantly received suggestions, and the constant repetition of the suggestions has taken hold of the German people."[90] These words were spoken by the Indian philosopher and yogi Sri Aurobindo in the course of a conversation on the last day of 1938. Sri Aurobindo was educated at St Paul's School in London and at Cambridge University; he was an accomplished classical scholar who remembered his Greek and Latin perfectly even in south India and at an advanced age; he had been one of the leading revolutionary politicians in his country and was at one time considered 'the most dangerous man

---

[90]Nirodbaran: *Talks with Sri Aurobindo*, p. 84.

in India'; he was a master of the English language who wrote more than thirty substantial volumes of philosophy, psychology and spirituality. He was thoroughly familiar with the Western as well as with the Eastern tradition and history, and proposed a global synthesis in which all levels of reality would be integrated.

The Swedish Academy was examining Sri Aurobindo's candidature for the Nobel Prize for literature in 1950, the year he expired. His nomination was seconded by Gabriela Mistral and Pearl S Buck. The former wrote about him: "Six languages have given the Master of Pondicherry a gift for co-ordination, a clarity free from gaudiness, and a charm that borders on the magical ... These are indeed 'glad tidings' that come to us: to know that there is a place in the world where culture has reached its tone of dignity by uniting in one man a supernatural life with a consummate literary style, thus making use of his beautifully austere and classical prose to serve as a handmaid of the spirit". As we shall see, Sri Aurobindo's involvement with Hitler and the Second World War is abundantly documented in his own writings and in the written reports of conversations with him.

14

SRI AUROBINDO'S VISION

Evolution is not finished; reason is not the last word nor the reasoning animal the supreme figure of Nature. As man emerged out of the animal, so out of man the superman emerges.

SRI AUROBINDO

A double ladder

Sri Aurobindo's vision is evolutionary and encompasses the standard scientific outlook while at the same time exceeding it. In his view matter is not the only and sufficient reality, nor is it capable of providing an adequate explanation of the evolutionary process. The appearance of the evolutionary principle, "the creation of forms of Matter, first of inconscient and inanimate, then of living and thinking Matter, the appearance of more and more organized bodies adapted to express a greater power of consciousness, has been studied from the physical side, the side of form-building, by Science", writes Sri Aurobindo in his major opus *The Life Divine*. "But very little light has been shed on the inner side, the side of consciousness, and what little has been observed is rather of its physical basis and instrumentation than of the progressive operations of Consciousness in its own nature.

"In the evolution, as it has been observed so far, although a continuity is there – for Life takes up Matter and Mind takes up submental Life, the Mind of intelligence takes up the mind of life and sensation – the leap from one grade of consciousness in the series to another grade seems to our eyes immense, the crossing of the gulf whether by bridge or by leap impossible; we fail to discover any concrete and satisfactory evidence of its accomplishment in the past or of the manner in which it was accomplished. Even in the outward evolution, even in the development of physical forms where the data are clearly in evidence, there are missing links that remain always missing; but in the evolution of consciousness the passage is still more difficult to account for, for it seems more like a transformation than a passage."[1]

The ground of all existence in whatever of its manifestations is *That*, the omnipresent Reality which cannot be limited or labelled with a name, but whose ultimate attributes are existence, consciousness-force and absolute joy. In the Indian tradition 'That' is often called 'Brahman'. "Brahman is in all things, all things are in Brahman, all things are Brahman". It is the absolute, indivisible Something in which there is neither centre nor circumference. "An omnipresent Reality is the truth of all life and existence whether absolute or relative, whether corporeal or incorporeal, whether animate or inanimate, whether intelligent or unintelligent; and in all its infinitely varying and even constantly opposed self-expressions, from the contradictions nearest to our ordinary experience to those remotest antinomies which lose themselves on the verges of the Ineffable, the Reality is one and not a sum or concourse. From that all variations begin, in that all variations consist, to that all variations return. All affirmations are denied only to lead to a wider affirmation of the same Reality. All antinomies confront each other in order to recognize one Truth in their opposed aspects and embrace by the

---

[1] Sri Aurobindo: *The Life Divine*, pp. 707-08.

way of conflict their mutual Unity. Brahman is the Alpha and the Omega. Brahman is the One besides whom there is nothing else existent."[2]

The evolutionary cycle of which we are a part takes place within That, its origin, essence and destiny. As there is no end to That, there is no end to its manifestations, the cosmic cycles and their extinctions. It is also self-evident that, where there is evolution, there must have been a previous involution. "Nothing can evolve out of Matter which is not already therein contained ... Evolution of Life in Matter supposes a previous involution of it there, unless we suppose it to be a new creation magically and unaccountably introduced in Nature ... The evolution of consciousness and knowledge cannot be accounted for unless there is already a concealed consciousness in things with its inherent and native powers emerging little by little."[3] There is "the mounting and descending hierarchy of planes of consciousness that like a double ladder lapse into the nescience of Matter and climb back again through the flowering of life and soul and mind into the infinity of the Spirit".[4]

This is how the gradations of existence as we know them came about: matter, life, mind, and the planes where all what surpasses the mind comes from. These gradations are also called 'the great chain of being'. Arthur Lovejoy writes in the preface of his book with the same title: "The phrase which I have taken for the title [*The Great Chain of Being*] was long one of the most famous in the vocabulary of Occidental philosophy, science and reflective poetry; and the conception which in modern times came to be expressed by this or similar phrases has been one of the half-dozen most potent and persistent presuppositions in Western thought. It was, in fact, until not much more than a century ago probably the most widely familiar conception of the general *scheme* of things, of the constitutive

---

[2] Id., p. 33.
[3] Id., pp. 42, 185, 612.
[4] Sri Aurobindo: *On Himself*, p. 23.

pattern of the universe; and as such it necessarily predetermined current ideas on many other matters."[5]

"Nothing can evolve out of Matter which is not already therein contained", writes Sri Aurobindo. "Each step of this graded existence prepares the next, holds in itself what appears in that which follows ... In the very atom there is something that becomes in us a will and a desire ... Every particle of what we call Matter contains [all the other principles] implicit in itself ... In fact, life, mind, Supermind are present in the atom." Ultimately "Matter is a form of Spirit, a habitation of Spirit, and here in Matter itself there can be a realization of Spirit." For "Matter itself is a substance and power of spirit and could not exist if it were anything else".[6]

Man is a transitional being

One of Sri Aurobindo's aphorisms says: "Evolution is not finished; reason is not the last word nor the reasoning animal the supreme figure of Nature. As man emerged out of the animal, so out of man the superman emerges."[7] In other words, the place of the human being is somewhere on the upward ladder, though not at the top. Man is not the king of creation but only its provisional leader, and the evolution ahead may be as long as was the past evolution, supposed it can be measured in time. "The animal is a living laboratory in which Nature has, it is said, worked out Man. Man himself may well be a thinking and living laboratory in whom and with whose conscious co-operation she wills to work out the superman, the god."[8] In both quotations 'superman' means the next evolutionary step or steps which will surpass us as much as we surpass the animal.

"Man is a transitional being, he is not final. He is too imperfect for that, too imperfect in capacity for knowledge, too imperfect in

---

[5] Arthur Lovejoy: *The Great Chain of Being*, p. vii.
[6] Sri Aurobindo: *The Life Divine*, pp. 42, 179, 183, 258, 711, 665, 761.
[7] Sri Aurobindo: *Thoughts and Aphorisms*, p. 27.
[8] Sri Aurobindo: *The Life Divine*, p. 3.

will and action, too imperfect in his turn towards joy and beauty, too imperfect in his will for freedom and his instinct for order. Even if he could perfect himself in his own type, his type is too low and small to satisfy the need of the universe. Something larger, higher, more capable of a rich all-embracing universality is needed, a greater being, a greater consciousness summing up in itself all that the world set out to be ... Man must evolve out of himself the divine superman: he was born for transcendence. Humanity is not enough."[9]

The human being occupies a special, awkward position in the cosmic process of evolution: it stands at its crossroads, it is the X, the incomplete, problematical, self-questioning being in between the hemispheres of lower and higher Nature. "Man is an abnormal who has not found his own normality – he may imagine he has, he may appear to be normal in his own kind, but that normality is only a sort of provisional order; therefore, though man is infinitely greater than the plant or the animal, he is not perfect in his own nature like the plant and the animal. This imperfection is not a thing to be at all deplored, but rather a privilege and a promise, for it opens out to us an immense vista of self-development and self-exceeding. Man at the highest is a half-god who has risen up out of the animal Nature and is splendidly abnormal in it, but the thing which he has started out to be, the whole god, is something so much greater than what he is that it seems to him as abnormal to himself as he is to the animal."[10]

Man's being is as complex as his evolutionary position, stretched out between a long and for the most part forgotten yesterday and a boundless tomorrow. His body "is not the whole even of our physical being; this gross density is not all of our substance. The oldest Vedantic knowledge tells us of five degrees of our being, the material, the vital, the mental, the ideal, the spiritual or beatific, and to each of these grades of our soul there corresponds a grade of our

---
[9] *Sri Aurobindo Archives and Research*, April 1983, p. 3.
[10] Sri Aurobindo: *The Human Cycle*, p. 220.

substance, a sheath as it was called in the ancient figurative language. A later psychology found that these five sheaths of our substance were the material of three bodies [contained within each other], gross physical, subtle and causal, in all of which the soul actually and simultaneously dwells, although here and now we are superficially conscious only of the material vehicle. But it is possible to become conscious in our other bodies as well and it is in fact the opening up of the veil between them and consequently between our physical, psychical and ideal personalities which is the cause of those 'psychic' and 'occult' phenomena that are now beginning to be increasingly though yet too little and too clumsily examined, even while they are too much exploited".[11] In other words, each human being contains all the degrees of the cosmic evolution within him. It is, as the traditions say, a 'microcosm'. "Man, the microcosm, has all these planes in his own being, ranged from the subconscient to his superconscient existence."[12]

'In Matter lies the crux'

It is significant that Sri Aurobindo often writes Matter with a capital M. In the cosmic 'world stair' of the degrees of substance and their corresponding realms, it was Matter on which his spiritual vision as well as his transforming yogic effort was focused. He had the courage to draw the logical conclusion of the Upanishadic statement that all is the Brahman; if so, then "Matter also is the Brahman and it is nothing other than or different from the Brahman". "Matter is a form of Spirit, a habitation of Spirit, and here in Matter itself there can be a realization of the Spirit."[13]

"In Matter undoubtedly lies the crux; that raises the obstacle [to the spiritual effort]: for because of Matter Life is gross and limited

---

[11]Id., p. 259.
[12]Sri Aurobindo: *The Synthesis of Yoga*, p. 604.
[13]Sri Aurobindo: *The Life Divine*, pp. 242, 665.

and stricken with death and pain; because of Matter Mind is more than half blind, its wings clipped, its feet tied to a narrow perch and held back from the vastness and freedom above of which it is conscious. Therefore the exclusive spiritual seeker is justified from his viewpoint if, disgusted with the mud of Matter, revolted by the animal grossness of Life or impatient of the self-imprisoned narrowness and downward vision of Mind, he determines to break from it all and return by inaction and silence to the Spirit's immobile liberty. But that is not the sole viewpoint, nor, because it has been sublimely held or glorified by shining and golden examples, need we consider it the integral and ultimate wisdom. Rather, liberating ourselves from all passion and revolt, let us see what this divine order of the universe means, and, as for this great knot and tangle of Matter denying the spirit, let us seek to find out and separate its strands so as to loosen it by a solution and not cut through it by a violence. We must state the difficulty, the opposition first, entirely, trenchantly, with exaggeration if need be, rather than with diminution, and then look for the issue."[14]

This is the Aurobindonian spiritual revolution. For it may be remembered that any spiritual effort in the course of humanity's existence has had the liberation from Matter, from this painfully burdensome world, as its aim. Sri Aurobindo, however, accords to Matter the recognition it intrinsically deserves as a form of the Spirit. In concrete terms: if the Divine has manifested this world, and if we are born in it, then there must be an intention behind both facts, for the consciousness of the Divine is an infallible Truth-Consciousness also in all of its manifestation. "The touch of Earth is always invigorating to the son of Earth, even when he seeks a supraphysical knowledge. It may even be said that the supraphysical can only be really mastered in its fullness – to its heights we can always reach – when we keep our feet firmly on the physical. 'Earth is His footing', says the Upanishad whenever it images the Self that

---

[14]Id., pp. 242-43.

manifests in the universe. And it is certainly the fact that the wider we extend and the surer we make our knowledge of the physical world, the wider and surer becomes our foundation for the higher knowledge, even for the highest, even for the Brahmavidya [knowledge of Brahman]."[15]

The evolutionary cosmos is one of 'the vast self-extensions of the Brahman' in a divine act of seeing which simultaneously is an act of creation. The mode of consciousness involved in this act of divine Self-manifestation Sri Aurobindo calls 'Truth-Consciousness' or 'Supermind', 'the real creative agency of the universal existence'. The Supermind is not an inflated or supreme degree of the human mental consciousness as we know it, and "lies far beyond the possibility of any satisfying mental scheme or map of it or any grasp of mental seeing and description. It would be difficult for the normal unillumined or untransformed mental conception to express or enter into something that is based on a consciousness; even if they were seen or conceived by some enlightenment or opening of vision, another language than the poor abstract counters [ie clichés] used by our mind would be needed to translate them into terms by which their reality could become at all seizable to us. As the summits of human mind are beyond animal perception, so the movements of Supermind are beyond the ordinary human mental conception ..."[16]

"Mental nature and mental thought are based on a consciousness of the finite; supramental nature is in its very grain a consciousness and power of the Infinite. Supramental nature sees everything from the standpoint of oneness and regards all things, even the greatest multiplicity and diversity, even what are to the mind the strongest contradictions, in the light of that oneness; its will, ideas, feelings, sense are made of the stuff of oneness, its actions proceed upon that basis. Mental nature, on the contrary, thinks, sees, wills, feels, senses with division as a starting-point and has only a constructed

---

[15] Id., p. 11.
[16] Id., pp. 919-20.

understanding of unity; even when it experiences oneness, it has to act from the oneness on a basis of limitation and difference. But the supramental, the divine life is a life of essential, spontaneous and inherent unity."[17]

According to Sri Aurobindo evolution cannot stop or be stopped in its tracks, and the appearance of the supramental being, the Aurobindonian superman, is inevitable. "The supramental change is a thing decreed and inevitable in the evolution of the earth-consciousness; for its upward ascent is not ended and mind is not the last summit."[18] Yet, as in all appearances of a new, higher species in evolution there will be transitional beings without which the gigantic leap from the human to the supramental being would not be possible.

Humanity is one

A precondition for the superman to be embodied on this earth is the realization of the oneness of humanity, which does not mean its uniformization but a sharing of its highest values in a common experience, making the acquisition of a superior consciousness possible. "All mankind is one in its nature, physical, vital, emotional, mental, and ever has been in spite of all differences of intellectual development ... and the whole race has, as the human totality, one destiny which it seeks and increasingly approaches in the cycles of progression and retrogression it describes through the countless millenniums of its history."[19] Seen in this light, the current globalisation with its inevitable confusion is the sure sign of the transition to a new global era, and many of the allegedly negative aspects of the present world can be seen as positive indications of the extremely intricate changes such a momentous process requires.

---

[17] Id., p. 965.
[18] Sri Aurobindo: *On the Mother*, p. 40.
[19] Sri Aurobindo: *The Human Cycle*, p. 59.

The present world is no longer a conglomerate of separate worlds or cultures on one planet, often unaware of each other's existence. "The whole world is now under one law", wrote Sri Aurobindo already during the First World War. And after the Second World War he wrote: "Mankind has a habit of surviving the worst catastrophes created by its own errors or by the violent turns of Nature and it must be so if there is any meaning in its existence, if its long history and continuous survival is not the accident of a fortuitously self-organizing Chance, which it must be in a purely materialistic view of the nature of the world. If man is intended to survive and carry forward the evolution of which he is at present the head and, to some extent, a half-conscious leader of its march, he must come out of his present chaotic international life and arrive at a beginning of organized united action; some kind of World-State, unitary or federal, or a confederacy or a coalition he must arrive at in the end; no smaller or looser expedient would adequately serve the purpose".[20]

Scholar and revolutionary

Aravinda Akroyd Ghose was born in Calcutta on 15 August 1872. His father, Civil Surgeon KD Ghose, was an anglophile who saw to it that in his house no Bengali but only English and a smattering of Hindustani were spoken. He had great ambitions for his sons and sent, in 1879, the three eldest to Great Britain. There Aravinda should study to prepare his entrance examination to the Indian Civil Service (ICS), the highest and highly valued position an Indian could attain under the colonial regime. At first the three brothers stayed with the family of a Congregational minister at Manchester, the centre and model of the industrial revolution, where Aravinda received an excellent private education. "I knew nothing of India and her culture", he would write later. In the young boy, a precocious poet, a very strong feeling arose when he read Shelley's *Revolt of Islam*.

---

[20]Sri Aurobindo: *The Ideal of Human Unity*, p. 315.

"I used to read it again and again – of course without understanding everything. Evidently it appealed to some part of the being ... I had a thought that I would dedicate my life to a similar world-change and take part in it."[21]

In 1885 Aravinda went to the esteemed St Paul's School in London. He became proficient in Greek and Latin, and in English literature. He also studied 'divinity' (the Bible), French and mathematics. His reports show that these subjects provided him with no difficulty, and he found time to study on the side Italian, German and Spanish in order to be able to read Dante, Goethe and Calderón in the original. At that time he led a life of poverty because his father, for unknown reasons, practically stopped sending money for him and his second brother, while most of their scanty resources went to the eldest one who was studying at Oxford. When growing up Aravinda had to survive during a whole year on "a slice or two of sandwich bread and butter and a cup of tea in the morning and in the evening a penny saveloy", some sort of sausage.

Aravinda took the scholarship examination for King's College at Cambridge University; he was elected to the first vacant open scholarship, which means that he was the best candidate. Known as AA Ghose, Aravinda studied at King's College from October 1890 to October 1892. The time of direst poverty was now over thanks to the scholarship. "As the recipient of a scholarship he had to prepare for the classical tripos [the equivalent of a BA], taking that difficult honours examination after two instead of the usual three years. At the same time, as an ICS probationer, he had to follow a completely different curriculum and demonstrate his mastery of half a dozen subjects in three periodical examinations."[22] He did very well on all fronts.

In addition to this there was the general education received at that famous university, concisely depicted by Peter Heehs as follows:

---

[21] AB Purani: *Evening Talks with Sri Aurobindo*, p. 378.
[22] Peter Heehs: *Sri Aurobindo – A Brief Biography*, p. 15.

"As a classical scholar, Aravinda was participating in an educational system whose traditions went back to the Renaissance. To master Greek and Latin, to read Homer and Sophocles, Virgil and Horace, to absorb the culture of classical Greece and Rome – this was considered the proper training of an English gentleman. And what one learned in the classroom and lecture hall was only part, and not the most important part, of the Cambridge experience. The university's atmosphere took hold of those who entered it and wrought a comprehensive change".[23] AA Ghose left Cambridge as a classical scholar and a gentleman; he would keep the knowledge acquired there for the rest of his life, both as a generally recognised master of the English language and as a man possessing a broad general knowledge.

But Aravinda did no longer want to join the Indian Civil Service. Influenced by his father, who sent him examples of colonial misrule from the press, he began to look at the British presence in India with new eyes and joined nationalist associations of Indian students. These organisations were infiltrated by government spies, who reported AA Ghose's revolutionary speeches. Moreover, he abhorred the routine and dreary paper work of the ICS administration. He was summoned three times for the horse-riding test and three times he failed to show up. He was disqualified and thereby eliminated as an ICS probationer.

As luck would have it, the Maharajah of Baroda, on one of his many visits to Europe, happened to be in London. He was delighted that he could hire a trained Cambridge and ICS man, higher qualified than most, for less than a reasonable salary. Aravinda sailed for India in February 1903. He set foot ashore in his motherland on the Apollo Bunder in Bombay and entered the service of Sayaji Rao Gaekwad III (1863-1939) two days later. It must have been an enormous change for Aravinda to find himself in the princely but culturally backward Baroda of the end of the nineteenth century

---

[23]Id., p. 14.

after having lived for more than thirteen years in places like Manchester, London and Cambridge. In due course he became at the Baroda College lecturer in French, professor of English and vice-principal. The prince also used him as his unofficial private secretary, especially for writing his speeches and the history of his reign.

Hardly six months after his arrival in India Aravinda was asked to contribute a series of articles to a newspaper called *Indu Prakash*. This may be considered his entrance into Indian politics. In this series, called 'New Lamps for Old', he lambasted the Indian National Congress Party (founded in 1885) for its submissive attitude towards the British masters in such hard-hitting prose that he was requested to tone down or write on less controversial topics. 'New Lamps for Old' remains proof of the precocious political maturity of AA Ghose and of the fire that burned in him. It is a historical fact that he was the first to take the standpoint of absolute independence for his motherland, even when the general atmosphere was one of 'apathy and despair' and absolute independence was still held to be 'an insane chimera'.

For a time Aravinda preferred to act behind the scenes. He was initiated in the Western Secret Society in Bombay, and administered in his turn the oath of secrecy and unconditional service of the Motherland to the *Anushilan Samiti*, "India's first true revolutionary society", in Calcutta. By now he had married a young girl from the city of his birth, which at that time was still the capital of British India – Delhi would become the capital in 1911 – and he travelled there almost every year during his holidays. These occasions he put to use for secret revolutionary activities, after a while helped by his younger brother Barin. It would be an exaggeration, though, to say that these efforts were even moderately successful.

But then Lord Curzon decreed the partition of Bengal (which would ultimately lead to the formation of what are now the Indian federal state of Bengal and Bangladesh). Such was the indignation of the Bengal people at the division of their holy land that they seemed to have caught a hot patriotic fever and that revolutionary action at last became possible. Their fervour was also fed by the victories of the Japanese over the Russians at Port Arthur (1904) and Mukden (1905), which proved for the first time that an Asian nation could beat the haughty Westerners. In 1906 a Bengal National College was founded in Calcutta. Aravinda took leave from the Maharajah's service and became the first principal of the College; that his payment was but a fraction of what he earned at Baroda was not an issue.

A period of hectic activity followed. Not only did Aurobindo – as he now spelled his name – have a full-time job in helping the National College afloat, he also supervised a revolutionary Bengali weekly, the organ of the militant extremists *Yugantar* (the changing age), edited by his brother Barin; he wrote for *Bande Mataram*, an English weekly which followed the line of the revolutionary nationalists and made Aurobindo Ghose's voice heard throughout India; and he even found time to write a play, *Perseus the Deliverer*. Aurobindo's articles were so skilfully written that they propagated the idea of unconditional independence and non-collaboration without ever crossing the line of sedition. Still he was put on trial in the *Bande Mataram* Sedition Case (1907), but as nothing could be proved against him the only result was that he shot to immediate all-India fame.

Aurobindo Ghose was now a recognised leader of the Extremists, the Congress faction dissatisfied with the docile political programme of the Moderates. He was in fact the most extreme Extremist, and brought matters to a head at the Surat congress in December 1907, where his insistence on full independence of his country from the colonial occupation led to a split between the two trends in the Congress. Political moderation gradually died a natural death. In 1929, more than twenty years after Aurobindo defined *swaraj* as 'full independence', Jawaharlal Nehru declared "the word 'swaraj' in article 1 of the Congress Constitution shall mean Complete Independence". Again eighteen years later the ideal was realised.

The year 1908 would become a landmark in Aurobindo's eventful life. First there was the decisive inner change which came about because of his search for a firm psychological foothold amid the fleeting stream of outer events. He met the yogi Vishnu Baskar Lele in Baroda shortly after the Surat congress. The event would prove determinative for Aurobindo's further life as, totally unexpected, he had the stunning experience of 'the silent Brahman' which he has described on several occasions. This was in fact more than an experience, it was a permanent realisation, for the state of inner silence never left him anymore. Along with it he followed Lele's recommendation to surrender himself unreservedly to his inner voice as the directive of his spiritual exploration called yoga, 'the art of conscious self-finding'.

But the British authorities knew what a dangerous man the politician Aurobindo Ghose was and they were looking for an occasion to get rid of him. This occasion came when, on 30 April 1908, Barin and his group of young militant patriots, of whom Aurobindo was the secret leader, bungled another of their bombing attempts. This time the colonial authorities came down with a heavy hand. Aurobindo Ghose was one of the first to be arrested. His trial and that of the other revolutionaries, mostly young students who had broken off their studies to fight for the Motherland, is known in Indian history as 'the Alipore Bomb Case', after Alipore Jail in Calcutta where the accused were imprisoned. The trial, presided over by a former Cambridge acquaintance of Aurobindo, lasted a full year. Barin and one companion were sentenced to death, but afterwards deported to the horrors of the jail in Port Blair, in the Andaman Islands; others were given prison sentences; Aurobindo was acquitted for lack of evidence as to his involvement in the attack.

Aurobindo's year-long stay in Alipore Jail was used by him as an intensive retreat which resulted in a series of ever widening spiritual realisations. The Aurobindo who left Alipore Jail on 6 May 1909 was not the same who had entered it with his hands tied together and a rope around his waist. He now saw his political work and the liberation of India as part of a spiritual tide which would carry the world into a new era. Nationalism, he said in his Uttarpara speech, had to be seen as part of the *sanatana dharma*, the eternal law.

But the British authorities did not forget Aurobindo Ghose; on the contrary, even the highest-placed among them, the Lieutenant-Governor of Bengal and the Viceroy called him in their correspondence 'the most dangerous man in India'. When once more a warrant for his arrest was signed, Aurobindo left Calcutta instantly at the command of his inner voice. He was taken in a rowing boat to Chandernagore, a French enclave to the north of Calcutta; shortly afterwards he sailed to Pondicherry, another French enclave on the Coromandel Coast below Madras. He thought of his stay there as temporary, but he would never leave Pondicherry again.

He was joined by a handful of the young Bengali revolutionaries who would become his first disciples. Once more he traversed, together with his companions, a period of extreme poverty. But no external circumstances could shake him anymore, nor could the constant presence of the British spies around the house where he was staying. His notebooks about the yoga he was practising, or for a great deal discovering, have been preserved. It was a full-time occupation which would soon make him 'the Master of Pondicherry' or the *Mahayogi* (great yogi), as he is still called today. More disciples came to stay with him, in some cases crossing the whole subcontinent in their quest. And then somebody arrived who had realised the same vision and who would help to initiate a new period in what Aurobindo called his 'integral yoga'.

A lady from Paris

Mirra Alfassa was born in Paris on 21 February 1878. Her father was Turkish and her mother Egyptian; they had settled in the French capital a few months before her birth. At that time Paris, refashioned by Baron Haussmann, was the cultural capital of the world. It was where the *haute couture* was created, the greatest concentration of artists lived, department stores, art exhibitions, circuses and cabarets like the *Moulin Rouge* were visited by an uninterrupted stream of tourists, and the world expositions of 1889 (when the Eiffel Tower was built) and 1900 took place. Paris set the tone in manners and fashion, and the French language was still the lingua franca in Europe, spoken by the educated people and the diplomats of all countries.

Mirra was born in a rather rich bourgeois family. Her brother would become governor-general of French Equatorial Africa. She herself showed a great independence of mind already at a young age and chose to become an artist in days when painting, together with playing the piano, was a great pastime for women but not a professional option. By enrolling at one of the painting *académies* in 1893, Mirra got fully involved in the intense artistic activity of that time and became acquainted with the artists. "I knew all the greatest artists of [the end of] the last century and the beginning of this century", among them Auguste Rodin and Henri Matisse. When Mirra entered the artistic world the heyday of Impressionism was already over, and the schools of Post-Impressionism, Pointillism and Fauvism set the tone. In 1897 she married the painter Henri Morisset.

Mirra's own work was appreciated. Some of her paintings would be selected by the jury of the *Salon de la Société Nationale des Beaux-Arts*, the yearly official grand exhibition, in 1903, 1904 and 1905. She considered herself nonetheless 'a very ordinary artist'. In the meantime, parallel to her outward activities, an inner life had been developing since her early childhood about which she could confide in nobody. Both her parents were materialists and atheists, and her husband does not seem to have been interested either. "I had such a need to know in me ... To know, know, *know*! You see, I knew nothing, but *nothing*, except the things of the ordinary life: the external knowledge. Whatever was given to me to learn, I had learned. I had learned not only what I was taught but also what my brother was taught, higher mathematics and all that! [Her brother was a *polytechnicien*.] And I learned and I learned and I learned – and it was nothing. *Nothing* gave me any explanation, I could not understand anything!"[24]

---

[24]Georges Van Vrekhem: *The Mother – The Story of Her Life*, p. 26.

Till she met an Indian on a visit to Paris who presented her with a copy of the *Bhagavad Gita*, saying: "Read the *Gita* and take Krishna as the symbol of the immanent God, the inner Godhead". This was all he told her. "But in one month the whole work was done. The first time I knew there was a discovery to be made within me, there was nothing else more important. I rushed headlong into it like a cyclone, and nothing could have stopped me."[25] Mirra was a headstrong character, and the floodgates were opened. Now she read all the spiritual literature she could lay her hands on, the *Dhammapada* and other Buddhist and Hindu texts. These were, besides, the decades of a general discovery of the art and the religions of the East, stimulated by writers like the Maupassant brothers and by an institution like the very active Guimet Museum in Paris.

On her search for knowledge that could provide her with an explanation of the surface reality she happened, in 1903, upon the *Revue cosmique*, the organ of *Le Mouvement cosmique*, founded by Max Théon (pseudonym of Louis Bimstein) and his wife. Contacts with the Théons led to her taking over the administration of the magazine, and to visits with the couple of occultists in Tlemcen (Algeria) in 1906 and 1907. There the Théons led a withdrawn life in a villa surrounded by a magnificent garden at the foot of the Atlas Mountains. Mirra found her appreciation of Théon's capacities confirmed, no less than her admiration for those of Madame Théon, for whom she always had the highest praise. Soon she herself learned everything there was to be learnt.

"To know these [occult] things and to bring their truths and forces into the life of humanity is a necessary part of its evolution", wrote Sri Aurobindo. "Science itself is in its own way an occultism; for it brings to light the formulas which Nature has hidden and it uses its knowledge to set free operations of her energies which she has not included in her ordinary operations and to organize and place at the service of man her occult powers and processes, a vast

---

[25]Id., p. 27.

system of physical magic – for there is and can be no other magic than the utilization of secret truths of being, secret powers and processes of Nature. It may even be found that a supraphysical knowledge is necessary for the completion of physical knowledge, because the processes of physical Nature have behind them a supraphysical factor, a power and action mental, vital or spiritual which is not tangible to any outer means of knowledge."[26]

Mirra approached occultism with the same scientific but open-minded spirit. "[Occultism] is a knowledge which in the modern world is hardly recognized as scientific", she said, "but which *is* scientific in the sense that it has precise procedures and that, if one reproduces the circumstances exactly, one obtains the same results."[27] "Occultism in the West ... never reached its majority, never acquired ripeness and a philosophic or sound systematic foundation. It indulged too freely in the romance of the supernatural or made the mistake of concentrating its major effort on the discovery of formulas and effective modes for using supernatural powers. It deviated into magic, white and black, or into romantic or thaumaturgic paraphernalia of occult mysticism and the exaggeration of what was after all a limited and scanty knowledge. These tendencies and this insecurity of a mental foundation made it difficult to defend and easy to discredit, a target facile and vulnerable." (Sri Aurobindo[28])

Mirra and Henri Morisset had grown apart. She was now living on her own in the bustling metropolis that was Paris and participated in its life in many ways, as we find in her reminiscences. She tells about its theatre: the popular *Grand Guignol* with spectacles like *Le Bossu* (the hunchback), in a way the James Bond capers of those days; the boulevard theatre with the comedies of Georges Feydeau, and the classical performances at the *Comédie française*. There were her meetings with famous people like the novelists Anatole France

---

[26]Sri Aurobindo: *The Life Divine*, p. 652.
[27]The Mother: *Questions and Answers 1954*, p. 38.
[28]Sri Aurobindo, op. cit., p. 876.

and Henryk Sienkiewicz, the author of *Quo Vadis*. There was the music of Richard Wagner, Camille Saint-Saëns, César Franck and Ambroise Thomas, the composer of *Mignon* and twenty-one other operas, and the concerts of Eugène Ysaye, the great Belgian violinist.

It is probable that Mirra met Paul Richard, somewhere in 1908, through the Théons, for he too had travelled to Tlemcen to meet them. Richard was a rather ambitious humanitarian, socialist and freethinker who had been a protestant pastor in Lille and became a barrister at the Paris Court of Appeals after having obtained his law degree. In 1910 he sailed to Pondicherry apparently to canvass for the candidate there of his socialist Party; for Pondicherry, as a French *comptoir*, was entitled to one member of the House of Representatives in Paris. What Richard really was looking for seems to have been a yogi who could initiate him in the occult and spiritual aspects of life which interested him above all else. When soon after his arrival in the sleepy South port town he started asking around, he was told that he was in luck, for a great yogi had just arrived from the north. And this is how Paul Richard met Sri Aurobindo, by whom he was very impressed.

It would take another four years before Richard, this time accompanied by Mirra, whom he had married in 1911, returned to Pondicherry, now to be himself a candidate in the elections for the House of Representatives. In the meantime Mirra had come to know the Sufi master and musician Inayat Khan, on a European tour with his 'Royal Musicians of Hindustan', and she had become especially well acquainted with Abdul Baha, the son and successor of Baha Ullah, the founder of the Baha'i faith.

Mirra had now become so well trained in spirituality and occultism, and she had assembled such an ample experience in these fields, that she might be considered an advanced *yogini* in her own right. Through her meetings with Eastern and Western masters, she had in fact discovered that a new synthesis was necessary which could lead to the advent of a new world. Her vision had much in common with what Paul Richard told her about the ideas of Sri Aurobindo. Having married Richard, she consented to accompany him to Pondicherry on the second lap of his adventures there, not suspecting what was awaiting her. They arrived in Pondicherry on 29 March 1914. Richard hurried to meet his yogi from Bengal, but Mirra waited till the afternoon of that Sunday, for she wanted to meet the yogi alone to see for herself who he was. The encounter must have been decisive, for she wrote in her diary on 1 April: 'A new phase has begun'.

Richard's electoral efforts were a fiasco; in the gangster world of Pondicherrian politics at that time he was but an unwitting lamb among wolves. He was more successful on another terrain, when he could convince Sri Aurobindo to make his revolutionary vision known to the world by publishing it in a philosophical magazine. The monthly periodical was called *Arya* and carried on its cover for the first time the name 'Sri Aurobindo' Ghose, together with the names of the other two editors, Paul and Mirra Richard. It was in this magazine that Sri Aurobindo published his major works from 1914 to 1921. Month after month he wrote simultaneously chapters of *The Life Divine*, *The Synthesis of Yoga*, *The Ideal of Human Unity*, *The Human Cycle*, *The Secret of the Veda*, and other works, each time managing to have his texts ready for the printer just ahead of the deadline. In some cases it took more than twenty years before these works were published in book form.

Soon Sri Aurobindo had to carry the burden of writing and publishing the magazine all by himself, for Paul Richard was expelled from French India because of his relations with the dreaded Aurobindo Ghose. Whenever a terrorist act against the colonial authorities was committed, Ghose, in spite of his fame as scholar and yogi, was still suspected of being the master brain behind it although he was no longer involved in this kind of actions. Paul and Mirra Richard sailed back to a Europe at war. In 1916 Paul Richard managed to obtain a trade commission in Japan, and the Richards again sailed eastward, this time on risky waters because of the German U-boats. Mirra will always remember Japan for the superb beauty she had encountered there time and again, but also for the mental rigidity of the people.

After a stay of four years at Tokyo and Kyoto, the Richards returned to India, closely watched by the British police. Mirra would never leave Pondicherry again. Paul, however great his admiration for Sri Aurobindo's knowledge, could not accept his spiritual superiority, for he had ambitions of his own; he would end as a professor at an American university.

In the first years of her life in Pondicherry, Mirra practically led a life of seclusion, discreetly creating a suitable material environment in which Sri Aurobindo could work out his yoga. When his yoga reached the point that, in 1926, he had to retire fully for its continuation, she came forward to take up the leadership of the community which had formed around Sri Aurobindo, and which was now called an 'ashram' for lack of a better than the traditional word. An ashram is a spiritual community around a guru. The 'Sri Aurobindo Ashram', however, was not conceived as a closed community, witness the presence of women on an equal footing with the men, and later of children. It was meant to be the seedbed of an integral life creative of a new world, and therefore had to remain open to the world, of which it had to accept the problems and try to find their solutions. It was symbolically situated in the middle of the town.

Mirra was now 'the Mother of the Sri Aurobindo Ashram' after Sri Aurobindo had started calling her the 'Mother'. Sri Aurobindo stopped seeing people and continued his great spiritual work unseen and unknown. The only glimpses we have of it from those years are passages in the stream of letters he wrote to the growing number of disciples, and in some poems. After the high tide of literary, philosophical and yogic creativity of the *Arya* period he wrote no other works, although he constantly continued rewriting and expanding his epic *Savitri*, begun at Baroda and finished in the last days of his life. The Mother was always present with the disciples and built up an exemplary community which was a world in miniature.

During the Second World War she would even set up a system of education for the children of the refugee families connected with the Ashram and who fled before an invasion by the Japanese.

About Golconde, a guest house constructed under the Mother's direction in a street near the main Ashram building, the following statement was made at the 'Solar World Congress' in Perth, Australia (1983): "In one of the most remote parts of India, one of the most advanced buildings in the world was constructed under the most demanding circumstances concerning material and craftsmen. This reinforced concrete structure was completed primarily by unskilled volunteers [ie Ashramites] with the most uncertain supplies [the work was interrupted by the Second World War and the prices of the materials increased tenfold], and with virtually every fitting custom-fabricated. Yet this handsome building has world-stature, both architecturally and in its bio-climatic response to a tropical climate, 13°N of the equator."[29]

The main effort of Sri Aurobindo's yoga consisted in realising a higher form of consciousness, called by him 'Supermind', and bringing it down into matter, so that it might work itself out and create a new, higher species. 'Matter' here signified in the first place his own material body, used as the part of the matter of humanity which would serve as the representative centre of descent. From his *Correspondence with Nirodbaran*, his frequent written exchanges with the Ashram doctor, we know that after all those years of uninterrupted effort this descent was imminent. But it was at that moment that forces adverse to his effort and the progress of humanity attacked him personally (he fell and broke his thigh) in order to postpone or even cancel the realisation. The same forces were mustering their legions in the world and caused the outbreak of the Second World War, to which Sri Aurobindo and the Mother attached so much importance that it interrupted their yoga for the duration.

---

[29]*Mother India*, Jan. 1989, p. 26. For more details about Golconde see Georges Van Vrekhem: *Beyond Man*, pp. 204 ff.

Even when the Second World War, or the second act of 'the Twentieth Century World War', was finished, Sri Aurobindo declared the global situation to be as grim as ever, if not more. Humanity had now acquired unprecedented destructive powers, and the attempts at world conquest by the communist block raised the fear of a third and final act of the Twentieth Century World War: Armageddon, the ultimate destruction. It was in these circumstances that Sri Aurobindo, for reasons unknown to his exegetes, left his body to work again behind the scenes, this time not of politics but of the perceptible world. The Mother continued the yoga in the body and announced in 1956 that the descent of the Supermind in the earth atmosphere had finally taken place. "A new world is born", she said. From conversations with disciples we can gather an idea of the work she then took up: the essay at transformation of the human body into the body of a new species. She reported having succeeded in building what one might call the 'archetype' of the new species, and laid down her old material body in 1973.

'The Titan kings attack ...'

Sri Aurobindo never considered his seclusion at the end of 1926 to be definitive. It was a necessity of his yoga, imposed upon him by the inner Voice which he obeyed unconditionally. His seclusion was misunderstood by many, and the temporary seal of secrecy on his yoga, as on all inner explorations, did not allow him to set things straight at once. "Those concerned with day-to-day politics deplored his retirement and thought that he was lost to India and the world, being interested only in his own spiritual salvation. So he was called a truant and escapist. Even now there is insufficient understanding of what led to his decision," Nirodbaran writes in *Twelve Years with Sri Aurobindo*.

In spiritual as in political matters Sri Aurobindo was a radical. The unconditional independence of India was thought to be a chimera when he was the first to demand it from the colonial occupant; now the integral transformation of Matter in its divine essence, with the formation of a new evolutionary species, was supposed to be equally chimerical. Sri Aurobindo had not started with this idea, or with any other idea. He had been gradually led to its revelation by his ever expanding realisations, and was at times daunted by them and by the effort they demanded from him. But he was stubborn and his surrender to the inner Guidance could be shaken but not eradicated. "Let all men jeer at me if they will or all Hell fall upon me if it will for my presumption – I go on till I conquer or perish. This is the spirit in which I seek the Supermind, no hunting for greatness for myself or others", he wrote in a letter.[30]

"The thing to be done is as large as human life, and therefore the individuals who lead the way will take all human life for their province. These pioneers will consider nothing as alien to them, nothing as outside their scope. For every part of human life has to be taken up by the spiritual – not only the intellectual, the aesthetic, the ethical, but the dynamic, the vital, the physical; therefore for none of these things or the activities that spring from them will they have contempt or aversion, however they may insist on a change of the spirit and a transmutation of the form." (*The Human Cycle*[31]) "Sri Aurobindo once wrote to a disciple: 'I think I can say that I have been testing day and night for years upon years' his spiritual knowledge and experience 'more scrupulously than any scientist his theory or his method on the physical plane'. The *Record of Yoga* bears this out in detail. It may be looked on as the laboratory notebook of an extended series of experiments of yoga." (Peter Heehs[32]) For he had no intention "of giving his sanction to a new edition of the old fiasco" by bringing a new yoga "with no true and radical change in the law of the outer nature".[33]

---

[30]Id., p. 144.
[31]Sri Aurobindo: *The Human Cycle*, p. 266.
[32]Peter Heehs, op.cit., pp. 99-100.
[33]Sri Aurobindo: *Letters on Yoga*, p. 1306.

If Sri Aurobindo's withdrawal from public life was not a retirement, it was still less a retreat in the sense of a separation from worldly matters. He read the newspapers and followed attentively what was going on in the world. There were also the yogic means of perception which he had developed: "I look across the world and no horizon walls my gaze ..."[34] And there was the daily chore of answering the letters from his disciples who could correspond freely with him and sometimes availed themselves rather indiscriminatingly of the privilege. "My dear sir", Sri Aurobindo wrote to Nirodbaran, "if you saw me nowadays with my nose to paper from afternoon to morning, deciphering, deciphering, writing, writing, writing, even the rocky heart of a disciple would be touched ..."[35] In these letters, published in the still increasing volumes of *Letters on Yoga*, all problems of the human condition are discussed, from the trivial to the sublime, and they reflect faithfully the political developments within and outside India.

Then there were the unceasing yogic battles he had to fight, for no yogic exploration or new effort at progress remains unchallenged, as the invisible powers-that-be want first and foremost to keep their grip on a world which is still under their rule. About this aspect of his work, at the time unknown to anybody, Sri Aurobindo wrote in 1935 one of the most wonderful poems in any language, *A God's Labour*. It is a kind of ballad in a light, almost nonchalant rhythm narrating the ordeal of the pioneers of evolution. "He who would bring the heavens here / Must descend himself into clay / And the burden of earthly nature bear / And tread the dolorous way ... My gaping wounds are a thousand and one / And the Titan kings assail, / But I cannot rest till my task is done / And wrought the eternal will ... I have delved through the dumb Earth's dreadful heart / And heard her black mass' bell. / I have seen the source whence her agonies part / And the inner reason of hell ..."[36]

---

[34]Sri Aurobindo: *Collected Poems*, p. 120.
[35]Nirodbaran: *Correspondence with Sri Aurobindo*, p. 525.
[36]Sri Aurobindo, op. cit., pp. 99 ff.

The 'Titan kings' attacked Sri Aurobindo in the very early hours of 24 November 1938, one of the four yearly darshan days on which disciples and visitors could come in his presence, with the Mother at his side, and receive their blessings. Sri Aurobindo fell heavily in his apartment and broke his right thigh. This happened at a time that, after years of continuous effort, the descent into matter of the higher, supramental Consciousness was expected. Now the circumstances of Sri Aurobindo's life changed drastically. Where before only the Mother and the faithful Champaklal had been regular visitors to his rooms, now doctors, medical assistants and one or two other helpers had to be admitted, for the fracture of the thigh had been nasty and took a long time to heal. The people present with Sri Aurobindo profited of the occasion to talk with him and ask questions. These conversations have been noted down by AB Purani in his *Evening Talks with Sri Aurobindo* and by Nirodbaran Talukdar in his *Talks with Sri Aurobindo*. Their notes remain a direct source of the involvement of Sri Aurobindo and the Mother in the Second World War.

To a disciple Sri Aurobindo will write in July 1942, when the outcome of the war was still in the balance: "You should not think of [the war] as a fight of certain nations against others or even for India; it is a struggle for an ideal that has to establish itself fully and against a darkness and falsehood that are trying to overwhelm the earth and mankind in the immediate future. It is the forces behind the battle that have to be seen and not this or that superficial circumstance ... It is a struggle for the liberty of mankind to develop, for conditions in which men have freedom and room to think and act according to the light in them and grow in the Truth, grow in the Spirit.

"There cannot be the slightest doubt that if one side wins, there will be an end of all such freedom and hope of light and truth and the work that has to be done will be subjected to conditions which would make it humanly impossible; there will be a reign of falsehood and darkness, a cruel oppression and degradation for most of the human race such as people in this country [i.e. India] do not dream of and cannot yet at all realize. If the other side that has declared itself for the free future of humanity triumphs, this terrible danger will have been averted and conditions will have been created in which there will be a chance for the Ideal to grow, for the Divine Work to be done, for the spiritual Truth for which we stand to establish itself on the earth. Those who fight for this cause are fighting for the Divine and against the threatened reign of the Asura."[37]

The human cycle

Sri Aurobindo's writings are not only based on a severely tested spiritual experience but also on a vast erudition. He was thoroughly familiar with the tradition and cultures of the East and the West and some of their principal languages, and he had imbibed the literature and the poetry of their epics and lyrics, Homer and Shelley as well as Vyasa and Kalidasa. He admired Plato greatly and classical Greek culture as a whole – 'where living itself was an education' – witness his essay on Heraclitus and the four thousand hexameters of his unfinished epic *Ilion*. He had the highest appreciation of the Buddha, "in his action the most powerful personality that we know of as having lived and produced results upon earth"[38], and referred to Nietzsche throughout his oeuvre.

It is a sign of his erudition (and excellent memory) that he used an idea of Karl Lamprecht as the starting point of *The Human Cycle*. Lamprecht (1856-1915) was a famous (Pan-) German historian, professor of history at Bonn and Leipzig, author of a *Deutsche Geschichte* (history of Germany) in twelve volumes and adviser to Chancellor Bethmann Hollweg. As "one of the first scholars to develop a systematic theory of psychological factors in history" he

---

[37] Sri Aurobindo: *On Himself*, p. 593.
[38] Sri Aurobindo: *The Life Divine*, p. 29.

gave Sri Aurobindo the idea of a cycle of humanity's development consisting of a symbolic, typal, conventional, individualistic and subjective stage.

The symbolic stage is predominantly religious and spiritual; life is the direct expression or symbol of an inner truth. The typal stage is predominantly psychological and ethical; spiritual truths become moral ideals or norms and psychological qualities 'typal' categories. "The conventional stage of human society is born when the external supports, the outward expressions of the spirit or the ideal become more important than the ideal, the body or even the clothes more important than the person." It is a stage of standardization and rigidity which gradually becomes 'a name, a shell, a sham' which "must either be dissolved in the crucible of an individualist period of society or else fatally affect with weakness and falsehood the system of life that clings to it".[39]

"The revolting individual flings off the yoke, declares the truth as he sees it and in doing so strikes inevitably at the root of the religious, the social, the political, momentarily perhaps even the moral order of the community as it stands, because it stands upon the authority he discredits and the convention he destroys and not upon a living truth which can be successfully opposed to his own. The champions of the old order may be right when they seek to suppress him as a destructive agency perilous to social security, political order or religious tradition; but he stands there and can no other [according to the famous statement of Martin Luther], because to destroy is his mission, to destroy falsehood and lay bare a new foundation of truth." With the individualistic stage "the Age of Protestantism has begun, the Age of Reason, the Age of Revolt, Progress, Freedom"[40] – the age of possible renewal and rebirth, renaissance and reformation.

---

[39] Sri Aurobindo: *The Human Cycle*, pp. 11, 12.
[40] Id., pp. 17, 14.

It is this age of breaking up of the petrified layers of human thought and society which allows humanity to see the world new again and to explore the living reality. It is the passage to "the subjective period of humanity through which man has to circle back towards the recovery of his deeper self and a new upward line or a new revolving cycle of civilization". The historical phases of this 'human cycle' will be clear after everything we have learned in our story about the end of the Christian Era in Europe, the beginning of a new cycle of searching possibilities with the Renaissance and the Age of Reason, and the importance of the great mutation, the *Wende*, starting around 1880 in which we are still fully involved at present and which has already produced such dramatic events. It should be added that Sri Aurobindo's cycles are never repetitive but the expression of an upward evolution, realising itself in an ever widening spiral.

"The Age of Reason is visibly drawing to an end", he wrote in 1916. "Novel ideas are sweeping over the world and are being accepted with a significant rapidity, ideas inevitably subversive of any premature typal order of economic rationalism, dynamic ideas such as Nietzsche's Will-to-live, Bergson's exaltation of Intuition above intellect or the latest German philosophical tendency to acknowledge a suprarational faculty and a suprarational order of truths. Already another mental poise is beginning to settle and conceptions are on the way to apply themselves in the field of practice which promise to give the succession of the individualistic age of society not to a new typal order, but to a subjective age which may well be a great and momentous passage to a very different goal. It may be doubted whether we are not already in the morning twilight of a new period of the human cycle."[41]

Sri Aurobindo was convinced of the importance of the change to which humanity was being subjected. Far from considering that the confusion and violence of this change was a negative omen, he valued it positively as the accelerated evolution into a new and

---

[41] Id., pp. 22-23.

greater era. "All these tendencies, though in a crude, initial and ill-developed form, are manifest now in the world and are growing from day to day with a significant rapidity. And their emergence and greater dominance means the transition from the rationalistic and utilitarian period of human development which individualism has created to a greater subjective age of society."[42] Yet so profound was the change, including the globalisation of mankind, that it led to the explosion of two 'hot' world wars and a potentially still more destructive 'cold' third one, the slaughter of millions, and the re-emergence of the darkest layers in the human personality.

Sri Aurobindo had clearly perceived the threatening aspect of the German national character before the First World War. "The military power, the political and commercial ambitions of Germany and her acute sense of her confined geographical position and her encirclement by an unfriendly alliance were the immediate moral cause of [the First World War]; but the real cause lay in the very nature of the international situation and the psychology of national life. The chief feature of this psychology is the predominance and worship of national egoism under the sacred name of patriotism." The national egoism of Germany had taken on excessive proportions leading to an irreversible course of its politics. "In Germany it was the aristocratic and the capitalist class combined that constituted the Pan-German party with its exaggerated and almost insane ambitions ... Pan-Germanism covered the longings of German industry for possession of the great resources and the large outlet into the North Sea offered by the countries along the Rhine. To seize African spaces of exploitation and perhaps French coal fields ... was the drift of its real intention."[43]

In *The Human Cycle* Sri Aurobindo presents Germany's conclusions of its dominant Darwinistic stance as follows: "The conquest of the world by German culture is the straight path of

---

[42]Id., p. 29.
[43]Sri Aurobindo: *The Ideal of Human Unity*, pp. 209, 219.

human progress. But culture is not, in this view, merely a state of knowledge or a system or cast of ideas and moral and aesthetic tendencies; culture is life governed by ideas, but ideas based on the truths of life and so organized as to bring it to its highest efficiency. Therefore all life not capable of this culture and this efficiency must be eliminated or trodden down, all life capable of it but not actually reaching to it must be taken up and assimilated. But capacity is always a matter of genus and species and in humanity a matter of race. Logically, then, the Teutonic race is alone entirely capable, and therefore all Teutonic races must be taken into Germany and become part of the German collectivity; races less capable but not wholly unfit must be Germanized, others, hopelessly decadent like the Latins of Europe and America or naturally inferior like the vast majority of the Africans and Asiatics, must be replaced where possible, dominated, exploited and treated according to their inferiority. So evolution would advance, so the human race grow towards its perfection."[44] It is all there, the German racial superiority complex and their future racial politics, summarised in a few lines.

Parallels and contrasts

There are striking parallels between the conceptions of Adolf Hitler and the vision of Sri Aurobindo. After all, Hitler saw himself as the announcer and initiator of a new era in human history which was succeeding the millennium of the Christian Era; it was his intention to create a race of supermen who were to be the lords of a new world; this race of supermen would create and rule their new world supported by their faith in their race and the mission of this race; their domination would ultimately be global and last a thousand years, in other words forever; the supermen would, moreover, become always purer and nobler because they would be freed of the peril of degradation by lower races and especially by the demonic race

---

[44] Sri Aurobindo: *The Human Cycle*, pp. 50-51.

that was the lowest of all, the Jews. As Sri Aurobindo's vision was that of a new era initiating the transformation of the human race into a race of higher beings he also called 'supermen', and as these higher beings would populate a new world, the expression of the higher consciousness which they would embody, it could be said that in broad outline Hitler's vision was the shadow of Sri Aurobindo's vision. Considerations of this sort have indeed led some to declare Hitler an 'avatar', i.e. a divine incarnation come to initiate a new age (cf. Miguel Sarrano: *Hitler – El ultimo Avatar*).

Yet, where Sri Aurobindo's vision is intrinsically progressive, Hitler's view and initiatives were retrograde, intending to lead humanity back to an era of barbarism which it was supposed to have left definitively behind. Hitler's 'new man' was educated to be blindly obedient and no longer subject to feelings or emotions; he was trained to behave in a superior, ruthless way towards people not of his kind, and to consider hardship and war as his element, death as his glorification. He took pride in being hardhearted and violent to the point of cruelty. His identity was expressed by his uniform, his usefulness to the Volk by his regimentation. What Hitler's superman would die for, he knew; what he would live for remains an enigma. Would racial pride, some resurrected folklore and a religion of the masses suffice? Could the life of a superior racial robot be satisfactory? And who would be their living god after Hitler had left the earthly stage?

In contrast with this terrible prospect of a world ruled by racial robots, Sri Aurobindo stressed the crucial importance of the individual, always of a higher consciousness than the group or the mass, and the centre or 'dynamo' of the cosmic forces in humanity. "The communal mind holds things subconsciously at first or, if consciously, then in a confused chaotic manner; it is only through the individual mind that the mass can arrive at a clear knowledge and creation of it held in its subconscient self. Thinkers, historians, sociologists who belittle the individual and would like to lose him in the mass or think of him chiefly as a cell, an atom, have got hold only of the obscurer side of the truth of Nature's workings in humanity. It is because man is not like the material formations of Nature or like the animal, because she intends in him a more and more conscious evolution, that individuality is so much developed in him and so absolutely important and indispensable."[45]

"The principle of individualism is the liberty of the human being regarded as a separate existence to develop himself and fulfil his life, satisfy his mental tendencies, emotional and vital needs and physical being according to his own desire governed by his reason; it admits no other limit to this right and this liberty except the obligation to respect the same individual liberty and right in others ... In this idea of life, as with the individual, so with the nation, each has the inherent right to manage its own affairs freely or, if it wills, to mismanage them freely and not to be interfered with in its rights and liberties so long as it does not interfere with the rights and liberties of other nations." In these formulations of Sri Aurobindo one hears a direct echo of Kant and the ideals of the Enlightenment.

As we have seen repeatedly, Fascism as a whole and Nazism in particular were a revolt against everything the Enlightenment stood for, especially the idea of 'progress'. The message of Sri Aurobindo lay precisely in the possibility and the necessity of an upward transformation of the human being, the only way of real progress. But this is a most difficult undertaking, which may be the reason why it was never tried out before. Now Mother Earth seemed to have reached a point in the human race where the conditions had grown opportune to try the impossible. Were not all indications around 1900 pointing towards a momentous change, for better or worse?

Sri Aurobindo strongly asserted the importance of the ideals of the Enlightenment to sustain the impetus of the forward movement in humanity. The new values – the 'democratic trinity' of liberty, equality and fraternity – had to be made permanent fixtures in the psychological structure of humanity. The ways of 'the forward

---

[45] Id., p. 246.

evolution' had to be kept open. "What we have to see is on which side men and nations put themselves; if they put themselves on the right side, they at once make themselves instruments of the Divine purpose in spite of all defects, errors, wrong movements and actions which are common to human nature and all human collectivities. The victory of one side (the Allies) would keep the path open for the evolutionary forces; the victory of the other side would drag back humanity, degrade it horribly and might lead even, at the worst, to its eventual failure as a race, as others in the past evolution failed and perished".[46]

A higher and a lower choice: what went wrong

And yet, seldom has a non-German shown a greater appreciation for the qualities and possibilities in the German people than Sri Aurobindo. "Germany was for the time the most remarkable instance of a nation preparing for the subjective stage because it had, in the first place, a certain kind of vision – unfortunately intellectual rather than illuminated – and the courage to follow it – unfortunately again a vital and intellectual rather than a spiritual hardihood – and, secondly, being master of its destinies, was able to order its own life so as to express its self-vision ... The real source of this great subjective force which has been so much disfigured in its objective action, was not in Germany's statesman and soldiers ... but came from her great philosophers, Kant, Hegel, Fichte, Nietzsche, from her great poet and thinker Goethe, from her great musicians, Beethoven and Wagner, and from all in the German soul and temperament which they represented. A nation whose master achievement has lain almost entirely in the two spheres of philosophy and music is clearly predestined to lead in the turn to subjectivism and to produce a profound result for good or evil on the beginnings of the subjective age.

---

[46]Sri Aurobindo: *On Himself,* p. 396.

"This was one side of the predestination of Germany; the other is to be found in her scholars, educationists, scientists, organizers. It was the industry, the conscientious diligence, the fidelity to ideas, the honest and painstaking spirit of work for which the nation has been long famous. A people might be highly gifted in the subjective capacities, and yet if it neglects to cultivate this lower side of our complex nature, it will fail to build that bridge between the idea and the imagination and the world of facts, between the vision and the force, which makes realisation possible ... In Germany the bridge was there ... For more than a half-century Germany turned a deep eye of subjective introspection on herself and things and ideas in search of the truth of her own being and of the world, and for another half-century a patient eye of scientific research on the objective means for organizing what she had or thought she had gained."

Then what went wrong? "[Germany] had taken her vital ego for herself; she had sought for her soul and found only her force. For she had said, like the Asura, 'I am my body, my life, my mind, my temperament', and became attached with a Titanic force to these; especially she had said, 'I am my life and body', and than that there can be no greater mistake for man or nation. The soul of man or nation is something more and diviner than that; it is greater than its instruments and cannot be shut up in a physical, a vital, a mental or a temperamental formula. So to confine it, even though the false formation be embodied in the armour-plated social body of a huge collective dinosaurus, can only stifle the growth of the inner Reality and end in decay or the extinction that overtakes all that is unplastic and unadaptable."[47]

This paragraph was written during the First World War; it would still more fully apply to the Germany that caused the outbreak of the Second World War. For a time Germany was the only nation in which there was a longing and a possibility to go beyond man, as

---

[47]Sri Aurobindo: *The Human Cycle*, pp. 40 ff. passim.

shown in the pages of our story about the projection of one kind of a superman or other, as well as in those about the knowledge that 'God' was to be met in one's own soul, and that this soul could communicate with the soul of the nation and the soul in all. What power distorted these perspectives and bend them back to the nether regions we will now have to find out.

15

'THE LORD OF THE NATIONS'

Only he can release me of my mission who has called me to it.
                                                    ADOLF HITLER

Our story has taken an unexpected turn with the introduction into it of India, and of two personalities who are generally associated with different terrains of interest, Sri Aurobindo and the Mother of the Sri Aurobindo Ashram. All the same, there were two and a half million Indians who fought in the combat theatres of the British army. India played an important role in Hitler's strategic thinking, as we will see below, and Japan tried to invade the Indian subcontinent. India was the central pillar of the British Empire, and as such one of the main stakes of the war despite the prevalent interest in Europe and the Pacific. And the constant interrelation with the war of the spiritual leaders in Pondicherry is extensively documented, perhaps the most convincing argument for its importance being the consistency of their endeavour.

Given the abundance of 'spurious' literature about Hitler, Nazism and the Order of the Death's Head, there would be no point to make if this presentation of new material, from however unfamiliar an angle, did not contribute to the elucidation of some fundamental questions which consensus history has not been able to answer. Respect for the historical facts is elementary. The new generation of German historians tackles facts which up to now were taboo, although essential for the understanding of Hitler and his revolutionary movement. Many of these newly evaluated facts are connected with the birth of National Socialism, others with the psychological involvement of the Germans with their Führer, the Reich and the war, and with the puzzling personality of that Führer which made National Socialism and the war possible. Our story too moves in this direction.

The four asuras

"When we say that Hitler is possessed by a vital power, it is a statement of fact, not a moral judgement. His being possessed is clear from what he does and the way he does it", said Sri Aurobindo* in January 1939. He confirmed this repeatedly: "One can say that Hitler is not a devil but that he is possessed by one".[1] As mentioned before, Sri Aurobindo followed the events in the world closely. The Mother will even say that the war interrupted their yogic work completely, as the global situation was so critical that they could not afford to turn away from it even for a moment.

One finds indications of Sri Aurobindo's growing concern with Nazism in his *Correspondence with Nirodbaran*, covering the middle 1930s. The run-up to the war and its initial stages were a daily subject of discussion with the small group of disciples gathered around him after he had broken his right thigh. He will even install a loudspeaker connected with an outside radio in his room to hear the BBC-news directly for himself. "I have not seen any other person who has followed the Asura with such extraordinary fidelity", he said about

---

*It should be remembered that Sri Aurobindo's words, quoted from the *Talks with Sri Aurobindo* and *Evening Talks with Sri Aurobindo*, are reported speech, although with great care noted down within hours after they were spoken.
[1] Nirodbaran: *Talks with Sri Aurobindo*, pp. 190, 575.

Hitler after his invasion of France. "He never considers possibilities. Possibilities don't matter. This is how he goes against all the generals ... All through he has been guided by inspiration and he has gone ahead depending on luck ... He has a most original mind because it is not his own mind."[2]

Hitler was, according to the Mother, 'very conscious of being the instrument' of the asura. We read in a letter to her son André written in October 1938, after the fate of Czechoslovakia was sealed at Munich: "Speaking of recent events, you ask me whether it was 'a dangerous bluff' or whether we 'narrowly escaped disaster'. To assume both at the same time would be nearer to the truth. Hitler was certainly bluffing ... Tactics and diplomacy were used, but on the other hand, behind every human will there are forces in action whose origin is not human and which move consciously towards certain goals. The play of these forces is very complex and generally eludes the human consciousness. But for the sake of explanation and easy understanding, they can be divided into two main opposing tendencies: those that work for the fulfilment of the Divine Work upon earth and those that are opposed to this fulfilment ... Hitler is a choice instrument of these anti-divine forces which want violence, upheavals and war, for they know that all this delays and hinders the action of the divine forces. That is why disaster was very close although no human government consciously wanted it."[3]

In one of the Mother's recorded talks to the children of the Ashram school, she said in 1951: "Hitler communicated with a being which he considered to be the Supreme. This being came and gave him advice, it told him everything he had to do. Hitler used to retire into solitude and remain there as long as necessary to come into contact with his 'guide' and receive from him the inspirations which afterwards he carried out very faithfully. This being, which Hitler took for the Supreme, was quite simply an *asura*, the one who is

---
[2] Id., pp. 817, 806.
[3] *Glimpses of the Mother's Life 2*, p. 157.

called 'the Lord of Falsehood' in occultism, and who has proclaimed himself 'the Lord of the Nations'. His appearance was resplendent, he could mislead anybody except those who had the real occult knowledge and could see what was there behind the appearance. He would have deceived anybody, he was really splendid.

"He generally appeared to Hitler wearing a silver cuirass and helmet; it was as if fire irradiated from his head, and there was an aura of dazzling light around him ... He told Hitler everything he wanted him to do: he played with him like with a little monkey or a mouse. He had clearly decided to make Hitler commit all possible excesses till the day he would break his neck – which was what happened ... Hitler was a very good medium. He had great mediumistic capacities but he lacked intelligence and discernment. That being could tell him anything whatsoever and he would swallow it all. It was he who pushed Hitler onward little by little. And he was doing this for fun, he did not take it at all seriously. For such beings humans are tiny things with which they play as cats play with mice, till they eat them up."[4]

"In his youth, [Hitler] was considered an amusing crank and nobody took any notice of him", said Sri Aurobindo. "It is the vital possession that gives him his size and greatness. Without this vital power he would be a crudely amiable fellow with some hobbies and eccentricities. It is in this kind of person, whose psychic is underdeveloped and weak, that possession is possible. There is nothing in the being that can resist the Power. In his latest photographs [in January 1939] I find that he is becoming more and more criminal and going down very fast." It was also in those days that Sri Aurobindo remarked: "It seems strange that the destiny of the whole world should depend on one man and yet it is so, for everybody looks up to him. From one point of view there never was a time when humanity came down so low as it has now. It looks as if a small

---

[4] La Mère: *Entretiens 1950-51*, pp. 207-08.

number of violent men are the arbiters of humanity and the rest of the world is ready to bow down before one man."[5]

"Hitler was quite simply a human being, and as a human being he was very soft, very sentimental," said the Mother. "He had the conscience of a simple workman, some said of a shoemaker – in any case of a simple workman or a little schoolmaster, something of that kind. But he was possessed ... He was a medium, a very good medium. Besides, *it was during spiritist séances that the possession took hold of him*. It was at such times [of possession] that he was seized by those fits which were said to be epileptic. They were not epileptic: they were crises of possession ... When he wanted to know something from that being, he went to his villa [on the Obersalzberg] to meditate. There he really made an intense appeal to what he called his god, his supreme god, who was the 'Lord of the Nations' ... Of course [that being] did not appear physically. Hitler was a medium, he 'saw', he had a certain power of clairvoyance. And it was at such times that he had his fits ... The people in his entourage knew that."[6]

Rumours of Hitler's perplexing crises seeped through to the public and were the reason why his opponents called him the *Teppichfresser*, the carpet chewer. The best known example of a description of this phenomenon is the last chapter of Hermann Rauschning's talks with Hitler, quoted in a previous chapter. The authenticity of Hitler's crises is still disputed. There are, however, many reports of his states of utter rage, especially in conferences with his generals, when he shrieked, his face became purple and foam appeared in the corners of his mouth; therefore the disposition was certainly present.

Ambassador François-Poncet also mentions that Hitler's entourage talked about crises he was subject to "which went from excesses of a devastating rage to the plaintive whimperings of a

---

[5]Nirodbaran, op. cit., pp. 194, 85.
[6]La Mère: *Entretiens 1953*, pp. 429-30 (emphasis added).

wounded animal ... What is sure is that he was not normal; he was a morbid man, near to being demented, a personage from Dostoyevsky, one of the 'possessed'."[7] And there is the following passage in Shirer's *Rise and Fall of the Third Reich* about the days of Hitler's meetings with Chamberlain, when the Führer was "in a highly nervous state": "He seemed to be, as I noted in my diary that evening, on the edge of a nervous breakdown. *'Teppichfresser!'* muttered my German companion, an editor who secretly despised the Nazis. And he explained that Hitler had been in such a maniacal mood over the Czechs the last few days that on more than one occasion he had lost control of himself completely, hurling himself to the floor and chewing the edge of the carpet. Hence the term 'carpet eater'. The evening before, while talking with some of the party hacks at [Hotel] Dreesen, I had heard the expression applied to the Führer – in whispers, of course."[8]

"To be a successful instrument of the Asuric forces is easy, because they take all the movements of your lower nature and make use of them, so that you have no spiritual effort to make." (Sri Aurobindo[9]) "There is always somebody to receive the influence [of the demonic forces] and who then immediately thinks that he is a very superior being. For this gives people the feeling that they are really, exceptionally remarkable ... This happens to ambitious people, especially to ambitious people who want power, who want to dominate others, who want to be great masters, great instructors, who want to perform miracles and acquire extraordinary powers." (The Mother[10]) Not only can opening to such a possession result in the soul's ruin, it usually also has a devastating physical effect – as shown by the stooping, slouching and trembling Hitler during the last days in the Berlin bunker.

---

[7] André François-Poncet: *Souvenirs d'une ambassade à Berlin*, p. 352.
[8] William Shirer: *The Rise and Fall of the Third Reich*, p. 391.
[9] Sri Aurobindo: *On Himself*, p. 395.
[10] La Mère: *Entretiens 1954*, pp. 283-84, passim.

"Hitler opened himself to forces which carried him onward, forces of dark and destructive power. When he still thought that he had the free choice of his decisions, he had already for a long time surrendered to an influence which one might call, on good grounds and not only metaphorically, demonic magic. And instead of a man who in his upward climb freed himself step by step from the remnants of a dark past, one saw a being that became more and more possessed, at every step more tightly bound, enslaved, incapacitated, the prey of powers who had him in their grip and did not let go of him anymore ... He choose the easier way, let himself go down and entrusted himself to the forces which carried him in his fall." (Hermann Rauschning[11])

"Hitler is a sort of a mystic", said Sri Aurobindo. "Hitler is a new type, an infra-rational mystic, representing the dark counterpart of what we are striving to arrive at: a supra-rational mysticism ... He is a mystic, only a mystic of the wrong kind! He goes into solitude for his messages and waits till they come."[12] This was the reason why Hitler asserted time and time again that "true knowledge was not to be sought in the examination of intellectual matters",[13] and that he insisted on unconditional *faith* in his leadership, for which the knowledge was given to him by a hidden but very powerful and irrefutable source. Most of what is stated here in occult terms was sensed, as we have seen, by perceptive contemporaries who lacked an adequate vocabulary to formulate their perceptions. They called Hitler a shaman, a being of light, a miracle man, a superman, a messiah endowed with the powers to accomplish his world-saving mission. This was how his magic influence and his oratorical and 'mesmeric' powers were explained.

---

[11]Hermann Rauschning: *Gespräche mit Hitler*, pp. 202-03.
[12]Nirodbaran, op. cit., pp. 84, 957, 919.
[13]Ralph Reuth: *Hitler*, p. 183.

Fallen angels

For centuries 'the devil' was one of the most feared presences in European civilization. Learned studies describe how this anti-divine being from the nether worlds originated in Chaldean Mesopotamia. The European imagination represented it as a repulsive replica of the great god Pan. The childishness of this representation was one of the main reasons of the devil's disappearance from the modern religious scene. He looked too ridiculous to be taken seriously by a mentality which now rated itself as scientific. As a result evil became unexplainable, and the boundless evil committed in the Second World War seemed no longer sufficiently substantial to be worthy of serious consideration by some leading historians, while its extreme forms left the theologians tongue-tied.

"The hostile forces exist and have been known to yogic experience ever since the days of the Veda and Zoroaster in Asia (and the mysteries of Egypt and the Cabbala) and in Europe also from old times", wrote Sri Aurobindo.[14] Yogic experience composed a much more detailed and complete repertory of the forces which have established their domain on earth and attack any aspiration in the human soul towards a goal that surpasses them and attempts to eliminate them. According to the Indian tradition there are in descending order the *asuras*, the great hostiles of the vital-mental plane, sometimes compared to the Titans of Greek mythology; then there are the *rakshasas*, the ugly ogres of the vital plane, which are nevertheless perfectly capable of taking on the most seductive appearance; and on the lowest level there are the *pishachas*, the little beings which revel in causing the greatest possible mischief and making life miserable for everybody. Why are these hostile forces there in the cosmos – in a world which after all is fully and totally Brahman?

---

[14]Sri Aurobindo: *Letters on Yoga*, p. 393.

To explain how the hostile forces had come about, the Mother told a story to the children of the Sri Aurobindo Ashram School, insisting that it was no more than a parable to clarify realities which transcend human understanding*. The Supreme Being is *sat-chit-ananda***, in other words Existence-Consciousness-Bliss in eternity, she said. As everything imaginable is contained in it, at one (eternal) moment there arose in it also the urge to manifest its being, and this urge was sufficient to manifest or 'create' the whole scale of the worlds, because what the Divine 'sees' instantly becomes reality. Thus the supercosmic tower of worlds was built, from the lowest to the highest, like a huge staircase of universes all peopled with countless beings. This tower of worlds exists in eternity, for there is never an end to the creative urge in the Divine, although in a simultaneous state He remains withdrawn and detached, self-existent in sempiternal self-contemplation and bliss. These worlds do not change, they do not evolve, and all beings in them are perfectly happy in the state in which they exist.

But as all possibilities are contained in the Divine, there was also the possibility of creating an evolutionary world, a world of total freedom. And because of this freedom it happened that the essential attributes or personalities of the Divine, in a supernal act of ego-centredness, saw themselves as the Supreme, each of them, and turned away from their one Origin. The Truth (*sat*) became Falsehood; Consciousness (*chit*) became Darkness and Ignorance; Life (*tapas*, the power of *chit*) turned into Death; Bliss and Love (*ananda*) changed into Suffering. They are the four great asuras, the Lords

---

*This 'parable' is closely paralleled in many traditions which hold that an 'accident' happened during the creation of the world, or that this world was created by a demiurge. The fallen angels, with Lucifer at their head, are also mentioned in the Bible. The difference with these dualistic conceptions of existence is that in the way the Mother tells the story the effects of the Fall are not permanent, but that there is an evolutionary process by which God's self-manifestation is being turned again into his likeness.

**Sanskrit does not have capital letters.

of Falsehood, Darkness, Death and Suffering – the four powers at the basis of our evolutionary universe, capable of multiplying themselves in cascades of lesser emanations, of lesser demons. They are "The iron dreadful Four who rule our breath, / Masters of falsehood, Kings of ignorance, / High sovereign Lords of suffering and death", as Sri Aurobindo wrote in a sonnet titled 'The Iron Dictators'.[15] They are also the four Horsemen of the Apocalypse, the four powers of hell.

Obviously something had gone wrong with this creation: the Supreme Being had turned into its contrary. And as asuras are absolute, implacable egos, this creation would remain forever a world of falsehood, ignorance, suffering and death. Who was responsible for the 'accident'? The creative Power of the Supreme Being, in other words the Universal Mother, the female Principle of all existence. Therefore she turned towards the Supreme Being for the permission to put forth a second wave of creation following on the first one, and she created the gods, as great as the asuras but less independent-minded. Because of the gods the original state of stagnation could begin to evolve again in a long-term movement which would lead back to the Divine Truth, Light, Life and Love. But the 'iron dictators' do not let go of their power over our universe easily. This is why evolution is a continuous battle between the divine and the asuric forces, as narrated in the traditional stories of all peoples, in their myths.

In the great Fall "the cosmic Intelligence separated itself from the light" of the divine Consciousness, which is a consciousness of unity and therefore of essential, infallible Truth. "As a result, instead of a world of integral truth and divine harmony created in the light of the divine Gnosis, we have a world founded on the part truths of an inferior cosmic Intelligence in which all is half-truth, half-error". Falsehood is an extreme result of this Ignorance. "It is created by an Asuric power which intervenes in the creation and is not only separated from the Truth and therefore limited in knowledge and

---

[15]Sri Aurobindo: *Collected Poems*, p. 136.

open to error, but in revolt against the Truth or in the habit of seizing the Truth only to pervert it. This Power ... puts forward its own perverted consciousness as true knowledge and its wilful distortions or reversals of the Truth as the verity of things."[16]

It was this Power, the Lord of Falsehood who calls himself 'the Lord of the Nations', by whom Hitler was possessed. At the time the nations were undergoing a decisive change towards a new, higher consciousness of truth and harmony, this asuric Power fought with all its might to conserve the status quo of its dominion over the earth. It was, according to Sri Aurobindo and the Mother, the initiator of the twentieth century wars, and prompted not only Hitler but all those who through falsehood and violence acted against the progressive movement of the world and the unification of humanity. It was also the Power by which Hitler was protected.

A charmed life

Hitler regularly visited the widow of his first favourite architect, Paul Troost. She asked him one day why he cared so little about his personal security. His answer was that he was following 'his inner voice' which had told him that he was destined to remain alive "as long as he was needed by the German people". When Germany did not need him any longer, he would be 'called back to his maker'.[17] Albert Speer writes: "The more events drove him into a corner, the more obstinately he opposed to them his certainty about the intentions of Fate. Naturally, he also soberly understood the military facts. But he transmuted them by his own faith and regarded even defeat as a secret guarantee, offered by Providence, of the coming victory. Sometimes he could realize the hopelessness of a situation, but he would not be shaken in his expectation that at the last moment Fate would suddenly turn the tide in his favour. If there

---

[16]Sri Aurobindo, op. cit., p. 381.
[17]David Clay Large: *Hitlers München*, p. 396.

was a fundamental insanity in Hitler, it was this unshakeable belief in his lucky star."[18]

It is a fact that Hitler's eventful life seemed to be protected on numerous occasions and in amazing ways. In the preface to his book about *Die 42 Attentate auf Adolf Hitler* Will Berthold writes: "It is difficult to say exactly how many attempts on Hitler's life there have actually been; the documentation remains incomplete, and the lines between wishful thinking and factual action in the eyewitnesses and executors have become blurred in the meantime." The forty-two attempts he narrates are the ones he could satisfactorily document, but "if one took all cases into account of what conspirators have plotted, agreed upon, tried out, started and initiated, the number of attempts would be considerably higher".[19] Some of these attempts are well known, like the one by Johann Elser in the Munich Bürgerbräukeller on 8 November 1939, when Hitler left early, and the Stauffenberg attempt on 20 July 1944 at the Rastenburg headquarters, when in the conference room the briefcase with the bomb was displaced behind a support of the oak table, away from Hitler, by an unsuspecting general.

During the four years of the First World War, Hitler performed the dangerous job of *Meldegänger*, a runner who had to carry messages from headquarters to the outposts and was, when zigzagging through the rubble and the bomb craters, the favourite target of enemy snipers. "That he always returned unhurt, although he tempted his luck rather brashly, increased his self-confidence immensely. After the ordeals of the first years and several sensational escapes from death, he felt himself more than ever an exceptional figure, one who is protected by the Lord himself – a conviction strengthened by the fact that his apparent invulnerability provided him with a kind of halo among his comrades: "If Hitler is present nothing will happen".[20]

---

[18] Albert Speer: *Inside the Third Reich*, p. 483.
[19] Will Berthold: *Die 42 Attentate auf Adolf Hitler*, p. 8.
[20] Ralph Reuth: *Hitler*, p. 48.

When the police opened fire on the marchers during the 1923 putsch, Hitler was lucky again. "He escaped by a whisker the deadly bullet which killed the man who marched at his right side, Erwin von Scheubner-Richter."[21] This, however, is an incomplete statement of Hitler's luck. For his bodyguard, Ulrich Graf (the burly moustached man one always sees with his Führer's shepherd dog in photos from the first Nazi years) was marching to his left. When the shots rang out, Graf threw himself upon Hitler, who had been pulled down by the weight of Scheubner-Richter, and was hit no less than eleven times. (He survived.)

Ernst Hanfstängl narrates how, during one of his propaganda tours, Hitler's plane, on its way from Königsberg to Kiel, nearly crashed in the Baltic. "The weather was very bad and overcast, but Bauer [Hitler's pilot] got above the clouds and we flew along in bright sunshine. What had not been taken into account was the increasing headwind and when we finally came down again we could see nothing but rain-lashed water. Bauer had the direction finding apparatus on, but for some reason the Berlin station had failed and Bremen and Lübeck were badly interrupted and kept giving us different readings. Fuel was starting to run low and the atmosphere got very tense ... I remembered that [Hitler] could not swim ... In the end he could stand it no longer and yelled at Bauer: 'You must turn south, it is the only way to hit land!' ... The situation was now really serious. The petrol tanks were as good as empty, but at the last moment we hit the coast over a small medieval town which none of us could recognize." The town was Wismar, and Bauer could land at a nearby airport with "literally no more than a few pints of fuel to spare. Hitler was quite groggy, and it was one of the few occasions when I saw him in a physical fright."[22]

After the Stauffenberg attempt on his life in July 1944, "Hitler displayed his tattered trousers like a trophy and did the same with

---

[21]Joachim Köhler: *Wagners Hitler*, p. 261.
[22]Ernst Hanfstängl: *Hitler – The Missing Years*, p. 180.

his jacket, which had a square hole ripped out of the back. His calm derived principally from the sense of a 'miraculous rescue'. It was as if he owned to this treacherous act his reinforced sense of his own mission. That, at any rate, was his interpretation of the event when Mussolini arrived in Rastenburg in the afternoon for a previously announced visit. As they looked at the devastated conference room, Hitler said: "When I call it all to mind again, I conclude that nothing is fated to happen to me, all the more so since this isn't the first time I've miraculously escaped death ... After my rescue from the peril of death today I am more than ever convinced that I am destined to carry on our great common cause to a happy conclusion."[23]

And then there is the peculiar phenomenon that took place in the Führerbunker, at the unhappy conclusion when Hitler had taken leave of his entourage and everybody knew that his suicide was imminent. "An unexpected thing happened", tells Trevor-Roper. "A great and heavy cloud seemed to roll away from the spirits of the bunker-dwellers. The terrible sorcerer, the tyrant who had charged their days with intolerable melodramatic tension, would soon be gone, and for a brief twilight moment they could play. In the canteen of the Chancellery, where the soldiers and orderlies took their meals, there was a dance. The news [of the imminent suicide] was brought, but no one allowed that to interfere with the business of pleasure. A message from the Führerbunker told them to be quieter, but the dance went on. A tailor who had been employed in the Führer's headquarters ... was surprised when Brigadeführer Rattenhuber, the head of the police guard and head of the SS, slapped him cordially on the back and greeted him with democratic cordiality ... 'I noticed that the mood had completely changed', he said. Then, from one of his equals, he learned the reason of this sudden and irregular affability. Hitler had said good-bye, and was going to commit

---

[23]Joachim Fest: *Hitler*, p. 709.

suicide'.[24] The instrument stopped functioning; the spell dropped off; the asuric influence vanished.

Convergences (continued)

During the Red revolution in Bavaria, the legal social-democratic Hoffmann government sought refuge in the town of Bamberg and remained there for some time even after Munich had been liberated in May 1919. This meant that the real authority in the federal state of Bavaria rested with the *Reichswehr* (as the post-war, reduced German defence forces were renamed), of which the commander was General Arnold von Möhl. This is one of the figures History has overlooked. For Möhl was a man with powerful connections not only in the higher command of the Army but also "with the Pan-Germans and especially with the Thule-Gesellschaft".[25] Knitting all facts together it becomes obvious that the commander of the Bavarian Reichswehr was involved in a Right-wing conspiracy to topple the social-democratic government.

Field Marshall Erich Ludendorff had regained his composure after Germany's defeat in the war, and appeared in München, looking for support in an eventual coup. (He would soon be involved in the Berlin 'Kapp Putsch'.) Captain Karl Mayr will later state that "Ludendorff and his friends were like talent spotters in Hollywood, looking for 'loyal' collaborators", and that Ludendorff soon had discovered the DAP, the political circle founded by the Thule Society. The DAP will not have been very hard to find, for Ludendorff met with other nationalist stalwarts, including General von Möhl, "every Wednesday in the smaller conference room of the Hotel Vier Jahreszeiten", the seat of the Thule Society.

The high point of Thule's activity was those critical months of 1918-19 in which the Society became a rallying centre of all rightists

---

[24]Id., pp. 227-28.
[25]Bruno Hipler: *Hitlers Lehrmeister*, p. 86, footnote.

in the Bavarian capital. Under the direction of Rudolf von Sebottendorff it not only founded two Free Corps, the *Kampfbund Thule* and the *Bund Oberland*, it also kept up a continuous contact with the government in exile. The organisations of the ruling Left were run so amateurishly that the Thule could penetrate them at will, putting on red armbands and falsifying identification papers. Unfortunately, Thule's organisation was not much better protected, and its negligence will cause the death of several members.

It was General von Möhl who created the intelligence apparatus of Reichswehr-commando Group 4, camouflaged as the Reichswehr's information and propaganda section, and who put Captain Karl Mayr in charge. "I selected some men who had stood out during the war. One of them was Hitler", Mayr recollected later.* We know that Hitler attended a meeting of the DAP on 12 September 1919 at the Sterneckerbräu on Mayr's instigation, and that he soon will join this secret Thule circle with the intention to use it as a launching pad for the realization of the mission he had received. Mayr reported about Hitler in a letter to Wolfgang Kapp, saying that the corporal "had become a moving force" in the DAP, animated by 'a glowing nationalism'. Hitler proved to be such an effective force that he was sent to Berlin, in Eckart's care and in a plane of the Reichswehr, as soon as it was known that Kapp and his co-conspirators had tried to overthrow the government. Alas, Kapp's bid for power was no more than a flash in the pan and they arrived too late.

---

*It is now an accepted fact that Corporal Adolf Hitler wore the red armband during the months of the socialist and communist regimes in Bavaria. Bruno Hilper, in his otherwise one-sided essay on Karl Haushofer, *Hitlers Lehrmeister*, is of the opinion that Hitler was a spy for the Thule Society. This theory, however farfetched at first sight, would agree with Hitler's deep-rooted nationalist feelings shown by him throughout the war, and with the fact that immediately after the defeat of the Republic of Councils he became a member of an inquiry commission to sift out the militant leftists from the Army. His temporary recruitment by Thule may have had no connection with his discovery by Captain Mayr.

It is a simple fact that the Reichswehr, the Pan-Germans and the Germanenorden, supported by the influential Wagner circle in Bayreuth, were conspiring all along to overthrow the social-democratic government. They will try again in November 1923, when Hitler hijacked the coup planned by the rather indecisive 'three vons' in Munich. In the literature one discovers with amazement how closely all the Rightist participants in this German power game were connected. They all knew each other because they were either related, had visited the same educational institutions or military academies, or had served in the same units during the war – if they were not brothers in the Germanenorden, fellow pan-Germans or accepted members of the Bayreuth circle.

Not less puzzling is the fact that the high-placed General von Möhl demanded that Hitler be introduced to him around the time of his first contacts with the DAP. The General 'had wanted that 'the Man' be presented to him', attested Mayr later. For a general in such a top position to meet at his own request a lowly and rather eccentric corporal, it must have been reported to him that there was something special about the man. It was also the general's decision to keep Hitler in the Reichswehr, even after he had become a member of a political party, the DAP, and to pay him a stipend.[26] All this took place only a short while after the lonesome Corporal had been feeding bread crumbs to the mice in his barracks.

The other important man who, in these months, joined his destiny with that of Adolf Hitler was of course Dietrich Eckart. It is remarkable how his reputation is improving among the younger German historians who at last begin to realise his crucial role in German history. Eckart is no longer seen as a 'coffeehouse intellectual and drug addict', but as 'the éminence grise of the DAP' (Hesemann), 'the founding father of the NSDAP' and 'a respected member of the better society in Munich' (Bärsch).

---

[26]Id., p. 86, footnote.

Eckart was after all a well-known playwright, personally acquainted with William II, and the editor and publisher of *In Plain German,* which counted practically all prominent nationalist authors among its collaborators. He was, moreover, immensely influential in Berlin as well as in Munich through his wide circle of acquaintances, something which would not have been possible if he had been nothing more than a drunk and a morphine addict. The misinterpretation of Eckart's personality rests apparently with non-German historical scholars who had no understanding of the Munich 'beer culture' – still very much alive – in which one can drink big mugs of the golden brew through the night and still be a respectable citizen.

Hitler's 'fatherly friend' was deeply interested in mysticism. He was in fact one of the foremost promoters of the idea that God was not the property of any Church but had to be found in the heart. As he wrote in one of his poems: "Awake, and you will feel that you have become God".

> You are like one who sleeps and dreams by day,
> Without suspecting that the brightest light surrounds you.
> You forget yourself in this world, like in the illusion of a dream,
> Without perceiving that another world enfolds you.
> Do understand at last: the other world is there already
> And was already there before your spirit met this world.[27]

One would not expect to read such lines from Hitler's mentor. But, as shown before, at the time there lived in many Germans a sincere longing for something more true and profound than what a confusing European culture-in-transition had to offer.

Regrettably, this purest and most soul-felt of urges was distorted by the general egocentric feeling of being *the* superior race. In this,

---

[27] In Claus-Ekkehard Bärsch: *Die politische Religion des Nationalsozialismus*, p. 68.

Eckart was not only not different, he was an active advocate of the idea. "The mission of the German people ends – this is my rock-solid conviction – at the last hour of humanity", for the German people have "to fulfil their destiny which consists in the salvation of the world ... The German power and strength and magnificence are needed to cure the world!"[28] And then follows an odd syllogism: "The soul is by nature Christian"; only the German people have a soul; therefore to be German and to be Christian is one and the same. And from this follows: "God-like – Christian – German" is the antithesis of "devilish – Jewish – anti-German".[29]

Fundamentally, Eckart saw himself as the champion of a new spirituality which would lead to a new man and a new world, as opposed to the materialistic world, which was how he (and the whole Volkisch movement) experienced the world around him. The worthy champions of the new spirituality were the Germans; the selfishly scheming promoters of materialism were the Jews. The latter had no idea of true spirituality, or of a soul, or of another world. Voltaire had written it long ago: "What is very singular is that in all the laws of god's people there is not a word about the spirituality and the immortality of the soul ... It is quite certain, it is indubitable that Moses nowhere promised the Jews rewards and punishments in another life, that he never talked to them about the immortality of their souls, that he never held out hopes of heaven, that he did not threaten them with hell: all is temporal."[30]

Eckart supported the DAP before 12 September 1919, for he had already given several talks in this 'workers' circle' of the Thule Society. He also knew Hitler before that date, for it was he, Eckart, who was scheduled to give another talk on that day; being prevented by illness he had himself replaced by Gottfried Feder and delegated Dr Gutberlet to report on the first appearance of the Austrian

---

[28] Id., pp. 77, 73.
[29] Ibid.
[30] Voltaire: *Philosophical Dictionary*, pp, 24-25.

corporal outside the Reichswehr. Eckart's initial encounters with Hitler must therefore have taken place before 12 September and after the first days of June, when Hitler was following the special course for Reichswehr propagandists at Munich University. The probable link was Captain Mayr; he knew Eckart personally, for he bought copies from him of *In Plain German* and distributed them clandestinely in the Reichswehr. Mayr, like many other military officers, had also connections with the Thule Society.

The point is that this leaves very little time for Eckart to coach the man whom he called 'my Adolf' and with whom he developed 'a very personal and intimate relation' (Bärsch), as it also left little time for a preparation of the resolute way in which Hitler took up the challenge. We know that Hitler had no doubts from the start about his vocation as the Leader of the German people, and that he entered the DAP with the explicit intention to use it for the realization of his ambitions. Eckart's writings and the historical information about him indicate that he saw his pupil from the very beginning as 'the man who will make Germany great again', which was the way in which he would soon introduce him to his circle of well-heeled acquaintances.

Captain Mayr's respectful address of his lowly subordinate, General von Möhl's special interest in the Austrian corporal, Eckart's support for 'a man from nowhere' whom he had known only shortly, and his introduction to a branch of the Thule Society with far-reaching albeit hidden ambitions, plus Hitler's career as 'the fulfilment of the task which Destiny has given to me' – all this adds up to the conclusion that in those summer months something decisive must have happened behind the scenes. The only explanation covering all these pointers is that Hitler must have been revealed as 'the Man' during séances of spiritism.

It has been shown elsewhere in our story that shortly after the war spiritism was a very common practice in Germany, not only because so many people wanted to keep the contact with their fallen near and dear ones, but also out of intellectual and spiritual interest.

We recall that the Thule was a secret society whose founder, Rudolf von Sebottendorff, was a many-sided and reputed occultist. The reading of his right hand man, Walter Nauhaus, "ranged from Guido von List's researches to astrology, chiromancy and the writings of Peryt Shou. In a letter to List he admitted to an interest in the Cabbala, and in Hindu and Egyptian beliefs. Like Sebottendorff, Nauhaus was fascinated by the mystical ideologies of ancient theocracies and secret cults".[31] Bronder characterizes the Thule as a secret loge with, as its esoteric core, 'a magic circle in which secret sciences were practised'. What the public knew as the Thule Society was only its 'exoteric circle'.[32]

There can be no doubt about the role of Dietrich Eckart as Hitler's 'fatherly friend', or more accurately as his 'godfatherly friend'. There was Hitler's reverence for him, even after Eckart's premature death and after 'his Adolf' had become Chancellor of Germany. Eckart's wide circle of notable acquaintances may have been the result of his fame as a writer, but also of his standing in the spiritist network. The way he had access to circles like the Bruckmanns, Bechsteins, Lehmanns and the Wagner family, as well as to the officer corps of the Reichswehr, tells of the emanation of an undeniable authority or 'charisma' from his person in spite of a delicate constitution. Eckart was the only one who really knew what was driving his pupil, and what Hitler never disclosed to anybody else (except perhaps to Hess).

Are there any indications of connections between Hitler and spiritism? When Timothy Ryback examined the books left over from Hitler's library, he was surprised by Hitler's 'serious exploration of spiritual matters' and his interest in occultism. He found books about Nostradamus, Nordic runes, the swastika and the Grail. And then there were books like *The Dead are Alive*. Hesemann mentions also *About Ghosts above and under the Earth; Death and Immortality in the World View of Indogermanic Thinkers* (a Christmas present

---

[31]Nicholas Goodrick-Clarke: *The Roots of Nazism*, p. 148.
[32]Dietrich Bronder: *Bevor Hitler kam*, p. 243.

from Heinrich Himmler); and *The Secret of Inspiration: From the Marvellous Realm of the Creative Power. For Subtle and Intelligent People of Genius Who are in Contact with the Genies and Intelligences, and with the Realm of the Spirit and the Spiritual Hosts*.[33]

"Most scholars dismiss the notion that Hitler seriously entertained the ideas of these cults", writes Ryback, "but the marginalia in several of his books confirm at least an intellectual engagement in the substance of Weimar-era occultism ... One of the most heavily marked books is *Magic: History, Theory and Practice* (1923), by Ernst Schertel ... Hitler's copy of *Magic* bears a handwritten dedication from Schertel, scrawled on the title page in pencil. A 170-page softcover in large format, the book has been thoroughly read and its margins scored repeatedly. I found a particularly thick pencil line beside the passage 'He who does not carry demonic seeds within him will never give birth to a new world' ...

"In the Fichte volumes given to him by [Leni] Riefenstahl", continues Ryback, "I encountered a veritable blizzard of underlines, question marks, exclamation points and marginal strikes that sweeps across a hundred pages of dense theological prose ... As I traced the pencilled notations, I realized that Hitler was seeking a path to the divine that lead to just one place. Fichte asked: 'Where did Jesus derive the power that has held his followers for all eternity?' Hitler drew a dense line beneath the answer: 'Through his absolute identification with God'. At another point Hitler highlighted a brief but revealing paragraph: 'God and I are One. Expressed simply in two identical sentences – His life is mine; my life is his. My work is his work, and his work is my work'." This reminds Ryback of a saying of Hitler's in December 1941: "If there is a God, then he gives us not only life but also consciousness and awareness. If I live my life according to my God-given insights, then I cannot go wrong, and even if I do, I know I have acted in good faith."[34]

---

[33]Michael Hesemann: *Hitlers Religion*, p. 30.
[34]Timothy W. Ryback, 'Hitler's Forgotten Library', in *The Atlantic Monthly*, May 2003.

Hesemann quotes, with reservations, Josef Greiner, a former companion of Hitler at the men's hostel in Vienna. "Hitler troubled his head about the fakirs and yogis in India, who can perform incredible wonders of human will power by turning away their senses from the outside world through concentration of the thought inwards and through self-punishment." According to Greiner, Hitler also attended several talks about occultism and was extremely interested in all kinds of occult phenomena.[35] Such interests would have been consistent with Hitler's religious adulation of Wagner's operas, which are peopled with beings from immaterial planes and in which the supernatural is the common way of experiencing reality.

According to the – trustworthy – Rudolf Olden, Hitler would have come into contact with spiritism after having arrived in Munich from the hospital in Pasewalk. "A Swedish countess would have introduced Hitler into a spiritist circle." Who might find this nutty ignores the fact that Carin von Kantzow – the first wife of Hermann Göring who was quasi canonized in Naziland after her untimely death – was also of Swedish nobility, and that there was a chapel at her family's castle dedicated to the spiritist religion and where séances were held.[36] "Among the spiritists, there were army officers." This too is probable, for we will see that Rudolf Hess, himself a lieutenant, was introduced to spiritist circles by officers from Karl Haushofer's former regiment. (During the First World War there were also Masonic "field lodges".) And Olden concludes: "It cannot be doubted that the disposition to receive inspiration from above was present in Hitler. But the facts, at present, are no more than rumours, as all tracks have been carefully wiped out"[37] – by the Nazi regime, that is.

If all this is rather vague, the following facts are historical. As we remember, in one of Hitler's books which survived the war, a German translation of Rabindranath Tagore's *Nationalism*, a

---

[35] Michael Hesemann, op. cit., pp. 30-31.
[36] Anna Maria Sigmund: *Die Frauen der Nazis I*, p. 37.
[37] Martin Sobieroj: *Der Stern des Abgrundes* (manuscript), pp. 128-29.

dedication was written. It went as follows: "*20.04.21. logapore, wodan wigiponar. Herrn Adolf Hitler, meinem lieben Armanenbruder. B. Steininger*". The last sentence, the one usually quoted, means: "To Mr Adolf Hitler, my dear Armanen-brother". The Armanen were Guido von List's present-day *Edelmenschen*, or supermen. "*Logapore, wodan wigiponare*" was an inscription in old Germanic on a precious stone found at Nordendorf, in Bavaria, and meant: "Logapore and Wotan, give divine protection". Babette Steininger has been identified as one of the first members of the NSDAP in Munich.[38]

"That she explicitly calls Hitler 'my dear Armanen-brother' can only mean that both Hitler and Steininger belonged to a chapter of a secret List society, or were closely connected with it, even when no further indications are available", writes Michael Hesemann. The Germanenorden, the Thule Society and societies like the Armanen took their oath of secrecy seriously. It is also relevant that the principal occult inspiration behind these secret societies was Guido von List, who relied for his revelations on clairvoyance and spiritism, and that several of their promoters were known spiritists.

The suicide of Geli Raubal, Hitler's niece, on 18 September 1931, is one of the most commented upon facts in his life and remains an unsolved mystery. Geli was the one passionate love in his life. (Eva Braun was much more a pleasant and steady companion.) The "vibrant, attractive young woman, who lived such an enviable life at the side of her famous uncle", is supposed to have taken Hitler's gun from a drawer on an impulse and fired a bullet into her chest after Hitler had left on a propaganda tour. "Buried beneath the layers of analysis are Hitler's own words that day to Detective Sauer", in his recorded testimony after a hurried return: "Some time ago, after she had in a certain circle participated in table turning [ie spiritism], she confided to me that she would not die a natural death."[39] No wonder that Ron Rosenbaum, who also mentions this

---

[38]Michael Hesemann: *Hitlers Religion*, pp. 111-12.
[39]Anna Maria Sigmund: *Des Führers bester Freund*, p. 175.

document, adds that "this remark struck Archivist Weber as very strange".[40] The jealous Hitler always had the activities of the girl closely watched and did not allow her to do anything without his knowledge. These words of his, spoken during an unprepared first testimony, do at least indicate that there were in his personal entourage some goings on of the table turning kind.

"The great world change is taking place now", Rauschning writes; "this was a theme which time and again cropped up in [Hitler's] conversations: a turnabout which we, ignorant people, were unable to comprehend in its full extent. On such occasions Hitler spoke like a seer and an initiate ... To acquire the 'magic vision' appeared to him the goal of human evolution. Personally, he felt that he had already reached the threshold of this magic knowledge, and he ascribed his successes and his future significance to it. A Munich savant had written, besides specialized works, some remarkable things about the primal world and the sagas of humanity, about humanity's capacity of dream-vision in olden times, about a way of knowledge of and a to us supernatural power over the rational laws of nature. There had been the eye of the Cyclops, the eye in the middle of the forehead, which was the organ of a magical perception of the All that had degenerated into the pineal gland. Such ideas fascinated Hitler. Sometimes he loved to investigate them passionately. He saw his own wondrous life as the confirmation of hidden powers."[41]

A friend

In documentary films of the Nuremberg NSDAP congresses, one can still see the Führer's deputy standing at attention on the rostrum high above the smartly lined up blocks of uniformed Germans, then suddenly turn to his left, raise his arm stiffly in salute to the arriving

---

[40]Ron Rosenbaun: *Explaining Hitler*, p. 102.
[41]Hermann Rauschning: *Gespräche mit Hitler*, pp. 229-3?.

Hitler, and announce, as chairman of the National Socialist Party: "The Party is in session and greets its Führer Adolf Hitler. The session continues. The Führer speaks!"

This man, proud to introduce his Leader to the world, was Rudolf Hess. He played a very special role in Hitler's life.

Hess was born in 1894, in the Egyptian town of Alexandria, where his father was a businessman. He studied at elite business schools in Europe, eg. the *École supérieure de commerce* at Neuchâtel, in Switzerland, and spoke English fluently. During the war he was at first a lieutenant in the infantry, but he switched over to the air force to become one of the proud and swaggering fighter pilots. He would remain a first rate pilot, capable enough to win a flying contest around the Zugspitze, Germany's highest mountain, and to execute some years later the complicated flight to Scotland. After the end of the First World War Hess was introduced by fellow officers of his regiment to the Thule Society, and became an active member 'of the inner circle'. He also fought in Thule's free corps, the *Kampfbund Thule*, during the Red revolution in Bavaria. Hesemann writes that Hess was "a close confidant of Rudolf von Sebottendorff"; this may explain why Hess, as the Führer's Deputy, helped his former Thule Master when he got in hot water with the Nazi authorities by publishing *Before Hitler Came* and trying to revive the Thule Society in 1933.

In April 1919 Hess, earning a living in the textile import, was personally introduced to Karl Haushofer (1869-1946), the former commander of his regiment. Out of interest for Haushofer's 'geopolitics', which the former major-general was teaching at Munich University, Hess soon became his student, and the master-disciple relation between the two men grew very close. Considering the fact that Hess was extremely interested in all aspects of occultism, and that Haushofer claimed to have second sight and was familiar with many aspects of the traditions of the East, especially those of Japan, the close relationship between the fifty and twenty-five year old may be supposed to have had an occult background. The diaries of

Haushofer's wife mention from 5 June onwards a sequence of nightly absences when the general purportedly was on 'guard duty' with the Reichswehr; but generals do not take up guard duty, and the situation in Bavaria had turned back to normal. The political and conspirational activities of the nationalists, however, were at their peak, and it was coincidentally on 5 June that the first course for propagandists of the Army started at Munich University, of which Haushofer knew all the organisers and lecturers.

Karl Haushofer was an ambitious man; he was, his son Albrecht would later write in tragic circumstances, 'blinded by the dream of power'. He was convinced that his theory of 'geopolitics' explained the fundamental political processes, including wars, and that it would help Germany conquer the place in the sun which it deserved. The field covered by geopolitics is very large and the theory has even been rehabilitated in recent years. Yet, all in all it seems to mean that the most developed and powerful peoples should appropriate anything which they find useful for their well-being. Its basis was 'scientific', in other words neo-darwinistic. It was not Haushofer's intention to grab power for himself, but to be the mentor of the men in power; his motto was (in English) 'let us educate our masters'. The 'professor-general' was extremely well connected in military and academic circles, and he had been close to the Pan-Germans from his boyhood.

He had, however, a handicap: his wife was the daughter of a rich Jewish businessman. It is therefore doubtful that he ever was a member of the Thule Society, for the Germanenorden demanded a signed declaration from its members that not a drop of Jewish blood ran in their veins. Haushofer also kept his distance from Hitler, even after Hess had discovered 'the Man', in May 1920, and convinced his professor to attend one of Hitler's speeches. 'Professor-General' Haushofer would not take the risk (as yet) of compromising himself with that outlandish political upstart, the Austrian corporal, who at that time was still in the Army. Moreover, as reported afterwards by Hess' wife, Haushofer resented Hitler's influence on his favourite student and close companion.

Hess' enthusiasm for Hitler was indeed boundless and developed into an 'enraptured fanaticism' (Hilpert). "This strange friendship" (Bärsch) will lead to Hess writing in some of his letters that Hitler was "a very dear friend, an exceptional human being!" and: "I am more than ever devoted to him! I love him!"[42] The relationship became especially close in the prison at Landsberg. Hess had actively participated in the Beerhall Putsch by rounding up the ministers of the government with his stormtroopers and putting them under arrest. After the debacle he was on the run for some time; then he found shelter in the house of Haushofer, who managed to convince him that he should give himself up to the police. Hess did this in May 1924 and was, to his delight, also sent to Landsberg. "I had the luck of landing here", he wrote to his mother, "where every day I can be together with that brilliant being: with Hitler".[43]

The situation in Landsberg prison has been described elsewhere. The relevance for our story at this juncture is that Hitler and Hess were staying not only on the same floor, but that they shared the same 'apartment'. This was an important period in Hitler's life, for he had now, as Hess put it, "again the time to concentrate and come to rest, and to gather fundamental knowledge".[44] Given the personality and the interests of both men, it seems obvious that they created an occult atmosphere around them. In every one of his letters Hess will henceforth call Hitler 'the Tribune', which is a reference to Hitler's *Rienzi* experience.

When Haushofer visited Hess, he necessarily met Hitler also. It has been established that the professor of geopolitics visited Landsberg eight times and met both men for a total duration of twenty-two hours. This was surely time enough for Haushofer to expound his theories to Hitler, and some results of this private tutoring are found in *Mein Kampf.* When later in difficulty because

---

[42]Claus-Ekkehard Bärsch, op. cit., p. 162.
[43]Bruno Hipler, op. cit., p. 155.
[44]Id., p. 159, footnote.

of Hess' flight to Scotland, Haushofer will remind the Nazi authorities that he had known the Führer since 1919 – which may be true but does not mean that he frequented him from that date – and that he went to visit him in Landsberg 'every Wednesday'.

Rudolf Hess was one of the three people, together with Dietrich Eckart and Albert Speer, with whom Hitler developed an intimate relationship, naturally with each one in his own way. Ernst Hanfstängl has described Hitler's reaction on the evening he had been released from jail. "The other strong impression he left me with that evening was the emotional quality of the friendship that had developed with Hess. *Ach, mein Rudi, mein Hesserl'*, he wailed as he stomped up and down. 'Isn't it appalling to think he's still there!' [Hess was not released from Landsberg until later] … It is probably not true to say that there was a physical homosexual relationship between the two, but in a passive way the attraction was there."[45]

Konrad Heiden, a rather matter-of-fact journalist, has the following intriguing paragraph: "Suddenly, in the midst of a conversation, Hitler's face grows tense as with an inner vision; these are the moments in which the humanly repulsive falls away from him and the unfathomable is intensified until it becomes truly terrible. His eyes peer into the distance, as though he were reading or gazing at something which no one else sees; and if the observer follows the direction of his gaze, sometimes, it has been claimed, Rudolf Hess can be seen in the far corner, with his eyes glued to the Führer, apparently speaking to him with closed lips … It is certain that in the decisive years of his career Hitler used his younger friend as a necessary complement to his own personality …"[46]

This puzzling statement is, in a way, supported by what the former Captain Karl Mayr wrote in his article 'I was Hitler's Boss': "Hess was Hitler's first and most successful mentor … A dabbler in mesmerism and faith healing, Hess certainly was most successful

---

[45]Ernst Hanfstängl, op. cit., p. 123.
[46]Konrad Heiden: *Hitler*, p. 285.

with Hitler. Before every important speech Hitler was, sometimes for days, closeted with Hess who in some unknown way got Hitler into that frenetic state in which he came forth to address the public".[47] During Hitler's speeches Hess may have repeated 'with closed lips' and in unison with Hitler some passages which he remembered from the rehearsals. As Mayr's article was written after his flight from Germany (and published after his internment in a concentration camp), he may have sought to involve only the Nazi potentates, conveniently forgetting Eckart and the role he himself had played at the time. And the 'unknown way' in which Hess 'got Hitler in that frenetic state' is easy to guess, for it must have been the same way in which the medium Hitler used to open himself to the Power that possessed him.

More friends

Observing the origins of National Socialism along the line followed in our story, one discerns two distinct groups among Hitler's paladins: the likes of Hess, Rosenberg, Streicher, Dinter, Göring, Röhm, Frank, Esser, Gürtner and Frick; and the likes of Himmler, Goebbels, von Schirach and Speer. The former were all men of the first hour who clearly had a common bond with Hitler which allowed them to survive the most dangerous crises in their relationship. Even in the case of Röhm, the main target in the Night of the Long Knives and the one exception in this group, Hitler needed a full day to decide that Röhm should die and gave him the choice of a honourable death by shooting himself. And Hess, who by flying to Scotland had given Hitler 'the second worst personal blow of his life'[48] (the first having been the death of Geli Raubal), was confident that Hitler would understand and forgive him in case they met again. The second

---

[47]Bruno Hipler, op. cit., p. 89, footnote.
[48]Gitta Sereny: *Albert Speer: His Battle with Truth*, p. 240.

group, however close to their Führer at certain times, came 'from elsewhere' and was, instead of having the personal bond with Hitler, simply possessed by him. In each of their cases, the process of their becoming dependent is known in detail. The convergence of these facts again leads to the conclusion of an occult secret behind the surface patterns known as history.

Alfred Rosenberg and his wife were fugitives from the Russian revolution; they landed in Munich towards the end of 1918 and became part of the Russian community there. During the troubled times in their country, most Russian intellectuals had been profoundly influenced by Theosophy (Madame Blavatsky was a Russian, after all) and many of them also by spiritism (remember Rasputin). The imperial court had set the example by its practice of spiritism and other forms of occultism, and there was an wide-ranging spiritist literature in the Russian language. These interests were brought with them by the numerous Russian communities in West European cities, also in Germany.

Shortly after his arrival in Munchen, Rosenberg went to meet the well-known Dietrich Eckart. They got along at once because of their common interest in mysticism, anti-Semitism and anti-Bolshevism, and Rosenberg became 'Eckart's right hand', assisting him with the writing and editing of *In Plain German*. Another of their common interests was occultism, and Eckart introduced the German Balt to the Thule Society in the spring of 1919. A few weeks later he introduced him also to Adolf Hitler, who was becoming a daily visitor at Eckart's house. Rosenberg's relation with Hitler was, at that time, 'very friendly' (Bärsch).

Rosenberg's whole personality was strongly focused on the occult, as may be deduced from his major opus, *The Myth of the Twentieth Century*, and more in particular from his obsession with Zionism and Freemasonry. It was he who translated *The Protocols of the Elders of Zion*, published them in the *Völkische Beobachter*, and commented upon them in a stream of anti-Semitic pamphlets. All this did not prevent him from being an admirer of the Indian scriptures, Christ and Meister Eckhart. Part of the world of this pale-faced, intellectual personality was his rootedness in the dream. "Rosenberg emphasized the importance for life of the dream explicitly, emphatically and energically", writes Bärsch. "Rosenberg ascribes to the dream and the myth practically the same attributes ... The dream is the activity of a power of the soul; the dream as such is cause as well as power 'and results finally in the creative act".[49]

Rosenberg was one of many who became instant Hitlerians after having experienced the man during one of his speeches, although he had remained unimpressed when meeting him personally beforehand. Another one was Julius Streicher, the notorious publisher of *Der Stürmer*, an anti-Semitic gutter publication which, after the coming to power of the Nazis, saw its circulation increase from 20,000 to over 400,000 copies. One of its most faithful readers was the Führer and Chancellor himself, and he will defend Streicher through thick and thin, also after having had to remove him as Gauleiter of Thuringia for recurrent misbehaviour and corruption. "There is, in spite of all his weaknesses, not a single full-blooded personality like him ... And the Jew is much more base, bloodthirsty and satanical than Streicher has depicted him", said Hitler in one of his monologues.[50]

He will never forget that in 1922, after his 'conversion', Streicher transferred in toto the German Socialist Party (DSP), of which he was the chairman, to the NSDAP. The reader may remember that the DSP was one of the two political parties which had been floated by the Thule Society to attract the working class to the nationalist cause, the other and considerably more successful being the DAP. From then onwards Streicher, sporting a whip just like his Führer, had been a most reliable Nazi. On photos taken during the Beerhall Putsch he can be seen addressing the crowd at the Marienplatz, the heart of Munich, when none of the participants knew how to

---

[49] Claus-Ekkehard Bärsch, op. cit., p. 204.
[50] *Monologe im Führerhauptquartier*, p. 158.

proceed further and Ludendorff gave the order to march on to the Feldherrnhalle, where the shoot-up would take place.

"Streicher associated the conviction of ultimate victory with the existence of Adolf Hitler, this in blatant contradiction with the empirical reality, for Hitler possessed hardly any power at the time", writes Claus-Ekkehard Bärsch. "Julius Streicher believed not only that Adolf Hitler was blessed by God, but also that he was the intermediary between God and humanity." Bärsch also points out that Streicher's faith in Hitler was not based upon race. "One reads nowhere in Julius Streicher, generally labelled a primitive racist, that Adolf Hitler is the Führer because in him the potential of the Aryan race has been actualized to perfection. The significance of Adolf Hitler does not come from below, from nature and race, but from above, in the struggle for a redeeming future against the evil enemy of the world."[51]

"Streicher had a close relationship with Dinter and was also befriended with Dietrich Eckart", notes Martin Sobieroj. "The overwhelming impression made by Hitler in the state of possession on those present [during spiritist séances] could explain why Streicher incorporated his followers nearly as one body into the NSDAP on 20.10.22." And it could explain why Streicher considered Hitler the saviour of the German people sent by God. Streicher himself acted as a basely possessed figure without any humane feelings. "He was considered disgusting even in the Third Reich", according to Speer, and Joseph Persico observed at Nuremberg that "the man had become a pariah, reviled by his captors and shunned by his fellow defendants".[52] But "Streicher spoke and acted aloud what Hitler secretly thought and desired", remarks Heiden. "Streicher was the embodiment of Hitler's subconscious."[53]

---

[51] Claus-Ekkehard Bärsch, op. cit., pp. 163 ff. passim.
[52] Joseph Persico: *Nuremberg*, p. 99.
[53] Konrad Heiden, op. cit., p. 457.

Arthur Dinter was the man who openly revolted against Hitler, accused him of betraying the original ideals of the NSDAP and demanded that he be deposed as Leader of the Party – all this when Hitler had already come to power and held the life of every German in his hand. As we have seen in an earlier chapter, Hitler did not even throw Dinter into a concentration camp; he simply isolated him in a way that he could no longer be heard and do no further harm.

Dinter acknowledged that he had been a practising spiritist. He had discovered spiritism shortly after the war when staying at a hotel in Luzern. There "a group of hotel guests began to make the tables turn after their repertoire of party games had been exhausted, all known aria's and popular songs had been sung, and a teenager had been repeating for the twelfth time a song with the refrain 'I love you'". Dinter maintained that he had studied spiritism and occultism in general from a scientific point of view. When he published *The Sin against the Spirit*, a sequel to his immensely successful anti-Semitic novel *The Sin against the Blood*, he dedicated it to the two mediums who had been channelling the communications of a spirit which were incorporated in the novel.

According to Sobieroj's sources, Dinter had been acquainted with Streicher and Eckhart, who had put him into contact with Hitler. Dinter, in his turn, should have put Hitler in contact with his main spirit whom called himself *Segensbringer*, literally meaning 'bringer of blessings'. If true, this spirit should have been the same as Hitler's Lord of the Nations, for it is improbable that the latter would have suffered another paranormal entity to exert an influence over his choice subject. "Dinter's influence upon Hitler, because of his spiritist foundation of racism and his practical spiritist experience, might therefore have been much more important than is commonly supposed", conjectures Sobieroj.[54] It would anyhow explain the extraordinary lenience Hitler showed towards a man who once had

---

[54]Martin Sobieroj, op. cit., p. 115, 59, 60.

been one of the Nazi trailblazers in the venerable town of Weimar, but who had also dared to defy him.

Was Karl Haushofer really 'an accomplished black magician' as one reads in certain 'spurious' authors? His ambitions as éminence grise behind the National Socialist movement were certainly limitless, but he will always see Rudolf Hess as the prime mover behind Hitler – even when he was applauding Hitler's first 'geopolitical' 'success quite loudly – with himself of course as the source of inspiration behind Hess. As indicated above, there can be little doubt that Haushofer and Hess were involved in occult and more specifically in spiritist activities. In the interrogations by the Allies in May 1945, after the war had ended, Haushofer will try to play down his part in defining Hitler's international war objectives; he will also insinuate that some chapters of *Mein Kampf* were written by Hess, which must have happened in his imagination. Hitler has always been his own man from the time he began to take his distance from Eckart, somewhere in 1923. And he was his own man because he had a direct contact with the highest inspiration, his god: the Lord of the Nations.

Hess always protected Karl Haushofer and his son Albrecht, dearer to him than his own relatives, even though the Haushofers belonged in the Jewish camp. Both were honoured with high educational positions, and Albrecht, widely travelled and well-connected in Great Britain, will even be a temporary consultant with the *Dienststelle Ribbentrop*, the think tank of the German Foreign Minister, and in this capacity assist Hitler at the infamous Munich conference of 1938. Only when the Haushofers found out that Hitler was going to march against Russia did they begin to question their opportunist pro-Nazi stance. They were certainly involved in Hess' plans to fly to Scotland in order to convince a fictional anti-Churchill faction to make peace and thus spare Germany a two-front war. Although Albrecht was a personal friend of the Duke of Hamilton, whom Hess wanted to meet, the way in which the political realities in London were misjudged is rather amazing.

Goebbels wrote in his diary: "The Haushofers, father and son, have the Hess case on their conscience".⁵⁵ They were interrogated by the secret police and their careers took a nosedive from that time onwards. Several Führer decrees were promulgated henceforth forbidding any form of occult activity (except secretly at the instance of high Nazi authorities). But Hitler still did not eliminate the Haushofers. An inwardly torn Albrecht will later be imprisoned on the accusation of complicity in the Stauffenberg plot to kill Hitler. A few days before the end of the war he will be executed on Himmler's orders by an SS-squad in the ruins of Berlin, clenching in his fist 80 remarkably spiritual sonnets.

Karl and Martha Haushofer will commit suicide after having learned that their other son had found and identified Albrecht's body. By that time Hess, simulating loss of memory, denied to Karl Haushofer's face that he had ever known him. To Speer he had however confided that the idea of flying to Scotland "had been inspired in him in a dream of supernatural forces".⁵⁶ This refers clearly to spiritist practice and is the only 'logical' explanation of Hess' undertaking. For the preparations for 'Operation Barbarossa' were already in an advanced phase on 10 May, the date of Hess' flight, and it is unimaginable that Hitler would have allowed an operation of this magnitude to depend on a circus act.

---

⁵⁵Joseph Goebbels: *Tagebücher*, volume IV, p. 1617.
⁵⁶Albert Speer, op. cit., p. 252.

16

Two poems

Ultimately the individual man is weak in all his nature and actions when he goes contrary to almighty Providence and its will, but he becomes immeasurably strong the moment he acts in harmony with this Providence! Then there pours upon him that force which has distinguished all the great men in the world.
Adolf Hitler

Judging from the this-side of existence, Sri Aurobindo could perhaps be seen in the first place as a poet, if poetry is understood in its original sense as an activity of the levels above the mind with the power to discover, to 'see', to act and to create. Words have power; being the seer who is inspired with the words of power and able to formulate them is to be a revealer of truth. "To us [people of the contemporary world] poetry is a revel of intellect and fancy", wrote Sri Aurobindo, "imagination a plaything and caterer for our amusement, our entertainer, the nautch-girl of the mind. But to the men of old the poet was a seer, a revealer of hidden truths, imagination no dancing courtesan but a priestess in God's house commissioned not to spin fictions but to image difficult and hidden truths; even the metaphor or simile in the Vedic style is used with a serious purpose and expected to convey a reality, not to suggest a pleasing artifice of thought. The image was to these seers a revelative symbol of the unrevealed and it was used because it could hint luminously to the mind what the precise intellectual word, apt only for logical or practical thought or to express the physical and the superficial, could not at all hope to manifest".[1]

Sri Aurobindo was one of the great poets of the twentieth century and its greatest spiritual poet. He stood aside from and above the poetic trends, although he was fully aware of them and kept himself informed about their developments even in his apparent seclusion. He greatly appreciated Mallarmé, Yeats, Whitman and Eliot, among others. But in him the poets of ancient Greece and Rome had also remained alive, as well as the 'hearers' of the Vedas and Upanishads and the classical Sanskrit poetry, and what he sought for was the adequate, irreplaceable expression of the inner experience in the adequate, irreplaceable form, without any concessions whatever.

Sri Aurobindo's major opus *in poeticis* was *Savitri*, his epic of nearly 24,000 lines on which he worked from his years in Baroda till a few days before his passing. From a story in the *Mahabharata* it grew into the creation of a poetical universe. "I used *Savitri* as a means of ascension. I began with it on a certain mental level; each time I could reach a higher level I rewrote from that level", confided Sri Aurobindo to Nirodbaran. The epic was revised eleven or twelve times, a labour which resembles metaphorically the multi-layered city of Troy. "*Savitri* has not been regarded by me as a poem to be written and finished, but as a field of experimentation to see how far poetry could be written from one's own yogic consciousness and how that could be made creative."[2]

Raymond Piper, professor at the University of Syracuse (USA), has rated *Savitri* as follows: "During a period of nearly fifty years ... [Sri Aurobindo] created what is probably the greatest epic in the

---

[1] Sri Aurobindo: *The Human Cycle*, pp. 10-11.
[2] Nirodbaran: *Correspondence with Sri Aurobindo*, pp. 543-44.

English language ... I venture the judgment that it is the most comprehensive, integrated, beautiful and perfect cosmic poem ever composed. It ranges symbolically from a primordial cosmic void, through earth's darkness and struggles, to the highest realms of Supramental spiritual existence, and illumines every important concern of man, through verse of unparalleled massiveness, magnificence and metaphysical brilliance."[3]

Yet, in Sri Aurobindo's poetry one finds not only the sublime. His attention, like his yoga, covered all aspects of human existence, and this open, all-embracing attitude is reflected in his poetry by concrete and even scientific statements, epigrams, the lyrical mood, humour, satire, rhythmical innovations, autobiographical facts, historical reconstructions and mythological interpretations.

'The Dwarf Napoleon'

Sri Aurobindo wrote two poems about Hitler and Nazism; both poems are reproduced in extenso below. The first, called 'The Dwarf Napoleon – Hitler, October 1939', is written in a polemical, scathing vein; it is an *ad hominem* attack on Adolf Hitler shortly after his invasion of Poland. The poetic quality of these lines is of secondary importance. The writing of 'The Dwarf Napoleon' was much more a yogic act, an act of yogic magic, to counter the aggression of a dictator who had already annexed Austria and Czechoslovakia and was therefore, now that Poland's turn had come, frequently compared with Napoleon. Sri Aurobindo has often stressed the importance of standing up against a spreading negative force, and in this case he doubtlessly wanted to inform the Asuric Power behind Hitler that the spiritual opposition had taken note.

> Behold, by Maya's fantasy of will
> A violent miracle takes sudden birth,

---

[3]In KR Srinivasan Iyengar: *Sri Aurobindo*, p. 636.

The real grows one with the incredible.
In the control of her magician wand
The small achieves things great, the base things grand.[4]

'Maya' is often understood to be Illusion. However, Maya is essentially the manifesting power of the Divine, in other words the supreme feminine principle or Universal Mother. She is 'Shakti', the inherent power of the Divine, or 'Prakriti', Nature as opposed to the Spirit. It should always be kept in mind that, in spite of the dualities for the working out of the Divine self-manifestation, the Spirit and its Shakti are inherently one and the same. She is He; He is She; both are the One.

In *The Human Cycle* and *The Ideal of Human Unity*, his two books most relevant to our story, Sri Aurobindo often uses the word 'Nature' for what in this poem he calls 'Maya'. He writes for instance: "There is nothing that can be set down as impossible in the chances of the future, and the urge in Nature always creates its own means".[5] Our universe is the work of Nature, and so is its evolution, 'moving with difficulty upward from Matter to Spirit'. The primal condition, responsible for the fact that this is an evolutionary universe, is the work of Nature, for so is the manifestation of the great negative beings, called 'asuras', and the great positive beings, called 'gods'. And all is the work of the One, for nothing can exist without That.

"When we speak indeed of the errors of Nature, we use a figure illegitimately borrowed from our human psychology and experience, for *in Nature there are no errors* but only the deliberate measure of her paces traced and retraced in a prefigured rhythm, of which each step has a meaning and its place in the action and reaction of her gradual advance ... For Nature tired of the obstinate immobility of an age-long resistance seems to care little how many beautiful and

---

[4]Sri Aurobindo: *Collected Poems*, p. 110.
[5]Sri Aurobindo: *The Ideal of Human Unity*, p. 288.

valuable things are destroyed so long as her main end is accomplished; but we may be sure that if destruction is done, it is because for that end the destruction was indispensable."[6]

> This puny creature would bestride the earth
> Even as the immense colossus of the past.
> Napoleon's mind was swift and bold and vast,
> His heart was calm and stormy like the sea,
> His will dynamic in its grip and clasp.
> His eye could hold a world within its grasp
> And see the great and small things sovereignly.
> A movement of enormous depth and scope
> He seized and gave coherence to its hope.

It is now usually forgotten how often Adolf Hitler, at the zenith of his glory, was favourably compared with Napoleon Bonaparte. The annexation of Austria, the cutting up of Czechoslovakia, the invasion of Poland and afterwards the surprise attacks on Denmark and Norway, and the invasion of France – all these were occasions of praising Hitler to the skies and calling him the greatest genius, military strategist and conqueror in history. This spontaneous appreciation of their Führer by the people of Naziland will continue till the first serious setbacks in Russia, when Goebbels' propaganda machine will be needed to carry it on.

Hitler had been the first to compare himself with the French Emperor. "What Napoleon did not accomplish, *I* will succeed in doing", he boasted to Rauschning in the 1930s.[7] "Hitler saw himself in a certain traditional line with the Corsican", writes Reuth.[8] Toland and Maser, in their biographies of Hitler, work out parallels between the Führer and the Emperor. John Lukacs writes: "The parallels –

---

[6]Id., p. 99, emphasis added.
[7]Hermann Rauschning, op. cit., p. 114.
[8]Ralf Reuth: *Hitler*, p. 479.

or, more precise, the similarities – between Napoleon's and Hitler's careers (their careers rather than their lives), should be apparent even to general readers who do not possess detailed historical knowledge ... but the differences are still more substantial".[9]

Thomas Mann saw Napoleon as the man who had to secure the ideals of the Enlightenment as formulated by the French revolutionaries, and who had to divulge these ideals everywhere in Europe.[10] Sri Aurobindo was very strongly of the same opinion. "If [Napoleon] had not risen at the time, the [reactionary] European powers would have crushed French democracy. What he did was to stabilize the French Revolution so that the world got the idea of democracy. Otherwise it would have been delayed by two or three centuries." Napoleon gave not only glory to France, "he gave peace and order, stable government and security in France. He was not only one of the greatest conquerors but also one of the greatest administrators and organizers the world has seen ... The only trouble was that he was not bold enough. If he had pushed on with the idea of unification of all Europe, which he had at the back of his mind, then the present Spanish struggle [the Spanish Civil War] would not have been necessary, Italy would have been united much earlier and Germany would have been more civilized. If instead of proclaiming himself Emperor he had remained the First Consul, he would have met with better success".[11]

"Hitler can't stand any comparison with Napoleon", said Sri Aurobindo. "Hitler is a man of one idea ... while Napoleon had many ideas: he was not only a military general, but also an administrator, organizer, legislator and many other things. It was he who organized France and Europe, [and who] stabilized the French Revolution. Besides being a legislator he established the bases of social laws, administration and finance which are followed even

---

[9] John Lukacs: *The Hitler of History*, pp. 243-44.
[10] Thomas Mann: *Deutschland und die Deutschen*, p. 55.
[11] Nirodbaran: *Talks with Sri Aurobindo*, pp. 150, 166.

today. He is not only the greatest military genius in history but one of the greatest men, with manifold capacities. Hitler is a man with no intellect and of one idea, which he applies with strong force and violence. He has no control over his emotions. He hesitates in his policies – which some call caution. And all his power comes from the Asura by whom he is possessed and guided while Napoleon was a normal human being acting through the power of his brain, which reached the highest development possible in a human being."[12]

> Far other this creature of a nether clay,
> Void of all grandeur, like a gnome at play,
> Iron and mud his nature's mingled stuff,
> A little limited visionary brain
> Cunning and skilful in its narrow vein,
> A sentimental egoist poor and rough,
> Whose heart was never sweet and fresh and young,
> A headlong spirit driven by hopes and fears,
> Intense neurotic with his shouts and tears,
> Violent and cruel, devil, child and brute...

Adolf Hitler was a 'solipsist'. The dictionaries define 'solipsism' as "the theory that the only thing you can be certain about is your own existence and your own thoughts and ideas" or "the extreme form of scepticism which denies the possibility of any knowledge other than of one's own existence". In other words: the solipsist is the sole protagonist in his own play of life and the world which he experiences is his stage. In psychology this is also called 'narcissism'. Hitler's biographer Reuth affirms that he was 'an egomaniacal loner', and Kershaw that he was 'a narcissistic egomaniac', suffering of 'an egomania of monumental proportions'. "He simply could not bear not to dominate any situation in which he found himself", Hanfstängl concurs.[13]

---

[12] Id., pp. 956-57.
[13] Ernst Hanfstängl: *Hitler – The Missing Years*, p. 60.

Examples of this attitude abound in Hitler's life. There was, at the age of sixteen-seventeen, his calf love for a girl in Linz, Stefanie, whom his imagination transformed into a Walkyrie but whom he never dared to approach. There was the time in Vienna when he began to write an opera on the theme of an old Germanic legend, 'Wieland the Smith', without as much as knowing how to write a musical score. "Hitler did not accept that the facts of reality should be an obstacle to his dreams and to his will", is the way his one-time close friend Kubizek puts it. The same Kubizek was also the first sufferer of Hitler's vehement and endless monologues, 'an unquenchable urge to launch into tirades', which was the only way Adolf could express himself and which was his manner of venting his inner turmoil in surges of verbalisation. Hitler would never be capable of normal conversation, in no company, and when he launched into one of his tirades he would address even a single individual as if it were a crowd.

"[Hitler] regarded life as a kind of permanent parade before a gigantic audience", writes Fest, who also mentions his inability to lead a life without posing. "This desire for theatre touches at the core of his being ... He had sought orientation and support against the world in a succession of new roles: from the early role of the son of good family and idling student, promenading in Linz with his cane and kid gloves, through the various roles of leader, genius and saviour, to the imitation Wagnerian end, where his aim was to enact an operatic finale. In every case he practised autosuggestion, presenting himself in disguises and borrowed forms of existence. And when after one of his successful foreign-policy coups he called himself, with naïve boastfulness, 'the greatest actor in Europe', he was expressing a need of his nature as well as an ability."[14]

Towards the end Hitler-the-solipsist was moving for months depleted or non-existing armies across his maps, sending 'with swiping gestures' thousands to a meaningless death. His doings became still

---

[14]Joachim Fest: *Hitler*, pp. 518, 520, 517.

more absurd during 'the imitation Wagnerian end' when there was no longer contact with the exhausted men in the field, and he did not hesitate to hasten the doomsday of a people which he deemed unworthy of him. "If the German nation is now defeated in this struggle, it has been too weak. That will mean it has not withstood the test of history and was destined for nothing but doom."[15] Besides, all had betrayed him. But "I'll fight this fight alone!" shouted theatrically the man who had become a physical wreck, and who for years had ordered to kill without himself ever firing a shot in anger.

The subconscious impulses of 'this creature of a nether clay' drove him to an existence of 'mud and iron'. Underneath all his actions there was his need to hate. Speer calls Hitler 'a pathological hater' and Heinrich Mann saw him as 'the high priest of hatred'. "Every conversation, however simple, seemed to prove that this man was possessed by boundless hate ... He always seemed to need something to hate", writes Rauschning.[16] Kubizek agrees: "In his thundering tirades of hate he, feeling abandoned and alone, shouted his rage against the existing world, against the whole of humanity which did not understand him, which did not give him a chance, by which he felt persecuted and cheated".[17] And from his hatred sprang his need to take revenge on anybody who had crossed his path. There is a long list of people who fell victim to his death sentences, and we have met several of them in our story.

"Hitler is terribly cruel", said Sri Aurobindo, "he has cruelty in his blood".[18] Sri Aurobindo found in January 1939 that Hitler was "becoming more and more criminal and going down very fast."[19] It was at this time that he decided upon 'the final solution' concerning the Jews, indirectly announcing this decision in his notorious

---

[15] Albert Speer: *Inside the Third Reich*, p. 529.
[16] Hermann Rauschning: *Gespräche mit Hitler*, p.83.
[17] August Kubizek: *Adolf Hitler, mein Jugendfreund*, p. 165.
[18] Nirodbaran, op. cit., p. 121.
[19] Id., p. 194.

Reichstag speech on 30 January. After coming to power he had exclaimed: "We are ruthless! I have no bourgeois scruples! They think I am uncultured, a barbarian. Yes, we are barbarians! We want to be. This is an honourable epithet."[20] Heartless, fearsome and cruel is how he wanted his youth to be. "In general the regime, contrary to its ideal of dispassionate sternness, displayed a remarkable cruelty, for which Hitler himself repeatedly gave the clues", states Fest rather coolly if one recalls the endless privation, torturing, killing and burning for which 'the regime' was responsible during the war.

Hitler's disdain for human life and for a human attitude towards it has been highlighted at the beginning of our story, when narrating the origins of the NSDAP and the SA. True, the times were chaotic and violent, but there is no doubt that the general inhuman character of the National Socialist movement is to be sought in the personality of its founder and sole decision maker, urged on by the Power that possessed him. "Things are not possible without the will to cruelty … Terror is absolutely indispensable for every foundation of a new power", he said.[21] And: "Our path is not clean. I know nobody who has not dirtied his feet on the path to greatness. We will leave it to our successors to construct something on clean foundations."[22] This may sound statesmanlike, but Hitler was also the man who revelled in the damage done to London and the devastation of Warsaw, Belgrade, Leningrad and Stalingrad, and who found pleasure in imagining the toppling of the Manhattan skyscrapers by his planned long-distance bombers. As he was the man who enjoyed the films shot on his orders of the first executions of conspirators in the Stauffenberg attempt on his life, some of whom, hanged with piano wires, took twenty minutes to die.

---

[20]Joachim Fest, op. cit., p. 412.
[21]Hermann Rauschning, op. cit., p. 257.
[22]Ernst Hanfstängl, op. cit., p. 136.

> This screaming orator with his strident tongue,
> The prophet of a scanty fixed idea,
> Plays now the leader of our human march;
> His might shall build the future's triumph arch.

These perceptions of Sri Aurobindo – it bears repetition – are dated October 1939, a time when the world held its breath but Hitler's intentions were as yet far from clear. Germany and Russia were still partners under their non-aggression pact; Mussolini had not yet taken his decisive step into Hitler's camp, staging many shows of 'everlasting' friendship with the Third Reich but also often making denigrating remarks about the Germans and their Führer, who to him was something like an epigone; and Japan seemed fully tied down in East Asia.

> Now is the world for his eating a ripe fruit.
> His shadow falls from London to Korea.
> Cities and nations crumble in his course.
> A terror holds the peoples in its grip:
> World-destiny waits upon that foaming lip.

Sri Aurobindo never had any doubt about the scope of Hitler's plans. "Hitlerism is the greatest menace the world has ever met", he said; and "the destiny of the world depends on one man... His aim is clearly world-empire." Or rather it was "the Asura who aims at world-domination. It is the descent of the Asuric world upon the human to maintain its own power on the earth." [23]

> A Titan Power supports this pigmy man,
> The crude dwarf instrument of a mighty Force.
> Hater of the free spirit's joy and light,

---
[23] Nirodbaran, op. cit., pp. 56, 20, 660, 669.

Made only of strength and skill and giant might,
A will to trample humanity into clay
And unify earth beneath one iron sway,
Insists upon its fierce enormous plan.
Trampling man's mind and will into one mould
Docile and facile in a dreadful hold,
It cries its demon slogans to the crowd.

The outcome of the apocalyptic drama, of which the prologue was being performed with the moustached 'strident' puppet in the centre of the spotlights, was nothing less than the destiny of humanity:

But if its tenebrous empire were allowed,
Its mastery would prepare the dismal hour
When the Inconscient shall regain its right,
And man who emerged as Nature's conscious power,
Shall sink into the deep original night
Sharing like all her forms that went before
The doom of the mammoth and the dinosaur.

Sri Aurobindo knew how the possession had come about and where Hitler's 'inspirations' came to him:

It is the shadow of the Titan's robe
That looms across the panic stricken globe.
In his high villa on the fatal hill
Alone he listens to that sovereign Voice,
Dictator of his action's sudden choice,
The tiger leap of a demonic skill.

However, those who feel inflated or aggrandised by being the instrument of a black power, and delight in being taken beyond their limits, often forget that they will have to pay the price. Not only are they selling their soul to the devil, as the saying goes, they usually also suffer in their body.

> Too small and human for that dreadful Guest,
> An energy his body cannot invest, –
> A tortured channel, not a happy vessel,
> Drives him to think and act and cry and wrestle.

We know now about the 'crises of possession' Hitler was subject to, but he was also going down physically from 1937 onwards, according to Werner Maser.[24] He started taking big quantities of drugs prescribed by his personal physician, Theo Morell. "He felt pressed by the idea that his career would be short, that it would not last longer than ten years, and by the worry to accomplish his work before the end of the time span provided to him by destiny." (François-Poncet[25]) He did not eat meat, drink alcohol or smoke, but he ate enormous quantities of cakes, so much so that in his last days somebody called him 'a cake-eating robot'.

"He has fears of being poisoned, fears of being assassinated, fears of losing his health, fears of gaining weight, fears of treason, fears of losing his mystical guidance, fears of anaesthetics, fears of premature death, fears that his mission will not be fulfilled", wrote Walter Langer, who had this information from people once close to the dictator. He also suffered from enormous **nervous** tension. At the time of the Munich pact Shirer observed: "The man is on the verge of a nervous breakdown", and again when awaiting the signing of the non-aggression pact with Moscow.[26] Goebbels noted that during the days leading up to the Russian invasion "the Führer lives in an indescribable state of tension". A similar tension had taken

---

[24] See the chapter *"Der kranke Führer, Reichskanzler..."* in Werner Maser: *Adolf Hitler – Legende, Mythos, Wirklichkeit.*
[25] André François-Poncet: *Souvenirs d'une ambassade à Berlin,* p. 13.
[26] William Shirer: *The Rise and Fall of the Third Reich,* pp. 343, 429.

hold of Hitler in April 1940, during the operations in Norway and a month later during the campaign in the West – "Hitler has got the jitters".[27]

Things became worse towards the end. "Physically [Hitler] represented a dreadful sight. He dragged himself about painfully and clumsily, throwing his torso forward and dragging his legs after him from his living room to the conference room of the bunker. He had lost his sense of balance; if he were detained on the brief walk (twenty to thirty meters), he had to sit down on one of the benches that had been placed along either wall for this purpose, or else cling to the person he was walking to ... He lay there completely torpid, filled with only one thought: chocolate and cake. His ferocious appetite for cake had become actually morbid."[28] The last documentary films, eg. the one taken when he pinned an Iron Cross on the chest of a few child heroes of the Hitler Youth, show how much his left hand was shaking, as was his leg when he sat down.

His fits of madness increased. He pronounced offhand one death sentence after the other, even of Eva Braun's brother-in-law. And sometimes, as his Chief of Staff tells it: "Cheeks flushed with rage, with raised fists, he stood before me with his whole body shaking, beside himself with fury and altogether out of control. After each eruption of wrath Hitler paced back and forth on the edge of the rug, then paused right in front of me and hurled the next reproach at me. He choked up with shouting; his eyes bulged from their sockets and the veins in his temples swelled". Yet, as we know, "he still preserved something of his magnetic powers".[29] "A nation in which there is even one righteous man will not perish", he said during those last days, and Speer comments: "There was no doubt that he regarded himself as this one righteous man".[30]

---

[27]Ralph Reuth: *Hitler,* pp. 343, 429.
[28]Joachim Fest: *Der Untergang,* pp. 34-35.
[29]Id., pp. 728, 729.
[30]Albert Speer: *Spandau – The Secret Diaries,* p. 19.

In October 1939, though, the dream of the Third Reich and German domination of the world was still alive – indeed it had never been more alive than then:

> Thus driven he must stride on conquering all,
> Threatening and clamouring, brutal, invincible,
> Until he meets upon his storm-swept road
> A greater devil – or thunderstroke of God.

Four-in-one

In the West, the Hindu religion is often mistakenly thought to be a superstitious idolatry of a pantheon of grotesque gods with eight arms, bulging eyes, a protruding tongue or an elephant trunk. Hinduism, however, is probably the oldest monotheism in the world. All Gods are aspects or cosmic powers of the One, which is the reason why above the main temple entrances one finds the glyph for OM, the sound which is the expression of the One and which is said to support the universe. But the human individual chooses his *ishta devata*, the God suited to his personal devotion, knowing full well that his God, like all the others, is an aspect of the One and represents it. Likewise one could say that each one of the four great Asuras represents the anti-One (which is also the One, as there is nothing else than That). The importance for our story lays in the fact that the Lord of Falsehood, who possessed Hitler, also represents Ignorance, Suffering and Death, and that these four aspects were therefore features of his personality.

Falsehood

One of Eckart and Hitler's recurrent themes was Schopenhauer's saying that the Jew was 'the great master of the lie'. When browsing through *Mein Kampf* we have found that Hitler systematically applied the methods of the fictional Elders of Zion, in which he was thoroughly instructed by Alfred Rosenberg, the promulgator of *The*

Protocols. In *Mein Kampf* Hitler professed openly that the lie was a primary means of political action: "In the big lie there is always a force of credibility, because the broad masses of a nation are always more easily corrupted in the deeper strata of their emotional nature than consciously or voluntarily, and thus in the primitive simplicity of their minds they more readily fall victims to the big lie than to the small lie." The German masses, in their 'primitive simplicity', proved him right.

Konrad Heiden said that Hitler was of 'a phenomenal untruthfulness' and called him 'a prophet of the Devil'. Günter Scholdt writes about his 'shamelessness in his relation with truth'. Hitler defined his own mental processes accurately when he wrote that to the Jew lying was an art. "[The Jew] speaks to hide his thoughts, or at least to disguise them, and what he really means is not to be found in what he says but between the lines".[31] His own language and that of Joseph Goebbels, the mouthpiece picked by him with such amazing discernment, soon spun Naziland into a cocoon of total illusion. It was as if Germany, in a very short while, became isolated from democratic Europe under a crystalline dome, a world with its own magic which bewitched its citizens.

Christian Zentner calls Hitler "a downright Machiavellian who considered every means as justified when it was useful to realize his objectives".[32] "Hitler became Chancellor by declaring his readiness not only to be a strictly parliamentary Chancellor, but also to tolerate continuous interference on the part of Hindenburg and to submit to every conceivable restriction".[33] As to his external politics, he set in 1930 a Frenchmen's mind at rest with the following words: "I think I can assure you that there is no one in Germany who will not with all his heart approve any honest attempt at an improvement of relations between Germany and France ... I regard the maintenance of peace

---

[31]Christian Zentner: *Adolf Hitler's "Mein Kampf"*, p. 49.
[32]Id., p. 29.
[33]Konrad Heiden: *The Fuehrer*, p. 421.

in Europe as especially desirable ... The young Germany, that is led by me and that finds its expression in the National Socialist Movement, has only the most heartfelt desire for an understanding with other European nations".[34] His appeasing speeches during the 1930s gave him the name *Friedenskanzler*, Chancellor of Peace. He even omitted verbally attacking the Jews for months on end during the period of successive elections preceding his coming to power, when he felt that the moment and the general mood were not appropriate.

Ignorance

We have seen time and again in our story how vehemently Romanticism and the neo-romantic Volkisch movement in Germany revolted against the intellect and its primacy during the Age of Reason, and that the political trends assembled under the common label of 'Fascism' were in fact nationalist-romanticist expressions of this spirit. Politics has always functioned by appealing to the lower strata of the human character, which were the only ones the masses had access to. And the intellectuals have always been the target of brute political force. Hitler, well informed by Eckart of the theories of Le Bon, Sorel, and similar-minded authors of that time, was aware of all this and wrote about it in *Mein Kampf*. It was his intention to go forward by setting the clock back and making humanity return to a pre-civilised, barbarian age; what in most cases had been a mainly mental exercise of certain hot-blooded reactionaries became with him one of the principal components of a world vision.

In the eyes of his German youth he wanted to see the look of the beast of prey, and upon their mind he wanted to imprint, in Burleigh's words, "an unfeeling form of neo-barbarism". As humanity's master race they had to become heartless, daring and cruel, trained for battle and the exertion of pitiless authority over the peoples subjected by them. A tough body came first, a cultured mind was of secondary importance. Their example was Sparta.

---

[34]Id., p. 327.

They found their ideal embodied in a person like Reinhard Heydrich, right-hand man of Himmler and chief of the secret police, called by some 'the Blond Bestie' and rumoured to be, before he was killed by Czech partisans, a candidate for Hitler's succession. "To the world he personified not only the boundless brutality and deliberate inhumanity which formed the foundation of the National Socialist state and the SS-system, but also the terrible characteristics of those who executed the National Socialist regime and Hitler's politics of annihilation. As long as Heydrich was alive he provided an idea of what Hitler's regime and the National Socialist new order of Europe would have become if the Third Reich had been victorious."[35]

The intellectual responsible for the implementation of Hitler's anti-intellectualism was Dr Joseph Goebbels. "He gave a voice to the madness", writes Guido Knopp,[36] and Goebbels saw himself as 'the smith of the German soul'. Ambassador François-Poncet found him 'one of the most redoubtable Hitlerians' whose mind had "something perverse and diabolical ... Nobody equals him in the art of skipping between truth and falsehood".[37] Speer too found him 'horribly dangerous' and called him "Hitler's cleverest and totally amoral disciple".[38] "The evil genius of the second half of Hitler's career was Goebbels", writes Hanfstängl. "I always likened this mocking, jealous, vicious, satanically gifted dwarf to the pilot-fish of the Hitler shark."[39] And Sri Aurobindo stated, in a talk with his disciples, that Goebbels, as well as Hitler, was "possessed by forces of the Life plane".[40]

Hermann Göring, Marshall of the Reich, potentate and drug addict, was the other Nazi leader whom Sri Aurobindo mentioned

---

[35] Charles Sydnor in Ronald Smelser and Enrico Seyring (ed.): *Die SS*, p. 218.
[36] Guido Knopp: *Hitlers Helfer*, p. 9.
[37] André François-Poncet, op. cit., p. 118.
[38] Gitta Sereny: *Albert Speer: His Battle with Truth*, pp. 324, 368.
[39] Ernst Hanfstängl, op. cit., p. 224.
[40] Nirodbaran, op. cit., p. 84.

by name as being possessed. Sri Aurobindo's opinion is confirmed by an unexpected source, a letter to Göring from his first wife, Carin von Kantzow. "To be a morphinist means the same as committing suicide – every day a small part of your body and your soul is lost. You are possessed by an evil spirit and by an evil power, and your body is gradually destroyed by its illness. Save yourself and by so doing save me too."[41]

In Nuremberg, Göring said to his counsel these revealing words: "If one really wants to bring about something new, good people won't be of any use. They are self-satisfied, lethargic, they have their dear Lord God and their own big head – one can't do anything with them ... What one needs is experienced criminals ... Those who have a lot on their slate will do what you tell them, they will listen when you give them a warning, for they know how things are done and how one gets at the spoils ... Give me experienced thugs, but on condition that I have the power, the unconditional power over life and death ... What do you people know about the possibilities of evil! You are always writing books and making up philosophies although all you know is something about virtue and the way it is acquired – while basically the world is moved by something altogether different!"[42]

Suffering

Falsehood and ignorance can be discussed, and death is a fact, but suffering remains intangible. Still, it is one of the elementary experiences of the human condition. The phenomenon of wilful, cruelly inflicted suffering was so typical of the Third Reich that 'Auschwitz' is the association it automatically evokes today. The physical and psychological suffering, administered for the most part by 'ordinary men' (the title of a much discussed book by Christopher

---

[41]Guido Knop, op. cit., p. 78.
[42]Dieter Wunderlich: *Göring und Goebbels*, p. 226.

Browning), was phenomenal. At its root we find, always, Adolf Hitler, the medium possessed by an asuric god. Most of the Germans did not know this. They glorified their Leader as the Messiah; he was pure and holy, he floated above all the filth. "If only the Führer knew", was a common expression in Naziland. But the Führer knew very well, for in practically all cases – certainly the most nasty and deadly – it was he who gave the initial orders.

If one feels the inclination to know about the suffering, one has to read what people who went through it have recounted, although the actual facts, of course, defy communication. Only those who belonged to the death commandos in Auschwitz, or who survived naked under a pile of naked corpses somewhere in a Russian field, or who miraculously lived to tell a medical experiment of the SS doctors at Buchenwald, or who were torn out their fingernails by the Gestapo in Paris – only those did *know*. Yet, as all this is an aspect of the capabilities of the species to which one belongs, one could read books like *Masters of Death* by Richard Rhodes, *The German Trauma* by Gitta Sereny, *Soldiers of Evil* by Tom Segev, *Orte des Grauens* (places of horror) by Gerd Ueberschär, *Annus Mundi* by Wieslaw Kielar, Léon Poliakovs *Bréviaire de la haine* (breviary of hate) or Anthony Beevors books on Stalingrad and the fall of Berlin, and many more.

The human ingenuity of finding ways to torture people is so horrifying. In *Annus Mundi,* a memoir of his five years in Auschwitz, Wieslaw Kielar tells about the *Stehbunker,* the 'standing-up bunker'. This was a shed which contained four cemented cells, each with hardly enough space for four men to stand up pressed against each other; one had to wriggle oneself into the cells through a small, low door. Some prisoners were locked into these cells for an indeterminate time, which meant until their death, without receiving any food or drink and having to relieve themselves where they stood. As they grew weaker, they gradually sank towards the bottom, making the ordeal still more agonising for their fellow-victims. Death took days to come.

Not less horrifying is the inhumanity of some citizens of a nation which prided itself on its superior human values. Martin Bormann, the eldest son of Hitler's sinister factotum, was named after his father. When as a young boy one day he visited the house of Heinrich Himmler in the company of his little brothers and sisters, Hedwig Potthast, Himmler's secretary and mistress, suddenly had an idea: she would show the children "something very interesting, a secret personal collection of her boss". She took them up the stairs and opened the door to the attic. "There stood tables and chairs made from parts of human skeletons." The seat of one chair was crafted from a human pelvis, the legs of another from human legs with the foot still attached. Then Miss Potthast showed the children a copy of *Mein Kampf* bound in the skin of a human back. Young Martin Bormann, who would become a catholic priest and missionary after the war, "still remembers how medically matter-of-fact she showed and explained everything."[43]

Death. "All things will pass away, nothing will remain but death and the glory of deeds." Walter Schellenberg writes in *The Labyrinth* that Hitler often quoted this sentence from the Hávamál, an old Nordic saga.[44] To Hermann Rauschning, Hitler said already in the 1930s: "We shall not surrender, never! We may perish, perhaps, but we shall take a world with us. *Muspilli.* The world on fire!"[45] A catastrophic end of the world was one of the main themes of the Nordic myths and a subconscious obsession with the Germanic-Nordic people. At the end of history there would inevitably be a *Götterdämmerung,* a twilight of the gods; or the world would die in the Fimbulwinter, when all would be covered with ice; or there would be the great world fire, Muspilli. 'Muspilli' is also the theme of a ninth century poem about the apocalyptic battle between Elijah and the Antichrist. "At the time of the Muspilli no clansman can help

---

[43]Norbert and Stephan Lebert: *Denn Du trägst meinen Namen,* pp. 102-03.
[44]Walter Schellenberg: *The Labyrinth,* p. 94.
[45]Hermann Rauschning, op. cit., p. 11.

another. When the whole world burns and fire and hot air devour everything, what remains then of the land for which one has fought together with one's clansmen?"[46]

Hitler had 'an abstract mania for destruction', writes Fest, who also mentions his 'craving for catastrophe'. Trevor-Roper calls him 'the Angel of destruction' and elsewhere in his *Last Days of Hitler* 'the God of destruction'. Kershaw ascribes to him 'an Asiatic will for destruction', and Spotts calls a whole section of his book on the Führer 'the Artist of Destruction'. Destruction was not only the result of Hitler's bid for world-supremacy, it was a primal Titanic inspiration and a conscious intention.

"According to an account by General Halder, [Hitler] opposed the opinions of his generals, insisting on the bombing and bombardment of Warsaw when the city was ready for surrender, and extracted aesthetic thrills from the images of destruction: the apocalyptically darkened sky, the walls pulverized by a million tons of bombs, people panic stricken and wiped out."[47] "I remember his reaction to the final scene of a newsreel on the bombing of Warsaw", writes Speer. "Hitler was fascinated ... His enthusiasm was unbounded. 'That is what will happen to them!' he cried out, carried away. 'That is how we will annihilate them!'"[48] The bombing of Rotterdam was totally unnecessary, but had to serve as an intimidating example of Teutonic terror.

London was bombed on 65 consecutive nights, in which 45,000 people died. "Have you looked at a map of London?" asked Hitler during one of his nightly gatherings with his inner circle. "It is so closely built up that one source of fire alone would suffice to destroy the whole city, as happened once before, two hundred years ago. Göring wants to use innumerable incendiary bombs of an altogether new type to create sources of fire in all parts of London. Fires everywhere. Thousands of them. Then they'll unite in one gigantic

---

[46] Otto Holzapfel: *Die Germanen*, p. 155.
[47] Joachim Fest, op. cit., p. 726.
[48] Albert Speer: *Inside the Third Reich*, pp. 317-18.

area conflagration. Göring has the right idea. Brisant bombs don't work, but it can be done with incendiary bombs – total destruction of London."[49]

Goebbels followed the bombings of England with ecstatic comments in his diary from 18 October onwards. "Horrible reports from London. A metropolis disappears from the surface of the earth ... The fires in the City must have been terrible ... We attack Plymouth extensively and with considerable results ... Reports from Coventry: it is pure hell ... Again we attack Plymouth massively ..." Hitler expected London to be 'a rubble heap' in three months. "I have not the slightest sympathy for the British civilian populace", he said.[50]

"When Yugoslavia attempted, as the result of an army officers' coup, to withdraw from the Tripartite Pact into which she had been forced, Hitler was so beside himself with fury that he ordered the defenceless capital of the country to be bombed systematically from low altitude for three full days. That was 'Operation Punishment'."[51] Belgrade "was razed to the ground. For three successive days and nights Göring's bombers ranged over the little capital at rooftop level ... killing 17,000 civilians, wounding many more and reducing the place to a mass of smouldering rubble."[52]

It was Hitler's 'firm decision' that Leningrad, Moscow, Stalingrad and Kiew would be 'razed to the ground'. As Goebbels wrote about Leningrad: "Once again the plough has to go over this city".[53] Henry Picker, one of the note takers of the *Tischgespräche*, comments: "On 8 September 1940, Leningrad was completely surrounded by German troops. Of the three million citizens only 400,000 could be evacuated. 632,000 starved to death."[54] "I can imagine that many are asking

---

[49] Id., p. 389.
[50] Albert Speer: *Spandau — The Secret Diaries*, p. 45.
[51] Joachim Fest, op. cit., p. 711.
[52] William Shirer, op. cit., p. 826.
[53] Joseph Goebbels: *Tagebücher* vol. IV, p. 1671.
[54] *Tischgespräche im Führerhauptquartier*, p. 270.

themselves in astonishment: how can the Führer destroy a city like Petersburg [i.e. Leningrad]!" Hitler mused. "Surely, I was educated in a very different way. I couldn't see anybody suffer and I couldn't harm anybody. But when I see that the species is endangered, then the ice-cold intellect takes over from the feelings. I see only the sacrifices which the future will claim if today no sacrifice is made."[55] Leningrad, though, would never be taken, and neither would Moscow or Stalingrad.

But Hitler saw further. "I never saw him so worked up as toward the end of the war, when in a kind of delirium he pictured for himself and for us the destruction of New York in a hurricane of fire", writes Speer. "He described the skyscrapers being turned into gigantic burning torches, collapsing upon one another, the glow of the exploding city illuminating the sky."[56] Speer also writes that he was sure that Hitler would not have hesitated for a moment to employ atom bombs against England, and consequently against other targets later in the war. To Rauschning he had already said: "We will weaken the physical health of our enemy and we will break his power of moral resistance. I can imagine that the bacterial weapon has a future."[57]

"Fire was Hitler's proper element, though what he loved about fire was not its Promethean aspect but its destructive force. That he set the world afire and brought fire and sword upon the Continent – such statements may be mere imagery. But fire itself, literally and directly, always stirred a profound excitement in him. I recall", continues Speer, "his ordering showings in the Chancellery of the films of burning London, of the sea of flames in Warsaw, of exploding convoys, and the rapture with which he watched those films."[58] Sri Aurobindo saw Hitler's fascination with fire as 'the real sign of the Asura' and expected from him more 'works of devilish ingenuity'.

---

[55] *Monologe im Führerhauptquartier*, p. 71.
[56] Albert Speer, op. cit., p. 80.
[57] Hermann Rauschning, op. cit., p. 10.
[58] Albert Speer, op. cit., p. 80.

Henriette von Schirach had known Hitler from nearby for many years, for she was the daughter of Hitler's photographer and the wife of the chief of the Hitler Youth. It was she who said on a certain occasion: "I believe that there are people who attract death, and Hitler was most certainly one of them".[59] It is a fact that several of the women who were closest to him tried to commit suicide. Mimi Reiter, in Berchtesgaden, tried to hang herself but was found by her brother before it was too late. Unity Valkyrie Mitford, the pompous British Nazi who had a crush on Hitler and whom he accepted in his Munich entourage, shot two bullets into her head but survived. Eva Braun tried to kill herself on two occasions, in November 1932 and May 1935; the first time she shot herself in the neck, the second time her sister found her before the sleeping tablets took their effect. Geli Raubal shot herself in the chest in September 1931.

Hitler himself suffered from 'a continuous readiness for suicide', as Sebastian Haffner puts it. His friend Kubizek recalls that he thought seriously of taking his own life during the period of his calf love for Stefanie in Linz. After the failed Beerhall Putsch, Hitler threatened to commit suicide at Hanfstängl's house in the Bavarian countryside, but was prevented from doing so by Hanfstängl's wife Helene. In Landsberg prison he went on hunger strike till he was talked out of it. He showed suicidal trends after the suicide of Geli Raubal. During the grave Party crisis in December 1932 when all seemed lost – although the tide would turn suddenly – Hitler is reported to have said: "If the Party falls apart, it won't take me more than three minutes to shoot myself".[60] He said on another occasion: "It is so simple to do it! The pistol – nothing is simpler than that!"[61] On 30 April 1945, it was for real. "The suicidal impulse that had accompanied him throughout his life and predisposed him to take maximum risks, was at last reaching its goal."[62]

---

[59]Guido Knopp, op. cit., p. 146.
[60]Joachim Fest, op. cit., p. 354.
[61]Erich Korsthorst: *Die Geburt der Tragödie aus dem Geist des Gehorsams*, p. 46.
[62]Joachim Fest, op. cit., p. 732.

When reaching his end, however, he had turned Germany into an Empire of Death. The Allied bombings reduced most of the German cities and towns to rubble. The skeletal, ghostlike prisoners of the concentration camps in their worn-out striped uniforms were seen everywhere, for the network of primary and secondary camps, like cancer metastases, now covered the whole country and had eaten itself even into the agglomerations. Allied armies were fighting their way towards the heart of the country against a resistance which, in its efficient desperation, increased the devastation. Columns of inmates of the eastern concentration camps, emaciated and soiled, were herded from one place to another, leaving behind a track of corpses. Waves of fugitives, fleeing before the Russian armies, tried to reach the Americans, British and French in the West.

And there he stood, the dilapidated Führer, in his bunker thirty feet under the ground, with his stomach full of cake and seeking support against the wall: he was going to fight this last battle alone. He ordered the formation of a *Fliegendes Standgericht*, a fully empowered, flying court martial which would pass sentence on deserters, plunderers and defeatists; they were hung by the roadside with on their chests a board mentioning their crime. He ordered that all German citizens had to flee before the Allied armies, on foot if need be, in the freezing cold through the snow. And then he issued a series of orders, the first of which was, on 19 March, the 'Nero Order', saying that "all military, transportation, communications, industrial and food-supply facilities, as well as all other resources within the Reich which the enemy might use either immediately or in the foreseeable future for continuing the war, are to be destroyed".[63]

Goebbels, 'Hitler's monkey', held on 21 April, in the ruined building of the Propaganda Ministry, the last of his daily staff conferences. "In the freezing cold sit two dozen gentlemen before

---

[63]Id., p. 731,

the Minister in an elegant dark suit. He asks them: 'What can I do with a Volk whose men are no longer fighting, even when their women are being raped?' The Germans deserve their lot, he snarls, they have chosen it themselves ... He crosses his arms before his chest and lets his eyes go over those present: 'I have forced nobody to be my collaborator, and neither have we forced the German people. It is the German people who have chosen us! Why have you worked together with me? Now your throat is going to be cut.' In the doorway he turns around a last time and shouts: 'But when we step down the whole earth will tremble!'"[64] Muspilli ...

'The Children of Wotan'

In the part of the globe which one may roughly call 'the West', the Christian Era and its civilisation were breaking up, and the West had become, since the Renaissance, a world in transition. "As the Christian view of the world loses its authority, the more menacingly will the 'blond beast' be heard prowling about in its underground prison, ready at any moment to burst out with devastating consequences", wrote CG Jung. "The memories of the old German religion have not been extinguished ... We are always convinced that the modern world is a reasonable world, basing our opinions on economic, political and psychological factors. But if we may forget for a moment that we are living in the Year of Our Lord 1936 [the year in which these words were written] ... we will find Wotan quite suitable as a causal hypothesis. In fact I venture the heretical suggestion that the unfathomable depths of Wotan's character explain more of National Socialism than all reasonable factors put together."[65]

In an earlier chapter of our story we have heard about Wotan, the one-eyed God with the green hat who rides at the head of his wild hunters, and who possesses the berserkers with his force and

---

[64]Dieter Wunderlich, op. cit., p. 213.
[65]Michael Baigent and Richard Leigh: *Secret Germany*, p. 226.

invulnerability. Nazism took pride in this revival of the ruthless Germanic warrior spirit. The Hitler Youth sang: "If all the world lies in ruins,/What the devil do we care?/We will still go on marching,/For today Germany belongs to us,/And tomorrow the world." And the SS-magazine *Das Schwarze Korps* saw, in 1940, the burning English cities as gigantic bonfires to celebrate the summer solstice; for it was the god Thor whose lightning (the exploding bombs) was taking revenge on Germany's enemies.[66]

This elementary force line in Hitler and Nazism has been sufficiently dealt with in our story to interpret Sri Aurobindo's poem: 'The Children of Wotan (1940)'. The date, part of the title, is relevant because at that time the further complexities and the outcome of the war still lay in an uncertain future and the destiny of humanity hung in the balance. It makes this forceful poem, written at that critical juncture of history by an Indian spiritual Master, all the more pregnant.

"Where is the end of your armoured march, O children of Wotan?
Earth shudders with fear at your tread, the death-flame laughs in your eyes."
"We have seen the sign of Thor and the hammer of new creation,
A seed of blood on the soil, a flower of blood in the skies.
We march to make of earth a hell and call it heaven.
The heart of mankind we have smitten with the whip of the sorrows seven;
The Mother of God lies bleeding in our black and gold sunrise."

"I hear the cry of a broken world, O children of Wotan."
"Question the volcano when it burns, chide the fire and bitumen!

---

[66]Rüdiger Sünner: *Schwarze Sonne*, p. 85.

Suffering is the food of our strength and torture the bliss of our entrails.
We are pitiless, mighty and glad, the gods fear our laughter inhuman.
Our hearts are heroic and hard; we wear the belt of Orion;
Our will has the edge of the thunderbolt, our acts the claws of the lion.
We rejoice in the pain we create as a man in the kiss of a woman."

"Have you seen your fate in the scales of God, O children of Wotan,
And the tail of the Dragon lashing the foam of far-off seas?"
"We mock at God, we have silenced the mutter of priests at his altar.
Our leader is master of Fate, medium of her mysteries.
We have made the mind a cipher, we have strangled Thought with a cord;
Dead now are pity and honour, strength only is Nature's lord.
We build a new world-order; our bombs shout Wotan's peace.

"We are the javelins of Destiny, we are the children of Wotan,
We are the human Titans, the supermen dreamed by the sage.
A cross of the beast and demoniac with the godhead of power and will,
We are born in humanity's sunset, to the Night is our pilgrimage.
On the bodies of perishing nations, mid the cry of the cataclysm coming,
To a presto of bomb and shell and the aeroplanes' fatal humming,
We march, lit by Truth's death-pyre, to the world's satanic age."[67]

---

[67] Sri Aurobindo: *Collected Poems*, p. 112.

17

A WORLD IN THE BALANCE

History very seldom records the things that were decisive but took place behind the veil; it records the show in front of the curtain.

SRI AUROBINDO

Sri Aurobindo's vision was traced out when he started writing the *Arya* in 1914 – although the working out of it would take the remainder of his and the Mother's lifetime. If we assume that the formation of his adult mind started around 1890, then the period of this formation in Western Europe coincides with the decades which were, as illustrated in our story, the time of the great change and expectation.

The essential difference with the other envisionings of a 'new world' and a 'new man' was that Sri Aurobindo found a system of effective fulfilment of his utopia while others – Marx, Nietzsche and George included – were unable to give theirs a concrete shape or even to suggest one. The making of a new man was the one condition for the making of a brighter tomorrow. "To hope for a true change of human life without the change of human nature is an irrational and unspiritual proposition; it is to ask for something unnatural and unreal, an impossible miracle."[1] The means to change the human being were available in the various yogic systems of the Indian tradition, used by Sri Aurobindo as his starting point. As 'man the microcosm' is a very complex entity, Sri Aurobindo had to achieve a synthesis of the existing systems and create an 'integral yoga' which would enable man to use his present nature as the basis for the realisation of a new species, for the aim of his yoga was no longer a hereafter but the appearance of a being beyond man on the earth.

It is generally presumed that the more spiritual something is the more unsubstantial and etheric it becomes. According to Sri Aurobindo, however, the right view would be that matter is not the only substance in the universe, and that the gradations of the density or 'reality' of a substance increase along with the level of their spirituality. This also means that an increase in spirituality equals an increase in power. "The more subtle is also the more powerful – one might say, the more truly concrete ... A powerless Spirit is no Spirit ... The supraphysical is as real as the physical; to know it is part of a complete knowledge", Sri Aurobindo wrote in *The Life Divine*.[2]

All traditions have warned against the use of spiritual powers, the reason being that they might cause an inflation of the ego and turn the subject away from his path. But an effort like the one by Sri Aurobindo and the Mother demanded a constant battle against the powers which dominate the earth. Against the use of black magic by the Black Forces there was no other option than the use of white magic by the White Forces. "Sri Aurobindo is neither an impotent moralist nor a weak pacifist",[3] he wrote about himself in the third person. His was not a yoga of 'world-shunning ascetism' but an effort to create a higher life in matter. "I am concerned with the earth, not with worlds beyond for their own sake", he wrote; "it is a terrestrial realization that I seek and not a flight to distant summits".[4]

---

[1] Sri Aurobindo: *The Life Divine*, p. 1059.
[2] Id., pp. 257, 1024, 651.
[3] Sri Aurobindo: *On Himself*, p. 22.
[4] Id., pp. 99, 124.

"... The experiences of Yoga belong to an inner domain and go according to a law of their own, have their own method of perception, criteria and all the rest of it which are neither those of the domain of the physical senses nor of the domain of rational or scientific inquiry ..." Still, "as in Science, so here you have to accumulate experience on experience ... you have to develop an intuitive discrimination which compares the experiences, see what they mean, how far and in what field each is valid, what is the place of each in the whole, how it can be reconciled or related with others that at first might seem to contradict it, etc., until you can move with a secure knowledge in the vast field of spiritual phenomena. That is the only way to test spiritual experience."[5] And he declared: "I think I can say that I have been testing day and night for years upon years more scrupulously than any scientist his theory or his method on the physical plane."[6]

"The invisible Force producing tangible results both inward and outward is the whole meaning of the Yogic consciousness ... It is not only in its results but in its movements that the Force is tangible and concrete." "It is neither a magician's wand nor a child's bauble, but something one has to observe, understand, develop, master before one can use it aright or else – for few can use it except in a limited manner – be its instrument." And, writing again in the third person, he disclosed about himself: "In his retirement Sri Aurobindo kept a close watch on all that was happening in the world and in India and actively intervened whenever necessary, but solely with a spiritual force and silent spiritual action ... It was this force which, as soon as he had attained to it, he used, at first only in a limited field of personal work, but afterwards in a constant action upon the world forces."[7] Our story will highlight in its next sections some of the focal points of Sri Aurobindo and the Mother's concerns with

---

[5]Id., p. 91.
[6]Id., p. 469.
[7]Id., pp. 197, 202, 38.

the historical events preceding and at the beginning of the Second World War.

The Munich Agreement (30 September 1938)

On 29 September 1938 Adolf Hitler, Benito Mussolini, Neville Chamberlain and Edouard Daladier met in Munich to decide on the fate of Czechoslovakia, which itself was barred from participation. Hitler wanted Czechoslovakia to be split up so that the Sudetenland with its majority German population could be incorporated into his Greater Germany, and he threatened to go to war on this issue. The Munich Conference is now held to be the high point of the 'appeasement' politics by which the non-German speaking West European nations tried to temper Hitler's ambitions, soft-pedalling on all hot issues and trying to talk the German dictator, aka the *Friedenskanzler*, into a more reasonable stance toward the situation. This attitude of appeasement, fully exploited by the sharp-sighted Führer, resulted on the following day in the signing of an agreement which gave Hitler complete satisfaction.

Czechoslovakia was forced to cede to Germany "11,000 square miles of territory in which dwelt 2,800, 000 Germans and 800,000 Czechs. Within this area lay all the vast Czech fortifications which hitherto had formed the most formidable defensive line in Europe, with the possible exception of the Maginot Line in France. But that was not all. Czechoslovakia's entire system of rail, road, telephone and telegraph communications was disrupted. According to German figures the dismembered country lost 66 percent of its coal, 80 percent of its lignite, 86 percent of its chemicals, 80 percent of its cement, 80 percent of its textiles, 70 percent of its iron and steel, 70 percent of its electric power and 40 percent of its timber. A prosperous industrial nation was split up and bankrupted overnight."[8]

---

[8]William Shirer: *The Rise and Fall of the Third Reich*, pp. 421-22.

Great Britain and France had omitted to defend Czechoslovakia, although they were in honour bound to do so by their international treaties. Moreover, as Field Marshal von Manstein would later explain: "If war had broken out, neither our western border nor our Polish frontier could really have been defended effectively by us, and there is no doubt whatsoever that if Czechoslovakia had defended herself, we would have been held up by her fortifications, for we did not have the means to break through". General Jodl, chief of the German High Command, would concur on this point at Nuremberg: "It was out of the question, with five fighting divisions and seven reserve divisions in the western fortifications, which were nothing but a large construction site, to hold out against 100 French divisions. That was militarily impossible."[9]

On his return from Munich Chamberlain was greeted as a hero. "Brandishing the declaration which he had signed with Hitler, the jubilant Prime Minister faced a large crowd that pressed into Downing Street ... He smilingly spoke a few words from a second-story window in Number 10. 'My good friends', he said, 'this is the second time in our history that there has come back from Germany to Downing Street peace with honour. [The first time had been Disraeli's return from the Congress of Berlin in 1878, during the Bismarck years.] I believe it is peace in our time.' The *Times* declared that 'no conqueror returning from a victory on the battlefield has come adorned with nobler laurels'."[10] The lonely voice of dissent, as it had been against appeasement all along, was that of Winston Churchill, who warned: "We have sustained a total and unmitigated defeat ... Silent, mournful, abandoned, broken, Czechoslovakia recedes into the darkness ... We are in the midst of a disaster of the first magnitude which has befallen Great Britain and France ... And do not suppose that this is the end. It is only the beginning of the reckoning."[11]

---

[9]Id., p. 424.
[10]Id., p. 420.
[11]David Cannadine (ed.): *The Speeches of Winston Churchill*, p 134.

Sri Aurobindo and the Mother condemned the Munich Agreement outright. A 'corrupt' France had 'backed out of her promise' and 'betrayed Czechoslovakia', thereby calling down upon her head her own future difficulties. "The Czechs could have offered good resistance but for the Allies who betrayed them. If the Allies had agreed to help them at that time in combination with Russia [a partner in the French treaty with Czechoslovakia], the Czechs could have given an effective fight to Hitler ... Blum and Daladier made the worst possible blunders, the one by his non-intervention policy [in the recently concluded civil war] in Spain, the other by betraying the Czechs."[12]

Chamberlain was "a crafty fool, thinking that he was dealing most diplomatically with Hitler while he did not see the reality of what he was doing ... So long as Chamberlain is at the helm, nothing will happen. He applies only business intelligence to politics".[13] (Shirer saw Chamberlain as "gullible almost beyond comprehension".) "In a photograph of the Munich Pact I saw Hitler with Chamberlain", said Sri Aurobindo. "This man with a great diabolical cunning in his eyes was looking at Chamberlain, who looked like a fly before a spider on the point of being caught – and he actually *was* caught."[14]

Sri Aurobindo explained the role Great Britain had played in Germany's military recovery. "It was England who thrust Germany into power. She saw that France was getting powerful in Europe after the war [i.e. the First World War]. As is her usual self-interested policy, she raised Germany in order to create a balance of power [on the European continent]. She didn't expect that Germany would aim her gun at her. At one time France and England came almost to the point of rivalry ... I have never seen such a bankruptcy of English diplomacy before."[15]

---

[12]Nirodbaran: *Talks with Sri Aurobindo*, pp. 603, 723.
[13]Id., pp. 741, 605.
[14]Id., p. 84.
[15]Id., p. 142.

"Western civilization is failing", remarked Sri Aurobindo. "Even the nineteenth century civilization with its defects was better than what we have now. Europe could not stand the test of the last world war ... From one point of view there never was a time when humanity came down so low as it has now. It looks as if a small number of violent men are the arbiters of humanity and the rest of the world is ready to bow down before one man ... The setback to the human mind in Europe is amazing ... We had thought during the last years of the nineteenth century that the human mind had attained a certain level of intelligence and that this would have to be satisfied before any new idea could find acceptance. But it seems one cannot rely on common sense to stand the strain."[16]

Now Hitler, convinced that he was pressed for time, loosened all the brakes. For a time he had gone easy on the Jews, heading straight for his world war and allowing nothing to come in between. In the back of his mind, though, the idea had taken shape that the war would be the right occasion to realise, unheeded by the outside world, one of the essential components of his fixed idea: the surgical removal of the Jewish race from the body of humanity. Hardly more than a month after the Munich Conference he used an incident of little importance to launch the *Kristallnacht,* an euphemism for the biggest pogrom in German history.

Soon a series of decrees gradually made life in Germany unbearable for the Jews – and not only for the Jews: Himmler issued his decree 'to fight the Gypsy plague' on 8 December. Whatever the half-measures Hitler had been forced to take not to offend world opinion too much, from now on he indubitably worked towards the genocide of the Jewish people in all territories within his power, with the ultimate aim to eradicate them (*ausmerzen*) in the whole world. Sri Aurobindo read his intentions and signalled the preparations for 'the deliberate cold-blooded murder of the Jews' as early as the last day of 1938.

---

[16] Id., pp. 82, 85, 154.

Hitler, the appearances notwithstanding, was sorely disappointed with the results of the Munich Conference. Raving against Chamberlain, he shouted: "That fellow has spoiled my entry into Prague!" But he would not stand much longer that his plans be frustrated. In an impertinent breach of the Munich Agreement the German army marched into Czechoslovakia in the night of 14 March 1939. When the next day Hitler was told that there are was no military riposte from the side of Great Britain and France he exclaimed jubilantly: "I knew it! In a fortnight nobody will talk about this anymore!" And again a day later the triumphant new master of Czechoslovakia entered the Hradshin, the famous castle and traditional seat of the government in Prague.

The beginning of the Second World War (1 September 1939)

Poland. It had been Hitler's steadfast intention to conquer Russia since the time he wrote *Mein Kampf*. To get there, however, he had to close the geographical gap which separated that country from Germany, for in between lay Czechoslovakia and Poland. Of Czechoslovakia he had made quick work, brashly and unhindered. Now, to invade Poland, he needed the compliance of Stalin – which means that to attack Stalin in the long term he had to befriend him in the short term.

A Non-Aggression Pact between Germany and Russia was concluded on 23 August, just in time to make the Polish invasion roll off as planned. This was perhaps the most cynical treaty in modern history, and a perfect illustration of Hitler's theories about the moral value of the relations between nations. For one of the main points of the Nazi doctrine and propaganda had been throughout that it was the aim of the Third Reich to obliterate Judeo-Bolshevism; on the other hand, for the Russians and for the Communist Parties all over the world Nazism represented the acme of imperialistic capitalism and was their much maligned enemy. Yet, after the news of the Non-Aggression Pact had struck them for a short while with complete consternation, the faithful in both blocs dapperly toed the party line again.

Sri Aurobindo will observe that "Hitler is getting remarkable inspiration from his Asura. He doesn't go by reason but only by the voice. He considers all possibilities and when he fixes on something he goes ahead. Only, he did not foresee the British and French intervention on behalf of Poland."[17] Indeed, the patience of the British and French Allies, and therewith the attitude of 'appeasement', had worn out. By now Chamberlain understood – and his government colleagues as well as the House of Commons had made him understand – that Hitler had tricked him. Great Britain and France both warned Hitler that this time they would not take any further aggressive action lying down. On 2 September they warned him by ultimatum that he had to withdraw his invasion force by 11 am the next day, or that their countries would be at war with Germany.

Paul Schmidt, Hitler's official interpreter, was present when the Führer received this news in the company of Joachim von Ribbentrop, his foreign minister. "When I entered the room Hitler was sitting at his desk and Ribbentrop stood by the window. Both looked up expectantly as I came in. [Schmidt had been handed the ultimatum by the British Ambassador.] I stopped at some distance from Hitler's desk, and then slowly translated the British ultimatum. When I finished there was complete silence. Hitler sat immobile, gazing before him ... After an interval which seemed an age he turned to Ribbentrop, who had remained standing by the window. 'What now?' asked Hitler with a savage look, as though implying that his Foreign Minister had misled him about England's probable reaction. Ribbentrop answered quietly: 'I assume that the French will hand in a similar ultimatum within the hour'."[18]

"Yes, he is getting remarkable guidance from his Asura", said Sri Aurobindo on another occasion. "Sometimes the Asuras have an

---

[17] Nirodbaran, op. cit., p. 709.
[18] William Shirer, op. cit., p. 613.

extraordinary foresight that comes true with perfect precision both on the vital and subtle-vital planes, just like that which is possible on the spiritual planes. Of course they are not always infallible. But Hitler committed only one mistake: when attacking Poland he thought that the Allies would not intervene. Napoleon did not have such guidance."[19] This was how, on the Western front, 'the phoney war' began, both sides occupying their positions from the North Sea to Switzerland, making loud propagandistic noises, watching each other through their binoculars, playing football, and shouting insults at each other. Then, on 10 May 1940, the *Sitzkrieg* (sitting war) turned into a *Blitzkrieg* (lightning war), when Hitler troops invaded the Netherlands, Luxemburg, Belgium and France.

Dunkirk

Hitler started this phase of his war with a daring manoeuvre: he attacked the Allied armies (Belgian, French and the British Expeditionary Force) at the one point which they had thought to be impracticable: through the Belgian wooded hills of the Ardennes. His inner guidance was again working wonders, also in the way he had fully supported the innovative ideas of his tank commanders. His strategy cut off the enemy armies in Belgium and the north of France, together more than a million men. The Belgians, under their enigmatic king Leopold III, soon surrendered, following the example of the Dutch. Suddenly the British Expeditionary Force, along with three French armies, found itself trapped and had to make the life-or-death effort of retreating posthaste towards Dunkirk, France's third biggest port.

When the retreating armies were completely encircled, Hitler gave the order to his tank divisions to stop. "That evening [of 24 May] four Panzer divisions were stopped at the AA Canal. The tank crews were astounded. No fire was coming from the opposite bank. Beyond they could make out the peaceful spires of Dunkirk. Had

---

[19]Nirodbaran, op. cit., p. 713.

Operations gone crazy? The division commanders were even more amazed. They knew they could take Dunkirk with little trouble since the British were still heavily engaged near Lille. Why weren't they allowed to seize the last escape port to England?"[20]

This Hitler order is briskly discussed to the present day and every historian has his own explanation. Hitler had special consideration for the British, who mainly consisted of tribes as Aryan as the Germans, and he wanted to gain their cooperation by sparing the encircled troops; he doubted that the tanks would be effective in a landscape cut by rivers and canals; the troops were tired and needed a rest; he feared an attack by the French on his southern flank; his military campaign had gone so well that he became nervous and feared it might turn sour; etc.

Given the military situation, with the hundreds of thousands of enemy soldiers inescapably trapped, and the fact that for Great Britain the continuation of the war depended on these troops, the real reason of Hitler's decision – possibly combined with one or other of the elements aforementioned – may have been Göring's eagerness and promise to pulverize the enemy armies, amassed in the harbour and on the beaches, with his Luftwaffe. Göring wanted his share in a victory which was driving the Germans wild with pride. If the Luftwaffe did the job, the tanks could be spared for the decisive turn towards the south and Paris. And it may have given Hitler great pleasure to visualize the bloody pulp to which his airplanes would reduce the helpless troops on the beaches. For from this time onward he was convinced that he was the master of the world – and the world better take notice.

When some troops of the BEF began to escape, Hitler realised that he had blundered and ordered the ground attack to restart on 26 May. This had given the Allies, commanded by the French Admiral Abrial, the time to organise a perimeter which they defended with heroism. Then, when Operation Dynamo took off, the transport of

---

[20] John Toland: *Adolf Hitler*, pp. 833-34.

thousands of soldiers by a fleet of vessels ranging from battle cruisers to small fishing and pleasure boats, something troubling for the Germans happened: their relentless aerial pounding of the Allies came at times practically to a standstill.

Survivors of the Operation as well as historians agree that the weather in those days was splendid: the sun shone in a blue sky and the sea was 'like glass' – luckily, for otherwise the soldiers, who had to wade through the water from the beach toward the vessels, would never have been able to embark. There was, however, another weather factor in play, this one preventing the German bomber planes from taking off because the airfields were covered with fog. "Fog came to the rescue of the British. Not only was Dunkirk itself enshrouded but all the Luftwaffe fields were blanketed by low clouds which grounded their three thousand bombers." (Toland[21]) Reuth and Kershaw too mention 'the bad weather', which can only have been prevalent inland; and Shirer quotes from the diary of the German General Halder: "The pocket would have been closed at the coast if only our armour had not been held back. The bad weather has grounded the Luftwaffe and we must now stand by and watch countless thousands of the enemy get away to England right under our noses."[22]

As soon as Belgium had surrendered, Sri Aurobindo, who closely kept track of the developments, commented: "The surrender means that Dunkirk – and also Calais – will fall to Germany ... There is no way out for [the BEF] unless Dunkirk can hold on or they can rush through the gap from the French line ... Ostend [a Belgian port town] was in the hands of the Belgian army. By their surrender Dunkirk will be vulnerable unless [the Allies] have sufficient troops there to defend it. Now escape also is difficult. They may try to dash through the gap and line up with the French on the Somme. Otherwise I don't see any way."[23]

---

[21]Id., p. 835.
[22]William Shirer: *The Nightmare Years*, p. 535.
[23]Nirodbaran, op. cit., pp. 672, 674, 678.

On 30 May, when Operation Dynamo was in full swing, a disciple observed: "Dunkirk is still in the hands of the Allies ... It will be a great feat if they can escape". Sri Aurobindo answered: "Yes, it can be called a great military feat". The next day Sri Aurobindo himself opened the talk with some relish by referring to the evacuation of the Allied troops: "So they are getting away from Dunkirk!" A disciple remarked: "Yes. It seems the fog helped the evacuation". Sri Aurobindo: "Yes. Fog is rather unusual at this time ..." According to Nirodbaran, who recorded these conversations, Sri Aurobindo's tone seemed to insinuate that the fog was caused by occult intervention.[24] The evacuation continued till 4 June, when the Germans finally succeeded in occupying the town of Dunkirk. Altogether 338,226 men were evacuated, of whom 123,095 were French and 16,816 Belgian.[25] "If the British Expeditionary Force had been lost, it is almost inconceivable that Churchill would have survived the growing pressure from those powerful forces within Britain that were ready to seek terms with Hitler."[26]

Sri Aurobindo would later write about himself, once more in the third person: "Inwardly he put his spiritual force behind the Allies from the moment of Dunkirk when everybody was expecting the immediate fall of England and the definite triumph of Hitler, and he had the satisfaction of seeing the rush of German victory almost immediately arrested and the tide of war began to turn in the opposite direction. This he did because he saw that behind Hitler and Nazism were dark Asuric forces and that their success would mean the enslavement of mankind to the tyranny of evil, and a setback to the course of evolution and especially to the spiritual evolution of mankind ..."[27] A few days after what has come to be named 'the miracle of Dunkirk' he said: "If England can win against the Germans,

---

[24] Id., pp. 680-81.
[25] Patrick Odone: *Dunkirk 1940*, p. 125.
[26] Ian Kershaw: *Hitler 1936-1945: Nemesis*, p. 297.
[27] Sri Aurobindo: *On Himself*, p. 39.

it would mean that she is specially protected"; and in December of the same year: "[The British] were saved by divine intervention ... They would have been smashed if Hitler had invaded England at the right time, just after the fall of France."[28]

It is noteworthy that Sri Aurobindo said on 20 June, i.e. before Hitler's western campaign was concluded: "I think the next war will be between Russia and Germany".[29] (In March, *before* the Blitzkrieg, he had already opined: "Hitler is the great danger to Russia".) Hitler had his first meeting about the invasion with some of his top generals on 31 July, and made his intentions known to attack Russia in the spring of the following year.[30] Toland describes how Field Marshall von Brauchitsch instructed his military staff, to their astonishment, to prepare the plans for what would become Operation Barbarossa.

Churchill

Hitler did not invade England and neither did Great Britain collapse, as was generally expected. The reason was one man: Winston Churchill, who had become Prime Minister on 10 May, the very day of the German attack. "In Churchill Hitler found something more than an antagonist. To a panic-stricken Europe the German dictator had appeared almost like invincible fate. Churchill reduced him to a conquerable power", writes Fest.[31] Before the invasion of France Sri Aurobindo had already said in passing: "England is quite unreliable under her present leadership"[32], and that he and the Mother were looking for a suitable person. If the Asura had his instrument in one camp, the White Forces needed theirs in the opposite camp once their decision had been taken to actively engage in the battle.

---

[28]Nirodbaran, op. cit., pp. 744, 998.
[29]Id., p. 733.
[30]Christoph Studt: *Das Dritte Reich in Daten*, p. 136.
[31]Joachim Fest: *Hitler*, p. 637.
[32]Nirodbaran, op. cit., p. 231.

It is now mostly forgotten what a chancy affair the coming to power of Winston Churchill actually was. For he was generally considered to be an adventurer, responsible for the debacles of Gallipoli in the First World War and recently, as the First Sea Lord, for the British misadventure in Norway. Besides, his dogged attitude of unconditional defiance toward Nazi Germany ran contrary to a widespread spirit which felt very much inclined to give in and ask for a peace settlement – which Hitler would have been delighted to accept. Hitler seems to have felt instinctively that Churchill would be the big obstacle for the realisation of his plans and hated him wholeheartedly. He called him 'an incompetent, alcoholic demagogue', 'a Yid-ridden half-American souse', 'a political whore', 'a characterless pig', and much more of the kind.

Was Churchill aware of the spiritual support provided to him? In the House of Commons he said on 13 October 1942: "I sometimes have a feeling, in fact I have it very strongly, a feeling of interference. I want to stress that I have a feeling sometimes that some guiding hand has interfered. I have the feeling that we have a guardian because we serve a great cause, and that we shall have that guardian so long as we serve that cause faithfully. And what cause it is!"[33] The greatness of the cause often echoed in his speeches, which at times took on Aurobindonian accents: "You ask: What is our aim? I can answer in one word: Victory ... for without victory, there is no survival ... no survival for the urge and impulse of the ages, that mankind will move forwards to its goal." "Behind them – behind us – behind the armies and fleets of Britain and France – gather a group of shattered States and bludgeoned races ... upon all of whom the long night of barbarism will descend ..." "If we can stand up to [Hitler], all Europe may be free and the life of the world may move forward into broad, sunlit uplands. But if we fail, then the whole world ... will sink into the abyss of a new Dark Age ..." "... I

---

[33]Maggi Lidchi-Grassi: *The Light that Shone into the Dark Abyss*, p. 72.

will say that he must indeed have a blind soul who cannot see that some great purpose and design is being worked out here below, of which we have the honour to be the faithful servants."[34]

Sri Aurobindo found Churchill's Ministry of National Cooperation 'a remarkable Ministry'. The British spirit of resistance, awakened by Churchill despite the desperate situation, had 'removed many dangers'. Even before the French armistice on 22 June 1940, when everybody expected that Hitler, following up on his successes, would cross over to England, Sri Aurobindo said: "I don't think an invasion is likely or possible", and a few days later: "I don't think any attack [on England] is likely now ... No, Hitler won't attack ..." After the armistice with France, when an invasion was thought to be imminent, Sri Aurobindo again weighed the chances and concluded: "Nobody knows what [Hitler] has up his sleeve, but I don't think that he can attack ... He never considers possibilities. If he gets the right inspiration, possibilities don't matter ... All through he has been guided by inspiration and he has gone ahead depending on luck. Regarding France, Poland and all other countries he had set out a plan beforehand and carried it out, but regarding England nobody knows what he has. He has a most original mind, because it is not his own mind."[35] Hitler set several dates for Operation Sea Lion in which the German forces would cross the Channel – but the attack, indeed, never happened.

Operation Sea Lion had to be preceded by an intensive action of Göring's Luftwaffe, which had to annihilate the RAF fighter force together with its bases. Hitler had blamed Göring for the evacuation of the BEF, which the Luftwaffe had not been able to prevent; this was Göring's chance to redeem himself. For *Operation Adlerangriff* (eagle attack) – which would develop into 'the Battle of Britain', the first air battle in history – he used everything at his disposal: 1039 fighters, 998 bombers and 316 dive-bombers.

---

[34]*The Speeches of Winston Churchill*, pp. 149, 154, 177, 233.
[35]Id., pp. 681, 693.

The odds were, as Churchill would recollect later, 'seven or eight to one'.

A few weeks before the attacks, one of Sri Aurobindo's disciples had asked: "Why does Hitler say that he wants to finish this campaign by 15 August?" Sri Aurobindo had answered: "That is a clear indication, if an indication was necessary, that he is the enemy of our work".[36] 15 August was Sri Aurobindo's birthday. Did Hitler ever say such a thing? In Shirer's *The Nightmare Years* we find the following: "On June 11, I had lunch at the Adlon [a hotel in Berlin] with Karl von Wiegand, the veteran Hearst correspondent, who was just back from interviewing Hitler at the front. The dictator had told him France would be finished by the middle of the month – four days from now! – and Great Britain by the middle of August – two months hence. Karl … said Hitler acted as if he had the world at his feet." A few pages further on, Shirer writes: "Making my rounds in the Wilhelmstrasse on August 1, I had taken two bets from Nazi officials: one, that the swastika would be flying over Trafalgar Square by August 15; the other, by September 7. I bet no."

Finally 15 August had come, and Shirer remembered: "Already excitement among our military guides was mounting. Coming into Calais from Dunkirk they had begun dropping hints that this day, Thursday, August 15, 1940, might be a historic one. The Luftwaffe might be carrying out, if the weather held, its most murderous attack yet against Britain. As it turned out, August 15 saw the biggest engagement of the Battle of Britain, with more planes in action than had ever been seen before. The Luftwaffe flew 1950 sorties, the RAF [Royal Air Force] nearly a thousand, as they joined battle over a front of five hundred miles. It was one of the decisive battles of history and, along with a similar one exactly a month later, on September 15, determined the fate of Britain and indeed of Nazi Germany."[37] The RAF won.

---

[36] AB Purani: *Evening Talks*, p. 710.
[37] William Shirer, op. cit., pp. 537, 580, 583-84.

In spite of this victory the situation remained very dark for Great Britain and any other leader but Churchill might have given in to the apparently hopeless situation. Britain had to stand up alone against a powerful and euphorically victorious enemy; it was bereft of most of its heavy military equipment, which the BEF had had to leave behind on the continent; and countless strategic problems were worsening day by day in its enormous empire in the East. Moreover, the British public, now heavily bombed in London and other places in the south of the country, had heard only bad news without a single ray of hope; and the military assistance of the United States remained uncertain because Roosevelt had to fight his internal political battles. Yet Churchill never vacillated, at least not in public, at a time when Hitler was 'sprawled over Europe' and Great Britain had "the honour to be the sole champion of the liberties of Europe". "If England can hold on for one year at least, or two winters, there is a chance", said Sri Aurobindo.[38]

The humiliation of France

The armistice between Germany and France was signed on 22 June 1940 at Compiègne. Hitler had staged the most humiliating ceremony possible, demanding that the signing take place at the exact spot where Germany had surrendered in 1918 and in the self-same railway car, which had been taken from a museum in Paris. Sri Aurobindo had already warned that Marshall Pétain was dangerous at the time that he became a member of the French war cabinet. Now he said, not mincing his words: "This fool of a Marshal Pétain has sold France," and "Pétain has killed the Revolution – the Revolution which had required three more revolutions to make it firm and established".[39] We know how essential Sri Aurobindo considered the ideals of the Enlightenment and the French Revolution for the future development of humanity, and how Hitler and Nazism represented the exact opposite.

---

[38]Nirodbaran, op. cit., p. 735.
[39]Id., pp. 747

"Hitler will see to it that France has no power to rise again ... France will be terribly impoverished", said Sri Aurobindo.[40] This was exactly what happened, although Pétain and his fascist collaborators thought they would be able to spare their country from Hitler's unspeakable contempt and greed. France was cut up into five parts. Alsace-Lorraine became once again German territory; the north of the country was joined with Belgium into a kind of temporary protectorate which in due time would also be incorporated into Greater Germany; the Atlantic coast with its precious ports and their hinterland were occupied; 'Vichy France' became so to speak independent under an own government; a fifth part, in the south, was occupied by Italy as its share of the spoils. Hitler had realised the *Kriegsziele* (war aims) of the First World War, and much more. In his mind there was never any doubt that France was there to be used, abused, and sucked dry. If he let Vichy France exist for the time being, it was only because he was too busy elsewhere and would be less distracted while others took care of it for the time being. As Robert Paxton puts it: "It was Pétain who wanted collaboration; Hitler wanted only booty".[41]

Sri Aurobindo feared that Hitler would want to destroy Paris. "Paris has been the centre of human civilization for three centuries. Now he will destroy it. That is the sign of the Asura. History is repeating itself. The Graeco-Roman civilization was also destroyed by the Germans ... It is not likely that Germany will preserve [Paris]. Destruction of Paris means the destruction of modern European civilization."[42] Knowledgeable people tell us that Sri Aurobindo saw correctly.

Speer quotes Hitler as saying: "In the past I often considered whether we would not have to destroy Paris". "Although I was accustomed to hearing Hitler make impulsive remarks", writes Speer,

---

[40] Id., p. 754.
[41] Robert Paxton: *Vichy France*, p. xxxvi.
[42] Nirodbaran, op. cit., pp. 707, 712.

"I was nevertheless shocked by this cool display of vandalism. He had reacted in a similar fashion to the destruction of Warsaw."[43] Hanfstängl testifies to the fact that the destruction of Paris was a kind of obsession with Hitler. "'We shall reach the decision in France', Hitler screamed. 'We will reduce Paris to rubble. We must break the chains of Versailles.' Oh! my God, I thought, Paris in ruins, the Louvre, all those art treasures gone. Each time Hitler got into this mood I felt almost physically sick."[44] And Fest writes in *Der Untergang*: "According to a report by Franz Halder, Chief of the General Staff, Hitler had already during the campaign against Poland insisted on the bombing of Warsaw, which was about to surrender, and found excitement in watching the destruction through his field glasses; later he had considered the destruction of Paris, and also of Moscow and Leningrad ..."[45]

The order for the destruction of Paris was finally given after the Allied invasion in Normandy, and is printed with all references in *Is Paris Burning?* by Larry Collins and Dominique Lapierre. It read: "Paris must not fall in the hands of the enemy, or, if it does he must find there nothing but a field of ruins". And the authors write that the day after the liberation of the cultural metropolis of the world "every Parisian looking out of his window on that night could gaze at one of the wonders of the war: Paris was unharmed ... All those peerless monuments which had made the city into a beacon of civilized man, had up to that day stood undamaged through five years of the most destructive war in history."[46]

A fifty per cent chance

After the Battle of Britain had been fought and won by the British, Sri Aurobindo still gave Hitler an even chance of success. "It is only

---

[43] Albert Speer: *Inside the Third Reich*, p. 249.
[44] Ernst Hanfstängl: *Hitler – The Missing Years*, p. 120
[45] Joachim Fest: *Der Untergang*, p. 153.
[46] Larry Collins and Dominique Lapierre: *Is Paris Burning?* p. 435.

the British navy that stands against Hitler's world domination ... He is practically master of Europe. If after the collapse of France he had invaded England, by now he would have been in Asia. Now another force has been set up against him. Still the danger has not passed. He has a fifty per cent chance of success. It is a question of balance of forces. Up to the time of the collapse of France he was extraordinarily successful because he sided with the Asuric Power behind him from which he received remarkably correct messages."[47]

Sri Aurobindo was not the only one who thought the scales were evenly balanced. Thomas Mann was of the same opinion in May 1941. John Lukacs writes that "in 1940 and 1941 Hitler came close to winning the war".[48] And HR Trevor-Roper said in a conversation with Ron Rosenbaum: "The fact is he nearly won the war. It was by a whisker he didn't".[49] We find this opinion similarly worded in Sri Aurobindo's 'postscript chapter' to his *Ideal of Human Unity*: "[The Germans] came for a time within a hair's breadth of success".[50]

A disciple said to Sri Aurobindo: "Gandhi writes that the non-violence tried by some people in Germany has failed because it has not been strong enough to generate sufficient heat to melt Hitler's heart". To this Sri Aurobindo answered: "It would have to be a furnace in that case. The only way to melt his heart is to bomb it out of existence."[51] This was before the war, when Sri Aurobindo also reflected: "There is no chance for the world unless something happens in Germany or else Hitler and Stalin quarrel. But there is no such likelihood at present."[52] The Non-Agression Pact between Germany and Russia still continued to be honoured. After the

---

[47] Nirodbaran, op. cit., p. 919.
[48] John Lukacs: *The Hitler of History*, p. 129.
[49] Ron Rosenbaum: *Explaining Hitler*, p. 268.
[50] Sri Aurobindo: *The Ideal of Human Unity*, p. 319.
[51] Nirodbaran, op. cit., pp. 120-21.
[52] Id., p. 553.

French surrender, Sri Aurobindo expressed his opinion trenchantly: "Hitler now becomes the master of Europe ... Now only Hitler's death can save the situation".[53]

When the world situation had become critical, Sri Aurobindo said: "It is only the British navy that stands against Hitler's world domination".[54] In fact, the only positive news in those dark months had been some gallant actions by the Navy, for instance in the Atlantic the battle with the *Graf Spee,* which had resulted in the scuttling of the 'pocket battle ship' and the suicide of its captain. When France surrendered, there was an imminent danger that the French fleet, the second in the world, would fall into Hitler's hands. Day by day Sri Aurobindo paid full attention to the development of the situation. "If the French navy falls into [Hitler's] hands, he will become tremendously strong ... If Pétain surrenders the navy and the colonies nothing can be more shameful and more disastrous ... The situation won't be safe if the French fleet falls into [Hitler's] hands ..."[55] "Article 8 of the Armistice prescribed that the French Fleet ... 'shall be collected in ports to be specified and there demobilised and disarmed under German or Italian control", writes Churchill. "But who in his senses would trust the word of Hitler after his shameful record and the facts of the hour? ... The life of the State and the salvation of our cause were at stake."[56]

Part of the French fleet, including the ultra-modern battle-cruisers *Dunkerque* and *Strasbourg,* was anchored at Mers-el-Kebir, the military harbour of Oran. Great Britain gave the admiral in charge three options: (*a*) join the British and continue to fight for victory against the Axis; (*b*) transfer the ships under control to a British port; (*c*) sail the ships under reduced crews to some French port in the West Indies, where they will be demilitarized and the crews repatriated.

---

[53] Id., p. 721.
[54] Id., p. 919.
[55] Id., pp. 738, 740, 759.
[56] Winston Churchill: *The Second World War,* p. 315.

If he refused this offer, his ships would be sunk within six hours. The Admiral did refuse and on 3 July most of the ships were sunk or damaged beyond repair, with the loss of 1250 lives.

"The elimination of the French Navy as an important factor almost at a single stroke by violent action produced a profound impression in every country", writes Churchill. "Here was this Britain which so many had counted down and out, which strangers had supposed to be quivering on the brink of surrender to the mighty power arrayed against her, striking ruthlessly at her dearest friends of yesterday and securing for a while to herself the undisputed command of the sea. It was made plain that the British War Cabinet feared nothing and would stop at nothing. This was true."[57]

But Britain remained 'at bay' for quite some time and its leaders really did have little else to offer to the population than 'blood, toil, tears and sweat'. Military catastrophes came in quick succession: North Africa, Greece, Crete … "On the map the sum of Hitler's conquests by September 1942 looked staggering. The Mediterranean had become practically an Axis lake, with Germany and Italy holding most of the northern shore from Spain to Turkey and the southern shore from Tunisia to within sixty miles of the Nile. In fact, German troops now stood guard from the Norwegian North Cape on the Arctic Ocean to Egypt, from the Atlantic at Brest to the southern reaches of the Volga River on the border of Central Asia." (William Shirer[58])

Sri Aurobindo had hoped that Great Britain would be able to hold out for a year or two winters; it did hold out and it was indeed in the second winter that the tide turned. 'Operation Torch', the Anglo-American invasion of North Africa, took place on 7/8 November 1942, just after Rommel and his *Afrika Korps* had had to retreat from El Alamein. When Stalingrad fell, on 31 January, the war was practically decided, for now the Red Army attained its full fighting capacity and the United States, shocked by the Japanese

---

[57]Id., p. 320.
[58]William Shirer: *The Rise and Fall of the Third Reich*, p. 914.

attack on Pearl Harbour, had entered the war on the side of the Allies. That from that time onward the outcome was certain, we know now; then, however, fighting raged all over the globe, continuing to cause suffering, destruction and death apparently without end.

Objective India

In his *Griff nach der Weltmacht* Fritz Fischer quotes several sources who state: "The Germans pursued in the Ukraine a precise economic and political goal. They wanted to keep permanent possession of the most secure way to Mesopotamia and Arabia, and to [the oilfields of] Baku and Persia, which they had won by their invasion of the Ukraine ... [One policy maker] went so far to postulate that, 'as long as England blocks Germany's expansion toward the West, the main interest of Germany must be directed via the Ukraine and the Krim towards India'." The efforts of the German foreign policy should be crowned by using the conquered Russian territories as a bridge with Central Asia.[59] This was during the First World War.

In the Second World War, as early as October 1940, when Yugoslavia had signed a protocol with made it completely dependent on Germany, Sri Aurobindo remarked: "If the news is true [it was true], that is the beginning of the end of the Balkans, because Bulgaria won't resist. Greece will be at its wits' end without Turkey's help, and what can Turkey do alone? So Hitler comes to Asia Minor and that means India. The Asura is up to his tricks again. Now Hitler's moves are quite clear. He will try to move towards the Mediterranean, taking possession of the Suez [Canal] and then Egypt ... "[60] Around the same time Sri Aurobindo said: "If England wouldn't stand in the way Hitler would settle first with Russia, then proceed to Asia and then to India".[61] Although England would not

---

[59]Fritz Fischer: *Griff nach der Weltmacht*, pp. 485-87, passim.
[60]Nirodbaran, op. cit., p. 939.
[61]Id., p. 815.

budge, Hitler took the fatal risk of turning against Russia and of engaging in a two-front war, sticking as always to the main ideas which buttressed his thinking, one of which was the conquest of *Lebensraum* in the East. The progress of the Afrika Korps towards Egypt and the Suez Canal and, simultaneously, of the southern Army Group in Russia towards the Caspian Sea and the Caucasus formed the pincer movement that was to break open Asia.

For Sri Aurobindo it had been an indubitable fact from the outset that Hitler aimed at world-domination. "His aim is clearly a world-empire ... God's front is the spiritual front, which is still lagging much behind. Hitler's Germany is not God's front. It is the Asuric front through which the Asura aims at world-domination. It is the descent of the Asuric world upon the human to establish its own power on the earth."[62] Moreover, according to Sri Aurobindo and the Mother India occupies a special place among the nations in the development of humanity. Towards this development every 'people' (nation or culture) should contribute the essential elements which constitute its unique character. As Sri Aurobindo saw it, India would have to share its highly developed spiritual knowledge, a treasure which it has guarded through the centuries. As the Lord of Falsehood wanted to bend the path of humanity back towards a 'satanic age', his intention was to use Hitler (and/or others) to attack one of the main elements that were to bring about a higher, spiritualised humanity.

Hitler's Asian plans remain generally unknown although they are well documented. "In [Hitler's] fantasies the campaign against Russia was transformed into the unexpected turning point which like a touch from a magic wand would solve all difficulties and open the way to world-dominion ... By a far-flung pincer movement over North Africa, the Near East and the Caucasus, in conjunction with the conquest of Russia, he would push forward to Afghanistan. That country would then be used as a base from which to strike the

---

[62]Id., 660, 669.

stubborn British Empire at its heart, in India. Rule of the world was, as he saw it, within his grasp." (Fest[63]) In the middle of August 1942, Hitler said: "As the next step we are going to advance south of the Caucasus and then help the rebels in Iran and Iraq against the English. Another thrust will be directed along the Caspian Sea toward Afghanistan and India. Then the English will run out of oil. In two years we will be on the borders of India. Twenty to thirty elite German divisions will do. Then the British Empire will collapse." (Speer[64])

In Hitler's mind India was always associated with Great Britain. "The birthplace of the English self-consciousness is India", he said in one of his monologues.[65] We read in Toland's Hitler biography: "Ribbentrop persistently pressed the Japanese, through Ambassador Oshima, to turn their major attack toward India, but to no avail. Nor was Hitler more successful when he invited Oshima to the *Wolfsschanze* and repeated the request. The Wehrmacht, he said, was about to invade the Caucasus and once that oil region was seized the road to Persia would be open. Then the Germans and Japanese could catch all the British Far East Forces in a giant pincer movement."[66] Ralph Giordano describes the same strategic plan in his essay *Wenn Hitler den Krieg gewonnen hätte* (if Hitler had won the war).

"A newspaper report from Moscow under the headline 'Hitler planned conquest of India, documents reveal' and dated 21 June 1986, was published the next day in the *Indian Express*. According to the documents on which this report is based, Germany, Italy and Japan had signed an agreement, in January 1942, on the division of the spheres. Hitler counted on a quick defeat of Russia to invade, in the spring of the same year, West Asia, which would then serve

---

[63] Joachim Fest: *Hitler*, p. 643.
[64] Albert Speer: *Spandau*, p. 47.
[65] *Monologe im Führerhauptquartier*, p. 54.
[66] John Toland, op. cit., p. 977.

as a springboard for reaching India."[67] "A Georgian historian, Professor Tskitishvili, mentions the *Sonderstab F* as a contingent that was given the task of marching to West Asia and India ... This special force, which was a highly mechanized contingent, had 1620 motor vehicles with its own artillery, tank and aviation units, intelligence and counter-intelligence. The corps mostly included students from eastern countries studying in German universities, who had undergone appropriate Fascist indoctrination. Many of them were also Germans who had lived in India and West Asia and knew the languages and customs."[68]

The Sri Aurobindo Ashram in peril

From the French armistice on 22 June 1940 onwards the French colonial territories were divided in their loyalties: some lined up behind Marshall Pétain, others behind General de Gaulle, even though the latter was still practically unknown. De Gaulle, whom Sri Aurobindo called 'a remarkable man', had formed a government in exile to save the honour of France and was therefore condemned to death in absentia by the Pétain government. Some French colonies, Pondicherry among them, kept their options open, anxiously following the day-to-day developments in Western Europe. There everything depended on the decision to be taken by Great Britain, under threat of an eventual invasion by Germany. If Winston Churchill had not become the premier of Great Britain, a peace settlement between Great Britain and Germany would have been a distinct possibility and the future of the world might have become quite different.

Pondicherry was a French *comptoir;* this means that it was one of the overseas places where the French ships could drop anchor, take in fresh water and provisions, and do business. Like that there were three more places on the east and west coast of the Indian

---

[67]Georges Van Vrekhem: *Beyond Man*, p. 238.
[68]Rudolf Hartog: *The Sign of the Tiger*, p. 58.

subcontinent, and one in the estuary of the Ganges. At Pondicherry France was represented by a governor who, at the time of our story, seems to have been one of the hedgers. His position was difficult, for Pondicherry was but a small port town surrounded on its land side by British territory. As the *comptoir* had to obtain most of it essential stuff from France (and was a notorious smugglers' den), the war had already made life there difficult and considerably more expensive; now the British could easily cut off this French enclave from the rest of the subcontinent.

"The Pondicherry Governor is sliding towards the Pétain Government", said Sri Aurobindo on 4 July 1940. The next day his comment on the situation was: "The French Governor is now frightened because the Pétain Government has issued orders to carry out government orders, as it is the duty of the *fonctionnaire* to obey the superior authority. Moreover, Hitler has threatened the admirals, officials and others [in the colonial territories] that, if they don't obey, their wives and children will be taken to the concentration camps." When a disciple reported that the British had forbidden their ships to touch Pondicherry, Sri Aurobindo replied: "Yes, they must have done that after learning of the Governor's attitude".

Two days later the same disciple had heard that, according to German sources, "France has cut off all diplomatic relations with England. In that case the [British] Indian Government will naturally take stern measures and they won't hesitate to take possession of Pondicherry". Sri Aurobindo: "Diplomatic relations are already cut off here". The situation became still more complicated by another threat to the existence of the Sri Aurobindo Ashram if the Pondicherry Governor opted for Vichy. For the Catholic Pétain Government was known for its firm adherence to its confessional values and for being inimical against anything not Catholic, especially 'idolatrous' religions and sects. Therefore, as Sri Aurobindo remarked, "if a Catholic government takes control, then our Ashram won't be allowed to exist".[69]

---

[69]Nirodbaran, op. cit., pp. 779, 781, 784, 794.

The most alarming threat in those uncertain days came, however, from within the Ashram, where a considerable part of patriotic sadhaks was anti-British and therefore pro-Hitler. On 11 May, Nirodbaran, the Ashram doctor, had already said to Sri Aurobindo: "In the Ashram the feeling is divided. Some are for the British and some for Hitler." Sri Aurobindo: "For Hitler?" A disciple: "Not exactly, but they are anti-British". Sri Aurobindo: "Not a rational feeling. How can India, who wants freedom, take sides with somebody who takes away freedom from other nations?"

The situation was quite serious, for about a week later Sri Aurobindo, against his habit, opened the daily conversation himself: "It seems it is not merely five or six of our people but more than half that are in sympathy with Hitler and want him to win!" A disciple, laughing: "Half?" Sri Aurobindo: "No, it is not a matter to laugh at. It is a very serious matter. The Government can dissolve the Ashram at any moment. In Indo-China all religious bodies have been dissolved. And here the whole of Pondicherry is against us. They cannot do anything only because Governor Bonvin is friendly towards us. But even he, if he hears that people in the Ashram are pro-Hitler, will be compelled to take steps, at least to expel those who are so. If these people want the Ashram to be dissolved, they can come and tell me and *I* will dissolve it instead of the police doing it.

"They have no idea about the world and talk like children. Hitler is the greatest menace the world has ever met. If Hitler wins, do they think India has any chance of being free? It is a well-known fact that Hitler has an eye on India. He is openly talking of world-empire. He will turn towards the Balkan, crushing Italy on the way, which would be a matter of three weeks, then Turkey and then Asia Minor. Asia Minor ultimately means India. If there he meets Stalin, then it is only a question as to who wins and comes to India. I hear K say that Russia can come now and conquer India. It is this kind of slave mentality that keeps India in bondage. He pretends to spirituality. Doesn't he know that the first thing that Stalin will do is to wipe out spirituality in India …?" And when he heard that a disciple had been jeered at by his fellow-sadhaks for admitting that he was sad at Holland's defeat, Sri Aurobindo said: "They are glad that Holland was occupied? Very strange, and yet they want freedom for India! This is one thing I can't swallow. How can they have sympathy for Hitler who is destroying other nations, taking away their liberty? It is not only pro-Ally sympathy but sympathy for humanity that they are jeering at."[70]

The increasingly complex and threatening situation made Sri Aurobindo, for a time, favour the Japanese. He had long been admiring this people for their samurai qualities. "The power of the Japanese for self-sacrifice, patriotism, self-abnegation and silence was remarkable … The Japanese are *kshatriyas* [the princely warrior caste], and their aesthetic sense is of course well-known." But soon Sri Aurobindo had to recognise that these values had deteriorated, especially after the frequent reports of cruelty during the Japanese military campaigns. "European influence has spoiled all that, and see now how brutal they have become – a thoroughly un-Japanese thing … A heroic people with wonderful self-control … but these things perhaps belong to the past. It is a great pity that people who have carried such ideals into practice are losing them through contact with European civilization … The Japanese have become bullies now. It is the new spirit of the Nazis and Fascists which they have got from the West."[71]

Still Sri Aurobindo, observing the simultaneous advance towards India by Germany from the west and Japan from the east, together with the age-old Russian threat to the country, would have preferred India to come under Japanese domination. His arguments were twofold. Firstly: "I don't want the Japanese to go down in the fight against the Chinese because they may be needed as a counterbalance against Germany and Russia when, in case England goes down, they

---

[70]Id., pp. 630, 641-42, 643.
[71]Id., pp. 25, 142, 852.

try to come to Asia ... Out of the three evils, [Japan] may be the best and I don't think she will annex India ... [Japan] won't like the 'barbarians' taking possession of Asia."[72] The second reason was spiritual: the religious-minded Japanese would tolerate an institution like the Sri Aurobindo Ashram, while Hitler and Stalin would, as Sri Aurobindo said, 'wipe it out'.

In India a whole range of attitudes towards the warring powers could be found, a situation which increased the pressure of the complexities Sri Aurobindo and the Mother had to deal with. The ultra-nationalist Vishva Hindu Parishad favoured collaboration with the British and their Indian army, mainly because enlisting would provide them with training and military know-how to rise up against the British after the war. (It may be recalled that the British Indian Army numbered two and a half million men, and that it saw action in all theatres where British troops were involved.) The Muslim League was also in favour of supporting the colonial authorities, hoping that they would agree to their demand of a partition of India along religious lines. Within the Congress party the opinions varied, sometimes in one and the same person. Some Congress members wanted India to side with the British, counting on a chance of obtaining the freedom of their country in return for their support in critical circumstances; others like SC Bose availed of the occasion to rise in armed rebellion against the colonial overlords.

Subhash Chandra Bose, a Bengali, was born in 1897; he followed an education similar to that of Sri Aurobindo, also renounced joining the Indian Civil Service, and became one of the top men of the Indian National Congress. When he could not see eye to eye with Mohandas K Gandhi, he founded his own Forward Block. In his resistance against the British – he was arrested eleven times in the course of his political career – he looked for inspiration in the examples of Mussolini and Hitler, and travelled to Europe to study

---

[72]Id., p. 810.

the elements of the success of these dictators while they were at the height of their power. At the end of January 1941 Bose escaped the watchful eye of the British and undertook a venturesome journey to Berlin via Kabul, Samarkhand and Moscow. In Germany he founded the Indian Legion with Indian soldiers from British armies taken prisoner by the Germans. Henceforth he was called *Netaji*, which like Führer, Duce and Caudillo means 'leader' in Hindustani.

Bose was sufficiently sensible to realise that he should not expect much from Hitler. In 1933 he had already said: "Today I regret that I have to return to India with the conviction that the new nationalism in Germany is not only narrow and selfish, but arrogant ... The new racial philosophy, which has a very weak scientific foundation, stands for the glorification of the white races in general and the German race in particular." Hitler deigned to receive him only once in what became a very tense encounter. Bose expected a declaration from the Führer that India would be fully independent, even if her independence would have come about with Germany's assistance. This was contrary to Hitler's character, racial ideas and political ambitions. When he began to proffer some advice to Bose, the latter said to the interpreter: "Tell his Excellency that I have been in politics all my life and that I don't need any advice from any side". Thereupon Hitler suggested that Bose try his luck in Japan.

And so it happened that SC Bose undertook another adventurous journey, this time by U-boat to Tokyo; he trans-shipped from a German unto a Japanese submarine in the middle of the Indian Ocean. The Japanese were more sympathetic towards his plans to liberate India from the British, although they too remained sceptical and kept all trump cards in their own hands. In Southeast Asia Bose formed his Indian National Army (INA) again with Indian prisoners of war and also with expatriate Indians who were living in what are now Indonesia, Malaysia, Myanmar (earlier Burma) and Singapore. The peak of this effort was the Imphal campaign in March 1944, when a Japanese army, including 3000 troops of Bose's INA, crossed the Indian border in the North-Western hills. That Imphal would fall despite the dogged British-Indian resistance was a foregone conclusion. But suddenly the monsoon set in, more than a month early, and "the Japanese chances of success were washed away", together with those of Bose's INA. It became, as Hugh Toye puts it, "a military catastrophe of the first magnitude".[73] Bose died on 18 August 1945 when the twin-engined bomber in which he was flying to Japan crashed on take-off at Taipei. In India he is officially honoured as a hero.

In the Sri Aurobindo Ashram, many of the pro-Hitler inmates were supporters of SC Bose. Considering these circumstances, Sri Aurobindo felt it necessary to take a public stance against Hitler and the Axis. During a considerable part of his life he had been fighting the British, often at the peril of his life; now the world-situation had evolved in a way with made it necessary for him to support them. "He always stood for India's complete independence which he was the first to advocate publicly and without compromise as the only ideal worthy of a self-respecting nation", wrote Sri Aurobindo about himself; now he had to support the colonial power which he once had described as a demon sucking the blood of Mother India.

The first time Sri Aurobindo and the Mother made their position public was on 19 September 1940, just after the Battle of Britain, when they sent 500 rupees, then a considerable sum, to the governor of Madras as a contribution to the Viceroy's War Purposes Fund. In an accompanying letter was written: "We feel that not only is this a battle waged in just self-defence and in defence of the nations threatened with the world-domination of Germany and the Nazi system of life, but that it is a defence of civilization and its highest attained social, cultural and spiritual values and of the whole future of humanity. To this cause our support and sympathy will be unswerving whatever may happen; we look forward to the victory of Britain and, as the eventual result, an era of peace and union

---

[73] Hugh Toye: *The Springing Tiger Subhash Chandra Bose*, p. 39.

among the nations and a better and more secure world-order".[74] When this public gesture was reported in the newspapers, the result was a wave of indignation, also among Aurobindonians within and without the Ashram.

The indignation would turn into a conflagration when Sri Aurobindo sent a message of support to Stafford Cripps on 31 February 1942. Cripps, former ambassador to Moscow and at present member of Churchill's War Cabinet, was sent on a mission to India by the British government, with a proposal for India's self-determination immediately after the war in exchange for her loyal support during the war. Sri Aurobindo saw at once that this would be equivalent to dominion status, which in turn would quasi automatically lead to complete self-determination and independence. He therefore sent the following message to Stafford Cripps: "... As one who has been a nationalist leader and worker for India's independence, though now my activity is no longer in the political but in the spiritual field, I wish to express my appreciation of all you have done to bring about this offer. I welcome it as an opportunity given to India to determine for herself, and organize in all liberty of choice, her freedom and unity, and take an effective place among the world's free nations. I hope it will be accepted, and right use made of it, putting aside all discords and divisions ... In this light, I offer my public adhesion, in case it can be of any help in your work."[75]

Sri Aurobindo also sent a trusted disciple to Delhi with a message for the leadership of the Congress party, recommending that they accept the Cripps proposal. The reaction was one of disdain, questioning the advice of a man who had withdrawn from politics and chosen to live in seclusion many years ago. None of those politicians, prejudiced by the common notions about religion, yoga and spirituality, had an idea of what Sri Aurobindo was really doing. The Working Committee of the Congress party rejected the Cripps

---

[74]Sri Aurobindo: *On Himself*, p. 393.
[75]Id., p. 399.

Offer by 7 voices to 5.[76] The long term consequences for the country would be catastrophic, leading among other things to its division into India and Pakistan.

Throughout the country the reactions against Sri Aurobindo's position were 'indignant and aggressive', as an Indian correspondent wrote recently to the author. "Shri MP, who has been a sadhak of [Sri Aurobindo's] yoga for more than 40 years now, this Sunday gave me a first hand account of the violent reaction that Sri Aurobindo's public support of the British war effort provoked among Indians. It seems that at that time MP was a young freedom fighter in Gujarat who idolized Gandhi, and who even tried to prepare himself for a possible armed struggle against the British. When news of Sri Aurobindo's support for the British war effort broke it apparently drove quite a few of these freedom fighters mad with rage. In their blind indignation many of them physically attacked Sri Aurobindo centres and places associated with him. MP himself was one of those who violently attacked such a centre in Gujarat including, it seems, any property as well as the very person of anyone who was identified as a sadhak or follower of Sri Aurobindo in the area."

'Where is Hitler now…?'

By this time the daily conversations Sri Aurobindo held with the small circle of disciples had gradually fizzled out. When three years back the author asked Nirodbaran for the reason, his answer was that he did not know. In his *Twelve Years with Sri Aurobindo* we find that "the original stream of abundance began to get thinner and thinner till in the last years there was practically a silent attendance on a silent Presence. Either we had exhausted all topics and a satiation had followed and dried up all our inspiration, or Sri Aurobindo had withdrawn his inner gesture of approval".[77]

---

[76]Simon Burgess: *Stafford Cripps – A Political Life*, p. 168.
[77]Nirodbaran: *Twelve Years with Sri Aurobindo*, p. 229.

The real reason may have been mentioned by Sri Aurobindo himself in a letter of 1942: "In these times of world-crisis I have to be on guard and concentrated all the time". In a conversation many years later, the Mother said that the war had brought their yoga to a complete halt. "For if we had continued the work personally, we would not have been assured of the time necessary to finish it before the other one [i.e. the Lord of the Nations] had made a mess of the earth – which would have put back the whole undertaking for centuries. *That* had to be stopped first: that action of the Lord of the Nations."[78]

The one thousand pages of the talks with Sri Aurobindo noted down in the first months of the war – Nirodbaran candidly confesses that "almost one third of the talks were not recorded for want of time or sheer laziness"[79] – provide us with some insight in the concerns of Sri Aurobindo and the Mother with the war. There can be no doubt that this concern continued during the rest of the worldwide tragedy, and many allusions in their writings or conversations confirm this. On 15 August 1945, Sri Aurobindo's birthday again, the Japanese Emperor Hirohito, for the first time in history addressing the nation directly, broadcast a message declaring the unconditional capitulation of his country, thus bringing the Second World War to an end. India will become independent in 1947, on the stroke of midnight of 15 August.

When the war was finished Sri Aurobindo wrote: "This is no time for patting the Germans on the back or embracing and consoling them. If they are allowed to get on their legs again without trouble or without making an atonement for the horror of darkness and suffering they have inflicted on the world, they will rise only to repeat their performance – unless something else forestalls them. The only help we can give to Germany now is silence."[80]

---

[78] *L'Agenda de Mère II*, p. 410.
[79] Nirodbaran, op. cit., p. 228.
[80] Sri Aurobindo: *On Himself*, p. 399.

The end of the war did not mean the end of danger for the world. The great Twentieth Century War did not terminate on 15 August 1945. Only one month later Sri Aurobindo wrote in a letter, commenting on a point made by his correspondent: "About the present human civilization. It is not this which has to be saved; it is the world that has to be saved and that will surely be done, though it may not be so easily or so soon as some wish or imagine, or in the way that they imagine. The present must surely change, but whether by destruction or a new creation on the basis of a greater Truth, is the issue. The Mother has left the question hanging and I can only do the same."

2 June 1946: "The better things that are to come are preparing or growing under a veil and the worse are prominent everywhere".[81] 19 October 1946: "I have never had a strong and persistent will for anything to happen in the world – I am not speaking of personal things – which did not eventually happen even after delay, defeat or even disaster. There was a time when Hitler was victorious everywhere and it seemed certain that a black yoke of the Asura would be imposed on the whole world; but where is Hitler now and where is his rule? Berlin and Nuremberg have marked the end of that dreadful chapter in human history. Other blacknesses threaten to overshadow or even engulf mankind, but they too will end as that nightmare has ended."

9 April 1947: "I know what is preparing behind the darkness and can see and feel the first signs of its coming". 18 July 1948, when the conflict between the two big blocs dividing humanity, Communism and Liberalism, was taking on drastic proportions: "Things are bad, are growing worse and may at any time grow worst or worse than worst if that is possible – and anything however paradoxical seems possible in the present perturbed world ... All this was necessary because certain possibilities had to emerge and be got

---

[81] Id., pp. 167, 168.

rid of, if a new and better world was at all to come into being; it would not have done to postpone them for a later time."[82]

4 April 1950: "For myself, the dark conditions do not discourage me or convince me of the vanity of my will to 'help the world'; for I knew they had to come; they were there in the world-nature and had to rise up so that they might be exhausted or expelled and a better world freed from them might be there. After all, something has been done in the outer field and that may help or prepare for getting something done in the inner field also ... So I am not disposed even now, in these dark conditions, to consider my will to help the world as condemned to failure."[83]

The year 1950 was when the war erupted in Korea – the Cold War was turning into a hot one. The editor of the Ashram magazine *Mother India* asked Sri Aurobindo for his assessment, since he intended to write an article on the subject. "The whole affair is as plain as a pikestaff", answered Sri Aurobindo. "It is the first move of the Communist plan of campaign to dominate and take possession first of these northern parts and then of South East Asia as a preliminary to their manoeuvres with regard to the rest of the continent – in passing, Tibet as a gate opening to India. If they succeed, there is no reason why domination of the whole world should not follow by steps until they are ready to deal with America ... For the moment the situation is as grave as it can be".[84] An ever more potentially destructive nuclear war seemed to become imminent, until the MAD point was reached, the point of 'mutual assured destruction.

We know now, more than half a century after the last quotation from Sri Aurobindo was written, that a third world conflagration, potentially the most destructive, did not happen. In this preservation of humanity there may also have been causes active 'behind the veil', for the events on the surface always have prolongations in realms

---

[82]Id., pp. 169, 170, 171.
[83]Id., p. 172.
[84]Id., pp. 416-17.

which constitute the total reality, and the human actors in front of the curtain are for the most part unconscious instruments of the Powers which really determine the course of history.

Hitler was very much aware of the occult gradations of existence and of the importance of the times in which he lived as one of the great changes in the destiny of humanity. It was his pride to be the chosen delegate of a being which considered itself the Lord of the Nations, Master of the Earth. He found his strength and guidance in accepting to realise the evil that would take humanity back to a former, lower phase of its evolution. Only this Power behind him explains how a man from nowhere could become the Führer and Messiah of the German people, as only this cosmic Power can be a norm for the enormity of the negative forces – falsehood, ignorance, suffering and death – which Hitler was instrumental in unleashing.

All ancient traditions tell us about the battle of good and evil which is the real key of the history of humanity. The evil is always very perceptible and easy to open oneself to; to adhere to the good requires discernment and effort, and humans soon become confused and tired. If there were not a Good Power, whatever its name, upholding the existence and evolution of humanity, our species might have disappeared on more than one occasion, just like so many other species on the globe.

The Second World War was one phase of the Great Twentieth Century War, itself the result of the changes in humanity preparing to take it a leap forward in its evolution. As such, this war can be seen as a crisis in the consciousness which dominated the world and which was still almost exclusively Western. But the Second World War was also a direct intervention of the Powers of Darkness, necessitating a reaction of the Powers of Light in order to assure the destiny of the planet and of humanity on it. Only this perspective and these dimensions are large enough to explain the scope of the terrible events.

The Powers of Darkness were not definitively conquered in 1945, we all know that. The ravages and horrors which were the results of their doings in the following decades are part of our life experience. The world is now subject to an enormous confusion. The cause of this general confusion, however, is the fact that humanity is becoming one for the first time in its existence, for this involves the friction of countless egoisms, most considered sacred, and the effort at overcoming them.

In 1947 Sri Aurobindo formulated what he called his 'five dreams', which were the five force lines required to take humanity up to the threshold of a new era. These five 'dreams' were essentially what he had expounded in his writings during the First World War, at a time when their fulfilment looked impracticable. They were: the freedom of India, which has an important role to play in humanity's future; the awakening of Asia; the formation of supranational conglomerates, like the European Union, which would lead to the unification of mankind; world unity; and the spreading of the Indian spirituality and its techniques of self-realisation, necessary for the change in the human being without which a better future is not possible. None of the five points is fully accomplished (the real India is still divided), but all five have arrived at a substantial degree of realisation, and this in a relatively short time.

The dead will not have suffered and died in vain if the living can see the light at the horizon and walk towards it.

Acknowledgments

The author thanks the Dutch Foundations *De Zaaier* and *Aurofonds;* without their financial help this book could not have been written. He also thanks Friederike Werner for providing him with essential texts, and Martin Sobieroj, who let him read the manuscript of his book on Hitler. Finally he thanks Norman Bowler, Gilles Guingan, Jason Inamorato, Guy Ryckaert, Wolfgang Schmidt-Reinecke and Martin Sobieroj for reading the manuscript.

INDEX

Abraham, 352
Abstract painting occult movement, 384
Abrial, French Admiral, 637
Abysmal evil use, 499-500
Ackermann, Marion, 384
Adolf meaning, 94
Age of Reason, 372, 553-554, 614
Age of possible retrieval and rebirth, 553
Age of Protestantism, 553
Age of Revolt, 553
Ahlwardt, Hermann *The Desperate Struggle between the Aryan Peoples and Judaism*, 322-323
Air Force Units strength, 463
Aksakov, Aleksander, 383
Albrecht, 596-597
Alfassa, Mirra
  birth, 540-541
  family background, 540-541
  headstrong character, 542
  involvement in artistic activity, 541
  married to Henri Morisset, 541
  meeting Paul Richard, 544
  occultism, 542-543
  her painting exhibitions, 541
  playing the piano, 541
  reading the *Bhagavad Gita*, 542
  stimulated by Maupassant brothers, 542
Allen, Martin, 169
Allies
  America enter's war, 129
  American troops help, 9
  bonding in Germany, 623
  conflict between France and Germany, 133-134
  France target, 133
  Second World War, 636
Amann, Max, 53-54, 113
American Revolution, 260
Amery, Chris, 38
Animals, German decent attitude, 301
  Hitler animal lover, 301
Anna, Miss, 126
Antarctica expedition, 472
  Anthroposophy teaching, 261
Anti-Semitism, 17, 19, 31, 63, 164-165, 157-158, 311, 349, 359, 362, 397, 429
  among Austro-Germans, 69
  and Volkisch Movement, 298
  development, 356
  examples, 323
  Fichte, father of, 317
  Hitler embracing, 298
  intensification, 325
  Martin Luther, 312-314
  movement, 321
  origin, 38
  slogans, 29

670 INDEX

Wagner's art of spreading, 327-328
without Christianity no, 304-307
widespread, 320
Anti-Semitic League launching, 319-320
Anti-Semitic People's Party (1889), 29
Apollonian light principle, 278, 325
Ariosophy teaching, 261
Armanenschaft revival, 25
Armistice with German signing, 117
Arminius story, 192-193
Army Group creation, 14
Arouet, Jean-Marie, 316
Artamanen Himmler member, 264-265
Aryan, 12, 63, 134, 146-147, 156-157, 236, 256, 427, 434, 439, 450, 472, 544, 637
  birthplace, 213-214
  enemies, 355
  friction between Jews and, 303, 329, 430
  future, 447-448
  Hitler writing in the *Mein Kamph*, 139-143
  Hitler preaching, 460
  Hitler views, 515
  instinct of self-preservation, 455
  Jews sexual intercourse, 142-143, 158-159, 272-273
  root language discovery, 212
  term, 139-140
  wisdom, 25
Aryan world empire, Hitler idea of establishing, 456
Aschheim, Peter, 406
Ascona, 403
Astrology, 261, 380, 582
  universalistic doctrine, 387
Asura, 640
  Hitler conscious of the instrument, 564, 568
  Hitler inspiration from, 634-635
  Lords of Falsehood, darkness death and suffering, 565
Asuras descending order, 569
Aurobindo Ashram, Pondicherry, 546-547
Austria, Napoleon annexation, 600, 602
Austrian *Antisemitenbund* (1889), founding, 322
Austrian pan-German movement, 70
Austrian state demonstration and riots, 69

Baba, Abdul, 544
Babarossa, Frederick, 200, 387
Bach, Walter, 300
Bachofen, Johann, 404
Back to Nature movement, 384
Baigent, Michael, 377, 415, 498-499
Baktashi sect of dervishes, 33
Balins, 333
Ball, George, 484
Baltic sea, 243
Barin (Aurobindo's brother), 537-539
Bärsch, Claus-Ekkehard, 440, 454, 594
Battle of Hastings (1066), 253
Battle of Stalingrad, 457
Baudelaire, 373
Bauer, Yehuda, 500
Baumann, 51
Bavaria history, 73-74
Bayle, Pierre, 315
Bayreuth, 74
Bechsteins, 582
Beethoven, 195, 559
Beevors, Anthony, 617
Bela Kun, 13
Belgium, 132
  battle, 4
  Hitler disdainful designation of neutrality with, 178

INDEX 671

Belgrade, 98
  damage, 607
Benn, Gottfried, 396
Berchtesgaden, 114
  discovery, 507
Berghof Hitler famous villa, 94
Bergson, Henri, 23, 291, 373
Berlin, Hitler plan of converting
  into a world capital, 189
Berlin-Baghdad railway
  construction, 132, 204, 289
Berlin Club of the Barons, 389
Bernhardi, 205
Beyschlag, Rudolf, 16
Bhagavad Gita, the, 426, 542
Bible, the, 312, 315
Bismark, Otto, 28, 46, 57, 101,
  178, 203-205, 208, 221, 294, 318,
  321, 631
Blavatsky, H.P., 142, 371, 381
  founder of the Theosophical
  society, 23
Blavatsky, Madame, 592
Blomberg, Walter, 482
Böhme, Jakob, 380
Bolle, Evald, 50
Bolshevik-Lenin takeover, 12
Bolshevik Revolution in Russia, 9,
  44, 99, 346
Bolshevism, 47, 238, 262
  fight against Nazism, 110-111
Book of Bundred Years, 181
Bonaparte, Napoleon, 73, 196, 228,
  294, 316-317, 429, 517, 599-603, 636
Bon, Le, 66
Bormann, Martin, 367, 426, 500, 618
Bose, Subash Chandra, account,
  657-659
Braun, Eva, 86, 611, 622
Brewer, Max, 237
British Army Indians fight in the
  combat theatres, 562
Broch, Hermann, 499
Bronder, Dietrich 212, 262, 350

Bruckmann, Frau Elsa, 95
Bruckmann, Hugo, 95
Bruno, Giordano, 190
Buchner, Frau, 95, 212
Buck, Pearl S., 524
Buddha, 552
Bruckmanns, 582
Bullock, Alan, 164, 500, 517, 520,
  522
Bund Oberland (Oberland League),
  73-74
Bürgerbräukeller, 114
Burleigh, Michael, 254, 331, 468

Caesar, 190, 237
Capitalism, 365
  alternative, 370
  Hitler's lecture, 17
  Jews creation, 344
Carlyle, 291
Catherine II of Russia, 195
Caudillo, 405
Chamberlain, Houston, 63, 66-67,
  107, 109-110, 227, 238, 247, 275,
  324, 390, 567
  a biologist, 234
  admirer of Gobineau, 235
  education, 206
  foundation of the *Ninteenth
    Century*, 161-172, 205-206, 233,
    235-236, 272, 323
  founder of the Third Reich, 233
  homage, 206-207
  married to Eva, 206
  racial theory, 234
Chamberlain, Lesley, 397
Chamberlain, Neville, 630-632,
  634-635
Charlemagne, Emperor, 508
Chatellier, Hildegard, 405
Chemanitz, 321
Chiang Kai-Sheik, 490
children of the African soldiers,
  sterilization, 134

'Children of Wotan' Sri Aurobindo poem, 624-626
Christ, Jesus, 110, 214, 272, 302, 304-305, 324, 336, 433, 441-442, 593
  Jews killing, 306
Christ, John, 237
Christian civilization end, 394
Christian era in Europe, end, 554, 556
Christian values, 404-405
  Cosmic Circle, 404
  George Circle, 406-409
  hotbed of the different groups, 403
  Orzechowski enumerates only philosophical religion and occult, 403
  spiritist seances common practice, 405-406
Christianity, 183, 404
  and anti-Semitism, 304-307
  friction between Jews and, 297-298, 309, 338
  Hitler views, 268-269, 449
  movement, 297-298
  teachings, 443-444
Christopher, 616
Church marriages prohibition, 470
Churchill, Winston, 596, 631, 639, 648-649, 660
Cicero, 190
Cistercian Order, 26
Cities and building Hitler plan, 186-187
Citizens Association Eckart founder, 61
Class, Heinrich, 227, 320
Cohn, Norman, 162-163, 178
Cohen, Hermann, 350
Colet, John, 190
Collins, Larry and Lapierre, Dominique *Is Paris Burning*, 646
Communications Hitler, youth strength, 463
Communism, Jews creation, 344
  rejection, 13

Communist uprising in Thuringia and Saxony and Hamburg putting down, 100
Comte, August, 377
Congress of Berlin (1878), 631
Constitutional monarch establishment on the British pattern plan, 136
Copernicans, 315
Cripps, stafford, 660
Cripps proposal, 660
Crookers William, 384
Cult of Wotan, 289
Cults, scholars dismiss the notion, 583
Curie, Pierre, 373
Czechoslovakia Allied betrayal, 632
  bankruptcy forced to cede to Germany, 630
  dismemberment, 630
  fate, 564, 630
  French Treaty, 632
  Germans fight, 24
  German army marching, 634
  Hitler plan of splitting, 630
  Napoleon annexation, 600, 602
  split, 630

d'Alembert, 195, 343
d'Holbach, 195
da Vinci, Leonardo, 189
Danzig, 482
Dante, 535
Darré, Walter, 180, 186, 265
Darwin, 66, 212, 219, 228, 397
Darwin Theory of Evolution (under the title *The Origin of Species*,
  account, 213, 217, 228
  Hitler's rejection, 219-220
Darwinism, 27-28, 109, 323
  in *Mein Kampf*, 143
Davies, Andrew, 383
Dawidowicz, Lucy, 314, 318, 357-359

INDEX 673

de Gobineau Joseph account, 228-231
  father of racial theory, 226
  death, 226
de la Mettrie, 195
de Lagarde, Paul, 177, 255, 321,
  335, 426
de Lapouge, Vacher, 216
  account, 231-233
  author of *The Social Selections*,
  231
  works, 231
de Maizière, Ulrich, 483, 500
Defence and Defiance League of
  the German Race, 74
Delitzsch, Friedrich, 111
Delpla, François, 56
Denmark attack, 602
Democracy (German democracy),
  427-428
  Hitler idea, 344
  use, 499
Demonic use, 499-500
Demosthenes, 190
Dannehl, 115
Derleth, Ludwig, 404
des Mousseaux, Gougenot, 111
Diderot, 195
Dietrich Eckart Homes, 58
Dietrich, Sepp, 469
Dietrich Eckart Societies, 58
Diederichs, Eugen, 39, 271, 420-421
Dinter, Arthur, 426, 591, 594
  brief sketch, 272
  famous for the hate of Jews, 273
  founder of Fighting League for
    the Completion of the
    Reformation, 272
  friendship with Eckart, 272
  influence on Hitler, 595
  practising spiritist, 595
  his religion thesis, 273-274
  revolt against Hitler, 595
  role in the formative years of
    Nazism, 272

study occultism, 595
The Sun Against the Blood novel,
  142, 592
Dinter-Bund
  foundation, 274
Disraeli, 631
Donitz, Admiral, 482
Donitz, Karl, 482, 500
Doyle, Arthur Conan, 384
Drexler, Anton, 48, 74, 77-79, 81,
  344
  founder of the Worker's
    Committee for a Just Peace, 48
  guest of the Thule, 48-49
  My Political Awaking, 48
Drexler, Thule, 116
Dreyfus affairs in France, 101
Duce, 432
Dühring, Eugen, 66, 319
Duke of Hamilton, 596
Duke of Windsor, 484
Dunkirk phase for Hitler, 636-637
'Dwarf Napoleon The', poem, 600-
  601

Ebert, Friedrich, 136-137
Eckart, Dietrich, 22, 46, 50-51,
  74-75, 78-81, 84-86, 90, 110,
  107-108, 161, 238, 356, 362, 401,
  403, 426, 433, 577-578, 590-591,
  594, 612, 614
  active advocate of the idea, 580
  admirer of Angelus Silesius, 62
  anti-Semite, 516
  and Dinter, 272
  association with the Thule
    Society, 516
  Before Hitler Came by, 115
  birth, 58
  *Bolshevism from Moses to Lenin:
    A Dialogue between Adolf
    Hitler and me*, 108
  brief biographical sketch, 61-62
  champion of new spirituality, 580

contact with Thule Society, 59
credit for his contribution of
  National Socialism, 56
death, 57, 114, 516, 582
depicting him as a Bavarian
  Stammtisch hero, 63
Dialogue, 110
different views, 55-56
dismissal from Landsberg prison,
  on heart problem, 114
dualism, 63
Editor, *In Plain German*, 157,
  579, 581
encounter with Hitler, 581
founder of a Citizens
  Association, 61
founding father of NSDAP, 578
frequent contacts with Hitler,
  112
genius and uncalculating man, 58
godfather, of Hitler, 55, 516
health problem, 58, 112
Hitler distancing from, 114
Hitler highlighting his name in
  Mein Kampf, 57
Hitler indebted to, 160
Hitler relations, 112-114, 390
illness, 580
Joachim Fest different
  impressions, 55
launching *In Plain German*
  magazine, 59-60
medical student, 58
law student, 58
Mosse views, 56
on Jews, 314
period of excile, 113
personality, 61-62
his plays, 58-59
Plewnia's biography, 56
poem *In Plain German*, 390
his poem *Awake*, 579
a poet, playwright and prolific
  publicist, 55, 516
replacement from the editorship
  of *Völkische Beobachter*, 112
role, 56, 75-77, 91, 112
Rosenberg description, 61
Rosenberg disparaging remark, 123
shifting from Berlin to Munich, 59
support DAP, 580-581
a staunch individualis, 516
well-known playwright, 579
writing his anti-Semitic *In Plain
  German*, 507
his writings, 111-112
Eckart, Drexler, 109, 148
Eckhart, Meister, 270, 380, 418-
  422, 593
Eckart-Hitler slogan, 138-139
Edelmensch experience, 459
Edward viii, 484
Egypt Biblical narration about
  Jews, 109-110
Egypt, Jews agricultural lists and
  colonisers, 337
Ehrhardt Brigade, 74, 78, 89, 93, 101
link between Hitler movement
  and, 90
organization council secret cabal
  within, 92
turned into the *Sturmabteilung
  Hitler*, 91
Eichmann, Adolf, 69, 600
Eicke, Theodor, 500
Einstein, Albert, 110, 234, 330
Eisner, Kurt, 10, 13, 43, 60, 72
  murder, 44
Eisner's socialist government, 12, 21
Elections of 1912 German Party
  position, 9
Elections before, 1914 Austro-
  Germans vote for anti-Semites, 69
Elisabeth, 400
Eliot, T.S., 85, 599
Elser, Johann, 573
Enlightenment ideals, 8-9, 24, 30,
  196-197, 214, 293-294, 323,

331-332, 372, 395-396, 405, 558, 591, 603, 644
  acquisitions, 22
  Hitler direct attack, 159-160
  Jews association, 343
  principles, 161, 315
  Sri Aurobindo assisted the importance, 558-559
Enlightenment thinkers, 316
Erasmus, Desiderius, 190
Erna, 85
Erzberger, Matthias, 130, 137-138
  murder, 92
Escherich organization, 74
Esser, Hermann, 84, 113, 591
Eva, 206
Evolution, Aurobindo vision, 525-528, 533

Fabricius, Johan-Christian, 213
Fackenheim, Emil, 499
Fascism, 196, 365-366, 396, 432, 558, 614
Feder, Gottfried, 50, 337, 580
Fest, Joachim, 6, 18-19, 55-56, 65-66, 102, 104, 124, 131, 156, 164, 176, 186, 189, 208, 250, 280, 289-290, 331, 346, 361, 367, 439, 476, 478, 481, 496, 619, 640, 646
Festpiele, the, 85
Feydeau, Georges, 543
Fischer, Engen, 301
Fischer, Fritz, 133, 167, 204, 209
Fichte, 195, 197-198, 317
  famous *Address to the German Nation*, 317
  father of modern German anti-Semitism, 317
Ficino, Marcello, 190
First World War, 3, 12, 23, 33, 129, 187, 262, 272, 306, 324, 331, 346, 369, 373, 432, 439, 459, 560, 573, 587, 632
  anti-Jewish feeling, 348
  Jews swarming into the army, 348
  background for catastrophic sequel to, 129-130
  debacle of Gallipoli, 641
  Fischer description, 207-210
  German teachers into the trenches, 367
  Jews women and children entering into army, 348-349
  list prophecy, 203
  occult interest, 378-379
  Ulrich Linge formation in post-war period, 379
First Zionist Congress, Basel (1897), 161
Flag of the Old Reich Association, 74
Flammarion, Camille, 383-384
Flemings, 468-469
Fletcher, Richard, 267
Food problem, 5, 13
Ford, Henry, 111
Forster, Bernhard, 400
Forster, Gauleiter, 482
Fourth estate (labourer class), account, 8
France, 133, 183
France battle, 4, 129
France German conflict, 132-135, 564
France, Anatole, 543
François-Poncet, André, 67, 282, 354, 355, 488, 500, 502, 508, 544, 566, 615
Frank, Hems, 425, 591
Frederick, 11, 178, 195, 369
Free Corps, 13, 41, 78, 89, 93, 100, 116, 263-264, 460, 577
Free Corps Brigade, 93
Free Corps Oberland, 116
Freemasonry, 30, 33, 379, 465
  Rosenberg obsession, 592
Freikorps Oberland, 44

French Revolution, 8, 200, 228, 260, 287, 294, 317, 343, 396, 603, 644
Freud, Sigmund, 23, 260, 373, 404
Friends of the Light Vikings, 253
Fritsch, Theodor, 29, 60, 63, 111, 325
  Der Hammer launching, 223
  founder of the *Germanenorden*, 222-223
  Handbook of the Jewish Question, 157
Führerprinzip notorious principle, 262
Fuhrer
  concept, 428, 450
  phrase, 486
  see also Hitler

Galilee, 237
Galileo, 315
Galton, Francis, 215
Gandhi, Mahatma, 647
Gebhardt, Dr Karl, 376
Germanenorden Philipp Stauff founder, 41
Geistchristliche Religionsgemeinschaft Dinter founder, 274
Gellately, Robert, 361, 452
Gemlich, Adlof, 18-19, 356
Gemütlichkeit, 24
Gentz, Friedrich, 340
George, Lloyd, 484
George, Stefan, 364, 368, 385, 406-410
George circle, 406, 410
Gerda (Bormann's wife), 265
German *Antisemitische Volkspartei*, birth, 322
German Army, 262
  Jew women and children entering into, 348
  number of casualties, 349
  reduction, 100
German Left split, 99
German musicians appreciation, 560

German nation or people
  before and during Hitler's time, 367-368
  discipline and self-sacrifice, 369
  Hitler contempt, 456-457
  ideal character, 366-367
  rules and discipline, 363
  Knights Templar or Teutonic Knights, 368-369
  new Temple order, 369
  possibility, 286-287
  non-German appreciation, the qualities, 559
  Sri Aurobindo perceived the threatening aspect, 555
German patriotism weakest point during pre-Hitler period, 182
German philosophers poet, 559
German princes, abdication, 4
German scholars and educationists appreciation, 560
German Socialist Party, 117, 129, 593
  launching, 46
  president, 47
  its new shapers, 47
  number of votes in 1912 elections, 9
German utopianism, 277, 280
German women sterilization, 133
German Workers Party (DAP), 19, 49, 72, 77, 88, 116, 148, 356, 515, 576, 578, 580-581, 593
  Hitler attends the meetings, 577
  Hitler first contact, 49
  Hitler in charge of *Werbeobmann*, 77
  Hitler joining, 51-52
  Hitler member, 77
  Karl Harrer founder, 74
  meeting, 50-51, 75
  twenty-five point programme, 78
  foundation, 48
  changing name into a National Socialist German Workers Party (NSDAP), 78

Germanhood spread of
  glorification, 25
Germany's Black Day, 9
German-Nordic Aryan race, 142,
  159, 468
Germanenorden, 14, 516
  birth, 28
  foundation, 220, 222
  Philipp Stauff member, 385
  goals, 36-37
  order of Germanic people,
    account, 27-32
  propagation of the literature, 142
  Theodor Fritsch founder, 60
Germanic origin, 139
Germany
  Allied bombing, 623
  Bavaria in open defiance of the
    Weimar Republic, 101
  birth, 203
  change, 204
  civil war, 46, 99-100
  economy, 204, 220
  compensation to industrialists
    and workers, 98
  Ehrhardt Brigade marching in, 78-79
  emergency, 101
  food problem, 5, 13
  formation, 203
  geographical distance between
    Munich and Berlin, 103
  Hitler an arch-opponent of
    Bavarian separatism, 103
  Hitler's appearance in beer hall
    in tailcoat, 105
  Hitler's financial problem, 104
  Hitler formation of national
    government, 105
  Hitler Putsch most comical
    events, 105
  Hitler's remarkable achievements,
    103
  Hohenzollern William I, king of
    Prussia, 203
  hungry people attacking shops
    and farms, 99
  "hyperinflation", 98
  industrial state, 204
  love lost (no) between the vons
    and Hitler, 103
  Marxist revolt, 13
  members of all social classes, 205
  from monarchy into a Republic, 46
  mysticism, 379-380
  occult interest, 378-380
  occupation of the Ruhr, 98
  Otto von Bismarck first
    chancellor, 203
  politics of Third Reich and
    blueprint, 126-127
  post-war period, 13
  printing money, 98
  prosperity, 436
  social-democratic governments
    coalition with the Liberals and
    Catholics of the centre, 100
  Spartcist revolt, 13
  split into left and right, 99
  strikes and riots, 99
  tension between Bavaria and the
    federal government, 101
  in turmoil, 7-13, 78-79
  territory, 203
  'three vons' formed a triumvirate
    with unlimited power in
    Bavaria, 102
  'three vons' planning another
    rightist coup against Weimar
    Republic, 102
  on the verge of political
    extinction, 102
  violence, 86-87
  wrong side, 560-561
Ghosh, Aravinda Akroyd or Sri
  Aurobindo, 534-540, 542, 562,
  621, 635, 642, 650-652
  admirer of classical Greek
    culture, 552

Alipore Conspiracy Case arrest and release, 538
arrive in Pondicherry, 540
Bande Matram sedition case, 538
Baroda college lecturer, 537
Cambridge experience, 536
on Battle of Britain, 643-644
on Belgium surrender, 638
birth, 534
call *Mahayogi*, 540
a classical scholar, 536
comment on Hitler, 565-566, 568
Congress split at Surat session, 538
contributing articles in *Indu Prakash*, 537
Correspondence with Nirodbaran, 563
conversation with Nirodbaran, 639
criticize the Indian National Congress, 537
education, 535
fame as a scholar and yogi, 545
family background, 534-535
first principal of the Bengal National College and payment problem, 538
first to take stand on absolute independence for his motherland, 537
France humiliation, 644-646
A God's Labour poem, 550
join the service of Sayaji Rao Gaekwad II, 536
leader of the extremists, 538
letter to Nirodbaran, 550
The Light Divine by, 628
marriage, 537
master of English Literature, 536
meeting yogi Vishnu Baskar Lele in Baroda, 539
misunderstanding his seclusion, 548
Munich agreement condemnation, 632
his speech in Uttarpara, 539-540
parallel between the concept of Hitler and, 556-559
a poet, 598
poem on 'The children of Wotan', 624-626
Postscript chapter of his *Ideal of Human Unity*, 647
proficiency in Greek, Latin and English Literature, 535
publications, 219, 545, 550
reading Shelly's *Revolt of Islam*, 534-535
revolutionary speeches, 536
right thigh broken, 563
Savitri, 599-600
scholarship examination for King's College at Cambridge University, 535
spell his name Aurobindo, 538
spiritual revolution, 531
spiritual knowledge and experience, 548-549, 552
yoga practice and experiments, 540, 548-549, 630
Yugantar magazine, 538
Western civilization failing, 633
withdrawal from public not retirement, 550
writing in *Arya*, 627
writing for *Bande Matram*, 538
Gilbhard, Hermann, 21, 43, 116-117, 250
Giordano, Ralph, 184
Gisevius, Hans, 128
Globocnik, Odilo, 501
Gobineau, 67, 212, 245, 265
Goebbels, Dr Joseph, 123, 146, 155, 206, 244, 272, 283, 302, 325, 344, 367, 390, 405, 415, 426, 431, 439, 442, 452, 481, 484, 488, 490, 498, 500, 522, 596, 600, 613, 615, 623
Goebbels' diaries, 362
Goethe, 80, 195, 253-254, 273, 390, 474, 535, 559

INDEX 679

Goldhagen, Daniel, 429
Gonen, Jay, 157
Gonen, Stanley, 507
Goodrick-Clarke, Nicholas, 24, 29, 36, 276, 374, 401
Goring, Hermann, 58, 431, 500, 591, 615-616, 637
Goring, Marshall, 300
Göth, Amon, 500
Götterdämmerung, 618
Gougenot, 118
Grand Central Station Hitler idea of building, 188-189
Grassinger, Hans, 48
Gregor, 97
Grillmeier, Sergeant Alois, 50
Gruppenkommando foundation, 17
Gumplowicz, 212
Gumppenberg, 405
Günther, Hans, 139
Gutbarlett, Dr, 41
Gürtner, 591
Gutberlet, Dr, 50, 75, 386, 580
Gurtner, 120

Habe, Hans, 177
Hadewych, 270, 418
Haffner Sebastian, 19, 82, 91, 95, 102, 176, 204, 314, 379, 388, 432, 500, 579
Hagen, 130
Haeckel, Ernst, 212, 335
 race theories, 224-225
Halder, General Franz, 500, 638
Hamann, Brigitte, 12, 17, 55, 66-67, 70, 92, 107, 112, 202, 327, 401, 512, 517
Hamann, 26
Hammer Associations, 29
Hammer Societies, 223
Handbook of the Hitler Youth (1937), 317
Hanfstängl, Ernst, 63, 85, 91, 103, 125, 160, 168, 238, 327, 437, 479, 507, 590, 615

Hapsburg Empire, 69
Harrer, Karl, 49, 77, 109, 148, 344,
 founder of DAP, 48, 74
Harrer, Thule-Brother, 116
Haushofer, Karl, 125, 426, 434, 584, 587, 597
 an ambitious man, 588
 brief sketch, 168-169
 founder of the Third Reich, 169
 close to the Pan-German, 588
 keeping distance from Hitler, 588
 involvement in occultism and spiritist, 596
 Haushofer know *Furher* since 1919, 590
 teaching profession, 587
 theory of geo-politics, 587-589
 well connected in military and academic circles, 588
Hauser, Otto, 110
Haushofer Albrecht, 329
Hegel, Friedrich, 195, 197, 199, 559
Heehs, Peter, 535
Heiden, Konrad, 55, 84, 88, 90, 92, 117, 162-163, 345, 354, 433, 477, 486, 499, 590, 613
Hedin, Sven, 206, 484
Helmuth von Moltke, 208
Heraclitus, 552
Herber, 195
Hertz, Heinrich, 372
Herodotus, 192
Hesemann, 584, 587
Hess, Rudolf, 41, 84, 116, 123, 168, 244, 385, 389, 434, 442, 584
Before Hitler Came publication, 587
 birth, 587
 career, 587
 chairman of the National Socialist Party, 587
 earning a living in the textile import, 587
 education, 587
 family background, 587

fly to Scotland, 596-597
homosexual relations with Hitler, 125-126, 590-591
in Landsberg prison, 589
involvement in occult and spiritism, 596
member of Thule Society, 22, 587
memory-loss, 597
participation in the beerhall Putsch, 589
role in Hitler's life, 587
shelter in the house of Haushofer, 589
Heydrich, Reinhard, 329, 615
Hilberg, Raul, 352
Himmelfarb, Milton, 500
Himmler, Heinrich, 242-243, 264, 278, 292, 301-302, 360-361, 386, 398, 431, 444, 470, 472-473, 467, 481, 500-501, 583, 618, 633
Himmler, Weisthor, 426
Hindenburg, 136, 138, 484
Hindenburg-Lundendorff, 9, 129
Hirohito, 662
Hitler Adolf,
abysmal evil, 499-500
achievements in regard to redeeming the economy, rebuilding German army, 103
an act of God, 437
agent in military intelligence, 50
amateurishness dominant trait, 67
and Karl Haushofer, 126
and Eckart, 112-114, 139, 390
and Karl Mayr, 117-118
and Kershaw, 15, 604
and Kubizek, 15
and Rosenberg, 592
and turmoil in Germany and flew to Berlin, 79
angel of destruction, 619
anti-Christian and anti-Enlightenment, 449
anti-Judaic ejaculations, 108-109
anti-Semitism, 72, 108, 157-158
Anton Drexler meeting, 74-75
his Asian plans, 650-653
Asura power behind, 600, 608, 622, 635, 640, 652, 656
Austrian by birth, 4
attempts on his life, 413-414, 573-576
attend Austrian Parliament Session, 15
attended several talks about occultism, 584
attitude within the party, 83-84
Bavarian coup by three vons, 387, 389
Bechstein, Bruckmanns and Wagners supporters of, 85-86
blessings from Chamberlain and Richard Wagner, 207
books in the Library of Congress, 441-442
borrow List's books and Tagor's book on Nationalism, 401
blue eyes, 488
building mausoleum for himself, 150
call himself a 'drummer', 82, 515
called 'Wolf' in his intimate circle, 94-95
career, 489
carpet eater applies to, 567
change in his life, 19
change into civil clothes, 5
his charisma, 522-523
chairman of the NSDAP, 81
chancellor of Germany, 5, 21, 46, 73, 411, 434, 448, 512, 582
his closest confidant's views, 475-480
a civilian, 117
compare with French Emperor, 602-603
compared with Luther in relation to Jews, 314
compare with Napoleon, 603-604

a consummate actor, 494
concious of the instrument of the asura, 564, 567
contrast between Sri Aurobindo and, 556-559
contact with Spiritism, 584
contact with the German Workers Party (DAP), 19
conqueror into Prague, Warsaw and Paris, 6
coup, 415
'crises of possession', 610
dangerous job of *Meldegänger* performance, 573
death, 416, 507
debacle of the November Putsch, 273
diatribes against Lenin and his Judeo-Bolshevism, 129
dictatorial powers, 430
difference between Nazism and, 435
discharge from the Pasewalk hospital, 11
disdain from human life, 607
distance from Eckart, 112-114
Eckart godfather, 516
Eckart frequent contact with, 112
Eckart introduce him circles in Berlin and in Bayreuth, 85
Eckart influence, 75
Eckart role in his political ideas, 75-77
an egomaniacal loner, 604
elected 'deputy battalion representative' under the regime of the communist soldiers councils, 14
elected representative of the lower ranks of the battalion, 11
embracing anti-Semitism, 298
enlist in the Bavarian Reserve Infantry Regiment, 4
enter into politics, 53

entry in the Harrer and Drexler circle, 109
entrance into politics, 19-20
escape from death on several occasions, 4
episode in the rise, 514
evil design, 92-93
evil genius, 615
excellent memory not a madman, 65
examples of his life, 605
experience of the fourteen year old girl shake hands with, 487
experienced the cult of the idol of the Pan-Germans, 70
expression of the full-blown Führer myth, 390-391
extraordinary dialectical ability, 68
fail in entrance examination to the Academy of Fine Arts for the second time, 66
his faith and will power, 446-447
his falsehood, 612-613
family background, 69
fakris and yogis in India, 584
fascination with fire as the real sign of Asura, 621-622
a fascist, 432
fears about his health, 187
fear the trial for his treason, 120
feeling of social inferiority, 54
financial crises, 104
first contact with DAP, 49, 148
first years of his public life, 82
first-Eckart encounter with, 75
first contact with DAP, 19
first steps on the political stage, 108
fits of madness, 611
frequent meetings with Eckart, 76
frequent outburst of oratory, 15-16

frequent visitor to the war ministry, 18
fond of natural joy in the theatre, 493-494
Freinberg experience, 519-520
his friends, 591-597
fulfilment of the dreams of many Germans, 388
Führer, 5, 104, 126, 155, 201, 388-392, 404, 412, 464-465, 489, 504, 563, 567, 427-428, 430, 447, 574, 594, 597, 623, 630
fundamental difference between the testimony of the direct witness and reactions, 486
genius but evil genius, 500
giving his name *Friedenskanzler* (chancellor of peace), 614
great Beings of Light term used, 390
George Von Schonerer influence, 69-70
German citizen in 1932, 507
Geli Raubal suicide impact, 585
global ambitions, 183-189
Gregor rival of Hitler, 96
grudge against educated people, 54
hate for his father, 69
hate for Jews, 17, 109, 156-157, 434, 515
see Jews
Haus Wahnfried visit in Bayreuth, 107
health problem, 440
Hess Call 'the Tribune', 589
historic mission, 437-438
honouring Pötsch, 71
a human being, 566
hypnotic effect, 486-488
Hans Wahnfried visit, 207
Head of the government and supreme executive chief, 6
his bodyguard Christian Weber presented German shepherd dog on his birthday, 94-95
homosexual relations with Rudolf Hess, 125-126, 590-591
hostage of his own propaganda, 104
idea of true democracy, 344
ideology of leadership, 362
his ignorance examples, 614-615
illness, 75, 107
imbibe the pan-Germanic ideas of his father and anti-Semitic, 15
in charge of *Werbeobmann*, 77
influence of Schönerer and, 72
Lueger as well List and Lanz von Liebenfels, 72
intellectual responsible for the implementation of anti-intellectualism, 615
interest in *In Plain German*, 75
interest in the technical aspects of stagecraft architecture
military equipment and war and German history, 66
intermediary between the Volk and God, 392
international war objectives, 596
intention to equate the party with the state, 427
introduction with the DAP, 72
Iron Cross Second and First Class for bravery awarded, 4, 72
Jews great master lie, 163
Jewish question, 76
join German workers party, 49, 51
join military guard unit of the Central Railway, 11
join and resign DAP, 515-516
Judgement day, 498
Karl Lueger influence, 69
Kubizek's narration about Wagner's Opera Rienzi, 510-512

INDEX 683

Landsberg prison, 107, 119-126, 168, 434
last days, 488
last days in the Berlin bunker, 567-568
The Last Days of Hitler, 485-486
last visit at the *Gralsburg*, 508
leader of the German Volk, 428
leader of the masses, 144-151, 494-497
leader of Munich's National Socialist Movement, 84
learning and reading newspapers, 67
Lechfeld mission, 16-17
his lectures, 15-16
lecture on capitalism, 17
lectures his readers on the art of reading, 68
his library, 582
Leopold Pötsch Dr indelible impression on, 71
link between the Ehrhardt Brigade and his movement, 90
liking Mussolini, 508
little sympathy with Himmler, 472-474
List Regiment, 16, 19, 514
'Lord of the Nations', 566
love-lost no between three vons, 103
low opinion of the racial purity of the Germans, 468
Münchener Post accusing him of misbehaviour within NSDAP, 81
Master of lie, 156-160
master of Europe, 648
Mayr advice to join DAP, 52
Mayr daily contact, 18
Mayr introduced to Eckart, 75
Mayr letter, 17-18
medium, 479, 521, 565-566, 617
a magnetic power, 480-486

Mein Kampt, 5
see Mein Kampt
meeting with Chamberlain, 567
member of the commission of inquiry, 14
member of the DAP, 50, 77
member of the propaganda section, 11
Messiah, 391, 430-445, 522, 568, 613
Messianic world view, 449
mindscape, 444
mountain retreat at Obersalzberg, 507
Mother's remarks, 566
at Munich University, 75
a mysterious stranger, 476
a national hero, 120
new message for the world, 150
November Putsch turning point, 117
his NSDAP programme, 430-431
not an accident of history, 175-178
not an anti-Semite, 75
obtain the blessings of Chamberlain, 107
occult occurrences in his life, 510
occult powers, 517
openly with the Ehrhardt Brigade, 91
oppose the opinion of his general on the Warsaw bombing, 619
opponents call him the *Teppichfresser*, the Carpet chewer, 566-567
orator, 492-493, 497-498, 568
Order of the Death, 473-474
on origin of the human race, 219-220
participation in a number of battles in France and Belgium, 4
Pasewalk experience, 517-520
Pasewalk hospital, 53, 517, 519

a pathological hater, 606
politics of annihilation, 615
poverty in life, 5
his powerful peroration, 121
praise by his audiences as a very passionate speaker, 16
as *primus inter pares*, 431
proclaim himself 'Lord of the Nation', 565
product of German consistency, 176-178
prophet of a new humanity, 458-464
propaganda tour 574, 585
prophet of world vision, 448-449
Providence guided, 440-443, 521-522
purchase *Haus Wachenfeld*, 507
public life at the age of thirty, 433
Rabindranath's nationalism in his library, 584-585
radical evil reign, 499
Rauschning compares him to a medium, 480
reader of *Ostara* during his Vienna years, 27
reason for not marrying, 438
reason for anti-Semitism, 164-165
reason of no longer, satisfied with Eckart's metaphysical anti-Semitism, 109
receive the French ambassador, 508
refuse to eat in the prison, 119
regularly visit widow of Paul Troost, 572
reject Darwin theory of evolution, 219
Rienzi revelation, 517
role in unification Austria with Germany, 6
Rosenberg influence, 160, 238, 434
Rudolf Hess secretary, 126

The Sagas of the German Heroes his favourite reading, 71
Satan, demon and demonic term use, 498-500
second speech of 1942, 218-219
a sharp division in his personality, 476
sharing Eckart beliefs, 76
sideline, 388-389
a social stranger, 476
a solipsist, 604-606
sort of mystic, 568
Speer meeting, 446-447
his speeches 'like sex murders', 496
Sri Aurobindo poem, 600, comment, 565-566,
stance against Enlightenment, 159-160
Stauffenberg plot of killing, 573, 597, 607
'strong One from Above' phrase used, 388-389
Supreme Commander of the Armed Forces, 5
Supreme judicial and leader of the NSDAP Party, 6
study of history, 71
suffering, 617-624
suicide attempts, 622-623
Supreme Being, 571
table talk, 218
his talent, 67
terribly cruel, 606-607
theory of worldwide, conspiracy under Eckart's influence, 76
three vons, coup plan, 578
thought of premature death, 439-440
try to commit suicide but prevented by Hanfstängl's, wife, 106
Vabanque Spieler, 522
Vienna years, 12, 65-66

views about, 388-393
vision, 436
vulgar mediocrity, 477
vs national socialism, 432
Wagner's opera, 327, 584
War records and his oratory, 11
wearing his grey army uniform, 77
well-read and well-informed, 72
Würzburg speech, 438
Hitler's birthday *Beobachter*
  publish a poem by Eckart titled
  'Führer of Germany', 113
Hitler youth education, 460-464
Hitlerism, 432-433, 465
Höhere Gewalt meaning, 437
Hobsbawm, Eric, 373
Höhne, Heinz, 90-91, 386, 425, 473
Hölderlin, 195
Hollow earth theory, 235
Hollweg, Bethmann, 132, 167, 223, 522
Homeopathy and naturapathy, 384
Homer, 536, 552
Horace, 536
Horlacher, Michael, 15
Horoscopes reading, 385
Höss Rudolf, 264, 426, 500
House of Commons, 641
Houston, 63
Huge meeting hall Hitler desire, 188
Hugenberg, Alfred, 82, 388
Hugo, Victor, 384
Hüftig, Hans, 474
human being or man, Aurobindo's view, 528-530
  principle of individualism in the theory, 558
human cycle, Sri Aurobindo idea, 555-556
humanity Aurobindo view, 533-534
Hume, David, 212, 315
Hyperborean, 214

Iceland expedition, 472
Indian subcontinent Japan invasion, 562
Iscariot, Judas, 305
Italian German fight, 24

Jäckel, Eberhard, 19, 127-128, 147, 150
Jeckeln, Friedrich, 501
Jackson, president of the
  Nuremberg Military Tribunal, 351
Jaspers, Karl, 370
Jews (German Jews), 13
  account of their life, 331-332
  accusations against international
    Jewry, 351-354
  agriculturalists and colonisers, 337
  Ahlwardt publications, 322-323
  an alien, 301
  anti-Jews atmosphere, 17-18, 297, 429-430
  Aryan propaganda, 324-325
  assimilation, 328-330
  banker, and the stock exchange
    Jobber, 303-304
  barbs against, 316
  beating, 104
  capitalist mentality, 304
  casualties, 307-308
  cause of Hitler's obsession with, 361
  Chamberlain views, 236
  conflict between Aryans and, 356-357, 361
  conspiracy against the Gentiles, 302
  contribution to the national
    efforts not appreciated, 349
  conversion, 332
  countless memories of
    harassment of German and
    Austrian teachers etc., 324
  crossbreeding in the ancient
    Middle East, 323

686 INDEX

crusades and Black Death, 310-311
debate in French National
  Assembly, 316
different in their beliefs, 332
different views, 313, 318, 320
division, 332-333
Dinter hate, 273
domination in banks and
  departmental stores, 330
domination in culture, 330
Enlightenment Treatment, 315
example of the betrayal by Prussian
  Protestant officers, 178
extermination, 109, 359-363
Fischer, Eugen rejects in every
  means, 301
forbidden to wear their war
  medals, 350
friction between Christianity and,
  338
Fritz Klein observation, 301
in German Army, 348-349
Goebbels observation, 302
great master of the lie (about
  Hitler), 157-160, 612-613
Himmler biologist standpoint,
  302
Hitler and Luther comparison, 314
Hitler beating and humiliating,
  351
Hitler omitted verbal attacking,
  614
Hitler's grudging admiration, 336
Hitler hate, 156-157, 230-231,
  306-307, 329, 434, 515
Hitler written order, 359-363
hunger for money with the lust
  for Aryan women, 303
influential in commerce, 330
intelligent, 340-343
intercourse with Aryan girls, 142-
  143, 158-159, 303
international speculation, 417
Jesus killing, 306

Jews writes that Hitler admire,
  156
lack of all human qualities, 298-299
Luther proposed programme,
  312-313
marriage, 333
massacre, 50, 380, 434, 633-634
materialistic intellectual, 62-63
misfortune, 30
money lending and charging high
  rates, 339-340
Nobel Prize winner, 331
notion, 335-336
number of casualties in First
  World War, 349
owner of the most important
  newspapers, 330
participation in past German
  Wars and highly honoured
  award in the First World War,
  350
paying taxes, 303
political choice, 333
population, 330, 349
pornographic contents, 303
portrayed in *The Protocol of the
  Wise Men of Zion*, 345
power and position, 330
powerful for, 323
problem, 17
professions, 337-338
relations between Christians and,
  309
Rosenberg hate, 329
as soldiers, 339, 350
stereotypes, 303-306
systematic operation of the mass
  murders, 360
*The Protocol of the Wise Men of
  Zion*, 351
Theodor Fritsch work, 321-322
title of chosen people, 184
in trade, 338-339
transfer to Sweden, 361

Treitschke's anti-Jews writings, 321
  ugly, dirty and stank with the
    foetor judaicus, 303
  unsecure, 307-308
  victims of Christianity, 297-298
  Volkisch Movement, 297
  vulgar and systematic
    suppression, 413-414
  Wagner, born enemy, 327-329
  war against, 357-359
  welcome the Reformation, 312
  Zionist protocol, 325
Joachimsen, Paul, 194
Joachimsthaler, Anton, 50-51
Jodl, General, 631
Jones, Stanley, 441
Jones, William, 140
Joseph, Emperor, Franz, 69
Judaism, 238, 242, 327, 358
  propagation, anti-Judaism in
    Germany, 298
Judeo-Bolshevism, 110, 346
Jung, Carl Gustav, 404, 501
Junge, Traudl, 438
Jünger, Ernst, 87, 90, 274, 396, 459-460

Kaiser, Ersatz, 3, 9, 136, 220, 389
Kalidasa, 552
Kamenev, 345
Kampfbund Thule formation, 44
Kandinsky, Vasili, 384-385
Kammler, Hans, 501
Kant, 80, 195, 558-559
Kapp, Wolfgang, 52, 60, 74, 78
Kapp Putsch (1920), 78, 227
Kardec, Allan, 384-385
Kaufmann, Walter, 397-398
Kehlstein peak, 508
Kehlsteinhaus building, 508
Kempowski, 489
Kerensky, Alexander, 12
Kershaw, Ian, 19, 51, 56, 66-67, 84, 355, 494, 501

Keynes, John Maynard, 378
Kielar, Wieslaw, 617
Kiev destruction, 620
Kirchhoff, Jochen, 380, 433, 436
Klages, Ludwig, 291, 406
Klein, Fritz, 301
Klemperer, Viktor, 329
Klintzsch, Lieutenant, 74, 92, 101
Knodn, Alois, 50
Knopp, Guido, 450, 486
Koch, Professor, 376
Kohler, Joachim 47, 119, 164, 227, 328, 362, 436
Kriebel, 106, 121
Kriemhild, 130
Kristallnacht launching, 633
Kruger, Hardy, 186
Kubizek, August, 15, 66-67, 71, 252, 494, 508-511, 517, 605
Kun, Bela, 112
Kyffhäuser mountain, 200, 387

Lamarck, 216
Lamprecht, Karl, 223, 552
Landsberg prison, 114, 119-126, 148, 168, 434, 589-590, 622
Langbehn, Julius, 177, 205
Langer, Walter, 476, 480, 506, 519, 610
Large, David Clay, 385, 404
Lawrence, D.H., 411
laws of Mendel rediscovery, 215
Le Bon, Gustav, 146
League of Loyalty for an Uplifting Life, 253
League of Young Girls, 463
Lebendo, Peter, 470
Lebensraum (living space) Theory, 166-172
Lechfeld Camp Hitler mission, 16-17
Lehmann, Julius, 85, 582
Leigh, Richard, 415, 498
Lenin, 12-13, 110-111, 136

688 INDEX

Leningrad destruction and damage, 607, 620-621
Levenda, Peter, 22, 372, 386
Leo Jogisches, 13
Leopold, 111, 636
Ley, Michael, 198, 254
Ley, Robert, 513
Liebknecht, Karl, 12, 136, 346
Lindbergh, Charles, 484
Linnaeus, 143, 216
Linse, 385
Lippman, Walter, 85
List Regiment, 75
List Societies in Austria, 25, 28
London bomb total casualties and damage, 607, 619-621
Longerich, Peter, 83, 90, 360
Lossow, 120
Louis XIV, 130, 203
Lovejoy, Arthur, 527
Ludwig III
  abdication, 10
Lüdecke, Kurt, 493, 497
Lueger, Karl role, 69-72, 322
Luftwaffe, 637
Lukacs, John, 19, 65, 362, 602, 647
Luke, 305
Ludendorff, Field Marshall Erich, 576
Luther, Martin, 25, 63, 177-178, 192, 237, 267-271, 293, 324, 371, 553
  Book of a Hundred Chapters in 1510, by, 178-179
  contribution, 193-194
  historical connection of his anti-Judaism with National Socialist anti-Semitism, 313-314
  programme for Jews, 312-313
Luxemburg, Rosa, 346

Machtergreifung, anniversary, 357
Mahabharata, the, 599
Mallarmé, 373, 599
Malthus, Thomas, 215

MAN, term, 140
Manheim, Ralph, 50
Mann, Heinrich, 606
Mann, Thomas, 175-177, 314, 405, 499, 505, 585
Marconi Giuglielmo, 373
Marine Brigade, 89
Mark, 305
Marshal, Field, 483
Marx, Karl, 66, 110, 347, 627
  The Jewish Question, 348
Marxism, 90, 365, 370, 396, 459
  Hitler different from, 344-345
Marxist doctrine, 9
Marxist German Independent Socialist Party, 9
Marxist Revolution in Hungary, 13
Marxist revolt, 13
Maser, Walter, 18, 476, 602
Masses comparison to a woman, 495-496
  Hitler leader, 494-497
Mathew, 305, 313
Matisse, Henri, 541
Matter, Aurobindo writings, 530-532
  form of spirit, 528, 530
Mauresberger, Volker narrating the surrender of the Nazis of Weimar, 254
Maurice Emil, 124, 729
  brief sketch, 336-337
Mauresberger, 137
Mayr, Karl, 16, 47, 50-52, 60, 68, 72, 75-80, 90, 362, 402, 514, 576, 581, 590-591
  adventure stories for Hitler, 72-73
  ambitious and intelligent, 14
  and Hitler, 117-118
  appointment chief of the propaganda section, 14
  background, 73
  death, 118

letter to Hitler, 17-18
radical Right, 14
Medium characteristics, 479-480
Mein Kampf, 12, 16, 54, 68-69, 71, 83, 87, 89, 126, 157, 185, 242, 246-247, 447-448, 450, 472, 517, 520, 612, 614
  about Aryans, 139, 143, 146-147
  about conspiracy, 416
  anti-Semitism, 164-165
  background for a catastrophic sequel to the First World War, 129-130
  cause of wrath, 130-131
  chapter on the German Worker's Party, 51
  conflict between Aryans and Jews, 361-361
  contempt for the German people, 456-457
  copy to be present at the ceremonies of baptism, marriages and death, 127
  demand for living space, 169-171
  dictating his co-prisoner Emil Maurice and type them later, 124
  on Dietrich Eckart, 56-57
  discovery of an Aryan root language, 212
  drive for Lebensraum (living space theory), 166-172
  English translation, 50
  fanatic faith in the Nationalist-Socialist movement, 284
  fanatical racist in Hitler, 134
  first part at Landsberg prison, 148
  food situation, 5
  German media study propaganda with quotations, 127
  German youth learn by heart whole passages from it, 127
  German-Nordic-Aryan race, 142-143
  Hitler-Hess connections 125
  Jews issue, 356
  Jews intercourse with Aryan girls, 303
  Jews intellectual powers, 340
  Karl Haushofer typing the dictates and helping with suggestions and corrections, 125
  Landsberg prison, 124, 589-590
  The Leader of the Masses, 144-148, 495
  legend of the stab in the back, a lie, 130
  magic power of Hitler, 491
  new testament, 391
  passage of Gobineau, 230
  peasant, 288
  prescribe study material in all educational institutions, 127
  propaganda mention, 451-452
  propaganda war, 451-452
  The Protocol of the Wise Men of Zion, 161-166
  public life at the age of thirty, 433
  racism and Darwinism, 143-144, 217-218
  racism thesis, 240-248
  reason for lack of understanding, 128
  Second World War, 624
  several untruthful statements, 20
  speech as a beer hall tribune, 130
  state a means to an end, 451
  Stempfle, one of the readers and made corrections in the manuscript, 116
  ten million copies of the first part printed till 1945, 127
  Thules concern, 47
  Treaty of Brest-Litovsk, 131-132
  Treaty of Versailles, 130-131
  Volk, 250-251
  war aims of the Germany, 132-134
  Weimar Republic Government and Weimar constitution system, 135-138

William Shirer opinion about the blueprint of the Third Reich, 126-127
written in 1924-25, 185
Meiners, Christoph, 212
Menshevik revolution, 12
'mentor' meaning, 55
Michelangelo, 189
Middle Ages, 380, 394, 418-419
Mirandola, Giovanni Pico della, 190
Mistral Gabriela, 524
Mitford, Unity, 484
Model-airplane clubs of the German youth strength, 463
Moltke, 208
Montmartre, 403
More, Thomas, 190
Morell, Dr, 440
Morisset, Henri, 541
Mosse, George, 56, 76, 176, 183, 206, 226-227, 231, 236, 249-250, 252, 282, 295, 298, 321, 365, 370, 387, 408-409, 603
Mother India ashram magazine, 664
Mother of the Sri Aurobindo ashram, 562
motorized Hitler Youth statistics, 463
Mozart, 195
Münchener Beobachter, the, 36, 48, 80
destruction, 81
Munich Agreement, 630
Sri Aurobindo and the Mother rejection, 632
Munich conference, 630, 633-634
Munich coup, 10
Munich pact, 610, 632
Munich Post, the, 45, 92, 117, 508
Munich Republic of Councils obliteration, 13-14
Munich University, 15, 17, 68-69, 389, 496, 581, 587
Mussolini, Benito, 103-104, 243, 275, 389, 432, 508, 575, 608, 630, 657

Muspilli, theme of the nineteenth century poem, 617-618
mysticism, 592

Napoleon code, 316, 343
National Socialism, 144, 155, 177-179, 183, 238, 241, 262, 282-283, 290, 300, 345, 380, 387, 412, 450, 458, 469, 498-499, 504
agenda, 436
birth, 357, 563
Christian current, 426
characterised as a Youth movement, 254
doctrine, 240
emergence, 426
a façade or masquerade, 426
Führerprinzip backbone, 427
Hitler's standpoint, 449
Luther inventor, 177
origins, 591
principles, 427-428, 465
programme, 425
a religion, 425, 453-458
rise, 358
socialist tendency, 426
National Association of Jews from Soldiers (1919)
foundation, 350
National Reich Church and *Mein Kampf*, 127
National Socialist movement, 359, 453, 596-597, 614
goal, 246
growth, 436
Hitler's faith, 284
NSDAP Hitler's National Socialist Worker's Party, 48, 55, 74, 88, 91, 93, 104, 116, 151, 274, 278, 300, 344, 359, 449, 489, 578, 585-587, 593-594
Anton Drexler founder, 74
defacto, 451
Eckart's contact, 113

elected chairman with dictatorial power, 81
first *Parteitag* in Munich, 113
Hitler-Eckart meetings at, 113-114
Hitler leader, 6
Hitler misbehaviour within, 81
Hitler seeking support from captain of German industry, 490
Hitler re-enter, 81
Hitler region, 81
inner tension, 490
July coup, 84
mass rally 282, 454
origins of, 607
programme, 20, 430, 464-465
rise in membership, 99, 103
Rosenberg incharge, 122
SA attack, 490
Schwabing headquarter, 78
Socialist accusing him, becoming bourgeois and betraying the party programme, 490
success, 152-154
Nature, generation contact, 259
  Fest, comment, 259-260
  peasant praise, 264
  Sri Aurobindo often uses, 601-602
  Youth Movement, 260-263
Nauhaus, Walter, 41, 582
Naval Hitler Youth, 463
Nazi movement, 425
  Luther influence, 177
  turning point, 117
Nazism, 22, 24, 27, 131, 147, 175, 196, 219, 235, 254, 262, 272, 282, 300, 317, 331, 356, 379, 384, 396, 400, 412, 504, 562, 634, 639, 641-642, 644-645
  amplification of Hitler's ideas, 433-434
  difference between Hitlerism and, 435

features, 431
fight against Bolshevism and capitalism, 110
form of fascism, 431
foundation of the Aryan world empire, 434
German's opponents, attitude towards, 435
Hitler plans and war aims, 433
leading personalities observations, 432-433
pageantry, 494
revival, 625
roots, 523
Sri Aurobindo concern, 563
Sri Aribindo poem, 600
as a Volkisch Movement, 110
Near East Jews agricultural and colonisers, 337
Neave, Airey, 498
Nebe, Arthur, 501
Nehru, Jawaharlal, 538
Nerthardt, George, 120
Netaji, 432
The New Age, 384
New-Man
  idea, 459
  Junger's view, 459-460
  Hitler explanation, 460-463
New Testament, 39, 304-305
New world and new mean Aurobindo differentiates, 627-628
New York destruction, 621
New York Times
  printing his political obituary, 120
Newton, Isaac, 377-378
Newton's Law, 315
Nietzsche, Friedrich, 23, 66-67, 204, 235, 254, 269, 274, 371, 373, 404, 411-412, 459, 559, 627
  attack Socrates, 395
  Christian civilization weakness, 395
  Christian God concept lost its acceptance in the west, 394

disdain from the masses, 396
The Gay Science, 394
hostile to Darwinism, 397
ideal of the superman, 398-400
importance to France, 395
marriage with Elisabeth, 400
pillars of the Nietzschean, perspectivism, 394
regard for the philosophers, 395
relationship with Richard Wagner, 397
suffer continuously from migraines, 395
suffering from migraines, 395
Volkisch thought in his writings, 394
Nirodbaran, 548, 563, 599, 639, 661
Nobel Prize
  Jews winner, 331
Noll, 280
Nolte, Ernst, 56, 108
non-aggression pact between Germany and Russia, 610, 634, 647-648
Nordau, Max, 215
Nordic race, 239
  definition, 425
Nordics term, 139
North Pole, 37
North-South divide, 180, 193, 266
Nostradamus, 582
Novak, Philip, 398
Novalis, 195, 253
Nudism and Orientalism, 384
Nuremberg, 5, 86, 272, 282, 303, 454, 487, 594, 616
  documentary films, 586
  party rally, 513
Nuremberg Laws, 357
Nuremberg trial, 24, 484, 498

Occult
  meaning, 516
  movement, 276
Obersalzberg account, 507-509

Occultism, 32-33, 426, 542-543, 565, 584, 592, 596
  abstract painting influence, 384
  age of reason, 372
  and theosophy, 372
  aspect of Volkisch, 275
  development parallel with industrialisation of Germany, 384-385
  flourishing, 275
  movement, 378
  myth, 401
  part of European culture, 372
  political motive, 275
  practitioners thrown in concentration camp, 386
  research, 383
  revival, 378
  re-emergence, 372
officers' association, *Eiserne Hand* (Iron Hard), 74
Ohlendorff, Walter, 501
Olcott, H.S., 23, 381
Old Testament, 275, 316
Olden, Rudolf, 584
Olympic Games talk about, 188
Operation Adlerangriff, 642
Operation Barbarossa, 201, 597, 640
Operation Dynamo, 637-639
Operation Michael, 129
Operation Punishment, 620
Operation Sea Lion, 642
Operation Torch, 649
Order of Young Germans, 253
Ordensburgen
  Hitler's highest Nazi elite school), 186, 461-462, 464
Organization Consul, 74, 92
Orzechowski, Peter, 25, 47, 52, 374, 405, 454
Otto, 490

Pacific Ocean, 169
Padfield, Peter, 386

INDEX 693

Pagels, Elaine, 304, 306
Pan-Germans, List guru of, 25
Pan-German League, 14, 47, 294
Pannwitz, Rudolf, 403
Paris account, 540-541
  destruction, 645-646
  threat, 129
Pasewalk hospital, 3, 53, 517
Pasha, Hussein, 33
Paul, 110
Paxton, Robert, 645
Peace Treaty of Brest-Litovsk, 9, 129, 132
Peace of Westphalia (1648), 182-183
peasant Spengler praise, 288
Pericles, 190
Persico, Joseph, 594
Pétain, Marshall, 644
Pichot, André, 212, 215, 232, 335-336
Picker, Henry, 218, 244, 451, 462, 620
Piaget, Jean, 383
Pilate, 305
Piper, Raymond, 599
Plato, 190, 552
Pletsch, Carl, 397
Plewnia, Margarete, 56, 62, 108, 114
Pliny, 192
Pohl, Hermann, 31-32, 34
Pol Pot, 341
Poland, 132
  extermination, camps, 501
  invasion, 352, 602, 634, 636
Poles German fight, 24
Poliakov, Leon, 182, 214, 270, 304, 310, 321, 326, 332, 334, 341, 348, 352
Pötsch, Leopold, 15, 70-71
Pondicherry, 544-545
Potthast, Miss, 618
Prinz, Rabbi, 349
Purani, AB, 551

Race concept, 425
racial purity documents, 468
  Hitler low opinion, 468
  steps, 468-469
Racism
  and Hitler, 592
  Gobineau racial theory, 226
  Chamberlain thesis, 233-237
  Darwin's theory, 214
  difference between whites and non-whites, 212
  different views, 212
  Dinter thesis, 273-275
  French biologist views, 214
  in Germany, 212
  Haeckel theories, 224-225
  Hitler thesis, 240-248
  Lapouge theory, 231-233
  in *Mein Kampf*, 143
  Nazi mythology, 214
  Rosenberg theory, 239-240
  spiritual movement, 271-272
  starting in France and England, 212
  views German, 222-223
Raphael, 189
Rathenau, Walter, 92, 328, 333
Rattenhuber, Brigadeführer, 575
Raubal, Geli, suicide, 329, 585, 591, 622
Rauschning, Hermann, 144, 147, 153, 156, 219, 241, 275, 285, 291, 344, 434, 456, 462, 464, 482, 488, 503, 505, 602
  brief sketch, 433, 433n
Reason Aurobindo views, 525, 528
Red Army, 12
Red Resistance crushing, 13
Redesdale, Lord, 484
Rees, Laurence, 88, 486-487
Reform centres, 384
Reformation, 369
  Jews welcome, 312
Reformation movement, 189
Reichshammerbund, founding, 29
Reichstage at Nuremberg events, 282-284

Reichswehr, 90, 103-104
Reinhardt, Max, 330
Reiter, Mimi, 622
Religion, 417-421
  Christian churches building, 267
  Christianisation of the heathen tribes, 267
  Christian commanders role, 267-268
  Hitler views, 268-269
  Martin Luther appeal, 269-270
  pagan temples distinction, 267
Religious wars analyses, 293-294
Religion of humanity launching, 377
Renaissance, 8, 178, 182, 314
  magic component, 377
  questioning, 370
Renaissance movement art, 189
  components, 190-191
  example of Ulrich Von Hutten, 192
  experiences, 190
  humanistic schools association, 189
  rediscovery the value of the individual and his family thinking, 191
Republic of Councils, 21, 44, 61, 72, 75, 111-112
  collapse, 73
Reuth, Ralph, 51, 76, 155, 425, 517, 602, 604, 638
Revolutionary of the Upper Rhine message, 178-180
Revolutions of 1830, 1848 and 1870, 8
Ribbentrop, 431
Richard, Paul, 594
Richet, Charles, 383
Riefenstahl Leni, 441, 497
Rienzi (Wanger opera Rienzi)
  Kubizek narration, 510-513
  story, 513, 584
Rilke, Rainer Maria, 385, 407
Rimbaud, 373, 384
Rissmann, Michael, 441
Rittlinger, Herbert, 117
Rodin, Auguste, 541
Rhodes, Richard, *Masters of Death* by, 617
Röhm, Ernst, 90-91, 93, 121, 426, 591
  homosexuals and scandalous letters published in the *Munich Post*, 117
Röhm's *Reichsflagge*, 117
Rohrmoser, Gunter, 328
Roman civilization, 266-267
Romantic Movement (Age of Reason), 22, 195-200, 294
  names, 195
  French culture domination, 197
  Napoleon of this period, 196-197
  role of the emotions, 196
Röntgen, Wilhelm, 373
Roosevelt, Franklin, 85, 644
Rose, Detlev, 374
Rosenbaum, Ron, 80, 92, 164, 306, 476, 500, 514, 518-519, 647
Rosenberg, 96, 109-110, 168, 180, 278, 330, 396, 434, 464, 566, 586, 591
  admirer of the Indian scriptures, 592-593
  anti-Communist and anti-Semitic, 161
  anti-Semitic pamphlets, 592
  Aryan-Nordic-German, 245
  birth, 161
  contribution to the *Volkische Beobachter*, 238
  describe about Eckart, 61
  disparaging conduct towards Drexler, 123
  Eckart introduce to Hitler, 161, 238
  editor of the *Volkische Beobachter*, 112
  education, 161
  fled Russia, 161

founder of the National
  Socialism, 238
influence on Hitler, 160
interest in mysticism, 592
member of the Thule Society, 238
meeting with Eckart, 592
Myth of the Twentieth Century by,
  142, 178, 238-239, 391, 420, 593
obsession with Zionism, 592
on race, 239-240
part of Russian refugees, 161
*The Protocol of the Wise Men of
  Zion*, 30, 61, 146, 161, 184,
  238, 297, 356, 385, 611-612
supervisor of the Third Reich, 39
writing and editing of *In Plain
  German*, 592
Roth, Joseph, 178, 504
Rothschilds, 304, 333
Rousseau, 195
Rupprecht, Crown Prince, 102
Russia or Soviet Union
  armed workers formation, 99
  bombardment. 201,646-647
  Communist Party Politburo, 99
  conquering plan, 634
  danger, 640
  events of 1917, 46
  example of change top socialist
    leadership, 345
  military command groups
    organization, 99
  revolutionary guards in
    Petersburg, 99
  setback, 602
Russian Jews, 172
  massacre, 314, 334, 347
  percentage and fled the county,
    347
Russian Kronstadt Revolt, example,
  42
Russian refugees in France and
  Germany, 166
  their tales, 9-10

Russian Revolution (1917), 12-13,
  100, 111, 116, 161, 438
  German Army High Command
    support, 8-9
Ruthenians Germans fight, 24
Ryback, Timothy, 441, 582-583

SS-system foundation, 615
Saint-Saëns, Camille, 544
Schacht, Hjalmar, 122, 500
Schafer Ernst, 472
Schellenburg, Walter, 41, 68, 500
Schickele René, 496
Schiller, 66
Scholdt, Günter, 392, 499
Schopenhauer, Arthur, 61-62, 66, 163
Schuler, Alfred, 405-406
Schellenberg, 469
Schworm, Karl, 388
Second World War, 117, 131, 175,
  208, 210, 222, 367, 474, 475, 574,
  524, 547-548, 560, 569
  account, 634-640
  Allied forces, 636
  Battle of Britain, 643, 646-647, 659
  beginning, 358, 634
  Belgium surrender, 638
  British Expeditionary Forces
    loosing, 639
  Churchill seeking terms with
    Hitler, 639
  evacuation, 639
  fall of England, 639
  France warning, 635
  France humiliation, 644-646
  French Navy destruction, 649
  Germany's defeat, 576
  Great Britain warning to Hitler,
    635
  Hitler troops invasion on
    Netherlands, Luxemburg,
    Belgium and France, 636
  Japanese Military campaigning,
    655-657

696 INDEX

Military catastrophes in North Africa, Greece, Crete, 6 49
Miracle of Dunkirk, 639-640
Moscow and Leningrad destruction, 646
Operation Dynamo, 637-639
Operation Torch, 649-650
RAF Victory, 643-644
total casualties, 416
Warsaw destruction, 646
secret Armanen loges, foundation, 25
Seeckt, 103
Schlegel, 195, 197
Scheidemann, Philipp, 136-137
Schellenberg Walter, 618
Schemann, Ludwig, 223, 226
Schiller, 253-254, 273
Schmidt Paul, 635
Scholdt, Gunter, 201, 613
Schopenhauer, 612
Schroeder Christa, 360
Schubert, 195
Schumann, 195
Seisser, 120
Sereny Gitta, 362, 469, 475, 485, 617
Serbo-Croats German fight, 24
Serpico, 513
Scythes, 192
Shelley, 552
Shirer, William, 126, 235-236, 452, 499
Siegfried, 130
Sienkiewicz, Henryk, 544
Sigmund, Anna Maria, 300
Silesius Angelus, 62, 270
Simon, Richard, 315, 484
Slovaks German fight, 24
Slovenes German fight, 24
Smith, Adam, 215
Social Darwinism, 233-234, 366
Socialism, 396
  Hitler's real feelings about, 344
  Jews creation, 344

Socialist and Communist movements Jews role, 344-348
solipsism definition, 604
Sombart Werner, 111
Sonderweg (Germany's 'road apart'), 24
Sophocles, 536
Sorel, 291
Spanish Civil War, 603, 632
Spartacist coup, 12
Spartacist revolt, 13, 78
Spartacists uprising, 346
Spartan totalitarianism Hitler plan of creation, 450
Spartacus party, 136
Speer, Albert, 67, 73, 186-188, 360, 367, 375-377, 431-432, 443, 445, 455, 457, 475, 481, 484-485, 490, 507, 508, 572, 591, 597, 611, 615, 619, 621, 645
Spengler Oswald, 205, 233, 263-266, 268, 284, 287, 395, 447-448, 482
Spiritist movement, 199, 405-406, 582, 592
  chief centres in Germany, 385
  conquering the problem of death and meaning of life, 382
  emergence in Anglo-Saxon countries, 381
  a feminist religion, 383
  Fox Sisters in USA, 383
  Hitler contact, 584
  influence, 384
  lectures, sermons and prayers holding, 381
  origin, 381
  practice, 261
  revival, 417-420
  roles, 380
  scientists interest, 382-383
  Sunday gathering, 381
Spiritist Publishing House, 385
Spiritual Movement, 271, 366

Sri Aurobindo Ashram School or Pondicherry Ashram, 657, 659
Stalin, 99, 341, 345, 450, 499, 517, 634, 647, 657
Stalingrad destruction, 607, 620
Stauff, Philipp, 31, 35, 41, 385
Stauffenberg, Clause, 607
  acknowledged leader of the conspiracy, 414-416
  an aristocrat and conscious of status, 410
  candidate for chief of general staff, 411
  driving force behind the attempts on Hitler's life, 409, 414
  engage in spiritual crusade, 410
  an extraordinary will power, 410
  impressed by Hitler's accomplishments, 413
  member of the George Circle, 410
  master-minded German armed warfare, 411
  meeting with George Mosse, 409-410
  serve in the armed forces, 411
  wounded in Africa, 413
Sportblatt Munchener Beobachter, the, 47
Steininger Babette, 585
Streicher Julius, 159, 236, 272-273, 303, 593-594
Steiner, George, 499
Steinert, 56, 142
Stennes, Hugo, 490-491
Stempfle, Berhard, 116
Stennes Revolt in 1930-31, 490
Stern, J.P., 363, 507, 515
Sternhell Zeev, 366
Stangl, Franz, 299
Strasser, Gregor, 274, 490
Strasser, Otto, 274, 426, 442, 492
Strauss, Richard, 327
Stresemann Gustav, 101, 122, 223

Striecher, 442
Stoakes, Geoffrey, 507
Sufism, 33
  Turkish aspect, 426
Suicide examples, 621-623
Sünner, Rüdiger, 251, 253, 258, 278-279, 473
superman meaning, 528
Swaraj Aurobindo define, 538
Swedish Academy, 524

Tacitus, 190
  Germania, 191
Tagore, Rabindranath, 401, 584
Talukar, Nirodbaran, 551
Tauler, Johannes, 426
Termudi family, 31
Theater, Hitler love and contact, 493-494
Theodor Mommsen, Latinist, 321
Théon, Max, 542
Theory of the superiority of the Aryan race, 238
Theory of the Teutonic origins, 215
Theosophical Society, 381, 592
  Blavatsky founder, 371
  deep impressionary, 24
  expansion of humanity, 371
  foundation, 23
  occultism, 372
  popularity, 23
  ideals, 24-25
  emergence in Anglo-Saxon countries, 381
  programme, 371
Theosophy spreading in Germany, 378-379
  spread, 371
  sweeping in Europe, 371
  teaching, 261
Theosophical Publishing House, 378
Third International, 9

Third Reich, 22, 39, 401, 426, 452, 469, 498, 513, 608, 615, 634
Thirty Years' War (1618-1648), 182-183, 293, 300
Thucydides, 190
Thule Society (Thule-Gesellschaft), 19, 21-22, 37-45, 51-52, 59, 74, 75, 85, 112, 116, 142, 280, 223, 344, 385, 426, 516, 576-577, 580, 582, 585, 587, 592
  foundation, 47
  gap between Right and Left, 46-47
  personal and ideological relationship between the Reichswehr and, 47
  try to win over the working from the nationalist idea, 47
Thule Kampfbund, Grassinger member, 48
Thule's emblem, 44
Tibet expedition, 472
Toland, John, 55, 56, 79, 94, 107, 125, 315, 425, 440, 460, 518, 602, 640
Tournier Michel, 499
Treaty of Brest Litovsk, 131, 224
Treaty of Bucharest, 131
Treaty of Versailles 7, 90, 98, 100, 130-131, 133, 137, 167, 429, 436, alwliton, 135-136
Treitschke, 205
Treitschke's *Handbuch des Judentums*, 199
Trevor-Roper, H.R., 6, 182, 475, 480, 485, 490, 619
Tripartite Pact, 620
Troost, Paul, 572
Trotsky, Leon, 111, 385
Tsar Nicholas II, 161
Twentieth Century War, 548, 663, 665

Ulrich Graf, Hitler's bodyguard, 106
Unemployment statistics, 489
Unification, Austria with Germany Hitler contribution, 6
USA Hitler's declaration of war on, 404
University of Berlin, 220-221
University of Montpellier, 231

Vacher, Georges, 231
Valéry, 373
Vegetarianism, 261, 384
Viking Bund, 92
Villiangen Dr Burger-, 236
Virgil, 536
Vishva Hindu Parishad, 657
Vitalist movements, 396
Vogt, 212
Volkisch concept, 250-251
  common with language, 250-251
  Hitler juggling with the words, 251
  meaning, 250, 297
  origin, 249n
  term, 27n
Volkisch movement, 34, 111, 142, 151, 183, 196, 242, 274, 322, 370, 580, 614
  aim, 297
  anti-semitism chief whip, 298
  Apollo and sun worship, 277-278
  attitude towards the Roman, 256
  Diederich's contribution, 270
  dimensions, 254
  examples of other groups, 253-354
  Fest denouncing, 290
  importance, 252
  justification and popularity, 252
  megalithic culture, 258
  National Socialism, 290
  occultism, 276
  rejection of reason, 289-292
  religion role, 266-275
  sacral character, 257-258
  sources, 256
  spirit, 254-255
  town and cities role, 288-289

trends, 384
youth role, 282-283, 298
Volkische Beobachter, the, 34, 84, 101, 103, 112, 390
Thules publication, 46
selling off, 79
Volkstum threat to, 18
Voltaire, 195, 316, 343
von Beneckendorff, Paul, 389
von Bothmer, Karl, 15
von Brauchitsch, Field Marshall, 640
von Freiburg Dietrich, 418
von Hindenburg, Paul, 83, 389, 416
von Hitler, Ulrich, 278
  German Renaissance and historical figure of Arminius, 192-193
von Kahr, Gustav, 73, 93-94, 101, 102
von Kantzow, Carin, 616
von Killinger, Manfred, 31
von Kluge, General, 488
von Krockow, Christian, 6, 126, 329
von Liebenfels Lanz, 34, 72, 202-203, 253, 238, 303, 401, 410-411
von List, Guido, 31, 34, 401, 200, 253, 257, 387, 400, 588
von Lossow, General Otto, 101-102, 105, 121
von Ludendorff, Erich, 74, 79, 83, 105,-106, 121-123, 129, 130, 136, 138, 178, 273, 389
von Luttwitz, General, 78-79
von Manstein Field Marshal, 631
von Mohl, General Arnold, 8, 14, 47, 576, 578, 581
von Muller, Karl Alexander, 15-16, 85, 496
von Ribbentrop, Joachim, 635
von Sebottendorff Rudolf, 38, 40-41, 45, 59, 112, 223, 302, 426, 385, 577, 582
  acquaintance of the Termudi family of Bursa, 33

adventuring search for gold, 32
Before Hitler Came by, 21-22
birth, 32
contact with Pohl, 32
engineering study, 32
home in Turkey, 21
Islamic mystism in Turkey, 33
join the Volkisch Movement, 34
marriage, 33, 36
mistakes, 115-116
rumour about, 117
reproduces his writings in the Thule Publications, 42
return to Germany from Turkey, 33
son of a locomotive driver, 32
speech to the members of Thule, 43
study of occultism, 32-33
suicide, 117
study an essay on the Baktashi dervishes, 33
views on Turkey, 33-34
visit the Cheops pyramid at El-Giza, 32
von Scheubner-Richter, Erwin, 166
von Scheubner-Richter, Erwin, 574
von Schirach, Henriette, 98, 622
von Schönerer, Georg, role, 15, 69-72, 222
von Schussnigg, 437
von Spaun, Fridolin, 486
Vondung, Klaus, 454
von See, Klaus, 253, 283, 425
von Seeckt, Hans, 100-101
von Seisser, 102
von Salomon, Pfeffer, 286
von Teuchert, Baron Karl, 44
von Tresckow, General Henning, 414-415
von Treitschke, 220-221, 320
  critisize Bismark, 221
  denouncing Jews, 224
  his writings, 222
  praise imprealism, 221
von Wiegand, Karl, 643

von Baden, Max, 136
von den Bruck, Möller, 365-366
Voroshilov, 345
Vyasa, 552

Wagner, Cosima, 227
Wagner, Richard, 22, 63, 66, 67, 71, 107, 110, 206-207, 227, 234, 252, 325-326, 329, 371, 397-398, 449, 544, 559, 578, 582
  his music, 327
Wagner, Siegfried, 85
Wagner, Winifred, 85, 107, 161, 513, 517
Wagner's *Tannhäuser*, 31
Wegener, Franz, 38
Walter, Bruno, 330
Wandervogel movement, 260, 262
War spiritual leader in Pondicherry against, 562-563
War Ministry, 18, 349
War propaganda, Hitler views 451-453
Warsaw bombing, 607, 619, 621
Weber, Christian, 113
  Hitler bodyguard, 94
Weber, Max, 223, 522
Weimar constitution, 138
Weiss, John, 69, 110, 220, 222, 249, 313, 331, 340, 342, 346, 347, 349, 429
  Ideology of Death by 177
Weltanschauung launching, 187
  programme, 87-88
Wervik, 13
Western civilization fall, 633
White, Charles, 213

Whitman, 599
wholism, 384
Wiechert, Ernst, 289
Wilhelm, Karin, 124
William I, Hohenzollern, 203
William II, Emperor, 10-11, 25, 59, 161, 170, 178, 204, 207, 210, 288
Wiligut, Karl Maria, 427, 471
Winock, Michel, 249
Wirth, 142
Wirtschaftswunder economic miracle, 167
Wissenschaft, concept, 204
Wistrich, Robert, 332, 352, 354
Wittgensteins, 333
Wolf Free Corps, 74
Wolfskehl, Karl, 405, 410
Women example of suicide, 622
Workers role, 8
Workers' circle Herrer founder, 49
Workers Committee for A Just Peace, Bremen, Anton Drexler founder, 48
Workers' Party, 76
World Hitler concept of achieving, 181-188
World Ice Theory, 220, 235
Wulff, Wilhelm, 386
Würzburg, 74

Yates, Frances, 190
Youth movement account, 260-263, 274
Youth organization 262-263, 298
Young Turks Revolution, 33

Zentner, Christian, 127, 128, 143, 147, 217, 351, 462, 613